THEIR MUSIC BROKE BOUNDARIES.

Photos l to r: © Erich Lessing/Art Resource, NY; © Getty Images; © Bettmann/CORBIS; © Phil Dent/Redferns/Getty Images; Courtesy Florida State University College of Music

© Bildarchiv Preussischer Kulturbesitz/Art Resource, NY

WE'RE BREAKING NEW ONES.

INTRODUCING **STREAMING MUSIC**, VIA OUR ALL-NEW PREMIUM WEBSITE AND INTERACTIVE EBOOK!

Wright gives you what you need!

- With this new edition, you have the option to listen to Wright's musical selections via streaming audio! No downloads necessary! If your instructor chose one of the following options as a package with your text, you'll **get** *streaming audio* **at no additional cost!**
  1) access to Wright's exceptional premium website
  2) access to the multimedia eBook
  3) either the complete 5-CD or core 2-CD set of the Western repertoire

  Open this insert to learn more about available CD sets, the jam-packed premium website (including Active Listening Guides), and the multimedia eBook!

- Use the FREE tools included in this text to help you get a good start in the first few weeks of class and beyond.
  ❖ A FREE "Introduction to Listening" CD includes all musical examples from the text's Part I, which will introduce you to the elements of music.
  ❖ Check out the FREE link to a complete online course taught by the author! **http://oyc.yale.edu/music**.
  ❖ Follow references in the margins to FREE iTunes, Rhapsody, and YouTube playlists.
  ❖ Use additional FREE online content to explore chapter quizzes, interactive Listening Exercises, flashcards, and chapter glossaries.

- Refine your listening skills with Wright's detailed Listening Exercises—available in the book and also online. These exercises, which ask questions like the ones your instructor is likely to ask in quizzes, will help you focus on important musical elements and do well in the course.

- If your instructor has selected Wright's *Listening to Western Music*, you'll learn the complete history of traditional Western music, from medieval to modern.

- If your instructor instead chose *Listening to Music*, you'll add on expanded coverage of popular music, including Broadway musicals, and even film and video game music. Wright will also introduce you to the music of the Far East, the Near East and Africa, and the Caribbean and Latin America in Part VIII (Global Music).

How better to learn to listen critically than with a wide array of music options?

Unfold this page to learn more about the many listening options—including streaming music—now available to you!

Receive exceptional value!

Every book comes with a free CD!
▼ The "Introduction to Listening" CD plays all music and musical examples from the text's Part I on the elements of music.

online course!
▼ Use our FREE link to a complete online course taught by the author himself and featuring in-class performances and demonstrations! Check it out now at **http://oyc.yale.edu/music**.

Watch a video of or download a recording of "Don't Stop the Music" (see box below) in the YouTube and iTunes playlists on the text website.

online playlists!
▲ Watch for marginal cues to related online playlists from iTunes, Rhapsody, and YouTube.

free online content!
Whether or not you purchased premium website access (see bottom of this page) you will receive free access to chapter quizzes, interactive Listening Exercises, YouTube, iTunes, and Rhapsody playlists, flashcards, and chapter glossaries.

Want even more music? Wright's got it!

Your instructor may have selected one or more CD sets to accompany your text. With a purchase of either the 2- or 5- CD set, you will receive **streaming music** at no extra cost!

See the inside front cover of this book for a comprehensive list of the musical selections.

CDs...and now streaming music!

5-CD set This complete set includes all Western music discussed in *Listening to Music* and *Listening to Western Music*.

2-CD set This streamlined set includes a core repertoire of Western music discussed in both books.

Popular and Global Music CD
Includes all music from Parts VII (American Popular Music) and VIII (Global Music) of *Listening to Music*.

---

ssons (downloadable mp3s), Musical Elements, rms and Genres, an Interactive Music Timeline, yles Quizzes, Britten's *Young Person's Guide* hestra videos, videos demonstrating keyboard ts, and

A Checklist of Musical Styles

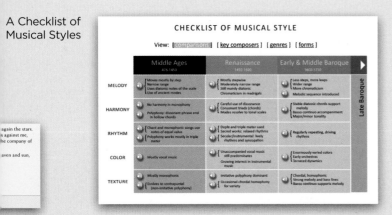

Multimedia eBook!

If your text purchase included a printed or an instant online access code for the multimedia eBook, you will receive everything on the premium website, as well as a corresponding multimedia-enabled eBook. It includes a page design identical to the print book as well as integrated links to much of the online content!

Streaming Audio!

State-of-the-art listening tools: the key to successful listening skills

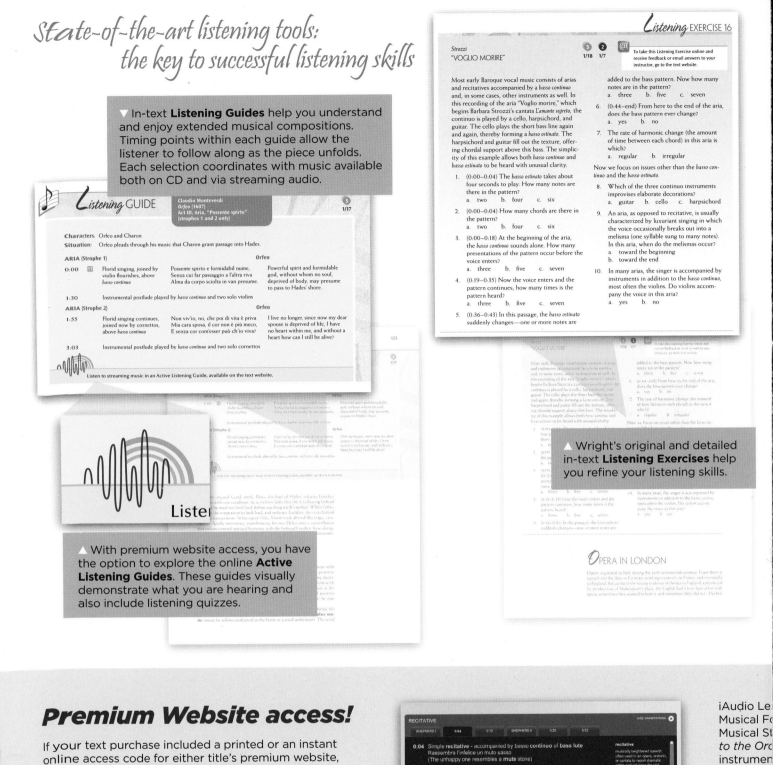

▼ In-text **Listening Guides** help you understand and enjoy extended musical compositions. Timing points within each guide allow the listener to follow along as the piece unfolds. Each selection coordinates with music available both on CD and via streaming audio.

Listening GUIDE

Claudio Monteverdi
Orfeo (1607)
Act III, Aria, "Possente spirto"
(strophes 1 and 2 only)

Characters: Orfeo and Charon
Situation: Orfeo pleads through his music that Charon grant passage into Hades.

ARIA (Strophe 1) — Orfeo

0:00 [17] Florid singing, joined by violin flourishes, above *basso continuo* — Possente spirto e formidabil nume, / Senza cui far passaggio a l'altra riva / Alma da corpo sciolta in van presume. — Powerful spirit and formidable god, without whom no soul, deprived of body, may presume to pass to Hades' shore.

1:30 Instrumental postlude played by *basso continuo* and two solo violins

ARIA (Strophe 2) — Orfeo

1:55 Florid singing continues, joined now by cornettos, above *basso continuo* — Non viv'io, no, che poi di vita è priva / Mia cara sposa, il cor non è più meco, / E senza cor com'esser può ch'io viva? — I live no longer, since now my dear spouse is deprived of life, I have no heart within me, and without a heart how can I still be alive?

3:03 Instrumental postlude played by *basso continuo* and two solo cornettos

Listen to streaming music in an Active Listening Guide, available on the text website.

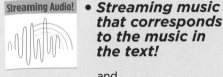

▲ With premium website access, you have the option to explore the online **Active Listening Guides**. These guides visually demonstrate what you are hearing and also include listening quizzes.

Listening EXERCISE 16

Strozzi
"VOGLIO MORIRE"

5 — 1/18   2 — 1/7

To take this Listening Exercise online and receive feedback or email answers to your instructor, go to the text website.

Most early Baroque vocal music consists of arias and recitatives accompanied by a *basso continuo* and, in some cases, other instruments as well. In this recording of the aria "Voglio morire," which begins Barbara Strozzi's cantata *L'amante segreto*, the continuo is played by a cello, harpsichord, and guitar. The cello plays the short bass line again and again, thereby forming a *basso ostinato*. The harpsichord and guitar fill out the texture, offering chordal support above this bass. The simplicity of this example allows both *basso continuo* and *basso ostinato* to be heard with unusual clarity.

1. (0:00–0:04) The *basso ostinato* takes about four seconds to play. How many notes are there in the pattern?
   a. two   b. four   c. six

2. (0:00–0:04) How many chords are there in the pattern?
   a. two   b. four   c. six

3. (0:00–0:18) At the beginning of the aria, the *basso continuo* sounds alone. How many presentations of the pattern occur before the voice enters?
   a. three   b. five   c. seven

4. (0:19–0:35) Now the voice enters and the pattern continues; how many times is the pattern heard?
   a. three   b. five   c. seven

5. (0:36–0:43) In this passage, the *basso ostinato* suddenly changes—one or more notes are

added to the bass pattern. Now how many notes are in the pattern?
   a. three   b. five   c. seven

6. (0:44–end) From here to the end of the aria, does the bass pattern ever change?
   a. yes   b. no

7. The rate of harmonic change (the amount of time between each chord) in this aria is which?
   a. regular   b. irregular

Now we focus on issues other than the *basso continuo* and the *basso ostinato*.

8. Which of the three continuo instruments improvises elaborate decorations?
   a. guitar   b. cello   c. harpsichord

9. An aria, as opposed to recitative, is usually characterized by luxuriant singing in which the voice occasionally breaks out into a melisma (one syllable sung to many notes). In this aria, when do the melismas occur?
   a. toward the beginning
   b. toward the end

10. In many arias, the singer is accompanied by instruments in addition to the *basso continuo*, most often the violins. Do violins accompany the voice in this aria?
   a. yes   b. no

▲ Wright's original and detailed in-text **Listening Exercises** help you refine your listening skills.

OPERA IN LONDON

Opera originated in Italy during the early seventeenth century. From there it spread over the Alps to German-speaking countries, to France, and eventually to England. But owing to the strong tradition of theater in England, epitomized by productions of Shakespeare's plays, the English had a love-hate affair with opera: sometimes they wanted to hear it, and sometimes they did not. The first

---

Premium Website access!

If your text purchase included a printed or an instant online access code for either title's premium website, you will receive:

- **Streaming music that corresponds to the music in the text!**

and

- **The premium website featuring:**

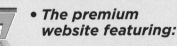

▶ Active Listening Guides (now redesigned to include listening quizzes and streaming music, available completely online with no need for either downloads or CDs!)

Listen to streaming music in an Active Listening Guide, available on the text website.

RECITATIVE

0:04 Simple recitative - accompanied by *basso continuo* of bass lute
Rassembra l'infelice un muto sasso
(The unhappy one resembles a mute stone)

recitative
musically heightened speech, often used in an opera, oratorio, or cantata to report dramatic action and advance the plot

continuo
a small ensemble of at least two

climbing to heaven causes flourish in high register — O, se ciò negherammi empio destino, / Rimarrò teco in compagnia di morte. — And, if cruel destiny would... / I will remain with you in death.

3:02 Growing conviction portrayed by chromatic ascent in vocal line — Addio terra, addio cielo e sole, addio. — Farewell earth, farewell heaven... farewell!

...rotti a riveder le stelle, — I will transport you to see...

iAudio Le...
Musical Fo...
Musical St...
to the Orc...
instrumen...

Listen to streaming music in an Active Listening Guide, available on the text website.

Listening to

WESTERN

MUSIC

Listening to WESTERN MUSIC

6th edition

CRAIG WRIGHT

Yale University

SCHIRMER
CENGAGE Learning™

Australia • Brazil • Japan • Korea • Mexico • Singapore • Spain • United Kingdom • United States

SCHIRMER
CENGAGE Learning

Listening to Western Music, Sixth Edition
Craig Wright

Publisher: Clark Baxter
Senior Development Editor: Sue Gleason
Assistant Editor: Nell Pepper
Editorial Assistant: Ashley Bargende
Senior Media Editor: Wendy Constantine
Marketing Manager: Mark Haynes
Marketing Coordinator: Josh Hendrick
Marketing Communications Manager:
   Heather Baxley
Senior Content Project Manager: Michael Lepera
Senior Print Buyer: Justin Palmeiro
Permissions Editor: Roberta Broyer
Text Designer: Marsha Cohen/Parallelogram
   Graphics
Photo Manager: Mandy Groszko
Photo Researcher: Abigail Baxter
Cover Image: Josef Danhauser (1805–1845). *Franz Liszt at the Piano.* 1840. Oil on canvas, 119 x 167 cm. Photo: Juergen Liepe. Nationalgalerie, Staatliche Museen zu Berlin, Berlin, Germany. © Bildarchiv Preussischer Kulturbesitz/Art Resource, NY.
Compositor: Thompson Type, Inc.

For product information and technology assistance, contact us at **Cengage Learning Customer & Sales Support, 1-800-354-9706**

For permission to use material from this text or product, submit all requests online at **www.cengage.com/permissions**. Further permissions questions can be emailed to **permissionrequest@cengage.com**.

Library of Congress Control Number: 2010921225

ISBN-13: 978-1-4390-8347-5
ISBN-10: 1-4390-8347-9

Schirmer
20 Channel Center Street
Boston, MA 02210
USA

Cengage Learning is a leading provider of customized learning solutions with office locations around the globe, including Singapore, the United Kingdom, Australia, Mexico, Brazil and Japan. Locate your local office at **international.cengage.com/region**.

Cengage Learning products are represented in Canada by Nelson Education, Ltd.

For your course and learning solutions, visit **www.cengage.com**.
Purchase any of our products at your local college store or at our preferred online store **www.CengageBrain.com**.

Printed in the United States of America
1 2 3 4 5 6 7 14 13 12 11 10

PART V

ROMANTICISM, 1820–1900 | 228

PART VI

MODERN AND POSTMODERN ART MUSIC, 1880–PRESENT | 318

PART IV

THE CLASSICAL PERIOD, 1750–1820 | 152

PART V

ROMANTICISM, 1820–1900 | 228

PART VI

Modern and Postmodern Art Music, 1880–Present | 318

31 IMPRESSIONISM AND EXOTICISM | 320

ABOUT THE AUTHOR

Craig M. WRIGHT received his Bachelor of Music degree at the Eastman School of Music in 1966 and his Ph.D. in musicology from Harvard University in 1972. He began his teaching career at the University of Kentucky and for the past thirty-six years has been teaching at Yale University, where he is currently the Henry L. and Lucy G. Moses Professor of Music. At Yale, Wright's courses include his perennially popular introductory course "Listening to Music," which is now part of the offerings of Open Yale Courses, and his selective seminar "Exploring the Nature of Genius." He is the author of numerous scholarly books and articles on composers ranging from Leoninus to Bach. Wright has also been the recipient of many awards, including a Guggenheim Fellowship, the Einstein and Kinkeldey Awards of the American Musicological Society, and the Dent Medal of the International Musicological Society. In 2004, he was awarded the honorary degree Doctor of Humane Letters from the University of Chicago. In addition to *Listening to Music* and *Listening to Western Music*, Wright has also published *Music in Western Civilization* (Schirmer Cengage Learning, 2010) with coauthor Bryan Simms. He is presently at work on a volume entitled *Mozart's Brain: Exploring the Nature of Genius.*

*L*istening to Western music is not just the title of this book and the theme of the painting incorporated in its cover. The aim of this textbook is to teach students to listen to Western classical music so that they, too, might become transfixed by its expressive power. As Josef Danhauser's scene on the cover suggests, music can be the most compelling of the arts.

Most music appreciation textbooks treat music not as an opportunity for personal engagement through listening but as a history of music. Students are required to learn something of the technical workings of music (what a tonic chord is, for example) and specific facts (how many symphonies Beethoven wrote), but are not asked to become personally engaged in the act of listening to music. What listening there is, is passive, not active. *Listening to Western Music*, however, is different. Here, students are encouraged—indeed required—to become active participants in a musical dialogue through a variety of means both within the covers of this book and beyond them.

*N*EW TO THIS EDITION

Although the goals of active listening have not changed, this edition of *Listening to Western Music* incorporates several significant improvements:

- For the first time, in this edition the complete musical selections and their Active Listening Guides (see below) are available *streaming* on the text's premium website.
- Twenty musical works are new to the Sixth Edition, spanning the centuries from Hildegard of Bingen to Prokofiev.
- Many more examples from popular culture enliven the entire text.
- Musical selections now have more conventional titling, employing original-language titles where those are more commonly used.
- Chapter 1's introduction to listening has been thoroughly rewritten, including additional exploration of the neurobiology of listening.
- Chapter 2 (Rhythm) provides expanded coverage and examples of syncopation, as well as a new Listening Guide on the basics of rhythm and a new box using Rihanna's "Don't Stop the Music" to illustrate rhythm in rap, hip hop, and current dance music.
- Chapter 3 (Melody) has a new Listening Guide introducing melody, added coverage of intervals, and new examples of antecedent and consequent phrases.
- Chapter 4 (Harmony) provides new coverage of cadences, including a new Listening Guide, and illustrates chord changes with a new, doo-wop example: "Duke of Earl."
- Chapter 5 (Dynamics and Color) includes a new section that explains why the different musical instruments sound the way they do.

- Chapter 6 (Musical Texture and Form) has rearranged homophony and polyphony to proceed more logically from simple to complex.
- Chapter 7 (Musical Style) is now abbreviated, providing all of the text's Checklists of Musical Style as interactive multimedia on the text's premium website.
- Chapter 8 provides expanded coverage of medieval musical instruments.
- The date separating the Middle Ages and the Renaissance has been changed to 1450.
- Chapter 9 features an additional selection of Renaissance dance music—a pavane and galliard.
- Chapter 14 now includes a fine example of a pastoral aria from an oratorio: Handel's "He Shall Feed His Flock," from *Messiah*.
- Chapter 17 provides further clarification of the difference between sonata and sonata–allegro form, as well as of the details of the form itself.
- Chapter 18 expands upon the definition of theme and variations, and introduces the concept of the Western canon.
- Chapter 21 includes a new box: "Beethoven and the Beatles: Breaking the Rules."
- Chapter 22 includes a new box: "Shelley and the Romantic Poets."
- Chapter 24 focuses on growth in the number and variety of instruments included in the Western symphony orchestra, through the program music of Berlioz and Tchaikovsky, as well as the ballet music of Tchaikovsky.
- Chapter 29 now showcases, in part, Dvořák's Symphony "From the New World."
- Chapter 30 focuses on the late Romantic concerto and symphony, featuring Brahms's Violin Concerto in D major and Mahler's Symphony No. 4.
- Chapter 31 now covers the mutually influential late-nineteenth-century movements of Impressionism and exoticism.

PEDAGOGICAL AIDS

Listening Exercises

Listening to Western Music is the only music appreciation text on the market that includes detailed Listening Exercises within the book, immediately following the appropriate musical selections. Using these, students will embrace hundreds of specific passages of music and make critical decisions about them. The exercises begin by developing basic listening skills—recognizing rhythmic patterns, distinguishing major keys from minor, and differentiating various kinds of textures. The exercises then move on to entire pieces in which students are required to become participants in an artistic exchange—the composer communicating with the listener, and the listener reacting over a long span of time. Ultimately, equipped with these newly developed listening skills, students will move comfortably to the concert hall, listening to classical and popular music with greater confidence and enjoyment. Although this book is for the present course, its aim is to prepare students for a lifetime of musical listening pleasure.

The instructor's enjoyment of the Sixth Edition has been enhanced as well. It is now possible for students to take the Listening Exercises online at the text's premium website (see below), to have them graded electronically, and to return the results to the instructor's electronic gradebook. Instructors will find additional drills and self-tests on the premium website.

Listening Guides

In addition to the Listening Exercises, more than 90 Listening Guides appear regularly throughout the text to help the novice enjoy extended musical compositions. Many of the Listening Guides and Listening Exercises in this edition have been reformatted to make them easier to follow.

Within each guide are an introduction to the piece's genre, form, meter, and texture, as well as a "time log" that allows the listener to follow along as the piece unfolds. The discussion in the text, the Listening Exercises, and the Listening Guides have been carefully coordinated, minute by minute, second by second, with the CDs. More important, for the first time in this edition the complete musical selections and their Active Listening Guides (see below) are available *streaming* on the text's premium website.

Because many more pieces now contain internal tracks to facilitate navigation to important points in the composition, the timings in both Listening Guides and Listening Exercises have been carefully keyed to help students find and keep their place. The sample Listening Guide on page xxii illustrates how these keys work. First, gold and blue disc symbols representing the 5-CD and 2-CD sets, respectively, appear at the upper right of the Listening Guide and Listening Exercise. Brown discs containing the word "intro" represent the Introduction to Listening CD bound into the textbook, and special 💿 symbols represent a separate Popular and Global Music CD. The first number below each symbol and before the slash indicates the appropriate CD number, and the number or numbers after the slash indicate track or tracks. (Intro and Popular/Global CD references contain only track numbers.) Students can thus choose the correct CD and locate the tracks that they need, regardless of which CD set they own. Within all the Listening Guides and the multitrack Listening Exercises, track number reminders appear in small squares, color-coded in gold for the 5-CD set, in blue for the 2-CD set, and in brown for the Intro and Popular/Global CDs.

For pieces with multiple tracks, there are two timing columns. Those on the left are total elapsed times from the beginning to the end of the piece. Those to the right of the track number reminders and next to the comments are the timings that appear on a CD player's or computer media player's display.

Over 150 additional Supplementary Listening Guides, including those from previous editions, may be downloaded from the text website and the instructor's PowerLecture.

The numbers in the discs indicate the 5-CD set and the 2-CD set. The numbers beneath them tell, first, the specific CD number within that set and, second, the appropriate tracks on that CD. Here, one needs CD 2, tracks 18–19, from the 5-CD set, or CD 1, tracks 21–22, from the 2-CD set.

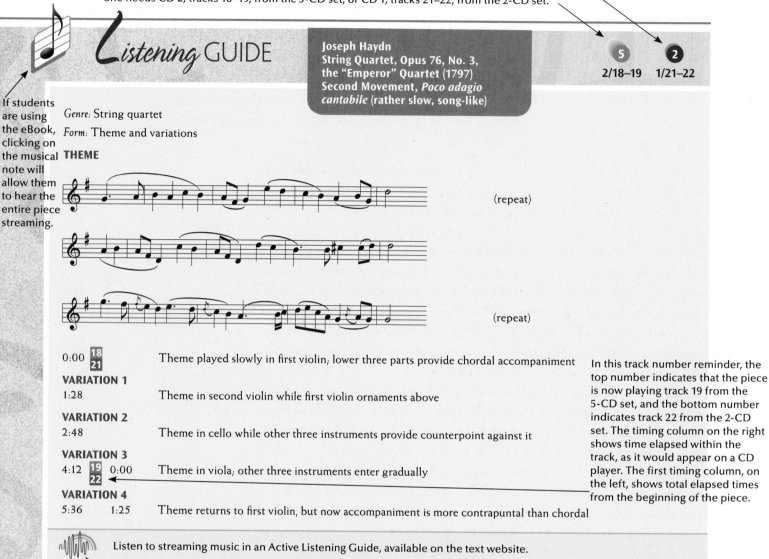

If students are using the eBook, clicking on the musical note will allow them to hear the entire piece streaming.

Listening GUIDE

**Joseph Haydn
String Quartet, Opus 76, No. 3,
the "Emperor" Quartet (1797)
Second Movement, *Poco adagio
cantabile* (rather slow, song-like)**

5 2/18–19   **2** 1/21–22

Genre: String quartet
Form: Theme and variations

THEME

(repeat)

(repeat)

0:00 **18/21**		Theme played slowly in first violin; lower three parts provide chordal accompaniment
VARIATION 1		
1:28		Theme in second violin while first violin ornaments above
VARIATION 2		
2:48		Theme in cello while other three instruments provide counterpoint against it
VARIATION 3		
4:12 **19/22**	0:00	Theme in viola; other three instruments enter gradually
VARIATION 4		
5:36	1:25	Theme returns to first violin, but now accompaniment is more contrapuntal than chordal

In this track number reminder, the top number indicates that the piece is now playing track 19 from the 5-CD set, and the bottom number indicates track 22 from the 2-CD set. The timing column on the right shows time elapsed within the track, as it would appear on a CD player. The first timing column, on the left, shows total elapsed times from the beginning of the piece.

Listen to streaming music in an Active Listening Guide, available on the text website.

Each Listening Guide reminds students that they may watch and listen to the music streaming in an Active Listening Guide on the text's premium website. If they are using the eBook, clicking on the waveform to the left allows them to play the Active Listening Guide directly from their book.

ANCILLARIES FOR STUDENTS

Introduction to Listening CD

Automatically packaged with each new copy of the book, and not sold separately, this CD contains all of the music discussed in Chapters 1–7 on the elements of music, as well as an interactive guide to instruments of the orchestra, which presents the instruments and then tests students' ability to recognize the instruments by themselves and in various combinations. Following a demonstration of the various instruments and instrumental techniques, students may undertake a series of graduated Listening Exercises (in Chapter 5) that test their ability to recognize the instruments.

2-CD Set

This includes a core repertoire of music discussed in the book. On the text's premium website, each selection may also be streamed by itself or in the context of an Active Listening Guide that demonstrates visually what students hear.

5-CD Set

This includes all of the classical Western repertoire discussed in the book. On the text's premium website, each selection may also be streamed by itself or in the context of an Active Listening Guide that demonstrates visually what students hear.

Active Listening Guides

The Active Listening Guides, now completely redesigned, feature full-color interactive and streaming listening guides for every selection on the CD sets, along with listening quizzes and background information. CDs or downloads are no longer required for the Active Listening Guides to work.

Website

The redesigned premium website (www.cengage.com/music/wright/ltm6e), prepared in part by Timothy Roden, of Ohio Wesleyan University, offers several challenging and interesting features. First, it allows for chapter-by-chapter self-study in which students can take a quiz to explore their knowledge of the topics presented in the chapter, as well as study appropriate flashcards, topic summaries, and demonstrations.

In addition, the website contains interactive versions of the text's Listening Exercises; a video of a performance of Britten's *Young Person's Guide to the Orchestra*, in whole and by instrument families; video demonstrations of keyboard instruments; a link to the Active Listening Guides; fifteen iAudio lessons on difficult musical concepts; an interactive music timeline; a checklist of musical styles with integrated musical styles comparisons; musical elements, genres, and forms tutorials; Supplementary Listening Guide pdfs for music beyond that provided with the text; classroom management for instructors; and a free link to a complete online course taught at Yale by the author and featuring in-class performances and demonstrations. In addition, marginal cues in the text direct readers to related online playlists from iTunes, Rhapsody, and YouTube—all housed on the website.

eBook

Also available is a multimedia-enabled eBook, featuring page design identical to the print book and links to all premium website media content, including streaming music and Active Listening Guides.

FOR INSTRUCTORS

PowerLecture with ExamView® and JoinIn on TurningPoint®

This includes the Instructor's Manual, Supplementary Listening Guides, ExamView® computerized testing, JoinIn on TurningPoint®, and Microsoft® PowerPoint® slides with lecture outlines and images that can be used as offered, or customized by importing personal lecture slides or other material. ExamView allows instructors to create, deliver, and customize tests and study guides (both print and online) in minutes with its easy-to-use assessment and tutorial system. It offers both a Quick Test Wizard and an Online Test Wizard that guide instructors step-by-step through the process of creating tests (up to 250 questions using up to 12 question types), while its "what you see is what you get" capability allows users to see the test they are creating on the screen exactly as it will print or display online. ExamView's complete word-processing capabilities allow users to enter an unlimited number of new questions or edit existing questions. The Test Bank now includes listening items, for which a bank of clips are available for instructors and/or students to download from the text website. JoinIn content (for use with most "clicker" systems) delivers instant classroom assessment and active learning opportunities such as in-class polling, attendance taking, and quizzing.

WebTutor™ for Blackboard and WebCT

This web-based teaching and learning tool is rich with study and mastery tools, communication tools, and course content. Use WebTutor™ to provide virtual office hours, post syllabi, set up threaded discussions, track student progress with the quizzing material, and more. For students, WebTutor™ offers real-time access to a full array of study tools, including flashcards (with audio), practice quizzes, online tutorials, and web links. Instructors can customize the content by uploading images and other resources, adding web links, or creating their own practice materials. WebTutor™ also provides rich communication tools, including a course calendar, asynchronous discussion, "real-time" chat, and an integrated email system. Visit webtutor.cengage.com to learn more.

ACKNOWLEDGMENTS

Part of the fun of teaching music appreciation comes from discussing with colleagues ways in which to introduce classical music to students who know little about music. What can students be reasonably expected to hear? What is the best terminology to use? Profs. Keith Polk (University of New Hampshire) and Tilden Russell (Southern Connecticut State University) have gently taken me to task for using the term *ternary form* where *rounded binary* is more correct; they are right, yet for fear of overloading the beginning student with too many new formal concepts, here I simplify and call both rounded binary and ternary forms just ternary. I am, nevertheless, grateful for their continuing support and attention to matters of detail. So, too, I am indebted to Profs. Anne Robertson and Robert Kendrick of the University of Chicago for their input on matters large and small. Six former students—Profs. David Metzer (University of British Columbia), Jess Tyre (SUNY at Potsdam), Marica Tacconi (Pennsylvania State University), Lorenzo Candelaria (University of Texas, Austin), Laura Nash (Fairfield University), and Nathan Link (Centre College)—continue to provide me with valuable criticism and suggestions. Several colleagues made suggestions for specific improvements in content, for which I am grateful, namely Profs. James Ladewig (University of Rhode Island), Carlo Caballero (University of Colorado, Boulder), Bryan Simms (University of Southern California), and James Sinclair (Orchestra New England). Finally, Prof. Timothy Roden (Ohio Wesleyan University), the author of much of the web materials, Instructor's Manual, and Test Bank, has corrected errors and saved me from myself on numerous occasions.

This edition has had the additional benefit of a stalwart editorial advisory board, who made themselves available to answer questions both large and small throughout the development of the book. They have my utmost gratitude:

Anthony J. Alms
College of New Jersey
Anthony DeQuattro
Quinnipiac University
Melissa Derechailo
Wayne State College
Mark Heidel
University of Iowa
David Johansen
Southeast Louisiana University
Charles Larkowski
Wright State University
Seow-Chin Ong
University of Louisville
Lynda Paul
Yale University
Heather Platt
Ball State University
Thomas J. Tacke
Arizona Western College
Scott Warfield
University of Central Florida

The following reviewers also evaluated material or provided helpful information during the writing of this book:
Adeline Bethany, *Cabrini College*; D. E. Bussineau-King, *University of the Incarnate Word*; Andrew Byrne, *Australian Music Center*; Ann B. Caldwell, *Georgia College and State University*; Cheong L. Chuah, *Cerro Cosso Community College*; Kyle Cheong Chuah, *Los Medanos College*; Ginger Covert, *Colla Modesto Junior College*; Joseph Darby, *Keene State College*; Willis Delony, *Louisiana State University*; Hollie Duvall, *Westmoreland County Community College*; Harry Faulk, *Fairmont State College*; Fenton G. Fly, *Alabama State University*; Holly J. Gaines, *Ursinus College*; Nancy M. Gamso, *Ohio Wesleyan University*; Cliff Ganus, *Harding University*; Benjamin K. Gish, *Walla Walla College*; Stephanie B. Graber, *University of Wisconsin, Stout*; Larry N. Graham, *Valencia Community College*; David Grayson, *University of Minnesota*; Mary-Jo Grenfell, *Salem State College*; Patricia L. Hales, *Purdue University, Calumet*; Robert Hansel, *University of Tennessee, Chattanooga*; Patricia Harden, *Rockingham Community College*; Tabitha Heavner, *Central Connecticut State University*; Marymal L. Holmes, *Bowie State University*; David Lee Jackson, *Baylor University*; Tido Janssen, *Hardin-Simmons University*; Benjamin M. Korstvedt, *University of St. Thomas*; Walter Kreiszig, *University of Saskatchewan*; Jonathan Kulp, *University of Louisiana, Lafayette*; Mark Latham, *Butte College*; Bernard C. Lemoine, *Mary Washington College*; Gary Lewis, *Midwestern State University*; Ed Macan, *College of the Redwoods*; Mary Macklem, *University of Central Florida*; Michael Moss, *Southern Connecticut State University*; Sharon H. Nelson, *Wright State University*; Mustak Zafer Ozgen, *Baruch College*; Diane M. Paige, *University of California, Santa Barbara*; Linda Pohly, *Ball State University*; Thomas C. Polett, *Culver-Stockton College*; Julia M. Quick, *South Carolina State University*; Ronald Rabin, *University of Michigan*; Daniel Ratelle, *San Diego Mesa College*; Laurie A. Reese, *Lebanon Community College*; Rebecca Ringer, *Collin County Community College*; Dan Robbins, *Truckee Meadows Community College*; Steven Roberson, *Butler University*; Karl Schmidt, *Towson University*; Christine Larson Seitz, *Indiana University, South Bend*; Richard Shillea, *Fairfield University*; John Sinclair, *Rollins College*; Jayme Stayer, *Owens Community College*; Lawrence Stomberg, *University of Delaware*; Larry Stuckenholtz, *St. Louis Community College*; Janet L. Sturman, *University of Arizona*; Gary R. Sudano, *Purdue University*; Jerry Ulrich, *Georgia Institute of Technology*; Timothy P. Urban, *Rutgers University*; Melva Villard, *Louisiana State University at Alexandria*; Susan Weiss, *Johns Hopkins University*; Carolyn Wilson, *Chipola College*; Graham Wood, *Coker College*; Barbara Young, *University of Wisconsin, Eau Claire*; Annette H. Zalanowski, *Pennsylvania State University, Altoona*; Ray H. Ziegler, *Salisbury State University*

I have also benefited from the help and good will of the staff of the Yale Music Library: Kendall Crilly, librarian; and Suzanne Lovejoy, Richard Boursy, and Evan Heater. Karl Schrom, record librarian at Yale, has been a source of good advice regarding the availability and quality of recordings for twenty years. The engineering of the audio was accomplished at the Yale Recording Studio by the capable hands of Jason Robins. And graduate student Nora Renka provided valuable assistance in checking the accuracy of proofs.

As always, it has been a privilege to work with publisher Clark Baxter and his experienced team at Schirmer Cengage Learning—Sue Gleason, Nell Pepper, Mark Haynes, Ashley Bargende, Wendy Constantine, Michael Lepera, and Tom Briggs—as well as Tom and Lisa Smialek, original developers of the Active Listening tools, and especially Tom Laskey, Director of A&R, Custom Marketing Group, at SONY. My heartiest thanks to all of you!

Finally, I thank my wife (Sherry Dominick) and four children (Evan, Andrew, Stephanie, and Chris), who did their best to keep the paterfamilias aware of popular culture, musical and otherwise.

INTRODUCTION TO LISTENING

LISTENING TO MUSIC

Why do you listen to music? What does it do for you? What do you hope to get out of the experience? Given a moment of free time, most people don't open a newspaper or a book of poetry; they turn on their iPods. Want proof of the allure of music? Next time you're riding on a bus, a train, or the subway, look around; you'll find that about twice as many people are listening to music as are reading. This is true pretty much everywhere around the developed world. But why does music have such universal appeal?

Simply said, music has power. "Music delights the ears, uplifts the mind, arouses fighters to go to war, strengthens the weak, and disarms bandits!" A medieval monk, John of St. Gall, said this about music nearly a thousand years ago, and little has changed since (except perhaps the part about the bandits). Music moves us, and not only to dance. We are moved at a parade more when the military band strikes up a tune than with the passage of silent troops. We tear up at weddings and funerals, not at the sight of the beautiful bride or the draped casket, but when the wedding processional or the funeral dirge begins. We get scared at horror films, not when the images become graphic, but when the music starts to get ominous. (If you want not to be scared, don't cover your eyes, plug your ears!)

For thousands of years, governments and institutions, both public and private, have tried to use the power of music to control our behavior. Think of the four-note "rally motive" played on the loudspeaker at professional sports events to get the crowd and home team energized. Think of the slow, calming classical music played in airports (the airlines don't want Ludacris or Metallica piped in during flight delays). And did you know that the state of Arizona recently passed a law banning the playing of powerful Beethoven symphonies on car stereos because it makes drivers too aggressive? (Not true, of course, but you get the point.) Sound perception is the most powerful sense we possess. A sudden noise can make us jump out of our seats. And organized sound—music—profoundly affects the way we feel and behave.

HEARING MUSIC

Briefly defined, **music** is the rational organization of sounds and silences passing through time. Tones must be arranged in some consistent, logical, and (usually) pleasing way before we can call these sounds "music" instead of just noise. A singer or an instrumentalist generates music literally by disturbing the environment, by creating vibrations that travel through the air as sound waves. Sound waves radiate out in a circle from their source, carrying with them two types of essential information: pitch and loudness. The speed of vibration within the sound wave determines what we perceive as high and low pitches; and the width (or amplitude) of the wave reflects its volume. When the music reaches our brain, that organ tells us how we should feel and respond to the sound. We tend to hear low, slow tones as relaxing, and high, rapid ones as

@

Watch a video of Craig Wright's Open Yale Course class sessions 1 and 2, "Introduction" and "Introduction to Instruments and Musical Genres," at the text website.

tension filled. If the sound waves contain strong, regular pulses, we might start to tap our foot or move in synch with the pulse or beat—the groove.

   Today the vast majority of music that we hear is not "live" music but recorded sound. Sound recording began in the 1870s with Thomas Edison's phonograph machine, which played what we now call "vinyl," or records. During the 1930s magnetic tape recorders appeared and grew in popularity until the early 1990s, when they were superseded by a new technology, digital recording. In digital recording all the components of musical sound—pitch, tone color, duration, volume, and more—are analyzed thousands of times per second, and that information is instantly stored as sequences of binary numbers. With equal speed this digital data can be reconverted to electrical impulses that are then changed back into analog sound that is amplified by speakers or earphones (Fig. 1-1). Most recorded music now is no longer stored and sold on discs (CDs) but distributed as MP3 files over the Internet.

FIGURE 1–1

A student listening to an MP3 file on an iPod.

MUSIC IN YOUR BRAIN

Given all the love songs in the world, we might think music is an affair of the heart. But both love and music are domains of a far more complex vital organ: the brain (Fig. 1-2). When sound waves reach us, our inner ear transforms them into electrical signals that go to various parts of the brain, each analyzing a particular component of the sound: pitch, color, loudness, duration,

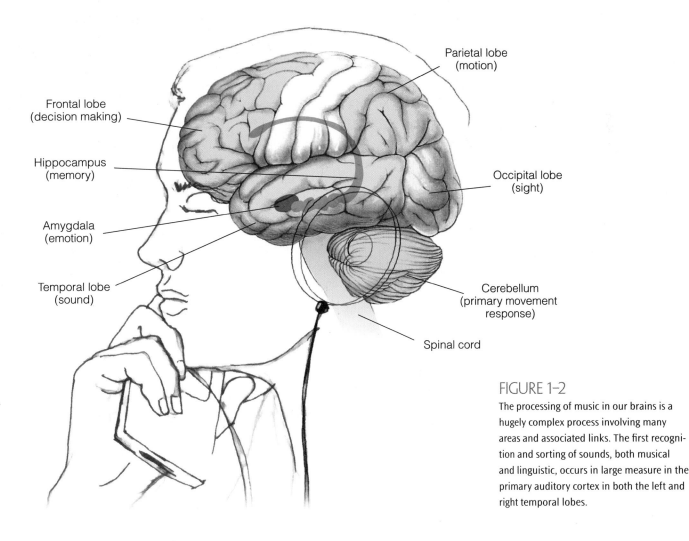

Frontal lobe
(decision making)

Hippocampus
(memory)

Amygdala
(emotion)

Temporal lobe
(sound)

Parietal lobe
(motion)

Occipital lobe
(sight)

Cerebellum
(primary movement
response)

Spinal cord

FIGURE 1–2

The processing of music in our brains is a hugely complex process involving many areas and associated links. The first recognition and sorting of sounds, both musical and linguistic, occurs in large measure in the primary auditory cortex in both the left and right temporal lobes.

@

To learn more about music and the brain, see a video of "Music and the Mind" in the YouTube playlist on the text website.

direction of source, relation to music we've already heard, and so on. Most processing of sounds (music as well as language) takes place in the temporal lobe. If we are imagining how the next line of a song will go, that decision is usually reached in the frontal lobe. If we are playing an instrument, we engage the motor center (parietal lobe) to move our fingers and the visual center (occipital lobe) to read the notes. As the music proceeds, our brain constantly updates the information it receives, hundreds of times per second. Associative neurons instantly integrate all the data into a single perception of sound.

How music makes us feel—happy or sad, energetic or relaxed—is determined partly by another part of the brain, the amygdala, and by other factors as well. Neurobiologists have observed increased levels of the chemical dopamine in the brain when pleasing music is heard, just as when, say, we eat chocolate. "It's not my fault that I like country music; it just sends a rush of dopamine to the part of my brain that controls emotion," your author confesses. Oddly, then, music alters the way we feel just as might a chemical substance, such as a candy bar, a medicine, or a drug. We can acquire the mechanism for a "mood-enhancing experience," it seems, either over the counter or over the Internet.

Have you ever had an old melody suddenly pop into your head, or had a really annoying tune get stuck there? Of course; it happens to us all. Errant data coursing around the hippocampus may be to blame! Although scientists are uncertain exactly how and where all musical data are stored, we know that music and memory are tightly linked. The songs we best remember are those from our adolescence, when hormonal changes caused sonic information to be engraved in our brain forever. Indeed, music is a powerful agent of memory. A familiar tune, whether heard externally or simply remembered, can cause us to think of the good times we have had or the loved ones we have lost. Therapy for Alzheimer's patients, who do not respond to verbal cues, now includes musical stimulation as a way to unlock their past experiences. The chance to relive our lives through music is another reason we choose to put on headphones.

LISTENING TO *WHOSE* MUSIC?

Popular Music

Most people prefer **popular music,** the music of all the people. Pop CDs and downloads outsell classical recordings by about twenty to one. But why are young people in particular attracted to popular music? Here are a few responses culled from a recent survey of one hundred college students. See if any of these answers resonate with your own experience:

- Patrick: "I use [popular] music to change my mood—to calm myself or focus."
- Rebecca: "Actually, I listen to [popular] music to avoid doing other types of work; it stimulates some parts of my brain while simultaneously relaxing other parts that may be exhausted."
- Amanda: "I hope its groove will drive me or its beauty will center me in some way. Or try to sing along with friends."
- Henry: "It synthesizes and clarifies the emotion that I already feel inside myself."
- Julio: "It's fun and I enjoy it."
- Rachel: "It allows me to share a spiritual and physical experience with fellow human beings."
- Sarah: "Decompression."

Mood enhancement, relaxation, focus, fun, bonding with friends—these seem to be the principal attractions of popular music. But what about classical music (Fig. 1-3)? What does it do for us, and what's the difference between popular and classical music?

Classical Music

Most of the music discussed in this book is what we call "classical" music, sometimes referred to as "art" music because a particular set of skills is needed to perform and appreciate it. **Classical music** is often regarded as "old" music, written by "dead white men." But this isn't entirely true: no small amount of it has been written by women, and many art composers, of both sexes, are very much alive and well today. In truth, however, much of the classical music we hear—the music of Bach, Beethoven, and Brahms, for example—*is* old. That is why, in part, it is called "classical." We refer to clothes, furniture, and cars as "classics" because they have timeless qualities of expression, proportion, and balance. So, too, we give the name "classical" to music with these same qualities, music that has endured the test of time.

Given the mass appeal of popular music, why would anyone *choose* to listen to classical music? To find out, National Public Radio (NPR) recently commissioned a survey of regular listeners of classical music. Summarized briefly below, in order of importance, are the reasons expressed by classical listeners:

- Classical music relieves stress and helps the listener to relax.
- Classical music helps "center the mind," allowing the listener to concentrate.
- Classical music provides a vision of a better world, a refuge of beauty and majesty in which we pass beyond the limits of our material existence.
- Classical music offers the opportunity to learn: about music, about history, and about people.

Oddly, except for the last response, the reasons for listening to classical music turn out to be very much the same as those for listening to popular music. But let's examine how classical music differs from popular music.

Classical Music and Popular Music Compared

Many cultures have their own styles of classical or art music—the much-respected classical music of China, Indian, and Japan, for example, dates back many centuries. Some cultures also have their own native brand of popular music, such as highlife, which emerged in the 1900s in Ghana, West Africa, or the more recent reggae from Jamaica. Today Western classical music is taught in conservatories in Beijing, Tokyo, and Singapore, and Western popular music, for good or for ill, has almost drowned out local popular music. But what are the essential differences between the Western classical and popular styles? Here is a brief summary:

- Classical music relies on **acoustic instruments** (whose sounds are not electronically altered), such as the trumpet, violin, and piano. Popular music often uses mechanically enhanced sounds such as those produced by electrically amplified guitars and basses, electronic synthesizers, and computers.
- Classical music relies greatly on preset written music, or musical notation, and so the work (a symphony, for example) is to some extent a "fixed entity," which will always be performed more or less the same way. Popular music relies more on oral and aural transmission, and the work can change

© Lynn Goldsmith/CORBIS

FIGURE 1–3

Classical music requires years of technical training on an instrument and knowledge of often-complicated music theory. Some musicians are equally at home in the worlds of classical and popular music. Juilliard School of Music–trained Wynton Marsalis can record a Baroque trumpet concerto one week and an album of New Orleans–style jazz the next. He has won nine Grammy awards—seven for various jazz categories and two for classical discs.

greatly from one performance to the next; never do we see performers reading from written music at a pop concert.

- Classical music is primarily, but by no means exclusively, instrumental, with meaning communicated abstractly through sound. Almost all popular music is vocal and makes use of a text, called the **lyrics,** from which the listener extracts the meaning of the music.
- In classical music the rhythmic "beat" often rests beneath the surface. Popular music foregrounds a recurring, heavy beat.
- Classical music offers the listener a chance to escape from the everyday world into a realm of abstract beauty. Popular music exists in the real world, its lyrics embracing such issues of contemporary life as love and rejection, racism and social inequality.

Why Listen to Classical Music?

Teachers of classical music sometimes use examples from the world of pop for instructional purposes—popular music may exhibit the basic elements of music in a less complex, more direct fashion. But the process can work the other way, too. Where better to learn about pop beat and rhythm, melody and harmony, and chord changes and textures than in the more challenging world of classical music? If you can learn to hear a bass line in a cantata by Bach, you will then easily hear one in a song by Kanye West!

But most important, classical music will reveal to you a brave new world of sound. The energy of a self-taught rock guitarist might be mind-boggling, but if it's real exhilaration you want, why not experience the prodigious speed and hand wizardry of a piano prodigy? Bono's band U2 has four members in it. Why not listen to the sound of sixty virtuosos all playing at once? This is what you get when the Cleveland Orchestra (or any professional orchestra, for that matter) plays a Beethoven symphony. Do you like the hot sound of Rihanna (Fenty)? Why not experience the rich, classically trained voice of the equally hot Renée (Fleming)? The power of all this music will transport you. You will hear new patterns and combinations that will transport you to far-off places, and perhaps even "blow you away." Exposure to classical music is, in fact, guaranteed to give you at least one new insight into whatever your current favorite type of music may be—whether hearing a theme from a classical opera in a classic rock song or recognizing a series of chords in a country ballad.

Classical Music All Around You

You might not think you listen to much classical music, but you do. Vivaldi concertos and Mozart symphonies are played regularly in Starbucks. Portions of Beethoven symphonies serve to animate segments of *The Simpsons;* a Puccini aria ("O mio babbino caro") sounds prominently in the best-selling video game *Grand Theft Auto,* no doubt for ironic effect. And Bizet's seductive "Habanera" from his opera *Carmen* (see Chapter 28) suggests the characters' secret intentions in a season 1 episode of *Gossip Girl.* What famous composer hasn't had one or more of his best-known works incorporated into a film score, to heighten the audience's emotional response? Similarly, classical music is employed for persuasive purposes in radio and television commercials. There it usually acts as a high-end marketing tool designed to encourage rich living: to sell a Mercedes automobile or a De Beers diamond, advertisers realize, they need Mozart, not Madonna, to create the mood.

Listen to an iAudio podcast on learning how to listen at the text website.

@

To be transported by the sound of Renée Fleming's voice as she sings Verdi's "Ave Maria" from *Otello,* see the video in the YouTube playlist on the text website.

ATTENDING A CLASSICAL CONCERT

There is no better way to experience the splendor of classical music than to attend a live concert. Compared to pop or rock concerts, however, performances of classical music can be rather staid affairs. For one thing, people dress "up," not "down": at classical events attendees wear "costumes" or "uniforms" (coat and tie, suit, or evening wear) of a very different sort than they do at, say, rock concerts (punk, grunge, or metal attire). For another, throughout the performance the classical audience sits rigidly, saying nothing to friends or performers. No one sways, dances, or sings along to the music. Only at the end of each composition does the audience express itself, clapping respectfully.

AP Images/Mark Humphrey

FIGURE 1–4

Schermerhorn Symphony Center, Nashville, Tennessee. Constructed in 2003–2006, the 1800-seat auditorium is home to the Nashville Symphony as well as concerts of pop, cabaret, choral, jazz, and blues. If that isn't enough for music lovers in Nashville, right across the street is the Country Music Hall of Fame.

But classical concerts weren't always so formal. In fact, they were more akin to professional wrestling matches. In the eighteenth century, for example, the audience talked during performances and yelled words of encouragement to the players. People clapped at the end of each movement of a symphony, and often in the middle of the movement as well. After an exceptionally pleasing performance, listeners would demand that the piece be repeated immediately in an **encore**. If, on the other hand, the audience didn't like what it heard, it might express its displeasure by throwing fruit and other debris at the stage. Our modern, more dignified classical concert was a creation of the nineteenth century (see p. 232), when the musical compositions came to be considered works of high art worthy of reverential silence.

Attending a classical concert requires familiarizing yourself with the music in advance. Nowadays this is easy. Go to YouTube and type in the titles of the pieces on the program. Enter "Beethoven Symphony 5," for example. Several recorded versions will appear, and you can compare different interpretations of the same piece. Should you need information about the history of the work and its composer, try to avoid Wikipedia, which is often unreliable. Instead, go to the more authoritative Oxford Music Online Grove Dictionary of Music (most colleges and universities have an online subscription) and search under the name of the composer.

Choosing the right seat at a concert is important, too. What is best for viewing might not be best for hearing. In some concert halls the sound sails over the front seats and settles at the back (Fig. 1-4). Often the optimal seat in terms of acoustics is at the back of the hall, in the first balcony. Sitting closer, on the other hand, allows you to watch the conductor and performers on stage. If you attend a concert of a symphony orchestra, sitting close allows you to follow the gestures that the conductor makes to the various soloists and sections of the orchestra; like a circus ringmaster, he or she turns directly to the soloist of a given moment. The conductor conveys the main ideas and the emotion of the music to the players, and they in turn communicate these themes and moods to the audience.

THE POWER OF CLASSICAL MUSIC: TWO FAMOUS BEGINNINGS

All right, let the music begin! As in all artistic media that unfold over time (music, poetry, novels, and film, for example), beginnings are crucial. If a composer, for example, doesn't capture your attention immediately, you may move on to the next track or hit the "off" button. To understand how classical music can grab and enthrall you, let's start with two famous beginnings, both of which are already well known to you.

Ludwig van Beethoven, Symphony No. 5 (1808)—Opening

The beginning of Beethoven's Symphony No. 5 is perhaps the best-known moment in all of classical music. Its "short-short-short-long" (SSSL) gesture (duh-duh-duh-DUHHH) is as much an icon of Western culture as is the "To be, or not to be" soliloquy in Shakespeare's *Hamlet*. Beethoven wrote this symphony in 1808 when he was thirty-seven and almost totally deaf (Fig. 1-5; see Chapter 21 for a biography of Beethoven). How could a deaf person write a symphony? Beethoven could do so because musicians can hear with an "inner ear," meaning that their brains can create and rework melodies without having to rely on externally generated sound. In this way the nearly deaf Beethoven fashioned a powerful thirty-minute symphony entirely inside his head.

A **symphony** is a genre, or type, of music for orchestra, divided into several independent pieces called **movements,** each possessing its own tempo and mood. A typical classical symphony will have four movements with the respective tempos of fast, slow, moderate, and fast. A symphony is played by an **orchestra,** a large ensemble of acoustic instruments such as violins, trumpets, and flutes. Although an orchestra might play a concerto, an overture, or a dance suite, historically it has played more symphonies than anything else, and for that reason is called a **symphony orchestra.** The orchestra for which Beethoven composed his fifth symphony was made up of about sixty players, including string, wind, and percussion instruments.

Beethoven begins his symphony with the musical equivalent of a powerful punch in the nose. The four-pitch rhythm (SSSL) is quick and abrupt. It is all the more startling because the music has no clear-cut beat or grounding harmony to support it. Our reaction is one of surprise, perhaps bewilderment, perhaps even fear. The brevity of the opening rhythm is typical of what we call a musical **motive,** a short, distinctive musical figure that can stand by itself. In the course of this symphony, Beethoven will repeat and reshape this opening (SSSL) motive, making it serve as the unifying theme of the entire symphony.

Having shaken, even staggered, the listener with this opening blow, Beethoven then begins to bring clarity and direction to his music. The motive sounds in rapid succession, rising stepwise in pitch, and the volume progressively increases. Beethoven uses the crescendo of sound here to suggest a continuous progression—he is taking us from point A to point B, what we call in music and film a "transition." Suddenly, the music stops: we have arrived. A French horn (a brass instrument; see p. 48) then blasts forth six pitches, as if to say, "And now for something new." Indeed, new material follows: a lovely, flowing melody played first by the strings and then by the winds. Its lyrical motion serves as a welcome contrast to the almost primitive opening

FIGURE 1–5

A portrait of Ludwig van Beethoven painted in 1818–1819 by Ferdinand Schimon (1797–1852).

motive (the musical "sucker punch"). Soon the motive reasserts itself, but it is gradually transformed into a melodic pattern that sounds more heroic than menacing, and with this Beethoven ends his opening section.

In sum, in the opening of Symphony No. 5, Beethoven shows us that his musical world includes many different feelings and states of mind, among them the fearful, the lyrical, and the heroic. When asked what the opening motive of the symphony meant, Beethoven is reported to have said, "There fate knocks at the door." In the course of all four movements of this symphony (all of which are included in the text's five-CD set), Beethoven opens the door, takes our hand, and leads us on a fateful journey that includes moments of fear, despair, and, ultimately, triumph.

Turn now to this opening section (intro /1) and to its Listening Guide below. Here you will see written music, or musical notation, representing the principal musical events. This notation may seem alien to you (the essentials of musical notation will be explained in Chapters 2 and 3). But don't panic! Millions of people enjoy classical music everyday without ever looking at a shred of written notation. For the moment simply play the music and follow along according to the minute and second counter on your player.

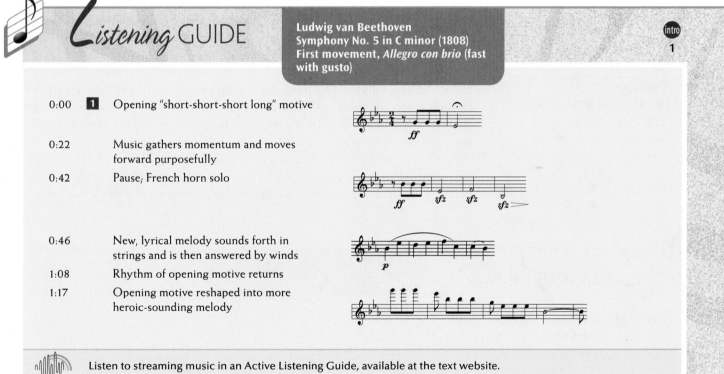

Listening GUIDE

**Ludwig van Beethoven
Symphony No. 5 in C minor (1808)
First movement, *Allegro con brio* (fast with gusto)**

intro
1

0:00	**1**	Opening "short-short-short long" motive
0:22		Music gathers momentum and moves forward purposefully
0:42		Pause; French horn solo
0:46		New, lyrical melody sounds forth in strings and is then answered by winds
1:08		Rhythm of opening motive returns
1:17		Opening motive reshaped into more heroic-sounding melody

Listen to streaming music in an Active Listening Guide, available at the text website.

Richard Strauss, Also Sprach Zarathustra (Thus Spoke Zarathustra; *1896)—Opening*

Richard Strauss's name is not a household word, as is Beethoven's. Obscuring things further, there were two important composers named Strauss. One, Johann Strauss, Jr. (1825-1899), was Austrian and is known as "the Waltz King" because he wrote mainly popular waltzes. The other, Richard Strauss (1864–1949), was German and composed primarily operas and large, spectacular compositions for orchestra called tone poems. A **tone poem** (also called a **symphonic poem**) is a one-movement work for orchestra that tries to capture in

Illustration after Cindy Davis

FIGURE 1–6

A fanciful depiction of the opening of Friedrich Nietzsche's *Also Sprach Zarathustra* with the rise of the all-powerful sun.

See a video of Strauss's theme in Kubrick's *2001* in the YouTube playlist on the text website.

music the emotions and events associated with a story, play, or personal experience. In his tone poem *Also Sprach Zarathustra*, Richard Strauss tries to depict in music the events described in a novel of that title by the German philosopher Friedrich Nietzsche (1844–1900). The hero of Nietzsche's story is the ancient Iranian prophet Zarathustra (Zoroaster), who foretells the coming of a more advanced human, a Superman who will rescue the common herd of humanity from its stupidity and sloth. (This strain in nineteenth-century German philosophy was later perverted by Adolf Hitler into the cult of a "Führer" or "Leader" and a "Master Race.") Strauss's tone poem begins with Zarathustra standing on the horizon at dawn (Fig. 1-6). This is the moment at which the sun, and the superhero, arises. As the sounds unfold, the listener senses the dawn of a new age.

While the imposing title *Also Sprach Zarathustra* may seem foreign, and the mention of German philosophy intimidating, Strauss's music is well known to you. It gained fame in the late 1960s when used as film music in Stanley Kubrick's *2001: A Space Odyssey*. Since then it has sounded forth in countless film spoofs, as well as radio and TV commercials, to convey a sense of high drama. The music begins with a low rumble, as if coming from the depths of the earth. From this darkness emerges a ray of light as four trumpets play a rising motive that Strauss called the "Nature Theme." The light suddenly falls dark—the hero has momentarily failed—and then the light rises again, ultimately to reach a stunning climax.

How do you describe a sunrise and the advent of a superhero through music? Strauss tells us. The music should ascend in pitch, get louder, grow in warmth (more instruments), and reach an impressive climax. Moreover, the leading instrument should be the trumpet, the sound of which has traditionally been associated with heroic deeds. Simple as these techniques may be, they are the means by which Strauss conveys musical meaning. The result is spectacular, overwhelming, a high point in the history of classical music. Nothing in the realm of classical or popular music can match it in terms of sheer sonic force.

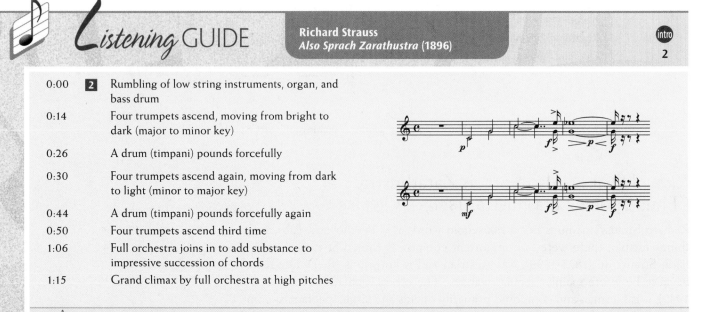

*L*istening GUIDE

Richard Strauss
***Also Sprach Zarathustra* (1896)**

intro
2

0:00	2	Rumbling of low string instruments, organ, and bass drum
0:14		Four trumpets ascend, moving from bright to dark (major to minor key)
0:26		A drum (timpani) pounds forcefully
0:30		Four trumpets ascend again, moving from dark to light (minor to major key)
0:44		A drum (timpani) pounds forcefully again
0:50		Four trumpets ascend third time
1:06		Full orchestra joins in to add substance to impressive succession of chords
1:15		Grand climax by full orchestra at high pitches

Listen to streaming music in an Active Listening Guide, available at the text website.

Listening EXERCISE 1

Musical Beginnings

This first Listening Exercise asks you to review two of the most famous "beginnings" in all of classical music.

To take this Listening Exercise online and receive feedback or email answers to your instructor, go to the text website.

Beethoven, Symphony No. 5 (1808)—Opening

1. **1** (0:00–0:05) Beethoven opens his Symphony No. 5 with the famous "short-short-short-long" motive and then immediately repeats it. Does the repetition present the motive at a higher or at a lower level of pitch?
   a. higher pitches
   b. lower pitches

2. (0:22–0:44) In this passage Beethoven constructs a musical transition that moves us from the opening motive to a more lyrical second theme. Which is true about this transition?
   a. The music seems to get faster and makes use of a crescendo.
   b. The music seems to get slower.

3. (0:38–0:42) How does Beethoven add intensity to the conclusion of the transition?
   a. A pounding drum (timpani) is added to the orchestra, and then a French horn plays a solo.
   b. A French horn plays a solo, and then a pounding drum (timpani) is added to the orchestra.

4. (0:46–1:00) Now a more lyrical new theme enters in the violins and is echoed by the winds. But has the opening motive (SSSL) really disappeared?
   a. Yes, it is no longer present.
   b. No, it can be heard above the new melody.
   c. No, it lurks below the new melody.

5. (1:17-1:26) *Student choice* (no "correct" answer): How do you feel about the end of the opening section, compared to the beginning?
   a. less anxious and more self-confident
   b. less self-confident and more anxious

Strauss, *Also Sprach Zarathustra* (1896)—Opening

6. **2** (0:00–0:13) Which is true about the opening sounds?
   a. The instruments are playing several different sounds in succession.
   b. The instruments are holding one and the same tone.

7. (0:14–0:20) When the trumpets enter and ascend, does the low, rumbling sound disappear?
   a. yes
   b. no

8. (0:14–0:22 and again at 0:30–0:40 and 0:49-0:57) When the trumpets rise, how many notes (different pitches) do they play?
   a. one
   b. two
   c. three

9. (1:18) At the very last chord, a new sound is added for emphasis—to signal that this is indeed the last chord of the climax. What instrument is making that sound?
   a. a piano
   b. an electric bass
   c. a cymbal

10. *Student choice:* You have now heard two very different musical openings, by Beethoven and Strauss. Which do you prefer? Which grabbed your attention more? Think about why.
    a. Beethoven
    b. Strauss

Key WORDS

music (2)	encore (7)	motive (8)
popular music (4)	symphony (8)	tone poem (symphonic
classical music (5)	movement (8)	poem) (9)
acoustic instrument (5)	orchestra (8)	
lyrics (6)	symphony orchestra (8)	

The materials on the text website will help you understand and pass tests on the content of this chapter. In addition, you may watch Craig Wright's own lectures at Open Yale Courses and complete this chapter's Listening Exercise interactively, as well as view Active Listening Guides and other materials that will help you succeed in this course.

2 RHYTHM

Music can be defined as sound that moves through time in an organized fashion. It involves, therefore, the interaction of time (expressed as rhythm, the subject of this chapter) and pitch (expressed as melody and harmony, the subjects of Chapters 3 and 4). Rhythm, melody, and harmony are the building blocks of music, and how they are arranged affects the color, texture, and form (the subjects of Chapters 5 and 6), and, ultimately, the meaning of every musical composition.

In discussing rhythm, melody, and harmony, we rely on terminology that developed alongside the practice of notating music. Musical notation is a system that allows us to represent sound on paper by means of special signs and symbols. In Western musical notation, the passing of time (rhythm) is represented by notes placed on a horizontal axis (moving left to right), with black (filled) notes moving more quickly than white (empty) notes. Pitch (melody and harmony) is shown on a vertical axis (top to bottom) with the higher-placed notes representing higher pitches. Example 2-1A shows low, slow sounds that become progressively higher and faster, while Example 2-1B shows the reverse:

Watch a video of Craig Wright's Open Yale Course class session 3, "Rhythm: Fundamentals," at the text website.

EXAMPLE 2–1A

EXAMPLE 2–1B

When we use musical notation, we in effect "freeze" a piece of music so that it can be reproduced exactly by performers at some later date. What is more, musical notation allows us to stop at any point. We can look at a composition as it "stands still," talk about its various parts, and learn something about how the music is put together. You can derive great pleasure from listening to music, of course, without being able to read musical notation. Indeed, musical notation is wholly absent from most musical cultures around the world. But the enjoyment of Western classical music in particular can be enhanced if you understand how this music works, and to see how it works, it helps to understand musical notation.

RHYTHM AND RHYTHMIC NOTATION

Rhythm is arguably the most fundamental element of music. Some rhythms are so recognizable that most of us don't need to hear the melody to identify the tune. Think of the opening of Beethoven's Fifth Symphony or "Happy Birthday," for instance, which are recognizable even when just clapped. The primacy of rhythm, neurobiologists believe, is caused by the fact that the body's tempo and timings are controlled largely by the cerebellum, the oldest and most primitive part of the brain (see Fig. 1-2). We have a direct, even physical, response to rhythm. We can move to it; we can dance to its pulse (Fig. 2-1).

Rhythm, in the broadest definition, is the organization of time in music. More specifically, rhythm divides time into long and short spans. It gives a profile to the pitches of a melody, just as it does to the syllables of a text, whether long (L) or short (S), as we see in the opening lines of "Every Breath You Take" by Sting and The Police:

> Every breath you take
>
> **S   S   L   L   L**
>
> Every move you make
>
> **S   S   L   L   L**

Musical rhythms are supported and clarified by a beat. The **beat** is an even pulse that divides the passing of time into equal units. It may be strongly felt, as in a waltz by Johann Strauss or a hard rock number by The Rolling Stones, or it may be only vaguely sensed (because no instrument plays it strongly), as often happens in classical music. Usually, no one instrument consistently plays the beat (except perhaps the bass drum); rather, our brains extract the beat from the mass of musical rhythms and accents we hear. But extract it we do. When we clap along with or tap our feet to music, we are reacting to what our brain says is the beat.

The beat in music is most often represented by a unit of measurement called the **quarter note** (♩), a basic duration in music. Normally, the quarter note moves along at roughly the rate of the average person's heartbeat, sometimes faster, sometimes slower. As you might suspect from its name, the quarter note is shorter in length than the half and the whole note, but longer than the eighth and the sixteenth note. These other note values account for durations that are longer or shorter than a single beat. Here are the symbols for the most-used musical notes, with an indication of how they relate to one another in length.

FIGURE 2–1

The fluid dance patterns of Michael Jackson show how rhythm can animate the body.

@

See Michael Jackson respond to and redefine the beat in the YouTube playlist on the text website.

EXAMPLE 2–2

(whole note) 𝅝 = ♩ ♩   (2 half notes = 4 beats)

      (half note) ♩ = ♩ ♩   (2 quarter notes = 2 beats)

           (quarter note) ♩ = ♪ ♪   (2 eighth notes = 1 beat)

                (eighth note) ♪ = ♪ ♪   (2 sixteenth notes = ½ beat)

To help the performer keep the beat when playing or singing, the smaller note values—specifically, those with flags on the vertical stem—are beamed, or joined together, in groups of two or four.

@

To see the power of rhythm to take control of the body, watch Christopher Walken in action in the YouTube playlist on the text website.

EXAMPLE 2–3

♩ ♪♪♪ ♪♪♪♪ becomes ♩ ♫♩ ♬

In vocal music, however, the beaming is broken when a syllable of text is placed below a note.

EXAMPLE 2-4

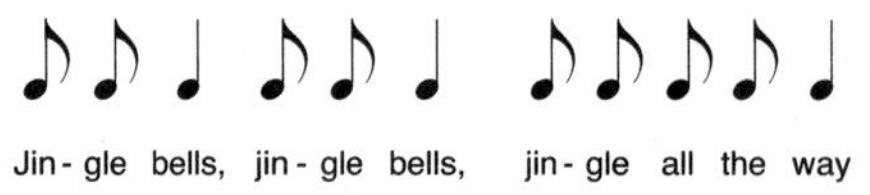

♪ ♪ ♩ ♪ ♪ ♩   ♪ ♪ ♪ ♪ ♩

Jin - gle bells, jin - gle bells,   jin - gle all the way

In addition to notes that signify the duration of sound, there are other signs, called rests, that indicate silence. For each note there is a corresponding rest of the same value.

EXAMPLE 2-5

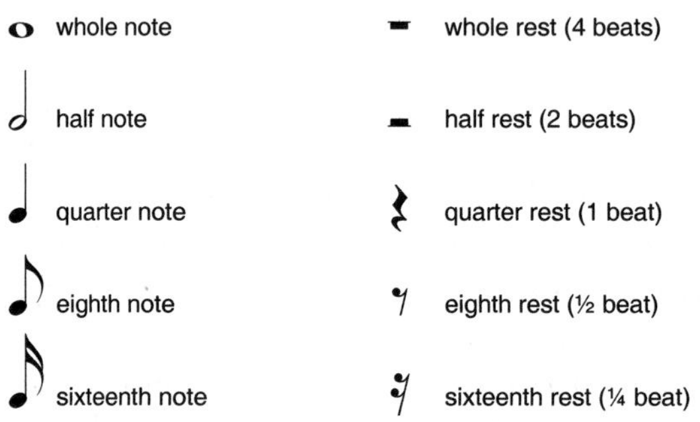

𝗼	whole note	▬	whole rest (4 beats)
𝅗𝅥	half note	▬	half rest (2 beats)
♩	quarter note	𝄽	quarter rest (1 beat)
♪	eighth note	𝄾	eighth rest (½ beat)
𝅘𝅥𝅯	sixteenth note	𝄿	sixteenth rest (¼ beat)

You will have noticed that, in their basic form, adjacent note values (and rests) in music all have a 2:1 ratio to each other: one half note equals two quarter notes, and so on. But triple relationships can and do exist, and these are created by the addition of a dot after a note, which increases the duration of the note to one and one-half its original length.

EXAMPLE 2-6

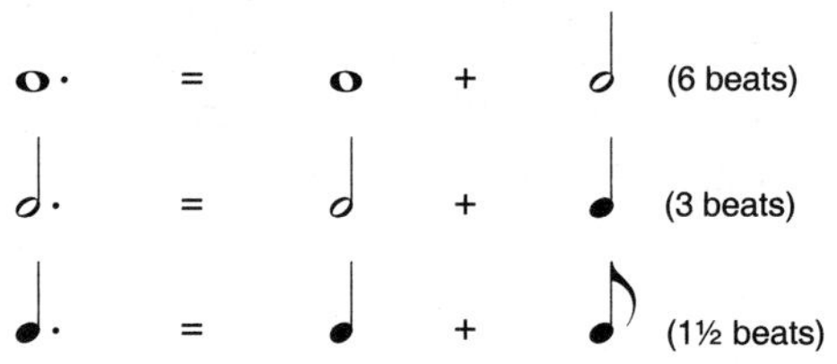

𝗼 · = 𝗼 + 𝅗𝅥 (6 beats)

𝅗𝅥 · = 𝅗𝅥 + ♩ (3 beats)

♩ · = ♩ + ♪ (1½ beats)

To see how the various note values indicate the rhythm of an actual piece of music, consider the well-known tune "Yankee Doodle." First, the text is given to refresh your memory. Next, the rhythm of the tune is indicated by horizontal lines of different lengths, to show how long each pitch lasts. Then, the rhythm (patterns of longs and shorts) is presented in musical notation. Finally, the position of each beat in "Yankee Doodle" is indicated by quarter notes.

EXAMPLE 2-7

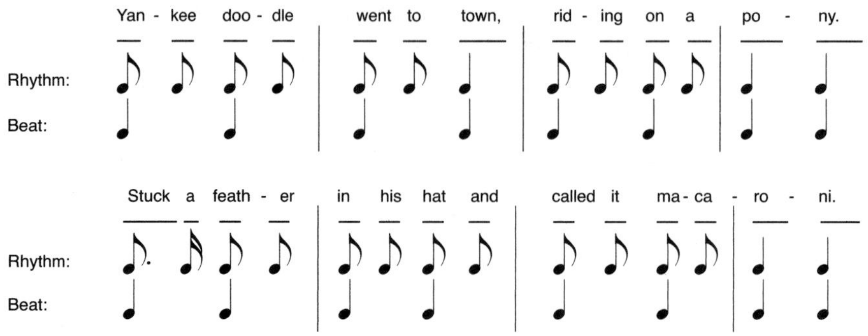

Here's the patriotic song "America" (first known in England and Canada as "God Save the King"—or "Queen") arranged the same way.

EXAMPLE 2–8

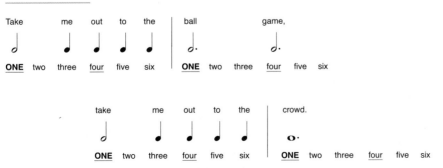

| My | coun - try | 'tis | of | thee, | sweet | land | of |

Rhythm:

Beat:

| lib - er - ty | of thee I | sing. |

Rhythm:

Beat:

Meter

Notice in the preceding examples how vertical lines divide the music into groups of two beats in the case of "Yankee Doodle" and into groups of three beats in "America." These strokes are called measure lines, or bar lines. A **measure,** or **bar,** is a group of beats. Usually, there are two, three, or four beats per measure, although in some cases there can be more. The gathering of beats into regular groups produces **meter.** A musical composition does not usually present a steady stream of equally loud beats. Instead, certain beats are given emphasis over others in a regular and repeating fashion. The stressed beats are called strong beats; the unstressed beats, weak beats.

If we stress every other beat—ONE two, ONE two, ONE two—we have two beats per measure and what is called **duple meter.** Similarly, if we emphasize every third beat—ONE two three, ONE two three—we have **triple meter. Quadruple meter** (four beats per measure) is common as well. Here is a familiar folk song notated in quadruple meter:

EXAMPLE 2–9

| Are you sleep - ing, | are you sleep - ing, | broth - er John, | broth - er John, |

ONE two three four **ONE** two three four **ONE** two three four **ONE** two three four

And here is an equally well-known tune in sextuple meter.

EXAMPLE 2–10

| Take | me out to the | ball | game, |

ONE two three four five six **ONE** two three four five six

| take | me out to the | crowd. |

ONE two three four five six **ONE** two three four five six

Most music, however, is written in duple ($\frac{2}{4}$), triple ($\frac{3}{4}$), or quadruple ($\frac{4}{4}$) meter.

Meter in music is indicated by a **meter signature** (also called a **time signature**)—two numbers, one on top of the other, placed at the beginning of the music to tell the performer how the beats of the music are to be grouped. The top number of the signature indicates how many beats there are per measure; the bottom number tells what note value receives the beat. Since, as we have said, the quarter note most often carries the beat, most time signatures have a "4" on the bottom. The three most frequently encountered time signatures are given here.

EXAMPLE 2–11

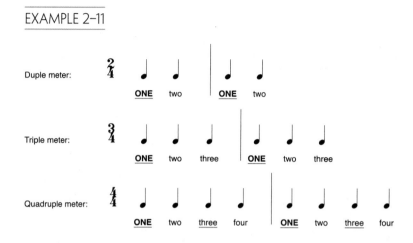

Most music, classical as well as popular, is written in $\frac{2}{4}$, $\frac{3}{4}$, or $\frac{4}{4}$. But because $\frac{4}{4}$ is in almost all ways merely a multiple or extension of $\frac{2}{4}$, there are really only two meters that the beginning listener need be aware of: duple meter $(\frac{2}{4})$ and triple meter $(\frac{3}{4})$—march meter and waltz meter, if you will. But how do we hear these and differentiate between them?

Hearing Meters

One way you can improve your ability to hear a given meter is to establish some sort of physical response to the music. As obvious as it might seem, it can be very helpful simply to tap your foot to the beat while moving along with the music in a way that groups the beats into measures of two or three beats. Perhaps the most precise way to move with the music is to adopt the same patterns of motion that conductors use to lead symphony orchestras and other musical ensembles. These patterns are cut in the air with the right hand (a baton is optional!). Here are the patterns that conductors use to show $\frac{2}{4}$ and $\frac{3}{4}$ meter.

EXAMPLE 2–12

Listen to an iAudio podcast about the basics of hearing meters at the text website.

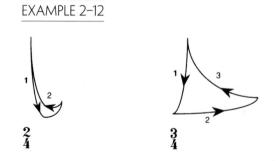

Notice that in both of these patterns, and indeed in all conducting patterns, the first beat is indicated by a downward movement of the hand. Accordingly, this first beat is called the **downbeat**. It represents by far the strongest beat in any given measure. In $\frac{2}{4}$ the downbeat is stronger, or more accented, than the **upbeat** (the beat signaled by an upward motion, which comes immediately before the downbeat); in $\frac{3}{4}$ the downbeat is more accented than either the middle beat (2) or the upbeat (3). When listening to a piece of music, then, tap the beat with your foot, listen for the downbeat, and try to get your conducting pattern synchronized with the music (move your hand down with the downbeat). If you hear only one weak beat between each strong beat, the music is in duple meter, and you should conduct in $\frac{2}{4}$ time. If you hear two weak beats between each downbeat, on the other hand, you are listening to a piece in triple meter and should use the $\frac{3}{4}$ pattern. Try conducting "Yankee Doodle" and "America" in $\frac{2}{4}$ and $\frac{3}{4}$, respectively.

EXAMPLE 2–13

Yan - kee doo - dle	went to town	rid - ing on a	po - ny.
ONE two	**ONE** two	**ONE** two	**ONE** two

My coun-try	'tis of thee,	sweet land of	lib - er-ty	of thee I	sing.
ONE two three	**ONE** two three	**ONE** two three	**ONE** two three	**ONE** two three	**ONE** two three

One final observation about meters and conducting patterns: Almost all music that we hear, and especially dance music, has a clearly identifiable meter and a strong downbeat. But not all music *starts* with the downbeat. Often a piece will begin with an upbeat. An upbeat at the very beginning of a piece is called a pickup. The **pickup** is usually only a note or two, but it gives a little momentum or extra push into the first downbeat, as can be seen in the following two patriotic songs.

EXAMPLE 2–14

Oh	beau-	ti-	ful	for	spa-	cious	skies
two	**ONE**	two	**ONE**	two	**ONE**	two	**ONE** two

Oh	say can you	see	by the	dawn's ear - ly	light
three	**ONE** two three	**ONE** two	three	**ONE** two three	**ONE** two

To sum up: To identify whether the meter of a piece is duple ($\frac{2}{4}$) or triple ($\frac{3}{4}$), try using this simple three-step approach. First, tap your foot or hand to the beat. Second, identify where the downbeat is falling—where do you hear strong beats instead of weak beats? Third, conduct with the music and decide if you hear one or two weak beats between each strong beat. If there is only one weak beat between the strong beats, then the piece is in duple meter; if there are two, then it is in triple meter.

Syncopation

One of the ways to add tension and excitement to music is by the use of syncopation. In most music, the **accent**, or musical emphasis, falls directly on the beat, with the downbeat getting the greatest accent of all. **Syncopation** places the accent either on a weak beat or between the beats. Picture in your mind a grid with the beats falling on the vertical lines; now picture notes—the syncopated notes—falling in between the lines. They contradict the prevailing beat, thereby adding tension to the music. A short example of syncopation can be heard in bar 2 of the chorus of The Beatles song "Lucy in the Sky with Diamonds." The arrows show the moments of syncopation.

Listen to an iAudio podcast about pickup notes at the text website.

Watch a video of Craig Wright's Open Yale Course class session 4, "Rhythm: Jazz, Pop, and Classical," at the text website.

EXAMPLE 2–15

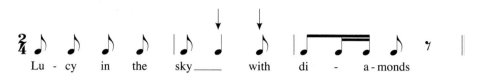

Lu - cy   in   the   sky____   with   di - a - monds

A far more complex example of syncopation can be found in the popular theme song to *The Simpsons*.

EXAMPLE 2–16

ONE two   ONE two   ONE two   ONE two   ONE two

Syncopation gives an unexpected bounce or lift to the music and is a prominent feature in Latin music and jazz.

Listening GUIDE   The Basics of Rhythm   (intro) 3

0:00	**3**	Music without strong sense of beat, meter, or rhythm
0:34		Music with strong sense of beat, meter, and rhythm
1:01		Succession of undifferentiated beats
1:15		Beats grouped into succession of strong-weak units, each forming measure (bar) in duple meter
1:26		Beats grouped into succession of strong-weak-weak units, each forming measure (bar) in triple meter
1:38		Duple-meter piece starting on downbeat (strong beat)
1:57		Triple-meter piece starting on downbeat
2:13		Triple-meter piece starting with pickup
2:25		Regular duple meter concluding with one measure of syncopation
2:35		Regular duple meter concluding with two measures of syncopation

Listen to streaming music in an Active Listening Guide, available on the text website.

Listening EXERCISE 2

Hearing Meters

(intro) 4

@ To take this Listening Exercise online and receive feedback or email answers to your instructor, go to the text website.

Now it's your chance to be the conductor! On your Intro CD, track 4, you have ten short musical excerpts, each played once. (You can replay them as many times as you wish.) Conduct the music and identify the meter of each excerpt. To do this, you should listen for the beat, count 1–2 or 1–2–3, and get your conductor's beat pattern in synchrony with the music (downbeat of the hand with downbeat of the music). If you do this correctly, the completion of each full conductor's pattern will equal one measure. All pieces are in duple ($\frac{2}{4}$) or triple ($\frac{3}{4}$) meter. Write "duple" or "triple" in the following blanks. There are five examples in duple meter and five in triple.

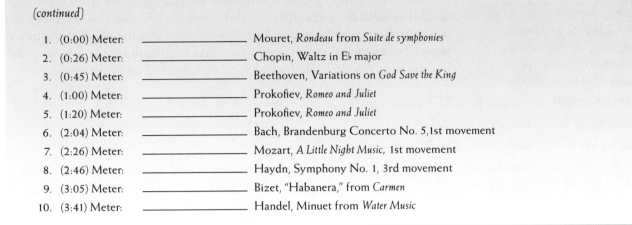

(*continued*)

1. (0:00) Meter: _____ Mouret, *Rondeau* from *Suite de symphonies*
2. (0:26) Meter: _____ Chopin, *Waltz in E♭ major*
3. (0:45) Meter: _____ Beethoven, *Variations on God Save the King*
4. (1:00) Meter: _____ Prokofiev, *Romeo and Juliet*
5. (1:20) Meter: _____ Prokofiev, *Romeo and Juliet*
6. (2:04) Meter: _____ Bach, *Brandenburg Concerto No. 5,*1st movement
7. (2:26) Meter: _____ Mozart, *A Little Night Music,* 1st movement
8. (2:46) Meter: _____ Haydn, *Symphony No. 1,* 3rd movement
9. (3:05) Meter: _____ Bizet, "Habanera," from *Carmen*
10. (3:41) Meter: _____ Handel, *Minuet from Water Music*

$\mathcal{T}$EMPO

The beat sets the basic pulse of the music. As beats are grouped into equal units, meter emerges. Rhythm is the durational pattern of longs and shorts superimposed over the meter. **Tempo,** finally, is the speed at which the beats progress. While the tempo of the beat can be fast or slow, it usually falls somewhere in the range of 60–90 beats per minute. We tend to feel slow tempos as relaxed or sad, and fast ones as energetic and happy. Tempo is indicated to the performer by means of a "tempo marking" placed at the beginning of the piece. Because tempo markings were first used in Italy, they are most often written in Italian. The following are the most common tempo indications, arranged from slow to fast:

grave (grave)	very slow
largo (broad)	
lento (slow)	slow
adagio (slow)	
andante (moving)	moderate
andantino (slightly faster than *andante*)	
moderato (moderate)	
allegretto (moderately fast)	fast
allegro (fast)	
vivace (fast and lively)	very fast
presto (very fast)	
prestissimo (as fast as possible)	

As you might imagine, general tempo terms such as these allow for a good deal of interpretive freedom. Conductors like Marin Alsop (Fig. 2-2) and Leonard Bernstein (Fig. 2-3), for example, have had very different notions of just how fast a movement by Beethoven marked *allegro* (fast) should go. A movement conducted by Bernstein can last two minutes longer than one directed by Alsop! In addition, composers often called

Listen to an iAudio podcast about hearing tempo at the text website.

FIGURE 2–2

Conductor Marin Alsop (1956–) in rehearsal with the Bournemouth Symphony Orchestra, Royal Albert Hall.

© ArenaPal/Topham/The Image Works

© Erich Auerbach/Getty Images

FIGURE 2–3

Leonard Bernstein (1918–1990), one of the most forceful, and flamboyant, conductors of the twentieth century.

@

Watch a video of or download a recording of "Don't Stop the Music" (see box below) in the YouTube and iTunes playlists on the text website.

for changes in tempo within a movement by placing in the score commands such as *accelerando* (getting faster) and *ritardando* (getting slower). From this last Italian term, we derive the English word for a slowing down of the music: **ritard**. Frequent changes in tempo can make it difficult for the listener to follow the beat, but they add much expression and feeling to the music.

*D*ON'T STOP THE MUSIC!
RHYTHM, RAP, HIP HOP, AND CURRENT DANCE MUSIC

Rhythm is an indispensable component of pop music. Some types of techno music repeat the same lyrics, melodies, and harmonies over and over—but the songs are still fun to listen to because the electronic rhythms shift and evolve over time. Certain traditional African musics feature relatively simple melodic and harmonic textures, but offer rhythmic complexity that surpasses that of most classical music.

Rap music is perhaps the most prominent popular musical genre to privilege rhythm over melody and harmony. In **rap,** the vocal line is delivered more like speech than like song, rarely offering discrete pitches that can be notated precisely. Rap, however, is not only a type of rhythmic speech-music; it is also a process commonly used in a larger genre called hip hop.

Hip hop features a wide variety of rhythmic devices. In addition to rapping, DJs "scratch" records in complex rhythmic patterns. They also "sample" (borrow) rhythms off older recordings and electronically manipulate them for new creative effects. Because of its strong emphasis on rhythmic processes, hip hop has been a primary influence on current dance music.

The following excerpt from Rihanna's dance tune "Don't Stop the Music" illustrates the way popular dance songs mix different rhythmic devices to create a pulsating musical texture. In this excerpt Rihanna uses syncopation, "samples" a rhythm from a famous pop song, and "layers" different rhythms on top of each other. The syncopation occurs from the very beginning. The upward-pointing arrows show the accent in the bass drum part, which plays every beat. The downward pointing arrows show where Rihanna syncopates the melody. Look at the way Rihanna's part falls *between*, rather than *on*, the beats in those measures.

The "sample" "ma ma se ma ma sa ma ma coo sa" is taken directly from Michael Jackson's "Wanna Be Startin' Somethin'" from *Thriller* (1982)—still the best-selling album of all time. But Jackson himself took this chant from Manu Dibango's *Soul Makossa* (1972), commonly considered the first disco album. In this way pop singers use the rhythms of other artists to create exciting new textures. In Rihanna's song, not only do the voices seem to integrate seamlessly, but they project a sense of "music history" to the sensitive listener who recognizes these references. In learning to listen to popular music as well as to classical, the more layers of music we understand, the greater our enjoyment.

Key WORDS

rhythm (13)
beat (13)
quarter note (13)
measure (bar) (15)
meter (15)
duple meter (15)
triple meter (15)

quadruple meter (15)
meter signature (time
   signature) (16)
downbeat (16)
upbeat (17)
pickup (17)
accent (17)

syncopation (17)
tempo (19)
ritard (20)
rap (20)
hip hop (20)

The materials on the text website will help you understand and pass tests on the content of this chapter. In addition, you may watch Craig Wright's own lectures at Open Yale Courses and complete this chapter's Listening Exercise interactively, as well as view Active Listening Guides and other materials that will help you succeed in this course.

MELODY

A **melody,** simply put, is the tune. It's the part we sing along with, the part we like and are willing to listen to again and again. TV pitchmen try to entice us to buy a CD set of "The Fifty All-Time Greatest Melodies," but not a similar collection of rhythms or harmonies. Rhythm and harmony are merely supporting actors; melody is the star. The more the melody shines, the more beautiful the music.

PITCH

Every melody is composed of a succession of pitches. **Pitch** is the relative position, high or low, of a musical sound. When an instrument produces a musical tone, it sets into motion vibrating sound waves that travel through the air to reach the listener's ears. A faster vibration will produce a higher pitch, and a slower one a lower pitch. The lowest key on the piano sets a string vibrating back and forth 27 cycles (times) per second, while the highest key does the same at a whopping 4186 times per second. Low pitches lumber along and sound "fuzzy," while high ones are fleetingly clear. A low note can convey sadness, a high one excitement (we don't usually hear a sad piccolo, for example). By grouping individual pitches so as to sweep forward, reach a climax, and then achieve repose, composers from Mozart to Beethoven to John Lennon create great melodies.

THE OCTAVE

Watch a video of Craig Wright's Open Yale Course class session 5, "Melody: Notes, Scales, Nuts and Bolts," at the text website.

Have you ever noticed, when singing a succession of tones up or down, that the melody reaches a tone that sounds like a duplication of an earlier pitch, but at a higher or lower level? That duplicating pitch is called an **octave,** for reasons that will become clear shortly. Pitches an octave apart sound similar because the frequency of vibration of the higher pitch is precisely twice that of the lower. The string that produces middle C on the piano vibrates 256 cycles per second, while the one generating the C an octave above does so 512 times per second. When men and women sing the same melody together, they almost invariably sing "at the octave" (an octave apart from each other). While it may sound as if all voices are singing the same pitches, the women are in fact singing an octave higher, with their vocal cords vibrating exactly twice as fast as those of their male counterparts.

All musical cultures, Western and non-Western, make use of the principle of octave duplication. But not all cultures divide the pitches within the octave the same way. In many traditional Chinese melodies, the octave is divided into five tones, resulting in wide spaces between pitches and giving the melodies an exotic, ethereal, "floating" sound to Western ears. Arabic melodies, by contrast, can divide the octave into up to twenty-four parts, resulting in extremely small spaces between pitches. This lends Arabic melodies their characteristic sound of "sliding" or "bending" between pitches. We in the West, however, beginning with Pythagoras and the ancient Greeks, have preferred melodies with seven unequally spaced pitches within the octave. The eighth pitch duplicates, or doubles, the sound of the first, and is thus called the octave.

During the early development of Western music, the seven notes within the octave corresponded to the white keys of the modern keyboard. Eventually, five additional notes were inserted, and these correspond to the black keys.

EXAMPLE 3–1

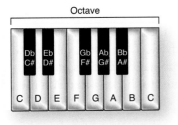

To get the sound of the octave in your ear, try singing "Over the Rainbow" and "Take Me Out to the Ball Game." Both immediately rise exactly an octave, regardless of what pitch you sing at the beginning.

EXAMPLE 3–2

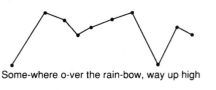

Some-where o-ver the rain-bow, way up high

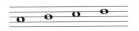

Take me out to the ball game, take me out to the crowd

Notating Melodies

The type of notation used for the two tunes in Example 3-2 is useful if you only need to be reminded of how a melody goes, but it is not precise enough to allow you to sing the tune from scratch. When the melody goes up, how *far* up does it go? More precision for musical notation began to appear in the West as early as the eleventh century, when people started to write notes on lines and spaces so that the exact distance between pitches could be judged immediately. This gridwork of lines and spaces, introduced in the previous chapter, came to be called a **staff.** The higher on the staff a note is placed, the higher its pitch.

EXAMPLE 3–3

The staff is always provided with a **clef** sign to indicate the range of pitch in which the melody is to be played or sung. One clef, called the **treble clef,** designates the upper range and is appropriate for high instruments like the trumpet and the violin, or a woman's voice. A second clef, called the **bass clef,** covers the lower range and is used for lower instruments like the tuba and the cello, or a man's voice.

EXAMPLE 3–4

For a single vocal part or a single instrument, a melody could easily be placed on either one of these two clefs. But for two-hand keyboard music with greater range, both clefs are used, one on top of the other. The performer looks at this combination of clefs, called the **great staff** (also **grand staff**), and relates the notes to the keys beneath the fingers. The two clefs join at middle C (the middle-most C key on the piano).

EXAMPLE 3–5

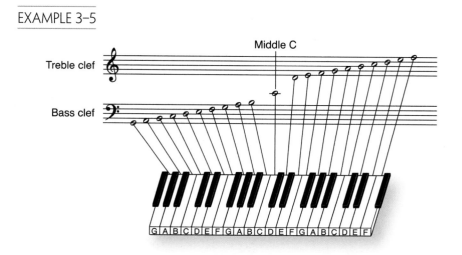

Each musical pitch can be represented by a letter name (like "C"), as well as by a particular line or space on the great staff. We use only seven letter names (in ascending order A, B, C, D, E, F, and G) because, as we have seen, melodies were made up of only seven pitches within each octave. (These seven pitches, once again, correspond to the seven white notes of the modern piano keyboard.) As a melody extends beyond the range of a single octave, the series of letter names repeats (see Ex. 3-5). The note above G, then, is an A, which lies exactly one octave above the previous A.

As music grew increasingly complex, the spaces between the white keys were divided and additional (black) keys were inserted (see Ex. 3-1). This increased the number of pitches within the octave from seven to twelve. Because they were not originally part of the staff, the five additional pitches were not represented by a line or space, nor were they given a separate letter name. Instead, they came to be indicated by a symbol, either a sharp or a flat, applied to one of the existing notes. A **sharp** (♯) raises the note to the piano key immediately above, usually a black one, whereas a **flat** (♭) lowers it to the next key below, again usually a black one. A **natural** (♮), on the other hand, cancels either of the two previous signs. Here, as an example of musical notation on the great staff, is a well-known melody as it might be notated for a chorus of male and female voices, the women an octave higher than the men. To keep things simple, the melody is notated in equal whole notes (without rhythm).

EXAMPLE 3–6

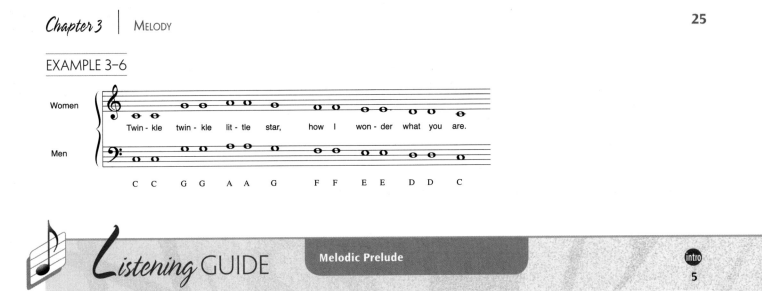

Listening GUIDE — Melodic Prelude

intro 5

Hearing melodies may be the single most important part of listening to music. Melodies contain the main themes and emotions that the composer wants to communicate. As a prelude to evaluating ten famous classical melodies, a preliminary drill will be helpful. Below you are given the bare melodic outline—the rhythm and harmony have been stripped away—of ten tunes and cues for their audio. Your goal is simply to match what you hear with these visual images. You can sit back and play the audio as you look at the melodic outlines. But why not be proactive? Try first singing the music, following the ups and downs of the notes, and then play the audio to hear how it actually sounds.

1. (0:00)
2. (0:13)
3. (0:25)
4. (0:41)
5. (1:00)
6. (1:15)
7. (1:32)
8. (1:50)

Listening EXERCISE 3

Hearing Melodies

intro 6

Pieces of classical music are sometimes long and complex. To keep track of everything that is going on, it helps to form a mental image, and maybe to make a quick sketch of the basic melodic contour. To familiarize you with this process, Listening Exercise 3 asks you to identify the melodic contour of ten famous classical melodies. Each is first performed as the composer originally intended and then played again in a more deliberate fashion to allow you to focus on the individual pitches. For each excerpt, select the pattern of notes that most accurately represents the pitches of the melody—the higher the note on the staff, the higher the pitch. Don't worry about rhythm for this exercise.

@ To take this Listening Exercise online and receive feedback or email answers to your instructor, go to the text website.

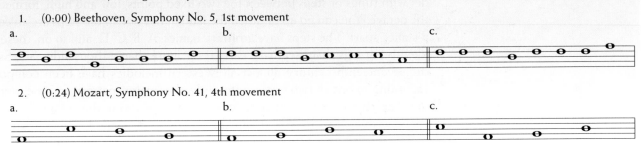

1. (0:00) Beethoven, Symphony No. 5, 1st movement
   a.   b.   c.

2. (0:24) Mozart, Symphony No. 41, 4th movement
   a.   b.   c.

(continued)

3. (0:44) Haydn, Symphony No. 94, 2nd movement
a.   b.   c.

4. (1:08) Schubert, Symphony No. 9, 1st movement
a.   b.   c.

5. (1:34) Beethoven, *Ode to Joy*
a.   b.   c.

6. (1:56) Vivaldi, Violin Concerto in E major, the "Spring," 1st movement
a.   b.   c.

7. (2:13) Beethoven, *Für Elise*
a.   b.   c.

8. (2:29) Mozart, *A Little Night Music*, 1st movement
a.   b.   c.

9. (2:48) Musorgsky, "Great Gate of Kiev" from *Pictures at an Exhibition*
a.   b.   c.

10. (3:16) Handel, "Hallelujah" chorus from *Messiah*
a.   b.   c.

SCALES, TONALITY, AND KEYS

When we listen to a pop or classical melody, our brain hears a succession of pitches spaced out on a grid. That grid is a **scale,** a fixed pattern of tones within the octave that ascends and descends. If you prefer, think of the scale as a ladder with rungs or steps between the two fixed points, low and high, formed by the octave. You can go up or down the ladder, but not all the steps are an equal distance apart. The steps have arbitrary names: A, B, C, D, and so on; these are identifying tags that they have carried for more than a thousand years. Since the seventeenth century almost all Western melodies have been composed according to one of two seven-note grids: the "major" pattern and the "minor" one. Each has its own arrangement of seven steps within the octave.

Now things get technical, but the image of the piano keyboard provided in Example 3-5 can help. Notice that there are no black keys between B and

C and between E and F—a "fault" attributable to the way the ancient Greeks constructed the first scales. All the adjacent white notes of the keyboard are not the same distance apart. A distance between two pitches in music is called an **interval.** The interval between B and C is only half the size of that between C and D. B to C is a "half step" (½), while C to D is a "whole step" (1). The factor that distinguishes the major scale from the minor is the position of the two half steps. The **major scale** follows a seven-note pattern moving upward 1–1–½–1–1–1–½. The **minor scale** goes 1–½–1–1–½–1–1. Once the eighth pitch (octave) is reached, the pattern can start over again.

Now the last piece of technical information: A major or minor scale may begin on any of the twelve notes within the octave, and thus there are twelve major and twelve minor scales. A major scale built on C uses only the white notes of the keyboard, as does a minor scale constructed on A. When begun on a note other than C (for the major scale) or other than A (for the minor scale), however, sharps and flats are needed to create the correct pattern of whole and half steps. Sharps and flats can be placed immediately before each note of the scale, or they can be grouped together at the beginning of the line in what is called a **key signature.** The key signature provides a "key" or guide, telling the musician which sharps or flats are to be applied throughout the piece. Here are the notes of the major and minor scales as they start on C and then on A.

Listen to an iAudio podcast on hearing intervals at the text website.

EXAMPLE 3–7

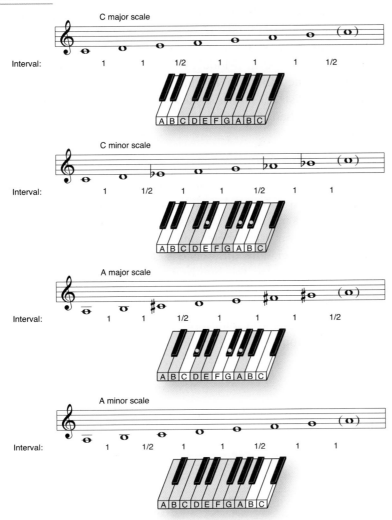

FIGURE 3–1

Planets rotate around and are pulled toward the sun, just as outlying pitches are pulled toward the tonic pitch.

To repeat: We Westerners have been accustomed to hear the pitches of a melody unfold within one of two seven-note grids—either the major or minor scale. But not all pitches in the grid are created equal. Our brain hears one pitch as central and the others as gravitating around it. That central, or home, pitch is called the tonic. The **tonic** is the first of the seven notes of the scale and, consequently, the eighth and last as well. Melodies almost invariably end on the tonic, as can be seen in *Twinkle, Twinkle Little Star* (see Ex. 3-6), which uses the C major scale and ends on C. The organization of music around a central pitch, the tonic, is called **tonality.** We can say that such and such a piece is written in the tonality of C major or of A minor, for example. More commonly, however, we say that the piece is written in the key of C or A. Thus, **key,** as with tonality, is something like a "gravitational field" that embodies both the scale of the melody and the strong pull of its tonic pitch (Fig. 3-1).

Modulation

Modulation is the change from one key to another. Most short popular songs don't modulate; they stay in one key from beginning to end. But longer pieces of classical music need to modulate so as not to bore the listener. Modulation lends a dynamic sense of movement to music. As the composer Arnold Schoenberg (1874–1951) said, "Modulation is like a change of scenery," like setting up camp in a new location. Modulations can be difficult to hear, however. The beginning listener may not know exactly where the music is going, but only sense that a change of key is occurring.

Hearing Major and Minor

The choice of scale, whether major or minor, greatly affects the mood and emotional quality of the music. A melody in a major key sounds decidedly different from one in a minor key. To Western ears, major-key melodies seem bright, cheery, and optimistic, whereas minor-key ones come across as dark, somber, and even sinister. This difference is caused, not by acoustics, but by culture—only during the last five hundred years have Westerners perceived melody in this "major = happy, minor = sad" way. By contrast, in many countries of the Near East, minor melodies are the happiest tunes—those played at weddings, for example. To establish firmly in your "mind's ear" the difference between major and minor, try singing the following familiar songs.

Listen to an iAudio podcast on hearing major and minor at the text website.

EXAMPLE 3–8

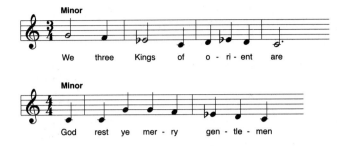

Composers over the centuries have manipulated the way we feel about their music by switching from major to minor (C major to C minor, for example) or minor to major (F minor to F major, for example). Changing from major to minor, or from minor to major, is called a change of **mode**—from the major mode to the minor, or vice versa. Changing the mode certainly affects the mood of the music. To prove the point, listen to the following familiar tunes (your instructor can play them for you). In each the mode has been changed from major to minor by inserting a flat into the scale near the tonic note (C), thereby switching from the beginning of the major (1–1–½) to that of the minor (1–½–1). Notice how this slight alteration sucks all the happiness, joy, and sunshine from these formerly major melodies.

EXAMPLE 3–9

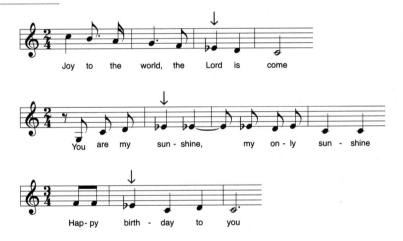

Now turn to Listening Exercise 4, which tests your ability to distinguish between melodies composed in major or minor.

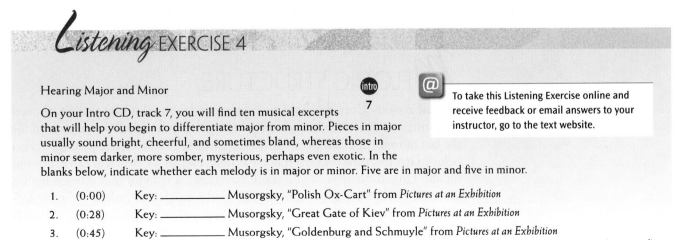

Listening EXERCISE 4

Hearing Major and Minor

On your Intro CD, track 7, you will find ten musical excerpts that will help you begin to differentiate major from minor. Pieces in major usually sound bright, cheerful, and sometimes bland, whereas those in minor seem darker, more somber, mysterious, perhaps even exotic. In the blanks below, indicate whether each melody is in major or minor. Five are in major and five in minor.

To take this Listening Exercise online and receive feedback or email answers to your instructor, go to the text website.

1. (0:00) Key: _____ Musorgsky, "Polish Ox-Cart" from *Pictures at an Exhibition*
2. (0:28) Key: _____ Musorgsky, "Great Gate of Kiev" from *Pictures at an Exhibition*
3. (0:45) Key: _____ Musorgsky, "Goldenburg and Schmuyle" from *Pictures at an Exhibition*

(continued)

4.	(1:05)	Key: _____	Tchaikovsky, "Dance of the Reed Pipes" from *The Nutcracker*
5.	(1:23)	Key: _____	Tchaikovsky, "Dance of the Reed Pipes" from *The Nutcracker*
6.	(1:39)	Key: _____	Mouret, *Rondeau* from *Suite de symphonies*
7.	(1:53)	Key: _____	Handel, Minuet from *Water Music*
8.	(2:07)	Key: _____	Prokofiev, "Dance of the Knights" from *Romeo and Juliet*
9.	(2:29)	Key: _____	Vivaldi, Violin Concerto, the "Spring," 1st movement
10.	(2:39)	Key: _____	Vivaldi, Violin Concerto, the "Spring," 1st movement

Other Scales

Most Western melodies, both classical and popular, are written in either the seven-note major or the seven-note minor scale. But there is a third scale that sometimes takes charge: the **chromatic scale,** which makes use of all twelve pitches, equally divided, within the octave. Chromatic (from the Greek *chroma*, "color") is a good word for this pattern because the additional five pitches do indeed add color and richness to a melody. In the chromatic scale all twelve pitches are just a half step apart (Ex. 3-10). Irving Berlin incorporates the chromatic scale at the beginning of his holiday song "White Christmas" (Ex. 3-11).

EXAMPLE 3–10

EXAMPLE 3–11

I'm dream-ing of a white Christ-mas

Although the major, minor, and chromatic scales regulate most of the music we hear, there are other melodic patterns in the West and elsewhere. The medieval Catholic Church once had a set of eight church modes for its religious music, and our own blues scale is essentially a six-note pattern. And, as we shall see in Chapters 29 and 31, other scalar arrangements of five, six, seven, and eight tones can be heard in the music of Russia and China, for example. As with food from around the world, so with scales—there are many local specialties.

MELODIC STRUCTURE

A great melody does not have to be a complex one. Ludwig van Beethoven demonstrated this when he fashioned his *Ode to Joy,* a melody he composed for the last movement of his Symphony No. 9 (1824). (You can hear it at intro /8.) So beloved has this tune become that it has been used as a Christmas carol, a hymn for the United Nations, a film score (*Die Hard*), a symbol in a science-fiction story (*A Clockwork Orange*), and background music in countless TV commercials. Below, the melody is notated in the bass clef in D major, the key in which Beethoven composed it, with the original German text translated into English.

EXAMPLE 3–12

(a) Praise to Joy the God de-scend-ed, Daugh-ter of E - ly - si-um.

(b) 5 Ray of mirth and rap-ture blend-ed, God-dess, to thy shrine wel-come.

(c) 10 By thy ma-gic is u - nit - ed what tra - di - tion kept a-part. All ___

(b) 15 ___ hu-mans are peo-ple plight - ed where thy gen-tle spi - rit darts.

We can make a few general observations about Beethoven's melody. First, notice that each pitch is very close to the next—the melody moves mainly by whole or half steps. Clearly, Beethoven wanted to keep this melody simple so that all the world could sing it. Next, notice that it starts in a strange way; it doesn't sound secure at the beginning because it commences on the third degree of the scale rather than the first—melodies don't have to begin on the tonic, they just have to end there. Now look at the overall structure of the tune. Beethoven has composed four melodic phrases, each four bars in length—symmetry at its best! A **phrase** in music functions much like a phrase or clause within a sentence, serving as an important part of a larger whole. The initial phrase (**a**) opens the melody and ends on a note *other* than the tonic (here the note E); the second phrase (**b**) answers this idea and returns the melody to the tonic (D). Two phrases that work in tandem this way are called **antecedent** and **consequent phrases**—one opens, the other closes. Beethoven then pushes off in a new direction (phrase **c**). The music gains momentum by means of a repeating rhythmic figure in measures 10–11 and reaches a musical climax in measure 12 with the only two large intervals (leaps) in the melody. The fourth and final phrase is an almost exact repeat of the second phrase (**b**), with the exception of one important detail (see * in Ex. 3-12). Beethoven brings the return of this phrase in one beat early—a bit of rhythmic syncopation—thereby confounding the symmetry and giving his melody an unexpected lift.

The melodic structure of Beethoven's *Ode to Joy*—balanced groups of four-bar phrases arranged as antecedent–consequent–expansion–consequent—is found frequently in the works of Haydn, Mozart, and Beethoven from the eighteenth and nineteenth centuries. Antecedent–consequent pairs also appear regularly in popular songs of nineteenth- and twentieth-century America. Think of the tune "When the Saints Go Marching In," for example.

Antecedent phrase: Oh when the saints, go marching in, oh when the saints go marching in;
Consequent phrase: Oh how I want to be in that number, when the saints go marching in.

Watch a video of Craig Wright's Open Yale Course class session 6, on what makes a great melody, "Melody: Mozart and Wagner," at the text website.

You may have been singing antecedent–consequent phrases all your life and not been aware of it. To prove the point, try singing a few phrases from Stevie Wonder's "You Are the Sunshine of My Life," The Who's "Pinball Wizard," or Billy Joel's "Piano Man."

Listening EXERCISE 5

Hearing Melodic Structure
Ludwig van Beethoven, *Ode to Joy* from Symphony No. 9 (1824)

(intro) 8

@ To take this Listening Exercise online and receive feedback or email answers to your instructor, go to the text website.

On your Intro CD, track 8, you have an excerpt from the last movement of Beethoven's Symphony No. 9, in which his famous *Ode to Joy* can be heard. You are probably familiar with the tune already, but look at it again as it is given on page 31. Try to get the antecedent (**a**), consequent (**b**), and expansion (**c**) phrases firmly in your ear. Now listen to the music on your CD. The melody is actually heard four times—stated and then repeated three times with a new and different orchestration for each repeat. As the four statements unfold, the music grows in power and majesty.

First presentation of the melody, just listen. 0:00 (**a** = antecedent), 0:09 (**b** = consequent), 0:17 (**c** = expansion), 0:24 (**b** = consequent), 0:33–0:47 (**c** and **b** repeated).

1. Second presentation (0:48–1:35): What happens during this second presentation of the melody?
   a. **a** and **b** repeat but **c** and **b** do not
   b. **c** and **b** repeat but **a** and **b** do not

2. Third presentation (1:36–2:21): What happens during this third presentation?
   a. **a** and **b** repeat but **c** and **b** do not
   b. **c** and **b** repeat but **a** and **b** do not

3. Fourth presentation (2:22–3:03): What happens during this fourth and final presentation?
   a. **a** and **b** repeat but **c** and **b** do not
   b. **c** and **b** repeat but **a** and **b** do not

4. What might we conclude from this?
   a. Beethoven wanted to achieve variety and thus changed the order of the repetition of the phrases in successive presentations.

   b. Beethoven knew he was onto a good thing and presented the phrases in the same order during each presentation.

Now listen more generally to *Ode to Joy*:

5. Does the tempo in each of the four presentations vary greatly from one to the next?
   a. yes   b. no

6.–7. Why is this melody, though inspiring, easy to remember? (Choose two.)
   a. It has many heroic leaps in it.
   b. It moves mostly in pitches a step apart.
   c. It is somewhat repetitious (there is only one phrase—**c**—that is completely different from the others).

8.–10. Why does *Ode to Joy* grow in power and majesty as Beethoven orchestrates it in the four successive presentations that you heard? (Choose three.)
   a. The tempo gets increasingly slower and grander.
   b. Each presentation is louder than the preceding one.
   c. It grows in richness as more and more instruments enter in each new presentation.
   d. A chorus enters to sing of the joy of unity and a common humanity.
   e. Heroic brass instruments enter in the fourth and final presentation.

Listen to an iAudio podcast on measures and phrases at the text website.

*H*EARING MELODIES AND PHRASES

As we have seen, melodies are made up of musical phrases. When listening to a piece of music, whether a classical symphony or a popular song, we tend to follow along with the phrases. For the most part, we do this intuitively—we instinctively hear where a phrase begins and where it ends. Beethoven's *Ode to Joy* is composed of four symmetrical phrases, each four measures, or bars, in length, as is typical of the music of the Classical period (1750–1820) in music history. But the same is true for most of our popular music. Look back over the musical examples we have seen thus far—"Over the Rainbow," "Take Me Out to the Ball Game," and Rihanna's "Don't Stop the Music," to choose just a few. Almost all of them are made up of four-measure phrases

© Michael Ochs Archives/CORBIS

FIGURE 3–2

Louis Armstrong at the age of thirty-two.

that are joined to other four-measure phrases to form longer units of eight or sixteen measures. The reason that so much of the music we hear sounds solid and pleasing to us is because of its four-square (or eight- or sixteen-square) structure. Whether in architecture, poetic meter, or music, a symmetrical structure makes us feel comfortable.

Having followed the phrase structure in Beethoven's *Ode to Joy*, now go on to do so in Louis Armstrong's version of the jazz song "Willie the Weeper" (also known as "Cocaine Lil and Morphine Sue"). Perhaps because of its highly symmetrical structure or simply because of its long-lasting popularity, this style of jazz is known as "classical" New Orleans jazz.

Listening EXERCISE 6

Counting Measures and Phrases

(intro)
9

@ To take this Listening Exercise online and receive feedback or email answers to your instructor, go to the text website.

Louis Armstrong was born in poverty in New Orleans in 1901 but went on to become the most famous jazz musician of the twentieth century (Fig. 3-2). Armstrong's powerful, "in-your-face" style of trumpet playing can be heard prominently in this 1927 recording of the song "Willie the Weeper." Your task here is to count the number of measures, or bars, in each musical phrase.

Armstrong's "Willie the Weeper" is in a straightforward duple meter ($\frac{2}{4}$ time). First, listen for a bit and tap your foot with the beat, which here goes slightly faster than your heartbeat. Every two of your taps forms one measure. Start counting the number of measures in each phrase. (The timings indicate the beginning of the phrase, and a new solo instrument plays for the duration of each phrase.) After the four-measure introduction, every phrase is either eight or sixteen measures in length, so fill in the blanks accordingly (write "8" or "16"). The answer for the first phrase is provided.

(0:00–0:03) Four-measure introduction

(0:04–0:24) Full band. Number of measures: ___16___

(0:25–0:45) Full band varies the tune. Number of measures: _____

(0:46–0:56) Trombone and tuba solo. Number of measures: _____

(0:57–1:06) Trombone and tuba repeat. Number of measures: _____

(1:07–1:27) Trombone solo. Number of measures: _____

(1:28–1:48) Extraordinary clarinet solo. Number of measures: _____

(1:49–1:58) Armstrong plays trumpet solo. Number of measures: _____

(1:59–2:08) Piano solo. Number of measures: _____

(2:09–2:28) Guitar solo. Number of measures: _____

(2:29–2:48) Armstrong plays trumpet solo. Number of measures: _____

(2:49–end) Trumpet, trombone, and clarinet improvise around tune. Number of measures: _____

Key WORDS

melody (22)
pitch (22)
octave (22)
staff (23)
clef (23)
treble clef (23)
bass clef (24)
great (grand) staff (24)
sharp (♯) (24)

flat (♭) (24)
natural (♮) (24)
scale (26)
interval (27)
major scale (27)
minor scale (27)
key signature (27)
tonic (28)
tonality (28)

key (28)
modulation (28)
mode (29)
chromatic scale (30)
phrase (31)
antecedent phrase (31)
consequent phrase (31)

@ The materials on the text website will help you understand and pass tests on the content of this chapter. In addition, you may watch Craig Wright's own lectures at Open Yale Courses and complete this chapter's Listening Exercises interactively, as well as view Active Listening Guides and other materials that will help you succeed in this course.

HARMONY

Melody provides a lyrical voice for music, rhythm gives vitality to that voice, and harmony adds depth and richness to it, just as the dimension of depth in painting adds a rich backdrop to that visual art. Although melody can stand by itself, it is most often supported by a harmony, an accompaniment that enriches it. Melody and harmony work gracefully together, the one carrying the central idea above, the other supporting it below. Sometimes, however, discord arises—as when a singer strumming a guitar fails to change the chord to make it agree with the melody. The melody and harmony now clash; they are out of harmony.

As the double sense of this last statement suggests, the term *harmony* has several meanings. In the broader sense, harmony is the peaceful arrangement of diverse elements (Fig. 4-1). When applied specifically to music, **harmony** is said to be the sounds that provide support and enrichment—an accompaniment—for melody. Finally, we often speak of harmony as if it is a specific event in the accompaniment; for example, we say the harmony changes, meaning that one chord in the accompaniment gives way to the next. Thus, we might say that the song "Oh, What a Beautiful Morning" from the musical *Oklahoma!* is a "harmonious" (pleasant-sounding) piece, "harmonized" (accompanied) in the key of C major, and that the "harmony" (the chords used to accompany the melody, which appear here below the tune) changes eight times.

FIGURE 4-1

Claude Monet, *Waterlily Pond: Pink Harmony* (1900). Monet's painting of this famous bridge at Giverny, France, reveals not only the harmonious qualities of nature, but also the painter's ability to harmonize various colors into a blend of pastels.

EXAMPLE 4–1

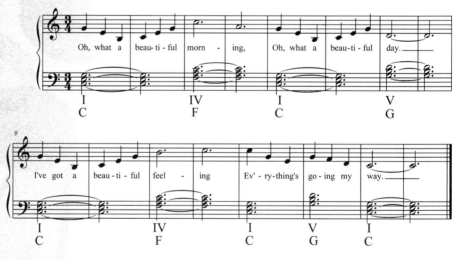

Watch a video of Craig Wright's Open Yale Course class session 7, "Harmony: Chords and How to Build Them," at the text website.

BUILDING HARMONY

Chords are the building blocks of harmony. A **chord** is simply a group of three or more pitches that sound at the same time. When we learn to play guitar or jazz piano, we first learn mainly how to construct chords. The basic chord in Western music is the **triad**, so called because it consists of three pitches arranged in a very specific way. Here is a C major triad.

EXAMPLE 4–2

Note that it comprises the first, third, and fifth pitches of the C major scale. The distance between each of the pitches is, again, called an **interval.** C to E, spanning three letter names (C, D, E), is the interval of a third. E to G, again spanning three letter names (E, F, G), is another third. Triads always consist of two intervals of a third placed one on top of the other. Here are triads built on every note of the C major scale.

EXAMPLE 4–3

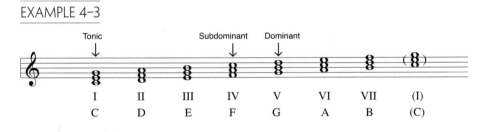

These triads provide all the basic chords necessary to harmonize a melody in C major.

Notice that each of the chords is given a Roman numeral, indicating on which note of the scale the triad is built, and that the triads built on I, IV, and V are called the tonic, subdominant, and dominant chords, respectively. We have already met the tonic note in our discussion of melody—it is the central pitch around which a tune gravitates and on which a melody usually ends. Similarly, the tonic chord, or triad, is the "home" chord of the harmony. It is the most stable and the one toward which the other chords move. The **dominant** triad, always built on the fifth note of the scale, is next in importance. A dominant triad is usually followed by a tonic one, especially at the end of a musical phrase, where such a movement (V–I) helps create a strong concluding statement. The **subdominant** triad is built on the fourth note of the scale and is called the "sub"-dominant because its pitch is just below the dominant. The subdominant often moves to the dominant, which in turn moves to the tonic, creating the succession IV–V–I. Just as words in a sentence must come in a certain order so as to conform to the rules of grammar, so chords in a musical phrase have a generally expected order and intent. A movement of chords in a purposeful fashion is called a **chord progression.** The individual chords in a chord progression seem to "pull" each other along, one giving way to the next, with all ultimately gravitating toward the powerful tonic harmony.

But why is it necessary for chords to change? The answer lies in the fact that the pitches of a melody continually change, sometimes moving through all the notes of a scale. But a single triadic chord can only be harmonious, or consonant, with the three notes of the scale that it contains. A tonic triad in C major, for example, can only "harmonize" with the melody notes C, E, and G (see Ex. 4-2). In order to keep the harmony consonant with the melody, then, chords must continually change. If they do not, dissonance results.

Listen to an iAudio podcast on hearing intervals at the text website.

Hear many pop songs built on just a I-V-VI-IV chord progression, in "Four Chords, 36 Songs," in the YouTube playlist on the text website.

Listen to an iAudio podcast on chord changes at the text website.

Finally, the notes of a triad need not always come in all at once, but can be spaced out over time. Such a broken, or staggered, triad is called an **arpeggio.** The name derives from *arpa,* the Italian word for "harp," because the harp often plays the notes of a chord not together, but in succession. Arpeggios can appear either as part of the melody or, more often, in the harmony that supports a melody. An arpeggio used in an accompaniment gives the listener the sense that the harmony is more active than it really is. In Example 4-4 the beginning of "Oh, What a Beautiful Morning" is harmonized with the supporting triads spaced out, and repeated, as arpeggios (beneath the brackets). These chords are the same as in Example 4-1, but now the harmony seems more active because one note of the accompanying triad is sounding on every beat.

EXAMPLE 4–4

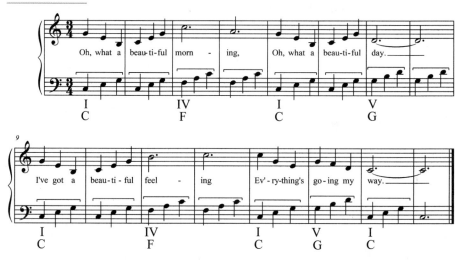

CONSONANCE AND DISSONANCE

You have undoubtedly noticed, when pressing the keys of the piano at one time or another, that some combinations of keys produce a harsh, jarring sound, while others are pleasing and harmonious. The former chords are characterized by **dissonance** (pitches sounding momentarily disagreeable and unstable), and the latter by **consonance** (pitches sounding agreeable and stable). In physical terms (acoustics), chords that contain pitches that are very close to one another, just a half or a whole step apart, sound dissonant. On the other hand, chords that involve a third, a somewhat larger interval, are usually consonant, as is the case for each triad in Example 4-3. But culture, and even personal taste, plays a role in dissonance perception, too—what is a disagreeable dissonance to one listener at one moment may be a delight to another at some other time. In fact, in the West our appreciation of dissonance has changed over the centuries; a chord that sounded wildly dissonant in the Renaissance (1450–1600) sounds consonant to modern ears. And, as bands such as Metallica have shown, we can get used to a lot of dissonance.

Dissonant chords add a feeling of tension and anxiety to music; consonant ones produce a sense of calmness and stability. As with tension-filled movements in life, dissonant chords seek out—want to move to—consonant resolutions. The continual flux between dissonant and consonant chords gives Western music a sense of drama, as a piece moves between moments of tension to longed-for resolution.

Listen to an iAudio podcast on consonance and dissonance at the text website.

CADENCES

In music as well as the other narrative arts, endings can be as important as beginnings; they tell us how things turned out and what we have learned from the experience. The end of a musical phrase usually finishes with a consonant chord; the end of an entire piece almost always ends so. We like happy endings. The portion of a musical phrase that leads to its last chord is called a **cadence.** Usually, a cadence encompasses the final two, three, four, or five notes of the melody and its accompanying chords. Just as there are often internal phrases within a long sentence, so there are internal phrases, each with a cadence, in a melody. Similarly, just like punctuation marks in written prose, the four main musical cadences express varying degrees of emphasis and finality. One cadence, sounding restful and peaceful, is called the *amen cadence*, for it is often heard in religious services (it moves IV–I). Another surprises us, indeed deceives us, and, appropriately, is called the *deceptive cadence* (I–VI). Another, the *half cadence* (usually IV–V), doesn't finish the phrase—doesn't end on the tonic (I)—but leaves us hanging, quizzical, waiting for more. And finally, and most emphatically, the *authentic cadence* (V–I) brings with it a feeling of real conclusion, as if to say, "THE END!" Cadences can come in any order, although pieces almost always end with an authentic cadence. A composer such as Bach, as might a great storyteller, lays out a succession of musical phrases that tell a lengthy tale, with moments of tranquility, uncertainty, and doubt, before arriving at an emphatic conclusion.

Listen to an iAudio podcast on cadences at the text website.

@

Watch comedian Dudley Moore parody a cadence (starting at 3:18) in the YouTube playlist on the text website.

Listening GUIDE

Consonance and Dissonance: Cadences

intro 10

0:00	**10**	Dissonant chords resolving into consonant ones
0:18		Chord progression in major key through entire phrase, followed by cadence of preceding phrase
0:35		Chord progression in minor key through entire phrase, followed by cadence of preceding phrase
0:50		Two amen cadences
1:07		Two deceptive cadences
1:20		Two phrases, each ending with a half cadence
1:41		Four authentic cadences
2:05		As warm-up for "Hearing the Harmony Change," bass line alone, followed by same bass line with melody and harmony it supports; harmony changes with each chord

Listen to streaming music in an Active Listening Guide, available at the text website.

HEARING THE HARMONY CHANGE

The first step in listening to harmony is to focus your attention on the bass, separating it from the higher melody line. Chords are often built on the bass note, and a change in the bass from one pitch to another may signal a change in chord. Concentrating on the bass might not be easy at first. Most of us have always thought that listening to music means listening to melody. Certainly, hearing melody is crucial. But the bass is next in importance, and it

Listen to an iAudio podcast on hearing the bass line at the text website.

rules supreme in a sort of subterranean world. It grounds the chords and determines where the harmony is going, more so than the higher melody. Baroque music (1600–1750) usually has a clear, driving bass line, and hard rock music perhaps even more so. Next time you listen to a rock song, follow the electric bass instead of the melody and lyrics (both Paul McCartney and Sting play bass guitar). See if you can sense when the chords are changing and when you have reached a chord that feels like the home key (the tonic triad). Listening Exercise 7 will help you follow the bass line as you enjoy the famous Pachelbel Canon. It is easy to hear in this piece because it repeats, again and again. Any element of music (rhythm, melody, or harmony) that continually repeats is called an **ostinato** (from the Italian, meaning "obstinate thing"). Pachelbel's ostinato bass has been used in popular songs by rapper Coolio ("C U When U Get There"), Blues Traveler ("Hook"), Vitamin C ("Graduation"), The Beatles ("Let It Be"), and others.

 EXERCISE 7

Hearing the Bass Line and Harmony
Johann Pachelbel, Canon in D major (c1690)
(For more on Pachelbel's Canon, see p. 118.)

(intro)
11

(@) To take this Listening Exercise online and receive feedback or email answers to your instructor, go to the text website.

When we listen to music, most of us naturally concentrate on the highest-sounding part, which is where the melody is usually to be found. To hear harmony, however, we need to focus on the lowest-sounding line, the bass. In Johann Pachelbel's famous four-part Canon in D major, there is a canon (a round) in the upper three parts. (Canon is explained more fully in Chapter 6.) Below this canon, however, Pachelbel writes a solitary bass part moving very slowly. This bass supports the canon that unfolds above. As with most bass lines, here the lowest part establishes the foundation for the harmony (chords) above each of its pitches. In this piece the bass with chords enters first, and then the canon (round) gradually unfolds. Focus now on the bass and answer the following questions.

1. The bass enters first. At what point does the first violin enter?
   a. 0:00   b. 0:12   c. 0:21

2. Listen again to the beginning. How many pitches do you hear before the violin enters and the bass begins to repeat? In other words, how many pitches are there in the bass pattern?
   a. 4   b. 6   c. 8

3. Are all the pitches within the pattern of the bass held for the same duration?
   a. yes   b. no

4. Therefore, the rate of harmonic change in Pachelbel's Canon is what?
   a. regular   b. irregular

5. Which diagram most accurately reflects the pitches (the pattern) of the bass line?
   a.   b.   c.

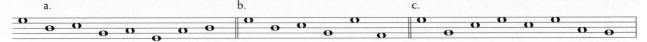

6. Listen now to more of the composition. The bass is highly repetitive as the pattern recurs again and again. Each statement of the pattern lasts approximately how long?
   a. 12 seconds   b. 15 seconds   c. 20 seconds

7. A melody, harmony, or rhythm that repeats again and again in music is called what (consult the glossary for the meanings of these terms)?
   a. a pizzicato   b. a legato   c. a tempo   d. an ostinato

8. Now listen up to 1:54 of the recording. Does the bass pattern ever change?
   a. yes   b. no

9. From the beginning of the piece (0:00) to this point (1:54), how many times do you hear the pattern?
   a. 8   b. 10   c. 12   d. 14

10. Listen all the way to the end of the work. Does Pachelbel ever vary his bass and his harmonic pattern?
    a. yes   b. no

Chord Changes in the Blues

The continually repeating bass line in Johann Pachelbel's Canon is unusual in classical music. In most classical pieces, the bass and the resulting chords do not repeat in a regular fashion, and that makes hearing the harmonic changes difficult. Yet in popular music, sensing when the harmony changes can be easier because it is more common for a succession of chord changes to repeat over and over again in exactly the same pattern. Rock music of the 1950s and 1960s frequently repeats three or four chords without varying their order. Similarly, harmonic repetition occurs in the **blues,** an expressive, soulful style of singing that unfolds above repeating chord changes. Although there are several variants, the standard harmony of the blues involves just three chords—tonic, subdominant, and dominant—which are spread out over twelve measures, or bars. Within the **twelve-bar blues** pattern, however, each chord does not sound for the same length of time. The first tonic holds for four bars, while all subsequent chords sound for just two bars. Once completed, the pattern repeats again and again, until the singer is finished.

Watch a video of Craig Wright's Open Yale Course class session 8, "Bass Patterns: Blues and Rock," at the text website.

For further explanation of the twelve-bar blues, watch "How to Learn Blues Chord Progressions: Vol. 1" in the YouTube playlist on the text website.

```
Chord: I _____IV_____I_____V_____I _____ (Repeat)
Bar:    1   2   3   4   5   6   7   8   9   10   11   12
```

Chord Changes in Doo-Wop

Finally, a bit of pure fun: Let's listen to chord changes in a special kind of soul music called doo-wop. **Doo-wop** emerged in the 1950s as an outgrowth of the gospel hymns sung in African-American churches in urban Detroit, Chicago, and New York. Often doo-wop was simply improvised on the street because it was direct and repetitive. The lyrics made use of repeating phrases, such as "doo wop, doo wah" or "shoo wop and shoo be doo," and such words were sung in a cappella (unaccompanied) harmony below the tune. Invariably, the harmony was a short chord progression, the most common of which went I–VI–IV–V and repeated over and over again (see the Listening Guide below). Because anyone could sing along, this sort of music became enormously popular, sweeping to the top of the "Hit Parade."

And you can sing it, too. In the doo-wop song "Duke of Earl" (1962) by Gene Chandler, you'll hear the bass voice lead, not with "doo, doo, doo," but with "duke, duke, duke," setting the foundation for the chords that soon enter in the other voices and instruments. The tempo is moderately fast, and each of the four chords lasts for one bar in $\frac{4}{4}$ meter. Thus, every fourth beat coincides with a new chord, and the pattern repeats approximately every nine seconds. Moreover, every time the harmony sings the word "Earl," the chords change. As you listen to this doo-wop classic, sing along with the bass, no matter what your vocal range. Anyone can hear these chord changes!

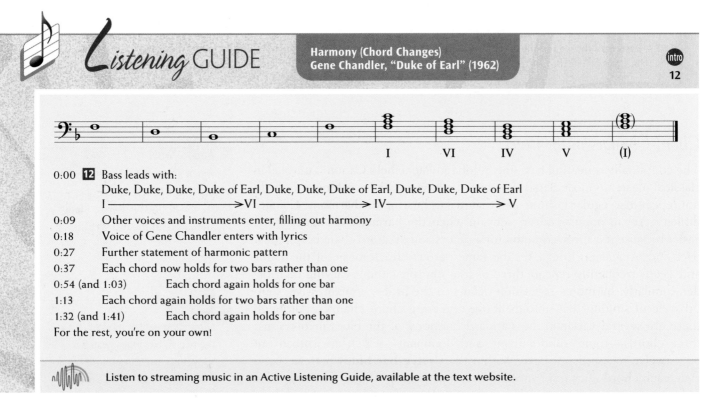

Listening GUIDE

Harmony (Chord Changes)
Gene Chandler, "Duke of Earl" (1962)

intro
12

0:00 **12** Bass leads with:
Duke, Duke, Duke, Duke of Earl, Duke, Duke, Duke of Earl, Duke, Duke, Duke of Earl
I ————————————→VI ————————→ IV————————→ V
0:09   Other voices and instruments enter, filling out harmony
0:18   Voice of Gene Chandler enters with lyrics
0:27   Further statement of harmonic pattern
0:37   Each chord now holds for two bars rather than one
0:54 (and 1:03)   Each chord again holds for one bar
1:13   Each chord again holds for two bars rather than one
1:32 (and 1:41)   Each chord again holds for one bar
For the rest, you're on your own!

Listen to streaming music in an Active Listening Guide, available at the text website.

The materials on the text website will help you understand and pass tests on the content of this chapter. In addition, you may watch Craig Wright's own lectures at Open Yale Courses and complete this chapter's Listening Exercise interactively, as well as view Active Listening Guides and other materials that will help you succeed in this course.

Key WORDS

harmony (34)	subdominant (35)	cadence (37)
chord (34)	chord progression (35)	ostinato (38)
triad (34)	arpeggio (36)	blues (39)
interval (35)	dissonance (36)	twelve-bar blues (39)
dominant (35)	consonance (36)	doo-wop (39)

DYNAMICS AND COLOR 5

As we have seen, rhythm, melody, and harmony constitute the primary elements of music. In order for a musical composition to be conveyed to a listener, however, these abstract concepts must be translated into concrete musical sounds. This is accomplished when musical instruments and voices transform the composer's ideas about rhythm, melody, and harmony into actual sound waves. We use the terms *dynamics* (loudness) and *color* (tone quality) to describe the particular character of these musical sounds as they are performed by the various instruments or voices.

Our response to dynamics and musical color is immediate. For example, we may be struck by a certain passage, not so much because of its pitches or rhythm, but because of a sudden, dynamic shift from very quiet to very loud, or because the melody is played by a brilliant-sounding trumpet. Dynamics and color, then, refer not so much to a musical idea itself, but instead to the way in which that musical idea is presented.

DYNAMICS

In all music **dynamics** are the various levels of volume, loud and soft, at which sounds are produced. Dynamics work together with tone colors to affect the way we hear and react to musical sound. For example, a high note in the clarinet has one quality—shrill and harsh—when played *fortissimo* (very loud) and quite another—vague and otherworldly—when played *pianissimo* (very soft). Figure 5-1 shows a computerized representation of the waveforms of a clarinet playing *pianissimo* and then *fortissimo*. Because they were first used by composers working in Italy, the terms for musical dynamics are traditionally written in Italian. Below are the most common terms and the musical symbols for them.

© Mateuz Zachowski

FIGURE 5-1

Computerized digital waveform of about ten seconds of sound of a clarinet playing soft and loud. The narrower the vertical lines, the softer the sound.

Term	Musical Symbol	Definition
fortissimo	*ff*	very loud
forte	*f*	loud
mezzo forte	*mf*	moderately loud
mezzo piano	*mp*	moderately soft
piano	*p*	soft
pianissimo	*pp*	very soft

Listen to an iAudio podcast on dynamics at the text website.

Dynamics sometimes change abruptly, for special effects. Most common among these quick changes is the **sforzando,** a sudden, loud attack on one note or chord. A famous *sforzando* occurs in the second movement of Joseph Haydn's "Surprise" Symphony (1792), for example, in which the composer interrupts a soft melody with a thunderous crash on a single chord (intro /25 at 0:32)—his intent was apparently to awaken those listeners who might have dozed off! In the world of pop music, Nirvana was known for using dynamic contrast in its songs, with soft, relaxed verses that explode into loud, raucous choruses. Listeners feel the immense excitement of these choruses partly because they are pitted against the more subdued verses. This exemplifies the importance of dynamic contrast in creating exciting pieces of music.

But changes in dynamics need not be sudden and abrupt. They can be gradual and extend over a long period of time. A gradual increase in the intensity of sound is called a **crescendo,** while a gradual decrease is called either a **decrescendo** or a **diminuendo.**

Term	Musical Symbol	Definition
crescendo		growing louder
decrescendo	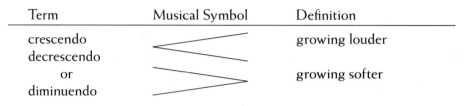	
or		growing softer
diminuendo		

Ludwig van Beethoven was a master at writing long crescendos. The transition to the last movement of his Symphony No. 5 comes upon the listener like a tidal wave of sound (5 3/10 at 3:10). An equally impressive crescendo can be heard at the beginning of Richard Strauss's *Thus Spoke Zarathustra* as the full orchestra gradually enters (intro /2). Spectacular moments such as these remind us that in music, as in marketing and communications generally, the medium (here dynamics and color) can be the message.

COLOR

Simply stated, **color** in music is the tone quality of any sound produced by a voice or an instrument. **Timbre** is another term for the tone quality of musical sound. Instruments produce sounds of different colors because they are constructed in different ways and from different materials. We need not understand the acoustical properties of the various instruments to appreciate that they sound different. We can all hear that the sound of a flute has a much different tone quality than does that of a trombone. Similarly, the voice of pop singer Rihanna has a different timbre than that of opera star Renée Fleming, even when the two produce the same pitches. Because the human voice was probably the first "instrument" to make music, it provides an appropriate starting point for our investigation of musical color.

THE VOICE

The human voice is an instrument of a very special sort that naturally generates sound without the aid of any kind of mechanical device. It is highly expressive, in part because it can produce a wide range of sounds and do so at greatly contrasting dynamic levels. Each voice has a distinctive timbre; we need hear only a few notes of a song to know that this is the sound, for example, of Pavarotti or Beyoncé or Bono.

When we sing we force air up through our vocal cords (two folds of mucous membrane within the throat), causing them to vibrate. Men's vocal cords are longer and thicker than women's, and for that reason the sound of the mature male voice is lower. (This principle is also at work with the string instruments: the longer and thicker the string, the lower the pitch.) Voices are classified by range into four principal parts. The two women's vocal parts are the **soprano** and the **alto,** and the two men's parts the **tenor** and the **bass.**

The soprano is the highest voice, and the bass the lowest. When many voices join together, they form a **chorus;** the soprano, alto, tenor, and bass constitute the four standard choral parts. In addition, the area of pitch shared by the soprano and alto is sometimes designated as a separate vocal range called the **mezzo-soprano,** just as the notes adjoining the tenor and bass are said to be encompassed by the **baritone** voice.

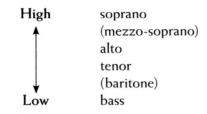

High   soprano
(mezzo-soprano)
alto
tenor
(baritone)
Low   bass

The voice is capable of producing many different styles of singing: the raspy sound of a blues singer, the twang of the country balladeer, the gutsy belt of a Broadway star, or the lyrical tones of an operatic soprano. We all try to sing, and we would like to sing well. How well we do, and what kind of sound we produce, depends on our training and our physical makeup—the lungs, vocal cords, throat, nose, and mouth are all involved in the production of vocal sound.

MUSICAL INSTRUMENTS

Why Do Musical Instruments Sound the Way They Do?

Have you ever wondered why a flute or violin sounds the way it does—why it has a distinctive timbre? The answer rests in a basic law of musical acoustics.

When a string vibrates or air rushes through a column in a wind instrument—or even in a Coke bottle—more than one sound is actually produced. We hear a basic sound, called the *fundamental.* But a string, for example, vibrates not only in its full (fundamental) length but simultaneously in parts of the string (halves, thirds, quarters, and so on), and these fractional vibrations produce many very, very faint sounds, called **overtones.** Generally, the larger the fraction (one-half rather than one-quarter, for instance), the louder the sound of the overtone. But each type of instrument—be it trumpet or

@

Watch a video of Craig Wright's Open Yale Course class session 2, "Introduction to Instruments and Musical Genres," at the text website.

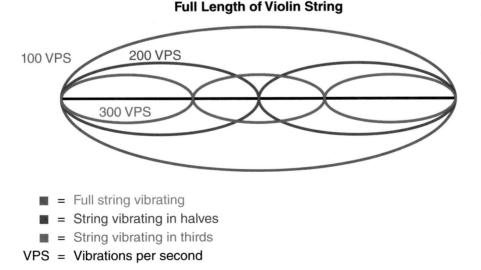

Full Length of Violin String

100 VPS

200 VPS

300 VPS

■ = Full string vibrating
■ = String vibrating in halves
■ = String vibrating in thirds
VPS = Vibrations per second

FIGURE 5–2

The diagram demonstrates that when a string (fundamental) vibrates, subsets of it also vibrate, thereby producing other faintly heard pitches called overtones.

FIGURE 5–3

The overtone series of a violin playing the G string arranged to show degree of loudness. It is the particular mix of the faint overtones that gives each type of instrument its distinctive sound.

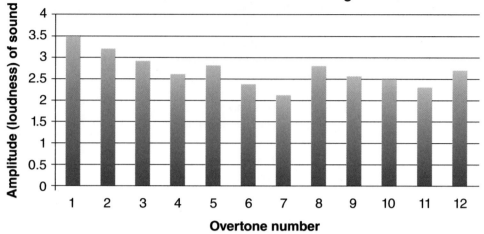

First Twelve Overtones of the G String of a Violin

oboe—manifests a distinctive pattern of overtones, depending on the instrument's material and design. The degree of prominence of particular overtones blending with the fundamental gives an entire family of instruments (see "Instrument Families" below) its distinctive sound. Figure 5-3 shows the overtone series of the G string of a violin. Notice how there is no straight-line descent as the overtones sound all at once. Overtone seven is faint but number eight asserts itself strongly. Although other issues are at play, the proportions of the overtones—just like the mix of various coffees in the "holiday blend" at Starbucks—gives each instrument its unique color.

Instrument Families

Musical instruments come in groups, or families—instruments of one general type that have similar materials and design. The Western symphony orchestra traditionally includes four such groups. The first is the string family, so called because sound is produced by plucking or bowing the strings of these instruments. The second and third groups are the woodwind and brass families. In both groups music is generated by blowing air through various pipes or tubes. In the fourth group, the percussion family, sound is produced by striking a suspended membrane (a drum), a block of wood, or a piece of metal with a stick of some kind. In addition, there is a fifth group of instruments, the keyboard instruments, which are not normally part of the symphony orchestra. The organ, harpsichord, and piano are the main keyboard instruments, and they make sound by means of keys and pipes (organ) or keys and strings (harpsichord and piano). The organ is usually played alone, while the piano is most often heard either by itself or as an accompaniment to another instrument or the voice.

STRINGS

Generally, when we speak of string instruments in Western music, we broadly include all instruments that produce sound by means of vibrating strings: the guitar, banjo, ukulele, and harp, as well as the violin and its close relatives, the viola, cello, and double bass. But the guitar, banjo, ukulele, and harp usually produce their sound when plucked, whereas the violin and its relatives are normally played with a bow, not just plucked. Indeed, it is their use of a bow, along with their distinctive shape, that identifies the four members of the violin group. We

See and hear a demonstration of the overtone series for a piano and a trumpet at "Timbre—Overtones and Pedal Tones" in the YouTube playlist on the text website.

See a video of all the instruments, in Benjamin Britten's *Young Person's Guide to the Orchestra*, as well as keyboard videos, at the text website.

Listen to an iAudio podcast on identifying the different instruments at the text website.

traditionally associate these instruments with classical music. The guitar, banjo, ukulele, and harp, on the other hand, have their origins in folk music.

VIOLIN GROUP

The violin group constituted the original core of the symphony orchestra when it was first formed during the Baroque era (1600–1750). In terms of numbers of players, the violins, violas, cellos, and double basses still make up the largest part of any Western symphony orchestra. A large orchestra can easily include as many as a hundred members, at least sixty of whom play one of these four instruments.

The **violin** (Fig. 5-4 center; see also p. 121) is chief among the string instruments. It is also the smallest—it has the shortest strings and therefore the highest pitch. Because of its high range and singing tone, it often is assigned the melody in orchestral and chamber music. The violins are usually divided into groups known as firsts and seconds. The seconds play a part slightly lower in pitch and subordinate in function to the firsts.

The sound of the violin is produced when a bow is pulled across one of four strings held tightly in place by tuning pegs at one end of the instrument and by a tailpiece at the other. The strings are slightly elevated above the wooden body by means of a supporting bridge. Different sounds or pitches are produced when a finger of the left hand shortens, or "stops," a string by pressing it against the fingerboard—again, the shorter the string, the higher the pitch. Because each of the four strings can be stopped quickly in many different places, the violin possesses both great range and agility. The strings themselves are made of either animal gut or metal wire. The singing tone of the violin, however, comes not so much from the strings as from the wooden body, known as the sound box, which amplifies and enriches the sound. The better the design, wood, glue, and varnish of the sound box, the better the tone. (For the sound of the violin, turn to (intro)/13 at 0:00.)

The **viola** (Fig. 5-4 left) is about six inches longer than the violin, and it produces a somewhat lower sound. If the violin is the string counterpart of the soprano voice, then the viola has its parallel in the alto voice. Its tone is darker, richer, and more somber than that of the brilliant violin. (For the sound of the viola, turn to (intro)/13 at 1:37.)

You can easily spot the **cello** (violoncello) in the orchestra because the player sits with the instrument placed between his or her legs (Fig. 5-4 right). The pitch of the cello is well below that of the viola. It can provide a low bass sound as well as a lyrical melody. When played in its middle range by a skilled performer, the cello is capable of producing an indescribably rich, expressive tone. (For the sound of the cello, turn to (intro)/13 at 2:10.)

The **double bass** (Fig. 5-5) gives weight and power to the bass line in the orchestra. Because at first it merely doubled the notes of the cello an octave below, it was called the double bass. As you can see, the double bass is the largest, and hence lowest-sounding, of the string instruments. Its job in the orchestra, and even in jazz bands, is to help set a solid base

© Christian Steiner/Courtesy Brentano String Quartet

FIGURE 5-4

This photo of the American group the Brentano String Quartet shows the relative size of the violin (center), viola (left), and cello (right).

FIGURE 5-5

Double bass player Israel "Cachao" Lopez.

© Alexander Tamargo/Getty Images

© Francisco Cruz/SuperStock

FIGURE 5–6
The harp's unique special effect is its glissando, a rapid run up and down the strings that seems to fill the atmosphere with energized sound.

for the musical harmony. (For the sound of the double bass, turn to (intro)/ 13 at 2:50.)

The members of the violin group all generate pitches in the same way: a bow is drawn across a tight string. This produces the traditional, penetrating string sound. In addition, a number of other effects can be created by using different playing techniques.

- **vibrato:** By shaking the left hand as it stops the string, the performer can produce a sort of controlled "wobble" in the pitch. This adds richness to the tone of the string because, in fact, it creates a blend of two or more pitches. (For an example of a violin playing without vibrato and then with vibrato, turn to (intro)/13 at 0:31 and at 0:51.)
- **pizzicato:** Instead of bowing the strings, the performer plucks them. With this technique, the resulting sound has a sharp attack, but it dies away quickly. (For an example of pizzicato, turn to (intro)/13 at 1:13.)
- **tremolo:** The performer creates a musical "tremor" by rapidly repeating the same pitch with quick up-and-down strokes of the bow. Tremolo creates a feeling of heightened tension and excitement when played loudly, and a velvety, shimmering backdrop when performed quietly. (For an example of tremolo, turn to (intro)/13 at 1:24.)
- **trill:** The performer rapidly alternates between two distinctly separate but neighboring pitches. Most instruments, not just the strings, can play trills. (For an example of a trill, turn to (intro)/13 at 1:30.)
- **mute:** If a composer wants to dampen the penetrating tone of a string instrument, he or she can instruct the player to place a mute (a metal or rubber clamp) on the strings of the instrument.

THE HARP

Although originally a folk instrument, one found in virtually every musical culture, the **harp** (Fig. 5-6) is sometimes added to the modern symphony orchestra. Its role is to add its distinctive color to the orchestral sound and sometimes to create special effects, the most striking of which is a rapid run up or down the strings called a **glissando.** (For the sound of the harp and an example of a glissando, turn to (intro)/13 at 3:35 and 3:44.)

Listening GUIDE   **Instruments of the Orchestra**
Strings   (intro)
                                                          13

0:00	**13**	Violin plays major scale	1:49		Viola solo: Haydn
0:13		Violin solo: Tchaikovsky	2:10		Cello plays major scale
0:31		Violin plays without vibrato: Haydn	2:30		Cello solo: Haydn
0:51		Violin plays with vibrato: Haydn	2:50		Double bass plays major scale
1:13		Violin plays pizzicato	3:13		Double bass solo: Haydn
1:24		Violin plays tremolo	3:35		Harp plays arpeggio
1:30		Violin plays trill	3:44		Harp solo: Tchaikovsky
1:37		Viola plays major scale			

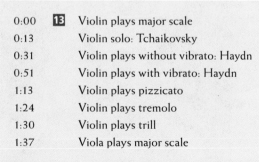

Listen to streaming music in an Active Listening Guide, available at the text website.

WOODWINDS

The name "woodwind" was originally given to this family of instruments because they emit sound when air is blown through a wooden tube or pipe. The pipe has holes along its length, and the player covers or uncovers these to change the pitch. Today, however, some of these woodwind instruments are made entirely of metal. Flutes, for example, are constructed of silver, and sometimes gold or even platinum. As with the violin group, there are four principal woodwind instruments in every modern symphony orchestra: flute, oboe, clarinet, and bassoon (Fig. 5-7). In addition, each of these has a close relative that is larger or smaller in size and that possesses a somewhat different timbre and range. The larger the instrument or length of pipe, the lower the sound.

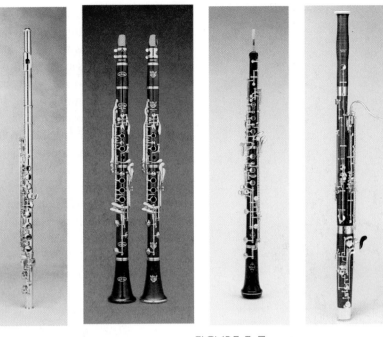

FIGURE 5–7

(from left to right) A flute, two clarinets, an oboe, and a bassoon. The flute, clarinet, and oboe are about the same length. The bassoon is nearly twice their size.

© Conn-Selmer, Inc.

The lovely, silvery tone of the **flute** is probably familiar to you. The instrument can be rich in the lower register and then light and airy on top. It is especially agile, capable of playing tones rapidly and moving quickly from one range to another. (For the sound of the flute, turn to (intro)/14 at 0:00.)

The smaller cousin of the flute is the **piccolo.** ("Piccolo" comes from the Italian *flauto piccolo,* meaning "little flute.") It can produce higher notes than any other orchestral instrument. And though the piccolo is very small, its sound is so piercing that it can always be heard, even when the full orchestra is playing loudly. (For the sound of the piccolo, turn to (intro)/14 at 0:38.)

The **clarinet** produces sound when the player blows against a single reed fitted to the mouthpiece. The tone of the clarinet is an open, hollow sound. It can be mellow in its low notes but shrill in its high ones. It also has the capacity to slide or glide smoothly between pitches, and this allows for a highly expressive style of playing. The flexibility and expressiveness of the instrument have made it a favorite with jazz musicians. (For the sound of the clarinet, turn to (intro)/14 at 0:54.) A lower, larger version of the clarinet is the bass clarinet.

The **oboe** is equipped with a double reed—two reeds tied together with an air space in between. When the player blows into the instrument through the double reed, the vibrations create a nasal, slightly exotic sound. It is invariably the oboe that gives the pitch at the beginning of every symphony concert. Not only was the oboe the first nonstring instrument to be added to the orchestra, but it is a difficult instrument to tune (regulate the pitch). Thus, it's better to have the other instruments tune to it than to try to have it adjust to them. (For the sound of the oboe, turn to (intro)/14 at 1:24.)

Related to the oboe is the **English horn.** Unfortunately, it is wrongly named, for the English horn is neither English nor a horn. It is simply a larger (hence lower-sounding) version of the oboe that originated on the continent of Europe. The English horn produces a dark, haunting sound, one that was especially favored by composers of the Romantic period (1820–1900). (For the sound of the English horn, turn to ▣4/18 at 0:40.)

The **bassoon** functions among the woodwinds much as the cello does among the strings. It can serve as a bass instrument, adding weight to the lowest sound, or, because of its very wide range, it can act as a soloist in its own right, playing high, lyrical passages. When playing moderately fast or rapid passages as a solo instrument, it has a dry, almost comic tone. (For the sound of the bassoon, turn to (intro)/14 at 1:54.)

There is also a double bassoon, usually called the **contrabassoon.** Its sound is deep and sluggish. Indeed, the contrabassoon can play notes lower than any other orchestral instrument. Because the keys are far apart, one has to have fairly large hands to play it.

The bassoon, contrabassoon, and English horn are all double-reed instruments, just like the oboe. Their tones, therefore, may sound more vibrant, even more exotic, than the mellow sounds of the single-reed instruments like the clarinet and saxophone.

Strictly speaking, the single-reed **saxophone** is not a member of the symphony orchestra, though it can be added on occasion. Its sound can be mellow and expressive but also, if the player wishes, husky, even raucous. The expressiveness of the saxophone makes it a welcome member of most jazz ensembles.

Listening GUIDE

Instruments of the Orchestra
Woodwinds

(intro) **14**

0:00	**14**	Flute plays major scale	1:02		Clarinet solo: Berlioz
0:11		Flute solo: Debussy	1:24		Oboe plays major scale
0:38		Piccolo plays major scale	1:33		Oboe solo: Tchaikovsky
0:47		Piccolo solo: Tchaikovsky	1:54		Bassoon plays major scale
0:54		Clarinet plays major scale	2:05		Bassoon solo: Stravinsky

Listen to streaming music in an Active Listening Guide, available at the text website.

FIGURE 5–8

Members of the Canadian Brass, with the French horn player at the left and the tuba player at the right.

BRASSES

Like the woodwind and string groups of the orchestra, the brass family consists of four primary instruments: trumpet, trombone, French horn, and tuba (Fig. 5-8). Brass players use no reeds, but instead blow into their instruments through a cup-shaped **mouthpiece** (Fig. 5-9). By adjusting valves or moving a slide, the performer can make the length of pipe on the instrument longer or shorter, and hence the pitch lower or higher.

Everyone has heard the high, bright, cutting sound of the **trumpet.** Whether in a football stadium or an orchestral hall, the trumpet is an excellent solo instrument because of its agility and penetrating tone. (For the sound of the trumpet, turn to (intro)/15 at 0:00.) The trumpet sounds forth with special brilliance at the beginning of Strauss's *Thus Spoke Zarathustra* ((intro)/2 at 0:14). When provided with a mute (a hollow plug placed in the bell of the instrument to dampen the sound), the trumpet can produce a softer tone that blends well with other instruments. (To hear a trumpet with a mute, turn to (intro)/15 at 0:22.)

Although distantly related to the trumpet, the **trombone** (Italian for "large trumpet") plays in the middle range of the brass family. Its sound is large and full. Most important, the trombone is the only brass instrument to generate sounds by moving a slide in and out, thereby producing higher or lower pitches. Needless to say, the trombone can easily slide from pitch to pitch, sometimes for comical effect. (For the sound of the trombone, turn to (intro)/15 at 0:35.)

The **French horn** (sometimes just called "horn") was the first brass instrument to join the orchestra, back in the late seventeenth century. Its sound is rich and mellow, yet somewhat veiled or covered. The French horn was especially popular during the Romantic period (1820–1900), because the horn's traditional association with the hunt and with Alpine mountains suggested nature, a subject dear to the hearts of the Romantics. (For the sound of the French horn, turn to (intro)/15 at 0:59.) It is easy to confuse the sound of the French horn with that of the trombone, because both are middle-range brass instruments and have a full, majestic tone. But the sound of the trombone is somewhat clearer and more focused, and its attack more direct, than that of the French horn, which can sound muffled. (For an immediate comparison of the trombone with the French horn, turn to (intro)/15, first at 0:45 and then at 1:17.)

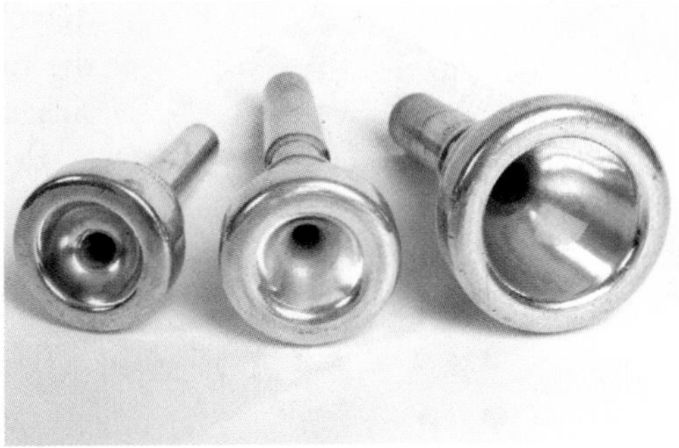

The **tuba** is the largest and lowest-sounding of the brass instruments. It produces a full, though sometimes muffled, tone in its lowest notes. Like the double bass of the violin group, the tuba is most often used to set a base, or foundation, for the melody. (For the sound of the tuba, turn to (intro)/15 at 1:39.) On occasion, the tuba itself is assigned a melodic line, as in Picture 4 of Musorgsky's *Pictures at an Exhibition* ([5] 4/15 at 0:02.) Here, the tuba demonstrates the melodious upper range of the instrument in a lengthy solo.

FIGURE 5–9
Three mouthpieces for brass instruments.

© Chris Stock/Lebrecht Music & Arts

*L*istening GUIDE

Instruments of the Orchestra Brasses

(intro) 15

0:00	15	Trumpet plays major scale	0:59	French horn plays major scale
0:09		Trumpet solo: Mouret	1:17	French horn solo: Copland
0:22		Trumpet solo with mute: Mouret	1:39	Tuba plays major scale
0:35		Trombone plays major scale	2:00	Tuba solo: Copland
0:45		Trombone solo: Copland		

Listen to streaming music in an Active Listening Guide, available at the text website.

PERCUSSION

Percussion instruments are those that are struck in some way, either by hitting the head of a drum with a stick or by banging or scraping a piece of metal or wood in one fashion or another. Some percussion instruments, like the timpani (kettledrums), produce a specific pitch, while others generate sound that, while rhythmically precise, has no recognizable musical pitch. It is the job of the percussion instruments to sharpen the rhythmic contour of the music. They can also add color to the sounds of other instruments and, when played loudly, can heighten the sense of climax in a piece.

The **timpani** (Fig. 5-10) is the percussion instrument most often heard in classical music. Whether struck in single,

FIGURE 5–10
Tympanist Jonathan Haas of the American Symphony Orchestra.

© Tim Wimborne/Reuters/CORBIS

detached strokes or hit rapidly to produce a thunderlike roll, the function of the timpani is to add depth, tension, and drama to the music. Timpani usually come in pairs, one instrument tuned to the tonic and the other to the dominant. Playing only these pitches, the timpani feature prominently at the beginning of Strauss's *Thus Spoke Zarathustra* ((intro)/2 at 0:26).

The rat-ta-tat-tat of the **snare drum,** the dull thud of the **bass drum,** and the crashing ring of the **cymbals** are sounds well known from marching bands and jazz ensembles, as well as the classical orchestra. None of these instruments produces a specific musical tone. (To hear all three in succession, turn to (intro)/16 at 0:11.)

The xylophone, glockenspiel, and celesta, however, are three percussion instruments that do generate specific pitches. The **xylophone** (Fig. 5-11) is a set of wooden bars that, when struck by two hard mallets, produce a dry, wooden sound. The **glockenspiel** works the same way, but the bars are made of metal so that the tone is brighter and more ringing. The **celesta,** too, produces sound when hammers strike metal bars, but the hammers are activated by keys, as in a piano; the tone of the celesta is bright and tinkling—a delightful, "celestial" sound, as the name of the instrument suggests. To hear the celesta playing in Tchaikovsky's *Nutcracker,* turn to [5]3/22 at 0:08.

FIGURE 5-11

The xylophone, a fixed-pitch percussion instrument on which can be played a fully chromatic scale of several octaves.

© C Squared Studios/Getty Images

*L*istening GUIDE   **Instruments of the Orchestra**
                          Percussion   (intro)
                                                                                    16

| 0:00 | **16** | Timpani | 0:19 | Bass drum |
| 0:11 | | Snare drum | 0:31 | Cymbal |

Listen to streaming music in an Active Listening Guide, available at the text website.

KEYBOARD INSTRUMENTS

Keyboard instruments, which are unique to Western music, boast highly intricate mechanisms. The pipe organ, harpsichord, and piano are the West's principal keyboard instruments, and they originated at markedly different times. The **pipe organ** (Fig. 5-12), which traces its origins back to ancient Greece, is by far the oldest. It works according to the following principle: the player depresses a key that allows air to rush into a pipe, thereby producing sound. The pipes are arranged in separate groups according to their shape and material. Each group produces a full range of musical pitches with one special timbre (the sound of the trumpet, for example). When the organist wants to add a particular musical color to a piece, he or she simply pulls a knob, called a **stop.** The most colorful, forceful sound occurs when all the stops have been activated (thus the expression "pulling out all the stops"). The several keyboards of the organ make it possible to play several musical lines at once, each with its own timbre. There is even a keyboard for the feet! The largest fully functioning pipe organ in the world is in the Cadet Chapel of the United States Military Academy at West Point, New York. It has 270 stops and 18,408 pipes.

FIGURE 5–12

A three-manual (keyboard) pipe organ with only small pipes visible. Notice the stops (small circular objects on either side of the manual keyboards) and the pedal keyboard below.

FIGURE 5–13

A two-manual harpsichord built by Pascal Taskin (Paris, 1770), preserved in the Yale University Collection of Musical Instruments, New Haven, Connecticut.

The **harpsichord** (Fig. 5-13) was played in northern Italy as early as 1400, but it reached its heyday during the Baroque era (1600–1750). It produces sound not by means of pipes but by strings. When a key is depressed, it drives a lever upward that in turn forces a pick to pluck a string. The plucking creates a bright, jangling sound. Some harpsichords are equipped with two keyboards so that the player can change from one group of strings to another, each with its particular tone color and volume of sound. The harpsichord has one important shortcoming, however: the lever mechanism does not allow the performer to control the force with which the string is plucked, so each string always sounds at the same volume. (For more on the harpsichord, see p. 100.)

The **piano** (Fig. 5-14) was invented in Italy around 1700, in part to overcome the dynamic limitations of the harpsichord. In a piano strings are not plucked; they are hit by soft hammers. A lever mechanism makes it possible for the player to regulate how hard each string is struck, thus producing softs and louds (the original piano was called the *pianoforte*, the "soft-loud"). During the lifetime of Mozart (1756–1791), the piano replaced the harpsichord as the favorite domestic musical instrument. By the nineteenth century every aspiring household had to have a piano, whether as an instrument for real musical enjoyment or as a symbol of affluence. Even today the piano stands as a domestic status symbol.

Whereas the organ's familiar home is the church, where it is heard in association with religious services, the versatile piano can be found almost everywhere. With equal success it can accompany a school chorus or an opera singer; it

FIGURE 5–14

Pianist Lang Lang.

@

View a video demonstration of the organ, harpsichord, and piano at the text website.

@

Watch a video of Craig Wright's Open Yale Course class session 12, "Guest Conductor: Saybrook Youth Orchestra," at the text website.

can harmonize with a rock band when in the hands of an Elton John or a Billy Joel; or it can become a powerful, yet expressive, solo instrument when played by a virtuoso such as Lang Lang (Fig. 5-14). The harpsichord, on the other hand, is used mainly to re-create the music of the time of Johann Sebastian Bach (1685–1750).

The Symphony Orchestra

The modern Western symphony orchestra is one of the largest and certainly the most colorful of all musical ensembles. It originated in the seventeenth century and has continually grown in size since then. When at full strength, the symphony orchestra can include upward of one hundred performers and nearly thirty different instruments, from the high, piping piccolo down to the rumbling contrabassoon. A typical seating plan for an orchestra is given in Figure 5-15. To achieve the best balance of sound, strings are placed toward the front, and the more powerful brasses at the back. Other seating arrangements are also used, according to the special requirements of the composition to be performed.

Surprisingly, a separate conductor was not originally part of the orchestra. Only around the time of Beethoven (1770–1827), when the orchestra was already two hundred years old, was it thought necessary to have someone stand before it and direct the players. Indeed, the conductor functions something like a musical traffic cop: he or she makes sure that the cellos don't crash into the violins and that the oboe yields to the clarinet at the proper moment so the melody can be heard. The conductor follows an **orchestral score**, a composite notation of all the instrumental parts for a particular piece. Figure 5-16 shows the orchestral score of the beginning of Beethoven's Symphony

FIGURE 5–15
Seating plan of a symphony orchestra.

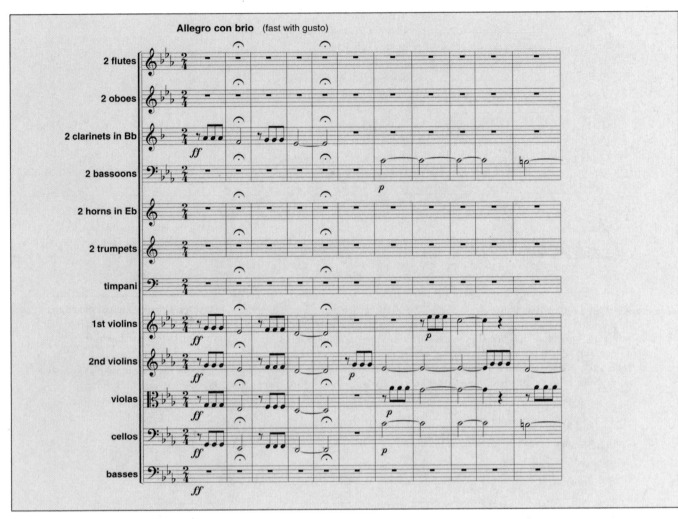

FIGURE 5–16

The orchestral score of the beginning of Beethoven's Symphony No. 5, first page, with instruments listed.

No. 5. Obviously, Beethoven had to put many notes on the page to achieve just a few seconds of music. It is the job of the conductor to follow, and perhaps memorize, the orchestral score and then pick out any incorrectly played pitches and rhythms in this complicated web of instrumental sounds. To do this, he or she must have an excellent musical ear.

You have now been introduced to the principal instruments of the Western symphony orchestra, as well as the West's three main keyboard instruments. Listening Exercises 8–10 test your ability to recognize orchestral instruments and are graduated in difficulty.

Listening EXERCISE 8

Hearing the Instruments of the Orchestra
Identifying a Single Instrument

(intro) 17

@ To take this Listening Exercise online and receive feedback or email answers to your instructor, go to the text website.

By listening to the Intro CD, tracks 13–16, you have heard all of the principal instruments of the Western symphony orchestra. Now it is time to test your ability to identify these instruments. The Intro CD, track 17, contains excerpts of performances of ten solo instruments. Write the name of the correct instrument in the blank by choosing one from the right-hand column.

(continued)

1. (0:00)   _____   Clarinet (Rimsky-Korsakov)
2. (0:14)   _____   Oboe (Tchaikovsky)
3. (0:38)   _____   Tuba (Berlioz)
4. (0:52)   _____   Bassoon (Rimsky-Korsakov)
5. (1:13)   _____   Violin (Tchaikovsky)
6. (1:30)   _____   French horn (Brahms)
7. (1:48)   _____   Flute (Tchaikovsky)
8. (2:09)   _____   Cello (Saint-Saëns)
9. (2:34)   _____   Double bass (Beethoven)
10. (2:50)   _____   Trombone (Ravel)

 EXERCISE 9

Hearing the Instruments of the Orchestra
Identifying Two Instruments

 intro 18   **@** To take this Listening Exercise online and receive feedback or email answers to your instructor, go to the text website.

Now things get more difficult. Can you identify two instruments playing at once, and which one is playing in a higher range? To keep you on track, a few instruments have been filled in. Choose from among the following instruments for the remaining blanks below: violin, viola, cello, double bass, flute (heard twice), clarinet, oboe (heard twice), bassoon, trumpet, and French horn.

		First Instrument	Second Instrument	Higher Instrument
(0:00)	Brahms	French horn	1. _____	2. _____
(0:40)	Mahler	3. _____	4. _____	5. _____
(1:08)	Lully	6. _____	clarinet	7. _____
(1:29)	Bach	8. _____	bassoon	9. _____
(1:44)	Bach	10. _____	11. _____	12. _____
(2:00)	Telemann	13. _____	viola	14. _____
(2:27)	Bartók	15. _____	16. _____	17. _____
(2:52)	Bach	18. _____	19. _____	20. _____

Listening EXERCISE 10

Hearing the Instruments of the Orchestra
Identifying Three Instruments

 intro 19   **@** To take this Listening Exercise online and receive feedback or email answers to your instructor, go to the text website.

Ready for the ultimate test? Now you need to identify three instruments. Choose from among the following instruments for the blanks below: violin, viola, cello, flute (twice), clarinet, bassoon, trumpet (twice), trombone, French horn, and tuba.

		First Instrument	Second Instrument	Third Instrument
(0:00)	Tchaikovsky	1. _____	French horn	2. _____
(0:18)	Tchaikovsky	3. _____	4. _____	5. _____
(0:40)	Lully	6. _____	bassoon	7. _____
(1:00)	Bach	8. _____	French horn	9. _____
(1:44)	Beethoven	10. _____	11. _____	12. _____

Finally, identify the highest and lowest sounding of the three instruments in four of the excerpts.

		Highest	Lowest
(0:40)	Lully	13. _____	14. _____
(0:00)	Tchaikovsky	15. _____	16. _____
(0:18)	Tchaikovsky	17. _____	18. _____
(1:44)	Beethoven	19. _____	20. _____

Key WORDS

dynamics (41)
forte (41)
piano (41)
sforzando (41)
crescendo (42)
decrescendo
    (diminuendo) (42)
color (42)
timbre (42)

soprano (42)
alto (42)
tenor (42)
bass (42)
chorus (43)
mezzo-soprano (43)
baritone (43)
overtone (43)
vibrato (46)

pizzicato (46)
tremolo (46)
trill (46)
mute (46)
glissando (46)
mouthpiece (48)
stop (50)
orchestral score (52)

@

The materials on the text website will help you understand and pass tests on the content of this chapter. In addition, you may watch Craig Wright's own lectures at Open Yale Courses and complete this chapter's Listening Exercises interactively, as well as view Active Listening Guides and other materials that will help you succeed in this course.

6

MUSICAL TEXTURE AND FORM

When a painter or weaver arranges material on a canvas or loom, he or she creates a texture: **texture** is the density and arrangement of artistic elements. Look at Vincent Van Gogh's *Branch of an Almond Tree in Blossom* (1890), shown in Figure 6-1. Though heavier at the bottom, the texture is generally light and airy, owing to the spaces between the lines (branches). And because the curving horizontal and vertical lines are more or less equally distributed across the blue background, the canvas conveys a feeling of balance and repose. Just as a painter can fabricate a particular texture—dense, heavy, light, or thin, with independent or interdependent strands—so, too, can the composer create similar effects with musical lines. The opening section of Richard Strauss's *Thus Spoke Zarathustra* (intro/2) begins with the bottom range of the orchestral palette (low organ pipe) in a sparse texture, then fills in the middle- (entering trumpet) and upper- (higher trumpet) range sounds, and concludes with the densest orchestral texture—all the instruments of the great nineteenth-century orchestra filling in the full sonic spectrum.

© Art Resource, NY

FIGURE 6-1

Branch of an Almond Tree in Blossom (1890), by Vincent Van Gogh.

Listen to an iAudio podcast on distinguishing the textures at the text website.

MONOPHONIC, HOMOPHONIC, AND POLYPHONIC TEXTURES

There are three primary textures in music—monophonic, homophonic, and polyphonic—depending on the number of musical lines and the way they relate to one another. Often we call these lines, or parts, voices even though they might not actually be sung.

Monophony is the easiest texture to hear. As the name "one sounding" indicates, **monophony** is a single line of music, with no harmony. When you sing by yourself, you are creating monophonic music. When a group of men (or women) sing the same pitches together, they are singing in **unison.** Unison singing is monophonic singing. Even when men and women sing together, doubling pitches at the octave, the texture is still monophonic. Thus, when we sing "Happy Birthday" with our friends at a party, and we all sing the exact same notes at the same time, we are singing in monophony. Monophonic texture is the sparsest of all musical textures.

Homophony means "same sounding." In this texture the voices, or lines, all move together to new pitches at roughly the same time. The most common type of homophonic texture is tune-plus-chordal-accompaniment. Here a melody is supported by the blocks of sound called chords. Notice in Example 6-1 how the melody, which by itself would be monophonic, now joins with vertical blocks of chords to create homophonic texture. Holiday carols, hymns, folksongs, and almost all pop songs invariably have this sort of tune-plus-chordal-accompaniment texture when sung with harmony. Can you hear in your mind's ear a band playing *The Star Spangled Banner?* That's homophonic texture. (Other examples can be heard in the following Listening Guide at intro/20 at 0:06 and 0:40.)

EXAMPLE 6–1 HOMOPHONY

As might be supposed from the meaning of its name, "many sounding," **polyphony** requires two or more lines in the musical fabric. In addition, the term *polyphonic* implies that each of the lines will be autonomous and independent, often entering at different times. Thus polyphonic texture has a strong linear (horizontal) thrust, whereas in homophonic texture the fabric is marked by lines that are more vertically conceived as blocks of accompanying chords (compare the arrows in Ex. 6-1 and Ex. 6-2). In polyphonic texture the voices are of equal importance, moving against one another to create what is called counterpoint. **Counterpoint** is simply the harmonious opposition of two or more independent musical lines. Because counterpoint requires polyphonic texture, the terms *counterpoint* and *polyphony* are often used interchangeably.

Finally, there are two types of counterpoint: free and imitative. In free counterpoint the voices are highly independent; they may begin all together or begin separately, but they then go their own ways. Much jazz improvisation is done in free counterpoint. To hear a fine example, turn to the end of Louis Armstrong's rendition of "Willie the Weeper" (intro /9 at 2:49). In imitative counterpoint, on the other hand, a leading voice begins followed by one or more other voices that duplicate what the first voice presented. If the followers copy exactly, note for note, what the leader plays or sings, then a **canon** results. Think of "Three Blind Mice," "Are You Sleeping?" ("Frère Jacques"), and "Row, Row, Row Your Boat," and remember how each voice enters in turn, imitating the first voice from beginning to end. These are all short canons, or rounds, a type of strictly imitative counterpoint popular since the Middle Ages. Example 6-2 shows the beginning of a brief canon for three voices.

EXAMPLE 6–2 POLYPHONY

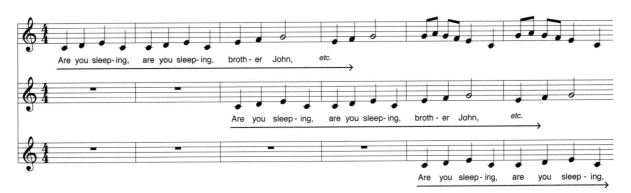

Among the most famous canons in music is Johann Pachelbel's Canon in D major (intro /11), written in Germany about 1690. This is not a short round like "Are You Sleeping?" but a lengthy work in which one violin begins and then two others in turn duplicate this line, note after note, for more than four minutes. As we saw in Listening Exercise 7, in Pachelbel's Canon a repeating bass line supports the three canonic upper parts; the bass sounds forth during the first two measures, and then the canon begins.

EXAMPLE 6–3 PACHELBEL'S CANON

Of course, composers are not limited to just one of these three musical textures—they can switch them within a given work. To get the sound of the various textures in your ear, as well as to hear changes of texture, listen to the famous "Hallelujah" chorus from George Frideric Handel's *Messiah.* Notice how rapidly, yet smoothly, the composer moves back and forth among homophonic, monophonic, and polyphonic textures.

Listening GUIDE

George Frideric Handel
"Hallelujah" chorus from *Messiah* (1741)

(intro) 20

0:06 **20**	"Hallelujah! Hallelujah!"	Homophony	1:27	"And He shall reign for ever and ever"	Polyphony
0:23	"For the Lord God Omnipotent reigneth"	Monophony	1:48	"King of Kings and Lord of Lords" together with "Hallelujah"	Homophony
0:30	"Hallelujah! Hallelujah!"	Homophony	2:28	"And He shall reign for ever and ever"	Polyphony
0:34	"For the Lord God Omnipotent reigneth"	Monophony			
			2:40	"King of Kings and Lord of Lords" together with "Hallelujah"	Homophony
0:40	"Hallelujah! Hallelujah!"	Homophony			
0:44	"For the Lord God Omnipotent reigneth" together with "Hallelujah"	Polyphony	2:48	"And He shall reign for ever and ever"	Polyphony
1:09	"The Kingdom of this world is become"	Homophony	2:55	"King of Kings and Lord of Lords" together with "Hallelujah"	Homophony

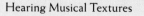 Listen to streaming music in an Active Listening Guide, available at the text website.

Listening EXERCISE 11

Hearing Musical Textures

(intro) 21

@ To take this Listening Exercise online and receive feedback or email answers to your instructor, go to the text website.

On your Intro CD, track 21, you have ten excerpts that exemplify the three basic textures of music. Monophonic texture, you will find, is easy to hear because it has only one line of music. More difficult is differentiating homophonic texture and polyphonic texture. Homophonic texture usually uses blocks of chords that accompany and support a single melody. Polyphonic texture, on the other hand, embodies many active, independent lines. Identify the texture of each of the excerpts by writing an M, H, or P in the appropriate blank.

1.	(0:00)	_____	Bach, Contrapunctus IX from *The Art of Fugue*
2.	(0:44)	_____	Beethoven, Symphony No. 5, 1st movement
3.	(0:52)	_____	Musorgsky, "Promenade" from *Pictures at an Exhibition*
4.	(1:02)	_____	Musorgsky, "Promenade" from *Pictures at an Exhibition*
5.	(1:12)	_____	Bach, Organ Fugue in G minor
6.	(2:03)	_____	Debussy, *Prelude to The Afternoon of a Faun*
7.	(2:22)	_____	Josquin Desprez, *Ave Maria*
8.	(2:48)	_____	Dvořák, Symphony No. 9, "From the New World," 2nd movement
9.	(3:17)	_____	Louis Armstrong, "Willie the Weeper"
10.	(3:41)	_____	Copland, "A Gift to Be Simple" from *Appalachian Spring*

FORM

Form in music is the arrangement of musical events. In architecture, sculpture, and painting, objects are situated in physical space so as to impose a formal design. Similarly, in music a composer places important sonic events in an order that creates a pleasing shape as sounds pass by in time.

To create form in music, a composer can employ four processes: statement, repetition, contrast, and variation. In other words, important musical ideas are stated, repeated, contrasted, or varied. A **statement,** of course, is the presentation of an important musical idea. **Repetition** works in tandem with a statement: it validates the statement by repeating it. Nothing would be more bewildering for a listener than a steady stream of ever-new music. How would we make sense of it? Repetition of a melody sets forth the formal markers, declaring each return an important musical event. Repetition also conveys a sense of comfort and security, of the musically familiar.

Contrast, on the other hand, takes us away from the familiar and into the unknown. A quiet melody in the strings can suddenly be followed by an insistent theme blasting from the French horns, as happens, for example, in the third movement of Beethoven's well-known Symphony No. 5 (**5** 3/9). Contrasting melodies, rhythms, textures, and moods can be used to serve as a foil to familiar material, to provide variety, and even to create conflict. In music, as in life, we need security, but we also need novelty and excitement—thus the interplay between repeating and contrasting musical units.

Variation stands midway between repetition and contrast. The original melody returns but is altered in some way. For example, the tune may now be more complex, or new instruments may be added against it to create counterpoint. The listener has the satisfaction of hearing the familiar melody, yet is challenged to recognize in what way it has been changed.

Needless to say, memory plays an important role in allowing us to hear musical form. Music is a most unusual art—we can't see it or touch it. As it wafts through the air, we use memory to make sense of it. We live forward but understand backward. Whether in history or in music, our memory puts the pieces together to show us relationships—patterns and forms. To help in this process, musicians have developed a simple system to visualize forms by labeling musical units with letters. The first statement of a musical idea is designated **A**. Subsequent contrasting sections are labeled **B, C, D,** and so on. If the first or any other musical unit returns in varied form, then that variation is indicated by a superscript number—A^1 and B^2, for example. Subdivisions of each large musical unit are shown by lowercase letters (**a**, **b**, and so on). How this works will become clear in the examples used throughout this book.

Five Favorite Musical Forms

Most musical forms are timeless—they are not unique to any one period in the history of music. The five forms discussed below have been favored by composers of both popular and classical music for many hundreds of years.

STROPHIC FORM

Listen to an iAudio podcast on distinguishing forms at the text website.

This is the most familiar of all musical forms because our hymns, carols, folksongs, patriotic songs, and pop tunes invariably make use of it. In **strophic form** the composer sets the words of the first poetic stanza and then uses the same entire melody for all subsequent stanzas. A good example is the 1960s pop favorite "The Weight" ("Take a Load off Annie"), originally created by the Canadian-American group The Band and then "covered" by at least thirty other artists, including the alternative rock group Travis. As is typical of many pop songs, each strophe begins with a verse of text and ends with a **chorus**—a textual refrain that repeats. Below is the text for the first two strophes of this five-strophe song. Again, in strophic form, each strophe has the same music.

Hear The Band sing this song in strophic form in the YouTube playlist on the text website.

Strophe 1
I pulled into Nazareth, I was feelin' about half past dead;
I just need some place where I can lay my head.
"Hey, mister, can you tell me where a man might find a bed?"
He just grinned and shook my hand, and "No!" was all he said.

(Chorus)
Take a load off Annie, take a load for free;
Take a load off Annie, And (and) (and) you can put the load right on me.

Strophe 2
I picked up my bag, I went lookin' for a place to hide;
When I saw Carmen and the Devil walkin' side by side.
I said, "Hey, Carmen, come on, let's go downtown."
She said, "I gotta go, but m'friend can stick around."

(Chorus)
Take a load off Annie, take a load for free;
Take a load off Annie, And (and) (and) you can put the load right on me.

Now listen to the first two stanzas of the equally well known *Wiegenlied* (*Lullaby*) of Johannes Brahms. Each stanza, again, is sung to the same music, but there is no chorus (refrain).

Listening GUIDE

Johannes Brahms
Lullaby (1868)

(intro)
22

0:00	**22**	Piano introduction		
0:05		Soprano sings strophe 1	Gut' Abend, gut Nacht,	Good evening, good night
			Mit Rosen bedacht,	Covered with roses,
			Mit Näglein besteckt	Adorned with carnations,
			Schlüpf unter die Deck':	Slip under the covers.
			Morgen früh, wenn Gott will,	Tomorrow early, if God so wills,
			Wirst du wieder geweckt.	You will awake again.

0:48	Repeat of piano introduction		
0:53	Soprano sings strophe 2 of text to same melody	Gut' Abend, gut Nacht,	Good evening, good night
		Von Englein bewacht,	Watched over by angels,
		Die zeigen im Traum	Who in dreams show
		Dir Christkindleins Baum:	You the Christ child's tree.
		Schlaf nun selig und süss,	Now sleep blissful and sweetly,
		Schau im Traum's Paradies.	Behold Paradise in your dreams.

Listen to streaming music in an Active Listening Guide, available at the text website.

A slightly varied version of strophic form, modified strophic form, can be heard in Clara Schumann's "Liebst du um Schönheit" ("If You Love for Beauty"); (intro)/23 and pp. 249–252.

THEME AND VARIATIONS

If, in the preceding example, the music of the first strophe, or stanza, is altered in some way each time it returns, then **theme and variations** form is present. The sort of changes that might occur include additions to the melody, new chords in the supporting accompaniment, and more density in the texture. The return of the basic musical unit (**A**) provides a unifying element, while the changes add variety. Theme and variations form can be visualized in the following scheme:

Statement of theme	Variation 1	Variation 2	Variation 3	Variation 4
A	**A^1**	**A^2**	**A^3**	**A^4**

FIGURE 6-2

Henri Matisse's *Jeannette 1–5* (1910) provides a clear example of theme and variations form applied to sculpture. Matisse first creates a sculpture of the head of his servant Jeannette (left) and then offers four progressively more abstract variations of it.

Digital Image © The Museum of Modern Art/ Licensed by SCALA/Art Resource, NY

When Mozart was a young man, he lived briefly in Paris, where he heard the French folksong *Ah, vous dirai-je Maman*. We know it today as *Twinkle, Twinkle, Little Star*. Upon this charming tune (**A**) he later composed a set of variations for piano, the first three of which are described in the following Listening Guide (for more on this piece, see p. 180).

Listening GUIDE

Wolfgang Amadeus Mozart
Variations on *Twinkle, Twinkle, Little*
***Star* (c1781)**

(intro)
24

0:00	**24**	A	Tune played without ornamentation; melody above, harmony below
0:30		A^1	Variation 1: Tune above decorated with florid, fast-moving figurations
0:59		A^2	Variation 2: Tune above undecorated; florid, fast-moving figurations now in bass
1:29		A^3	Variation 3: Tune above decorated with graceful arpeggios

Listen to streaming music in an Active Listening Guide, available at the text website.

FIGURE 6-3

(left) The essence of binary form, or **AB** form, can be seen in this Japanese wood carving. Here the two figures are distinctly different, yet mutually harmonious. (right) Ternary form, or **ABA** form, can clearly be seen in the architecture of the cathedral of Salzburg, Austria, where Mozart and his father frequently performed.

BINARY FORM

As the name indicates, **binary form** consists of two contrasting units, A and B. In length and general shape, A and B are constructed so as to balance and complement each other (Fig. 6-3). Variety is usually introduced in B by means of a dissimilar mood, key, or melody. Sometimes in binary form, both A and B are immediately repeated, note for note. Musicians indicate exact repeats by means of the following sign: ‖: :‖. Thus, when binary form appears as ‖: A :‖ ‖: B :‖ it is performed AABB.

Joseph Haydn created a perfect example of binary form in music for the second movement of his Symphony No. 94. Here an eight-bar musical phrase (A) is balanced by a different but corresponding eight-bar phrase (B). First A and then B are repeated. Notice that the repeats involve slight alterations. In the repeat of A, Haydn adds a sudden *sforzando* to startle sleepy listeners. From this musical gesture the symphony derives its name: the "Surprise" Symphony. In the repeat of B, flutes are added to the melody to enrich it.

Listening GUIDE

**Joseph Haydn
Symphony No. 94, the "Surprise"
Symphony
Second movement, *Andante* (moving)**

(intro)
25

| 0:00 | 25 | A presented by strings | | 0:33 | B presented by strings |
| 0:17 | | A repeated with surprise *sforzando* at end | | 0:50 | B repeated with flutes added to melody |

With this charming binary-form melody now in place, Haydn proceeds to compose a set of variations on it. The movement is discussed in full on pages 181–183.

Listen to streaming music in an Active Listening Guide, available at the text website.

TERNARY FORM

Ternary form in music is even more common than binary. It consists of three sections. The second is a contrasting unit, and the third is a repeat of the first—hence the formal pattern is **ABA**. As we will see (p. 168), ternary form has appeared many times in the history of music.[1] It is an especially satisfying arrangement because it is simple yet rounded and complete.

Listen now to the "Dance of the Reed Pipes" from Peter Tchaikovsky's famous ballet *The Nutcracker*. The **A** section is bright and cheery because it makes use of the major mode as well as silvery flutes. However, **B** is dark and low, even ominous, owing to the minor mode and the insistent ostinato (repeated pattern) in the bass. The return of **A** is shortened because the melody is not repeated.

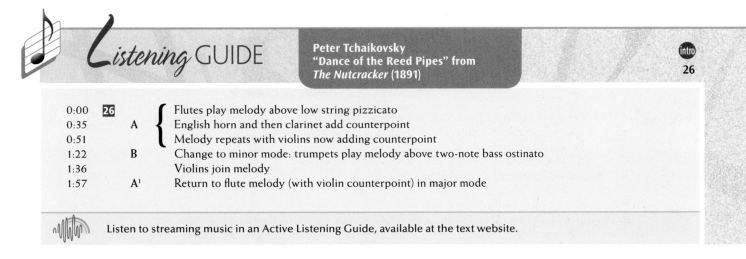

Listening GUIDE

Peter Tchaikovsky
"Dance of the Reed Pipes" from
The Nutcracker (1891)

intro
26

0:00	26		Flutes play melody above low string pizzicato
0:35	A	{	English horn and then clarinet add counterpoint
0:51			Melody repeats with violins now adding counterpoint
1:22	B		Change to minor mode: trumpets play melody above two-note bass ostinato
1:36			Violins join melody
1:57	A[1]		Return to flute melody (with violin counterpoint) in major mode

Listen to streaming music in an Active Listening Guide, available at the text website.

RONDO FORM

Rondo form involves a simple principle: a refrain (**A**) alternates with contrasting music. Usually in a rondo, there are at least two contrasting sections (**B** and **C**). Perhaps because of its simple, but pleasing design (Fig. 6-4), rondo form has been favored by musicians of every age—medieval monks, classical symphonists such as Mozart and Haydn, and even contemporary pop artists like Sting (see p. 186). Although the principle of a recurring refrain is a constant, composers have written rondos in several different formal patterns, as seen below. The hallmark of each, however, is a refrain (**A**).

ABACA   ABACABA   ABACADA

---

[1]On the difference between ternary and rounded binary form, see the Preface.

© Charles & Josette Lenars/CORBIS

FIGURE 6-4

The château of Chambord, France, has a formal design equivalent to **ABACABA** structure, a pattern often encountered in music in rondo form.

You may already be familiar with a rondo composed by Jean-Joseph Mouret (1682–1738), made famous as the theme music for *Masterpiece Theatre* (now *Masterpiece*), America's longest-running prime-time drama series, on PBS. Mouret was a composer at the French court during the reign of Louis XV (1715–1774), and his well-known *Rondeau* typifies the ceremonial splendor of the royal household during the Baroque era (1600–1750). Here the refrain (**A**), played by full orchestra with brilliant trumpets and drums, alternates with two contrasting ideas (**B** and **C**) to form a neatly symmetrical pattern.

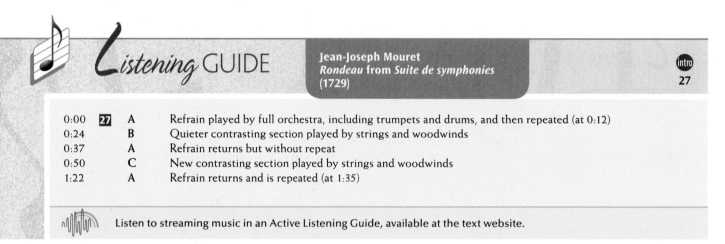

Listening GUIDE

Jean-Joseph Mouret
***Rondeau* from *Suite de symphonies* (1729)**

(intro) **27**

0:00	**27**	A	Refrain played by full orchestra, including trumpets and drums, and then repeated (at 0:12)
0:24		B	Quieter contrasting section played by strings and woodwinds
0:37		A	Refrain returns but without repeat
0:50		C	New contrasting section played by strings and woodwinds
1:22		A	Refrain returns and is repeated (at 1:35)

Listen to streaming music in an Active Listening Guide, available at the text website.

To sum up: Form in music is the purposeful arrangement of important musical elements. It offers a user-friendly guide—a road map, if you will—to the passage of music through time. Strophic form involves the repetition of the same short piece again and again, each time with a new text. In theme and variations form, a single idea continually returns but is varied in each presentation. Binary form involves two contrasting sections, whereas ternary form calls for statement, contrast, and return. Finally, in rondo form a predominant theme returns at regular intervals. These five forms are basic to all kinds of music in many parts of the world. In Western classical music there are other, more complex forms, such as sonata–allegro and fugal form. These we will meet in the subsequent parts of this book.

@

The materials on the text website will help you understand and pass tests on the content of this chapter. In addition, you may complete this chapter's Listening Exercise interactively, as well as view Active Listening Guides and other materials that will help you succeed in this course.

Key WORDS

texture (56)
monophony (56)
unison (56)
homophony (56)
polyphony (57)
counterpoint (57)
canon (57)

form (59)
statement (59)
repetition (59)
contrast (59)
variation (59)
strophic form (60)
chorus (60)

theme and variations (61)
binary form (62)
‖:‖ (indication to performer to repeat the music) (62)
ternary form (62)
rondo form (63)

MUSICAL STYLE

7

One of the challenges of listening to music is evaluating what we hear. Consciously or not, we do this every day. For example, sometimes when turning on the car radio or flipping through a playlist, we land in the middle of an unrecognized piece. Immediately, we try to make an educated guess as to the style. If pop, is it rap or reggae? If classical, is it Romantic or Baroque? As to the composer or artist, is the style that of Bach, Beethoven, or Bono? But what is style generally in music, and what is style specifically in classical music?

Style in music generally is the distinctive sound created by an artist, composer, or performing group. The voice of Norah Jones, for example, has a distinctive style that is soft and velvety. Classical composers, too, have distinctive styles. Take a work by Mozart (1756–1791), for example. A trained listener will recognize it as a piece from the Classical period (1750–1820) because of its generally symmetrical melodies, light texture, and dynamic ebb and flow. A truly experienced ear will identify Mozart as the composer, perhaps by recognizing the sudden shifts to minor keys, the intensely chromatic melodies, or the colorful writing for the woodwinds, all hallmarks of Mozart's personal musical style.

Classical music in general, and indeed each period in its history, also has a distinctive style. Here style is determined by the particular presentation and arrangement of the basic elements of music—rhythm, melody, harmony, texture, and so on. A concerto from the Baroque era (1600–1750), for example, will likely be marked by a strong bass, direct chord progressions, and an energetic but repetitive rhythm. A symphony from the Romantic period (1820–1900), on the other hand, will typically exhibit long, sweeping melodies; chromatic harmonies; and a relaxed, free rhythm. Every musical era has such telltale markers of style.

Human activity—artistic or otherwise—cannot always be neatly categorized. When does an infant become a child, or the child the adult? Similarly, musical styles do not change overnight; they evolve and overlap. Historians of music, however, like historians of art, have divided the development of Western music into eight style periods. This allows us to break the long continuum of human creativity into shorter, more manageable units.

Middle Ages: 476–1450	Classical: 1750–1820	Modern: 1900–1985
Renaissance: 1450–1600	Romantic: 1820–1900	Postmodern: 1945–present
Baroque: 1600–1750	Impressionist: 1880–1920	

FIGURE 7–1

Portions of the East Wing of the National Gallery of Art in Washington, built in 1978 to a design by I. M. Pei, stand in contrast to the United States Capitol in the background. Pei's building, with its flat surfaces and unadorned geometric shapes, is representative of the modern style in architecture, while the Capitol reflects the neoclassical style of the eighteenth century.

@ Complete Checklists of Musical Style can be found at the text website.

Key WORD

style (65)

@ View and hear comparisons of and quizzes on musical styles of all periods in the history of music, at the text website.

PART II

THE MIDDLE AGES AND RENAISSANCE, 476–1600

400	500	600	700	800	900	1000	1100	1200	1300	1400

MIDDLE AGES

● 476 Fall of Rome to Visigoths

● c530 Benedict of Nursia founds monastic order

 ← Hildegard of Bingen (1098–1179), musician, poet, visionary

● c1150 Beatriz of Dia and other troubadours flourish in southern France

● c1160 Gothic Cathedral of Notre Dame begun in Paris

● c700 *Beowulf*

c1170–1230 Leoninus and Perotinus develop polyphony in Paris

1348–1350 Black Death

c1360 Guillaume ● de Machaut (c1300–1377) composes *Messe de Nostre Dame* at Reims

● 800 Charlemagne crowned Holy Roman Emperor

c1390 Geoffrey ● Chaucer (c1340–1400) writes *Canterbury Tales*

● c880 Vikings invade Western Europe

1430s Guillaume ● Dufay (c1397–1474) composes chansons for Court of Burgundy

● 1066 William the Conqueror invades England

Historians use the term *Middle Ages* as a catchall phrase to refer to the thousand years of history between the fall of the Roman Empire (476) and the dawn of the Age of Discovery (mid-1400s, culminating in the voyages of Christopher Columbus). It was a period of monks and nuns, of knightly chivalry and brutal warfare, of sublime spirituality and deadly plagues, and of soaring cathedrals amidst abject poverty. Two institutions vied for political control: the Church and the court. From our modern perspective, the medieval period appears as a vast chronological expanse dotted by outposts of dazzling architecture, stunning stained glass, and equally compelling poetry and music.

Renaissance means literally "rebirth." Historians use the term to designate a period of intellectual and artistic flowering that occurred first in Italy, then in France, and finally in England, during the years 1350–1600. Music historians apply the term more narrowly to musical developments in those same countries during the period 1450–1600. The Renaissance was an age in which writers, artists, and architects looked back to classical Greece and Rome to find models for personal and civic expression. It was an important period for music as well. Among the most significant musical developments of the Renaissance was a newfound desire to use music to amplify the meaning of a given text. Finally, attributing creativity to human accomplishment as well as to God, Renaissance composers began to fashion secular music for the home as well as traditional religious music for the church.

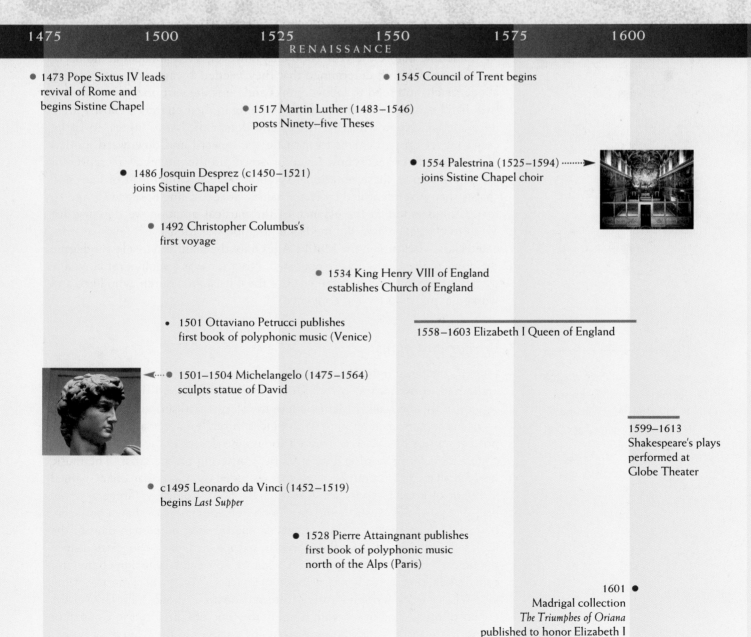

| 1475 | 1500 | 1525 | 1550 | 1575 | 1600 |

RENAISSANCE

- 1473 Pope Sixtus IV leads revival of Rome and begins Sistine Chapel

- 1545 Council of Trent begins

- 1517 Martin Luther (1483–1546) posts Ninety–five Theses

- 1554 Palestrina (1525–1594) joins Sistine Chapel choir

- 1486 Josquin Desprez (c1450–1521) joins Sistine Chapel choir

- 1492 Christopher Columbus's first voyage

- 1534 King Henry VIII of England establishes Church of England

- 1501 Ottaviano Petrucci publishes first book of polyphonic music (Venice)

1558–1603 Elizabeth I Queen of England

- 1501–1504 Michelangelo (1475–1564) sculpts statue of David

1599–1613 Shakespeare's plays performed at Globe Theater

- c1495 Leonardo da Vinci (1452–1519) begins *Last Supper*

- 1528 Pierre Attaingnant publishes first book of polyphonic music north of the Alps (Paris)

1601
Madrigal collection
The Triumphes of Oriana
published to honor Elizabeth I

MEDIEVAL MUSIC, 476–1450

Music in the Monastery

Pop musicians around the world today have no use for musical notation. Instead, they pass along tunes aurally—one singer, or group, hears and copies another. Music is not fixed on paper in quarter notes and meter signatures but is captured in digital recordings, whether MP3 files or discs. So, too, in the Middle Ages, one soldier, farmer, weaver, or minstrel heard a tune and passed it on. Needless to say, there were no digital recordings in the Middle Ages; what's more, there was little musical notation. Most music was not written down in a formal language of notation symbols. Why would anyone want to "write down" sounds?

Sometime before the year 1000 C.E., however, a few influential monks of the Western Church determined that they needed a way to organize, speak about, teach, and send to fellow monks and nuns the vast body of chant that they had learned by ear and had been singing in their churches. Slowly, they developed a system whereby dashes and dots, called *notae* (notes) in Latin, could be set on parchment to indicate the upward and downward motion of a melody. But exactly how *far* up or down did the pitch go? To represent melodic distance, these notational symbols were put on a grid of lines and spaces that were identified by letter names (space A, line B, space C, and so forth). Thus emerged the essence of the musical notation we now use for Western classical music. But medieval notation was for a select few—an educated class—because in the Middle Ages only the men, and to a lesser degree the nuns, of the Church were educated. Notation was a semisecret language used by those initiated into the ways of the Christian Church, who lived and worked in monasteries and convents.

Watch a video of Craig Wright's Open Yale Course class session 15, "Benedictine Chant and Music in the Sistine Chapel," at the text website.

Gregorian Chant

Life in a medieval monastery or convent was not easy. Monks and nuns generally had to rise at four o'clock in the morning to attend the first religious service of the day, called Matins. Here the clergy read scripture, prayed, and sang, and so, too, at eight other observances throughout the day. The most important service was Mass, celebrated about nine o'clock in the morning, which commemorated in word and song Christ's suffering on the cross. The music heard at all medieval churches was what we today call Gregorian chant, named in honor of Pope Gregory the Great (c540–604). Ironically, Gregory wrote little, if any, of this music. Being more a church administrator than a musician, he merely decreed that certain chants should be sung on certain days of the liturgical year. Melodies for the Christian service, had, of course, existed since the time of Christ's Apostles. In truth, what we now call **Gregorian chant** (also called **plainsong**) is really a large body of unaccompanied vocal music, setting sacred Latin texts, written for the Western (Roman Catholic) Church over the course of fifteen centuries, from roughly the time of Christ to the Council of Trent (1545–1563), which brought sweeping changes to the Church of Rome.

Gregorian chant is like no other music. It has a timeless, otherworldly quality that arises, no doubt, because Gregorian chant has neither meter nor regular rhythms. True, some notes are longer or shorter than others, but they do not recur in obvious patterns that would allow us to clap our hands or tap our feet. Free of tension and drama, chant is far more conducive to pious meditation than to dancing. Because all voices sing in unison, Gregorian chant is considered monophony, or music for one line. There is no instrumental accompaniment, nor, as a rule, are men's and women's voices mixed. Finally, Gregorian chant has a uniform, monochromatic sound. Any contrasts that occur are of the mildest sort. Sometimes a soloist will alternate with a full choir, for example. Occasionally, a passage of **syllabic singing** (only one or two notes for each syllable of text) will give way to **melismatic singing** (many notes sung to just one syllable), as in Example 8-1.

Example 8-1 shows most of a lengthy chant, *Viderunt omnes (All the Ends of the Earth)*, sung during Mass on Christmas Day. We know that it dates from the fifth century C.E., but we know nothing about its creator. (Not in jest do we say that "Master Anonymous" was the most prolific artist of the medieval period; this was a religious age in which creative individuals did not step forward to take credit for their accomplishments—the honor belonged to God.) Notice that although the pitches are clearly indicated, no rhythmic information is provided. The notes are generally of one basic value, something close to our eighth note in length. Notice also the presence of syllabic singing on the words "Viderunt" (They have seen) and "jubilate" (sing joyfully) and, conversely, the melismatic singing, particularly on the final syllable "ra" of "terra" (earth).

@ Download Supplementary Listening Guides for three more chants—*Dies irae, Puer natus est nobis,* and *Vidimus stellam*—at the text website.

EXAMPLE 8–1

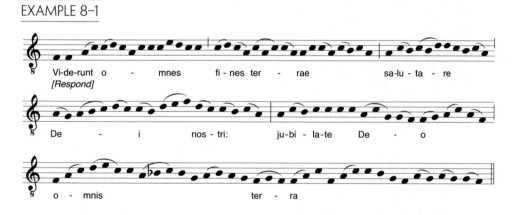

Vi-de-runt o - mnes fi-nes ter - rae sa-lu-ta - re
[Respond]

De - i nos - tri: ju-bi-la-te De - o

o - mnis ter - ra

All the ends of the earth have seen the salvation of our God; sing joyfully to God, all the earth.

Listening GUIDE   **Anonymous Gregorian chant, *Viderunt omnes* (fifth century)**   5 1/1

Texture: Monophonic

0:00	**1**	**Soloist:**	Viderunt omnes	All the ends of the earth have seen
		Choir:	fines terrae salutare Dei nostri;	the salvation of our God; sing
			jubilate Deo omnis terra.	joyfully to God, all the earth.

Listen to streaming music in an Active Listening Guide, available at the text website.

The Gregorian Chant of Hildegard of Bingen (1098–1179)

Gregorian chant was composed by churchwomen as well as churchmen. One of the most remarkable contributors to the repertoire of Gregorian chant was Hildegard of Bingen (1098–1179), from whose pen we received seventy-seven chants (Fig. 8-1). Hildegard was the tenth child of noble parents who gave her to the Church as a tithe (a donation of a tenth of one's worldly goods). She was educated by Benedictine nuns and then, at the age of fifty-two, founded her own convent near the small town of Bingen, Germany, on the west bank of the Rhine. Over time, Hildegard manifested her extraordinary intellect and imagination as a playwright, poet, musician, naturalist, pharmacologist, and visionary (Fig. 8-2). Ironically, then, the first "Renaissance man" was really a medieval woman: Hildegard of Bingen.

Hildegard's *O rubor sanguinis* (*O Redness of Blood*) possesses many qualities typical of her chants, and of chant generally (Ex. 8-2). First, it sets a starkly vivid text, which Hildegard herself created. Honoring St. Ursula and a group of 11,000 Christian women believed slain by the Huns in the fourth or fifth century, the poem envisages martyred blood streaming in the heavens and virginal flowers unsullied by serpentine evil. Each phrase of text receives its own phrase of music. And although it sweeps along melodically, having an unusually wide range for a chant, the melody sounds grounded tonally, each phrase ending with the first (tonic) or fifth (dominant) degree of the scale, with D or A. Notice that after an initial jump (D to A) in the first two pitches, the chant proceeds mostly in stepwise motion (neighboring pitches). This was, after all, choral music to be sung by the full community of musically unsophisticated nuns or monks, so it had to be easy. Finally, as with most chants, this piece has no overt rhythm or meter. The unaccompanied, monophonic line and the absence of rhythmic drive allow a restful, meditative mood to develop. Hildegard did not see herself as an "artist" as we think of one today, but in the spirit of medieval anonymity only as a vessel through which divine revelation came to earth. Indeed, she styled herself simply "a feather floating on the breath of God."

© Erich Lessing/Art Resource, NY

FIGURE 8–1

A twelfth-century illumination depicting Hildegard of Bingen receiving divine inspiration, perhaps a vision or a chant, directly from the heavens. To the right, her secretary, the monk Volmar, peeks in on her in amazement.

© The Art Archive/Biblioteca Civica, Lucca, Italy/Gianni Dagli Orti

FIGURE 8–2

(upper frame) A vision of Hildegard revealing how a fantastic winged figure of God the Father, the Son, and the Mystical Lamb killed the serpent Satan with a blazing sword. (lower frame) Hildegard (center) receives the vision and reports it to her secretary (left). This manuscript dates from the twelfth century.

EXAMPLE 8-2 Hildegard of Bingen, *O rubor sanguinis*

O   ru - bor san - gui - nis   /   qui   de ex - cel - so

CHANT AT THE TOP OF THE CHARTS

S·HILDEGARDIS·PROPHETISSA

In recent years Gregorian chant has become surprisingly popular. The excitement began in 1994 with the release, appropriately enough by Angel Records, of the CD *Chant*, which sold one million copies within the first two months of its appearance. That success spawned sequels, leading eventually to *Chant IV* (Angel 56373). More recently (2008), the album *Chant: Music for Paradise* shot to number 7 in the British pop charts, outselling releases from Amy Winehouse and Madonna. Much of the popularity of Gregorian chant can be attributed to the fact that it has stylistic traits in common with New Age music. Both project smooth, uniform, rhythmically fluid sounds that are decidedly nonassertive and nonconfrontational—the ultimate formula for relaxation and stress relief.

Hildegard, too, has been popularized as something of a New Age cult figure. She is a fixture on the Internet, where you can study her chants in the original notation, find translations of her poetry, view spectacular medieval depictions of her visions, and order the latest CDs or DVDs. A Google search will return more than 320,000 results for "Hildegard of Bingen." Most recently, her chant *O rubor sanguinis* featured prominently in the score of the 2006 Academy Award–winning film *Crash*. More than half of her chants can now be seen and heard on YouTube, and tens of thousands of listeners have done so. Could the visionary nun have foreseen that this intensely spiritual music would become such an overtly commercial success?

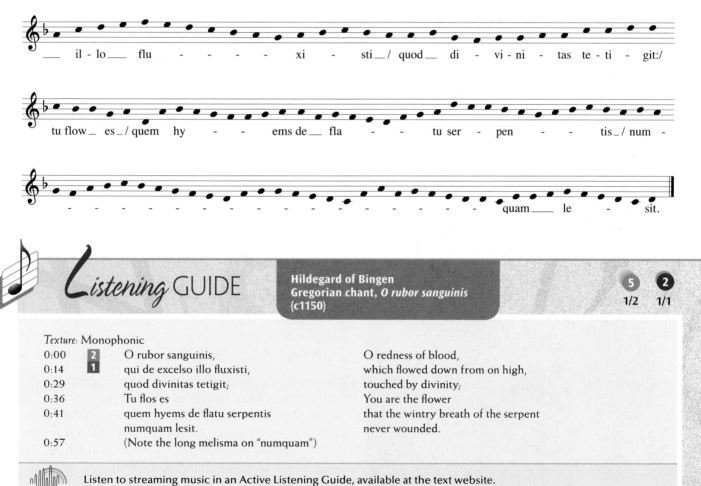

___ il - lo __ flu - - - - xi - sti _/ quod __ di - vi - ni - tas te - ti - git:/_

_tu flow __ es _/ quem hy - - ems de __ fla - - tu ser - pen - - - tis _/ num -_

_- - - - - - - - - - - - - - quam __ le - sit._

Listening GUIDE

**Hildegard of Bingen
Gregorian chant, *O rubor sanguinis*
(c1150)**

5 1/2   **2** 1/1

Texture: Monophonic

Time		Latin	English
0:00	**2**	O rubor sanguinis,	O redness of blood,
0:14	**1**	qui de excelso illo fluxisti,	which flowed down from on high,
0:29		quod divinitas tetigit;	touched by divinity;
0:36		Tu flos es	You are the flower
0:41		quem hyems de flatu serpentis numquam lesit.	that the wintry breath of the serpent never wounded.
0:57		(Note the long melisma on "numquam")	

Listen to streaming music in an Active Listening Guide, available at the text website.

Download Supplementary
Listening Guides for three
more pieces by Hildegard of
Bingen—*Columba aspexit,*
O successores, and *Ordo*
virtutum—at the text website.

MUSIC IN THE CATHEDRAL

Gregorian chant arose primarily in secluded monasteries and convents around Western Europe. The future of art music within the Church, however, rested not in rural monasteries, but rather in urban cathedrals. Every cathedral served as the "home church" of a bishop, and the bishop could minister to the largest flock by locating himself within the increasingly large urban centers. During the twelfth century, cities such as Milan, Paris, and London, among others, grew significantly, as trade and commerce increased. Much of the commercial wealth generated in the cities was used to construct splendid new cathedrals that served as both houses of worship and monuments of civic pride. So substantial was this building campaign that the period 1150–1350 is often called the "Age of the Cathedrals." Most were constructed in what we now call the Gothic style, with pointed arches, high ceiling vaults, supporting buttresses, and richly colored stained glass.

Notre Dame of Paris

Gothic architecture began in northern France, in the region that now has Paris as its capital. The cathedral of Paris (Fig. 8-3), dedicated to Notre Dame (Our Lady), was begun about 1160, yet not completed until more than a hundred years later. Throughout this period Notre Dame was blessed with a succession of churchmen who were not only theologians and philosophers but poets and musicians as well. Foremost among these were Master Leoninus (flourished 1169–1201) and Master Perotinus, called the Great (fl. 1198–1236). Leoninus wrote a great book of religious music (called, in Latin, the *Magnus liber organi*). Perotinus revised Leoninus's book and also composed many additional pieces of his own.

Leoninus and Perotinus created a new style of composition. They wrote polyphony (two or more voices, or lines, sounding simultaneously) and not merely monophonic (one-voice) Gregorian chant. In truth, earlier composers had written polyphony, but this earlier music rarely had voices or lines that were fully separate from the chant. The novelty of the new music arising in Paris rested in the fact that Parisian composers added one or more wholly independent voices above the existing chant. In this musical development we see an early instance of a creative spirit breaking free of the ancient authority (the chant) of the Church.

FIGURE 8-3

The cathedral of Notre Dame of Paris, begun c1160, was one of the first to be built in the new Gothic style of architecture. The polyphony of Master Leoninus and Master Perotinus was composed as the building was being constructed.

Perotinus: Organum Viderunt omnes

The surviving documents from Paris suggest that Perotinus the Great served as director of the choir at Notre Dame of Paris. To lend special splendor to the celebration of Mass on Christmas morning in the year 1198 Perotinus composed a four-voice **organum,** the name given to early church polyphony. He took the centuries-old chant for the Mass, *Viderunt omnes (All the Ends of the Earth;* see p. 69), and added three new voices above it (Fig. 8-4). Compared to the new upper voices, the old borrowed chant moved very slowly, drawing out or holding each pitch. Because of this, the sustaining line with the chant came to be called the **tenor** voice (from the Latin *teneo*, French *tenir*, "to hold"). As you listen to the work of Perotinus, you will clearly hear the sustaining chant that provides a harmonic support for the upper voices, just as a massive pillar in a Gothic church might support the delicate movement of the arches above (see Fig. 8-5). Equally audible is the jaunty triple rhythm, often seeming to move in two-bar units in a fast tempo. By 1200 musicians had devised a system to notate and control not only pitch, but also rhythm. Significantly, all early polyphony written in rhythmic notation was composed in triple meter. As the music theorists of the time tell us, this was done to honor the Holy Trinity.

Ms. Pluteus 29, Bibiloteca laurenziana, Florence/Photo © Craig Wright

FIGURE 8–4

Perotinus's four-voice *Viderunt omnes* for Christmas Day. Note how the chant in the tenor voice (lines 4, 8, and 12) provides a long-note foundation for the three voices above.

Download a Supplementary Listening Guide for Perotinus, *Diffusa est gratia*, at the text website.

*L*istening GUIDE

Master Perotinus the Great
Organum built on Gregorian chant
***Viderunt omnes* (1198)**

5

1/3

Texture: Polyphonic

Because Perotinus sustains the chant in long notes in his setting of *Viderunt omnes* (see Ex. 8-1), a composition of great length—eleven to twelve minutes—results. Thus only the beginning of his organum is given here. The singers relate that all the ends of the earth have seen ("Viderunt") the Christian Savior.

0:00	**3**	Syllable "Vi-" of "Viderunt"; all voices hold on open sound of fifth and octave
0:06		Upper three voices proceed in rocking triple meter as tenor sustains first note of chant, all voices singing syllable "Vi-"
0:47		Tenor changes to next pitch, and all change to syllable "-de-" of "Viderunt"
1:10		Tenor changes to next pitch, and all change to syllable "-runt" of "Viderunt"
2:06		End of word "Viderunt"

(Continuing organum not included on CD)

Listen to streaming music in an Active Listening Guide, available at the text website.

Notre Dame of Reims

Notre Dame of Paris was not the only important cathedral in northern Europe devoted to Our Lady. The city of Reims, one hundred miles east of Paris in the Champagne region of France, was graced with a monument equally large and impressive (Fig. 8-5). In the fourteenth century, it, too, benefited from the service of a poetically and musically talented churchman, Guillaume de Machaut (c1300–1377). Judging by his nearly 150 surviving works, not only was Machaut (pronounced "ma-SHOW") the most important composer of his day, he was equally esteemed as a lyric poet. Today, historians of literature place him on a pedestal next to his slightly younger English counterpart, Geoffrey Chaucer (c1340–1400), author of the *Canterbury Tales*. Indeed, Chaucer knew and borrowed heavily from the poetic works of Machaut.

Machaut: Messe de Nostre Dame

Machaut's *Messe de Nostre Dame (Mass of Our Lady)* is deservedly the best-known work in the entire repertoire of medieval music. It is impressive for its twenty-five minute length and the novel way it applies music to the texts of the **Mass**—the central and most important service of the Roman Catholic Church. Before Machaut's time, composers writing polyphony for the Mass had set only one or two sections of what is called the **Proper of the Mass** (chants whose texts changed to suit, or "be proper for," the feast day in question). Perotinus's *Viderunt omnes*, for example, is a setting of the Gradual (see box on p. 75) of the Proper of the Mass for Christmas Day.

Machaut, on the other hand, chose to set all of the chants of the **Ordinary of the Mass** (chants with unvarying texts that were sung virtually every day). (The term *Mass* henceforth replaced *organum* to indicate a polyphonic setting of the Ordinary of the Mass.) Setting the Ordinary had the obvious practical advantage that the composition could be heard on more than just one feast day of the church year. Machaut's *Mass of Our Lady,* for example, could be sung any time a Mass in honor of the Virgin Mary was celebrated. The accompanying box lists the musical portions of the Mass and the order in which they are sung. From Machaut's work onward, composing a Mass meant setting the five texts of the Ordinary (Kyrie, Gloria, Credo, Sanctus, and Agnus Dei) and finding some way to shape them into an integrated whole. Palestrina, Bach, Mozart, and Beethoven were just a few of the later composers to follow Machaut's lead and set the five parts of the Ordinary of the Mass.

To construct his Mass, Machaut added three new voices to a preexisting chant, but in a way different from that used by Perotinus before him. Whereas Perotinus had placed all three new voices above the tenor line, Machaut added just two voices above (Ex. 8-3). These came to be called the *superius* and the *contratenor altus*, whence we get our terms *soprano* and *alto*. The voice added below the tenor was called the *contratenor bassus*, whence our term *bass*. And unlike Perotinus, who bunched his voices all together in the same range around middle C, Machaut spread his voices out over two and a half octaves, making him the first composer to exploit nearly the full vocal range of a chorus. But as you will hear, this polyphony is often dissonant and biting, resolving to open, consonant chords only at the ends of phrases. These chords sound especially rich in an echo-filled medieval cathedral where the open sonorities can swirl and endlessly rebound around bare stone walls.

FIGURE 8–5

Interior of the cathedral of Reims looking from floor to ceiling. The pillars carry the eye up to the ribbed vaults of the roof, creating a feeling of great upward movement, just as the Mass of Machaut, with four superimposed voices, has a new sense of verticality.

© Craig Wright

@

Download Supplementary Listening Guides for three more pieces by Machaut—*Agnus Dei* of *Messe de Nostre Dame* and the secular songs *Puis qu'en oubli* and *Quant en moy*—at the text website.

EXAMPLE 8–3

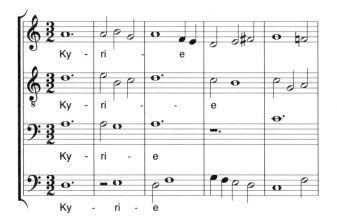

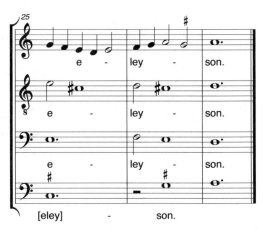

MUSICAL PORTIONS OF THE MASS

Proper of the Mass	Ordinary of the Mass
1. Introit (an introductory chant for the entry of the celebrating clergy)	
	2. Kyrie (a petition for mercy)
	3. Gloria (a hymn of praise to the Lord)
4. Gradual (a reflective chant)	
5. Alleluia or Tract (a chant of thanksgiving or penance)	
	6. Credo (a profession of faith)
7. Offertory (a chant for the offering)	
	8. Sanctus (an acclamation to the Lord)
	9. Agnus Dei (a petition for mercy and eternal peace)
10. Communion (a chant accompanying communion)	

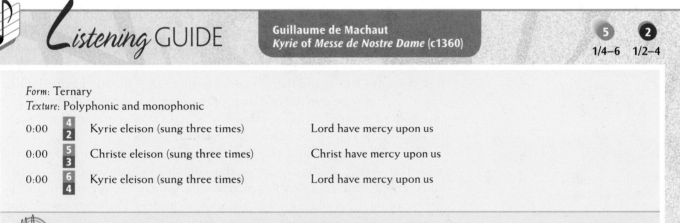

Listening GUIDE

Guillaume de Machaut
***Kyrie* of *Messe de Nostre Dame* (c1360)**

5 1/4–6   **2** 1/2–4

Form: Ternary
Texture: Polyphonic and monophonic

0:00	**4/2**	Kyrie eleison (sung three times)	Lord have mercy upon us
0:00	**5/3**	Christe eleison (sung three times)	Christ have mercy upon us
0:00	**6/4**	Kyrie eleison (sung three times)	Lord have mercy upon us

Listen to streaming music in an Active Listening Guide, available at the text website.

Listening EXERCISE 12

Machaut
KYRIE OF MESSE DE NOSTRE DAME

5 1/4–6   **2** 1/2–4

To take this Listening Exercise online and receive feedback or email answers to your instructor, go to the text website.

The *Kyrie* of the Ordinary of the Mass is a threefold petition for mercy (*Kyrie eleison* means "Lord have mercy upon us"). In Machaut's setting the composer makes use of preexisting monophonic chant in two ways: he sets it in the tenor voice in long notes and builds polyphony around it (see Ex. 8-3); and he requires that sections of the *Kyrie* be sung in chant alone. On this recording, when the chant alone is heard, it is sung by men in unison. Your task in this Listening Exercise is straightforward: identify which sections are composed in four-voice polyphony and which make use of monophonic

Gregorian chant by writing either "polyphony" or "chant" in the blanks below.

1. **4/2** (0:00)   Kyrie eleison: _____
2.   (0:59)   Kyrie eleison: _____
3.   (1:17)   Kyrie eleison: _____
4. **5/3** (0:00)   Christe eleison: _____

(continued)

5.   (0:15)   Christe eleison: _____

6.   (1:07)   Christe eleison: _____

7. **6/4** (0:00)   Kyrie eleison: _____

8.   (0:40)   Kyrie eleison: _____

9.   (0:56)   Kyrie eleison: _____

10. Finally, notice that each of the polyphonic sections takes longer to perform than the monophonic ones. Why is that the case?

    a. because the soloists singing polyphony have more words to sing in each section

    b. because singing the tenor in longer notes in the polyphony causes the music to be drawn out

Music at the Court

Outside the walls of the cathedral, there was yet another musical world: one of popular song and dance centered at the court. Indeed, the court embraced forms of public entertainment not permitted by church authorities. Itinerant actors, jugglers, jesters, and animal acts all provided welcome diversions. Minstrels wandered from castle to castle, bringing the latest tunes, along with news and gossip. Churchmen, too, sojourned at court. Guillaume de Machaut, for example, enjoyed a double career as cleric and courtier. He composed liturgical music for the cathedral of Reims, yet at various times in his life, he served at the court of the king of Bohemia, the king of Navarre, and the duke of Berry. While it may seem strange that a clergyman like Machaut was active in worldly affairs at court, during the Middle Ages learned churchmen were much in demand for their ability to read and write. And because of their skill with letters and their knowledge of musical notation gained in the church, clerics were inevitably drawn to the poetry and music of the courtly song. Indeed, most of the polyphonic love songs emanating from the court in the late Middle Ages were written by ordained priests.

The court emerged as a center for the patronage of the arts during the years 1150–1400, as the power of the church gradually declined. Kings, dukes, counts, and lesser nobles increasingly assumed responsibility for the defense of the land and the administration of justice. The aristocratic court became a small, independent city-state, but one that could move from place to place. To enhance the ruler's prestige and show that he or she was a person of refinement and sensibility, nobles often engaged bands of trumpeters to herald an arrival, instrumentalists to provide dance music for evening entertainment, and singers and poets to create lyric verse. Some poems were meant to be recited, but most were sung.

Troubadours and Trouvères

Southern France was the center of this new courtly art, though it extended into northern Spain and Italy as well. The poet-musicians who flourished there were known as **troubadours** (men) and **trobairitz** (women). Both terms derived from the verb *trobar*, which meant "to find" in the vernacular tongue of medieval southern France. Thus the troubadours and *trobairitz* were "finders" or inventors of new modes of verbal and vocal expression. Their art was devoted mainly to the creation of songs of love that extolled the courtly ideals of faith and devotion, whether to the ideal lady, the just seigneur (lord), or the knight crusading in the Holy Land. Their songs were not in the Latin of the Church, but in the vernacular tongue: medieval Italian, Catalan, and Provençal (medieval French of the south). The origins of the troubadours were equally varied. Some were sons of bakers and drapers, others were members of the nobility, many were clerics living outside the Church, and not a few were women.

In the Middle Ages, and later during the Renaissance (1450–1600), women were not allowed to sing in church, except in convents, owing to the biblical command of St. Paul ("A woman must be silent in the church"). But at court, women often recited poetry, sang, and played musical instruments, performing on instruments like the harp, flute (recorder), and vielle or rebec (medieval fiddles; Fig. 8-6). Moreover, *trobairitz* were not merely performers, but creators in their own right. One such composer was Beatriz, Countess of Dia (Fig. 8-7), who lived in southern France in the mid-twelfth century. She was married to Count William of Poitiers but fell in love with a fellow troubadour, Raimbaut d'Orange (1146–1173). Her song *A chantar m'er* (*I Must Sing*) laments her failure in love, despite her self-proclaimed charms. It is composed of five strophes, or stanzas, each with seven lines of text and seven musical phrases. The seven-phrase melody displays a clear music form: **ABABCDB** (the use of letters to indicate musical form is explained on p. 59). As with the chant of the Church, troubadour song has no clearly articulated meter and rhythm, but is sung in notes of more or less equal length.

FIGURE 8–6

A thirteenth-century Spanish miniature showing a medieval fiddle (the rebec or vielle) on the left and a lute on the right. Both instruments were brought into Spain by the Arabs and then carried northward into the lands of the troubadours and *trouvères*.

Listening GUIDE

Countess of Dia
Troubadour song, *A chantar m'er* (c1175)

5
1/7

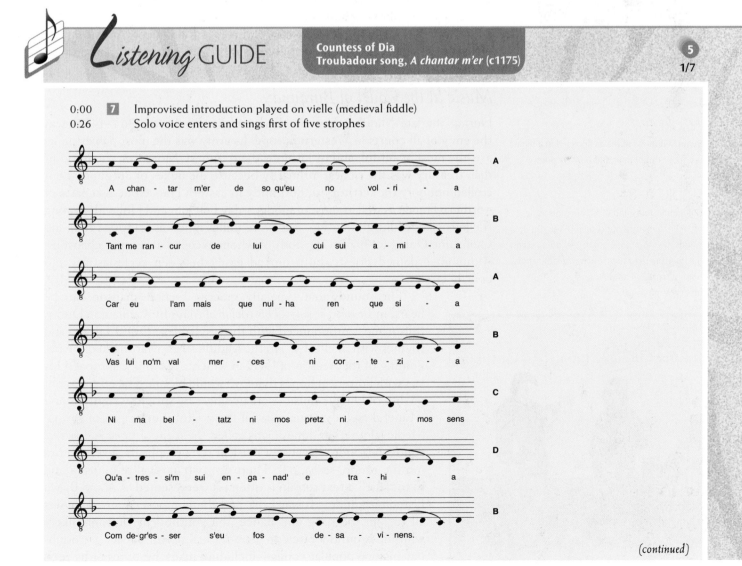

0:00 **7** Improvised introduction played on vielle (medieval fiddle)
0:26 Solo voice enters and sings first of five strophes

A chan - tar m'er de so qu'eu no vol - ri - a   A

Tant me ran - cur de lui cui sui a - mi - a   B

Car eu l'am mais que nul - ha ren que si - a   A

Vas lui no'm val mer - ces ni cor - te - zi - a   B

Ni ma bel - tatz ni mos pretz ni mos sens   C

Qu'a - tres - si'm sui en - ga - nad' e tra - hi - a   D

Com de - gr'es - ser s'eu fos de - sa - vi - nens.   B

(continued)

I must sing of that which I'd rather not,
So bitter do I feel toward him
Whom I love more than anything.
But with him kindness and courtliness get me nowhere,
Neither my beauty, nor my worth, nor my intelligence.
In this way am I cheated and betrayed,
Just as I would be if I were ugly.

Listen to streaming music in an Active Listening Guide, available at the text website.

Bibliothèque nationale de France

FIGURE 8-7

Beatriz Countess of Dia as depicted in a manuscript of troubadour and *trouvère* poetry.

FIGURE 8-8

Guillaume Dufay and Gilles Binchois as depicted in a manuscript copied c1440. Dufay stands next to a small organ, the quintessential instrument of the church, while Binchois holds a harp, one of the principal instruments of the court.

© Giraudon/The Bridgeman Art Library International

Gradually, the musical traditions created by the troubadours were carried to the north of France, where such composer-performers came to be called **trouvères,** and even to Germany, where they were called **Minnesingers** (singers of love). Around 1300 some of the *trouvères* began to mix the traditions of the troubadours with the learned vocal polyphony coming from the Church. Soon churchmen such as Guillaume de Machaut (see p. 73) adopted the musical forms and poetic style of the *trouvères* to fashion a new genre of music, the polyphonic **chanson** (French for "song"). The chanson is simply a love song, normally in French, for two, three, or four voices. At its best the chanson is a small jewel of poignant lyricism.

Music at the Court of Burgundy

During the late Middle Ages, the Court of Burgundy (fl. 1364–1477) was the envy of all courts in Western Europe. Its army was the most powerful, its arts the most beautiful, and its fashions the trendiest. Moreover, the Burgundian treasury was the richest, primarily because the dukes of Burgundy controlled not only the territory of Burgundy in eastern France but also parts of northern France as well as most of modern-day Belgium and Holland. Among the musicians of Burgundy (Fig. 8-8) were Gilles Binchois (c1400–1460) and Guillaume Dufay (c1397–1474), both of whom excelled at writing chansons. Although ordained priests, both moved easily between ecclesiastical and courtly circles.

The sounds that typically grace a French chanson can be heard in *Ce moys de may (This Month of May)* by Guillaume Dufay. (His name is pronounced with three syllables: "DOO-fah-ee" and rhymes with "mel-od-y.") In the Middle Ages, May marked the beginning of the "season of love" in which a lad might approach his lass with flowers in hopes that love would bloom. The effervescent quality of Dufay's music—created here by sprightly rhythms and a tuneful melody—suggests all the youthful optimism of spring. Medieval poets and musicians called the form of *Ce moys de may* a **rondeau** (rondo) because a musical refrain appears several times (on the rondo, see p. 63). There are two musical sections (**a** and **b**) to which a text refrain is often set (represented as **A** and **B**; see Listening Guide). Toward the end the composer himself invites all to join the song and dance, the youthful participants likely whirling around a circle in a traditional round dance. Throughout history popular songs—including many by tunesmiths such as Dufay, Machaut, and Michael Jackson—were conceived as much as dance numbers as they were as vocals.

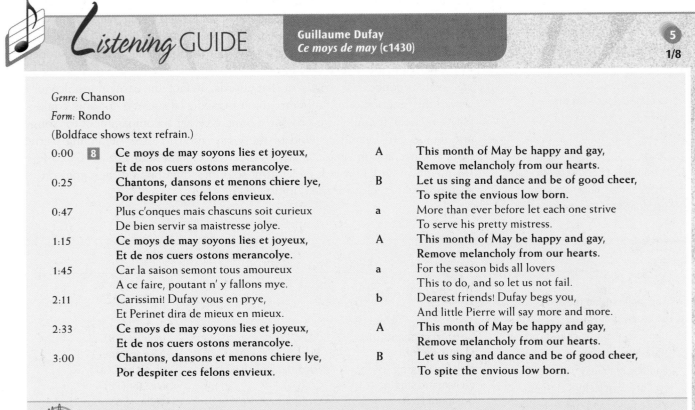

Listening GUIDE

Guillaume Dufay
Ce moys de may (c1430)

5
1/8

Genre: Chanson

Form: Rondo

(Boldface shows text refrain.)

0:00	8	**Ce moys de may soyons lies et joyeux,** **Et de nos cuers ostons merancolye.**	A	This month of May be happy and gay, Remove melancholy from our hearts.
0:25		**Chantons, dansons et menons chiere lye,** **Por despiter ces felons envieux.**	B	Let us sing and dance and be of good cheer, To spite the envious low born.
0:47		Plus c'onques mais chascuns soit curieux De bien servir sa maistresse jolye.	a	More than ever before let each one strive To serve his pretty mistress.
1:15		**Ce moys de may soyons lies et joyeux,** **Et de nos cuers ostons merancolye.**	A	This month of May be happy and gay, Remove melancholy from our hearts.
1:45		Car la saison semont tous amoureux A ce faire, poutant n' y fallons mye.	a	For the season bids all lovers This to do, and so let us not fail.
2:11		Carissimi! Dufay vous en prye, Et Perinet dira de mieux en mieux.	b	Dearest friends! Dufay begs you, And little Pierre will say more and more.
2:33		**Ce moys de may soyons lies et joyeux,** **Et de nos cuers ostons merancolye.**	A	This month of May be happy and gay, Remove melancholy from our hearts.
3:00		**Chantons, dansons et menons chiere lye,** **Por despiter ces felons envieux.**	B	Let us sing and dance and be of good cheer, To spite the envious low born.

Listen to streaming music in an Active Listening Guide, available at the text website.

To take Listening Exercise 13 for this musical selection online and receive feedback or email answers to your instructor, go to the text website.

MEDIEVAL MUSICAL INSTRUMENTS

In the late Middle Ages the principal musical instrument of the monastery and cathedral was the large pipe organ. Indeed, the organ was the only instrument admitted by church authorities. At court, however, a variety of instrumental sounds could be heard. Some, such as the trumpet and early trombone, were rightly identified as loud (*haut*). Others, such as the fiddle, harp, lute, flute (recorder), and small portable organ, were classified as soft (*bas*).

Figure 8-9 shows a group of angels playing musical instruments of the late medieval period. While this vision of loveliness may be alluring, we must proceed with caution: Never trust a musical angel! How are we to know what instruments angels played? And certainly, any attempt to form an ensemble combining a straight trumpet, rudimentary trombone, harp, portative organ, and fiddle would have been doomed to

FIGURE 8–9

Hans Memling (c1430–1491), musical angels painted for the walls of a hospital in Bruges, Belgium. The depiction of the instruments is remarkably detailed.

Download Supplementary Listening Guides for two more pieces by Dufay—*Ave maris stella* and *Lamentatio Sanctae Matris Ecclesiae Constantinopolitanae (Lament of the Holy Mother Church of Constantinople)*—at the text website.

A complete Checklist of Musical Style for the Middle Ages can be found at the text website.

The materials on the text website will help you understand and pass tests on the content of this chapter. In addition, you may watch Craig Wright's own lecture at Open Yale Courses and complete this chapter's Listening Exercises interactively, as well as view Active Listening Guides and other materials that will help you succeed in this course.

failure. The loud brasses would have overwhelmed the soft organ and strings. Nevertheless, from such a painting we can extract precise information about the size, construction, and method of playing of each instrument.

Take, for example, the **vielle**, the medieval fiddle—to the far right, a distant ancestor of the modern violin. Like all medieval bowed string instruments (and unlike the modern violin), it was played off the shoulder. Looking more carefully, we see five strings, the standard number for the vielle. They were tuned in a way that made it very easy to play block chords, just the way guitars today can easily produce basic triads, or "bar chords." In fact, the easily portable vielle served the function of our modern guitar in medieval society: not only could it play a melody, it could also provide a basic chordal accompaniment for songs and dances. To hear the sound of the vielle, return to the beginning of the troubadour chanson *A chantar m'er* by Beatriz, Countess of Dia (**5**1/7). Here the medieval fiddle provides a lengthy solo introduction and then goes on to accompany the voice for the duration of the song.

Key WORDS

Gregorian chant (68)	Mass (74)	*trouvère* (78)
plainsong (68)	Proper of the Mass (74)	Minnesinger (78)
syllabic singing (69)	Ordinary of the Mass	chanson (78)
melismatic singing (69)	(74)	*rondeau* (78)
organum (72)	troubadour (76)	vielle (80)
tenor (73)	*trobairitz* (76)	

RENAISSANCE MUSIC, 1450–1600

Historians use the term *Renaissance* to designate the period 1350–1600 during which Western Europe experienced a rebirth of interest in classical antiquity and a reawakening of interest in the fine arts generally. Music historians, however, usually apply the term more narrowly, to indicate the time span from 1450 to 1600. In these years composers began to think of themselves as independent artists, rather than servants of the Church, and music theorists rediscovered ancient Greek treatises on music, which changed the way musicians created and thought about music.

Ancient Greece and Rome, of course, were pagan, non-Christian cultures. As a result, the Renaissance, while still a religious period in many ways, was decidedly more worldly, or secular, in its outlook. The surviving music of the Middle Ages is overwhelmingly religious in character (Gregorian chant and sacred polyphony). By contrast, the music of the Renaissance is more or less equally divided between religious music, used in worship, and secular music, serving as popular entertainment for private music-making at home.

The Renaissance originated in Italy, in large measure because the manuscripts and ruins of classical antiquity lay all around. Greek and Roman design showed how buildings might be constructed (Fig. 9-1) and what sort of statues might be placed in them (see Fig. 9-4 on p. 82). Similarly, Greek and Roman literature suggested how poetry should be written and public speeches composed. So, too, the ancient philosophers provided guidelines as to how leaders should act, as well as a new way of thinking about the fine arts.

The ancient Greek writers, especially Homer and Plato, had spoken of the great emotional power of music. Their stories told how music had calmed the agitated spirit or made brave the warrior. Musicians in the Renaissance eagerly embraced this notion that music could sway the emotions, and even the behavior, of listeners. Consequently, composers of the Renaissance began to intensify the vocabulary of musical expression. Music, they believed, should underscore and heighten the meaning of each and every phrase of the text. If the verse depicted birds soaring gracefully in the sky, the accompanying music should be in a major key and ascend into a high range; if the text lamented the pain and sorrow of sin, the music ought to be in a minor key, and dark and dissonant. As a result, the Renaissance produced a greater range of musical styles, mirroring the development of the visual arts of the Renaissance, which now likewise allowed for a greater range of emotional expression. Compare, for example, the highly contrasting moods of two paintings created within a few years of each other—the peaceful serenity of Leonardo da Vinci's *Madonna, Child, Saint Anne, and a Lamb* (Fig. 9-2) and the painful intensity of Mathias Grünewald's *Saint John and the Two Marys* (Fig. 9-3).

FIGURE 9–1

Andrea Palladio's Villa Rotunda (c1550) near Vicenza, Italy, clearly shows the extent to which classical architecture was reborn during the Renaissance. Elements of the ancient style include the columns with capitals, triangular pediments, and central rotunda (compare Fig. 15-1).

FIGURE 9-2

Leonardo da Vinci's *Madonna, Child, Saint Anne, and a Lamb* (c1508–1517). Notice the warm, human expression and the near-complete absence of religious symbolism, as well as the highly formalistic composition of the painting; the groupings of figures form successively larger triangles.

FIGURE 9-3

The expressive grief of the Virgin, Saint John, and Mary Magdalene mark this portion of an altarpiece (1510–1515) painted by Mathias Grünewald.

FIGURE 9-4

Michelangelo's giant statue of David (1501–1504) expresses the heroic nobility of man in near-perfect form. Like Leonardo da Vinci, Michelangelo made a careful study of human anatomy.

Attending the rebirth of the arts and letters of classical antiquity was a renewed interest in humankind itself. We have come to call this enthusiastic self-interest humanism. Simply said, **humanism** is the belief that people are something more than a mere conduit for gifts descending from heaven, that they have the capacity to create many things good and beautiful—indeed, the ability to shape their own world. The culture of the Middle Ages, as we have seen, was fostered by the Church, which emphasized a collective submission to the almighty, hiding the individual human form beneath layers of clothing. The culture of the Renaissance, by contrast, rejoiced in the human form in all its fullness (Fig. 9-4). It looked outward and indulged a passion for invention and discovery.

True to the humanistic spirit, composers in the Renaissance began to think of themselves not merely as anonymous churchmen, but as talented artists, and they sought credit for their musical creations. Composers now worked their own names into the texts of their compositions, just as painters painted their own faces among the crowd on their canvases. A composition or a painting came to be viewed as a tangible record of the individual creative genius, and the artist was eager to take a bow. Moreover, he wanted to be paid, and paid well. Medieval craftsmen had traditionally belonged to guilds, which regulated both what type of work they could accept and what they might earn. In the Renaissance, however, this system began to break down. Now a gifted artist might vie for the highest-paying commission, just as a sought-after composer might play one patron off against another for the highest salary. Money, it seems, could prime the pump of creativity, leading to greater productivity. This productivity, in turn, was in some cases richly rewarded—the prolific Michelangelo left an estate worth some $10 million in terms of money today.

If artists were paid more in the Renaissance, it was because art was now thought to be more valuable. For the first time in the Christian West, there emerged the concept of a "work of art": the belief that an object might not only serve as a religious symbol but also be a creation of purely aesthetic value and enjoyment. Music in the Renaissance was composed by proud artists who aimed to give pleasure. Their music conversed, not with eternity, but with the listener. It was judged good or bad only to the degree that it pleased fellow human beings. Music and the other arts could now be freely evaluated, and composers and painters could be ranked according to their greatness. Artistic judgment, appreciation, and criticism entered Western thought for the first time in the humanistic Renaissance.

JOSQUIN DESPREZ (c1455–1521) AND THE RENAISSANCE MOTET

FIGURE 9–5
The only surviving portrait of Josquin Desprez.

FIGURE 9–6
Interior of the Sistine Chapel. The high altar and Michelangelo's *Last Judgment* are at the far end, the balcony for the singers, including Josquin Desprez, at the lower right. The congregants could stand and listen from the near side of the screen.

Josquin Desprez (pronounced "josh-CAN day-PRAY") was one of the greatest composers of the Renaissance or, indeed, of any age (Fig. 9-5). He was born somewhere near the present border between France and Belgium about 1455, and died in the same region in 1521. Yet, like so many musicians of northern France, he was attracted to Italy to pursue professional and monetary gain. Between 1484 and 1504, he worked for various dukes in Milan and Ferrara, and for the pope in his Sistine Chapel in Rome (Fig. 9-6). Evidence suggests that Josquin (he was known universally just by his first name) had a temperamental, egotistical personality, one typical of many artists of the Renaissance. He would fly into a rage when singers tampered with his music; he composed only when he, not his patron, wished; and he demanded a salary twice that of composers only slightly less gifted. Yet Josquin's contemporaries recognized his genius. Martin Luther said of him: "Josquin is master of the notes, which must express what he desires; other composers can do only what the notes dictate." And Florentine humanist Cosimo Bartoli compared him to the great Michelangelo (1475–1564):

Josquin may be said to have been a prodigy of nature, as our Michelangelo Buonarroti has been in architecture, painting, and sculpture; for just as there has not yet been anyone who in his compositions approaches Josquin, so Michelangelo, among those active in his arts, is still alone and without a peer. Both Josquin and Michelangelo have opened the eyes of all those who delight in these arts or are to delight in them in the future.

Josquin composed in all of the musical genres of his day, but he excelled in writing motets, some seventy of which survive under his name. The Renaissance **motet** can be defined as a composition for a choir, setting a Latin text on a sacred subject, and intended to be sung either in a church or chapel, or at home in private devotion. While composers of the Renaissance continued to set the prescribed text of the Mass, they increasingly sought more dramatic texts in the Old Testament of the Bible—specifically, in the expressive Psalms and the mournful Lamentations. A vivid text cried out for an equally vivid musical setting, allowing the composer to fulfill a mandate of Renaissance humanism: use music to heighten the meaning of the word.

Download Supplementary Listening Guides for two more pieces by Josquin Desprez—*Kyrie* and *Gloria* of *Missa Pange lingua*—at the text website.

Most motets in the Renaissance, as well as most Masses for the Church, were sung **a cappella** (literally, "in the chapel"), meaning that they were performed by voices alone, without any instrumental accompaniment. (Instruments other than the organ were generally not allowed in churches during the Middle Ages and the Renaissance.) This, in part, accounts for the often serene quality of the sound of Renaissance sacred music. Indeed, the Renaissance has been called the "golden age of a cappella singing."

Josquin's motet *Ave Maria (Hail, Mary)* was written about 1485 when the composer was in Milan, Italy, in the service of the Duke of Milan. Composed in honor of the Virgin Mary, it employs the standard four voice parts: soprano, alto, tenor, and bass (S, A, T, and B in Ex. 9-1). As the motet unfolds, the listener hears the voices enter in succession with the same musical motive. This process is called **imitation,** a procedure whereby one or more voices duplicate in turn the notes of a melody.

EXAMPLE 9–1

Josquin also sometimes has one pair of voices imitate another—the tenor and bass, for example, imitating what the alto and soprano have just sung.

EXAMPLE 9–2

In Josquin's imitative writing, each voice is given equal opportunity to present the melodic material; thus, all four voices are of equal importance. Josquin and his contemporaries favored this texture of four equal voices in part because of its potential to yield symmetry and balance. Agreeable proportions were prized not only in Renaissance music but also in the arts generally during this period (see Figs. 9-1 through 9-4). As the four voices enter independently they invariably create counterpoint—individual voices working with and against one another in harmonious fashion. In Josquin's *Ave Maria*, sections in imitative counterpoint (polyphony) alternate with passages of chordal writing (homophony) to achieve variety and thereby maintain the listener's interest.

Josquin organizes the overall structure of *Ave Maria* in much the same manner that a humanistic orator would construct a persuasive speech or address. It begins with a salutation to the Virgin, sung in imitation. Thereafter, a key word, "Ave" ("Hail"), sparks a succession of salutes to the Virgin, each making reference to one of her principal feast days during the church year (Conception, Nativity, Annunciation, Purification, and Assumption). At the end of this series of "hails" comes a final exclamation, "O Mother of God, be mindful of me. Amen." These last words are set to striking chords, with each syllable of text receiving its own chord. The chordal, homophonic treatment allows this final text to stand out with absolute clarity, again observing the principle of musical humanism: text and music must work together to persuade and move the listener. Here they must persuade the Virgin Mary as well, for they plead with her to intercede on behalf of the needy soul at the hour of death.

@ Watch a video of Craig Wright's Open Yale Course class session 15, "Benedictine Chant and Music in the Sistine Chapel," at the text website.

*L*istening GUIDE

Josquin Desprez
Motet, *Ave Maria* (c1485)

5   2
1/9   1/5

Genre: Sacred motet

Texture: Mostly imitative counterpoint (polyphony)

Time		Description	Latin	English
0:00	9/5	All four voices present each two-word phrase in turn	Ave Maria, gratia plena. Dominus tecum, virgo serena.	Hail Mary, full of grace. The Lord be with you, serene Virgin.
0:46		Soprano and alto are imitated by tenor and bass; then all four voices work to peak on "laetitia" ("joy")	Ave cujus conceptio, Solemni plena gaudio, Coelestia, terrestria, Nova replet laetitia.	Hail to you whose conception, With solemn rejoicing, Fills heaven and earth With new joy.
1:20		Imitation in pairs; soprano and alto answered by tenor and bass	Ave cujus nativitas Nostra fuit solemnitas, Ut lucifer lux oriens, Verum solem praeveniens.	Hail to you whose birth Was to be our solemnity, As the rising morning star Anticipates the true sun.
1:58		More imitation by pairs of voices; soprano and alto followed by tenor and bass	Ave pia humilitas, Sine viro foecunditas, Cujus annuntiatio, Nostra fuit salvatio.	Hail pious humility, Fruitful without man, Whose annunciation Was to be our salvation.
2:26		Chordal writing; meter changes from duple to triple	Ave vera virginitas, Immaculata castitas, Cujus purificatio Nostra fuit purgatio.	Hail true virginity, Immaculate chastity, Whose purification Was to be our purgation.
3:03		Return to duple meter; soprano and alto imitated by tenor and bass	Ave praeclara omnibus Angelicis virtutibus, Cujus fuit assumptio Nostra glorificatio.	Hail shining example Of all angelic virtues, Whose assumption Was to be our glorification.
3:58		Strict chordal writing; clear presentation of text	O Mater Dei, Memento mei. Amen.	O Mother of God, Be mindful of me. Amen.

Listen to streaming music in an Active Listening Guide, available on the text website.

Listening EXERCISE 14

Josquin Desprez
AVE MARIA

5 1/9   **2** 1/5

@ To take this Listening Exercise online and receive feedback or email answers to your instructor, go to the text website.

Josquin's *Ave Maria* is a fine example of a motet that employs imitation, the musical technique favored by Renaissance composers for church music. What follows is mainly an exercise in hearing the four voices unfold in imitative counterpoint and identifying how Josquin clarifies the meaning of the text. On this modern recording, the soprano part is sung by women, and the alto, tenor, and bass parts by men.

1. (0:00–0:26) As the four voices enter, which texture gradually emerges?
   a. monophonic
   b. homophonic
   c. polyphonic

2. (0:00–0:26) What is the term for the musical procedure in which the voices replicate in turn the notes of a melody?
   a. imitation
   b. replication
   c. modulation

3. (0:00–0:44) The opening stanza of *Ave Maria* contains eight words divided into four syntactical units (units of meaning): Ave Maria—gratia plena—dominus tecum—virgo serena. Josquin clarifies the meaning of the text by grouping the words in pairs, and he does so how?
   a. by assigning each pair of words first to the soprano and then to the other voices
   b. by assigning each pair of words first to the bass and then to the other voices

4. (1:05–1:20) Now the voices work toward a joyful climax on the word "laetitia" ("joy"), and Josquin expresses the meaning of this passage by writing music that does what?
   a. ascends and then descends in an excited fashion
   b. forcefully reiterates the same pitches
   c. emphatically descends to a lower range

5. (1:18) Which voice joyfully sings the final "laetitia"?
   a. soprano   b. male alto   c. bass

6. (2:15–2:40) A new stanza of text appears, and the meter and texture change for the sake of variety. Which is correct?
   a. Triple-meter polyphony gives way to duple-meter homophony.
   b. Duple-meter homophony gives way to triple-meter polyphony.
   c. Duple-meter polyphony gives way to triple-meter homophony.

7. (4:23–end) The final word of the motet is "Amen," which is Hebrew for "and so be it." Josquin declaims the meaning of this word by having the voices sing what with emphasis?
   a. "A" and "men" to two different pitches
   b. "A" and "men" to the same pitches

8. Which is true throughout this motet?
   a. In the imitative sections, the soprano and alto always enter before the tenor and bass.
   b. In the imitative sections, the tenor and bass always enter before the soprano and alto.

9. Do instruments accompany the voices on this performance? If not, what is this style of performance called?
   a. imitative   b. a cappella   c. Vatican style

10. Most listeners would agree that Josquin's *Ave Maria* is a soothing auditory experience, an appropriate companion for the image of the Virgin Mary within the Roman Catholic Church. Which single answer best suggests why?
   a. The voices are equal in importance.
   b. The dynamics stay in the middle range of loud and soft.
   c. There is no strongly emphasized beat.
   d. There is no strong element of dissonance in the counterpoint.
   e. All of the above
   f. None of the above

*T*HE COUNTER-REFORMATION AND PALESTRINA (1525–1594)

On October 31, 1517, an obscure Augustinian monk named Martin Luther nailed to the door of the castle church at Wittenberg, Germany, ninety-five complaints against the Roman Catholic Church—his famous ninety-five theses. With this defiant act Luther began what has come to be called the Protestant Reformation. Luther and his fellow reformers sought to bring an end to corruption within the Roman Catholic Church: the selling of indulgences (forgiveness of sin in exchange for money), the unholy lives of leading churchmen (at least two popes admitted to having illegitimate children), and the abuse of power in church appointments (one pope rewarded the fifteen-year-old keeper of his pet monkey by making him a cardinal). By the time the Protestant Reformation had run its course, most of Germany, Switzerland, and the Low Countries, and all of England, as well as parts of France, Austria, Bohemia, Poland, and Hungary, had gone over to the Protestant cause. The established Roman Catholic Church was shaken to its very foundations.

In response to the Protestant Reformation, the Church of Rome began to clean its own house. The cleansing applied not only to matters of spirituality and church administration but also to art, liturgy, and music. A list of offending books was compiled, and often they, along with their authors, were publically burned. Nudity in religious paintings, musical instruments within the church, popular tunes and catchy rhythms in the midst of polyphonic Masses, and married church singers—all of these "transgressions" were now deemed inappropriate to a truly pious environment. The reform movement that promoted a more conservative, austere approach to art is called the **Counter-Reformation,** and the musician whose music most embodies its spirit is Giovanni Pierluigi da Palestrina.

Palestrina (1525–1594; Fig. 9-7) was born in the small town of that name outside Rome and spent almost his entire professional life as a singer and composer at various churches in and around the Vatican: Saint Peter's Basilica, Saint John Lateran, Saint Mary Major, and the **Sistine Chapel,** the pope's private chapel within his Vatican apartments (see Fig. 9-6). But in 1555, Paul IV, one of the more zealous of the reforming popes, dismissed Palestrina from the Sistine Chapel because he was a married layman not conforming to the strict rule of celibacy. Later, under a new pope, Palestrina returned to papal employment at Saint Peter's, holding the titles *maestro di cappella* (master of the chapel) and ultimately *maestro compositore* (master composer).

Palestrina's tenure at the Sistine Chapel coincided with the **Council of Trent** (1545–1563), a two-decade-long conference at which leading cardinals and bishops undertook a reform of the Roman Catholic Church. What bothered the reformers most about the sacred music of the Church was that the incessant entry of voices in musical imitation obscured the text—excessively dense counterpoint was burying the word of the Lord. As one well-placed bishop said mockingly:

In our times they [composers] have put all their industry and effort into the writing of imitative passages, so that while one voice says "Sanctus," another says "Sabaoth," still another says "Gloria tua," with howling, bellowing, and stammering, so that they more nearly resemble cats in January than flowers in May.

Initially, the assembled prelates considered banning music altogether from the service or limiting it to just the old, monophonic Gregorian chant. But the timely appearance of a few sacred compositions by Palestrina showed the council that sacred polyphony for four, five, or six voices could still be written in a clear, dignified manner. For his role in maintaining a place for composed polyphony within the established church, Palestrina came to be called, perhaps with some exaggeration, the "savior of church music."

Most famous of all Counter-Reformation compositions is Palestrina's *Missa Papae Marcelli* (*Mass for Pope Marcellus;* 1555), which the composer said

FIGURE 9–7

Portrait of Giovanni Palestrina, the first important composer of the Church to have been a layman rather than a member of the clergy.

Download a Supplementary Listening Guide for the *Kyrie* of Palestrina's *Missa Papae Marcelli* at the text website.

MALE CHOIRS: THE CASTRATO

As mentioned in our discussion of medieval music (Chapter 8), women were allowed to sing in the early Roman Catholic Church in convents but not in any public church. Similarly, women were not allowed to appear in public in theatrical productions within territories under strict Church control. Thus most church choirs in the Middle Ages and Renaissance were exclusively male. But who, then, sang the soprano and alto parts when polyphony was performed? The most common practice was to assign these parts to adult males who sang in what is called "head voice," or **falsetto**. Alternatively, choirboys might be used, but they were expensive to house and educate. Finally, beginning in 1562, the **castrato** (castrated male) voice was introduced into the papal chapel, mainly as a money-saving measure. A single castrato could produce as much volume as two falsettists or three or four boys. Castrati were renowned for their power and their great lung capacity, which allowed them to execute unusually long phrases in a single breath. Surprisingly, castrati sopranos remained a hallmark of the papal chapel until 1903, when they were officially banned by Pope Pius X. Nevertheless, the voice of one castrato, Alessandro Moreschi, known as the "Last Castrato," was captured on phonograph recording between 1902 and 1904 and is readily available for listening today.

On our recording of sections of Palestrina's *Missa Papae Marcelli*, women take the soprano line, while male

© Scala/Art Resource, NY

All-male choir with choirboys for the soprano part as depicted in a sixteenth-century Italian fresco.

falsettists and women share the alto part. To make their sound as close as possible to that of a choirboy, the women sing with almost no vibrato.

Hear Alessandro Moreschi, the "Last Castrato," in the YouTube playlist on the text website.

© British Library Board. All Rights Reserved/The Bridgeman Art Library International

FIGURE 9–8

Although public church choirs in the Middle Ages and Renaissance were all-male ensembles, women could be heard at court and in the home singing secular genres, such as the chanson and madrigal. And women, too, sang in churches, specifically in convents, where they performed all the chant and, when required, polyphony. In this illumination from a fifteenth-century English liturgical manuscript, nuns sing from their choir stalls.

was written "in a new manner." By this Palestrina meant that he had set the text of the Mass with exceptional clarity, allowing the music to inspire the listener to greater piety and devotion. To see how Palestrina imposed this clarity of expression through music, let us explore two contrasting sections of his Mass. The first is the *Gloria* of the Mass, a lengthy hymn of praise in honor of the majestic Christ; here Palestrina commands the singers to declaim the text triumphantly, mostly in block chords, with the rhythm of the music emphasizing the accents in the Latin text. Who could possibly miss the meaning of the words as the singers seemingly spit out the text? By contrast, the *Agnus Dei* of the Mass commemorates the tender, merciful Lamb of God; now Palestrina deploys imitation with peacefully overlapping lines, but each phrase of text is kept separate from the next and remains clearly audible. What Palestrina proved to the prelates of the Council of Trent remains true for us today: clarity of expression and beauty are not mutually exclusive.

*L*istening GUIDE

Giovanni Pierluigi da Palestrina
Gloria and *Agnus Dei* of the *Missa Papae Marcelli* (1555)

5
1/10–11

Genre: Sacred Mass

Texture: Mostly homophonic in *Gloria;* mostly polyphonic in *Agnus Dei*

Gloria Part I

0:00	**10** Priest chants opening phrase	Gloria in excelsis Deo,	Glory to God in the highest,
0:10	Six-voice choir completes phrase	et in terra pax hominibus bonae voluntatis.	and on earth peace to men of good will.
0:26	Four similar Latin phrases clearly declaimed	Laudamus te. Benedicimus te. Adoramus te. Glorificamus te.	We praise you. We bless you. We worship you. We glorify you.
0:44	Loud choral exclamation	Gratias agimus tibi propter magnam gloriam tuam.	We give thanks to you because of your great glory.
1:04–2:19	Varying combinations of four of six voices address the Lord	Domine Deus, rex caelestis Deus Pater omnipotens Domine, Fili unigenite, Jesu Christe; Domine Deus, Agnus Dei,	Lord, God, king of heaven God the almighty Father Lord, only begotten Son, Jesus Christ; Lord God, Lamb of God,
2:20	Full cadence	Filius Patris.	Son of the Father.

Agnus Dei Part I

0:00	**11** All six voices enter in turn in imitation	A - gnus De - - [i]	Lamb of God,
0:50	Imitation quietly continues with new phrase	qui tol - lis pec - - ca - ta	Who takes away the sins [of the earth]
1:52	Imitation quietly continues with new phrase	mi - se - re - re no - [bis]	Have mercy upon us.

Listen to streaming music in an Active Listening Guide, available on the text website.

Palestrina's serene music best captures the somber, restrained spirit of the Counter-Reformation, embodying in its quiet simplicity all that Roman Catholic authority thought proper church music should be. After his death in 1594, the legend of Palestrina, "savior of church music," continued to grow. Later composers such as Bach (*Mass in B minor,* 1733) and Mozart (*Requiem Mass,* 1791) incorporated elements of Palestrina's style into their sacred compositions. Even in our universities today, courses in counterpoint for advanced music students usually include some practice in composing in the pure, contrapuntally correct style of Palestrina. Thus the spirit of the Counter-Reformation, distilled into a set of contrapuntal rules, has continued to influence musicians long after the Renaissance came to an end.

*P*OPULAR MUSIC IN THE RENAISSANCE

The Masses and motets of Josquin and Palestrina represent the "high" art of the Renaissance—learned music for the church. But secular, popular music flourished in the Renaissance as well. Indeed, the sixteenth century witnessed an increase in commerce and trade, and with it came a growing middle class.

Though it constituted only about 6 percent of the population, the middle class was concentrated in the cities, where the new technology of music printing was beginning to flourish. Naturally, the urban middle class had different, more popular musical tastes than did the high churchmen and the nobles.

In truth, there had always been popular music for the less exalted members of society. Dance music and popular songs, for example, are indigenous to all classes in all societies. But like rock musicians today, popular musicians in the Middle Ages performed without benefit of written musical notation. Most people couldn't read—text or music—and manuscripts (by definition copied by hand) were exceedingly expensive.

All this changed, however, with Johann Gutenberg's invention of printing by movable type around 1460. Printing revolutionized the world of information in the late fifteenth century no less than did the computer in the late twentieth century. Hundreds of copies of a book could be produced quickly and cheaply once the type had been set. The first printed book of music appeared in Venice in 1501, and to this important event can be traced the origins of today's music business. The standard press run for a printed book of music then was usually five hundred copies. Mass production put the music book within reach of the banker, merchant, lawyer, and shopkeeper. "How to" manuals encouraged ordinary men and women to learn to read musical notation, so as to sing and to play an instrument at home. The learned amateur had arrived.

Dance Music

Our fascination with dance didn't begin with *Dancing with the Stars*. Music and dance are likely as old as human life itself. But most dance music before the Renaissance is lost in the mists of time because it, like much popular culture, was not preserved in written form. With the increase in literacy generally—and musical literacy in particular—publishers in sixteenth-century Europe issued collections of dances, assuming that the musically inclined middle class was now ready to dance at home. Dances went by the name of a dance type, such as basse dance, pavane, galliard, or branle, or by the name of a dance type plus the title of the tune—"Basse Dance the Admiral," for example. Printers suggested which instruments were most appropriate; flutes, lutes, various keyboard instruments, and even the newly emerging violin are named. Not wishing to lose a single sale, however, publishers would often conclude an advertisement with the all-inclusive encouragement "or suitable for any similar sort of instrument." As visual evidence from the period shows (Fig. 9-9), a group of several shawms (predecessor of the modern-day oboe) and perhaps a sackbut (parent of our trombone), along with a drum, formed the most common dance band.

By far the most popular type of dance of the mid-sixteenth century was the **pavane,** a slow, gliding dance in duple meter performed by couples holding hands. It was often followed by a contrasting **galliard,** a fast, leaping dance in triple meter. (For a painting believed to show Queen Elizabeth I leaping in a galliard, see Figure 9-11.) Around 1550 the French publisher Jacques Moderne issued a collection of twenty-five anonymous dances that included several pavanes and galliards. Moderne titled this collection *Musicque de Joye*—listen and you'll understand why.

FIGURE 9-9

Musicians in a procession as painted by Denis van Alsloot, c1600. The instruments are, from right to left, a sackbut, two shawms, a cornetto, another shawm, and an early bassoon.

© Prado, Madrid/The Bridgeman Art Library International

Listening GUIDE

**Jacques Moderne, publisher, *Musique de Joye* (c1550)
Anonymous, Pavane and Galliard**

5

1/12–13

Genre: Instrumental dance

Texture: Homophonic

Moderne printed these dances in four separate parts (SATB), and on this recording by the American early music group Piffaro, the parts are played on four shawms (see Fig. 9-9). Like most dances, the musical phrasing is square, to allow the dancers to coordinate foot patterns easily with beats. Here both pavane and galliard have three phrases, each of which is 4 + 4 measures in length and immediately repeated.

Pavane (slow duple meter)		**Galliard (fast triple meter)**	
0:05 **12**	Phrase 1	0:00 **13**	Phrase 1
0:21	Phrase 1 repeated but with top line ornamented	0:11	Phrase 1 repeated
0:37	Phrase 2	0:19	Phrase 2
0:53	Phrase 2 repeated but with top line ornamented	0:27	Phrase 2 repeated
1:09	Phrase 3	0:34	Phrase 3
1:26	Phrase 3 repeated but with top line ornamented	0:42	Phrase 3 repeated

Listen to streaming music in an Active Listening Guide, available on the text website.

The Madrigal

About 1530, a new kind of popular song took Europe by storm: the madrigal. A **madrigal** is a piece for several solo voices (usually four or five) that sets a vernacular poem, most often about love, to music. The madrigal arose in Italy but soon spread to northern European countries. So popular did the madrigal become that by 1630 some 40,000 pieces had been printed by publishers eager to satisfy public demand. The madrigal was a truly social art, one that both men and women could enjoy (Fig. 9-10).

Of all the musical genres of the Renaissance, the madrigal best exemplifies the humanist requirement that music express the meaning of the text. In a typical madrigal each word or phrase of poetry receives its own musical gesture. Thus, when the madrigal text says "chase after" or "follow quickly," the music becomes fast, and one voice chases after another in musical imitation. For words such as "pain," "anguish," "death," and "cruel fate," the madrigal composer almost invariably employs a twisting chromatic scale or a biting dissonance. This practice of depicting the text by means of a descriptive musical gesture, whether subtly or jokingly as a musical pun, is called **word painting.** Word painting became all the rage with madrigal composers in Italy and England. Even today such musical clichés as a falling melody for "swoon" and a dissonance for "pain" are called **madrigalisms.**

Although the madrigal was born in Italy, popular favor soon carried it over the Alps to Germany, Denmark, the Low Countries, and England. The first madrigals to be printed in England appeared in a 1588 publication titled *Musica transalpina* (*Music from Across the Alps*), a collection of more than fifty madrigals, mainly by Italian composers, with the texts translated into English. Soon English composers—all contemporaries of William Shakespeare (1564–1616)—were writing their own madrigals to new English poems. One of the best of the English madrigalists was Thomas Weelkes (1576–1623), an organist who spent

Download Supplementary Listening Guides for additional madrigals—by Weelkes (*O Care Thou Wilt Dispatch Me*) and by John Farmer (*Fair Phyllis*)—at the text website.

FIGURE 9–10

Singers of a four-part madrigal during the mid-sixteenth century. Women were very much a part of this secular, nonreligious music-making.

© Giraudon/The Bridgeman Art Library International

FIGURE 9–11

A painting believed to show Queen Elizabeth dancing with the Duke of Leicester.

A complete Checklist of Musical Style for the Renaissance can be found at the text website.

most of his career in rural Chichester but ended his days in London, an honorary Gentleman of the Chapel Royal.

In 1601, Weelkes and twenty-three other English composers each contributed a madrigal to a collection titled *The Triumphes of Oriana*, an album of music compiled in honor of the Virgin Queen Elizabeth (1533–1603). (Oriana, a legendary British princess and maiden, was used as the poetic nickname of Queen Elizabeth.) Weelkes's contribution to *The Triumphes of Oriana* was the six-voice madrigal *As Vesta Was from Latmos Hill Descending*. Its text, likely fashioned by Weelkes himself, is a rather confused mixture of images from classical mythology: the Roman goddess Vesta, descending the Greek mountain of Latmos, spies Oriana (Elizabeth) ascending the hill; the nymphs and shepherds attending the goddess Diana desert her to sing the praises of Oriana. The sole virtue of this verse is that it provides frequent opportunity for word painting in music. As the text commands, the music descends, ascends, runs, mingles imitatively, and offers "mirthful tunes" to the maiden queen. Elizabeth herself played lute and harpsichord, and loved to dance (Fig. 9-11). Weelkes saw fit to end his madrigal with cries of "Long live fair Oriana." Indeed, the fair queen did enjoy a long and glorious reign—thus our term "Elizabethan Age."

Madrigals such as Weelkes's *As Vesta Was from Latmos Hill Descending* were popular because they were fun to sing. Vocal lines were written within a comfortable range, melodies were often triadic, rhythms were catchy, and the music was full of puns. When Vesta descends the mountain, so too her music moves down the scale; when Oriana (Queen Elizabeth) ascends, her music does likewise; when Diana, the goddess of virginity, is all alone—you guessed it, we hear a solo voice. With sport like this to be had, no wonder the popularity of the madrigal endured beyond the Renaissance. Even today the madrigal remains a staple of a cappella singing groups and university glee clubs.

Listening GUIDE

Thomas Weelkes
As Vesta Was from Latmos Hill Descending (1601)

5   2
1/14   1/6

Genre: Madrigal

Texture: Changes according to dictates of text

Time		Description	Text
0:00	14 6	Opening homophonic chords give way to falling pitches on "descending"	As Vesta was from Latmos Hill descending,
0:12		Imitation falls, then rises on word "ascending"	She spied a maiden Queen the same ascending,
0:32		Simple repeating notes suggest simple country swains	Attended on by all the shepherds' swain;
0:49		All voices come "running down amain"	To whom Diana's darlings came running down amain,
1:13		Two voices exemplify "two by two," then three "three by three"	First two by two, then three by three together,
1:23		Solo voice highlights "all alone"	Leaving their goddess all alone, hasted thither;
1:35		Imitative entries suggest "mingling"	And mingling with the shepherds of her train,
1:42		Light, rapid singing produces "mirthful tunes"	With mirthful tunes her presence did entertain.
1:58		Stark chords announce final acclamation	Then sang the shepherds and nymphs of Diana:
2:10		Long life to the queen is declaimed endlessly	Long live fair Oriana.

Listen to streaming music in an Active Listening Guide, available at the text website.

Listening EXERCISE 15

Weelkes

AS VESTA WAS FROM LATMOS HILL DESCENDING

 5 2 @ 1/14 1/6

To take this Listening Exercise online and receive feedback or email answers to your instructor, go to the text website.

So striking is the depiction of the text through music in the madrigal of the Renaissance that these instances of musical word painting are called madrigalisms. Often the music depicts the text by its motion (up, down, or stationary) or by its texture (polyphonic, monophonic, or homophonic). At these moments the word painting is so obvious as to be amusing, and that makes several of the following questions easy to answer.

1. (0:00–0:11) The text sets the scene of this madrigal at the top of Latmos Hill, a mountain in Greek mythology. At the beginning, we hear sounds that are what?
   a. generally low with male voices predominating
   b. generally high with female voices predominating

2. (0:00–0:31) Which is true about the direction of the music for the words "descending" and "ascending"?
   a. It descends for "descending" and ascends for "ascending."
   b. It ascends for "descending" and descends for "ascending."
   c. There is no clear direction, and word painting is not present.

3. (0:33–0:47) Which is true about the music for the words "attended on"?
   a. It ascends.
   b. It descends.
   c. The singers mostly repeat the same pitches, so the music sounds static.

4. (0:54–1:10) For the word "running," what does the music do?
   a. It goes faster and ascends.
   b. It goes faster and descends.
   c. It goes slower and remains stationary in pitch.

5. (1:22–1:28) What is the texture of the music at the words "Leaving their goddess"?
   a. monophony
   b. homophony
   c. imitative polyphony

6. (1:29–1:31) What is the texture of the music at the words "all alone"?
   a. monophony
   b. homophony
   c. imitative polyphony

7. (1:59–2:07) What is the texture at the words "Then sang the shepherds"?
   a. monophony
   b. homophony
   c. imitative polyphony

8. (2:10–end) What is the texture at the words "Long live fair Oriana"?
   a. monophony
   b. homophony
   c. imitative polyphony

9. (2:16–end) When the bass enters with a presentation of "Long live fair Oriana," what is the nature of the musical line?
   a. The bass sings long, steady notes to emphasize the word "long."
   b. The bass sings rapid notes, joining the many acclamations of the upper voices.

10. Which of the following is true?
   a. The performance of this madrigal is a cappella with one singer to a part.
   b. The performance of this madrigal is a cappella with two singers to a part.
   c. The performance of this madrigal is not a cappella.

Key WORDS

humanism (82)
motet (83)
a cappella (84)
imitation (84)
Counter-Reformation (87)

Sistine Chapel (87)
Council of Trent (87)
falsetto (88)
castrato (88)
pavane (90)
galliard (90)

madrigal (91)
word painting (91)
madrigalism (91)

@ The materials on the text website will help you understand and pass tests on the content of this chapter. In addition, you may watch Craig Wright's own lecture at Open Yale Courses and complete this chapter's Listening Exercises interactively, as well as view Active Listening Guides and other materials that will help you succeed in this course.

PART III *T*HE BAROQUE PERIOD, 1600–1750

© Bridgeman-Giraudon/Art Resource, NY

1600	1610	1620	1630	1640	1650	1660	1670

BAROQUE

● 1607 Claudio Monteverdi's opera *Orfeo* premiers in Mantua

1618–1648 Thirty Years' War in Europe

● 1626 Saint Peter's Basilica completed

● 1643 Louis XIV becomes king of France

● 1650s Barbara Strozzi publishes chamber cantatas in Venice

● c1660 Antonio Stradivari begins to make violins in Cremona

● 1669 King Louis XIV begins construction of Versailles

The dominant style of architecture, painting, sculpture, music, and dance in the period 1600–1750 is called Baroque. It originated first in Rome, as a way to glorify the Counter-Reformation Catholic Church, and then spread beyond Italy to Spain, France, Germany, Austria, the Low Countries, and England. The artists who created Baroque art worked mainly for the pope and important monarchs throughout Europe. Thus Baroque art is akin to the "official" art of the ruling establishment. Whereas the art and music of the Renaissance was marked by classical balance and rational restraint, that of the Baroque era is full of grandeur, extravagance, drama, and overt sensuality. This is as true for the music of Claudio Monteverdi at the beginning of the Baroque period as it is of that of Bach and Handel at the end. During the Baroque period, several new musical genres emerge: opera, cantata, and oratorio enter the realm of vocal music, and sonata and concerto appear among the instrumental types.

| 1680 | 1690 | 1700 | 1710 | 1720 | 1730 | 1740 | 1750 |

BAROQUE

- 1685 Johann Sebastian Bach and George Frideric Handel born in Germany

- c1685 Johann Pachelbel composes his Canon in Germany

- 1687 Isaac Newton publishes his masterpiece *Mathematical Principles*

- c1689 Henry Purcell composes opera *Dido and Aeneas* in London ·······▶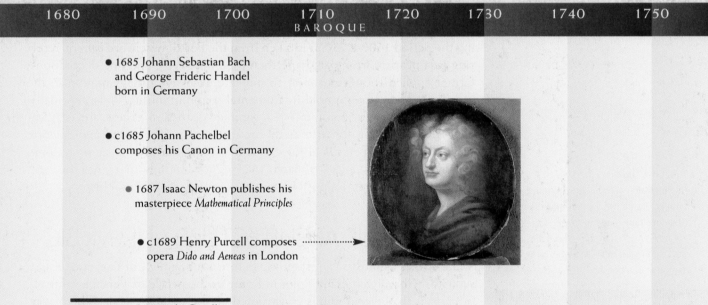

c1681–1700 Arcangelo Corelli publishes violin sonatas in Rome

c1700–1730 Antonio Vivaldi composes concertos in Venice

- 1711 Handel moves to London and writes operas

◀·············· ● 1723 Bach moves to Leipzig and writes cantatas

- 1741 Handel composes oratorio *Messiah*

10

INTRODUCTION TO BAROQUE ART AND MUSIC

Music historians agree, with unusual unanimity, that Baroque music first appeared in Italy in the early seventeenth century. To be sure, around 1600, certain qualities of the Italian madrigal—virtuosic solo singing, for example—came to be emphasized in a way that created an entirely new sound. The older equal-voiced choral polyphony of the Renaissance receded in importance as a new, more flamboyant style gained in popularity. Eventually, the new style was given a new name: Baroque.

Baroque is the term used to describe the arts generally during the period 1600–1750. It is taken from the Portuguese word *barroco*, referring to a pearl of irregular shape then used in jewelry and fine decorations. Critics applied the term *baroque* to indicate excessive ornamentation in the visual arts and a rough, bold instrumental sound in music. Thus, originally, *baroque* had a negative connotation: it signified distortion, excess, and extravagance. Only during the twentieth century, with a new-found appreciation of the painting of Peter Paul Rubens (1577–1640) and the music of Antonio Vivaldi (1678–1741) and J. S. Bach (1685–1750), among others, has the term *baroque* come to assume a positive meaning in Western cultural history.

FIGURE 10-1

The high altar at Saint Peter's Basilica, Rome, with baldachin by Gian Lorenzo Bernini. Standing more than ninety feet high, this canopy is marked by twisted columns and curving shapes, color, and movement, all typical of Baroque art.

© Scala/Art Resource, NY

BAROQUE ARCHITECTURE AND MUSIC

What strikes us most when standing before a monument of Baroque design, such as the basilica of Saint Peter in Rome or the palace of Versailles outside of Paris, is that everything is constructed on the grandest scale. The plazas, buildings, colonnades, gardens, and fountains are all massive. Look at the ninety-foot-high altar canopy inside Saint Peter's, designed by Gian Lorenzo Bernini (1598–1680), and imagine how it dwarfs the priest below (Fig. 10-1). Outside the basilica, a circle of colonnades forms a courtyard large enough to encompass several football fields (Fig. 10-2). Or consider the French king's palace of Versailles, constructed during the reign of Louis XIV (1643–1715), so monumental in scope that it formed a small independent city, home to several thousand court functionaries (see Fig. 12-2).

The music composed for performance in such vast expanses could also be grandiose. While at first the Baroque orchestra was small, under King Louis XIV, it sometimes swelled to more than eighty players. Similarly, choral works for Baroque churches sometimes required twenty-four, forty-eight, or even fifty-three separate lines or parts. These compositions for massive choral forces epitomize the grand or "colossal" Baroque.

Once the exteriors of the large Baroque palaces and churches were built, the artists of the time rushed in to fill these expanses with abundant, perhaps even excessive, decoration. It was as if the architect had created a large vacuum, and into it raced the painter, sculptor, and carver to fill the void. Examine again the interior of Saint Peter's (see Fig. 10-1) and notice the ornamentation on the ceiling, as well as the elaborate twists and turns of Bernini's canopy. Or consider the Austrian monastery of Saint Florian (Fig. 10-3); there are massive columns, yet the frieze connecting them is richly decorated, as is the ceiling above. Here elaborate scrolls and floral capitals add warmth and humanity to what would otherwise be a vast, cold space.

FIGURE 10-2

Saint Peter's Square, designed by Bernini in the mid-seventeenth century. The expanse is so colossal it seems to swallow people, cars, and buses.

Similarly, when expressed in the music of the Baroque era, this love of energetic detail within large-scale compositions took the form of a highly ornamental melody set upon a solid chordal foundation. Sometimes the decoration almost seems to overrun the fundamental harmonic structure of the piece. Notice in Figure 10-4 the abundance of melodic flourishes in just a few measures of music for violin by Arcangelo Corelli (1653–1713). Such ornaments were equally popular with the singers of the early Baroque period, when the cult of the vocal virtuoso first emerged.

BAROQUE PAINTING AND MUSIC

Many of the principles at work in Baroque architecture are also found in Baroque painting and music. Baroque canvases are usually large and colorful. Most important, they are overtly dramatic. Drama in painting is created by means of contrast: bold colors are pitted against one another; bright light is set against darkness; and lines are placed at right angles to one another, which suggests tension and energetic movement. Figure 10-5 shows Peter Paul Rubens's *The Horrors of War*. The large canvas swirls with a chaotic scene that is extravagant yet sensual, typical qualities of Baroque art. Barely visible in the right lower foreground is a woman with a broken lute,

FIGURE 10-3

Church of the monastery of Saint Florian, Austria (1686–1708). The powerful pillars and arches set a strong structural framework, while the painted ceiling and heavily foliated capitals provide decoration and warmth.

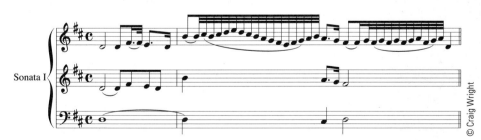

Sonata I

FIGURE 10-4

Arcangelo Corelli's sonata for violin and *basso continuo*, Opus 5, No. 1. The bass provides the structural support, while the violin adds elaborate decoration above.

FIGURE 10-5

Rubens's *The Horrors of War* (1638) is a reaction to the Thirty Years' War (1618–1648) that ravaged Europe at this time. Here Mars, the god of war (center, wearing a military helmet), is pulled to the right by Fury and to the left by a mostly naked Venus, goddess of love. Beneath these figures, the populace suffers.

FIGURE 10-6

Judith Beheading Holofernes (c1615) by Artemisia Gentileschi. The grisly scene of Judith slaying the tyrant general was painted several times by Gentileschi, perhaps as a vivid way of demonstrating her abhorrence of aggressive male domination.

which symbolizes that harmony (music) cannot exist beside the discord of war. Figure 10-6 paints an even more horrific scene: the woman Judith visiting retribution upon the Assyrian general Holofernes, as depicted by Artemisia Gentileschi (1593–1652). Here the play of light and dark creates a dramatic effect, the stark blue and red colors add intensity, while the head of the victim, set at a right angle to his body, suggests an unnatural motion. Baroque art sometimes delights in the pure shock value of presenting gruesome events from history or myth in a dramatic way.

Music of the Baroque is also highly dramatic. We observed in the music of the Renaissance (1450–1600) a growing awareness of the capacity of this art to sway, or affect, the emotions. This led in the early seventeenth century to an aesthetic theory called the Doctrine of Affections. The **Doctrine of Affections** held that different musical moods could and should be used to influence the emotions, or affections, of the listener. A musical setting should reinforce the intended "affection" of the text. Yet each work of Baroque art in general confines itself to one specific emotion, keeping each unit of space and expression separate and distinct from the next. There is a unity of mood within each scene. So, too, musicians spoke of the need to dramatize the text yet maintain a single affection—be it rage, revenge, sorrow, joy, or love—from beginning to end of a piece. Not surprisingly, the single most important new genre to emerge in the Baroque period was opera. Here the drama of the stage joined with music to form a powerful new medium.

*C*HARACTERISTICS OF BAROQUE MUSIC

Perhaps more than any other period in the history of music, the Baroque (1600–1750) gave rise to a remarkable variety of musical styles, ranging from the expressive monody of Claudio Monteverdi (1567–1643) to the complex polyphony of J. S. Bach (1685–1750). It also saw the introduction of many new musical genres—opera, cantata, oratorio, sonata, concerto, and suite—each of which is discussed in the following chapters. Yet despite the quick stylistic changes and all the new types of music created, two elements remain constant throughout the Baroque period: an expressive melody and a strong supporting bass.

Expressive Melody

Renaissance music, as we saw in Chapter 9, was dominated by polyphonic texture, in which the voices spin out a web of imitative counterpoint. The nature and importance of each of the lines is about equal, as the following graphic suggests:

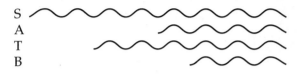

In early Baroque music, however, the voices are no longer equal. Rather, a polarity develops in which the musical emphasis gravitates toward the top and bottom lines:

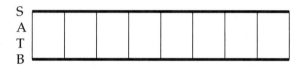

Renaissance vocal music was mostly ensemble music—motets, Masses, and madrigals for groups of vocalists, even if there was only one singer on a part. In the early Baroque, however, the musical focus shifts from vocal ensemble to accompanied solo song. A choir might be a useful medium to convey the abstract religious thoughts of the multitudes, but to communicate raw human emotions, direct appeal by an individual soloist now seemed more appropriate. The new kind of solo singing was at first called **monody** (from Greek terms meaning "to sing alone"). A single singer stepped forward, accompanied by a very few supporting instruments, to project a highly charged text. Within the medium of monody, the vocal virtuoso would soon emerge, the star of the court theater and the operatic stage.

The Basso Continuo

Monody emphasizes a solo melody, but one supported by chords springing up vertically from the bass. In simple terms, the soprano carries the melody while the bass provides a strong harmonic support. In between, the middle voices do little more than fill out the texture. If Renaissance music was conceived polyphonically and horizontally, line by line, that of the early Baroque period is organized homophonically and vertically, chord by chord.

The bass-driven, chordal support in Baroque music is called the **basso continuo,** and it is played by one or more instruments. Figure 10-7 shows a woman singing to the accompaniment of a large plucked string instrument called the theorbo. This instrument has

FIGURE 10–7

A Woman Playing the Theorbo-Lute and a Cavalier (c1658) by Gerard ter Borch. The bass strings are at the top of the instrument and off the fingerboard. The theorbo was often used to play the *basso continuo* in the seventeenth century.

© Image Asset Management Ltd./SuperStock

FIGURE 10-8

Antonio Visentini (1688–1782), *Concert at the Villa.* Notice how the double bass player at the left turns his head to read the bass (bottom) line in the score on the harpsichord; together they provide the *basso continuo.*

more low strings than its close cousin the lute, which allows it to not only strum chords but also play low bass notes. In the early seventeenth century, a theorbo or some other kind of bass lute often played the *basso continuo.* Figure 10-8 shows a solo singer, two violinists, and a violist, accompanied by two other instruments: a large double bass (to the left), which plays the bass line, and a harpsichord, which improvises chords built above that bass line. The singer, viola, and violins project an expressive melody while the other two instruments provide the *basso continuo.* Harpsichord and low string instrument formed the most common *basso continuo* in the Baroque period. Indeed, it is the continual tinkling of the harpsichord, in step with a strong bass line, that signals the listener that the music being played comes from the Baroque ((intro)/11, for example). Coincidentally, this top-bottom makeup of monodic singing in Baroque music is not structurally different from the straight-ahead rock 'n' roll music of today with electric bass; in both styles, an expressive soloist sings above a rock-solid bass, while a keyboardist (or guitar player), building on the bass line, improvises chords in the middle of the texture.

What chords did the Baroque harpsichordist play? These were suggested to the performer by means of **figured bass**—a numerical shorthand placed below the bass line. A player familiar with chord formations would look at the bass line, such as that given in Example 10-1a, and improvise chords along the lines of those given in Example 10-1b. These improvised chords, generated from the bass according to the numerical code, support a melody above. Here, too, there is a modern parallel. Figured bass is similar in intent to the alphanumerical code found in "fake books" used by jazz musicians today, which suggest which chords to play beneath the written melody.

EXAMPLE 10-1

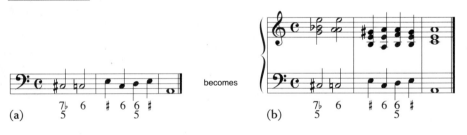

ℰLEMENTS OF BAROQUE MUSIC

Baroque music, as we have seen, is marked by grandeur, by passionate expression, and by drama. It is held together by a chordal framework and a strong bass line, both supplied by the *basso continuo.* These qualities can be heard in all three chronological divisions of Baroque music: early Baroque (1600–1660), middle Baroque (1660–1710), and late Baroque (1710–1750). In the music of the early Baroque in particular, the artistic expression of the voice and the richness of the harmony were especially intense. In the late

Baroque, some of the excessively exuberant qualities of early Baroque music would be smoothed out and regularized by Bach and Handel (see Chapters 13 and 14). The following elements, however, are common to all periods of Baroque music.

Melody

In the Renaissance, melody was more or less all of one type. It was a direct, uncomplicated line that could be performed by either a voice or an instrument. But in early Baroque music, beginning about 1600, two different melodic styles begin to develop: a dramatic, virtuosic style in singing, and a more mechanical style, full of figural repetitions, in instrumental music. Vocal melody in the Baroque is marked by quick shifts from long notes to very short ones, which creates an excited, exuberant sound. From time to time, the voice will luxuriate in a long flourish as it projects a single syllable in long melisma (Ex. 10-2). Below are two melodies, one from Monteverdi's opera *Orfeo* from the beginning of the Baroque and the other from Handel's oratorio *Messiah* from the end of the period.

EXAMPLE 10–2

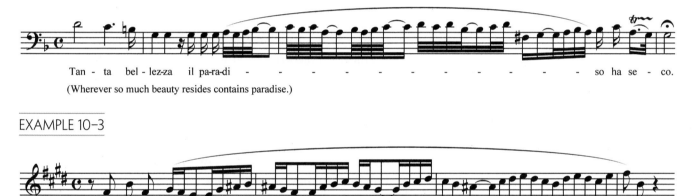

Tan - ta bel - lez-za il pa-ra-di - - - - - - - - - - - so ha se - co.
(Wherever so much beauty resides contains paradise.)

EXAMPLE 10–3

[Every valley] shall be ex - alt - - - - - - - - - - - - ed,

Generally, Baroque melody does not unfold in short, symmetrical units, but expands luxuriantly, and often unpredictably, over long musical phrases.

Harmony

Baroque harmonies are chordally conceived and tightly bound to the *basso continuo.* Composers in the early seventeenth century sometimes placed their chords in an order that sounds arbitrary to our modern ears. But as the century progressed, harmonies unfold more and more in patterns familiar to us, and standard harmonic progressions emerge; in other words, chord progressions as we know them come into being. The shortest and most frequent of these is the V-I (dominant-tonic) cadence (see p. 35). The advent of standard harmonic progressions like the V-I cadence gives added direction and cohesion to the music.

Attending this development is the growing importance—and eventual total domination—of the major and minor keys. These two scale patterns, major and minor, replaced the dozen or so scales (or "modes," as they were called) employed during the Renaissance and before. Moreover, as music was reduced to just two very different qualities of sound, the composer could play the dark minor off against the bright major, just as a painter might contrast light and dark (see Fig. 10-6), for particular effect.

Rhythm

Rhythm in Baroque music is characterized by uniformity, not flexibility. Just as a single mood, or affect, is carried from the beginning to the end of a piece of Baroque music, so, too, the rhythmic patterns heard at the beginning will surface again and again, right to the end. Moreover, in Baroque music—especially instrumental music—a strong recurring beat is usually clearly audible, which pushes the music forward and creates, in contemporary terms, a "groove." This tendency toward rhythmic clarity and drive becomes more and more pronounced as the Baroque period proceeds. It culminates in the rhythmically propulsive music of Vivaldi and Bach.

Texture

Baroque composers approached musical texture in ever-changing ways. Texture in the early Baroque is overwhelmingly homophonic, the *basso continuo* providing a wholly chordal framework. Indeed, composers of the early seventeenth century rebelled against the predominantly polyphonic, imitative texture of the Renaissance. This initial hostility toward polyphony gradually diminished, however. In the late Baroque, composers such as Bach and Handel returned to contrapuntal writing, in part to add richness to the middle range of the standard top-bottom (soprano-bass)–dominated texture.

Dynamics

Before the Baroque era, musicians did not put dynamic marks in the score. That doesn't mean that there were no louds or softs in music, but simply that performers intuited what they were to do without being told. In the early seventeenth century, however, composers began to dictate the dynamic level they wished by inserting two very basic terms: *piano* (soft) and *forte* (loud). Sudden contrasts of dynamics were more prized than gradual crescendos and diminuendos. This practice of shifting the volume of sound suddenly from one level to another is called **terraced dynamics.** Terraced dynamics went hand in hand with clear contrasts between major and minor keys, as well as with abrupt changes in orchestration. By contrasting distinctly different dynamics, moods, and colors, composers of the Baroque created the one thing prized above all others in Baroque art: drama.

@

The materials on the text website will help you understand and pass tests on the content of this chapter.

Key WORDS

Baroque (96)	monody (99)	figured bass (100)
Doctrine of Affections (98)	*basso continuo* (99)	terraced dynamics (102)

EARLY BAROQUE VOCAL MUSIC

/ /

⟨OPERA

Given the popularity of opera today—and the fact that there had been opera in China and Japan since the thirteenth century—it is surprising that this genre of music emerged comparatively late in the history of Western European culture. Not until around 1600 did opera appear in Europe, and its native soil was Italy.

Opera requires a union of music, drama, scenery, costumes, and often dance. It demands singers who can act or, in some cases, actors who can sing. In opera, all lines are sung, unlike in a Broadway musical, for example, in which the dialogue is spoken and only the emotional high points are sung. The text of an opera is called the **libretto** (little book), and it is normally written by a poet working in collaboration with the composer. Because all the text must be sung, opera creates a somewhat unnatural art. We don't usually sing to our roommate, "Get out of the bathroom, I need to get to class this morning." The advantage of communication in song, however, lies in the increased potential for expressive intensity, as the flexible sung melody amplifies the nuances of the text. By combining orchestrally accompanied song, scenic design, and dramatic action to make opera, composers of the seventeenth century created for their day a genre not unlike the multimedia films of today. In opera, however, everything unfolds live on stage and in "real time."

The term *opera* means literally "work." The word was first employed in the early seventeenth century in the Italian phrase *opera drammatica in musica* (dramatic work set to music). Early Baroque opera rejected the Renaissance belief that emotions could best be expressed by a group of singers gathered in a choir. The individual, not the multitude, was now deemed the best vehicle to convey heartfelt personal feelings. From its inception, then, opera placed the solo singer at center stage. Then, as now, three laws ruled the opera house: (1) all parts of the drama are sung, mainly by soloists; (2) the major roles go to the best singers; and (3) these star singers demand and receive huge appearance fees (the highest among classical musicians); thus the cost of opera is enormous.

The origins of opera can be traced to late sixteenth-century Italy—specifically, to progressive musicians and intellectuals in the cities of Florence, Mantua, and Venice (Fig. 11-1). Here, a number of visionary thinkers continued to pursue a goal of late Renaissance humanism—recapture the expressive

FIGURE 11-1

The major musical centers in northern Italy in the seventeenth century.

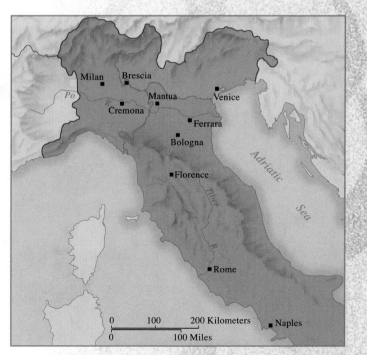

© Erich Lessing/Art Resource, NY

FIGURE 11–2

Portrait of Claudio Monteverdi by Bernardo Strozzi (1581–1644). Strozzi also painted the singer and composer Barbara Strozzi (see page 110).

FIGURE 11–3

Piazza San Marco painted by Gentile Bellini, c1500. Saint Mark's was the focal point of all religious and civic activities in Venice. In the 1630s, Venice became home to the first public opera houses.

power of ancient Greek music. Florence in particular was home to several outstanding musical intellectuals, including Vincenzo Galilei (1533–1591), the father of the famous astronomer Galileo Galilei (1564–1642). The elder Galilei and his followers believed that the power of Greek drama owed much to the fact that every line was sung, not spoken. In an attempt to imitate the ancient Greeks, the fathers of Western opera strove to create a theatrical medium in which the drama might be projected through intensified vocal recitations sung to the plainest of accompaniments. While various composers tried their hand at this new genre in the years around 1600, it was not until 1607, with Claudio Monteverdi's *Orfeo*, that the first great opera emerged.

Claudio Monteverdi (1567–1643)

Claudio Monteverdi was a musical genius who could manifest his enormous talents equally well in a madrigal, a Mass, a motet, or an opera (Fig. 11-2). He was born in the northern Italian town of Cremona in 1567 and moved to the larger city of Mantua (see Fig. 11-1) about 1590 to serve Duke Vincenzo Gonzaga as a singer and a performer on string instruments. In 1601, Monteverdi was appointed director of music, and in this capacity, he composed two operas for the court, *Orfeo* (1607) and *Arianna* (1608). But the duke failed to pay Monteverdi what he had promised. "I have never in my life suffered greater humiliation of the spirit than when I had to go and beg the treasurer for what was mine," said the composer some years later. Thus disenchanted with Mantua, Monteverdi accepted the much-coveted position of *maestro di cappella* at Saint Mark's in Venice (Fig. 11-3). Although called to Venice ostensibly to write church music for Saint Mark's, Monteverdi continued to compose opera as well. Among his important later works in this genre are *The Return of Ulysses* (1640) and *The Coronation of Poppea* (1642). He died in Venice in 1643 after thirty years of faithful service.

Monteverdi's first opera—and the first important opera in the history of Western music—is his *Orfeo*. Because the aim of early opera was to reproduce elements of ancient Greek drama, it was only natural that the libretto for

© Scala/Ministero per i Beni e le Attività culturali/Art Resource, NY

Orfeo drew on a tale from classical Greek mythology. The leading character is Orfeo (Orpheus), the son of Apollo, the Greek god of the sun and of music. (Indeed, the very word *music* comes from the artistic Muses who attended Apollo.) Orfeo, himself a demigod, finds love in the form of the beautiful Euridice, a mortal. No sooner are they married than she is killed by a poisonous snake and carried off to Hades (the ancient world's version of Hell). Orfeo vows to descend into the Underworld to rescue his beloved. This he nearly accomplishes by means of his divine musical powers, for Orfeo can make trees sway, calm savage beasts, and overcome demonic forces with the beauty of his song alone. The theme of *Orfeo*, then, is the divine power of music.

Monteverdi advances the drama in *Orfeo* mainly through **monody** (expressive solo singing to simple accompaniment), a medium thought to approximate the singing of the ancient Greek theater. The simplest type of monody was recitative. **Recitative,** from the Italian word *recitativo* (something recited), is musically heightened speech, through which the plot of the opera is communicated to the audience. Generally, recitative is performed without a perceptible meter or beat—you can't tap your foot to it. And because recitative attempts to mirror the natural rhythms of everyday speech, it is often made up of rapidly repeating notes followed by one or two long notes at the ends of phrases, as in the following recitative from Act II of *Orfeo*.

EXAMPLE 11–1

Al l'a-ma - ra no-vel-la Ras-sem-bra l'in-fe-li - ce un mu-to sas-so
(At the bitter news the unhappy one resembles a mute stone)

Recitative in Baroque opera is accompanied only by the *basso continuo*, which consists, as we have seen, of a bass line and accompanying chords (Fig. 11-4). Such sparsely accompanied recitative is called **simple recitative** (*recitativo semplice* in Italian). (In the nineteenth century, recitative accompanied by the full

FIGURE 11–4

The beginning of the second act of Monteverdi's *Orfeo* (1607), from an early print of the opera. The vocal part of a messenger appears on the odd-numbered staffs above the slower-moving bass line of the *basso continuo* (even-numbered staffs).

orchestra, called *recitativo accompagnato*, would become the norm.) A good example of simple recitative can be heard at the beginning of the vocal excerpt from Act II of *Orfeo*, discussed later in the Listening Guide.

In addition to recitative, Monteverdi made use of a more lyrical type of monody called aria. An **aria** (Italian for "song" or "ayre") is more passionate, more expansive, and more tuneful than a recitative. It also tends to have a clear meter and more regular rhythms. If a recitative tells what is happening on stage, an aria conveys what the character *feels* about those events. Similarly, whereas a recitative advances the plot, an aria usually brings the action to a halt so as to focus a spotlight on the emotional state of the singer. Finally, whereas a recitative often involves a rapid-fire delivery of text, an aria will work through text at a more leisurely pace; words are repeated to heighten their dramatic effect, and important vowels are extended by means of vocal melismas, as can be seen, for example, in Orfeo's aria "Possente spirto" ("Powerful Spirit").

EXAMPLE 11–2

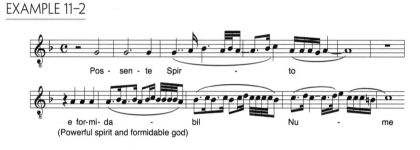

Pos - sen - te Spir - - to

e for-mi- da - bil Nu - me
(Powerful spirit and formidable god)

An aria is an important, self-contained unit, both textually and musically. Whereas recitative is normally written in blank verse (has meter but no rhyme), an aria is usually composed with meter and rhyme—in other words, an aria text is a short, rhyming poem of one or more stanzas. The text of Orfeo's aria "Possente spirto" consists of three three-line stanzas, each with a rhyme scheme **aba**. Moreover, the music for each stanza begins and ends in the same key (G minor). Finally, operatic arias are nearly always accompanied not merely by the *basso continuo* but also by all or part of the orchestra. Monteverdi gives special prominence to the violins, cornettos (see Fig. 9-9), and harps in "Possente spirto" to give added weight to the aria, as well as to show how music can charm even the guards of Hell (Fig. 11-5).

Recitative and aria are the two main styles of singing in Baroque opera, and in opera in general. In addition, there is a third style called **arioso,** a manner of singing halfway between aria and recitative. It is more declamatory than an aria but has a less rapid-fire delivery than a recitative. The lament that Orfeo sings on learning of the death of Euridice, "Tu se' morta" ("Thou Art Dead"; see Listening Guide below), is a classic example of arioso style.

Like all operas, *Orfeo* begins with a purely instrumental work that serves as a curtain raiser. Such instrumental introductions are usually called overtures, preludes, or sinfonias, but Monteverdi called his musical preamble a toccata. The term **toccata** (literally, "a touched thing") refers to an instrumental piece, for keyboard or other instruments, requiring great technical dexterity of the performers. It is, in other words, an instrumental showpiece. Here the trumpet races up and down the scale while many of the lower parts rapidly articulate repeating pitches. Monteverdi instructs that the toccata be sounded three times. Brief though it may be, this toccata is sufficiently long to suggest the richness and variety of instrumental sounds available to a composer in the early

FIGURE 11–5

Orfeo charms the guardians of Hades with his voice and lyre—a detail from a painting by Nicolas Poussin (1594–1665).

© Erich Lessing/Art Resource, NY

Baroque period. Its theatrical function, of course, is to call the audience to attention, to signal that the action is about to begin.

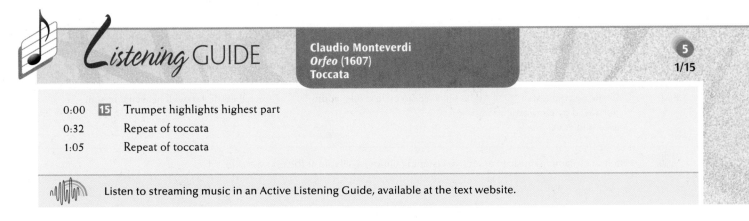

*L*istening GUIDE

Claudio Monteverdi
Orfeo (1607)
Toccata

5
1/15

0:00	**15**	Trumpet highlights highest part
0:32		Repeat of toccata
1:05		Repeat of toccata

Listen to streaming music in an Active Listening Guide, available at the text website.

Although Monteverdi divided his *Orfeo* into five short acts, this ninety-minute opera was originally performed at Mantua without intermission. The first dramatic high point occurs midway through Act II, when the hero learns that his new bride, Euridice, has been claimed by the Underworld. In a heart-felt arioso, "Tu se' morta," Orfeo laments his loss and vows to enter Hades to reclaim his beloved. Listen especially to the poignant conclusion in which Orfeo, by means of an ascending vocal line, bids farewell to earth, sky, and sun, and thus begins his journey to the land of the dead.

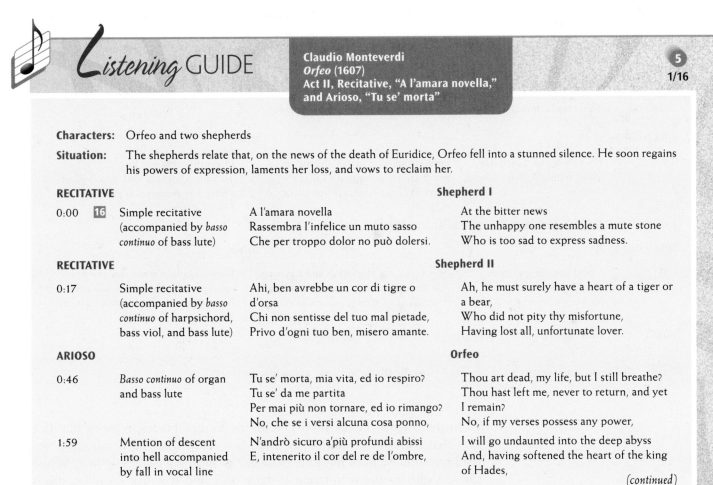

*L*istening GUIDE

Claudio Monteverdi
Orfeo (1607)
**Act II, Recitative, "A l'amara novella,"
and Arioso, "Tu se' morta"**

5
1/16

Characters: Orfeo and two shepherds

Situation: The shepherds relate that, on the news of the death of Euridice, Orfeo fell into a stunned silence. He soon regains his powers of expression, laments her loss, and vows to reclaim her.

RECITATIVE			**Shepherd I**
0:00 **16**	Simple recitative (accompanied by *basso continuo* of bass lute)	A l'amara novella Rassembra l'infelice un muto sasso Che per troppo dolor no può dolersi.	At the bitter news The unhappy one resembles a mute stone Who is too sad to express sadness.

RECITATIVE			**Shepherd II**
0:17	Simple recitative (accompanied by *basso continuo* of harpsichord, bass viol, and bass lute)	Ahi, ben avrebbe un cor di tigre o d'orsa Chi non sentisse del tuo mal pietade, Privo d'ogni tuo ben, misero amante.	Ah, he must surely have a heart of a tiger or a bear, Who did not pity thy misfortune, Having lost all, unfortunate lover.

ARIOSO			**Orfeo**
0:46	*Basso continuo* of organ and bass lute	Tu se' morta, mia vita, ed io respiro? Tu se' da me partita Per mai più non tornare, ed io rimango? No, che se i versi alcuna cosa ponno,	Thou art dead, my life, but I still breathe? Thou hast left me, never to return, and yet I remain? No, if my verses possess any power,
1:59	Mention of descent into hell accompanied by fall in vocal line	N'andrò sicuro a'più profundi abissi E, intenerito il cor del re de l'ombre,	I will go undaunted into the deep abyss And, having softened the heart of the king of Hades,

(continued)

ARIOSO   **Orfeo**

| 2:22 | Vision of Euridice climbing to heaven causes flourish in high register | Meco trarrotti a riveder le stelle; O, se ciò negherammi empio destino, Rimarrò teco in compagnia di morte. | I will transport you to see again the stars. And, if cruel destiny works against me, I will remain with you in the company of death. |
| 3:02 | Growing conviction portrayed by chromatic ascent in vocal line | Addio terra, addio cielo e sole, addio. | Farewell earth, farewell heaven and sun, farewell! |

Listen to streaming music in an Active Listening Guide, available at the text website.

Having descended to the shores of Hades, Orfeo now invokes all his musical powers to gain entry. In the aria "Possente spirto," he addresses Charon, the spirit that controls access to the kingdom of the dead. Orfeo's elaborate, florid vocal style, aided by an exotic instrumental accompaniment, soon disarms the frightful guard. After stanza 2, for example, we hear the cornetto (see Fig. 9-9), the now-extinct wind instrument of the Renaissance and Baroque that sounded something akin to a cross between a trumpet and a clarinet.

Listening GUIDE

Claudio Monteverdi
Orfeo (1607)
Act III, Aria, "Possente spirto"
(strophes 1 and 2 only)

5

1/17

Characters: Orfeo and Charon

Situation: Orfeo pleads through his music that Charon grant passage into Hades.

ARIA (Strophe 1)   **Orfeo**

| 0:00 [17] | Florid singing, joined by violin flourishes, above *basso continuo* | Possente spirto e formidabil nume, Senza cui far passaggio a l'altra riva Alma da corpo sciolta in van presume. | Powerful spirit and formidable god, without whom no soul, deprived of body, may presume to pass to Hades' shore. |
| 1:30 | Instrumental postlude played by *basso continuo* and two solo violins | | |

ARIA (Strophe 2)   **Orfeo**

| 1:55 | Florid singing continues, joined now by cornettos, above *basso continuo* | Non viv'io, no, che poi di vita è priva Mia cara sposa, il cor non è più meco, E senza cor com'esser può ch'io viva? | I live no longer, since now my dear spouse is deprived of life, I have no heart within me, and without a heart how can I still be alive? |
| 3:03 | Instrumental postlude played by *basso continuo* and two solo cornettos | | |

Listen to streaming music in an Active Listening Guide, available at the text website.

In the original Greek myth, Pluto, the lord of Hades, releases Euridice to Orfeo with one condition: he is to have faith that she is following behind him, and he must not look back before reaching earth's surface. When Orfeo yields to the temptation to look back and embrace Euridice, she is reclaimed by Pluto forevermore. In his opera *Orfeo*, Monteverdi altered this tragic conclusion: Apollo intervenes, transforming his son Orfeo into a constellation that radiates eternal spiritual harmony with the beloved Euridice. In so doing, Monteverdi established what was to become a convention for seventeenth- and eighteenth-century opera: the *lieto fine,* or "happy ending."

CHAMBER CANTATA

Seventeenth- and eighteenth-century Venice had much in common with modern Las Vegas. It was a tourist destination where gambling and prostitution flourished, and because the citizens were accustomed to wearing masks, "What happened in Venice stayed in Venice." In 1613, Claudio Monteverdi moved to this very worldly city in the sea to become director of music at the basilica of Saint Mark, then perhaps the most prestigious musical position in the world. But Monteverdi not only wrote religious music there; he also composed opera and a new genre: the chamber cantata.

Whereas opera was the dominant form of public theater music during the Baroque period, the cantata became the primary genre of vocal **chamber music** (music for soloists performed in the home or a small auditorium). The word **cantata** literally means "something sung," as opposed to sonata, "something sounded" (played on a musical instrument). Because it was usually performed before a select group of listeners in a private residence, this genre is called the chamber cantata. Like opera, the seventeenth-century **chamber cantata** emphasized accompanied solo singing, and the subject matter usually concerned unrequited love or the heroes and heroines of ancient history and mythology. (Later, Bach would transform the secular chamber cantata into the sacred church cantata; see Chapter 13.) A typical chamber cantata lasts eight to fifteen minutes and is usually divided into contrasting sections that alternate between recitative and aria. Although it lacks costumes and scenery, a chamber cantata might be considered a "mini-opera," but for a single soloist. The most prolific composer of chamber cantatas in the early Baroque was the Venetian Barbara Strozzi.

Barbara Strozzi (1619–1677) was steeped in the traditions of Claudio Monteverdi. Her teacher, Francesco Cavalli, was a pupil of Monteverdi, and her father, Giulio Strozzi, wrote librettos for him. The younger Strozzi excelled in composing chamber cantatas, works for solo voice and *basso continuo* that she herself could sing in the fashionable homes of Venice's elite. Her cantata *L'amante segreto* (*The Secret Lover*) treats the eternal subject of unrequited love. The hopeless lover is too timid to reveal her passion to the object of her desire, preferring to plead for a merciful death. The petition for death, "Voglio morire" ("I want to die"), comes in the form of a brief aria accompanied by a *basso continuo.* The bass line of the *basso continuo* sounds a stepwise descent that repeats again and again.

EXAMPLE 11–3

BARBARA STROZZI: PROFESSIONAL COMPOSER

Until the twentieth century, very few women earned a living as professional composers. In the Middle Ages, for example, a few *trobairitz* wrote chansons, but to a woman, they were all members of the lesser nobility and not financially dependent on the success of their creations. So, too, a few women composed during the late Renaissance and early Baroque, but most were cloistered nuns who received their sustenance from the Church. The reason for the scarcity of independent women composers in the Baroque era is simple: only performance within the home was then thought to be an appropriate musical activity for ladies. Musical activities outside the home were not deemed proper because they smacked of "professionalism." Women did not go to university, nor did they engage in income-earning professions or trades.

There were, however, a few notable exceptions. Adriana Basile, an associate of Monteverdi at Mantua, carved out for herself a highly successful career as a virtuoso soprano, thereby laying claim to the title "the first diva." In 1678, Elena Piscopia became the first woman to receive a university degree, when she earned the title Doctor of Philosophy at the University of Padua, Italy, following a rigorous public examination carried out in Latin. We have seen the work of Artemisia Gentileschi (see Fig. 10-6), a Florentine painter who became the first woman to be admitted to the prestigious Accademia del Disegno (Academy of Design) and who went on to become a court painter for King Charles I of England. And to this list of illustrious women artists and intellectuals should be added the name of Barbara Strozzi.

Barbara Strozzi was born out of wedlock in 1619, the daughter of a Venetian man of letters, Giulio Strozzi, who encouraged her musical development. Giulio Strozzi not only provided his daughter with lessons in composition but also organized domestic gatherings where her works could be heard. When Giulio Strozzi died in 1652, Barbara was left both destitute and desperate—she had four children but was unmarried. Over the next six years, she published six collections of cantatas, more than any other composer of the early Baroque. Each collection was dedicated to a member of the high nobility, and according to custom, the dedicatee paid for the honor. Barbara Strozzi may have been unique as a professional woman composer, but she had to deal with economic reality just like her male counterparts. Throughout the Baroque era, composers earned handsome sums from dedicatory fees paid by wealthy patrons, but nothing from royalties generated by sales of the music itself. Payment of royalties, to both male and female composers, would not come until the twentieth century.

A portrait of Barbara Strozzi painted in the 1630s by Bernardo Strozzi, perhaps a relative.

© Erich Lessing/Art Resource, NY

A melody, harmony, or rhythm that repeats continually throughout a musical composition is an **ostinato.** When the repetition occurs in the bass, it is called a ***basso ostinato.*** The term *ostinato* comes from an Italian word meaning "obstinate," "stubborn," or "pig-headed." In Baroque operas and cantatas, performers often sang laments accompanied by a *basso ostinato* that descended, as here, in stepwise motion. Such a descending bass consequently became a symbol for grief or lamentation. Consider the title of Barbara Strozzi's aria: Could any sentiment be more lamentable than "I want to die"?

Listening GUIDE

Barbara Strozzi
L'amante segreto (1651)
Aria, "Voglio morire," Part 1

5　　2
1/18　1/7

Genre: Chamber cantata
Form: Ostinato

0:00	**18** **7**	*Basso continuo* begins, with *basso ostinato* played by cello
0:19		Soprano enters as *basso continuo* proceeds
0:41		*Basso ostinato* extended by one note to accommodate cadence
0:45		*Basso continuo* alone
0:50		Soprano reenters; *basso continuo* proceeds to end

Voglio, voglio morire,	I want to die,
più tosto ch'il mio mal venga a scoprire;	rather than have my pain discovered;
ò disgrazia fatale,	oh, fatal misfortune,
quanto più miran gl'occhi il suo bel volto	the more my eyes admire his beautiful face
più tien la bocca il mio desir sepolto.	the more my mouth keeps my desire hidden.

Listen to streaming music in an Active Listening Guide, available at the text website.

Listening EXERCISE 16

Strozzi
"VOGLIO MORIRE"

5 **2**   **@**
1/18 1/7

To take this Listening Exercise online and receive feedback or email answers to your instructor, go to the text website.

Most early Baroque vocal music consists of arias and recitatives accompanied by a *basso continuo* and, in some cases, other instruments as well. In this recording of the aria "Voglio morire," which begins Barbara Strozzi's cantata *L'amante segreto*, the continuo is played by a cello, harpsichord, and guitar. The cello plays the short bass line again and again, thereby forming a *basso ostinato*. The harpsichord and guitar fill out the texture, offering chordal support above this bass. The simplicity of this example allows both *basso continuo* and *basso ostinato* to be heard with unusual clarity.

1. (0:00–0:05) The *basso ostinato* takes about five seconds to play. How many notes are there in the pattern?
   a. two   b. four   c. six

2. (0:00–0:05) How many chords are there in the pattern?
   a. two   b. four   c. six

3. (0:00–0:18) At the beginning of the aria, the *basso continuo* sounds alone. How many presentations of the pattern occur before the voice enters?
   a. three   b. five   c. seven

4. (0:19–0:35) Now the voice enters and the pattern continues; how many times is the pattern heard?
   a. three   b. five   c. seven

5. (0:36–0:43) In this passage, the *basso ostinato* suddenly changes—one or more notes are added

to the bass pattern. Now how many notes are in the pattern?
   a. three   b. five   c. seven

6. (0:44–end) From here to the end of the aria, does the bass pattern ever change?
   a. yes   b. no

7. The rate of harmonic change (the amount of time between each chord) in this aria is which?
   a. regular   b. irregular

Now we focus on issues other than the *basso continuo* and the *basso ostinato*.

8. Which of the three continuo instruments improvises elaborate decorations?
   a. guitar   b. cello   c. harpsichord

9. An aria, as opposed to recitative, is usually characterized by luxuriant singing in which the voice occasionally breaks out into a melisma (one syllable sung to many notes). In this aria, when do the melismas occur?
   a. toward the beginning
   b. toward the end

10. In many arias, the singer is accompanied by instruments in addition to the *basso continuo*, most often the violins. Do violins accompany the voice in this aria?
   a. yes   b. no

*O*PERA IN LONDON

Opera originated in Italy during the early seventeenth century. From there it spread over the Alps to German-speaking countries, to France, and eventually to England. But owing to the strong tradition of theater in England,

FIGURE 11–6

Henry Purcell, by an anonymous painter.

epitomized by productions of Shakespeare's plays, the English had a love-hate affair with opera: sometimes they wanted to hear it, and sometimes they did not. The first important opera written in English, Henry Purcell's *Dido and Aeneas*, dates from 1689. Chronologically, it falls outside the boundaries of the "early Baroque." But because English opera at this time was heavily influenced by earlier Italian opera, Purcell's opera belongs stylistically to the earlier period.

Henry Purcell (1659–1695)

Henry Purcell (Fig. 11-6) has been called the "greatest of all English composers." Indeed, only the late-Baroque composer George Frideric Handel (who was actually German-born) and pop songwriters John Lennon and Paul McCartney can plausibly challenge Purcell for this title. Purcell was born in London, the son of one of the king's singers. In 1679, the younger Purcell obtained the position of organist at Westminster Abbey, and then, in 1682, he became organist for the king's Chapel Royal as well. But London has always been a vital theater town, and although an employee of the court, Purcell increasingly devoted his attention to works for the public stage.

Purcell's *Dido and Aeneas* was among the first operas written in the English language. Yet it was apparently created for neither the king's court nor a public theater, but for a private girls' boarding school in the London suburb of Chelsea. The girls presented one major stage production annually, something like the senior class play of today. In *Dido and Aeneas*, they sang the numerous choruses and danced in the equally frequent dance numbers. All nine solo parts save one (the role of Aeneas) were written for female voices. The libretto of the opera, one appropriate for a school curriculum steeped in classical Latin, is drawn from Virgil's *Aeneid*. Surely the girls had studied this epic poem in Latin class, and likely they had memorized parts of it. Surely, too, they knew the story of the soldier-of-fortune Aeneas, who seduces proud Dido, queen of Carthage, but then deserts her to fulfill his destiny—sailing on to found the city of Rome. Betrayed and alone, Dido vents her feelings in an exceptionally beautiful aria, "When I am laid in earth," and then expires. In Virgil's original story, Dido stabs herself with the sword of Aeneas (Fig. 11-7). Here in Purcell's opera, she dies of a broken heart: her pain is poison enough.

Dido's final aria is introduced by a brief example of simple recitative (accompanied by *basso continuo* only): "Thy hand, Belinda." Normally, simple recitative is a businesslike process that moves the action along through direct declamation. In this passage, however, recitative transcends its typically perfunctory role. Notice the remarkable way Purcell sets the English language. He understood where the accents fell in the text of his libretto, and he knew how to replicate these effectively in music. In Example 11-4, the stressed words in the text generally appear in long notes and at the beginning of each measure. Equally important, notice how the vocal line descends a full octave, passing through chromatic notes along the way. (Chromaticism is another device composers use to signal pain and grief.) As the voice

FIGURE 11–7

A detail from the painting *The Death of Dido* by Guercino (1599–1666). The servant Belinda bends over the dying Dido, who has fallen on her formidable sword.

twists chromatically downward, we feel the pain of the abandoned Dido. By the end, she has slumped into the arms of her servant Belinda.

EXAMPLE 11–4

Thy hand, Be - lin - da! Dark - - ness shades me; on thy bo - som let me

rest. More I would, but Death in - vades me: Death is now a wel - come guest.

From the recitative "Thy hand Belinda," Purcell moves imperceptibly to the climactic aria "When I am laid in earth," where Dido sings of her impending death. Because this high point of the opera is a lament, Purcell chooses, in the Baroque tradition, to build it upon a *basso ostinato*. English composers called the *basso ostinato* the **ground bass,** because the repeating bass provided a solid foundation, or grounding, on which an entire composition could be built. The ground bass Purcell composed for Dido's lament consists of two sections (see the Listening Guide): (1) a chromatic stepwise descent over the interval of a fourth (G, F♯, F, E, E♭, D) and (2) a two-measure cadence returning to the tonic G (B♭, C, D, G).

In the libretto, Dido's lament consists of a brief one-stanza poem with an **aba** rhyme scheme:

> When I am laid in earth, may my wrongs create
> No trouble in thy breast.
> Remember me, but ah! Forget my fate.

Each line of text is repeated, as are many individual words and pairs of words alike. (Such repetition of text is typical of an aria but not of recitative.) In this case, Dido's repetitions are perfectly appropriate to her emotional state—she can communicate in fragments, but cannot articulate her feelings in complete sentences. Here the listener cares less about grammatical correctness, however, and more about the emotion of the moment. No fewer than six times does Dido plead with Belinda, and with us, to remember her. And, indeed, we do remember, for this plaintive aria is one of the most moving pieces in all of opera.

@

Watch a video of Craig Wright's Open Yale Course class session 14, "Ostinato Form in the Music of Purcell, Pachelbel, Elton John, and Vitamin C," at the text website.

$\mathcal{L}$*istening* GUIDE

Henry Purcell
***Dido and Aeneas* (1689)**
Aria, "When I am laid in earth"

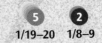
1/19–20 1/8–9

Characters: Dido, queen of Carthage; Belinda, her servant

Situation: Having been deserted by her lover, Aeneas, Dido sings farewell to Belinda (and to all) before dying of a broken heart.

BRIEF RECITATIVE

0:00   **19**
       8   Continuo played by large lute and cello

Thy hand, Belinda! Darkness shades me; on thy bosom let me rest. More I would, but Death invades me: Death is now a welcome guest.

(continued)

ARIA

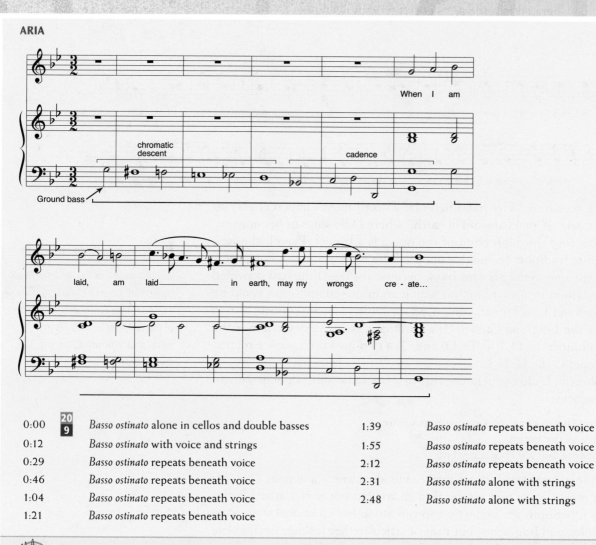

0:00	**20 9**	*Basso ostinato* alone in cellos and double basses
0:12		*Basso ostinato* with voice and strings
0:29		*Basso ostinato* repeats beneath voice
0:46		*Basso ostinato* repeats beneath voice
1:04		*Basso ostinato* repeats beneath voice
1:21		*Basso ostinato* repeats beneath voice

1:39	*Basso ostinato* repeats beneath voice
1:55	*Basso ostinato* repeats beneath voice
2:12	*Basso ostinato* repeats beneath voice
2:31	*Basso ostinato* alone with strings
2:48	*Basso ostinato* alone with strings

Listen to streaming music in an Active Listening Guide, available at the text website.

Listening EXERCISE 17

Purcell   **5**   **2**   **@**

"WHEN I AM LAID IN EARTH"   1/19–20   1/8–9

To take this Listening Exercise online and receive feedback or email answers to your instructor, go to the text website.

Henry Purcell begins the climactic scene of *Dido and Aeneas* with an expressive recitative and follows it with a lamenting aria built on a *basso ostinato*. To avoid a fitful "start-and-stop" melody, which the short, repeating bass would seem to dictate, Purcell composes melodic phrases that span more than one statement of the bass pattern. In this suicide aria, emotion carries the voice beyond the constraining form inscribed in the bass.

1. **19 8** (0:00–0:57) Is the recitative a simple recitative (accompanied only by the instruments of the *basso continuo*) or an accompanied recitative?
   a. simple   b. accompanied

2. (0:00–0:57) What is the trajectory of the voice in this recitative?
   a. It ascends to reflect Dido's exalted mood.
   b. It descends to reflect the depressed spirit of Dido.

3. **20 9** (0:00–0:11) How many statements of the *basso ostinato* sound before the voice enters?
   a. one   b. two   c. three

4. (0:12–) When the voice enters, does the rest of the orchestra (strings) enter then as well?
   a. yes   b. no

5. (0:12–1:20) How many times does the voice sing the lines "When I am laid in earth, may my wrongs create no trouble in thy breast"?
    a. once   b. twice   c. three times

6. (0:12–1:20) During this same passage, how many statements of the *basso ostinato* are performed?
    a. one   b. two   c. three   d. four

7. (1:21–2:30) How many times does the voice sing *the musical phrase* "Remember me, but ah! Forget my fate," and how many statements of the *basso ostinato* accompany it?
    a. once, one   c. three times, three
    b. twice, two   d. twice, four

8. (1:21–2:30) The emotional highpoint in this aria (and the opera) comes when the singer reaches her highest notes and loudest dynamic. When does this occur?

    a. at the first statement of "Remember me" (1:21–1:56)
    b. at the second statement of "Remember me" (1:57–2:30)

9. Which of the following, as appropriate for a lament, is true of this aria?
    a. It is in a major key and a fast tempo.
    b. It is in a major key and a slow tempo.
    c. It is in a minor key and a fast tempo.
    d. It is in a minor key and a slow tempo.

10. Dido singing a lament over a ground bass has much in common with which popular song over a repeating bass?
    a. Rihanna singing "Don't Stop the Music" (see p. 20)
    b. Elton John singing "Sorry Seems to Be the Hardest Word" (see below)
    c. Louis Armstrong's rendition of the tune "Willie the Weeper" (see p. 33)

ELTON JOHN AND *BASSO OSTINATO*

For an up-to-date example of ostinato bass, we can look at a modern aria-lament by a more recent English composer, Elton John. Although not built exclusively on an ostinato figure, John's song "Sorry Seems to Be the Hardest Word" (*Live in Australia,* 1987) nonetheless has one striking affinity to the aria by Purcell—it, too, makes use of a *basso ostinato,* incorporating a chromatically descending fourth as a way of setting a very, very sad text. The ostinato pattern begins on G, with a chromatically descending fourth followed by a one-measure cadence:

It's sad (so sad), it's a sad, sad situation
Bass
G   F♯   F   E

   And it's getting more and more absurd
   E♭   D   F♯GAD
       (cadence)

This *basso ostinato,* and a slightly varied form of it, is then repeated several times for this and other lines of text.

© DMI/Time Life Pictures/Getty Images

Elton John (Sir Reginald Dwight). Was the pop artist, who studied at the Royal Academy of Music in London, inspired by the famous aria of his equally well-coiffed countryman (see Fig. 11-6)?

Listen to Elton John, "Sorry Seems to Be the Hardest Word" in the iTunes and Rhapsody playlists at the text website.

Compare Elton John's bass line with Purcell's *basso ostinato* (see p. 114), and note that both laments are set in the key of G minor.

Key WORDS

TOWARD LATE BAROQUE INSTRUMENTAL MUSIC

When we think of classical music today, we usually think of instrumental music and instrumental performing groups—a symphony orchestra or a string quartet, for example. The equation classical = instrumental, while certainly not entirely true, nonetheless has some validity—about 80 percent of the Western classical repertoire is instrumental. The seventeenth century was the period in which instrumental music came to rival, and indeed surpass, vocal music in popularity, and statistics prove the point. During the Renaissance, the number of prints of vocal music outsold those of instrumental music by almost ten to one; by the end of the seventeenth century, on the other hand, instrumental publications outnumbered vocal ones by about three to one.

Much of this new-found desire for instrumental music can be attributed directly to the growing popularity of the violin and other instruments of the violin family. While the violin originated around 1520 as an instrument played solely by professionals, by 1650, it had become a favorite of talented amateurs. Composers such as Corelli, Vivaldi, and (later) Bach responded to the growing demand for music for the violin and other string instruments by writing sonatas and concertos for them.

Accompanying the growth of instrumental music was the emergence of a distinctly instrumental sound. During the Renaissance, melody was all of one generic type—a direct, uncomplicated line that could be performed by either a voice or an instrument. Around 1600, however, instrumental and vocal styles began to diverge. Composers increasingly became aware that the Baroque trumpet, for example, could easily leap an octave but could not run quickly up a scale and stay in tune. Accordingly, they began to write idiomatic (well-suited) music not only for voice but also for instruments, so as to take advantage of their special abilities and colors. **Idiomatic writing,** then, exploits the strengths and avoids the weaknesses of particular voices and instruments.

Finally, during the Baroque era, the vocabulary of expressive gestures that had developed for vocal music came to be applied to instrumental music as well. Composers realized that the Doctrine of Affections (see p. 98) was valid for instrumental music, too. By adopting devices used in vocal music, composers made it possible for purely instrumental music to express rage (with tremolos and rapidly racing scales, for example), despair (as with a swooning melody above a lament bass), or a bright spring day (by such means as trills and other "chirps" high in the violins and flutes). Even without the benefit of a text, instrumental music could tell a tale or paint a scene. As we shall see, it was by means of such expressive devices that Antonio Vivaldi was able to depict the four seasons of the year.

THE BAROQUE ORCHESTRA

The symphony orchestra as we know it today had its origins in seventeenth-century Italy and France. At first, the term *orchestra* referred to the area for musicians in the ancient Greek theater, between the audience and the stage; eventually, it came to mean the musicians themselves. At the beginning of the seventeenth century, the orchestra was something of a musical Noah's ark—it included an impressive variety of instruments, but usually no more than one or two of each type. The small orchestra that accompanied Monteverdi's *Orfeo* (1607), for example, consisted of fourteen different instruments. By the mid-seventeenth century, however, many of the older instruments from the late Renaissance—viol, sackbut (trombone), cornetto, shawm, and theorbo—had begun to disappear. Into their place stepped the four instruments of the violin family—violins, violas, cellos, and the related double bass. The violin family formed a core string ensemble, one that would henceforth dominate the orchestra. To this string nucleus were added woodwinds: first flute and oboes, and then bassoons, usually in pairs. Occasionally, a pair of trumpets would be included to provide extra brilliance. When trumpets appeared, so, too, often did timpani, although the parts for these drums were usually not written out but simply improvised as the music seemed to require. Finally, by the end of the seventeenth century, a pair of French horns was sometimes added to the orchestra to give it more sonic resonance. Supporting the entire ensemble was the ever-present *basso continuo*, one usually consisting of a harpsichord to provide chords and one or two low string instruments to play the bass line (Fig. 12-1). The **orchestra** for Western classical music, then, can be said to be an ensemble of musicians, organized around a core of strings, with added woodwinds and brasses, playing under a leader.

Most Baroque orchestras were small, usually with no more than twenty performers, and none of the parts was doubled—that is, no more than one instrumentalist was assigned to a single written line. Yet while the typical Baroque orchestra had no more than twenty players, there were exceptions, especially toward the end of the seventeenth century. At some of the more splendid courts around Europe, the orchestra might swell to as many as eighty instrumentalists for special occasions. Foremost among these was the court of French king Louis XIV.

Of all the courts of Baroque Europe, that of King Louis XIV (reigned 1643–1715) was the most splendid. Louis styled himself the "Sun King," after Apollo, the god of the sun and of music. Outside of Paris, near the small town of

FIGURE 12–1

Detail of an orchestra playing for a Baroque opera, as seen in Pietro Domenico Olivero's *Interior of the Teatro Regio*, Turin (1740). From left to right are a bassoon, two French horns, a cello, a double bass, a harpsichord, and then violins, violas, and oboes.

FIGURE 12-2
This standard view of the front of Versailles gives a sense of the grandeur of the palace that King Louis XIV began there in 1669.

© The Gallery Collection/CORBIS

Versailles, Louis built himself a palace, the largest court complex ever constructed (Fig. 12-2). There Louis not only shone forth in all his glory but also ruled absolutely: as he famously said, "I *am* the state" ("L'État, c'est moi").

To direct music at the court, Louis XIV engaged another domineering figure, Jean-Baptiste Lully (1632–1687), who controlled the court orchestra. Lully built his orchestra around a nucleus of twenty-four string players. To these he added flutes, oboes, and bassoons. Lully was the first composer to require that strings and woodwinds always play together in an orchestra, though he often asked the woodwinds to do no more than double the notes of the strings. For his increasingly large orchestra, Lully selected the players, led rehearsals, and made sure they all executed the notes exactly and in strict time. If necessary, he instilled discipline by force; in one instance, he hit a violinist with his large conducting stick, and in another, he broke a violin over the owner's back. Ironically, Lully's penchant for musical discipline killed him. Late in 1686, while thumping the floor with his conducting stick (the method of the day for keeping the beat), he stabbed himself in the foot and died of gangrene a few weeks later.

Besides setting in place the core of the modern orchestra, Jean-Baptiste Lully can claim credit for another innovation: the French overture. An **overture** is an instrumental piece that precedes and thus "opens" some larger composition, such as an opera, oratorio, ballet, or suite of dances. As perfected by Lully, the distinctly **French overture** consists of two sections. The first is set in a slow duple meter, with stately dotted rhythms suggesting a royal procession; the second is in a fast triple meter and features much imitation among the various musical lines. Although developed at the court of Louis XIV, the French overture spread to England and Germany. Handel wrote one, for example, to begin his *Messiah,* and Bach did likewise to open each of his orchestral suites.

PACHELBEL AND HIS CANON

Today most of us remember the name Johann Pachelbel (rhymes with Taco Bell) only because of a single musical composition, the famous "Pachelbel Canon" in D major. In his day, however, Pachelbel was known as a composer of a great deal of instrumental music, some of it for small orchestra but most for organ or harpsichord. Pachelbel's Canon is the first movement of a two-movement instrumental suite (on the suite, see p. 144), the second being a lively contrapuntal dance called a gigue. The odd thing about Pachelbel's Canon is that we don't even hear the imitative canon, or at least we don't focus on it. The three canonic voices are all in the same range and all played by a violin. Because the lines don't stand out from one another by range or color, the unfolding of the canon is difficult to follow.

What we hear instead is the bass line churning inexorably in the low strings, which, together with the harpsichord, form the *basso continuo* (Ex. 12-1). A strong bass is typical of Baroque music generally, but Pachelbel's bass is unforgettable in part because it has a pleasing intervallic pattern to it (fourths alternate with steps) and because it gravitates strongly around the subdominant, dominant, and tonic chords. Pachelbel knew he was onto a good thing, so he gives us this bass line twenty-eight times, a classic example of a *basso ostinato.* The allure of the bass is such that later classical composers borrowed it (Handel, Haydn, and Mozart

Watch a video of Craig Wright's Open Yale Course class session 14, "Ostinato Form in the Music of Purcell, Pachelbel, Elton John, and Vitamin C," at the text website.

among them), as well as pop musicians in recent times, such as Blues Traveler, Vitamin C, and Coolio. The full composition has served as background music in numerous TV commercials and films. Why such popularity? Likely the reason is a play of opposites that we find appealing: the regular, almost plodding bass provides a rock-solid foundation for the free flights of fancy that unfold in the soaring violins.

EXAMPLE 12–1

 Listening GUIDE

Johann Pachelbel
Canon in D major (c1685)

intro
11

Texture: Polyphonic

Form: Canon

0:00	**11**	*Basso continuo* begins
0:12		Violin 1 enters
0:24		Violin 2 enters in imitation
0:35		Violin 3 enters in imitation
0:57		Violin 1 followed by violins 2 and 3 at two-bar intervals
1:44		Violin 1 followed by violins 2 and 3 at two-bar intervals
2:30		Violin 1 followed by violins 2 and 3 at two-bar intervals
3:18		Violin 1 followed by violins 2 and 3 at two-bar intervals
4:04		Violin 1 followed by violins 2 and 3 at two-bar intervals

Listen to streaming music in an Active Listening Guide, available at the text website.

During the 1680s, about the time he composed his Canon, Pachelbel worked in central Germany where, among other things, he became the teacher of Johann Christoph Bach, the older brother and only known teacher of Johann Sebastian Bach. Pachelbel's use of counterpoint here (the three-voice canon) is suggestive of a return to favor of polyphony and contrapuntal texture in instrumental music generally at the end of the seventeenth century. The greatest proponent of late Baroque instrumental counterpoint, as we shall see in the next chapter, would be J. S. Bach himself.

CORELLI AND THE TRIO SONATA

The melody of Pachelbel's Canon is carried by three violins. As the Baroque era progressed, the popularity of the violin continued to grow and so, too, did the demand for string music that talented amateurs might play in the home. This demand, in turn, encouraged the growth of a new genre of instrumental music: the sonata. A **sonata** is a type of instrumental chamber music (music for the home with just one player per part). When the term *sonata* originated in early sixteenth-century Italy, it connoted "something sounded" in distinction to a cantata (see p. 109), which meant "something sung." A Baroque sonata consists of a collection of movements, each with its own mood and tempo, but all in the same key. In the Baroque era, the movements usually carried such names as "allemande," "sarabande," "gavotte," or "gigue"—all named after dances. A Baroque sonata with dance movements was normally called a **chamber sonata** (*sonata da camera*) and consisted of four movements with alternating tempos: slow-fast-slow-fast.

In the Baroque era, there were two types of sonatas: the solo sonata and the trio sonata. A **solo sonata** might be written either for a solo keyboard instrument, such as the harpsichord, or for a solo melody instrument, such as the violin, in which case three musicians were actually needed: the violinist and the two *basso continuo* performers. A **trio sonata** consists of three musical lines (two melody instruments plus bass). Yet here, too, the term is somewhat misleading, for when a harpsichord joins with the bass to form the *basso continuo*, four players actually perform. The sonata originated in Italy and then spread to the rest of Europe, in large measure through the published works of Arcangelo Corelli.

Arcangelo Corelli (1653–1713)

The composer-virtuoso who made the Baroque solo and trio sonatas internationally popular was Arcangelo Corelli. Corelli was born in 1653 near Bologna, Italy, then an important center for violin instruction and performance. By 1675, he had moved to Rome, where he remained for the duration of his life as a teacher, composer, and performer on the violin (Fig. 12-3). Corelli was one of the first superstars of the violin, and he remains today the only musician buried in Rome's Pantheon—as its name implies, a "hall for the gods" (hall of fame) of Italian culture.

Although Corelli's musical output was small, consisting of only five sets of sonatas and one of concertos, his works were widely admired. Such diverse composers as Johann Sebastian Bach in Leipzig, François Couperin (1668–1733) in Paris, and Henry Purcell in London either borrowed his melodies directly or more generally studied and absorbed his style.

The most remarkable aspect of Corelli's music is its harmony: it sounds modern to our ears. We have heard so much classical and popular music that we have come to possess an almost subconscious sense of how a succession of

FIGURE 12-3

Arcangelo Corelli looks placid enough in this print. But when playing the violin, according to a contemporary, "his eyes turn red as fire, his face becomes distorted, and his eyeballs roll as if in agony."

chords—a harmonic progression—should sound. Corelli was the first composer to write this kind of harmony, one that we call "functional" harmony, in which each chord has a specific role, or function, in the overall succession of chords. Not only does the individual chord constitute an important sound in itself, but it also draws us toward the next, thereby helping to form a tightly linked chain of chords, which sounds directed and purposeful. The most basic link in the chain is the V-I (dominant-tonic) cadence (see p. 35). In addition, Corelli often constructs bass lines that move upward chromatically by half step. This chromatic, stepwise motion pulls up and into the next-higher note, increasing the sense of direction and cohesiveness we feel in Corelli's music.

TRIO SONATA IN C MAJOR, OPUS 4, NO. 1 (1694)

The Trio Sonata in C major, Opus 4, No. 1, is a chamber sonata written by Corelli in 1694 for two violins and *basso continuo,* here played by a harpsichord and cello. Corelli called this sonata Opus 4, No. 1. (Composers frequently use **opus,** the Latin word meaning "work," to enumerate and identify their compositions; this was the first piece in Corelli's fourth published collection.) This chamber sonata is in four movements, the second and fourth of which are dance movements in binary form (**AB**), the most common musical form for Baroque dances. No one danced, however. These movements were stylized pieces that aimed only to capture in music the spirit of the dance in question. As one musician of the day observed, they are written "for the refreshment of the ear alone."

Corelli begins sonata Opus 4, No. 1 with a *preludio* (prelude), which gives the players a chance to warm up and also establishes the general musical mood of the sonata. Notice that the prelude makes use of what is called a **walking bass,** a bass that moves at a moderate, steady pace, mostly in equal note values and often stepwise up or down the scale.

EXAMPLE 12–2

The second movement, a dance called the *corrente* (from the Italian *correre,* "to run"), is rather fast and in triple meter. Here the first violin engages in a rapid dialogue with the cello. The second violin is scarcely audible as it helps fill in the chords, literally playing "second fiddle" to the first violin. The short *adagio* ("slow" movement) serves merely as a bridge that links the *corrente* with the final movement—the brisk, duple-meter *allemanda* (literally, "the German dance"). This last movement, too, has a walking bass, but the tempo is so fast (*presto*) that it sounds more like a running or a sprinting bass.

FIGURE 12–4

The violin came to be the most important string instrument of the orchestra during the Baroque period—up to that point it had been mainly a "low-class" instrument for playing dances in taverns. Compared to the earlier viol, the violin (from *violino* = "little viol") had only four strings, no frets, and a louder, more penetrating sound. The best of the Baroque violin makers was Antonio Stradivari (1644–1737), whose instruments today, as seen in this photo, have sold for as much as $4 million at auction.

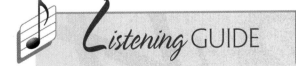

Listening GUIDE

Arcangelo Corelli
Trio Sonata in C major, Opus 4, No. 1
(1694)

5

1/21–24

Ensemble: Two violins, cello, and harpsichord

PRELUDE

0:00	**21**	"Walking bass" descends stepwise below dotted rhythms in violins
0:35		Bass now moves twice as fast
0:45		Bass returns to original slow pace

(continued)

CORRENTE

0:00	22	First violin and cello lead lively dance in triple meter
0:14		Repeat of **A**
0:28		**B** section begins with sequences in cello and violins
0:46		Rhythmic syncopation signals arrival of final cadence
0:52		Repeat of **B** including syncopation (1:10)

ADAGIO

0:00	23	Stationary chords in violins; only cello moves in purposeful fashion
1:36		Cadential chords prepare way to next movement

ALLEMANDA

0:00	24	Two violins move together above racing bass
0:22		Repeat of **A** and pause
0:43		**B** section begins and includes sudden shift to minor key (0:56)
1:03		Repeat of **B** including sudden shift to minor key (1:16)

Listen to streaming music in an Active Listening Guide, available on the text website.

$\mathcal{V}$IVALDI AND THE BAROQUE CONCERTO

The concerto was to the Baroque era what the symphony would later become to the Classical period: the showpiece of orchestral music. A Baroque concerto emphasizes abrupt contrasts within a unity of mood, just as striking change between the zones of light and darkness often characterizes a Baroque painting (see, for example, Fig. 10-6).

A **concerto** (from the Latin *concertare*, "to strive together") is a musical composition marked by a friendly contest or competition between a soloist and an orchestra. When only one soloist confronts the orchestra, the work is a **solo concerto.** When a small group of soloists works together, performing as a unit against the full orchestra, the piece is called a **concerto grosso.** A concerto grosso consists of two performing forces who work together, a larger group forming the basic orchestra called the concerto grosso (big concert) and a smaller one of two, three, or four soloists called the **concertino** (little concert). Playing together, the two groups constitute the full orchestra, called the **tutti** (meaning "all" or "everybody"). A typical concerto grosso had a concertino of two violins and continuo. The soloists were not highly paid masters imported from afar, but rather the regular first-chair players who, when they were not serving as soloists, joined with the others to form the tutti. The resulting contrast was desirable, said a contemporary, "so that the ear might be astonished by the alternation of loud and soft . . . as the eye is dazzled by the alternation of light and shade."

As written by Vivaldi and Bach, the solo concerto and the concerto grosso usually had three movements: fast-slow-fast. The serious first movement is composed in a carefully worked-out structure called ritornello form (see p. 124); the second movement is invariably more lyrical and tender; while the third movement, though often using ritornello form, tends to be lighter, more dancelike, sometimes even rustic in mood. Both the solo concerto and the concerto grosso originated in Italy toward the end of the seventeenth century. Solo concertos for violin, flute, recorder, oboe, trumpet, and harpsichord were especially popular. The vogue of the concerto grosso peaked about 1730 and then all but ended around the time of Bach's death (1750). But the solo concerto continued to be cultivated during the Classical and Romantic periods, becoming increasingly a showcase in which a single soloist could display his or her technical mastery of an instrument.

Antonio Vivaldi (1678–1741)

No composer was more influential, and certainly none more prolific, in the creation of the Baroque concerto than Antonio Vivaldi (Fig. 12-5). Vivaldi, like Barbara Strozzi a native of Venice, was the son of a barber and part-time musician at the basilica of Saint Mark (see Fig. 11-3). Young Vivaldi's proximity to Saint Mark's naturally brought him into contact with the clergy. Although he became a skilled performer on the violin, he also entered Holy Orders, ultimately being ordained a priest. Vivaldi's life, however, was by no means confined to the realm of the spirit. He concertized on the violin throughout Europe; he wrote and produced nearly fifty operas, which brought him a great deal of money; and he lived for fifteen years with an Italian opera star. The worldly pursuits of *il prete rosso* (the red-haired priest) eventually provoked a response from the authorities of the Roman Catholic Church. In 1737, Vivaldi was forbidden to practice his musical artistry in papally controlled lands. This ban affected his income as well as his creativity. He died poor and obscure in 1741 in Vienna, where he had gone in search of a post at the imperial court.

FIGURE 12–5

Portrait of a violinist and composer believed by some to be the musician Antonio Vivaldi.

From 1703 until 1740, Vivaldi worked in Venice at the *Ospedale della Pietà* (Hospice of Mercy), first as a violinist and music teacher, and then as musical director. The Hospice of Mercy was an orphanage for the care and education of young women. It was one of four such charitable institutions in Venice that accepted abandoned, mostly illegitimate girls, who, as several reports state, "otherwise would have been thrown in the canals." By 1700, music had been made to serve an important role in the religious and social life of the orphanage. Each Sunday afternoon, its orchestra of young women offered public performances for the well-to-do of Venice (see Fig. 12-6). Also attending these concerts were foreign visitors—Venice was already a tourist city—among them a French diplomat, who wrote in 1739:

FIGURE 12–6

Foreign visitors attend a concert performed by orphan girls assembled from various orphanages around Venice, as depicted by Gabriele Bella about 1750. The Hospice of Mercy was the most musically intense of the Venetian orphanages. Here girls who showed a special talent for music were placed within a prestigious ensemble of forty musicians. Their musical education included tutelage in singing, ear training, and counterpoint, as well as instruction on at least two musical instruments. Antonio Vivaldi was one of the teachers.

These girls are educated at the expense of the state, and they are trained solely with the purpose of excelling in music. That is why they sing like angels and play violin, flute, organ, oboe, cello, and bassoon; in short, no instrument is so big as to frighten them. They are kept like nuns in a convent. All they do is perform concerts, always in groups of about forty girls. I swear to you that there is nothing as pleasant as seeing a young and pretty nun, dressed in white, with a little pomegranate bouquet over her ears, conducting the orchestra with all the gracefulness and incredible precision one can imagine.

VIOLIN CONCERTO IN E MAJOR, OPUS 8, NO. 1, THE "SPRING" (EARLY 1700s)

During the early 1700s, Vivaldi composed literally hundreds of solo concertos for the all-female orchestras of the Hospice of Mercy in Venice. In 1725, he gathered twelve of the more colorful of these together and published them under the title "Opus 8." (This set of concertos was thus Vivaldi's eighth published work.) In addition, he called the

first four of these solo concertos *The Seasons*. What Vivaldi meant by this was that each of the four concertos in turn represents the feelings, sounds, and sights of one of the four seasons of the year, beginning with spring. So that there be no ambiguity as to what sensations and events the music depicts at any given moment, Vivaldi first composed a poem (an "illustrative sonnet" as he called it) about each season. Then he placed each line of the poem at the appropriate point in the music where that particular event or feeling was to be expressed, even specifying at one point that the violins are to sound "like barking dogs." In so doing, Vivaldi showed that not only voices, but instruments as well, could create a mood and sway the emotions. Vivaldi also fashioned here a landmark in what is called instrumental program music—music that plays out a story or a series of events or moods (for more on program music, see p. 253).

It is fitting that *The Seasons* begins with the bright, optimistic sounds of spring. In fact, the "Spring" Concerto for solo violin and small orchestra is Vivaldi's best-known work. The fast first movement of this three-movement concerto is composed in ritornello form, a form that Vivaldi was the first to popularize. (The Italian word *ritornello* means "return" or "refrain.") In **ritornello form**, all or part of the main theme—the ritornello—returns again and again, invariably played by the tutti, or full orchestra. Between the tutti's statements of the ritornello, the soloist inserts fragments and extensions of this ritornello theme in virtuosic fashion. Much of the excitement of a Baroque concerto comes from the tension between the reaffirming ritornello played by the tutti and the fanciful flights of the soloist.

The jaunty ritornello theme of the first movement of the "Spring" Concerto has two complementary parts, the second of which returns more often than the first. Between appearances of the ritornello, Vivaldi inserts the music that represents his feelings about spring. He creates the songbirds of May by asking the violin to play rapidly and staccato (very short notes) in a high register. Similarly, he depicts the sudden arrival of thunder and lightning by means of a tremolo and shooting scales, then returns to the cheerful song of the birds. Thereafter, in the slow second movement, a vision of a flower-strewn meadow is conveyed by an expansive, tender melody in the violin. Finally, during the fast finale, a sustained droning in the lower strings invokes "the festive sounds of country bagpipes." The full text of Vivaldi's "program" for the first movement of the "Spring" Concerto is given in the Listening Guide.

Vivaldi's "Spring" Concerto is marked by a stylistic trait that is often prominent in his music: melodic sequence. A **melodic sequence** is the repetition of a musical motive at successively higher or lower degrees of the scale. Example 12-3 shows a sequence from the middle of the first movement of this work. In this sequence, the motive is repeated twice, each time a step lower.

EXAMPLE 12–3

Although melodic sequence can be found in music from almost all periods, it is especially prevalent in the Baroque. It helps propel the music forward and create the energy we associate with Baroque style. However, because hearing the same melodic phrase time and again can become a tedious listening experience, Baroque composers usually follow the "three strikes and you're out" rule: the melodic unit appears, as in Example 12-3, three times, but no more.

Vivaldi composed more than 450 concertos and thus is known as "the father of the concerto." Widely admired as both a performer and a composer in his day, within a few years of his death, he was largely forgotten, a victim of rapidly changing musical tastes. Not until the revival of Baroque music in the 1950s were his scores resurrected from obscure libraries and dusty archives. Now his music is loved for its freshness and vigor, its exuberance and daring. More than 200 professional recordings have been made of *The Seasons* alone. So often is the "Spring" Concerto played that it has passed from the realm of art music into that of "classical pops"—a staple at Starbucks.

A complete Checklist of Musical Style for the Early and Middle Baroque can be found at the text website.

Listening GUIDE

Antonio Vivaldi
Violin Concerto in E major, Opus 8,
No. 1 (the "Spring"; early 1700s)
First movement, *Allegro* (fast)

⑤ ②
1/25   1/10

Meter: Duple

Texture: Mainly homophonic

Form: Ritornello

0:00 **25** **10**	Ritornello part 1 played by tutti	
0:11	Ritornello part 1 repeated by tutti *pianissimo*	
0:19	Ritornello part 2 played by tutti	
0:27	Ritornello part 2 repeated by tutti *pianissimo*	
0:36	Solo violin (aided by two violins from tutti) chirps on high	"Spring with all its festiveness has arrived And the birds salute it with happy song"
1:10	Ritornello part 2 played by tutti	
1:18	Tutti softly plays running sixteenth notes	"And the brooks, kissed by the breezes, Meanwhile flow with sweet murmurings"
1:42	Ritornello part 2 played by tutti	
1:50	Tutti plays tremolo and violins shoot up scale	"Dark clouds cover the sky Announced by bolts of lightning and thunder"
1:58	Solo violin plays agitated, broken triads while tutti continues with tremolos below	
2:19	Ritornello part 2 played by tutti	
2:28	Solo violin chirps on high, adding ascending chromatic scale and trill	"But when all has returned to quiet The birds commence to sing once again their enchanted song"
2:47	Ritornello part 1, slightly varied, played by tutti	
3:00	Solo violin plays rising sixteenth notes	
3:16	Ritornello part 2 played by tutti	

Listen to streaming music in an Active Listening Guide, available on the text website.

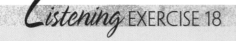 EXERCISE 18

Vivaldi
"SPRING" CONCERTO   **5** **2**   1/25   1/10

@ To take this Listening Exercise online and receive feedback or email answers to your instructor, go to the text website.

The opening movement of Vivaldi's "Spring" Concerto is a traditional favorite with listeners everywhere, in part because its musical gestures are clear and its ritornello form straightforward.

1. Vivaldi was a virtuoso on this instrument, which dominates the sound of this concerto.
    a. harpsichord
    b. violin
    c. cello
    d. organ

2. How would you describe the rhythmic pulse of this movement?
    a. energetic and regularly repeating patterns
    b. languid with no clear sense of a downbeat

3. (0:00–0:35) Ritornello part 1 is immediately repeated *pianissimo*, as is ritornello part 2. Abrupt shifts in dynamics, typical of the Baroque era, are called what?
    a. terrain dynamics
    b. terraced dynamics
    c. terra cotta dynamics

4. (0:36–1:09) Does the *basso continuo* play during this solo section?
    a. yes
    b. no

5. (1:42–1:49) Vivaldi has modulated to a new key and brings back ritornello part 2. Does it sound at a higher or lower pitch compared to its first appearance (0:19–0:35)?
    a. higher
    b. lower

6. (1:58–2:07) Is the pattern in this melodic sequence rising or falling?
    a. rising
    b. falling

7. (2:19–2:29) When the ritornello returns, in what mode is it?
    a. major
    b. minor

8. (2:28–2:47) During this passage and beyond, what does the cello do?
    a. It rises by step.
    b. It falls by step.
    c. It plays a pedal point (holds one bass note).

9. Which of the following is true about the "Spring" Concerto?
    a. It has both a *basso continuo* and a *basso ostinato*.
    b. It has a *basso continuo* but no *basso ostinato*.
    c. It has a *basso ostinato* but no *basso continuo*.
    d. It has neither a *basso ostinato* nor a *basso continuo*.

10. Finally, how did Vivaldi communicate his "program" to his listeners?
    a. He wrote onomatopoeic music that mimicked in sound the words of his own poem.
    b. He had created a poem about spring, and a narrator read it as the music sounded.
    c. He held up cue cards as the music sounded.

@ The materials on the text website will help you understand and pass tests on the content of this chapter. In addition, you may watch Craig Wright's own lecture at Open Yale Courses and complete this chapter's Listening Exercise interactively, as well as view Active Listening Guides and other materials that will help you succeed in this course.

 WORDS

idiomatic writing (116)
orchestra (117)
overture (118)
French overture (118)
sonata (120)
chamber sonata (120)

solo sonata (120)
trio sonata (120)
opus (121)
walking bass (121)
concerto (122)
solo concerto (122)

concerto grosso (122)
concertino (122)
tutti (122)
ritornello form (124)
melodic sequence (124)

THE LATE BAROQUE
BACH

13

The music of the late Baroque period (1710–1750), represented by the two great figures Johann Sebastian Bach and George Frideric Handel, stands as a high-water mark in Western musical culture. Among the marvels of late Baroque music, we might also include the works of Antonio Vivaldi, treated in the previous chapter, because some of his most distinctive concertos, such as the "Spring," were written around 1710. But late Baroque music, typified by the works of Bach and Handel, is usually characterized by great length and contrapuntal complexity. Generally, the most noteworthy compositions of Bach and Handel are large-scale works full of dramatic power, broad gestures, and, often, complex counterpoint. At the same time, they convey to the listener a sense of technical mastery—that Bach and Handel could compose seemingly effortlessly in a variety of musical forms, techniques, and styles, building on the innovations of previous Baroque composers.

Earlier Baroque composers had created many new musical genres, such as opera, chamber cantata, sonata, solo concerto, and concerto grosso. The late Baroque, by contrast, is not a period of musical innovation, but one of refinement. Bach and his contemporaries did not, in the main, invent new forms, styles, techniques, or genres, but rather gave greater weight, length, and polish to those established by their musical forebears. Arcangelo Corelli (1653–1713), for example, had introduced functional harmony in his sonatas, but Bach and Handel expanded Corelli's harmonic template to create much longer, and often more compelling, works of art. Bach and Handel approached the craft of composition with unbounded self-confidence. Their music has a sense of rightness, solidity, and maturity about it. Each time we choose to listen to one of their compositions, we offer further witness to their success in bringing a hundred years of musical innovation to a glorious culmination.

ASPECTS OF LATE BAROQUE MUSICAL STYLE

During the years 1710–1750, Bach, Handel, and their contemporaries continued to build upon the distinctive elements of musical style that appeared earlier in the Baroque era (see pp. 98–126). Melody is governed by the principle of progressive development; an initial theme is set forth and then continually expanded, spun out over an ever-lengthening line. Melodies are typically long and asymmetrical, and often the notes are propelled forward by melodic sequence, as exemplified by this passage in the overture to Bach's first orchestral suite.

EXAMPLE 13–1

© Erich Lessing/Art Resource, NY

FIGURE 13–1

The only authentic portrait of Johann Sebastian Bach, painted by Elias Gottlob Haussmann in 1746. Bach holds in his hand a six-voice canon, or round, which he created to symbolize his skill as a musical craftsman.

FIGURE 13–2

The organ presently in the choir loft of Saint Thomas's Church, Leipzig. It was from this loft that Bach played and conducted.

© Foto Beck/Photolibrary

Rhythm in late Baroque music is also ruled by the principle of progressive development. A piece typically begins with one prominent rhythmic idea (see Ex. 13-1), and it or a complementary one continues uninterrupted to the very end of the movement, pushed along by a strong, clearly audible beat. Indeed, beat and meter are more easily recognized in late Baroque music than in the music of any other period. Thus, if an overture or concerto by Bach or Handel seems to "chug along" with irrepressible optimism and vitality, it is usually owing to a strong beat, a clearly articulated meter, and a continually recurring rhythmic pattern.

Finally, the music of Bach and Handel is usually denser in texture than that of the early Baroque era. Recall that around 1600, composers of the early Baroque rebelled against what they perceived to be the excessively polyphonic style of Renaissance music, with its constant overlapping points of imitation (see p. 84). As a result, early Baroque music is not polyphonic, but rather homophonic, in texture. By the heyday of Bach and Handel around 1725, however, composers had returned to polyphonic writing, mainly to add richness to the middle range of what had been in the early Baroque a top-bottom (soprano-bass)–dominated texture. German composers of the late Baroque were particularly fond of counterpoint, perhaps owing to their traditional love of the organ, an instrument with several keyboards, thus well suited to playing multiple polyphonic lines at once. The gradual reintegration of counterpoint into the fabric of Baroque music culminates in the rigorously contrapuntal vocal and instrumental music of J. S. Bach.

*J*OHANN SEBASTIAN BACH (1685–1750)

In the creations of Johann Sebastian Bach (Fig. 13-1), the music of the Baroque reaches its greatest glory. Bach was born into a musical dynasty, though one originally of common standing. For nearly 200 years, members of the Bach family served as musicians in small towns in Thuringia, a province in central Germany. Johann Sebastian was merely the most talented of the ubiquitous musical Bachs, though he himself had four sons who achieved international fame. Aside from some initial instruction from his brother Johann Christoph, Bach was largely self-taught. To learn his craft, he studied, copied, and arranged the compositions of Corelli, Vivaldi, Pachelbel, and even Palestrina. He also learned to play the organ, in part by emulating others, once traveling 200 miles each way on foot to hear a great performer. Bach's first position of importance was in the town of Weimar, Germany, where he served as organist to the court beginning in 1708. It was here that he wrote many of his finest works for organ. Soon Bach became the most renowned organ virtuoso in Germany, and his improvisations on that instrument became legendary.

Of all instruments, the organ is the most suitable for playing polyphonic counterpoint. Most organs have at least two separate keyboards for the hands, in addition to one placed on the floor, which the performer plays with the feet (see Figs. 5-12 and 13-2). This gives the instrument the capacity to play several lines simultaneously. More important, each of these keyboards can be set to engage a different group (rank) of pipes, each with its own color, and thus the ear can more readily hear the individual musical lines. For these reasons, the organ is the instrument *par excellence* for playing fugues.

Fugue

Bach was the master of counterpoint—the art of combining completely independent melodies in imaginative ways—and rich, complex counterpoint lies at the heart of the fugue. Fugue is a contrapuntal form and procedure that flourished during the late Baroque era. The word *fugue* itself comes from the Latin *fuga*, meaning "flight." Within a fugue, one voice presents a theme and then "flies away" as another voice enters with the same theme. The theme in a fugue is called the **subject.** At the outset, each voice presents the subject in turn, and this successive presentation is called the **exposition** of the fugue. As the voices enter, they do not imitate or pursue each other exactly—this would produce a canon or a round such as "Row, Row, Row Your Boat" (see p. 57). Rather, passages of exact imitation are interrupted by sections of free writing in which the voices more or less go their own ways. These freer sections, where the subject is not heard in its entirety, are called **episodes.** Episodes and further presentations of the subject alternate throughout the remainder of the fugue.

Fugues have been written for from two to as many as thirty-two voices, but the norm is two to five. These may be actual human voices in a chorus or choir, or they may simply be lines or parts played by a group of instruments, or even by a solo instrument like the piano, organ, or guitar, which has the capacity to play several "voices" simultaneously. Thus, a formal definition of a **fugue** might be as follows: a composition for two, three, four, or five parts played or sung by voices or instruments, which begins with a presentation of a subject in imitation in each part (exposition), continues with modulating passages of free counterpoint (episodes) and further appearances of the subject, and ends with a strong affirmation of the tonic key. Fortunately, the fugue is easier to hear than to describe: the unfolding and recurrence of one subject makes it easy to follow.

ORGAN FUGUE IN G MINOR (C1710)

Bach has left us nearly a hundred keyboard fugues, about a third of which are for organ. The organ was Bach's favorite instrument, and in his day, he was known more as a performer and improviser on it than as a composer. Bach's G minor organ fugue was composed rather early in his career, sometime between 1708 and 1717, when he was in Weimar. It is written for four voices, which we will refer to as soprano, alto, tenor, and bass, and it begins with the subject appearing first in the soprano.

EXAMPLE 13–2

As fugue subjects go, this is a rather long one, but it is typical of the way Baroque composers liked to "spin out" their melodies. It sounds very solid in tonality because the subject is clearly constructed around the notes of the G minor triad (G, B♭, D), not only in the first measure but on the strong beats of the following measures as well. The subject also conveys a sense of gathering momentum. It starts moderately with quarter notes and then seems to gain speed as eighth notes and finally sixteenth notes are introduced. This, too, is typical of fugue subjects. After the soprano introduces the subject, it is then

Download a Supplementary Listening Guide for Bach, Toccata and Fugue in D minor, at the text website.

See a hilarious video on the building of a fugue in the style of Bach, upon a subject of Britney Spears's, in the YouTube playlist on the text website.

Watch a video of Craig Wright's Open Yale Course class session 13, "Fugue: Bach, Bizet, and Bernstein," at the text website.

FIGURE 13-3

Fugue (1925) by Josef Albers. Albers's design suggests the "constructivist" quality of the fugue, one full of repeating and reciprocal relationships. The black-and-white units seem to allude to subject and episode, respectively.

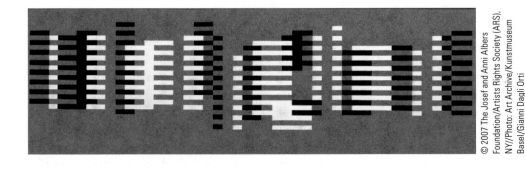

presented, in turn, by the alto, the tenor, and the bass. The voices need not appear in any particular order; here Bach simply decided to have them enter in succession from top to bottom.

When each voice has presented the subject and joined the polyphonic complex, Bach's exposition is at an end. Now a short passage of free counterpoint follows—the first episode—which uses only bits and pieces of the subject. Then the subject returns, but in a highly unusual way: it begins in the tenor, but continues and ends in the soprano. Thereafter, Bach's G minor fugue unfolds in the usual alternation of episodes and statements of the subject. The episodes sound unsettled and convey a sense of movement, modulating from one key to another. The subject, on the other hand, doesn't modulate. It is *in* a key—here the tonic G minor, or the dominant D minor, or some other closely related major key. The tension between settled music (the subject) and unsettled music (the episodes) creates the exciting, dynamic quality of the fugue.

Finally, because Bach wrote many fugues for organ, they often make use of a device particularly well suited to the organ—the pedal point. A **pedal point** is a note, usually in the bass, that is sustained (or repeated) for a time while harmonies change around it. Such a sustaining tone in the bass derives its name, of course, from the fact that on the organ the note is sounded by a foot holding down a key on the pedal keyboard. After a pronounced pedal point and additional statements of the subject, Bach modulates back to the tonic key, G minor, for one final statement of the subject in the bass to end his fugue. Notice that, although this fugue is in a minor key, Bach puts the last chord in major. This is common in Baroque music, with composers preferring the brighter, more optimistic, sound of the major mode in the final chord. Given all its complexities and the fact that it is full of reciprocating, almost mathematical relationships (see Fig. 13-3), it is not surprising that the fugue has traditionally appealed to listeners with scientific interest. Fugues are music for the eye and mind, as much as for the ear and heart.

Listening GUIDE

Johann Sebastian Bach
Organ Fugue in G minor (c1710)

5
1/26

2
1/11

Texture: Polyphonic

26
11

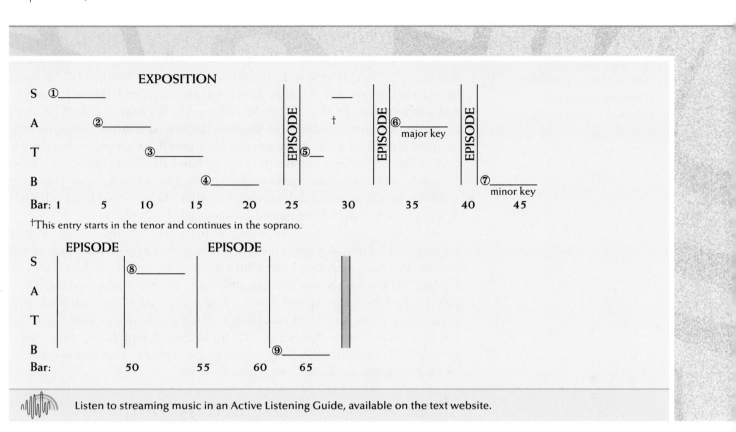

†This entry starts in the tenor and continues in the soprano.

🎵 Listen to streaming music in an Active Listening Guide, available on the text website.

Listening EXERCISE 19

Bach
ORGAN FUGUE IN G MINOR

5 **2**
1/26 **1/11**

@ To take this Listening Exercise online and receive feedback or email answers to your instructor, go to the text website.

Bach's Fugue in G minor is composed for four voices. In the exposition, the subject appears four times, once in each voice, and it returns five times thereafter. The first skill needed to enjoy a fugue is the ability to differentiate the subject from the episodes. To assure that you are hearing the presentations of the subject, questions 1–5 ask you to identify the moments at which the subject enters after the exposition. The remaining questions explore the complexities that typically reside within a fugue.

1. Statement 5 of the subject begins at what time?
   a. 1:24   b. 1:42

2. Statement 6 of the subject begins at what time?
   a. 1:52   b. 2:00

3. Statement 7 of the subject begins at what time?
   a. 2:11   b. 2:20

4. Statement 8 of the subject begins at what time?
   a. 2:54   b. 3:02

5. Statement 9 of the subject begins at what time?
   a. 3:40   b. 3:49

6. (1:04–1:11) During this passage, as the bass plays the end of the subject, what does the soprano execute against it?
   a. a pedal point
   b. a descending melodic sequence
   c. a trill
   d. a long, rising scale

7. (1:35–1:44) During this passage, what does the bass play?
   a. a pedal point
   b. a descending melodic sequence
   c. a trill
   d. a long, rising scale

8. (2:13–2:18) During this passage, what does the soprano play?
   a. a pedal point
   b. a descending melodic sequence
   c. a trill
   d. a long, rising scale

9. (3:26–3:35) During this passage, what does the tenor play?
   a. a pedal point
   b. a descending melodic sequence
   c. a trill
   d. a long, rising scale

10. Bach intended this four-voice fugue to be played by how many performers on the organ?
    a. one   b. two   c. three   d. four

@

Download Supplementary
Listening Guides for Bach,
Orchestral Suite No. 3, Air,
Gavottes I and II, and Gigue, at
the text website.

Bach's Orchestral Music

After nine years as organist in Weimar, Bach, then a young man with a wife and four children, determined to improve his station in life. In 1717, he auditioned for the position of music director at the court of Cöthen, Germany, and was awarded the post. When he returned to Weimar to collect his family and possessions, the Duke of Weimar, displeased that the composer had "jumped ship," had Bach thrown in jail for a month. (Composers before the time of Beethoven were not like "free agent" baseball players today; they were little more than indentured servants who needed to obtain a release from one employer before entering the service of another.) When freed from jail, Bach fled to Cöthen, where he remained for six years (1717–1723).

At Cöthen, Bach turned his attention from organ music for the church to instrumental music for the court. It was here that he wrote the bulk of his orchestral scores, including more than a dozen solo concertos. The Prince of Cöthen had assembled something of an "all-star" orchestra, drawing many top players from the larger city of Berlin. He also ordered a large two-keyboard harpsichord from Berlin and sent Bach to fetch it. About this time, Bach began his *Well-Tempered Clavier* (see p. 142) for keyboard, and during these years, he completed six concertos of the concerto grosso type. This set has come to be called the Brandenburg Concertos.

THE BRANDENBURG CONCERTOS (1715–1721)

In 1721, still in Cöthen, Bach began to look for yet another job in the politically more important city of Berlin—specifically, at the court of Margrave Christian Ludwig of Brandenburg. To impress the margrave, Bach gathered together a half-dozen of his best concertos and sent them to his prospective employer. Although no job offer was forthcoming, Bach's autograph manuscript survives (Fig. 13-4), and in it are six superb examples of the concerto grosso.

The concerto grosso, as we have seen (p. 122), is a three-movement work involving a musical give-and-take between a full orchestra (tutti) and a much smaller group of soloists (concertino), consisting usually of just two or three violins and continuo. In the first movement, the tutti normally plays a recurring musical theme, called the ritornello. The soloists in the concertino play along with the tutti; but when the ritornello stops, they go on to present their

FIGURE 13-4

The autograph manuscript of the opening of Bach's Brandenburg Concerto No. 5.

Lebrecht Music & Arts

own musical material in a flashy, sometimes dazzling show of technical skill. Each of the six Brandenburg Concertos calls for a different group of soloists in the concertino. Together, these works constitute an anthology of nearly all instrumental combinations known to the Baroque era.

Bach's aim in the Brandenburg Concertos was to show his ability to write challenging music for any and all instruments. A listener cannot fail to be impressed by the brilliant writing for the harpsichord in Concerto No. 5, for example. Here the full orchestra (tutti) is pitted against a concertino consisting of solo violin, flute, and, most important, harpsichord. In principle, the tutti plays the ritornello, and the soloists play motives derived from it. In practice, however, the separation between tutti and concertino is not as distinct with Bach as it was in the earlier concertos of Vivaldi (see p. 124). In Bach's more refined treatment of ritornello form, the line between the large (loud) ensemble and the small (soft) group of soloists is less obvious. Notice here that Bach's ritornello (see the Listening Guide) possesses many characteristics of Baroque melody: it is idiomatic to the violin (having many repeated notes); it is lengthy and somewhat asymmetrical (spinning out over many measures); and it possesses a driving rhythm that propels the music forward.

While the sound of violins dominates the ritornello in this opening movement, gradually the solo harpsichord steals the show. In fact, this work might fairly be called the first keyboard concerto. In earlier concertos, the harpsichord had appeared only as part of the *basso continuo*, not as a solo instrument. But here, toward the end of the movement, all the other instruments fall silent, leaving the harpsichord to sound alone in a lengthy section full of brilliant scales and arpeggios. Such a showy passage for soloist alone toward the end of a movement in a concerto is called a **cadenza.** One can easily imagine the great virtuoso Bach performing Brandenburg Concerto No. 5 in the Hall of Mirrors at Cöthen (Fig. 13-5), the principal concert hall of the court. There, seated at the large harpsichord he had brought from Berlin, Bach would have dazzled patron and fellow performers alike with his bravura playing.

Finally, note the length of this movement: more than nine minutes! Typical of Bach's grand musical vision, his movement is three times longer than a typical concerto movement by Vivaldi.

Download a Supplementary Listening Guide for Bach, Brandenburg Concerto No. 2, first movement, at the text website.

See a video of Bach's Brandenburg Concerto No. 5, first movement, in the YouTube playlist on the text website.

© Craig Wright

FIGURE 13–5

The Hall of Mirrors at the court of Cöthen, Germany, in which most of Bach's orchestral music was performed while he resided in that town. The bust on the pedestal at the right is of Bach.

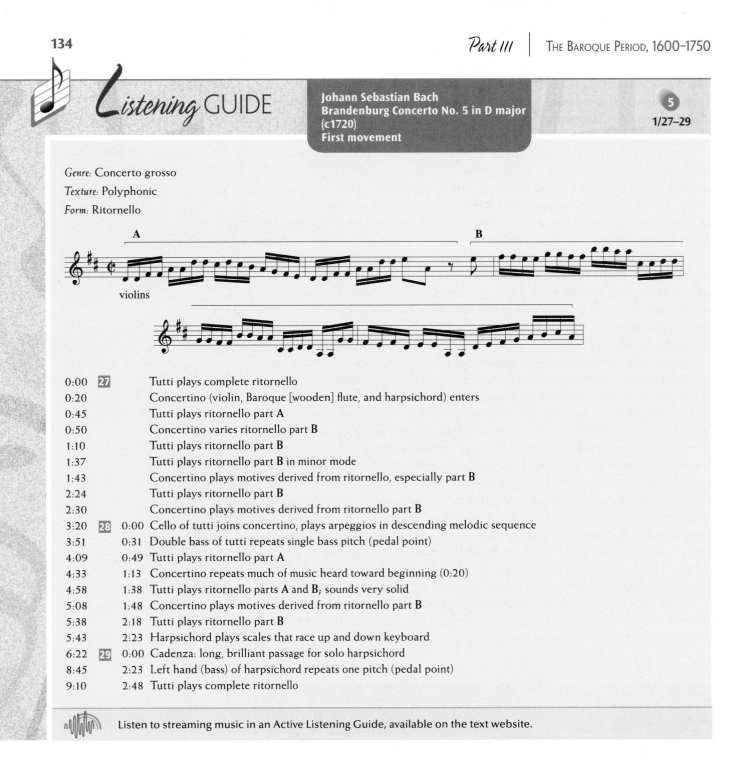

Listening GUIDE

Johann Sebastian Bach
Brandenburg Concerto No. 5 in D major
(c1720)
First movement

5
1/27–29

Genre: Concerto grosso

Texture: Polyphonic

Form: Ritornello

0:00	**27**		Tutti plays complete ritornello
0:20			Concertino (violin, Baroque [wooden] flute, and harpsichord) enters
0:45			Tutti plays ritornello part **A**
0:50			Concertino varies ritornello part **B**
1:10			Tutti plays ritornello part **B**
1:37			Tutti plays ritornello part **B** in minor mode
1:43			Concertino plays motives derived from ritornello, especially part **B**
2:24			Tutti plays ritornello part **B**
2:30			Concertino plays motives derived from ritornello part **B**
3:20	**28**	0:00	Cello of tutti joins concertino, plays arpeggios in descending melodic sequence
3:51		0:31	Double bass of tutti repeats single bass pitch (pedal point)
4:09		0:49	Tutti plays ritornello part **A**
4:33		1:13	Concertino repeats much of music heard toward beginning (0:20)
4:58		1:38	Tutti plays ritornello parts **A** and **B**; sounds very solid
5:08		1:48	Concertino plays motives derived from ritornello part **B**
5:38		2:18	Tutti plays ritornello part **B**
5:43		2:23	Harpsichord plays scales that race up and down keyboard
6:22	**29**	0:00	Cadenza: long, brilliant passage for solo harpsichord
8:45		2:23	Left hand (bass) of harpsichord repeats one pitch (pedal point)
9:10		2:48	Tutti plays complete ritornello

Listen to streaming music in an Active Listening Guide, available on the text website.

The fingers of the harpsichordist get a much-deserved rest in the slow second movement of Brandenburg Concerto No. 5. Now an elegiac mood envelops the music as the violin and flute engage in a quiet dialogue. The fast finale is dominated by fugal writing, a style in which Bach excelled above all other composers.

The Church Cantata

In 1723, Bach moved yet again, this time to assume the coveted position of cantor of Saint Thomas's Church and choir school in Leipzig, Germany (Fig. 13-6), a post he retained until his death in 1750. He seems to have been attracted to Leipzig, then a city of about 30,000 inhabitants, because of its excellent university where his sons might enroll at no cost.

Although prestigious, the post of cantor of the Lutheran church of Saint Thomas was not an easy one. As an employee of the town council of Leipzig, Bach was charged with superintending the liturgical music of the four principal churches of that city. He also played organ for all funerals, composed any music needed for ceremonies at the university, and sometimes taught Latin grammar to the boys at the choir school of Saint Thomas. But by far the most demanding part of his job as cantor was to provide new music for the church each Sunday and religious holiday, a total of about sixty days a year. In so doing, Bach brought an important genre of music, the church cantata, to the highest point of its development.

Like the opera, the sonata, and the concerto, the cantata first appeared in Italy during the seventeenth century in the form we call the chamber cantata (see p. 109). Typically written for a solo singer and small accompanying orchestra, the chamber cantata treated subjects of love or history and was performed in the home. During the early eighteenth century, however, composers in Germany increasingly came to see the cantata as an appropriate vehicle for religious music in the church. Bach and his contemporaries created the **church cantata,** a multimovement sacred work including arias, ariosos, and recitatives, performed by vocal soloists, a chorus, and a small accompanying orchestra. The church cantata became the musical core of the Sunday service of the Lutheran Church, the Protestant religion that then dominated spiritual life in German-speaking lands.

In Bach's time, Saint Thomas's Church in Leipzig (Fig. 13-7) celebrated a Sunday Mass, as prescribed by Martin Luther (1483–1546) nearly two centuries earlier. The service began at seven o'clock in the morning and lasted nearly four hours. The musical high point, the cantata, came after the reading of the Gospel and provided a commentary on the Gospel text, allowing the congregation to meditate on the word of the Lord. The preacher then delivered an hour-long sermon, which also expounded on the scriptural theme of the day. Bach wrote almost 300 cantatas (five annual cycles) for the citizens of Leipzig, though only about 200 of these survive. His musical forces consisted of about a dozen men and boy singers from the Saint Thomas choir school (see Fig. 13-6) and an equal number of instrumentalists from the university and town. The ensemble was placed in a choir loft above the west door (see Fig. 13-2), and Bach himself conducted the group, beating time with a roll of paper.

WACHET AUF, RUFT UNS DIE STIMME (*AWAKE, A VOICE IS CALLING,* 1731)

Bach was a devoted husband, a loving father to twenty children in all, and a respected burgher of Leipzig. Yet above all, he was a religious man who composed not only for self-expression but also for the greater glory of God. His cantata *Wachet auf, ruft uns die Stimme* (*Awake, a Voice Is Calling*) reveals his abiding faith in the religious traditions of his German Lutheran community. Bach composed it in 1731 for a service on a Sunday immediately before the beginning of Advent (four Sundays before Christmas). The text of the cantata announces the coming of a bridegroom toward his hopeful bride. Christ is the groom. A group of ten virgins, whose story is recounted in the Gospel of Matthew (25:1–13),

© Bettmann/Corbis

FIGURE 13–6

Leipzig, Saint Thomas's Church (center) and choir school (left) from an engraving of 1723, the year in which Bach moved to the city. Bach's large family occupied 900 square feet of the second floor of the choir school.

FIGURE 13–7

Looking across the parishioner's pews and toward the high altar at Saint Thomas's Church, Leipzig, as it was in the mid-nineteenth century. The pulpit for the sermon is at the right. In Bach's day, nearly 2,500 people would crowd into the church.

Lebrecht Music & Arts

@

Download Supplementary Listening Guides for Bach, cantatas *Christ lag in Todesbanden* and *Ein feste Burg,* as well as the chorale prelude *Christ lag in Todesbanden,* at the text website.

@

Watch a video of Craig Wright's Open Yale Course class session 16, "Baroque Music: The Vocal Music of Johann Sebastian Bach," at the text website.

symbolizes the bride and the entire community. Here is the Gospel of Matthew as it was read to the congregation at Saint Thomas's Church immediately before Bach's cantata was performed:

Then shall the kingdom of heaven be likened unto ten virgins, which took their lamps, and went forth to meet the bridegroom. And five of them were wise, and five were foolish. They that were foolish took their lamps, but took no oil with them. . . . And at midnight there was a cry made, Behold, the bridegroom cometh; go ye out to meet him. Then all those virgins arose, and trimmed their lamps. And the foolish said unto the wise, Give us of your oil; for our lamps are gone out. But the wise answered, saying, Not so; lest there be not enough for us and you: but go ye rather to them that sell, and buy for yourselves. And while they went to buy, the bridegroom came; and they that were ready went in with him to the marriage: and the door was shut. . . . Watch therefore, for ye know neither the day nor the hour wherein the Son of man cometh.

The message to every good Lutheran of Leipzig was clear: get your spiritual house in order so as to receive the coming Christ. Thus Bach's cantatas were intended not as concert pieces but as religious instruction for his community—sermons in music.

The cantata *Wachet auf* is made up of a succession of seven independent movements. Those for chorus provide a structural framework, coming at the beginning, the middle, and the end. They make use of the three stanzas of text of a sixteenth-century Lutheran hymn, *Wachet auf, ruft uns die Stimme,* from which this cantata derives its name. The text of the recitatives and arias, on the other hand, is a patchwork of biblical quotations cobbled together by a contemporary of Bach's. Thus the chorus sings the verses of the traditional hymn, while the soloists present the biblical excerpts in the recitatives and arias. Notice how the structure of the cantata creates a formal symmetry: recitative–aria pairs surround the central choral movement, and are preceded and followed in turn by a chorus.

Movement

1	2	3	4	5	6	7
Chorus chorale 1st stanza	Recitative	Aria (duet)	Chorus chorale 2nd stanza	Recitative	Aria (duet)	Chorus chorale 3rd stanza

Wachet auf is a built upon a **chorale,** a spiritual melody or religious folksong of the Lutheran Church—what other denominations would simply call a hymn. Most chorale tunes were centuries old by Bach's time and belonged to the religious tradition of the community; most Lutherans knew these melodies by heart. Chorales are easy to sing because they have clear-cut phrases and a steady beat with one syllable of text per note. The structure of the chorale tune *Wachet auf* is typical of this genre (see the Listening Guide). The music unfolds in **AAB** form, and the seven musical phrases are allocated in the following way: **A** (1, 2, 3) **A** (1, 2, 3) **B** (4–7, 3). The last phrase of section **A** returns at the end of **B** to round out the melody.

Movement 1. Of the seven movements of the cantata *Wachet auf,* the most remarkable is the first, a gigantic chorale fantasy that displays a polyphonic mastery exceptional even for Bach. Here Bach creates a multidimensional spectacle surrounding the coming of Christ. First, the orchestra announces Christ's arrival by means of a three-part ritornello that conveys a sense of growing anticipation. Part **a** of the ritornello, with its dotted rhythm, suggests a steady march; part **b,** with its strong downbeat and then syncopations, imparts a tugging urgency; part **c**, with its rapid sixteenth notes, implies an unrestrained race toward the object of desire (Christ). Now the chorale melody enters high in the sopranos, the voice of tradition, perhaps the voice of God. In long, steady notes placed squarely on downbeats, it calls the people to prepare themselves to receive God's Son. Beneath this the voices of the people—the altos, tenors, and basses—scurry in rapid counterpoint, excited by the call to meet their savior. Lowest of all is the bass of the *basso continuo*. It plods along, sometimes in a dotted pattern, sometimes in rapid eighth notes, but mostly in regularly recurring quarter notes falling on the beat. The enormous complexity of a movement such as this shows why musicians, then and now, view Bach as the greatest contrapuntalist who ever lived.

Listening GUIDE

Johann Sebastian Bach
**Cantata, *Wachet auf, ruft uns die Stimme*
(1731)**
First movement

5
1/30–31

Texture: Polyphonic

Form: **AAB**

chorale tune

Wa-chet auf! ruft uns die Stim - me der Wäch-ter sehr hoch auf der Zin - ne: wach'
Mit - ter - nacht heisst die-se Stun - de; sie ru - fen uns mit hel-lem Mun-de: wo

auf, du Stadt Je - ru - sa - lem! Wohl - auf! der Bräut'gam kommt, steht auf! die Lam-pen nehmt.
seid ihr klu-gen Jung-frau - en?

Al - le - lu - ja! macht euch be - reit zu der Hoch-zeit, ihr müs-set ihm ent-ge-gen gehn!

A section of chorale tune

0:00 **30**   Ritornello parts   **a**

0:07   **b**

0:14   **c**

Chorale phrases sung by sopranos accompanied by horn, instrument of watchmen

0:28	Chorale phrase 1	Wachet auf, ruft uns die Stimme	Awake, a voice is calling
0:43	Ritornello part **a**		
0:50	Chorale phrase 2	Der Wächter sehr hoch auf der Zinne	From the watchmen from high in the tower
1:07	Ritornello part **b**		
1:14	Chorale phrase 3	Wach' auf, du Stadt Jerusalem!	Awake, Jerusalem!

* *

(continued)

WHAT DID MRS. BACH DO?

Actually, there were two Mrs. Bachs. The first, Maria Barbara, died suddenly in 1720, leaving the composer with four young children (three others had died in infancy). The second, Anna Magdalena, he married in 1722, and she would bear him thirteen more. Anna Magdalena Bach was a professional singer, earning about as much as her new husband at the court of Cöthen. But when the family moved to Leipzig and the Saint Thomas Church, Anna Magdalena curtailed her professional activities. Women did not perform publicly in the Lutheran Church at this time; the difficult soprano lines in Bach's religious works were sung by choirboys. Consequently, Anna Magdalena put her musical skills to work as manager of what might be called "Bach Inc."

For almost every Sunday throughout the year, J. S. Bach was required to produce a cantata, about twenty to twenty-five minutes of new music, week after week, year after year. Writing the music was only part of the high-pressure task. Rehearsals had to be set and music learned by the next Sunday. But composing and rehearsing paled in comparison to the amount of time needed to copy all the parts—these were the days before photocopy machines and software programs to notate music. Each of the approximately twelve independent lines of the full score had to be copied, entirely by hand, for each new cantata, along with sufficient copies (parts) for all the singers and players. For this, Bach turned to the members of his household—namely, his wife and children (both sons and daughters), as well as the nephews, and other fee-paying private students who resided in the cantor's quarters at the Saint Thomas school (see Fig. 13-6). In 1731, the year he composed the cantata *Wachet auf, ruft uns die Stimme,* the roof was taken off the building and two more stories added to accommodate the Bach family and its "music industry."

When Bach died in 1750, he left his most valuable assets (his musical scores) to his eldest sons. The performing parts to many of his cantatas, however, he left to his wife with the expectation that she would rent or sell them in the course of time—her old-age pension in the days before social security. In the end, however, the income from these cantata manuscripts did not prove sufficient, and Anna Magdalena Bach finished her days in 1760 as a ward of the city of Leipzig.

Repeat of **A** section of chorale tune (0:00–1:30) with new text as required by repeat in chorale tune

1:31	Ritornello parts **a**, **b**, and **c**		
2:00	Chorale phrase 1	Mitternacht heisst diese Stunde	Midnight is the hour
2:15	Ritornello part **a**		
2:21	Chorale phrase 2	Sie rufen uns mit hellem Munde	They call us with a clarion voice
2:38	Ritornello part **b**		
2:46	Chorale phrase 3	Wo seid ihr klugen Jungfrauen?	Where are the Wise Virgins?

* * ** * * ** ** * * * * * * * * * * * * * ** * * * * * ** * * *

B section of chorale tune

3:05 **31**	0:00	Variation of ritornello parts **a**, **b**, and **c** leads to new keys		
3:24	0:19	Chorale phrase 4	Wohl auf, der Bräutgam kommt	Get up, the Bridegroom comes
3:37	0:31	Ritornello part **a**		
3:42	0:36	Chorale phrase 5	Steht auf, die Lampen nehmt	Stand up and take your lamps
3:57	0:51	Altos, tenors, and basses enjoy extended imitative fantasy on "Alleluja"		
4:23	1:17	Chorale phrase 6	Alleluja	Alleluia
4:34	1:27	Ritornello part **a**		
4:44	1:37	Chorale phrase 7 begins	Macht euch bereit	Prepare yourselves
4:52	1:45	Ritornello part **a**		
4:58	1:52	Chorale phrase 7 ends	Zu der Hochzeit	For the wedding
5:07	2:00	Ritornello part **b**		
5:16	2:09	Chorale phrase 3	Ihr müsset ihm entgegen gehn!	You must go forth to meet him!
5:33	2:26	Ritornello parts **a**, **b**, and **c**		

Listen to streaming music in an Active Listening Guide, available on the text website.

Movement 2. In this recitative, the Evangelist (the narrator) invites the daughters of Zion to the wedding feast; there is no use of chorale tune. In Bach's religious vocal music, the Evangelist is invariably sung by a tenor.

Movement 3. In this aria (duet) between the Soul (soprano) and Jesus (bass), there is also no use of chorale tune. It is traditional in German sacred music of the Baroque era to assign the role of Christ to a bass.

Movement 4. For this meeting of Christ and the daughters of Zion (true believers), Bach fashioned one of his loveliest creations. Again the chorale tune serves as a unifying force, now carrying stanza 2 of the chorale text. Once more Bach constructs a musical tapestry for chorus and orchestra, but a less complex one than the first movement. Here we hear only two central motives. One is the chorale melody sung by the tenors, who represent the watchmen calling on Jerusalem (Leipzig) to awake. The other is the exquisite melody played by all the violins and violas in unison—their togetherness symbolizes the unifying love of Christ for his people. This unison line is a perfect example of a lengthy, ever-expanding Baroque melody, and one of the most memorable of the entire era. Beneath it we hear the measured tread of the ever-present *basso continuo.* The bass plays regularly recurring quarter notes on the beat. As we have seen, a bass that moves at a moderate, steady pace, mostly in equal note values and often stepwise up or down the scale, is called a walking bass. The walking bass in this movement enhances the meaning of the text, underscoring the steady approach of the Lord. This movement was one of Bach's own favorites and the only cantata movement that he published—all the rest of his Leipzig cantata music was left in handwritten scores at the time of his death.

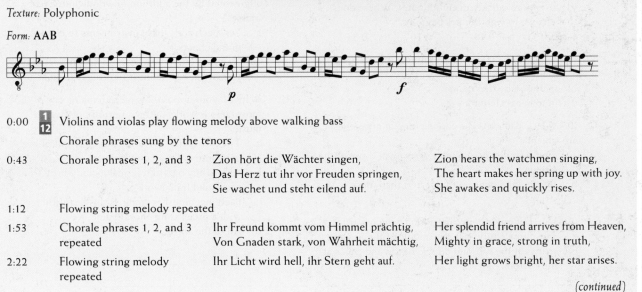

Listening GUIDE

Johann Sebastian Bach
Wachet auf, ruft uns die Stimme
Fourth movement

5 · 2/1   2 · 1/12

Texture: Polyphonic

Form: AAB

Time				
0:00	1/12	Violins and violas play flowing melody above walking bass		
		Chorale phrases sung by the tenors		
0:43		Chorale phrases 1, 2, and 3	Zion hört die Wächter singen,	Zion hears the watchmen singing,
			Das Herz tut ihr vor Freuden springen,	The heart makes her spring up with joy.
			Sie wachet und steht eilend auf.	She awakes and quickly rises.
1:12		Flowing string melody repeated		
1:53		Chorale phrases 1, 2, and 3 repeated	Ihr Freund kommt vom Himmel prächtig,	Her splendid friend arrives from Heaven,
			Von Gnaden stark, von Wahrheit mächtig,	Mighty in grace, strong in truth,
2:22		Flowing string melody repeated	Ihr Licht wird hell, ihr Stern geht auf.	Her light grows bright, her star arises.

(continued)

2:47	Chorale phrases 4, 5, and 6	Nun komm, du werte Kron, Herr Jesu, Gottes Sohn! Hosanna!	Now come, you worthy crown, Lord, Jesus, Son of God! Hosanna!
3:09	String melody continues in minor		
3:28	Chorale phrases 7 and 3	Wir folgen all zum Freudensaal Und halten mit das Abendmahl.	We will follow all to the banquet hall And share in the Lord's supper.
3:56	String melody concludes movement		

Listen to streaming music in an Active Listening Guide, available at the text website.

Listening EXERCISE 20

Bach

WACHET AUF, RUFT UNS DIE STIMME

2/1   1/12

To take this Listening Exercise online and receive feedback or email answers to your instructor, go to the text website.

The most famous section of Bach's cantata *Wachet auf* is in the middle (fourth) movement. Here the composer creates for the strings a lovely melody to be used as a counterpoint to the chorale tune. Let us begin by considering the string melody and its accompaniment, and then the chorale.

1. (0:00–0:42) How many musical lines or parts do you hear at the beginning of the movement?
   a. one   b. two   c. three

2. (0:00–0:42) A bass that plods along in equal note values moving in predominantly stepwise motion is called what?
   a. a *basso continuo*
   b. a *basso ostinato*
   c. a walking bass

3. (0:00–0:42) The basses (double basses and cellos) play only quarter notes on the beat until they begin to move more quickly in eighth notes. Where does that change to eighth notes begin?
   a. 0:10   b 0:18   c. 0:26   d. 0:34

4. (0:43) When the chorale tune enters, how is it sung?
   a. in unison by the sopranos
   b. in unison by the tenors
   c. in four-part harmony

5. (0:43–1:11) Bach sets the chorale tune in notes that are which?
   a. longer (and hence sound slower) than those of the strings
   b. shorter (and hence sound faster) than those of the strings

6. (0:43–1:11) Throughout this section, which is true?
   a. The chorale tune is in the middle of the texture, strings at the top, and double basses and cellos at the bottom.

   b. The chorale tune is at the top of the texture, strings in the middle, and double basses and cellos at the bottom.

7. (1:12–2:52, repeat of section **A** of the movement) Do the relative positions of the string melody and the chorale tune change during this repeat?
   a. yes   b. no

8. (2:53–end) Which is true about the nature of the string melody during the **B** section?
   a. It is an entirely new melody.
   b. Sometimes it repeats phrases from the **A** section.

9. At any time throughout this movement, is the three-line texture (bass, choral tune, string melody) augmented by the addition of woodwinds and brasses?
   a. Yes; Bach adds these instruments to create a grand climax.
   b. No; once Bach decides upon his three-strand texture, he maintains it rigorously to the end.

10. Why do you suppose this piece remains one of the most famous works in the repertoire of classical music?
    a. The lilting string melody has clear-cut phrases yet continually presses forward.
    b. The strong bass and lyrical melody provide a rock-solid framework.
    c. Bach ingeniously combines this beautiful melody with a preexisting chorale tune.
    d. All of the above.

Movement 5. In this recitative for Christ (bass), there is no use of chorale tune. Christ invites the anguished Soul to find comfort in Him.

Movement 6. In this aria (duet) for bass and soprano, again there is no use of chorale tune. The form is ternary (**ABA**), which for an aria is often called **da capo form** because the performers, when reaching the end of **B**, "take it from the head" and repeat **A**. Here Christ and the Soul sing a passionate love duet. A religious man who did not compose operas, Bach most closely approaches the world of the popular theater in this ardent duet.

Movement 7. Bach's cantatas usually end with a simple four-voice homophonic setting of the last stanza of the chorale tune. In his closing movements, he always places the chorale melody in the soprano part, harmonizing and supporting it with the other three voices below. The instruments of the orchestra have no line of their own and merely double the four vocal parts. But more important, the members of the congregation join in the singing of the chorale melody. Martin Luther had ordained that the community should not merely witness but also participate in communal worship. At this moment, all of the spiritual energy of Leipzig was concentrated into this one emphatic declaration of faith. The coming Christ reveals to all true believers a vision of life in the celestial kingdom.

@

Download a Supplementary Listening Guide for Bach, Prelude and Fugue in C minor, from *The Well-Tempered Clavier*, at the text website.

Listening GUIDE

Johann Sebastian Bach
Wachet auf, ruft uns die Stimme
Seventh and last movement

5
2/2

Texture: Homophonic

Form: **AAB**

0:00	**2**	Phrase 1	Gloria sei dir gesungen	May Glory be sung to you
		Phrase 2	Mit Menschen und englischen Zungen	With the tongues of man and the angels
		Phrase 3	Mit Harfen und mit Zimbeln schon.	And harps and cymbals too.
0:24		Phrase 1	Von zwölf Perlen sind die Pforten,	The gates are of twelve pearls,
		Phrase 2	An deiner Stadt, wir sind Konsorten	In your city, we are consorts
		Phrase 3	Der Engel hoch um deiner Thron.	Of the angels high above your throne.

(continued)

0:48	Phrase 4	Kein Aug hat je gespürt,	No eye has ever seen,
	Phrase 5	Kein Ohr hat je gehört	No ear has ever heard
	Phrase 6	Solche Freude.	Such joy.
	Phrase 7	Des sind wir froh,	Let us therefore rejoice,
		Io, io!	Io, io!
	Phrase 3	Ewig in dulci jubilo.	Eternally in sweet jubilation.

Listen to streaming music in an Active Listening Guide, available on the text website.

FIGURE 13–8

When Bach died in 1750 he was buried in an outlying parish church, and he and his music soon forgotten. But during the nineteenth century the world came to realize that the citizens of Leipzig had had in their midst a musical genius. So in 1895 they dug him up to measure his skull to see if it were abnormally large or small (it was not), photographed his remains, and repositioned them beneath the high altar of his Saint Thomas Church (Saint Bach!). Sometimes genius is recognized only belatedly.

"Gesammtansicht des Bach-Skeletts" In: W. His, Anatomische Forschungen über Johann Sebastian Bach's Gebeine und Antlitz S. Leipzig: S. Hirzel, 1895

@

Download a Supplementary Listening Guide for Bach, Contrapunctus 5, from *The Art of Fugue*, at the text website.

In the last decade of his life, Bach gradually withdrew from the world to dwell in the contrapuntal realm of his own mind. He finished the best-known of his large-scale contrapuntal projects, *The Well-Tempered Clavier* (1720–1742), a "clavier" simply being a general term for keyboard instruments. (It is called "Well-Tempered," or "Well-Tuned," because Bach was gradually adopting a keyboard in which all the half steps were equidistant in pitch, something that had not been universally true before this time.) *The Well-Tempered Clavier* consists of two sets of twenty-four preludes and fugues. The **prelude** is a short preparatory piece that sets a mood and serves as a technical warm-up for the player before the fugue. In both sets of twenty-four, there is one prelude and fugue in each of the twelve major and twelve minor keys. Today every serious pianist around the world "cuts his or her teeth" on what is affectionately known as the "WTC."

Bach's last project was **The Art of Fugue** (1742–1750), an encyclopedic treatment of all known contrapuntal procedures set forth in nineteen canons and fugues. The final fugue, one in which Bach combines four related subjects, was broken off by his death in 1750. *The Art of Fugue* was thus Bach's valedictory statement of a musical form he brought to supreme mastery. It remains a fitting testimony to this composer's stylistic integrity, grand vision, and superhuman craftsmanship.

@

The materials on the text website will help you understand and pass tests on the content of this chapter. In addition, you may watch Craig Wright's own lectures at Open Yale Courses and complete this chapter's Listening Exercises interactively, as well as view Active Listening Guides and other materials that will help you succeed in this course.

Key WORDS

subject (129)	pedal point (130)	*da capo* form (141)
exposition (129)	cadenza (133)	prelude (142)
episode (129)	church cantata (135)	*The Art of Fugue* (142)
fugue (129)	chorale (136)	

THE LATE BAROQUE
HANDEL

14

Bach and Handel were born in the same year, 1685, in small towns in central Germany. Other than that commonality, however, their careers could not have been more different. While Bach spent his life confined to towns in the region of his birth, the cosmopolitan Handel traveled the world—from Rome, to Venice, to Hamburg, to Amsterdam, to London, to Dublin. If Bach was most at home playing organ fugues and conducting church cantatas from the choir loft, Handel was a musical entrepreneur working in the theater, by training and temperament a composer of opera. And if Bach fell into obscurity at the end of his life, retreating into a world of esoteric counterpoint, Handel's stature only grew larger on the international stage. He became during his lifetime the most famous composer in Europe and a treasured national institution in England.

GEORGE FRIDERIC HANDEL (1685–1759)

George Frideric Handel was born in the town of Halle, Germany, in 1685, and died in London in 1759 (Fig. 14-1). Although his father had decreed a program of study in law, the young Handel managed to cultivate his intense interest in music, sometimes secretly in the attic. At the age of eighteen, he left for the city of Hamburg, where he took a job as second violinist in the public opera (he was later promoted to *continuo* harpsichordist). But because the musical world around 1700 was dominated by things Italian, he set off for Italy to learn his trade and broaden his horizons. He moved between Florence and Venice, where he wrote operas, and Rome, where he composed mainly chamber cantatas. In 1710, Handel returned to North Germany to accept the post of chapel master to the Elector of Hanover, but on the condition that he be given an immediate leave of absence to visit London. Although he made one final voyage back to his employer in Hanover in 1711 and many subsequent visits to the Continent, Handel conveniently "forgot" about his obligation to the Hanoverian court. London became the site of his musical activity and the place where he won fame and fortune.

London in the early eighteenth century was the largest city in Europe, boasting a population of 500,000. It was also the capital city of a country in the process of forming an empire for international trade and commerce. London may not have possessed the rich cultural heritage of Rome or Paris, but it offered opportunity for financial gain. As the eighteenth-century saying went: "In France and Italy there is something to learn, but in London there is something to earn."

Handel soon found employment in the homes of the aristocracy and became the music tutor to the English royal family. As fate would have it, his continental employer, the Elector of Hanover, became King George I of England in 1714, when the Hanoverians acceded to the throne on the extinction of the Stuart line.

FIGURE 14–1

Thomas Hudson's portrait (1749) of Handel with the score of *Messiah* visible in the composer's left hand. Handel had a quick temper, could swear in four languages, and liked to eat.

Lebrecht Music and Arts

Fortunately for Handel, the new king bore his truant musician no grudge, and he was called on frequently to compose festival music to entertain the court or mark its progress. For these events, Handel produced such works as *Water Music* (1717), *Music for the Royal Fireworks* (1749), and the Coronation Service (1727) for King George II and Queen Caroline, parts of which have been used at the coronation of every English monarch since then.

Handel and the Orchestral Dance Suite

The English royal family, which has historically had a problem with its image, has sometimes given concerts of popular music to win favor with the public. Queen Elizabeth II did so in 2002 by inviting Ozzy Osbourne and Paul McCartney to play at Buckingham Palace with simulcasts around the parks of London. Handel's *Water Music* was created for an earlier bit of royal image building. In 1717, King George I, a direct ancestor of the present queen, was an unpopular monarch. He refused to speak a word of English, preferring his native German. He fought with his son, the Prince of Wales, even banning him from court. His subjects considered George dimwitted—"an honest blockhead," as one contemporary put it.

To improve his standing in the eyes of his subjects, the king's ministers planned a program of public entertainments, including an evening of music on the Thames River for the lords of Parliament and the lesser people of London (Fig. 14-2). Thus, on July 17, 1717, the king and his court left London, accompanied by a small armada of boats, and progressed up the Thames to the strains of Handel's orchestral music. An eyewitness describes this nautical parade in detail:

About eight in the evening the King repaired to his barge, into which were admitted the Duchess of Bolton, Countess Godolphin, Madam de Kilmansech (the king's mistress), Mrs. Were and the Earl of Orkney, the Gentleman of the Bedchamber in Waiting. Next to the King's barge was that of the musicians, about 50 in number, who played on all kinds of instruments, to wit trumpets, horns, hautboys [oboes], bassoons, German flutes, French flutes [recorders], violins and basses; but there were no singers. The music had been composed specially by the famous Handel, a native of Halle [Germany], and His Majesty's principal Court Composer. His Majesty so greatly approved of the music that he caused it to be repeated three times in all, although each performance lasted an hour—namely twice before and once after supper. The evening weather was all that could be desired for the festivity, the number of barges and above all of boats filled with people desirous of hearing the music was beyond counting.

The score played for King George and the crowd of music lovers moving on the Thames River was, of course, Handel's *Water Music*. *Water Music* belongs to a genre called the **dance suite**: a collection of dances, usually from two to seven in number, all in one key and for one group of instruments, be it full orchestra, trio, or solo. (The term derives from the French word *suite*, meaning "a succession of things or pieces.") Listeners usually did not dance to the music of a suite; these were

FIGURE 14-2
View of London, Saint Paul's Cathedral, and the Thames River by Canaletto (1697–1768). Notice the large barges. Crafts such as these could have easily accommodated the fifty musicians reported to have played behind the king as he moved upstream in 1717, listening to Handel's *Water Music*.

stylized, abstract dances intended only for the ear. But it was the job of the composer to bring each one to life, to make it recognizable to the audience by incorporating the salient elements of rhythm and style of each particular dance. Among the dances found in a typical late-Baroque suite are the allemande (literally, "German dance"; a moderate or brisk, stately dance in duple meter), the saraband (a slow, sensual dance of Spanish origin in triple meter), and the minuet (a moderate, elegant dance in triple meter).

Almost all dances of the Baroque period were composed in one musical form: binary form (**AB**), the two sections of which could be repeated. Some dance movements are followed by a second, complementary dance, called a trio (**CD**) because it was originally played by only three instruments. When a minuet, for example, is followed by a trio and the minuet repeated, a large-scale ternary arrangement results: **AB|CD|AB**. What make the dance movements of *Water Music* so enjoyable and easy to follow are their tuneful themes and formal clarity. Notice in the Minuet and Trio how Handel asks the French horns and trumpets first to announce both the **A** and **B** sections before passing this material on to the woodwinds and then the full orchestra. Here instrumentation makes the form clearly audible.

Listening GUIDE

George Frideric Handel
Water Music (1717)
Minuet and Trio

5
2/3–4

Genre: Dance from dance suite

Form: Binary (**AB**) within larger ternary (**ABCDAB**)

MINUET (triple meter, major key)

0:00	**3** A		French horns introduce part A
0:12	B		Trumpets introduce part B
0:29	A		Winds and continuo play A
0:42			Full orchestra repeats A
0:55	B		Winds and continuo play B
1:08			Full orchestra repeats B

TRIO (triple meter, minor key)

1:28	**4** C	0:00	Strings and continuo play part C
1:43	D	0:15	Strings and continuo play part D

MINUET

2:19	A	0:51	Full orchestra plays A
2:31	B	1:03	Full orchestra plays B

Listen to streaming music in an Active Listening Guide, available on the text website.

Handel and Opera

George Frideric Handel emigrated from Germany to England in 1710 not for the chance to entertain the king, and certainly not for the cuisine or the climate. Rather, he went to London to make money producing Italian opera.

With the rare exception of a work such as Purcell's *Dido and Aeneas* (see p. 112), there was no opera in London at this time. English audiences preferred spoken plays, with an occasional musical interlude. Handel aimed to change this. London audiences, he reasoned, were daily growing wealthier and more cosmopolitan, and would welcome the "high art" form provided by Italian opera. Guaranteeing himself a healthy share of the profits, Handel participated in the formation of an opera company, the Royal Academy of Music. He composed the music, engaged high-paid soloists from Italy, led the rehearsals, and conducted the finished product from the harpsichord in the orchestra pit. His first opera, *Rinaldo* (1711), was first performed at the Queen's Theatre, the same theater in which Andrew Lloyd Webber's *Phantom of the Opera* premiered in 1986.

The type of Italian opera Handel produced in London is called **opera seria** (literally, serious, as opposed to comic, opera), a style that then dominated the operatic stage throughout continental Europe. Glorifying the nobility, *opera seria* chronicles the triumphs and tragedies of kings and queens, gods and goddesses. Much of the action occurs off stage and is simply reported in the form of recitatives. The principal characters react to these unseen events by means of arias that express stock emotions—hope, anger, hate, frenzy, and despair, to name a few. In Handel's day, the leading male roles were sung by castrati (castrated males with the vocal range of a female); Baroque audiences associated high social standing on stage with a high voice, male or female. From 1710 until 1728, Handel had great artistic and some financial success, producing two dozen examples of Italian *opera seria*. Foremost among these was *Giulio Cesare* (*Julius Caesar*, 1724), a recasting of the story of Caesar's conquest of the army of Egypt and Cleopatra's romantic conquest of Caesar (Fig. 14-3).

But opera is a notoriously risky business, and in 1728, Handel's Royal Academy of Music went bankrupt, a victim of the exorbitant fees paid the star singers and the fickle tastes of English theatergoers. Handel continued to write operas into the early 1740s, but he increasingly turned his attention to a musical genre similar in construction to opera: oratorio.

Handel and Oratorio

An **oratorio** is literally "something sung in an oratory," an oratory being a hall or chapel used specifically for prayer and sometimes prayer with music. Thus the oratorio in seventeenth-century Italy had something in common with today's gospel music: it was sacred music sung in a special hall or chapel and was intended to inspire the faithful to greater devotion. By the time it reached Handel's hands, however, the oratorio had become close to an unstaged opera with a religious subject.

Both Baroque oratorio and opera begin with an overture, are divided into acts, and are composed primarily of recitatives and arias. Both genres are also long, usually lasting two to three hours. But there are a few important differences between opera and oratorio, aside from the obvious fact that oratorio treats a religious subject. Oratorio, being a quasi-religious genre, is performed in a church, a theater, or a concert hall, but it makes no use of acting, staging, or costumes. Because the subject matter is almost always sacred, there is more of an opportunity for moralizing, a dramatic function best performed by a chorus. Thus the chorus assumes greater importance in an oratorio. It sometimes serves as a narrator but more often functions, like the chorus in ancient Greek drama, as the voice of the people commenting on the action that has transpired.

FIGURE 14–3

Title page of an early English edition of Handel's opera *Julius Caesar*. The musicians form a *basso continuo*.

By the 1730s, oratorio appeared to Handel as an attractive alternative to the increasingly unprofitable opera in London. He could do away with the irascible and expensive castrati and prima donnas. He no longer had to pay for elaborate sets and costumes. He could draw on the ancient English love of choral music, a tradition that extended well back into the Middle Ages. And he could exploit a new, untapped market—the faithful of the Puritan, Methodist, and growing evangelical sects in England, who had viewed the pleasures of foreign opera with distrust and even contempt. And in contrast to the Italian opera, the oratorio was sung in English, contributing further to the appeal of the genre to a large segment of English society.

MESSIAH (1741)

Beginning in 1732 and continuing over a twenty-year period, Handel wrote upward of twenty oratorios. The most famous of these is his *Messiah*, composed in the astonishingly short period of three-and-a-half weeks during the summer of 1741. It was first performed in Dublin, Ireland, the following April as part of a charity benefit, with Handel conducting. Having heard the dress rehearsal, the local press waxed enthusiastic about the new oratorio, saying that it "far surpasses anything of that Nature, which has been performed in this or any other Kingdom." Such a large crowd was expected for the work of the famous Handel that ladies were urged not to wear hoopskirts and gentlemen were admonished to leave their swords at home. In this way, an audience of 700 could be squeezed into a hall of only 600 seats.

Buoyed by his artistic and financial success in Dublin, Handel took *Messiah* back to London, made minor alterations, and performed it in Covent Garden Theater. In 1750, he offered *Messiah* again, this time in the chapel of the Foundling Hospital, an orphanage in London (Fig. 14-4), and again there was much popular acclaim for Handel, as well as profit for charity. This was the first time one of his oratorios was sung in a religious setting rather than a theater or a concert hall. The annual repetition of *Messiah* in the Foundling Hospital chapel during Handel's lifetime and long after did much to convince the public that his oratorios were essentially religious music to be performed in church.

In a general way, *Messiah* tells the story of the life of Christ. It is divided into three parts (instead of three acts): (I) the prophecy of His coming and His Incarnation, (II) His Passion and Resurrection, and the triumph of the Gospel, and (III) reflections on the Christian victory over death. Most of Handel's oratorios recount the heroic deeds of characters from the Old Testament; *Messiah* is exceptional because the subject comes from the New Testament, though much of the libretto is drawn directly from both the Old and New Testaments. There is neither plot action nor "characters" in the dramatic sense. The music consists of fifty-three numbers: nineteen choruses, sixteen solo arias, sixteen recitatives, and two purely instrumental pieces.

FIGURE 14–4

The chapel of the Foundling Hospital, London, where *Messiah* was performed annually for the benefit of the orphans. Handel himself designed and donated the organ seen on the second story at the back of the hall.

@

Download Supplementary
Listening Guides for more parts
of *Messiah*—French overture,
recitative "Comfort ye my
people," aria "Ev'ry valley shall
be exalted," and chorus "And
the glory of the Lord"—at the
text website.

There are many beautiful and stirring arias in *Messiah*, including "Ev'ry valley shall be exalted" and "O thou that tellest good tidings to Zion." But perhaps the loveliest of all is the pastoral aria "He shall feed his flock," which comes at the end of Part I and alludes to the birth of Christ. A **pastoral aria** has several distinctive characteristics, all of which suggest the movement of simple shepherds attending the Christ Child: it glides along mainly in stepwise motion; it projects a lilting rhythm in which a slow-moving beat is subdivided into three easily flowing eighth notes; and it grounds itself upon a harmony that changes slowly (in imitation of shepherds' bagpipes). Even the key of F major is suggestive, for F major was traditionally heard as a relaxed tonality, and composers from Bach to Beethoven and beyond employed its particular sound to evoke shepherds and pastoral scenes. (Before the mid-nineteenth century, each key was tuned a slightly different way from the next and had its own particular associations.) But let's not kill a beautiful melody with too much analysis and history. Just listen to what is arguably the most relaxing aria ever written, an anthem for peace.

*L*istening GUIDE

George Frideric Handel
***Messiah*, Aria, "He shall feed His flock" (1741)**

5

2/5–6

Genre: Pastoral aria from an oratorio

Form: Strophic (two stanzas with vocal ornamentation applied to the second, some written by
Handel, some added by the singer of this recording)

0:00	**5**	Instrumental introduction	
STANZA 1			
0:20		Undulating melody unfolds above slowly changing harmony	He shall feed His flock like a shepherd And He shall gather the lambs with His arm.
0:50		Repeat of first lines with slight ornamentation	
1:17		Modulation to minor key	And carry them in His bosom,
1:40		Return to tonic major key	And gently lead those that are with young.
2:01		Instruments lead modulation to higher range (dominant key)	
STANZA 2			
2:13	**6** 0:00	Melody of stanza 1 in higher range; ornaments added to melodic line	Come unto Him all ye that labour, Come unto Him that are heavy laden and He will give you rest.
2:43	0:30	Repeat of first lines with increased ornamentation	
3:11	0:58	Modulation to minor key	Take His yoke upon you, and learn of Him
3:33	1:18	Return to tonic major	For He is meek and lowly of heart and ye shall find rest unto your souls.
3:56	1:41	Repeat of last lines with increased ornamentation	
4:42	2:27	Instruments conclude with reminiscence of beginning	

Listen to streaming music in an Active Listening Guide, available on the text website.

Despite the beauty of the arias, the true glory of *Messiah* is to be found in its choruses. Handel is arguably the finest composer for chorus who ever lived. As a world traveler with an unsurpassed ear, he absorbed a variety of musical styles from throughout Europe: in Germany, he acquired knowledge of the fugue and the Lutheran chorale; in Italy, he immersed himself in the styles of the oratorio and the chamber cantata; and during his years in England, he became familiar with the idioms of the English church anthem (essentially an extended motet). Most important, having spent a lifetime in the opera theater, Handel had a flair for the dramatic.

Nowhere is Handel's choral mastery more evident than in the justly famous "Hallelujah" chorus that concludes Part II of *Messiah*. We have moved from peaceful adoration to triumphant resurrection, and now a variety of choral styles are displayed in quick succession: chordal, unison, chorale, fugal, and fugal and chordal together. The opening word "Hallelujah" recurs throughout as a powerful refrain, yet each new phrase of text generates its own distinct musical idea. The vivid phrases speak directly to the listener, making the audience feel like a participant in the drama. So moved was King George II when he first heard the great opening chords, as the story goes, that he rose to his feet in admiration, thereby establishing the tradition of the audience standing for the "Hallelujah" chorus—for no one sat while the king stood. Indeed, this movement would serve well as a royal coronation march, though in *Messiah*, of course, it is Christ the King who is being crowned.

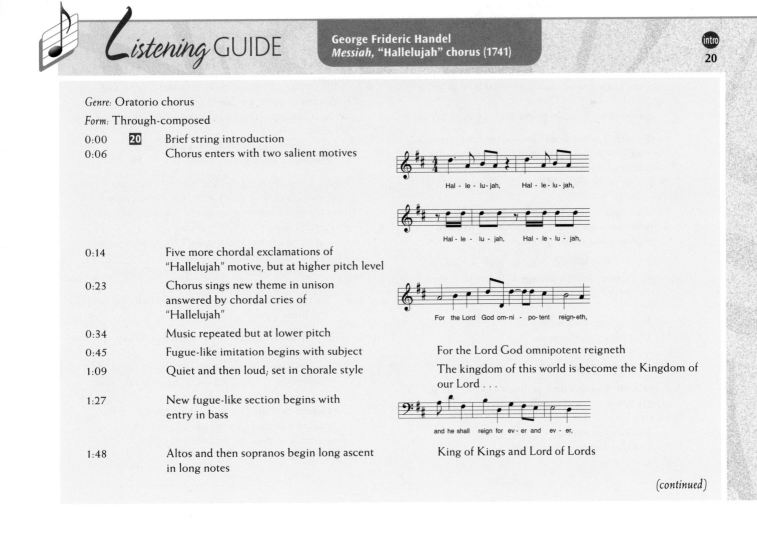

*L*istening GUIDE

George Frideric Handel
***Messiah*, "Hallelujah" chorus (1741)**

intro
20

Genre: Oratorio chorus

Form: Through-composed

Time		Description	Text
0:00	**20**	Brief string introduction	
0:06		Chorus enters with two salient motives	Hal-le-lu-jah, Hal-le-lu-jah, / Hal-le-lu-jah, Hal-le-lu-jah,
0:14		Five more chordal exclamations of "Hallelujah" motive, but at higher pitch level	
0:23		Chorus sings new theme in unison answered by chordal cries of "Hallelujah"	For the Lord God om-ni-po-tent reign-eth,
0:34		Music repeated but at lower pitch	
0:45		Fugue-like imitation begins with subject	For the Lord God omnipotent reigneth
1:09		Quiet and then loud; set in chorale style	The kingdom of this world is become the Kingdom of our Lord . . .
1:27		New fugue-like section begins with entry in bass	and he shall reign for ev-er and ev-er,
1:48		Altos and then sopranos begin long ascent in long notes	King of Kings and Lord of Lords

(continued)

2:28	Basses and sopranos reenter	And he shall reign for ever and ever
2:40	Tenors and basses sing in long notes	King of Kings and Lord of Lords
2:55	Incessant major tonic chord	King of Kings
3:20	Broad final cadence	Hallelujah

Listen to streaming music in an Active Listening Guide, available at the text website.

Listening EXERCISE 21

Handel

MESSIAH, "HALLELUJAH" CHORUS

 intro 20

To take this Listening Exercise online and receive feedback or email answers to your instructor, go to the text website.

As a man of the theater, Handel was the master of the dramatic gesture. Sometimes, as we shall see, he would even insert a "thundering silence" for special effect. This exercise asks you to hear the frequent changes of texture in the "Hallelujah" chorus. It is by means of striking textural changes that Handel creates the grand effects of this classical favorite.

1. (0:06–0:22) In what kind of musical texture do the voices sing when they enter with "Hallelujah"?
   a. monophonic   b. homophonic   c. polyphonic

2. (0:23–0:28; "For the Lord God omnipotent reigneth") As the chorus sings in unison and the violins double (play the same line as) their part, what kind of texture is created?
   a. monophonic   b. homophonic   c. polyphonic

3. (0:45–1:09; "For the Lord God omnipotent reigneth") Now we have a passage of imitative, contrapuntal writing in which a subject is presented in succession in the voices. In what order do the voices enter with this subject?
   a. alto, male voices, soprano
   b. soprano, male voices, alto (men and women)
   c. soprano, alto, male voices

4. (1:27–1:47; "And he shall reign for ever and ever") Again, Handel offers a passage of imitative writing, with a new subject. In what order do the voices enter?
   a. bass, tenor, soprano, alto
   b. bass, alto, tenor, soprano
   c. bass, tenor, alto, soprano
   d. bass, soprano, alto, tenor

5. Polyphonic passages such as this (1:27–1:47) most closely approximate the style and musical texture found where?
   a. in a Gregorian chant
   b. in a chorale tune
   c. in a fugue

6. (2:01–2:25) What are the sopranos doing here on "King of Kings and Lord of Lords"?
   a. rising in an arpeggio
   b. rising by leap
   c. rising by step

7. (2:49–end) What brass instruments, associated with kings through history, sound forth here along with "King of Kings"?
   a. trombones   b. trumpets   c. tubas

8. (3:17–3:19) In a brilliant stroke, Handel sets off and highlights the final statement of "Hallelujah" (and the final cadence) by inserting a new kind of texture. Which is correct?
   a. He inserts a homophonic brass fanfare.
   b. He inserts the texture of silence.

9. Which correctly identifies the ways in which our modern recording of the "Hallelujah" chorus differs from the performance practices of Handel's time (see paragraph below)?
   a. An orchestra has been added to support what was only a chorus in Handel's original.
   b. The chorus is much larger, and women sing the alto and soprano chorus parts.
   c. Castrati would have been used in Handel's original chorus.

10. What perhaps accounts for the eternal popularity of the "Hallelujah" chorus?
    a. Handel draws upon a deep wellspring of English national pride, skillfully manipulating a chorale tune to create a variety of exciting textures and styles.
    b. Handel exploits a clear, emphatic setting of the English text and a few powerful gestures to create a variety of exciting textures and styles.
    c. Both the above.

The "Hallelujah" chorus is a strikingly effective work mainly because the large choral force creates a variety of exciting textures. In fact, however, Handel's chorus for the original Dublin *Messiah* was much smaller than those used today. It included about four singers on the alto, tenor, and bass parts and six choirboys singing the soprano (Fig. 14-5). The orchestra was equally slight. For the Foundling Hospital performances of the 1750s, however, the orchestra grew to thirty-five players. Then, over the next hundred years, the chorus progressively swelled to as many as 4,000 with a balancing orchestra of 500 in what were billed as "Festivals of the People" in honor of Handel.

And just as there was a continual increase in the performing forces for his *Messiah*, so too Handel's fortune and reputation grew. Toward the end of his life, he occupied a squire's house in the center of London; bought paintings, including a large and "indeed excellent" Rembrandt; and, on his death, left an enormous estate of nearly 20,000 pounds, as the newspapers of the day were quick to report. More than 3,000 persons attended his funeral in Westminster Abbey on April 20, 1759, and a sculpture of the composer holding an aria from *Messiah* was erected above his grave and is still visible today (Fig. 14-6). As a memento of Handel's music, *Messiah* was an apt choice, for it is still performed each year at Christmas and Easter by countless amateur and professional groups throughout the world.

FIGURE 14-5

Eighteenth-century London was a place of biting satire. Here, in William Hogarth's *The Oratorio Singer* (1732), the chorus of an oratorio is the object of parody. But there is an element of truth here: the chorus for the first performance of *Messiah*, for example, numbered about sixteen males, with choirboys (front row) taking the soprano part. Women, however, sang soprano and alto for the vocal solos.

FIGURE 14-6

Handel's funeral monument at Westminster Abbey. The composer holds the aria "I know that my Redeemer liveth" from *Messiah*. When Handel was buried, the gravedigger left room to cram in another body immediately adjacent. That space was later filled by the corpse of Charles Dickens.

@ A complete Checklist of Musical Style for the late Baroque can be found at the text website.

Key WORDS

dance suite (144)	oratorio (146)	pastoral aria (148)
opera seria (146)		

@ The materials on the text website will help you understand and pass tests on the content of this chapter. In addition, you may complete this chapter's Listening Exercise interactively, as well as view Active Listening Guides and other materials that will help you succeed in this course.

PART IV *T*HE CLASSICAL PERIOD, 1750–1820

© The Art Archive/Gianni Dagli Orti

1750	1755	1760	1765	1770	1775	1780	1785

CLASSICAL

1756–1763 Seven Year's War
(French and Indian War)

● 1759 Voltaire publishes Enlightenment novel *Candide*

● 1761 Joseph Haydn takes first job at Esterházy court

● 1762 Rousseau publishes outline for
just government in *The Social Contract*

1763–1766 Mozart family tours and
performs around Western Europe

● 1776 American Declaration of Independence
signed in Philadelphia

● 1781 Mozart moves to
Vienna and composes operas,
symphonies, concertos, and
quartets

During the years 1750–1820, music manifested a style called "Classicism," often termed "Neoclassicism" in the other fine arts. In art and architecture, for example, Neoclassicism aimed to reinstitute the aesthetic values of the ancient Greeks and Romans by incorporating balance and harmonious proportions while avoiding ornate decoration, all leading to a feeling of quiet grace and noble simplicity. When expressed in music, these same tendencies appeared as balanced phrases, lucid textures, and clear, easily audible musical forms. Although composers in cities such as Milan, Paris, and London all wrote symphonies and sonatas with these qualities, the music of this period is often referred to as the "Viennese Classical style." Vienna, Austria, was the capital city of the Holy Roman Empire and the most active center of Classical music in Central Europe. The three principal composers of the Classical era—Joseph Haydn (1732–1809), Wolfgang Amadeus Mozart (1756–1791), and Ludwig van Beethoven (1770–1827)—chose to make Vienna their home because of the city's vibrant musical life. In many ways, Mozart and Haydn created the Classical style while Beethoven extended it. The majority of the works of Beethoven fall within the time frame of the Classical era, but they also sometimes exhibit stylistic characteristics of the succeeding Romantic period.

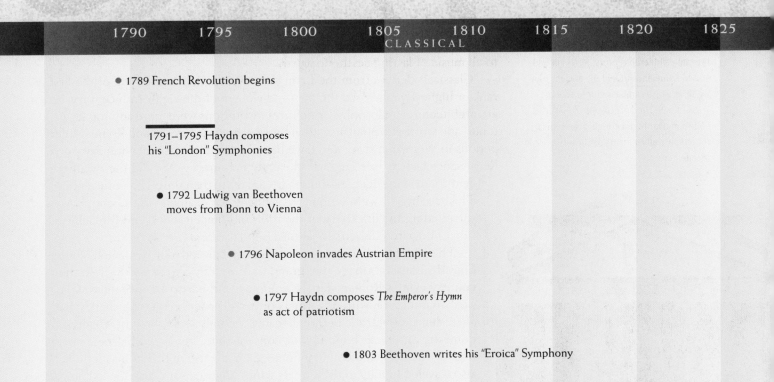

| 1790 | 1795 | 1800 | 1805 | 1810 | 1815 | 1820 | 1825 |

CLASSICAL

● 1789 French Revolution begins

1791–1795 Haydn composes his "London" Symphonies

● 1792 Ludwig van Beethoven moves from Bonn to Vienna

● 1796 Napoleon invades Austrian Empire

● 1797 Haydn composes *The Emperor's Hymn* as act of patriotism

● 1803 Beethoven writes his "Eroica" Symphony

● 1815 Napoleon defeated at Waterloo

●
1824 Beethoven composes his ninth and last symphony

15

CLASSICAL STYLE

Classical as a musical term has two separate, though related, meanings. We use the word *classical* to signify the "serious" or "art" music of the West as distinguished from folk music, popular music, jazz, and the traditional music of various ethnic cultures. We call this music "classical" because there is something about the excellence of its form and style that makes it enduring, just as a finely crafted watch or a vintage automobile may be said to be a "classic" because it has a timeless beauty. Yet in the same breath, we may refer to "Classical" music (now with a capital C), and by this we mean the music of a specific historical period, 1750–1820, a period of the great works of Haydn and Mozart and the early masterpieces of Beethoven. The creations of these artists have become so identified in the public mind with musical proportion, balance, and formal correctness—with standards of musical excellence—that this comparatively brief period has given its name to all music of lasting aesthetic worth.

"Classical" derives from the Latin *classicus*, meaning "something of the first rank or highest quality." To the men and women of the eighteenth century, no art, architecture, philosophy, or political institutions were more admirable, virtuous, and worthy of emulation than those of ancient Greece and Rome. Other periods in Western history also have been inspired by classical antiquity—the Renaissance heavily (see Fig. 9-1), the early Baroque less so, and the twentieth century to some degree—but no period more than the eighteenth century. This fascination with antiquity is evident, for example, in the enthusiasm surrounding the discovery of the ruins of Pompeii (1748) and the publication of Edward Gibbon's *Decline and Fall of the Roman Empire* (1788).

The eighteenth century was also the period during which young English aristocrats made the "grand tour" of Italy and carted back to their country estates Roman statues, columns, and parts of entire villas. Classical architecture, with its formal control of space, geometric shapes, balance, and symmetrical design, became the only style thought worthy for domestic and state buildings of consequence. European palaces, opera houses, theaters, and country homes all made use of it. Thomas Jefferson also traveled to Italy in these years while American ambassador to France, and later brought Classical design to the United States (Figs. 15-1 and 15-2). Our nation's Capitol, many state capitols, and countless other governmental and university buildings abound with the well-proportioned columns, porticos, and rotundas of the Classical style.

FIGURES 15-1 AND 15-2

(top) The second-century Pantheon in Rome. (bottom) The library of the University of Virginia, designed by Thomas Jefferson in the late eighteenth century. Jefferson had visited Rome and studied the ancient ruins while serving as ambassador to France (1784–1789). The portico, with columns and triangular pediment, and the central rotunda are all elements of Classical style in architecture.

THE ENLIGHTENMENT

The Classical era in music, art, and architecture coincides with the period in philosophy and letters known as the **Enlightenment**. During the Enlightenment, also referred to as the Age of Reason, thinkers gave free rein to the pursuit of truth and the discovery of natural laws. This is the era that saw the rise of a natural religion called Deism, the belief that a Creator made the world, set it in motion, and has left it alone ever since. This is also the age of such scientific advances as the discovery of electricity and the invention of the steam engine. The first *Encyclopedia Britannica* appeared in 1771, and the French *Encyclopédie* between 1751 and 1772, a twenty-four-volume set whose authors discarded traditional religious convictions and superstitions in favor of more rational scientific, philosophical, and political beliefs. In France, the encyclopedists Voltaire (1694–1778) and Jean-Jacques Rousseau (1712–1778) espoused the principles of social justice, equality, religious tolerance, and freedom of speech. These Enlightenment ideals subsequently became fundamental to democratic government and were enshrined in the American Constitution.

Needless to say, the notion that all persons are created equal and should enjoy full political freedom put the thinkers of the Enlightenment on a collision course with the defenders of the existing social order. The old political structure had been built on the superstitions of the Church, the privileges of the nobility, and the divine right of kings. Voltaire attacked the habits and prerogatives of both clergy and aristocracy, and championed middle-class virtues: honesty, common sense, and hard work. The extravagant gestures and powdered wigs of the frivolous courtier were easy targets for his pen. A more natural appearance, one appropriate to a tradesman, merchant, or manufacturer, now became the paradigm (Fig. 15-3). Spurred on by economic self-interest and the principles of the Enlightenment philosophers, an expanding, more confident middle class in France and America rebelled against the monarchy and its supporters. The American colonists issued a Declaration of Independence in 1776, and French citizens stormed the Bastille in 1789 to gain weapons, thereby precipitating a civil war among classes. The Age of Reason gave way to the Age of Revolution.

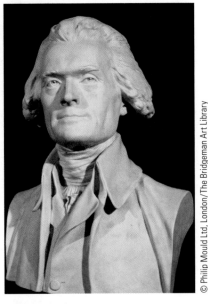

FIGURE 15-3

Thomas Jefferson, by the French sculptor Houdon, done in 1789, the year of the French Revolution.

$\mathcal{M}$USIC AND SOCIAL CHANGE: COMIC OPERA

Music was affected by these profound social changes, and in some ways, it helped to precipitate them. A new form of opera, comic opera, proved to be a powerful vehicle for social reform. Opera in the Baroque period had been dominated by *opera seria* (see p. 146). It was beautiful, grandiose, somewhat stiff, and expensive to mount. Portraying the deeds of mythological gods and goddesses, and historical emperors and kings, it glorified the deeds of the aristocracy. By contrast, the new **comic opera,** called **opera buffa** in Italy, championed middle-class values. It made use of everyday characters and situations; it typically employed spoken dialogue and simple songs in place of recitatives and *da capo* (**ABA**) arias; and it was liberally spiced with sight gags, slapstick antics, and bawdy humor. The librettos, such as they were, either poked fun at the nobility for its pomposity and incompetence or criticized it for being heartless.

Like seditious pamphlets, comic operas appeared across Europe; among them were John Gay's *The Beggar's Opera* (1728) in England, Giovanni Pergolesi's *La serva padrona* (*The Maid Made Master*, 1733) in Italy, and Rousseau's *Le Devin du village* (*The Village Soothsayer*, 1752) in France. Even composers of greater stature were seduced by the charms of this more middle-class entertainment and its anti-aristocratic leanings. Mozart, who was treated poorly by the nobility during his adult life, wrote one opera *Le nozze di Figaro* (*The Marriage of Figaro*,

Watch a video of Craig Wright's Open Yale Course class session 17, "Mozart and His Operas," at the text website.

1786), in which a barber and a maid outsmart a count and hold him up to public ridicule, and in his *Don Giovanni* (1787) the villain is a leading nobleman of the town. The nobility took seriously the threat that such works posed to the established social order; indeed, the play that served as the basis for Mozart's *Figaro* was initially banned by the king of France and the Holy Roman Emperor. By the time of the French Revolution (1789), comic opera, a rebellious upstart, had nearly driven the established *opera seria* off the eighteenth-century stage.

PUBLIC CONCERTS

The social changes of the eighteenth century, in turn, affected who listened to classical music. In an earlier day, the average citizen might have heard sacred vocal music in a church, and that was about all. But by mid-century, the bookkeeper, physician, cloth merchant, and stock trader collectively had enough disposable income to organize and patronize their own concerts. In Paris, then a city of 450,000 residents, one could attend, as proclaimed, "the best concerts every day with complete freedom." The most successful Parisian concert series was the *Concert spirituel* (founded in 1725), at which the West's first noncourt orchestra played a regular schedule of performances, all open to the public. The *Concert spirituel* advertised its performances by means of flyers distributed in the streets. To make its offerings accessible to several strata of society, it also instituted a two-tiered price scheme for a subscription series (four livres for boxes and two livres for the pit; roughly $200 and $100 in today's money). Children under fifteen were admitted for half price. Thus we can trace to the middle of the eighteenth century the tradition of middle-class citizens paying an admission fee and attending a public performance. The institution of the "concert," as we know it today, dates from this time.

In London, entrepreneurs offered concerts in the Vauxhall Gardens, an eighteenth-century amusement park drawing as many as 4,500 paying visitors daily. Here symphonies could be heard inside in the orchestra room, or outside, when the weather was good. When Leopold Mozart took his young son Wolfgang to concerts there in 1764, he was surprised to see that the audience was not segregated by class. Likewise in Vienna, the Burgtheater (City Theater) opened in 1759 to any and all paying customers, as long as they were properly dressed and properly behaved. Although the nobility still occupied the best seats (Fig. 15-4), the doors of the concert hall were now open to the general public, fostering a leveling between classes with respect to all the fine arts. The middle class was seizing control of high culture from the aristocracy. Classical music was becoming public entertainment.

FIGURE 15–4

A performance at the Burgtheater in Vienna in the late 1700s. The nobility occupied the front-most seats on the floor, but the area behind them was open to all. So, too, in the galleries, the aristocracy bought boxes low and close to the stage, while commoners occupied higher rungs, as well as the standing room in the fourth gallery. Ticket prices depended, then as now, on proximity to the performers.

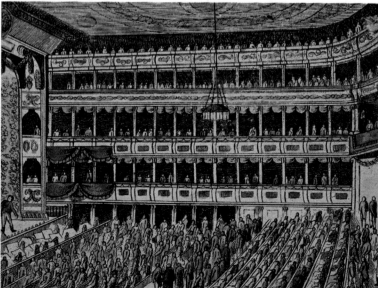

THE ADVENT OF THE PIANO

The newly affluent middle class wished not only to listen to music but also to play it.

Most of this music-making was centered in the home and around an instrument that first entered public consciousness in the Classical period: the piano. Invented in Italy about 1700, the piano gradually replaced the harpsichord as the keyboard instrument of preference (Fig. 15-5)—and with good reason, for the piano could play at more than one dynamic level (hence the original name **pianoforte,** "soft-loud"). Compared with the harpsichord, the piano could produce gradual dynamic changes, more subtle contrasts, and—ultimately—more power.

Those who played this new domestic instrument were mostly amateurs, and the great majority of these were women. A smattering of French, an eye for needlepoint, and some skill at the piano—these were signs of status and gentility that rendered a young woman suitable for marriage. For the nonprofessional woman to play in the home, however, a simpler, more homophonic style of keyboard music was needed, one that would not tax the presumed technical limitations of the performer. The spirit of democracy may have been in the air, but this was still very much a sexist age. It was assumed that ladies would not wish, as one publication said, "to bother their pretty little heads with counterpoint and harmony," but would be content with a tuneful melody and a few rudimentary chords to flesh it out. Collections such as *Keyboard Pieces for Ladies* (1768) were directed at these new musical consumers.

FIGURE 15–5

Marie Antoinette, in 1770 at the age of fifteen, seated at an early piano. In 1774, this Austrian princess became queen of France, but in 1793, at the height of French Revolution, she was beheaded.

ELEMENTS OF CLASSICAL STYLE

Much has been written about the Classical style in music: its quiet grace, noble simplicity, purity, and serenity. It is certainly "classical" in the sense that emphasis is placed on formal clarity, order, and balance. Compared with the relentless, often grandiose sound of the Baroque, Classical music is lighter in tone, more natural, yet less predictable. It is even capable of humor and surprise, as when Joseph Haydn explodes with a thunderous chord in a quiet passage in his "Surprise" Symphony (1791). But what in precise musical terms creates the levity, grace, clarity, and balance characteristic of Classical music?

Melody

Perhaps the first thing that strikes the listener about the music of Haydn or Mozart is that the theme is often tuneful, catchy, even singable. Not only are melodies simple and short, but the phrases tend to be organized in antecedent–consequent, or "question–answer," pairs (see p. 31). (Think of the first two phrases of *Twinkle, Twinkle Little Star,* a folksong set by Mozart.) Indeed, antecedent–consequent phrases appear in significant number for the first time in the history of music during the Classical period. The melody usually progresses by playing out these short phrases in symmetrical groups of two, three, four, eight, twelve, or sixteen bars. The brevity of the phrase and the frequent cadences allow for ample light and air to penetrate the melodic line.

At the top of the next page is the theme from the second movement of Mozart's Piano Concerto in C major (1785). It is composed of two three-bar phrases—an antecedent and a consequent phrase. The melody is light and airy, yet perfectly balanced. It is also singable and quite memorable—indeed, it has been turned into a popular movie theme (the "love song" from *Elvira Madigan*). Contrast this to the long, asymmetrical melodies of the Baroque that were often instrumental in character (see pp. 127, 129, and 134).

EXAMPLE 15–1

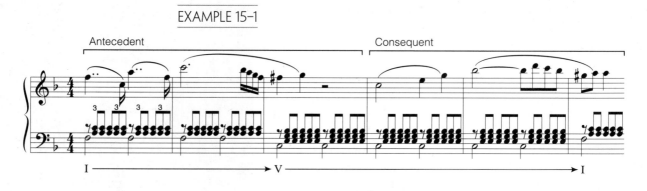

Harmony

After about 1750, all classical music assumed a more homophonic, less polyphonic character. The new tuneful melody was supported by a simple harmony. Note that in Example 15-1 only two chords—tonic (I) and dominant (V)—support Mozart's lovely melody. The heavy *basso continuo* of the Baroque era has disappeared entirely. The bass still generates the harmony, but it does not always move in the regular, constant fashion typified by the Baroque walking bass. Rather, the bass might sit on the bottom of one chord for several beats, even several measures, then move rapidly, and then stop again. Thus, the rate at which chords change—the "harmonic rhythm," as it is called—is much more fluid and flexible with Classical composers.

To avoid a feeling of inactivity when the harmony is static, Classical composers invented new patterns for accompaniment. Sometimes, as in Example 15-1, they simply repeat the accompanying chord in a uniform triplet rhythm. More common is the pattern called the **Alberti bass,** named after the minor Italian keyboard composer Domenico Alberti (1710–1740), who popularized this figure. Instead of playing the pitches of a chord all together, the performer spreads them out to provide a continual stream of sound. Mozart used an Alberti bass at the beginning of his famous C major piano sonata (1788).

EXAMPLE 15–2

The Alberti bass serves essentially the same function as both the modern "boogie-woogie" bass and the process of "tapping" on a guitar (made famous by Metallica). It provides an illusion of harmonic activity for those moments when, in fact, the harmony is stationary.

Rhythm

Rhythm, too, is more flexible in the hands of Haydn and Mozart than it was in the music of the Baroque era, animating the stop-and-go character of Classical melody and harmony. Rapid motion may be followed by repose and then further quick movement, but there is little of the driving, perpetual motion of Baroque musical rhythm.

Texture

Musical texture was also transformed in the latter half of the eighteenth century, mainly because composers began to concentrate less on writing dense counterpoint and more on creating charming melodies. No longer are independent polyphonic lines superimposed, layer upon layer, as in a Baroque fugue of Bach or a polyphonic chorus of Handel. This lessening of counterpoint made for a lighter, more transparent sound, especially in the middle range of the texture (see Ex. 15-1, where chords repeat quietly in the middle between melody and bass). Mozart, after a study of Bach and Handel in the early 1780s, infused his symphonies, quartets, and concertos with greater polyphonic content, but this seems to have caused the pleasure-loving Viennese to think his music too dense!

THE DRAMATIC QUALITY OF CLASSICAL MUSIC

What is perhaps most revolutionary in the music of Haydn, Mozart, and their younger contemporary, Beethoven, is its capacity for rapid change and endless fluctuation. Recall that in earlier times, a work by Purcell, Corelli, Vivaldi, or Bach would establish one "affect," or mood, to be rigidly maintained from beginning to end—the rhythm, melody, and harmony all progressing in a continuous, uninterrupted flow. Such a uniform approach to expression is part of the "single-mindedness" of Baroque art. Now, with Haydn, Mozart, and the young Beethoven, the mood of a piece might change radically within a few short phrases. An energetic theme in rapid notes may be followed by a second one that is slow, lyrical, and tender. Similarly, textures might change quickly from light and airy to dense and more contrapuntal, adding tension and excitement. For the first time, composers began to call for crescendos and diminuendos, a gradual increase or lessening of the dynamic level, so that the volume of sound might continually fluctuate. When skilled orchestras made use of this technique, audiences were fascinated and rose to their feet. Keyboard players, too, now took up the crescendo and diminuendo, assuming that the new, multidynamic piano was at hand in place of the older, less flexible harpsichord. These rapid changes in mood, texture, color, and dynamics give to Classical music a new sense of urgency and drama. The listener feels a constant flux and flow, not unlike the continual swings of mood we all experience.

© Mary Evans Picture Library/The Image Works

FIGURE 15-6

Many major artists of the eighteenth century journeyed to Rome to absorb the ancient classical style, and what they created in painting and architecture we now call "Neoclassicism." Among such classically inspired painters was the Englishwoman Angelica Kauffmann (1741–1807), whose *The Artist [Angelica Kauffmann] in the Character of Design Listening to the Inspiration of Poetry* (1782) shows classical balance (two women and two columns) and ancient symbols (Design holds a drawing board; Poetry holds a lyre and wears the wreath of the poet laureate). The simplicity, balance, and static quality of the painting create a feeling of calm, serenity, and repose, sentiments often felt in Classical music as well.

FIGURE 15–7

Bryn Terfel as the combative and cunning Figaro performs in an English National Opera production of *The Marriage of Figaro*.

An Example of Classical Style

To experience the essence of the Classical style in music, let us turn to an aria from Mozart's comic opera *Le nozze di Figaro* (1786). Recall that the libretto of this opera was taken from a revolutionary play that criticized the aristocracy (see pp. 155–156). It was Mozart's idea to set this play to music, softening only slightly its call for a new social order.

Social tension is immediately apparent at the beginning of the opera. The main character is Figaro (Fig. 15-7), a clever, mostly honest barber and manservant who outwits his lord, the philandering, mostly dishonest Count Almaviva. We first meet Figaro as he discovers that he and his betrothed, Susanna, have been assigned a bedroom next to the Count's. The Count wishes to exercise his ancient *droit de seigneur*—the lord's claim to sexual favors from the servant's fiancée. Figaro responds with a short aria "Se vuol ballare" ("If you want to dance"). Here he calls the Count by the diminutive "Contino," translated roughly as "Count, you little twerp," and vows to outwit his master.

Example 15-3 shows the simplicity, clarity, and balance typical of the Classical style. The texture is light and homophonic—really only supporting chords—as if Figaro were accompanying himself on the guitar. The melody begins with a four-bar phrase that immediately repeats at a higher level of pitch. Formally, the aria consists of four sections: **A**, **B**, **C**, and **D**, with a return to **A** at the end. Section **A** has five four-bar phrases, and so do sections **B** and **C**, while section **D** has twice that number. Although the sections are connected by a measure or two of purely instrumental music, the vocal sections of this aria thus have the proportions 20 + 20 + 20 + 40 + 20—a balanced, "classical" arrangement indeed.

EXAMPLE 15–3

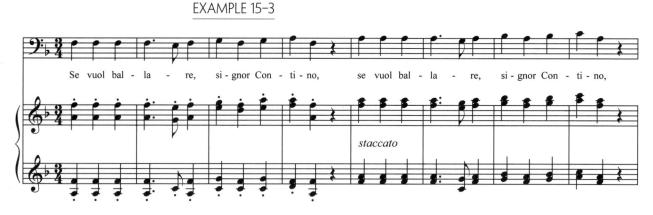

Se vuol bal - la - re, si - gnor Con - ti - no, se vuol bal - la - re, si - gnor Con - ti - no,

staccato

(If you want to dance, Count, you little twerp . . .)

The dynamic quality of Classical music—its capacity to encompass changes of mood—is also evident in Figaro's "Se vuol ballare." Figaro begins in a calm, measured manner, but the more he thinks about the Count's lechery and treachery, the more anxious he becomes. Musically, we hear Figaro's agitation grow throughout sections **A**, **B**, **C**, and **D**, each gaining in intensity. Only at the end does the barber regain his composure, as signaled by the return of **A**. Mozart casts the aria "Se vuol ballare" within the context of a dance—specifically, the courtly minuet. Here dance serves as a metaphor for a shuffling of social order—if the Count wants to "dance" (fool around), Figaro, the servant, will call the tune.

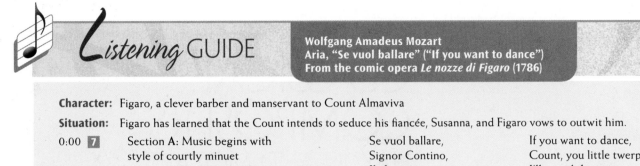

Listening GUIDE

Wolfgang Amadeus Mozart
Aria, "Se vuol ballare" ("If you want to dance")
From the comic opera *Le nozze di Figaro* (1786)

5
2/7

Character: Figaro, a clever barber and manservant to Count Almaviva

Situation: Figaro has learned that the Count intends to seduce his fiancée, Susanna, and Figaro vows to outwit him.

0:00 **7**	Section A: Music begins with style of courtly minuet	Se vuol ballare, Signor Contino, Il chitarrino Le suonerò.	If you want to dance, Count, you little twerp, I'll sound the guitar. (I'll call the tune.)
0:28	Section B: Music becomes slightly more agitated with fluttering strings	Se vuol venire Nella mia scuola, La capriola Le insegnerò.	If you want to come To my dancing school, I'll teach you How to caper.
0:55	Section C: Music becomes much more agitated with racing strings	Saprò . . . ma piano Meglio ogni arcano	I know . . . but quietly All his secrets
1:13	Music assumes dark, sinister tone, changing to minor	Dissimulando Scoprir potrò.	Better by trickery I can discover.

me - glio_o - gni_ar - ca - no dis - si - mu - lan - do sco - prir po - trò.

(I can discover all his secrets better by trickery.)

1:25	Section D: Tempo increases and meter changes to duple	L'arte schermendo, L'arte adoprando, Di qua pungendo, Di là scherzando, Tutte le maccine	Sometimes concealing, Sometimes revealing, Punching here, Feigning there, All your schemes
1:45	Mozart slows down music	Rovescierò.	I'll turn against you.
1:52	Music of section A returns	Se vuol ballare, Signor Contino, Il chitarrino Le suonerò.	If you want to dance, Count, you little twerp, I'll sound the guitar. (I'll call the tune.)
2:18	Orchestral conclusion		

Listen to streaming music in an Active Listening Guide, available on the text website.

@ To take Listening Exercise 22 for this musical selection online and receive feedback or email answers to your instructor, go to the text website.

Key WORDS

Enlightenment (154)	*opera buffa* (155)	Alberti bass (158)
comic opera (155)	*pianoforte* (157)	

@

The materials on the text website will help you understand and pass tests on the content of this chapter. In addition, you may watch Craig Wright's own lecture at Open Yale Courses and complete this chapter's Listening Exercise interactively, as well as view Active Listening Guides and other materials that will help you succeed in this course.

16

CLASSICAL COMPOSERS
HAYDN AND MOZART

We tend to think of the music of the Classical era as the work of just three composers: Haydn, Mozart, and Beethoven. There were, of course, others. At the very beginning of the Classical period, Haydn was greatly influenced by Carl Philipp Emanuel Bach, then residing in Berlin, just as Mozart was by this Bach's half-brother Johann Christian Bach, living in London. (Both Bachs were sons of Baroque master Johann Sebastian Bach.) In the 1790s, the symphonies of Mozart were not as well known in Paris and London as those of Haydn's pupil, Ignace Pleyel. Mozart once played a piano competition against Muzio Clementi, whose sonatas are still studied by beginning pianists today. Haydn's younger brother Michael, who worked in Salzburg, composed a Symphony in G (1783) that was long thought (mistakenly) to be Mozart's. As this confusion suggests, there were other musicians in Europe during the Classical era whose compositional skills were not so much less than those of the three great masters. The best compositions of Haydn, Mozart, and Beethoven, however, belong in a class all their own.

*V*IENNA: A CITY OF MUSIC

FIGURE 16–1
A map of eighteenth-century Europe showing the Holy Roman Empire and the principal musical cities, including Vienna, Austria.

New Orleans jazz, Hollywood film music, and the Broadway musical—these are all names that suggest that a particular locale became the epicenter for the development of a distinctive kind of music. So, too, with the Viennese Classical style. The careers of Haydn, Mozart, Beethoven, and the young Franz Schubert all unfolded in Vienna, and from Vienna radiated their powerful musical influence. For that reason, we often refer to them collectively as the **Viennese School** and say that their music epitomizes the "Viennese Classical style."

Vienna was then the capital of the old Holy Roman Empire, a huge expanse covering much of Western and Central Europe (Fig. 16-1). In 1790, the heyday of Haydn and Mozart, Vienna had a population of 215,000, which made it the fourth-largest city in Europe, after London,

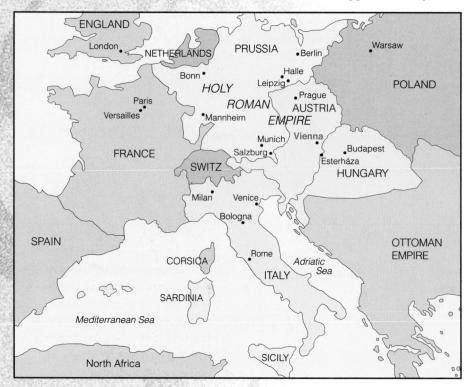

Paris, and Naples. Vienna served as the administrative center for portions of modern-day Germany, Italy, Croatia, Bosnia, Serbia, Slovakia, Poland, Czech Republic, and Hungary, in addition to all of Austria. It was bordered to the east by vast agricultural lands, with no other large city for hundreds of miles. The landowning aristocracy from even as far away as Russia congregated in Vienna, especially during the long winter months when there was little agricultural work to be supervised. The nobles patronized music, often enjoying it together with middle-class citizens at public concerts. There were theaters for German and Italian opera, concerts in the streets on fine summer nights, and ballroom dances (see Fig. 17-1) where as many as 4,000 persons might sway to a minuet or a waltz by Mozart or Beethoven.

With so much musical patronage to offer, Vienna attracted musicians from throughout Europe. Haydn moved there from Lower Austria, Mozart from Upper Austria, his rival Antonio Salieri from Italy, and Beethoven from Bonn, Germany. Later, in the nineteenth century, in addition to native-born Franz Schubert, outsiders such as Anton Bruckner, Johannes Brahms, and Gustav Mahler spent many of their most productive years there. Even today Vienna remains the capital of a nation (Austria) that spends nearly as much money on its state opera as it does on national defense.

$\mathcal{F}$RANZ JOSEPH HAYDN (1732–1809)

Joseph Haydn was the first of the great composers to move to Vienna, and his life offers something of a "rags-to-riches" story (Fig. 16-2). Haydn was born in 1732 in a farmhouse in Rohrau, Austria, about twenty-five miles east of Vienna. His father, a wheelwright, played the harp but could not read music. When the choir director of Saint Stephen's Cathedral in Vienna happened to be scouting

FIGURE 16-2

Portrait of Joseph Haydn (c1762–1763) wearing a wig and the blue livery of the Esterházy court.

for talent in the provinces, he heard the boy soprano Haydn sing and, impressed by his musicianship, brought him back to the cathedral in Vienna. Here Haydn remained as a choirboy, studying the rudiments of composition and learning to play the violin and keyboard. After nearly ten years of service, his voice broke and he was abruptly dismissed. For most of the 1750s, Haydn eked out a "wretched existence," as he called it, working as a freelance musician around Vienna. He gave keyboard lessons, accompanied singers, and sang or played violin or organ at three churches each Sunday, moving quickly from one to the next. In 1761, Haydn's years of struggle ended when he was engaged as director of music at the Esterházy court.

The **Esterházy family** was the richest and most influential among the German-speaking aristocrats of Hungary, with extensive landholdings southeast of Vienna and a passionate interest in music. At the family seat at Esterháza (see Fig. 16-1), Prince Nikolaus Esterházy (1714–1790) constructed a palace (Fig. 16-3) influenced by that of King Louis XIV at Versailles. Here he maintained an orchestra, a chapel for singing religious music, and a theater for opera. As was typical of the period, Prince Nikolaus engaged Haydn to be a musical servant at the court and wear servants' dress (see Fig. 16-2). Haydn also was required to sign a contract of employment, one that suggests the subservient place of the composer in eighteenth-century society:

© Imagno/Getty Images

FIGURE 16–3

The palace of the Esterházy family southeast of Vienna, where Joseph Haydn lived until 1790. The elements of Neoclassical architectural style include the triangular pediment over the entryway, the columns, and the Ionic capitals atop the flat columns.

[He] and all the musicians shall appear in uniform, and the said Joseph Haydn shall take care that he and all the members of the orchestra follow the instructions given, and appear in white stocking, white linen, powdered, and with either a pigtail or a tiewig. . . .

The said [Haydn] shall be under obligation to compose such music as his Serene Highness may command, and neither to communicate such compositions to any other person, nor to allow them to be copied, but he shall retain them for the absolute use of his Highness, and not compose for any other person without the knowledge and permission of his Highness.

Haydn was thus prohibited from circulating his music without the express permission of his patron. But somehow his symphonies, quartets, and sonatas began to make their way to Vienna and other foreign capitals, much like "file sharing" today. In the 1770s, they surfaced in Amsterdam, London, and Paris in unauthorized editions. Since there was no international copyright law in those years, a publisher could simply print a work from a copyist's score without the composer's knowledge or consent and without paying royalties. When Haydn signed another contract with Prince Nikolaus in 1779, there was no such "exclusive use" provision, and he began to sell his works to various publishers, sometimes consigning the same piece to two or three at the same time!

For a period of nearly thirty years, Haydn served Nikolaus Esterházy, writing symphonies and divertimentos for evening entertainment, operas for the court theater, and string trios in which the prince himself might participate. When Nikolaus died in 1790, the Esterházy orchestra was dismissed in favor of a smaller concert band. Haydn retained his title as court composer, as well as his full salary, but he was now free to travel as he wished. After settling briefly in Vienna, he journeyed to London, where he had been engaged at a substantial fee to compose and conduct. From this commission resulted the twelve **London Symphonies** (Nos. 93–104), which were first performed in the Hanover Square Rooms (see Fig. 18-2), a large public concert hall built in part with capital supplied by Johann Christian Bach, old Bach's youngest son. Haydn stayed in London during 1791–1792 and returned again for the concert season in 1794–1795. He was presented to the king and queen, received the honorary degree of doctor of music at Oxford, and was generally accorded the status of a visiting celebrity, as a letter written within two weeks of his arrival attests:

Everyone wants to know me. I had to dine out six times up to now, and if I wanted, I could have an invitation every day; but first I must consider my health and second my work. Except for the nobility, I admit no callers 'til 2 o'clock in the afternoon.

In the summer of 1795, Haydn returned from London to Vienna a wealthy man. From his activities in London, he had netted 24,000 Austrian gulden, the equivalent about 1.2 million U.S. dollars in money of today—not bad for the son of a wheel maker. Haydn also returned from England with an abiding love of the oratorios of Handel, and among his last completed works are his own two oratorios, *The Creation* (1798) and *The Seasons* (1801). When he died on May 31, 1809, at the age of seventy-seven, he was the most respected composer in Europe.

Haydn's long life, commitment to duty, and unflagging industry resulted in an impressive number of musical compositions: 104 symphonies, about 70 string quartets, nearly a dozen operas, 52 piano sonatas, 14 Masses, and 2 oratorios. He began composing before the death of Bach (1750) and did not put down his pen until about the time Beethoven set to work on his Fifth Symphony (1808). Thus, Haydn not only witnessed but, more than any other composer, helped to create the mature Classical style.

Despite his accomplishments, Haydn did not rebel against the modest station assigned to him in traditional eighteenth-century society: "I have associated with emperors, kings, and many great people," he said, "and I have heard many flattering things from them, but I would not live in familiar relations with such persons; I prefer to be close to people of my own standing." And though keenly aware of his own musical gifts, he was quick to recognize talent in others, especially Mozart: "Friends often flatter me that I have some genius, but he [Mozart] stood far above me."

© Alinari/The Bridgeman Art Library

FIGURES 16–4 AND 16–5

(top) An unfinished portrait of Mozart painted by his brother-in-law Joseph Lange during 1789–1790. (bottom) The child Mozart at the keyboard, with his sister Nannerl and his father Leopold, in Paris in 1764 during their three-year tour of Europe.

WOLFGANG AMADEUS MOZART (1756–1791)

Indeed who, except possibly Bach, could match Mozart's diversity, breadth of expression, and perfect formal control? Wolfgang Amadeus Mozart (Fig. 16-4) was born in 1756 in the mountain town of **Salzburg,** Austria, then a city of about 20,000 residents. His father, Leopold Mozart, was a violinist in the orchestra of the archbishop of Salzburg and the author of a best-selling introduction to playing the violin. Leopold was quick to recognize the musical gifts of his son, who by the age of six was playing the piano, violin, and organ, as well as composing. In 1762, the Mozart family coached off to Vienna, where Wolfgang and his older sister Nannerl displayed their musical wares before Empress Maria Theresa (1717–1780). They then embarked on a three-year tour of Northern Europe that included extended stops in Munich, Brussels, Paris, London, Amsterdam, and Geneva (Fig. 16-5). In London, Wolfgang sat on the knee of Johann Christian Bach (1735–1782) and improvised a fugue. And here, at the age of eight, he wrote his first two symphonies. Eventually, the Mozarts made their way back to Salzburg. But in 1768, they were off again to Vienna, where the now twelve-year-old Wolfgang staged a production of his first opera, *Bastien und Bastienne,* in the home of the famous Dr. Franz Anton Mesmer (1734–1815), the inventor of the theory of animal magnetism (hence, "to mesmerize"). The next year father and son visited the major cities of Italy, including Rome, where, on July 8, 1770, the pope dubbed

©British Library Board, London/The Bridgeman Art Library

AMADEO WOLFGANGO MOZART ACCAD. FILARMON: DI BOLO VERONA.

© Alinari/The Bridgeman Art Library

FIGURE 16–6

Young Mozart proudly wearing the collar of a Knight of the Order of the Golden Spur, an honor conferred upon him for his musical skills by Pope Clement XIV in July 1770.

Wolfgang a Knight of the Order of the Golden Spur (Fig. 16-6). Although the aim of all this globe-trotting was to acquire fame and fortune, the result was that Mozart, unlike Haydn, was exposed at an early age to a wealth of musical styles—French Baroque, English choral, German polyphonic, and Italian vocal. His extraordinarily keen ear absorbed them all, and ultimately, they increased the breadth and substance of his music.

A period of relative stability followed: for much of the 1770s, Mozart resided in Salzburg, where he served as organist, violinist, and composer to the archbishop. But the reigning archbishop, Colloredo, was a stern, frugal man who had little sympathy for Mozart, genius or not (the composer referred to him as the "Archboobie"). Mozart was given a place in the orchestra, a small salary, and his board. Like the musicians at the court of Esterházy, those at Salzburg ate with the cooks and valets. For a Knight of the Golden Spur who had hobnobbed with kings and queens across Europe, this was humble fare indeed, and Mozart chafed under this system of aristocratic patronage. After several unpleasant scenes in the spring of 1781, the twenty-five-year-old composer goaded the archbishop into firing him and set out to make his living as a freelance musician in Vienna.

Mozart chose Vienna partly because of the city's rich musical life and partly because it was a comfortable distance from his overbearing father. In a letter to his sister written in the spring of 1782, Wolfgang spells out his daily regimen in the Austrian capital:

My hair is always done by six o'clock in the morning and by seven I am fully dressed. I then compose until nine. From nine to one I give lessons. Then I lunch, unless I am invited to some house where they lunch at two or even three o'clock. . . . I can never work before five or six o'clock in the evening, and even then I am often prevented by a concert. If I am not prevented, I compose until nine. Then I go to my dear Constanze.

Against the advice of his father, Wolfgang married his "dear Constanze" (Weber) in the summer of 1782. But, alas, she was as romantic and impractical as he, though less given to streaks of hard work. In addition to his composing, teaching, and performing, Mozart now found time to study the music of Bach and Handel, play chamber music with his friend Joseph Haydn, and join the **Freemasons.** Although still very much a practicing Catholic, he

FIGURE 16–7

This still from the spectacularly good Academy Award–winning film *Amadeus* (1985) shows "Mozart" composing at a billiard table. Mozart did in fact keep a billiard table in his bedroom. But in most other ways, the portrayal of Mozart in *Amadeus* is largely fictitious. Mozart was not an irresponsible idiot-savant who died penniless, but a highly intelligent entrepreneur whose income fluctuated wildly from year to year; moreover, he was not poisoned by his rival, composer Antonio Salieri (1750–1825). But *Amadeus* does pose an intriguing question: What does a mediocre or even somewhat gifted person (Salieri) do when faced with an absolute genius (Mozart)?

Saul Zaentz Company/The Kobal Collection

was attracted to this fraternity of the Enlightenment because of its belief in tolerance and universal brotherhood. His opera *Die Zauberflöte* (*The Magic Flute,* 1791) is viewed by many as a hymn in praise of Masonic ideals.

The years 1785–1787 witnessed the peak of Mozart's success and the creation of many of his greatest works. He had a full complement of pupils, played several concerts a week, and enjoyed lucrative commissions as a composer. Piano concertos, string quartets, and symphonies flowed from his pen, as did his two greatest Italian operas, *The Marriage of Figaro* and *Don Giovanni.*

But *Don Giovanni,* a huge success when first performed in Prague in 1787, was little appreciated when mounted in Vienna in the spring of 1788. "The opera is divine, perhaps even more beautiful than *Figaro*," declared Emperor Joseph II, "but no food for the teeth of my Viennese." Mozart's music was no longer in vogue with the nobility. His style was thought to be too dense, too intense, and too dissonant. One publisher warned him: "Write in a more popular style or else I cannot print or pay for more of your music."

In his last year (1791), despite declining health, Mozart was still capable of creating the greatest sort of masterpieces. He composed a superb clarinet concerto and *The Magic Flute,* and began work on a Requiem Mass, one he was never to finish (it was completed by a pupil, Franz Süssmayr). Mozart died unexpectedly on December 5, 1791, at the age of thirty-five. The precise reason for his death has never been determined, though rheumatic fever and kidney failure, made worse by needless blood-letting, are the most likely causes. No single event in the history of music is more regrettable than the premature loss of Mozart. We might think that Michael Jackson died young, but he outlived Mozart by fifteen years.

Key WORDS

Viennese School (162)
Esterházy family (163)
London Symphonies (164)
Salzburg (165)
Freemasons (166)

The materials on the text website will help you understand and pass tests on the content of this chapter.

17

CLASSICAL FORMS
TERNARY AND
SONATA–ALLEGRO

How did composers of the Classical period reconcile the Classical principles of order and balance with their urge to create a more dramatic style of music—music with more contrast in volume, color, and tempo? They did so, in a word, by means of form. In the Classical period, more than any other in the history of music, a small number of forms—ternary, sonata–allegro, rondo, and theme and variations—regulated nearly all art music. At the same time, none of these forms was unique to the Classical period. Ternary form can be found in the earliest examples of Gregorian chant and in the Baroque *da capo* aria. The rondo had its origins in the popular dances of the Middle Ages, and its repetitive structure has made it attractive to such diverse musicians as Mozart, Beethoven, Elton John, and Sting (see boxed essay on p. 186). Only sonata–allegro form actually came into being in the Classical period. It dominated musical structure during the time of Mozart and Haydn, and remained a potent force in the works of most composers of the Romantic era (1820–1900) and in the creations of some twentieth-century musicians as well. Thus, the forms discussed in this chapter should be thought of not as belonging to the Classical period alone, but in the broader meaning of "classical music." With the single exception of sonata–allegro form, all recur in eras and genres throughout the history of Western music.

Watch a video of Craig Wright's Open Yale Course class session 9, on ternary and sonata–allegro forms, at the text website.

TERNARY FORM

Ternary structure is a simple arrangement (**ABA**—"home-away-home") that can serve as a useful introduction to the more complex sonata–allegro form discussed later in this chapter. Classical composers favored **ternary form** for its simplicity and directness. Everyone is familiar with the music of the French folk song *Ah, vous dirai-je, Maman* (*Ah, Let Me Tell You, Mama*), though we recognize the tune as *Twinkle, Twinkle, Little Star* (also the tune of *Baa, Baa, Black Sheep* and *A, B, C, D, E, F, G*). Wolfgang Amadeus Mozart came to know the melody when he toured France as a youth, and he composed a setting for keyboard.

EXAMPLE 17–1

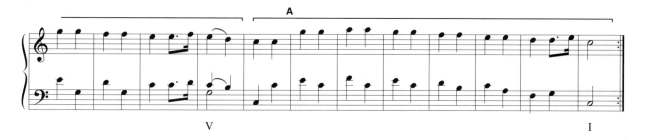

Notice that both units (**A** and **BA**) are repeated (see repeat sign). Observe also that **A** is in the tonic, **B** emphasizes a contrasting key (here the dominant), and the returning **A** is again in the tonic (these harmonies are indicated by the roman numerals I and V). If a piece in ternary form is in a minor key, the contrasting **B** section is usually in what is called the **relative major.*** Needless to say, most pieces in ternary form are more complex than *Twinkle, Twinkle*. Most have more contrast of melody, key, and/or mood between the **B** section and the surrounding units of **A**.†

Minuet and Trio

Sometimes popular dance music grows so popular that it becomes stylized to the point that it evolves into classical music—in a word, "dance music" becomes "listening music." That is the history of the **minuet,** a stately dance in triple meter, which began in the Baroque era as a popular dance (Fig. 17-1) and ended as a stylized (for listening only) movement within a classical symphony or string quartet. At the time of Haydn and Mozart, the minuet served for both dancing (Fig. 17-2) and listening. What in 1670 had been a dance in binary form (**AB**) by 1770 had grown into a ternary (**ABA**) movement, and the return home to **A** had become a major listening event. Traditionally, one minuet was grouped with a second possessing a much lighter texture. Because this second minuet had originally been played by only three instruments, it was called the **trio,** a name that persisted into the nineteenth century, no matter how many instrumental lines were required. Once the trio was finished, convention dictated a return to the first minuet, now performed without repeats. Because the trio also was composed in ternary form, an **ABA** pattern was heard three times in succession. (In the following, the **ABA** structure of the trio is represented by **CDC**, to distinguish

FIGURE 17–1

A ball at the Redoutensaal (dancing hall) in the emperor's palace in Vienna, c1800. Mozart, Haydn, and, later, Beethoven composed minuets and "German dances" for these events, which sometimes attracted nearly 4,000 fee-paying dancers. The orchestra can be seen in the gallery to the left. The Redoutensaal still provides a venue for concerts and balls today.

© Erich Lessing/Art Resource, NY

---

*Relative keys are keys that share the same key signature—E♭ major and C minor (both with three flats), for example.
†Note for instructors: on the designation "ternary form" for this and other pieces, see the Preface of this book.

it from the minuet.) And, because the trio was different from the surrounding minuet, the entire minuet–trio–minuet movement formed an **ABA** arrangement:

A (minuet)   B (trio)   A (minuet)

‖: A :‖ ‖: BA :‖   ‖: C :‖ ‖: DC :‖   ABA

Mozart's *Eine kleine Nachtmusik* (*A Little Night Music*), written in the summer of 1787, is among his most popular works. It is a **serenade,** a light, multimovement piece for strings alone or small orchestra, one intended for an evening's entertainment and often performed outdoors. Although we do not know the precise occasion for which Mozart composed it, we might well imagine *Eine kleine Nachtmusik* providing the musical backdrop for a torch-lit party in a formal Viennese garden. The *Menuetto* appears as the third of four movements in this serenade and is a model of grace and concision.

FIGURE 17–2

Couples in the late eighteenth century dancing the stately minuet. In some areas of Europe at this time, women were forbidden to dance the minuet because it was thought to involve excessive body contact!

EXAMPLE 17–2

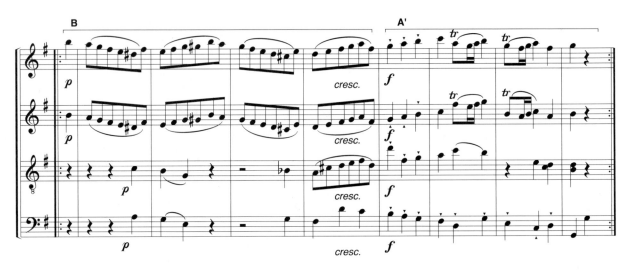

As you can see, the **B** section is only four measures long, and the return to **A** does not reproduce the full eight bars of the original but only the last four—thus, this pattern might be viewed as **ABA´**. In the trio that follows, a lighter texture is created as the first violin plays a solo melody quietly above a soft accompaniment in the lower strings. The **D** section of the trio is distinguished by a *forte* stepwise run up and down the scale, and then the quiet melody of **C** returns to complete the ternary form. Finally, the minuet appears once again, but now without repeats.

Listening GUIDE

Wolfgang Amadeus Mozart
Eine kleine Nachtmusik (*A Little Night Music*, 1787)
Third movement, Minuet and Trio

⑤ ②
2/11 1/16

Genre: Serenade

Form: Ternary

MINUET

				Number of Bars
0:00	11 16	A	Strong violin melody with active bass	8
0:09			Repeat of A	
0:19		B	Softer violin scales	4
0:24		A´	Return of violin melody	4
0:28			Repeat of B and A´	

TRIO

0:38		C	Soft, stepwise melody in violin	8
0:49			Repeat of C	
1:00		D	Louder violins	4
1:05		C	Return of soft stepwise melody	8
1:17			Repeat of D and C	

MINUET

1:33		A	Return of A	8
1:43		B	Return of B	4
1:48		A´	Return of violin melody A´	4

Listen to streaming music in an Active Listening Guide, available on the text website.

We have said that Classical music is symmetrical and proportional. Note here how both minuet and trio are balanced by a return of the opening music (**A** and **C**) and how all the sections are either four or eight bars in length.

If Mozart's *Menuetto* represents the minuet in its most succinct form, the minuet of Haydn's Symphony No. 94 (the "Surprise" Symphony) offers a more typically symphonic presentation of this ternary design. The form is considerably extended, in part because Haydn was writing for a full orchestra rather than the small string ensemble of Mozart's serenade. (It is axiomatic in music that the larger the performing force, the more extended the musical form.) Notice at the end of **B** how Haydn builds up great expectation—and holds us back by means of a static pedal point (at 0:50)—before delivering the longed-for return home to **A**. This is the central "emotional event" of the movement.

Listening GUIDE

Franz Joseph Haydn
Symphony No. 94, the "Surprise"
Symphony (1791)
Third movement, Minuet and Trio

5

2/12–13

Genre: Symphony

Form: Ternary

MINUET [   ] = repeats

0:00	12		A	Rollicking dance in triple meter begins
0:17				Repeat of A
0:34		[1:21]	B	Imitation and lighter texture
0:43		[1:30]		Strong harmonic movement
0:50		[1:37]		Bass sits on dominant pedal point
0:56		[1:43]	A´	Return of A
1:03		[1:50]		Pause on dominant chord
1:13		[1:59]		Gentle rocking over tonic pedal point

TRIO

2:08	13	[0:00]	C	Light descending scales for violins and bassoon
2:16		[0:08]		Repeat of C
2:26		[0:17] [0:37]	D	Two-voice counterpoint for 1st and 2nd violins
2:35		[0:27] [0:47]	C	Bassoon reentry signals return of C

MINUET

3:06		[0:58]	A	Return to minuet
3:22		[1:14]	B	Return of B
3:43		[1:35]	A´	Return of A

Listen to streaming music in an Active Listening Guide, available on the text website.

SONATA–ALLEGRO FORM

Most stories and plays have a stereotypical form: setup, complication, resolution. So, too, with sonata–allegro form, which came into being around 1750 as a means of incorporating more drama and conflict into a single movement of music. Like a great play, a movement in sonata–allegro form has the potential for dramatic presentation (**A**), conflict (**B**), and resolution (**A**). Sonata–allegro form would continue to serve composers into the Romantic period and beyond. Thus, there is no way around it: to understand the core of classical music, we must understand sonata–allegro form.

At the outset, however, it is important to distinguish between the general term *sonata* and the more specific *sonata–allegro form*—that is, between the multimovement genre, the sonata, and the single-movement form, sonata–allegro. When a solo piano or some other solo instrument accompanied by piano plays a three- or four-movement work (fast-slow-fast, for example), that genre in classical music is called a sonata. By contrast, when a string quartet or an orchestra plays a three- or four-movement work, the genre is not referred to as a sonata but rather as a quartet or a symphony. Sonata, then, is a *genre* for solo instrument; sonata–allegro, however, is a *form* giving structure to a single movement of any one of several genres: sonata, string quartet, symphony, even a one-movement overture.

Let's take a typical four-movement symphony of the Classical period. The form of the first movement is almost invariably composed in **sonata–allegro**

form. The first half of the term ("sonata") derives, obviously, from the fact that most sonatas feature this form in their first movement, while the second ("allegro") refers to the standard practice of setting this first movement to a fast tempo. Although the slow second movements and fast finales of Classical compositions are sometimes written in sonata–allegro form as well, they often make use of other forms, such as rondo or theme and variations (both discussed in Chapter 18). If there are four movements, the third is usually a minuet with trio, and thus in ternary form. To make sense of this, consider the movements and forms of Mozart's *Eine kleine Nachtmusik* and Haydn's Symphony No. 94:

Mozart, *Eine kleine Nachtmusik* (1787)

Fast	Slow	Minuet and Trio	Fast
Sonata–allegro	Rondo	Ternary	Rondo

Haydn, Symphony No. 94 (1791)

Fast	Slow	Minuet and Trio	Fast
Sonata–allegro	Theme and variations	Ternary	Sonata–allegro

The Shape of Sonata–Allegro Form

To get a sense of what might happen in a typical first movement of a sonata, string quartet, symphony, or serenade, look at the diagram below. As with all models of this sort, this one is an ideal, an abstraction of what commonly occurs in sonata–allegro form. It is not a blueprint for any composition. Composers have exhibited countless individual solutions to the task of writing in this and every other form. Yet such a model can be of great use to the listener because it gives a clear picture of what we might expect to hear. Ultimately, once we have embraced the form and are familiar with its workings, we will take as much delight in having our musical expectations foiled or delayed as in having them fulfilled.

SONATA–ALLEGRO FORM

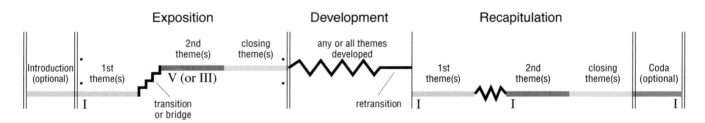

In its broad outline, sonata–allegro form looks much like ternary form. It consists of an **ABA** plan, with the **B** section providing contrast in mood, key, and thematic treatment. The initial **A** in sonata–allegro form is called the exposition, the **B** the development, and the return to **A** the recapitulation. In the early Classical period, the exposition (**A**) and the development and recapitulation (**BA**) were each repeated, as in ternary form. But Haydn and Mozart eventually dropped the repeat of the development and recapitulation, and composers of the Romantic period gradually dispensed with the repeat of the exposition. Let's examine each of these sections in turn and learn what we are likely to hear.

EXPOSITION

In the **exposition,** the composer presents the main themes (or musical personalities) of the movement. It begins with the first theme or theme group and is always in the tonic key. Next comes the **transition,** or **bridge** as it is sometimes called, which carries the music from the tonic to the dominant (from tonic to relative major if the movement is in a minor key) and prepares for the arrival of the second theme. Often the transition is composed of rapid figural patterns—scales, arpeggios, and melodic sequences—giving us a feeling of movement. The second theme typically contrasts in character with the first; if the first is rapid and assertive, the second may be more languid and lyrical. The exposition usually concludes with a closing theme (or group of themes), often simply oscillating between dominant and tonic chords—not much is happening harmonically, so we must be near the end. After the final cadence, the exposition is repeated in full. We've now met all the "characters" of the piece; let's see how things develop.

DEVELOPMENT

If sonata–allegro is a dramatic musical form, most of the drama comes in the **development.** As the name indicates, a further working out, or "developing," of the thematic material occurs here. The themes can be extended and varied, or wholly transformed; a character we thought we knew can turn out to have a completely different personality. Dramatic confrontation can occur, as when several themes sound together, fighting for our attention. The contrapuntal possibilities lurking within a theme might emerge, with the composer using it as the subject of a brief fugue. (A fugue within a movement of a sonata is called a **fugato.**) Not only are developments dramatic, they are unstable and unsettling, the harmony typically modulating quickly from one key to the next. Only toward the end of the development, in the passage called the **retransition,** is tonal order restored, often by means of a stabilizing pedal point on the dominant note. When the dominant chord (V) finally gives way to the tonic (I), the recapitulation begins.

RECAPITULATION

After the turmoil of the development, the listener greets the return of the first theme and the tonic key of the exposition with welcome relief. Though the **recapitulation** is not an exact, note-for-note repetition of the exposition, it nonetheless presents the same musical events in the same order. The only change that regularly occurs in this restatement is the rewriting of the transition, or bridge. Because the movement must end in the tonic, the bridge does not modulate to the dominant (or relative major) as before, but stays at home in the tonic key. Thus, the recapitulation imparts to the listener not only a feeling of return to familiar surroundings but also an increased sense of harmonic stability, as all themes are now heard in the tonic key. We've gone on a great musical (and emotional) journey and are now back home safe and sound.

The following two elements are optional to sonata–allegro form, functioning something akin to a preface and an epilogue.

INTRODUCTION

About half the mature symphonies of Haydn and Mozart have brief introductions before the exposition begins. (That the introduction is not part of the

exposition is shown by the fact that it is never repeated.) These are, without exception, slow and stately, and usually filled with ominous or puzzling chords designed to get the listener wondering what sort of musical excursion he or she is about to undertake.

CODA

As the name **coda** (Italian for "tail") indicates, this is a section added to the end of the movement to wrap things up. Like tails, codas can be long or short. Haydn and Mozart wrote relatively short codas in which a motive might simply be repeated again and again in conjunction with repeating dominant-tonic chords. Beethoven, however, was inclined to compose lengthy codas, sometimes introducing new themes even at the end of the movement. But no matter how long the coda, most will end with a final cadence in which the harmonic motion slows down to just two chords, dominant and tonic, played over and over, as if to say "the end, the end, the end, THE END." The more these repeat, the greater the feeling of conclusion.

FIGURE 17–3

Jazz artist and improv singer Bobby McFerrin conducting the St. Paul Chamber Orchestra. McFerrin has conducted orchestras around the world and issued several recordings of Mozart, including his *Eine kleine Nachtmusik*, heard in the Listening Guide.

Hearing Sonata–Allegro Form

Why all this attention to sonata–allegro form? First, because it is absolutely central to the core repertoire of Classical music and beyond—Haydn, Mozart, Beethoven, Schubert, Tchaikovsky, Brahms, Mahler, Shostakovich: they all used it. And second, because sonata–allegro form is the most complex and difficult of the classical forms to follow. A sonata–allegro movement tends to be long, lasting anywhere from four minutes in a simple composition from the Classical period, to twenty minutes or more in a full-blown movement of the Romantic era.

Listen to a series of iAudio podcasts on hearing sonata–allegro form at the text website.

How does one tame this musical beast? First, be sure to memorize the diagram of sonata–allegro form given on page 173. Next, sharpen your ability to grasp and remember melodies. (If necessary, return to Chapter 3 and practice recognizing melodies by redoing Listening Exercise 3.) Finally, think carefully about the four distinctive styles of writing found in sonata–allegro form: thematic, transitional, developmental, and cadential. A thematic passage has a clearly recognizable theme, often a singable tune. The transition is full of motion, with melodic sequences and rapid chord changes. The development sounds harmonically active, is full of counterpoint, and makes use of a recognizable theme (or themes), albeit either extended in length or reduced to short motives. Finally, a cadential passage, coming at the end of a section or the end of the piece, sounds repetitious because the same chords are heard again and again in a harmony that seems to have stopped moving forward. Each of these four styles has a specific function within sonata–allegro form: to state, to move, to develop, or to conclude.

See a fascinating interaction between Mozart's *Eine kleine Nachtmusik* and the musical style of Bobby McFerrin in the YouTube playlist on the text website.

To test our ability to follow along in a movement composed in sonata–allegro form, we turn to the first movement of Mozart's *Eine kleine Nachtmusik*. The following Listening Guide is not typical of this book. It is unusually lengthy so as to lead you through the difficult process of hearing sonata–allegro form. First, read the description in the center column; then listen to the music, stopping where indicated to rehear each of the principal sections of the form. Likely this movement, one of the favorites in the classical repertoire, will seem like an old friend. Its sophisticated sounds have been used as background music in countless radio and TV commercials to suggest that the product is "high end"—we associate expensive items with Classical elegance.

*L*istening GUIDE

Wolfgang Amadeus Mozart
Eine kleine Nachtmusik (1787)
First movement, *Allegro* (fast)

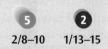

2/8–10   1/13–15

Genre: Serenade

Form: Sonata–allegro

FIRST THEME GROUP [ ] = repeats

0:00   **8** **13**   [1:37]   The movement opens aggressively with a leaping, fanfare-like motive. It then moves on to a more confined, pressing melody with sixteenth notes agitating beneath, and ends with a relaxed, stepwise descent down the G major scale, which is repeated with light ornamentation.

STOP: LISTEN TO THE FIRST THEME GROUP AGAIN

TRANSITION

0:30   [2:08]   This starts with two quick turns and then races up the scale in repeating sixteenth notes. The bass is at first static, but when it finally moves, it does so with great urgency, pushing the modulation forward to a cadence. The stage is then cleared by a brief pause, allowing the listener an "unobstructed view" of the new theme that is about to enter.

0:30	[2:08]	Rapid scales
0:40	[2:18]	Bass moves
0:45	[2:21]	Cadence and pause

STOP: LISTEN TO THE TRANSITION AGAIN

SECOND THEME

0:48   [2:24]   With its *piano* dynamic level and separating rests, the second theme sounds soft and delicate. It is soon overtaken by a light, somewhat humorous closing theme.

STOP: LISTEN TO THE SECOND THEME AGAIN

CLOSING THEME

1:01   [2:37]   The light quality of this melody is produced by its repeating note and the simple rocking of dominant-to-tonic harmony below. Toward the end, more substance is added when the music turns *forte*, and counterpoint appears in the bass. The bass's closing theme is then repeated, and a few cadential chords are tacked on to bring the exposition to an end.

1:07	[2:44]	Loud; counterpoint in bass
1:14	[2:51]	Closing theme repeated
1:33	[3:09]	Cadential chords

STOP: LISTEN TO THE CLOSING THEME AGAIN

1:37–3:12   The exposition is now repeated.

DEVELOPMENT

3:13   **9** **14**   0:00   Just about anything can happen in a development, so the listener had best be on guard. Mozart begins with the fanfare-like first theme again in unison, as if this were yet another statement of the exposition. But abruptly the theme is altered and the tonal center slides up to a new key. Now the closing theme is heard, but soon it, too, begins to slide tonally, down through several keys that sound increasingly remote and bizarre. From this arises a unison scale (all parts move up stepwise together) in a dark-sounding minor key. The dominant note is held, first on top in the violins and then in the bass (0:33). This is the retransition. The

0:00	First theme developed
0:04	Quick modulation
0:07	Closing theme developed
0:16	More modulations
0:24	Rising scale in unison
0:33	Retransition: held note (dominant) in violins and then bass

mode changes from dark minor to bright major, and the
first theme returns forcefully in the tonic key, signaling the
beginning of the recapitulation.

STOP: LISTEN TO THE DEVELOPMENT AGAIN

RECAPITULATION

3:48 🔟 0:00   It is this "double return" of both the tonic key and the first theme that makes the arrival of this and all recapitulations so satisfying. We expect the recapitulation to more or less duplicate the exposition, and this one holds true to form. The only change comes, as usual, in the transition, or bridge, where the modulation to the dominant is simply omitted—there's no need to modulate to the dominant since tradition demands that the second theme and the closing theme appear in the tonic.

0:00	Loud return of first theme
0:30	Transition much abbreviated
0:44	Second theme
0:57	Closing theme
1:11	Closing theme repeated
1:29	Cadential chords

CODA

5:26   1:31   After the cadential chords that ended the exposition are heard again, a brief coda begins. It makes use of a fanfare motive that strongly resembles that of the opening theme, but this one is supported below by a pounding tonic chord that drives home the feeling that the movement has come to an appropriate end.

Listen to streaming music in an Active Listening Guide, available on the text website.

What we have just heard is an example of sonata–allegro form in miniature. Rarely has this design been produced in less time, or space, and almost never as artfully.

In the Classical era, sonatas, quartets, symphonies, and serenades typically began with a movement in sonata–allegro form. So, too, did operas. That is, a Classical opera often commenced with an overture, performed by full orchestra, composed in sonata form. A case in point is Mozart's overture to *Don Giovanni* (1787). (The full opera will be discussed in Chapter 20.) Mozart begins this dramatic overture with a slow introduction in a minor key that incorporates some of the musical motives we hear later in the opera. This slow, ominous beginning soon changes to a fast tempo and a major key at the start of the exposition. Because this is an overture to an opera, and not a symphony, the exposition is not repeated.

Listening GUIDE

**Wolfgang Amadeus Mozart
Overture to the opera *Don Giovanni*
(1787)**

5
2/23–26

Genre: Opera overture

Form: Sonata–allegro

INTRODUCTION

0:00   23   Slow, sinister chords give way to twisting chromaticism and finally to writhing scales, all of which suggest the evil nature of Don Giovanni

(continued)

EXPOSITION

1:57	24	0:00	First theme moves ahead rapidly

2:20		0:23	Transition starts with scalar theme
			presented in melodic sequence
2:30		0:33	Continues with unstable chords that build tension
2:35		0:38	Transition ends with strong cadence
2:39		0:41	Second theme marked by scalar descent and
			"birdlike fluttering" in woodwinds

3:00		1:02	Light closing theme

DEVELOPMENT

3:18	25	0:00	Themes from exposition are heard in unexpected order
			(Material discussed in Listening Exercise 23)
4:15		0:57	Retransition: gradual return to first theme

RECAPITULATION

4:23	26	0:00	Themes return in same order as in exposition
			(Material discussed in Listening Exercise 23)

CODA

5:43		1:19	No loud cadential chords to produce
			"big bang" ending; rather, orchestral
			fadeout designed to coincide with raising
			of curtain and beginning of first scene.

Listen to streaming music in an Active Listening Guide, available on the text website.

@ To take Listening Exercise 23 for this musical selection online and receive feedback or email answers to your instructor, go to the text website.

A discussion of another Classical movement in sonata–allegro form (Mozart's Symphony No. 40 in G minor, first movement) can be found on pages 190–193, along with a Listening Guide and Listening Exercise.

Finally, if you like the overture to *Don Giovanni,* you'll love the opera (see pp. 203–208). The central character, Don Giovanni, has all the amoral charm of psychopath Patrick Bateman of *American Psycho* (2000).

@
The materials on the text website will help you understand and pass tests on the content of this chapter. In addition, you may watch Craig Wright's own lecture at Open Yale Courses and complete this chapter's Listening Exercise interactively, as well as view Active Listening Guides and other materials that will help you succeed in this course.

Key WORDS

ternary form (168)	sonata–allegro form	fugato (174)
relative major (169)	(172–173)	retransition (174)
minuet (169)	exposition (174)	recapitulation (174)
trio (169)	transition (bridge) (174)	coda (175)
serenade (170)	development (174)	

CLASSICAL FORMS
THEME AND VARIATIONS, RONDO

18

In addition to sonata–allegro and ternary, there were other important musical forms during the Classical period—most notably, theme and variations, and rondo. Both of these forms are simple and straightforward, emphasizing just one theme, in contrast to the multiplicity of themes present in sonata–allegro form. A composition in theme and variations or rondo form may exist as a movement within a multimovement sonata or symphony, or it may stand alone as a one-movement, independent piece.

*T*HEME AND VARIATIONS

In the film *Amadeus*, Mozart is shown composing variations on a theme of another composer (Salieri), tossing them off effortlessly like a magician pulling handkerchiefs from his sleeve. The capacity, indeed need, of a great artist for substantive change or modification is called the "transformational imperative"; Leonardo da Vinci continually transforms one and the same face just as Shakespeare endlessly riffs on a metaphor for a sunrise. In music, it is not an image or a vision that is varied, but usually a melody. **Theme and variations** occurs when a melody is altered, decorated, or adorned in some way by changing pitch, rhythm, harmony, or even (major or minor) mode. The object is still recognizable but somehow doesn't seem to sound the same. For theme and variations to work, the theme must be well known or easy to remember. Traditionally, composers have chosen to vary folk songs and, especially, patriotic songs. Those so treated include *God Preserve Franz the Emperor* (Haydn), *God Save the King* (Beethoven), *Rule Britannia* (Beethoven), and later *Yankee Doodle* (Vieuxtemps) and *America* (Ives). Such tunes are popular, in part, because they are simple, and this, too, is an advantage for the composer. Melodies that are spare and uncluttered can more easily be dressed in new musical clothing.

Broadly speaking, a variation can be affected in either of two ways: (1) by changing the primary theme itself, or (2) by changing the context around that theme (the accompaniment)—again, dressing it up in new finery. The accompaniment can be modified, for example, by adding figural or contrapuntal embellishment. Changing the theme itself, a more radical transformation, is accomplished by alterations to the theme's melodic or rhythmic profile. Sometimes, these two techniques are used simultaneously. As the variations proceed one to the next, they typically grow in complexity, with the original theme becoming progressively more obscure (see Fig. 18-1).

The two examples that follow—one by Mozart and one by Haydn—illustrate

@

Watch a video of Craig Wright's Open Yale Course class session 10, "Sonata–Allegro and Theme and Variations," at the text website.

FIGURE 18–1

Henri Matisse's classically inspired series of bronze sculptures of the head of his model, Jeannette Vaderin, executed in 1910, allows us to visualize the process of theme and variations. The image becomes progressively more distant from the original as we move left to right.

Digital Image © The Museum of Modern Art/ Licensed by SCALA/Art Resource, NY

a number of techniques for altering or embellishing a melody. The primary task of the listener, of course, is to keep track of the tune throughout its various permutations.

Mozart: *Variations on* Twinkle, Twinkle, Little Star *(c1781)*

In the Classical period, it was common for a composer-pianist to improvise in concert a set of variations on a well-known tune, perhaps one requested by the audience. Contemporary reports tell us that Mozart was especially skilled in this art of spontaneous variation. In the early 1780s, Mozart wrote down a set of such improvised variations built on the French folk song *Ah, vous dirai-je, Maman*, which we know as *Twinkle, Twinkle, Little Star*. With a tune as well known as this, it is easy to follow the melody, as it is increasingly ornamented and altered in the course of twelve variations. (Only the first eight bars of the theme are given here; for the complete melody, see p. 168–169; the music through the first five variations can be heard on (intro)/24.)

EXAMPLE 18–1A: *TWINKLE, TWINKLE, LITTLE STAR*, BASIC THEME (0:00)

Variation 1 ornaments the theme and almost buries it beneath an avalanche of sixteenth notes. Would you know that *Twinkle, Twinkle* lurks herein (see the asterisks) if you did not have the tune securely in your ear?

EXAMPLE 18–1B: VARIATION 1 (0:30)

In variation 2, the rushing ornamentation is transferred to the bass, and the theme surfaces again rather clearly in the upper voice.

EXAMPLE 18–1C: VARIATION 2 (0:59)

In variation 3, triplets in the right hand alter the theme, which is now only recognizable by its general contour.

EXAMPLE 18–1D: VARIATION 3 (1:29)

After the same technique has been applied to the bass (variation 4; 2:00), a thematic alteration again occurs in variation 5. Here the rhythm of the melody is "jazzed up" by placing part of it off the beat, in syncopated fashion.

EXAMPLE 18–1E: VARIATION 5 (2:29)

Of the remaining seven variations, some change the tune to minor, while others add Bach-like counterpoint against it. The final variation presents this duple-meter folk tune reworked into a triple-meter waltz! Yet throughout all of Mozart's magical embroidery, the theme remains clearly audible, so well ingrained is *Twinkle, Twinkle* in our musical memory.

Haydn: Symphony No. 94 (the "Surprise" Symphony, 1792), Second movement

Joseph Haydn (1732–1809) was the first composer to take theme and variations form and use it for a movement within a symphony. To be sure, Haydn was an innovative composer—he could "surprise" or "shock" like no other composer of the Classical period. In his "Surprise" Symphony, the shock comes in the form of a sudden *fortissimo* chord inserted, as we shall see, in the second movement in the middle of an otherwise serene theme. When Haydn's Symphony No. 94 was first heard in London in 1792, the audience cheered this second movement and demanded its immediate repetition (Fig. 18-2). Ever since, this surprising movement has been Haydn's most celebrated composition.

The famous opening melody of the second movement (*Andante*) is written in binary form (**AB**), and to this simple sixteen-bar theme, Haydn adds four variations. Notice how the beginning of the theme is shaped by laying out in succession the notes of a tonic triad (I) and then a dominant chord (V) in C major (see the first notated example

FIGURE 18–2

The Hanover Square Rooms in London, the hall in which Haydn's "Surprise" Symphony was first performed in 1792. Designed for an audience of 800–900, nearly 1,500 crowded in for the performances of these London Symphonies.

in the Listening Guide). The triadic nature of the tune accounts for its folk song–like quality and makes it easy to remember during the variations that follow. These first eight bars (**A**) are stated and then repeated quietly. And just when all is ending peacefully, the full orchestra, including a thunderous timpani, comes crashing in with a *fortissimo* chord, as if to shock the drowsy listener back to attention. What better way to show off the latent dynamic power of the larger Classical orchestra? The surprise *fortissimo* chord is a dominant chord that leads into the **B** section of the theme (second example in the Listening Guide), another eight-bar phrase, which is also repeated but with added flute and oboe accompaniment. With the simple yet highly attractive binary theme now in place, Haydn proceeds to compose four variations on it, adding a superb coda at the end. In his memoirs, dictated in 1809, Haydn explains that he included the surprise blast as something of a publicity stunt, "to make a début in a brilliant manner" and thereby call further attention to his concerts in London.

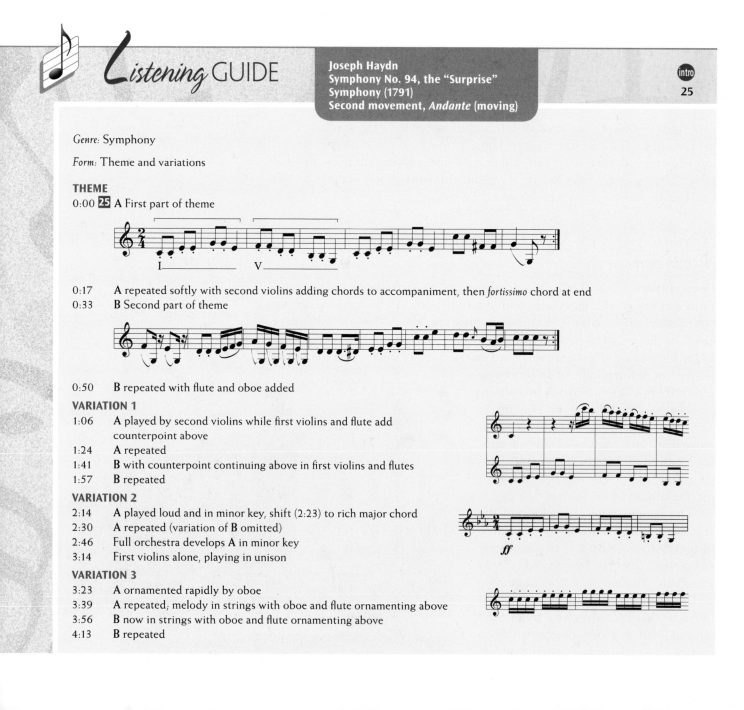

Listening GUIDE

Joseph Haydn
Symphony No. 94, the "Surprise"
Symphony (1791)
Second movement, *Andante* (moving)

intro
25

Genre: Symphony

Form: Theme and variations

THEME

0:00 **25** **A** First part of theme

0:17 **A** repeated softly with second violins adding chords to accompaniment, then *fortissimo* chord at end
0:33 **B** Second part of theme

0:50 **B** repeated with flute and oboe added

VARIATION 1
1:06 **A** played by second violins while first violins and flute add counterpoint above
1:24 **A** repeated
1:41 **B** with counterpoint continuing above in first violins and flutes
1:57 **B** repeated

VARIATION 2
2:14 **A** played loud and in minor key, shift (2:23) to rich major chord
2:30 **A** repeated (variation of **B** omitted)
2:46 Full orchestra develops **A** in minor key
3:14 First violins alone, playing in unison

VARIATION 3
3:23 **A** ornamented rapidly by oboe
3:39 **A** repeated; melody in strings with oboe and flute ornamenting above
3:56 **B** now in strings with oboe and flute ornamenting above
4:13 **B** repeated

VARIATION 4

4:29	A loud, in full orchestra, with violins playing running arpeggios
4:45	A repeated with theme rhythmically varied
5:03	B varied further by violins
5:20	B repeated loudly by full orchestra
5:37	Transition to coda, pause (5:45)

CODA

5:51	Reminiscences of theme in its original form

 Listen to streaming music in an Active Listening Guide, available on the text website.

After listening to this movement by Haydn, you can understand that hearing theme and variations form requires listening to discrete units of music. Each block (variation) is marked by some new treatment of the theme. In the Classical period, all the units are usually the same size, that is, have the same number of measures. The variations become progressively more complicated as more ornamentation and transformation are applied, but each unit remains the same length. The addition of a coda after the last variation gives extra weight to the end, so the listener feels that the set of variations has reached an appropriate conclusion. If such extra bars were not appended, the audience would be left hanging, expecting yet another variation to begin.

RONDO FORM

Of all musical forms, the rondo is perhaps the easiest to hear, because a single, unvaried theme (the refrain) returns again and again. The rondo is also one of the oldest forms, having existed since the Middle Ages in the guise of the vocal *rondeau* (see p. 78) and since the Baroque era in the ritornello form of the concerto (see p. 124). A true Classical **rondo** must have at least three statements of the refrain (**A**) and at least two contrasting sections (at least **B** and **C**). Often the placement of the refrain creates symmetrical patterns such as **ABACA**, **ABACABA**, or even **ABACADA**. Haydn and Mozart infused the rondo with musical processes found in sonata–allegro form—specifically, transitional and developmental writing. They thereby created a more elastic, flexible rondo "environment" in which the refrain (**A**) and, more often, the contrasting sections (**B**, **C**, or **D**) might develop and expand dramatically.

As in the following piece by Mozart, the rondo is typically light, quick, and jovial in nature. Classical composers most often chose the rondo form for the **finale** (Italian for "end") of a sonata, quartet, or symphony. The carefree tune and the easily grasped digressions lend to the rondo finale an "upbeat" feeling, the musical equivalent of a happy ending.

Mozart: *Horn Concerto in E♭ major (1786), K. 495, Third movement (finale)*

In his short lifetime, Mozart wrote more than 650 compositions, an enormous amount of music. To help us keep track of them, a musicologist in the nineteenth century, Ludwig von Köchel, published a list of Mozart's works in

FIGURE 18–3

A portrait of Joseph Haydn at work. His left hand is trying an idea at the keyboard while his right is ready to write it down. Haydn said about his compositional process: "I sat down at the keyboard and began to improvise. Once I had seized upon an idea, my whole effort was to develop and sustain it."

© The Art Archive/Eileen Tweedy

Watch a video of Craig Wright's Open Yale Course class session 11, "Form: Rondo, Sonata–Allegro, and Theme and Variations (cont.)," at the text website.

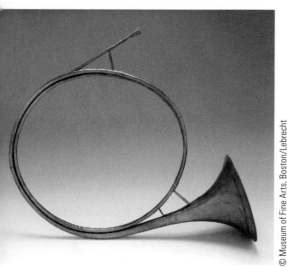

FIGURE 18-4

A natural French horn of the late eighteenth century, the sort of horn that would have been used in the Classical orchestras of Mozart, Haydn, and Beethoven.

approximate chronological order, and even today we identify Mozart's compositions by a **Köchel (K) number.** This is especially handy in the case of Mozart's four concertos for the French horn, three of which he composed in E♭: How else could we differentiate them without a number? Thus, the concerto in E♭ written in Vienna in 1786 is identified as K. 495.

The fact that Mozart wrote three of his four horn concertos in E♭ major tells us something about the French horn in the Classical era. It was a "natural" horn (one without valves or keys), and it was set to play in only a few tonal centers, usually in keys with flats (Fig. 18-4). Because the French horn then had no valves or mechanical keys, it also had difficulty playing a fully chromatic scale in tune. For that reason, composers wrote for the horn what it could play easily: repeated notes, as well as triads spun out as arpeggios.

Mozart conceived all four of his horn concertos with one performer in mind, Joseph Leutgeb (1732–1811). Mozart had grown up with Leutgeb in Salzburg and counted him among his best friends, one at whom he could poke fun. Thus, the inscription to the first horn concerto in E♭ (K. 417) reads: "Wolfgang Amadé Mozart has taken pity on Leutgeb, ass, ox, and fool." All four horn concertos by Mozart end with a movement in rondo form. The horn had something of a light-hearted, playful sound in Mozart's day, one well suited to the similarly light-hearted, playful quality of the Classical rondo.

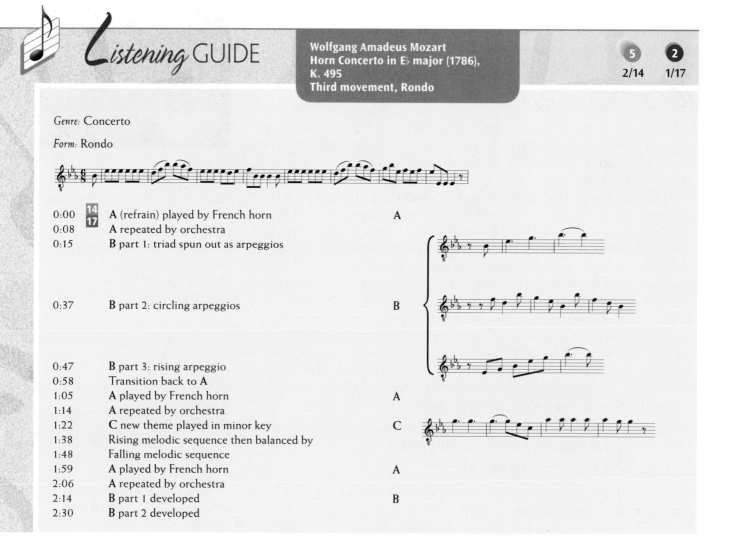

Listening GUIDE

**Wolfgang Amadeus Mozart
Horn Concerto in E♭ major (1786), K. 495
Third movement, Rondo**

5   2
2/14 1/17

Genre: Concerto

Form: Rondo

Time		Description	
0:00	14 17	A (refrain) played by French horn	A
0:08		A repeated by orchestra	
0:15		B part 1: triad spun out as arpeggios	
0:37		B part 2: circling arpeggios	B
0:47		B part 3: rising arpeggio	
0:58		Transition back to A	
1:05		A played by French horn	A
1:14		A repeated by orchestra	
1:22		C new theme played in minor key	C
1:38		Rising melodic sequence then balanced by	
1:48		Falling melodic sequence	
1:59		A played by French horn	A
2:06		A repeated by orchestra	
2:14		B part 1 developed	B
2:30		B part 2 developed	

2:49	**B** part 3 ends with pause, and brief horn cadenza (2:59)	
3:08	**A** played by horn	**A**
3:15	Orchestra begins to repeat **A** but then launches into	
3:17	Coda: Reminiscences of **A** and descending arpeggios	**Coda**

Listen to streaming music in an Active Listening Guide, available on the text website.

Listening EXERCISE 24

Mozart
HORN CONCERTO IN E♭ MAJOR

5 **2**

2/14 **1/17**

@ To take this Listening Exercise online and receive feedback or email answers to your instructor, go to the text website.

The key to hearing rondo form is to recognize the refrain and know when it has returned. Sometimes it is useful to make a simple melodic graph (as in question 1) to help differentiate between the refrain and the contrasting material.

1. Which of the three melodic graphs most closely approximates the beginning of the refrain (**A**)?
   a.   b.   c.

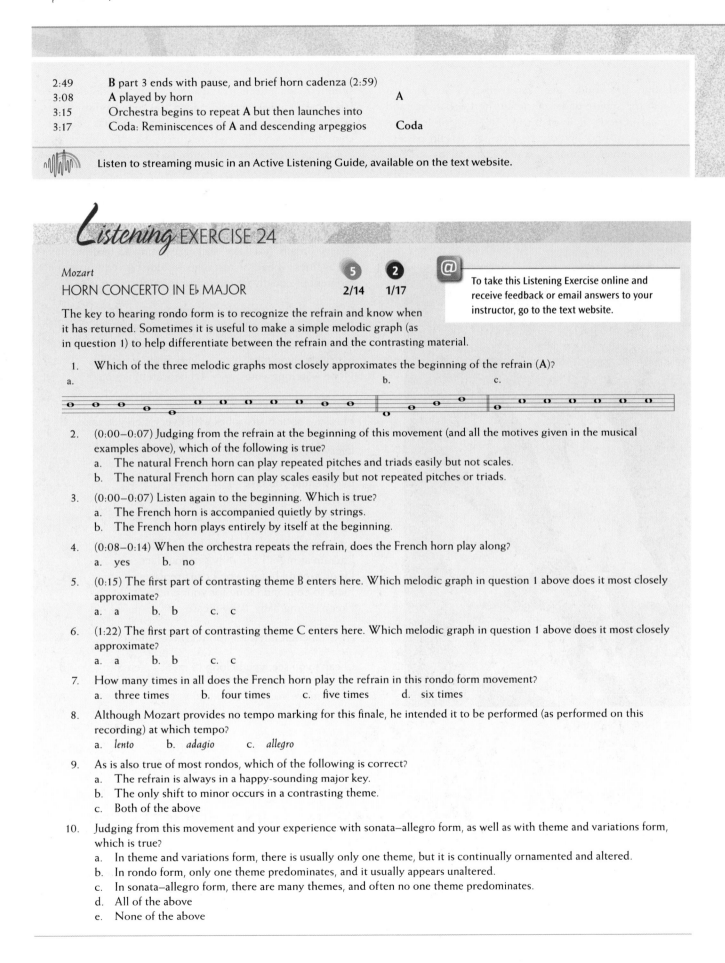

2. (0:00–0:07) Judging from the refrain at the beginning of this movement (and all the motives given in the musical examples above), which of the following is true?
   a.   The natural French horn can play repeated pitches and triads easily but not scales.
   b.   The natural French horn can play scales easily but not repeated pitches or triads.

3. (0:00–0:07) Listen again to the beginning. Which is true?
   a.   The French horn is accompanied quietly by strings.
   b.   The French horn plays entirely by itself at the beginning.

4. (0:08–0:14) When the orchestra repeats the refrain, does the French horn play along?
   a.   yes   b.   no

5. (0:15) The first part of contrasting theme B enters here. Which melodic graph in question 1 above does it most closely approximate?
   a.   a   b.   b   c.   c

6. (1:22) The first part of contrasting theme C enters here. Which melodic graph in question 1 above does it most closely approximate?
   a.   a   b.   b   c.   c

7. How many times in all does the French horn play the refrain in this rondo form movement?
   a.   three times   b.   four times   c.   five times   d.   six times

8. Although Mozart provides no tempo marking for this finale, he intended it to be performed (as performed on this recording) at which tempo?
   a.   *lento*   b.   *adagio*   c.   *allegro*

9. As is also true of most rondos, which of the following is correct?
   a.   The refrain is always in a happy-sounding major key.
   b.   The only shift to minor occurs in a contrasting theme.
   c.   Both of the above

10. Judging from this movement and your experience with sonata–allegro form, as well as with theme and variations form, which is true?
   a.   In theme and variations form, there is usually only one theme, but it is continually ornamented and altered.
   b.   In rondo form, only one theme predominates, and it usually appears unaltered.
   c.   In sonata–allegro form, there are many themes, and often no one theme predominates.
   d.   All of the above
   e.   None of the above

A RONDO BY STING

Although the rondo may have enjoyed its greatest favor in the sphere of art music during the Baroque and Classical periods, it lived on in the realm of folk and popular song, undoubtedly because the refrain pattern has such universal appeal. Traditional ballads such as "Tom Dooley" make use of it, and so do more recent pop songs. "Every Breath You Take," composed by Sting and recorded in 1983 by his New Wave group The Police, produces a rondo pattern (**ABACABA**) that in its symmetrical, indeed palindromic, shape would do any Classical composer proud. Indeed, this song has now been around for more than twenty-five years and has become something of a classic itself, reborn as the title track of the Police's greatest-hits compilation *Every Breath You Take: The Classics* (A & M Records). The song has also crossed over into the classical-pop repertoire, having been recorded in 2000 by the Royal Philharmonic Orchestra of London. It crossed back in 2002, becoming hip hop in the hands of Sean "Puffy" Combs. According to Wikipedia, the rondo "Every Breath You Take" still earns Sting $2,000 per day in royalties. What the rest of us wouldn't give for just one moment of equally lucrative inspiration!

Sting (Gordon Sumner)

Every breath you take	Every single day	
Every move you make	Every word you say	
Every bond you break	Every game you play	**A**
Every step you take	Every night you stay	
I'll be watching you.	I'll be watching you.	

O can't you see you belong to me?
How my poor heart aches with every step you take.   **B**

Every move you make
Every vow you break
Every smile you fake   **A**
Every claim you stake
I'll be watching you.

Since you've gone I've been lost without a trace
I dream at night I can only see your face
I look around but it's you I can't replace   **C**
I feel so cold and I long for your embrace
I keep crying baby, baby please.

[Instrumental interlude (no text) to **A** music]   **A**

O can't you see, you belong to me? . . . (etc.)   **B**

Every move you make . . . (etc.)   **A**

Coda (fade out)

F ORM, MOOD, AND THE LISTENER'S EXPECTATIONS

When today we attend a concert of classical music—of a symphony orchestra, for example—most of the music on the program (perhaps an overture by Wagner, a symphony by Haydn, and a concerto by Beethoven) will have been played by that orchestra and in that hall many times over the years. These favorite overtures, symphonies, and concertos belong to the **canon** (standard repertoire, or "chestnuts") of Western classical music. When concertgoers stepped into a hall in the late eighteenth century, however, they expected all of the music to be new and up to date—why would anyone want to hear old music? But while the late-eighteenth-century audience didn't know the pieces in advance, listeners did come with certain expectations, not only about the musical form but also about the mood of the music. For the Classical period, we might summarize these as follows:

	Movement			
	1	2	3	4
Tempo	Fast	Slow	Lively	Fast
Form	Sonata–allegro	Large ternary, theme and variations, or rondo	Minuet and trio in ternary form	Sonata–allegro, theme and variations, or rondo
Mood	Serious and substantive despite fast tempo	Lyrical and tender	Usually light and elegant, sometimes spirited	Bright, light-hearted, sometimes humorous

Ludwig van Beethoven (1770–1827) and later composers of the Romantic era (1820–1900) modified somewhat this conventional format—the third movement, for example, was often treated as a boisterous scherzo (see p. 222) rather than an elegant minuet. Yet the Classical model of what was good and what should be expected endured. Succeeding generations not only wanted to hear "new" music but increasingly wanted to return to the tried-and-true works of Haydn, Mozart, and their later contemporary Beethoven. The beginnings of the canon of Western music—and the forms these pieces should follow—were the product of the Classical era.

Key WORDS

theme and variations (179)
rondo (183)

finale (183)
Köchel (K) number (184)

canon (of Western music) (187)

19

CLASSICAL GENRES
INSTRUMENTAL MUSIC

In music, the term **genre** simply means the type or class of music to which we listen. The string quartet is a genre of music just as is the country music ballad, the twelve-bar blues piece, the military march, and the rap song. When we listen to a piece of music, we come armed with expectations as to how it will sound, how long it will last, and how we should behave. We may even go to a special place—an opera house or a bar—and dress a certain way—in gown and diamond earrings or black leather jacket and nose rings, for example. It all depends on the genre of music we expect to hear. If you change the genre, you change the audience, and vice versa.

In the age of Mozart, there were five main genres of art music: the symphony, string quartet, sonata, concerto, and opera. Opera, of course, had been around since the early Baroque era. The sonata and concerto, too, had existed during the Baroque, but they underwent such change at the hands of Haydn and Mozart that each became essentially a new genre. The symphony and string quartet were entirely new to the Classical period, created in no small part by Haydn.

THE SYMPHONY AND THE SYMPHONY ORCHESTRA

Download a Supplementary Listening Guide for Haydn's Symphony No. 95, movements 1–4, at the text website.

During the Classical era, the symphony became the preeminent genre of instrumental music. The fact that Haydn composed so many (106), and Mozart (given his short life) an even more astonishing number (41), shows that the symphony had become, and would remain, a staple of concert life.

The symphony traces its origins to the late-seventeenth-century Italian opera overture called the **sinfonia** (literally, "a harmonious sounding together"). Around 1700, the typical Italian *sinfonia* was a one-movement instrumental work in three sections: fast-slow-fast. Soon, Italian musicians and foreigners alike took the *sinfonia* out of the opera house and expanded it into three separate and distinct movements. A fourth movement, the minuet, was inserted by composers north of the Alps beginning in the 1740s. Thus, by midcentury the **symphony** had emerged as a major instrumental genre and assumed its familiar four-movement format: fast-slow-minuet-fast.

The public favor that the symphony came to enjoy was tied to progressive social changes that swept Europe during the Enlightenment, including the appearance of public concerts (see p. 156). The center of musical life in such cities as London, Paris, and, to a lesser degree, Vienna gradually shifted from the aristocratic court to the newly constructed or refurbished public concert hall. Among these halls were the Hanover Square Rooms in London (see Fig. 18-2), where Haydn's London Symphonies premiered, and the Burgtheater (City Theater) in Vienna (see Fig. 15-4), where many of Mozart's symphonies

FIGURE 19–1

The New Market in Vienna in the late 1700s. The building on the far right (today the Ambassador Hotel) housed the casino, and it was here that Mozart's G minor symphony was apparently first performed in 1788. Even today, famous musicians, such as Placido Domingo and Sting, perform in casinos, because that's where the money is!

and concertos were first heard. All but a few of Haydn's last twenty symphonies were composed for public performance in Paris and London, and Mozart wrote no symphonies for a court patron during the last ten years of his life. His famous G minor symphony (1788) was apparently first performed in a casino in central Vienna (Fig. 19-1)—that's where the people were and that's where the money was to be found.

The audiences at these public concerts in the capital cities of Europe increasingly came to hear the symphony and the large ensemble that played it. A symphony usually opened and closed each concert. Indeed, so closely did the genre of the symphony come to be linked with the performing force called the "orchestra," that the instrumental group came to be called a "symphony orchestra."

The Classical Symphony Orchestra

As the place of performance of the symphony orchestra moved from the private salon to the public auditorium, the size of both orchestra and audience increased. During the 1760s and 1770s, the orchestra at the court of Haydn's patron, Prince Nikolaus Esterházy, was never larger than twenty-five, and the audience at court was often only the prince and his staff (Fig. 19-2). But when Haydn went to London in 1791, his orchestra and audiences alike were much larger. By 1795, Haydn's orchestra had more than doubled in size, now consisting of some sixty players. He conducted his London Symphonies in the public Hanover Square Rooms, which typically held 800–900 people but sometimes more—for one concert in the spring of 1792, nearly 1,500 eager patrons crowded the hall.

FIGURE 19–2

A watercolor of 1775 shows Haydn leading the small orchestra at the court of the Esterházy princes during a performance of a comic opera. The composer is seated at the keyboard, surrounded by the cellos. The higher strings and woodwinds are seated in two rows at the desk.

Mozart's experience in Vienna was similar. For the public concerts he mounted in the Burgtheater in the mid-1780s, he engaged an orchestra of 35–40 players. But in a letter of 1781, he mentions an orchestra of 80 instrumentalists including 40 violins, 10 violas, 8 cellos, and 10 double basses. While this was an exceptional ensemble brought together for a special benefit concert, it shows that at times a very large group could be assembled. It also reveals that a large number of string players could be assigned to play just one string part—as many as 20 might "double" each other on the first violin line, for example.

To balance the growth in the string section, and to increase the variety of color in the orchestra, more winds were added. Now, instead of just one oboe or one bassoon, there were usually pairs. And a new woodwind, the clarinet, was welcomed into the orchestra. Mozart was especially fond of the clarinet and introduced it into his symphonies as early as 1778. Moreover, Mozart began to write independent lines for his woodwinds, not being satisfied with simply using them to double the string parts, as often happened in Baroque scores. Independent woodwind lines added not only color but also contrapuntal density to the orchestral fabric. By the 1790s, a typical symphony orchestra in a large European city might include the instrumentalists listed below. Compared to the Baroque orchestra, this ensemble of up to forty players was larger, more colorful, and more flexible.

Strings   1st violins, 2nd violins, violas, cellos, double basses (about 27 players in all)
Woodwinds   2 flutes, 2 oboes, 2 clarinets, 2 bassoons
Brasses   2 French horns, 2 trumpets (for festive pieces)
Percussion   2 timpani (for festive pieces)

Mozart: *Symphony No. 40 in G minor* (1788), K. 550

Mozart's celebrated Symphony in G minor requires all the full instrumental sound and disciplined playing the late-eighteenth-century orchestra could muster. This is not a festive composition (hence no trumpets and drums), but rather an intensely brooding work that suggests tragedy and despair. While we might be tempted to associate the minor key and despondent mood with a specific event in Mozart's life, apparently no such causal relationship exists. This was one of three symphonies, his last three, that Mozart produced in the incredibly short span of six weeks during the summer of 1788, and the other two are sunny, optimistic works. Rather than responding to a particular disappointment, it is more likely that Mozart invoked the tragic muse in this G minor symphony by drawing on a lifetime of disappointments and a premonition—as his letters attest—of an early death, to come three years later.

FIRST MOVEMENT (*MOLTO ALLEGRO*)

Exposition   Although Mozart begins his G minor symphony with a textbook example of Classical phrase structure (four-bar antecedent, four-bar consequent phrases), an unusual sense of urgency is created by the repeating, insistent eighth-note figure at the beginning. This urgent motive is immediately grasped by the listener and becomes the most memorable theme in the work. Embedded in the motive is a falling half step (here E♭ to D), a tight interval used throughout the history of music to denote pain and suffering.

EXAMPLE 19–1

Not so quickly seized, but still contributing equally to the sense of urgency, is the accelerating rate of harmonic change. At the outset, chords are set beneath the melody at an interval of one chord every four measures, then one every two bars, then one every measure, then two chords per measure, and finally four. Thus, the "harmonic rhythm" is moving sixteen times faster at the end of this section than at the start. This is how Mozart creates the sense of drive and urgency we all feel yet may be unable to explain. After this quickening start, the first theme begins once again but soon veers off its previous course, initiating the transition. Transitions take us somewhere, usually by means of running scales, and this one is no exception. What is unusual is that a new motive is inserted, one so distinctive that we might call it a "transition theme" (see the example in the following Listening Guide). As if to reciprocate for an extra theme here, Mozart dispenses with one toward the end of the exposition, at the point where we would expect a closing theme to appear. Instead, as closing material, he uses the persistent motive and rhythm from the beginning of the first theme, which rather nicely rounds off the exposition. Finally, a single, isolated chord is heard, one that first leads back to a repeat of the exposition and then, after the second statement of the exposition, launches into the development.

Development   In the development, Mozart employs only the first theme (and then only the first four bars), but subjects it to a variety of musical treatments. He first pushes it through several distantly related keys, next shapes it into a fugue subject for use in a fugato, then sets it as a descending melodic sequence, and finally inverts the direction of the half-step motive.

EXAMPLE 19–2

becomes

The retransition (return to the main theme and tonic key) is suddenly interrupted by *sforzandi* (loud attacks). But soon a dominant pedal point sounds in the bassoons, and above it, the flute and clarinets cascade like a musical waterfall down to the tonic pitch. This use of colorful, solo woodwinds in the retransition is a hallmark of Mozart's symphonic style.

Recapitulation   As expected, the recapitulation offers the themes in the same order in which they appeared in the exposition. But now the transition theme, which Mozart has left untouched since its initial appearance, receives extended treatment, creating something akin to a second development section as it charges through one new key after another, only to end up right back in the original tonic minor. When the lyrical second theme finally reappears, now in the minor mode, its mood is somber and plaintive. Because the repeating figure of the first theme rounds off the recapitulation by way of a closing theme, only the briefest coda is needed to end this passionate, haunting movement.

Listening GUIDE

**Wolfgang Amadeus Mozart
Symphony No. 40 in G minor (1788),
K. 550
First movement, *Molto allegro* (very fast)**

⑤ 2/15–17   ② 1/18–20

Genre: Symphony

Form: Sonata–allegro

EXPOSITION   [ ] = REPEAT

0:00	**15** [1:49]		Urgent, insistent first theme
0:21	**18** [2:10]		First theme begins to repeat but is cut short
0:30	[2:18]		Transition
0:36	[2:23]		Rapid, ascending scales
0:44	[2:32]		Strong cadence ending transition; pause to clear air
0:47	[2:35]		Lyrical second theme, major key contribute to brighter mood
0:57	[2:44]		Second theme repeated with new orchestration
1:07	[2:54]		Crescendo leads to closing material (taken from first theme); abrupt stop

DEVELOPMENT

3:34	**16**	0:00	First theme modulates through several distant keys
3:51	**19**	0:17	First theme used as fugue subject in fugato in basses and then violins
4:12		0:38	First theme reduced to just opening motive
4:32		0:58	*Sforzandi* (loud attacks) give way to retransition
4:39		1:05	Retransition: dominant pedal point in bassoons as music cascades downward

RECAPITULATION

4:45	**17**	0:00	First theme returns
5:06	**20**	0:21	First theme begins to repeat but is cut off by transition
5:15		0:30	Transition theme returns but is greatly extended
5:41		0:56	Rapid, ascending scales
5:49		1:04	Cadence and pause
5:52		1:07	Second theme now in (tonic) minor
6:01		1:16	Second theme repeated with new orchestration
6:12		1:27	Return of crescendo, which leads to closing material (taken from first theme)

CODA

6:51		2:05	Begins with rising chromatic scale
6:56		2:10	Opening motive returns, then three final chords

Listen to streaming music in an Active Listening Guide, available on the text website.

Listening EXERCISE 25

Mozart

SYMPHONY NO. 40 IN G MINOR

⑤ 2/15–17   ② 1/18–20

@ — To take this Listening Exercise online and receive feedback or email answers to your instructor, go to the text website.

As mentioned, Mozart was the first composer to integrate colorful writing for independent woodwinds, including the clarinet, into his symphonic scores. Yet the strings remained the core of the Classical symphony orchestra. The following exercise asks you to consider the relationship between woodwinds and strings in one of Mozart's most famous symphonic movements.

0:00–1:52 **Exposition**

1. 15 18 Which instruments begin by playing the haunting melody?
    a. violins   b. clarinets   c. cellos

2. When do the woodwinds first enter?
    a. 0:08   b. 0:16   c. 0:22

3. (0:38–0:46) What do the French horns do in this transition, something that is typical of the horns in orchestras during the Classical period?
    a. They stand out by playing independent solo melodies as in a horn concerto.
    b. They add "background" resonance by quietly repeating one or two pitches.

4. (0:47–1:05) Which is true about the orchestration of the second theme?
    a. The strings begin with the theme, and then the woodwinds take it over.
    b. The woodwinds begin with the theme, and then the strings take it over.

5. (1:20–1:30) Echoes of the first theme close the exposition. Which woodwind instrument plays a main motive of the first theme?
    a. French horn
    b. clarinet
    c. bassoon
    d. oboe

1:49–3:33 **Repeat of exposition**

6. 16 19 (0:00–0:30) Which family of instruments dominates the first section of the development?
    a. woodwinds   b. strings   c. brasses

7. (1:06–1:11) Which family of instruments dominates the end of the development, the retransition?
    a. woodwinds   b. strings   c. brasses

8. 17 20 (0:04–0:08) At the beginning of the recapitulation, Mozart reorchestrates his score (compare the exposition, 0:05–0:09). Which of the following is true?
    a. The melody is now assigned to the woodwinds.
    b. A flute plays a new contrapuntal line against the melody.
    c. A bassoon plays a new contrapuntal line against the melody.

9. (0:47–1:02) Which is true about Mozart's reorchestration of the second theme?
    a. The woodwinds begin with the theme, and then the strings take it over.
    b. The strings begin with the theme, and then the woodwinds take it over.

10. In sum, which of the following is true about this movement (and Mozart's symphonies generally)?
    a. The woodwinds introduce all themes, the violins add color and counterpoint, and the brasses play sustaining pitches in the background.
    b. The violins introduce all themes, the woodwinds add color and counterpoint, and the brasses play sustaining pitches in the background.
    c. The brasses introduce all themes, the woodwinds add color and counterpoint, and the violins play sustaining pitches in the background.

SECOND MOVEMENT (*ANDANTE*)

After the feverish excitement of the opening movement, the slow, lyrical *Andante* comes as a welcome change of pace. What makes this movement exceptionally beautiful is the extraordinary interplay between the light and dark colors of the woodwinds against the constant tone of the strings. If there is no thematic contrast and confrontation here, there is, nonetheless, heartfelt expression brought about by Mozart's masterful use of orchestral color.

THIRD MOVEMENT (*MENUETTO: ALLEGRETTO*)

We expect the aristocratic minuet to provide elegant, graceful dance music. But much to our surprise, Mozart returns to the intense, somber mood of the opening movement. This he does, in part, by choosing to write in the tonic minor key—a rare minuet in minor. This again demonstrates how the minuet had changed from "dance music" to "listening music."

FOURTH MOVEMENT (*ALLEGRO ASSAI*)

The finale starts with an ascending "rocket" that explodes in a rapid, *forte* flourish—and only carefully rehearsed string playing can bring off the brilliant effect of this opening gesture. The contrasting second theme of this sonata–allegro form movement is typically Mozartean in its grace and charm, a proper foil to the explosive opening melody. Midway through the development, musical compression takes hold: there is no retransition, only a pregnant pause before the recapitulation; the return dispenses with the repeats built into the first theme; and a coda is omitted. This musical foreshortening at the end produces the same psychological effect experienced at the very beginning of the symphony—a feeling of urgency and acceleration.

*T*HE STRING QUARTET

The symphony is the ideal genre for the public concert hall, for it aims to please a large listening public. The string quartet, on the other hand, typifies chamber music—music for the small concert hall, for the private chamber, or, often, just for the enjoyment of the performers themselves. Unlike the symphony, which might have a dozen violinists joining on the first violin line, the **string quartet** has only one player per part: first violinist, second violinist, violist, and cellist (Fig. 19-3). Moreover, there is no conductor. All performers function equally and communicate directly among themselves. No wonder the German poet Johann Wolfgang von Goethe (1749–1832) compared the string quartet to a conversation among four intelligent people. All chamber music, whether for string quartet, solo piano or violin, wind quintet, or even string octet, employs just one player on a part. Of these chamber media, the string quartet is historically the most important.

Joseph Haydn is rightly called "the father of the string quartet." In the 1760s and 1770s, he took the trio sonata (see p. 120), the staple of Baroque chamber music, and made it into something new. He removed the old *basso continuo* and replaced it with a more melodically active bass played by an agile cello alone. And he enriched the middle of the texture by adding a viola, playing immediately above the cello. If the Baroque trio sonata had a "top-and bottom-heavy" texture, the newer Classical string quartet shows a texture covered evenly by four instruments, each of which participates more or less equally in a give-and-take of theme and motive.

The string quartet, of course, is not only a performing force but also a musical genre. The Classical string quartet has four movements that are identical to those of the Classical symphony: fast-slow-minuet-fast. Moreover, in a set of quartets he wrote in 1772, Haydn dubbed each minuet a **scherzo** (Italian for "joke"), aptly characterizing the high-spirited style of playing intended for this third movement.

It was the chance to play string quartets together that gave rise to a lasting friendship between Haydn and Mozart. During 1784–1785, the two men met in Vienna, sometimes at the home of an aristocrat, and other times in Mozart's own apartment. In their quartet, Haydn

FIGURE 19-3

A representation of a string quartet at the end of the eighteenth century. The string quartet was at first an ensemble for playing chamber music in the home. Not until 1804 did a string quartet appear in a public concert in Vienna, and not until 1814 in Paris.

played first violin, and Mozart viola. As a result of this experience, Mozart was inspired to dedicate a set of his best works in this genre to the older master, which he published in 1785 (Fig. 19-4). Yet in this convivial, domestic music-making, Haydn and Mozart merely joined in the fashion of the day. For whether in Vienna, Paris, or London, aristocrats and members of the well-to-do middle class were encouraged to play quartets with friends, as well as to engage professional musicians to entertain their guests.

Haydn: Opus 76, No. 3, the "Emperor" Quartet (1797)

Haydn's "Emperor" Quartet, written in Vienna during the summer of 1797, numbers among the best works of the string quartet genre. It is known as the "Emperor" because it makes liberal use of *The Emperor's Hymn*, a melody that Haydn composed in response to the military and political events of his day.

In 1796, the armies of Napoleon invaded the Austrian Empire, which ignited a firestorm of patriotism in Vienna, the Austrian capital. But the Austrians were at a musical disadvantage: the French now had the *Marseillaise*, and the English had their *God Save the King*, but the Austrians had no national anthem. To this end, the ministers of state approached Haydn, who quickly fashioned one to the text "Gott erhalte Franz den Kaiser" ("God Preserve Franz the Emperor"), in honor of the reigning Austrian Emperor Franz II (Fig. 19-5). Called *The Emperor's Hymn*, it was first sung in theaters throughout the Austrian realm on the emperor's birthday, February 12, 1797. Later that year, Haydn took the tune and worked it into a string quartet.

In truth, when Haydn fashioned quartet Opus 76, No. 3, he made use of his imperial hymn mainly in the slow, second movement, where it serves as the basis of a theme and variations set. The theme (see the example in the following Listening Guide) is first presented by the first violin and harmonized in simple chords. Four variations follow in which the theme is ornamented but never altered. All four instruments are given equal opportunity to hold forth with the tune. Even the cello, more flexible and lyrical than the double bass of the orchestra, can participate as an equal partner. Example 19-3 shows how in the Classical string quartet the melodic profile of each of the lines is more or less the same, a far cry from the melody/walking-bass polarity that typified the earlier Baroque trio sonata.

FIGURES 19–4 AND 19–5

(top) Title page of six string quartets by Mozart dedicated to Haydn (1785). Mozart offers them to Haydn as "six children," asking Haydn to be their "father, guide, and friend." (bottom) Franz II (1765–1835), last Holy Roman Emperor, first emperor of Austria. Haydn composed *The Emperor's Hymn* in his honor.

EXAMPLE 19–3

Listening GUIDE

Joseph Haydn
String Quartet, Opus 76, No. 3,
the "Emperor" Quartet (1797)
Second Movement, *Poco adagio cantabile* (rather slow, song-like)

5   **2**
2/18–19   1/21–22

Genre: String quartet

Form: Theme and variations

THEME

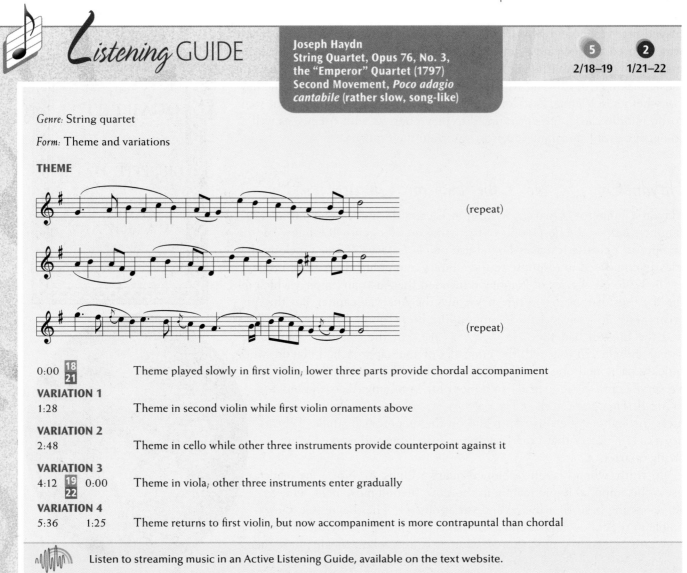

(repeat)

(repeat)

0:00 | **18** / **21** | Theme played slowly in first violin; lower three parts provide chordal accompaniment

VARIATION 1
1:28   Theme in second violin while first violin ornaments above

VARIATION 2
2:48   Theme in cello while other three instruments provide counterpoint against it

VARIATION 3
4:12 | **19** / **22** | 0:00   Theme in viola; other three instruments enter gradually

VARIATION 4
5:36   1:25   Theme returns to first violin, but now accompaniment is more contrapuntal than chordal

Listen to streaming music in an Active Listening Guide, available on the text website.

Listening EXERCISE 26

Haydn
"EMPEROR" QUARTET

5   **2**
2/18–19   1/21–22

@   To take this Listening Exercise online and receive feedback or email answers to your instructor, go to the text website.

In a symphony, two or more players can join together ("double") on just one line. Similarly, with a large ensemble, various sorts of crowd-pleasing special effects are possible. A string quartet, on the other hand, produces a purer, more abstract, more exposed sound, one that requires very careful playing and equally careful listening. The following exercise encourages you to think about the difference between the genres of symphony and quartet.

1. How many performers play on each of the four parts of a string quartet?
   a. one   b. two   c. three   d. four

0:00–1:26   **Theme**

2. **18** / **21**   Listen to the theme. Why does it sound so secure and firm—an appropriate musical vehicle to represent a national identity?

a. because all the notes are the same length
b. because the theme starts low and ends high
c. because each phrase is the same length and each ends on a dominant or tonic note

1:28–2:46   **Variation 1**

3. The second violin has the theme while the first violin rapidly ornaments above. Do the viola and cello (the lowest two instruments) play at all during this variation?
   a. yes   b. no

2:48–4:11   **Variation 2**

4. The cello has the theme in this variation. Would you say the instrument is playing in the higher or the

lower part of its range? (Listen especially to the last section of the melody.)
    a. higher   b. lower

0:00–1:23   Variation 3

5. The viola has the melody but is gradually joined by the other instruments. Which instrument is the last to enter in this variation?
    a. first violin   b. second violin   c. cello

6. The musical texture in this variation is what?
    a. homophonic (chordal)
    b. polyphonic (contrapuntal)

1:25–2:51   Variation 4

7. This last variation sounds "otherworldly" or ethereal. How is it that the quartet makes it sound this way?
    a. They play with no vibrato.
    b. They play with a great deal of vibrato.
    c. They have slowed the tempo down to a crawl.

2:52–end   A brief coda

8. In what way does Haydn conclude the movement?
    a. He has the players execute a "fadeout" by means of a ritard and diminuendo.
    b. He produces a special effect by having the players drive toward a grand *fortissimo* climax.

9. Which ensemble might we say is a more democratic institution (or at least one in which the voices are heard more or less equally)?
    a. a symphony orchestra   b. a string quartet

10. If you were a violinist prone to playing wrong notes (and didn't want to embarrass yourself), in which ensemble would you be more comfortable performing?
    a. a symphony orchestra   b. a string quartet

The popularity of *The Emperor's Hymn* did not end with the defeat of Napoleon in 1815 or the death of Emperor Franz II in 1835. So alluring is Haydn's melody that with altered text it became a Protestant hymn (*Glorious Things of Thee Are Spoken*), as well as the national anthem of Austria (1853) and Germany (1922). It was also Haydn's own favorite piece, and he played a piano arrangement of it daily. In fact, *The Emperor's Hymn* was the last music Haydn played before he died in the early hours of May 31, 1809.

THE SONATA

Most children who study a Western musical instrument (piano, flute, violin, or cello, for example) will play a sonata at one time or another. Like the symphony and the string quartet, the sonata was a genre of classical music that took its definitive shape (usually three movements, fast-slow-fast) during the Classical era. And, as with these other genres, each movement of a sonata usually makes use of one or another of the forms favored by Classical composers: sonata–allegro, ternary, rondo, or theme and variations.

The sonata came to enjoy great popularity during the Classical period. According to publishers' inventories from the end of the eighteenth century, more sonatas were printed than any other type of music. The explanation for this sudden vogue is tied to the equally sudden popularity of the piano. Indeed, the word *sonata* has become so closely associated with the piano that unless otherwise qualified as "violin sonata," "cello sonata," or the like, we usually assume that "sonata" refers to a three-movement work for piano.

Who played this flood of new sonatas for the piano? Amateur musicians, mostly women, who practiced and performed for polite society in the comfort of their own homes. (Oddly, men in this period usually played not the piano but string instruments such as the violin or cello.) As we have seen (p. 157), in Mozart's time, the ability to play the piano, to do fancy needlework, and to utter a few selected words of French were thought by male-dominated society all that was necessary to be a cultured young lady. To teach the musical handicraft, instructors were needed. Mozart, Haydn, and Beethoven

Watch a video of Craig Wright's Open Yale Course class session 18, "Piano Music of Mozart and Beethoven," at the text website.

all served as piano teachers in fashionable circles early in their careers. The piano sonatas they composed for their many pupils were not intended to be played in the public concert halls. Rather, sonatas were to provide students with material that they might practice to develop technique and that they might play as musical entertainment in the home. Even among the thirty-two splendid piano sonatas that Beethoven composed, only one was ever performed at a public concert in Vienna during his lifetime.

(An example of a Classical piano sonata by Beethoven, his *"Pathétique"* Sonata, is found on **5**3/1–3 and **2**1/23–25. It is discussed in detail on pages 211–214.)

THE CONCERTO

With the genre of the concerto, we leave the salon or private chamber and return to the public concert hall. The Classical concerto, like the symphony, was a large-scale, three-movement work for instrumental soloist and orchestra intended for a public audience. While the symphony might have provided the greatest musical substance at a concert, audiences were often lured to the hall by the prospect of hearing a virtuoso performer play a concerto. Then as now, audiences were fascinated with personal virtuosity and all the derring-do that a stunning technical display might bring. Gone was the Baroque tradition of the concerto grosso, in which a group of soloists (concertino) stepped forward from the full orchestra (tutti) and then receded back into it. From this point forward, the concerto was a **solo concerto,** usually for piano but sometimes for violin, cello, French horn, trumpet, or woodwind. In the new concerto, the soloist commanded all the audience's attention.

Credit for the creation of the Classical piano concerto must go to Wolfgang Amadeus Mozart alone. Just as Haydn can be said to have created the string quartet, so Mozart can be dubbed the father of the modern piano concerto. Indeed, Mozart wrote more piano concertos than any other important composer in history: twenty-three in all. And his motivation was money. After cutting himself loose from the patronage of the archbishop of Salzburg in 1781 and establishing residence in Vienna, Mozart no longer had an annual salary on which to rely. The Viennese were eager to hear brilliant passagework and dazzling displays of keyboard virtuosity. The piano concerto was for Mozart the perfect vehicle for such a display. At each of the public concerts he produced, Mozart offered one or two of his latest concertos. But he had to do more: he was responsible for renting the hall, hiring the orchestra, leading rehearsals, attracting an audience, and selling tickets from his apartment (Fig. 19-6)—all this in addition to composing the music and appearing as solo virtuoso. But when all went well, Mozart could make a killing, as a music journal of March 22, 1783, reported:

Today the celebrated Chevalier Mozart gave a musical concert for his own benefit at the Burgtheater in which pieces of his own music, which was already very popular, were performed. The concert was honored by the presence of an extraordinarily large audience and the two new concertos and other fantasies which Mr. Mozart played on the Forte Piano were received with the loudest approval. Our Monarch [Emperor Joseph II], who contrary to his custom honored the entire concert with his presence, joined in the applause of the public so heartily that one can think of no similar example. The proceeds of the concert are estimated at sixteen hundred gulden.

Sixteen hundred gulden was the equivalent of about $140,000 today, and more than five times the annual salary of Mozart's father. With a take such as this, young Mozart could, at least for a time, indulge his expensive tastes.

FIGURE 19-6

One of the few surviving tickets to a concert given by Mozart in Vienna. These were sold in advance, not from a ticket agency, but from Mozart's own apartment!

Mozart: Piano Concerto in A major (1786), K. 488

We derive our term "concerto" from the Italian word *concertare*. It means above all else "to strive together," but it also resonates with a sense of "to struggle against." In a piano concerto, the piano and orchestra engage in a spirited give-and-take of thematic material—the piano, perhaps more than any instrument, can compete on an equal footing with the orchestra (Fig. 19-7). Mozart composed his Piano Concerto in A major of 1786 for one of his star pupils, Barbara Ployer.

FIRST MOVEMENT (*ALLEGRO*)

As with all of Mozart's concertos, this one is in three movements (there is never a minuet or scherzo in a concerto). And, as is invariably the case, the first movement is written in sonata–allegro form. Here, however, it is modified to meet the special demands and opportunities of the concerto. What results is **double exposition form,** an extension of sonata–allegro form in which the orchestra plays one exposition and the soloist then plays another. First, the orchestra presents the first, second, and closing themes, all in the tonic key. Then the soloist enters and, with orchestral assistance, offers the piano's version of the same material, but modulating to the dominant before the second theme. After the piano expands the closing theme, part of the first theme group returns, a throwback to the ritornello principle of the old Baroque concerto grosso.

Then a surprise: Just when we expect this second exposition to end, Mozart inserts a lyrical new melody played by the strings. This is another feature of the Classical concerto—a melody held back for last-minute presentation, a way of keeping the listener "on guard" during the second exposition.

FIGURE 19–7

Mozart's piano, preserved in the house of his birth in Salzburg, Austria. The keyboard spans only five octaves, and the black-and-white color scheme of the keys is reversed, both typical features of the late-eighteenth-century piano. Mozart purchased the instrument in 1784, two years before he composed his A major piano concerto.

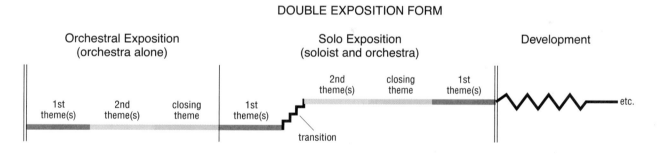

DOUBLE EXPOSITION FORM

The development here is concerned exclusively with exploiting the new theme that appeared at the end of the second exposition. The recapitulation compresses the two expositions into one, presenting the themes in the same order as before but now all in the tonic key. Finally, toward the end of the movement, the orchestra suddenly stops its forward motion and comes to rest on a single chord for several moments. Using this chord as a point of departure, the pianist plunges headlong into

FIGURE 19–8

A young woman performs a keyboard concerto in 1777. When Mozart moved to Vienna in 1781 he was forced to earn a living, so he gave composition lessons (mostly to men) and piano lessons (mostly to women). Among his best female students was Barbara Ployer (1765–1811) for whom he wrote the piano concerto in A minor (K. 488) discussed here.

a flight of virtuosic fancy called a "cadenza." In a **cadenza,** the soloist, playing alone, mixes rapid runs, arpeggios, and snippets of previously heard themes into a fantasy-like improvisation. Indeed, Mozart didn't write down this cadenza when he himself performed it, but improvised it on the spot, just as in our own century a talented jazz musician might improvise an extended solo. After a minute or so of this virtuosic dazzle, the pianist plays a trill, a signal to the orchestra that it is time for it to reenter the competition. From here to the end, the orchestra holds forth, making use of the original closing theme. There is much to absorb in the long Listening Guide that follows, but the glorious music of Mozart will amply reward the attentive listener.

*L*istening GUIDE

Wolfgang Amadeus Mozart
Piano Concerto in A major (1786)
First movement, *Allegro* (fast)

5

2/20–22

Genre: Concerto

Form: Sonata–allegro

EXPOSITION 1 (orchestra)

0:00 **20**	Strings present first theme	
0:16	Woodwinds repeat first theme	
0:34	Full orchestra presents first theme, part **b**	
0:59	Strings present second theme, part **a**	
1:15	Woodwinds repeat second theme, part **a**	
1:30	Strings present second theme, part **b**	
1:32	Strings present closing theme, part **a**	
1:57	Woodwinds present closing theme, part **b**	

EXPOSITION 2 (piano and orchestra)

2:11	Piano enters with first theme
2:40	Orchestra plays first theme, part **b**
3:11	Piano plays second theme, part **a**
3:27	Woodwinds repeat second theme, part **a**
3:44	Piano plays and ornaments second theme, part **b**
3:53	Piano and orchestra in dialogue play closing theme, part **a**
4:24	Piano trill heralds return of first theme, part **b**
4:39	Strings quietly offer lyrical new theme

DEVELOPMENT

5:05 **21** 0:00	Woodwinds transform new theme as piano interjects scales and then arpeggios
5:35 0:30	Woodwinds offer new theme in imitative counterpoint
5:49 0:44	Pedal point on dominant note in low strings signals beginning of retransition
6:04 0:59	Piano takes over dominant pedal point
6:18 1:13	Piano flourish above sustained dominant chord leads to recapitulation

RECAPITULATION

6:30 **22** 0:00	Orchestra plays first theme, part **a**
6:47 0:17	Piano repeats first theme, part **a**

7:00	0:30	Orchestra plays first theme, part **b**
7:10	0:40	Scales in piano signal beginning of transition
7:30	1:00	Piano plays second theme, now in tonic, part **a**
7:46	1:16	Woodwinds repeat second theme, part **a**
8:02	1:32	Piano plays second theme, part **b**
8:06	1:36	Piano and orchestra divide closing theme, part **a**
8:35	2:05	Piano plays new theme
8:48	2:18	Woodwinds play new theme while piano offers scales and arpeggios against it
9:17	2:47	Trill in piano announces return of first theme, part **b**
9:46	3:16	Orchestra stops and holds chord
9:50	3:20	Cadenza for piano
10:53	4:23	Trill signals reentry of orchestra
11:05	4:35	Orchestra plays closing theme, parts **a** and **b**
11:27	4:57	Final cadential chords

Listen to streaming music in an Active Listening Guide, available on the text website.

SECOND MOVEMENT (*ANDANTE*)

The essence of this movement rests in Mozart's exquisitely crafted lines and coloristic harmonies. This is the only work the Viennese master ever wrote in the remote key of F♯ minor, and the daring harmonic changes it contains prefigure those of the Romantic era. Musicians who have lived with Mozart's music from childhood to old age continue to be profoundly moved by this extraordinary movement. It is at once sublimely beautiful and distantly remote, its ending as cold and desolate as death itself.

THIRD MOVEMENT (*PRESTO*)

The sublime pessimism of the *Andante* is suddenly shattered by a boisterous rondo refrain in the piano. As Mozart was well aware, this movement, not the previous slow one, had the kind of music the fun-loving Viennese would pay to hear. And in this rondo, his subscribers got more than they bargained for; the soloist and orchestra do not simply "speak in turn," but rather banter back and forth in the most playful and pleasing way. "Anything you can do, I can do better," "No you can't," "Yes I can," the antagonists seem to say. In Mozart's contest between interactive forces, there is no winner—except the listener.

Download a Supplementary Listening Guide for another Mozart piano concerto, Concerto No. 17 in G major, at the text website.

Key WORDS

genre (188)
sinfonia (188)
symphony (188)

string quartet (194)
scherzo (194)
solo concerto (198)

double exposition form (199)
cadenza (200)

The materials on the text website will help you understand and pass tests on the content of this chapter. In addition, you may watch Craig Wright's own lecture at Open Yale Courses and complete this chapter's Listening Exercises interactively, as well as view Active Listening Guides and other materials that will help you succeed in this course.

20

CLASSICAL GENRES
VOCAL MUSIC

While it would be wrong to overlook the many wonderful Masses for the Roman Catholic liturgy written by Haydn, Mozart, and Beethoven, nonetheless opera rightly commands our attention when we consider the vocal music of the Classical period. Then as now, the public embraced opera because, in addition to beautiful music, it had glamour, star appeal, and all the excitement of the theater.

CLASSICAL OPERA

Opera is drama, yes, but drama propelled by music. In the Classical period, opera maintained the essential features it had developed during the Baroque era. It still began with an overture, was divided into two or three acts, and made use of a succession of arias and recitatives, along with an occasional choral number. And, of course, it still was performed in a theater large enough to accommodate both an orchestra and elaborate stage sets.

Opera in the eighteenth century was marked by the rise of comic opera, a powerful voice for social change during the Enlightenment (see p. 155). The statue-like gods, goddesses, emperors, and queens of the old Baroque *opera seria* gradually departed the stage, making room for more natural, realistic characters drawn from everyday life—a barber and a maid, for example. Where Baroque opera posed magnificently, Classical opera moves fluidly. Arias and recitatives flow easily from one to another, and the mood of the music changes rapidly to reflect the quick-moving, often comic, events on stage.

Comic opera introduces a new element into the opera house, the **vocal ensemble,** which allows the plot to unfold more quickly. Instead of waiting for each character to sing successively, three or more characters can express their own particular emotions simultaneously. One might sing of her love, another of his fear, another of her outrage, while a fourth pokes fun at the other three. If an author does that in a play, what results is a jumble; if a composer does that in an opera, what results is a vocal ensemble. Composers often placed vocal ensembles at the ends of acts to help spark a rousing conclusion, one in which all the principals might appear on stage. The vocal ensemble typifies the more democratic spirit, and better dramatic pacing, of the late eighteenth century.

MOZART AND OPERA

The master of Classical opera, and of the vocal ensemble in particular, was Wolfgang Amadeus Mozart (1756–1791). While Haydn wrote more than a dozen operas and conducted others (see Fig. 19-1), he lacked Mozart's instinct for what was effective in the theater and what was not. Beethoven wrote only one opera, *Fidelio*, and he labored mightily on it, working through several revisions over the course of nearly ten years. Neither Haydn nor Beethoven had Mozart's talent for lightning-quick changes in mood or his capacity for equally quick exchanges in musical dialogue, the sort of banter in music that we heard in his piano concerto (see pp. 199–201). Mozart's music is inherently dramatic and perfectly suited to the stage.

Mozart wrote Italian *opera seria* of the old Baroque sort as well as German comic opera, which was called *Singspiel*. Like a Broadway musical, a **Singspiel** is made up of spoken dialogue (instead of recitative) and songs. Mozart's best work of this type is *Die Zauberflöte* (*The Magic Flute*, 1791). But Mozart also wrote Italian comic operas. These include his masterpieces *Le nozze di Figaro* (*The Marriage of Figaro*, 1786), *Don Giovanni* (1787), and *Così fan tutte* (*Thus Do They All*, 1790), all three with text (libretto) by Lorenzo da Ponte.

Mozart: Don Giovanni (1787), K. 527

Don Giovanni has been called not only Mozart's greatest opera but also the greatest opera ever written. It tells the tale of an amoral philanderer, a Don Juan, who seduces and murders his way across Europe before being pursued and finally dragged down to Hell by the ghost of a man whom he has killed. Because the seducer and mocker of public law and morality is a nobleman, *Don Giovanni* is implicitly critical of the aristocracy, and Mozart and da Ponte danced quickly to stay one step ahead of the imperial censor before production. Mozart's opera was first performed on October 29, 1787, in Prague, Czech Republic, a city in which his music was especially popular. As fate would have it, the most notorious Don Juan of the eighteenth century, Giacomo Casanova (1725–1798), was in the audience that first night in Prague. It turns out that he had a small hand in helping his friend da Ponte shape the libretto.

The overture to *Don Giovanni*, as we have seen (**5** 2/23–26; Listening Exercise 23), is a fine example of sonata–allegro form. It begins with a slow introduction that incorporates several themes or motives important later in the opera. Just as an author may postpone writing a preface until after the book is finished, so a composer typically saves the overture for the end of the creative process. In this way, the overture can not only prefigure important themes in the opera but also characterize the overall tone of the work. Mozart, as was his tendency, postponed much of the writing of *Don Giovanni* until the last minute, and the overture was not completed until the night before the premiere, the copyist's ink still wet on the pages as the music was handed to the orchestra.

Don Giovanni is a rare mix of serious (*opera seria*) and comic (*opera buffa*), and we begin with the latter. As the last strains of the overture die away, the curtain rises on the comic figure Leporello, Don Giovanni's faithful, though reluctant, servant. Leporello has been keeping a nocturnal vigil outside the house of Donna Anna while his master is inside attempting to satisfy his sexual appetite. Grumbling as he paces back and forth, Leporello sings about how he would gladly trade places with the fortunate aristocrat ("Notte e giorno faticar" ["I would like to play the gentleman"]; **5** 2/27). Immediately, Mozart works to establish Leporello's musical character. He sets this opening aria in F major, a traditional key for the pastoral in music (see p. 148), showing that Leporello is a rustic fellow; he gives him a narrow vocal range without fancy chromaticism; and he has him sing quick, repeated notes, almost as if he were stuttering. This last technique, called "patter song," is a stock device used to depict low-caste, inarticulate characters in comic opera.

As Leporello concludes his complaint, the masked Don Giovanni rushes onstage, chased by the virtuous Donna Anna. Here the strings rush up the

Watch a video of Craig Wright's Open Yale Course class session 17, "Mozart and His Operas," at the text website.

FIGURE 20–1

The man who wrote the librettos for Mozart's most important operas of the 1780s, including *Don Giovanni*, was Lorenzo da Ponte. Da Ponte was an Italian priest who, after the death of Mozart and a stay in London, emigrated to America in 1805. Once there, he ran a dry goods store in Sunbury, Pennsylvania, and worked as a trader, distiller, and occasional gunrunner during the War of 1812. Eventually, he moved to New York City, becoming the first professor of Italian literature at Columbia University in 1825. In 1826 he sponsored a performance of *Don Giovanni*, the first opera by Mozart to be performed in America.

© Tristram Kenton/Lebrecht Music & Arts

FIGURE 20-2

Don Giovanni (Roderick Williams) tries to seduce Donna Anna (Suzannah Glanville) at the beginning of a 2005 British production of Mozart's *Don Giovanni*. Note the similarity in approach to *The Phantom of the Opera* by Andrew Lloyd Webber. Lloyd Webber drew heavily from Mozart's *Don Giovanni*. For example, the opera that the Phantom composes in Act II is called *Don Juan [Giovanni] Triumphant*, which tries to tell this timeless tale of seduction from Don Juan's point of view.

scale and the music modulates up a fourth (at 1:40) to signify that we are now dealing with the highborn. The victim of Don Giovanni's unwanted sexual advances, Donna Anna wants her assailant captured and unmasked (Fig. 20-2). While the gentleman and lady carry on a musical tug-of-war in long notes above, the cowering Leporello patters away fearfully below. This excellent example of vocal ensemble makes clear the conflicting emotions of each party.

Now Donna Anna's father, the Commandant, enters to confront Don Giovanni. The listener senses that this bodes ill—there is a troubling tremolo in the strings, and the music shifts from major to minor mode (3:04). Our fear is immediately confirmed as the Don, first refusing to duel, draws his sword and attacks the aging Commandant. In the brief exchange of steel, Mozart depicts the rising tension by means of ascending chromatic scales and tight, tense chords (3:55). At the very moment Don Giovanni's sword pierces the Commandant, the action stops and the orchestra sustains on a painful **diminished chord** (4:00)—a chord comprised entirely of minor thirds. Mozart then clears the air of discord with a simple texture and accompaniment as Don Giovanni and Leporello gaze in horror on the dying Commandant.

In this vocal ensemble, three very different sentiments are conveyed simultaneously: surprise and satisfaction (Don Giovanni), the desire to flee (Leporello), and the pain of a violent death (Commandant). At the end, the listener can feel the Commandant expire, his life sinking away through the slow descent of a chromatic scale (0:56). In its intensity and compression, only the opening scene of Shakespeare's *King Lear* rivals the beginning of *Don Giovanni*.

♪ *Listening* GUIDE

Wolfgang Amadeus Mozart
Opera, *Don Giovanni* (1787), K. 527
Act I, Scene 1

5

2/27–28

Characters: Don Giovanni, a rakish lord; Leporello, his servant; Donna Anna, a virtuous noblewoman; the Commandant, her father, a retired military man

ARIA

			Leporello	
0:00 [27]		The pacing Leporello grumbles as he awaits his master Don Giovanni	Notte e giorno faticar, per chi nulla sa gradir, piova e il vento sopportar, mangiar male e mal dormir. Voglio far il gentiluomo e non volgio più servir . . .	On the go from morn 'til night for one who shows no appreciation, sustaining wind and rain, without proper food or sleep. I would like to play the gentleman and no more a servant be . . .

(Leporello continues in this vein.)

1:40		Violins rush up scale and music modulates upward as Don Giovanni and Donna Anna rush in

ENSEMBLE (TRIO)

			Donna Anna	
1:46		Donna Anna tries to hold and unmask Don Giovanni while Leporello cowers on side	Non sperar, se non m'uccidi, ch'io ti lasci fuggir mai.	Do not hope you can escape unless you kill me.

Don Giovanni

| Donna folle, indarno gridi, chi son io tu non saprai. | Crazy lady, you scream in vain, you will never know who I am. |

Leporello

Che tumulto, oh ciel, che gridi	What a racket, heavens, what screams,
il padron in nuovi guai.	my master in a new scrape.

Donna Anna

Gente! Servi! Al traditore!	Everyone! Help! Catch the traitor!
Scellerato!	Scoundrel!

Don Giovanni

Taci et trema al mio furore!	Shut up and get out of my way!
Sconsigliata!	Fool!

Leporello

Sta a veder che il malandrino	We will see if this malefactor
mi farà recipitar. . . .	will be the ruin of me. . . .

(The trio continues in this manner with liberal repeats of text and music.)

3:04	String tremolo and shift from major to minor as the Commandant enters		

ENSEMBLE (TRIO)

	The Commandant comes forward to fight; Don Giovanni first refuses, then duels; Leporello tries to flee	**Commandant**

Lasciala, indegno!	Let her go, villain!
Battiti meco!	Fight with me!

Don Giovanni

Va! non mi degno	Away, I wouldn't deign
di pugnar teco!	to fight with you!

Commandant

Così pretendi	So you think
da me fuggir!	you can get away thus?

Leporello (aside)

Potessi almeno	If I could only
di qua partir!	get out of here!

Don Giovanni

Misero! attendi	You old fool! Get ready then,
se vuoi morir!	if you wish to die!

3:55	Musical duel (running scales and tense diminished chords)
4:00	Climax on intense diminished chord (the Commandant falls mortally wounded), then pause

ENSEMBLE (TRIO)

4:06 **28**	0:00	Don Giovanni and Leporello look upon dying Commandant; "ticking" sound in strings freezes time	**Commandant**

Ah, soccorso! son tradito.	Ah, I'm wounded, betrayed.
L'assassino m'ha ferito,	The assassin has run me through,
e dal seno palpitante	and from my heaving breast
sento l'anima partir.	I feel my soul depart.

Don Giovanni

Ah, gia cade il sciagurato,	Ah, already the old fool falls,
affannoso e agonizzante,	gasping and writhing in pain,
già del seno palpitante	and from his heaving breast
Veggo l'anima partir.	I can see his soul depart.

(continued)

Leporello

Qual misfatto! qual eccesso!	What a horrible thing, how stupid!
Entro il sen dallo spavento	I can feel within my breast
palpitar il cor mi sento.	my heart pounding from fear.
Io non so che far, che dir.	I don't know what to say or do.

5:02   0:56   Slow, chromatic descent
as last breath seeps out of
the Commandant

Listen to streaming music in an Active Listening Guide, available on the text website.

@

Download a Supplementary
Listening Guide for Mozart,
"Madamina," a patter-song aria in
which Leporello later shares Don
Giovanni's book of conquests with
Donna Anna, at the text website.

@

Download a Supplementary
Listening Guide for Mozart, "Ho
capito," Masetto's aria in response
to Don Giovanni's advances on his
fiancée, at the text website.

When we next meet the unrepentant Don Giovanni, he is in pursuit of the country girl Zerlina. She is the betrothed of another peasant, Masetto, and the two are to be married the next day. Don Giovanni quickly dismisses Masetto and turns his charm on the naive Zerlina. First, he tries verbal persuasion carried off in simple recitative (the harpsichord is still used to accompany simple recitatives in Classical opera, a vestige of the older Baroque practice). Zerlina, he says, is too lovely for a country bumpkin like Masetto. Her beauty demands a higher state: she will become his wife.

Simple recitative now gives way to more passionate expression in the charming duet "Là ci darem la mano" ("Give me your hand, o fairest"). During this duet, Don Giovanni persuades Zerlina to extend her hand (and the prospect of a good deal more). He begins with a seductive melody (**A**) cast squarely in the Classical mold of two four-bar antecedent–consequent phrases (see the following Listening Guide). Zerlina repeats and extends this, but she still sings alone and untouched. The Don becomes more insistent in a new phrase (**B**), and Zerlina, in turn, becomes flustered, as her quick sixteenth notes reveal. The initial melody (**A**) returns but is now sung together by the two principals, their voices intertwining—musical union accompanies the act of physical touching that occurs on stage. Finally, as if to further affirm this coupling through music, Mozart adds a concluding section (**C**) in which the two characters skip off, arm in arm ("Let's go, my treasure"), their voices linked together, mainly in parallel-moving thirds to show unity of feeling and purpose. These are the means by which a skilled composer like Mozart can underscore, through music, the drama unfolding on the stage.

Listening GUIDE

Wolfgang Amadeus Mozart
Opera, *Don Giovanni* (1787), K. 527
Act I, Scene 7

2/29–30

Characters: Don Giovanni and the peasant girl Zerlina

Situation: Don Giovanni apparently succeeding in the seduction of Zerlina

RECITATIVE

Don Giovanni

0:00   29   Alfin siam liberati, Zerlinetta gentil,
da quel scioccone.
Che ne dite, mio ben, sò far pulito?

At last, gentle Zerlina,
we are free of that clown.
And say, my love, didn't I handle it well?

Zerlina

Signore, è mio marito.

Sir, he is my fiancé.

Don Giovanni

Chi? Colui?	Who? Him?
Vi par che un onest'uomo,	Do you think that an honorable man,
un nobil cavalier, qual io mi vanto,	a noble cavalier as I believe I am,
possa soffrir che quel visetto d'oro,	could let such a golden face,
quel viso inzuccherato	such a sweet beauty,
da un bifolcaccio vil sia strapazzato?	be profaned by that clumsy oaf?

Zerlina

Ma, signor, io gli diedi parola di	But sir, I have already given my word to
sposarlo.	marry him.

Don Giovanni

Tal parola non vale un zero.	Such a promise counts for nothing.
Voi non siete fatta per esser paesana;	You were not made to be a peasant girl,
un altra sorte vi procuran quegli	a higher fate is in store for those
occhi bricconcelli, quei labretti sì belli,	mischievous eyes, those beautiful lips,
quelle dituccia candide e odorose,	those milky, perfumed hands,
par me toccar giuncata e fiutar rose.	so soft to touch, scented with roses.

Zerlina

Ah! . . . Non vorrei . . .	Ah! . . . I do not wish . . .

Don Giovanni

Che non vorreste?	What don't you wish?

Zerlina

Alfine ingannata restar.	In the end to be deceived.
Io sò che raro colle donne voi	I know that rarely are you noblemen
altri cavalieri siete onesti e sinceri.	honest and sincere with women.

Don Giovanni

Eh, un'impostura della gente plebea!	A vile slander of the low classes!
La nobiltà ha dipinta negli occhi l'onestà.	Nobility can be seen in honest eyes.
Orsù, non perdiam tempo;	Now let's not waste time.
in questo istante io ti voglio sponsar.	I will marry you immediately.

Zerlina

Voi?	You?

Don Giovanni

Certo, io. Quell casinetto è mio.	Certainly I. That villa over there is mine.
Soli saremo, e là, gioiello mio,	We will be alone, and there, my little jewel,
ci sposeremo.	we will be married.

ARIA (DUET)

Don Giovanni

Antecedent   Consequent

Là ci da-rem la mano,   là mi di-rai di sì;   ve-di, non è lon - ta-no, par - tiam, ben — mio, da — qui.

0:00 **30** A	Là ci darem la mano,	Give me your hand, o fairest,
	là mi dirai di sì.	whisper a gentle "yes."
	Vedi, non è lontano:	See, it's not far:
	partiam, ben mio, da qui.	let's go, my love.

Zerlina

0:20	Vorrei, e non vorrei,	I'd like to but yet I would not.
	mi trema un poco il cor;	My heart will not be still.
	felice, è ver, sarei,	'Tis true I would be happy,
	ma può burlarmi ancor.	yet he may deceive me still.

(continued)

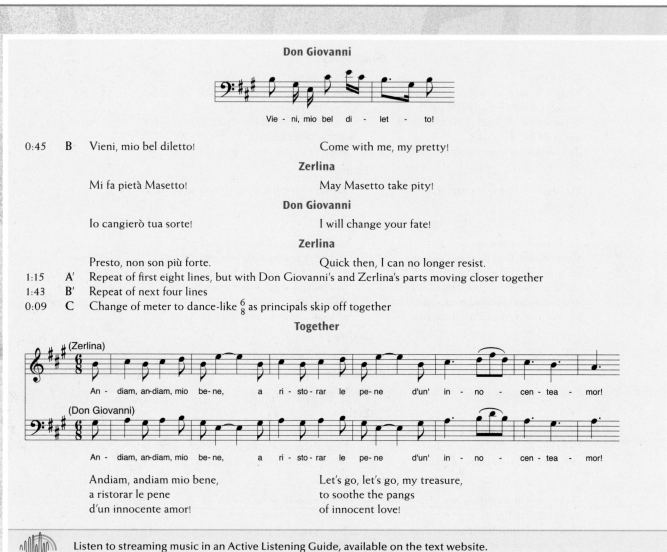

Don Giovanni

Vie - ni, mio bel di - let - to!

0:45	B	Vieni, mio bel diletto!	Come with me, my pretty!

Zerlina

Mi fa pietà Masetto!   May Masetto take pity!

Don Giovanni

Io cangierò tua sorte!   I will change your fate!

Zerlina

Presto, non son più forte.   Quick then, I can no longer resist.

1:15	A′	Repeat of first eight lines, but with Don Giovanni's and Zerlina's parts moving closer together
1:43	B′	Repeat of next four lines
0:09	C	Change of meter to dance-like $\frac{6}{8}$ as principals skip off together

Together

(Zerlina)

An - diam, an-diam, mio be-ne,   a ri-sto-rar le pe-ne   d'un' in - no - cen-te a - mor!

(Don Giovanni)

An - diam, an-diam, mio be-ne,   a ri-sto-rar le pe-ne   d'un' in - no - cen-te a - mor!

Andiam, andiam mio bene,   Let's go, let's go, my treasure,
a ristorar le pene   to soothe the pangs
d'un innocente amor!   of innocent love!

Listen to streaming music in an Active Listening Guide, available on the text website.

In the end, the frightful ghost of the dead Commandant confronts Don Giovanni and orders him to repent. Ever defiant, Don Giovanni cries, "No, no," and is dragged down to Hell to the sounds of Mozart's most demonic music. It is the admixture of divine beauty and sinister power that makes *Don Giovanni* a masterpiece of the highest order. No wonder Andrew Lloyd Webber paid homage to it in his long-running *Phantom of the Opera*.

@

The materials on the text website will help you understand and pass tests on the content of this chapter. In addition, you may watch Craig Wright's own lecture at Open Yale Courses and view Active Listening Guides and other materials that will help you succeed in this course.

Key WORDS

vocal ensemble (202)   *Singspiel* (203)   diminished chord (204)

BEETHOVEN
BRIDGE TO ROMANTICISM

21

No composer looms larger as an iconic figure than Ludwig van Beethoven (1770–1827). When we imagine the "musician as artist," most likely it is the angry, defiant, disheveled Beethoven (Fig. 21-1) who comes to mind. Is it not the bust of Beethoven, rather than the elegant Mozart or the stalwart Bach, that sits atop Schroeder's piano in the comic strip *Peanuts*? Is it not Beethoven who is the namesake of nearly a dozen popular kids' films (*Beethoven, Beethoven's 2nd,* and *Beethoven Lives Upstairs,* for example). And, is it not Beethoven's Fifth Symphony that, in one episode of *The Simpsons,* inaugurates Springfield's new concert hall? Such observations are not mere trivialities. Beethoven is deeply ingrained in our popular culture.

Even in his own day, Beethoven had a cult-like following, embraced as both mad genius and popular hero. Oblivious to the world, he walked about Vienna humming and scribbling music in a notebook. When he died in March 1827, 20,000 people turned out for the funeral. Schools closed, and the army mobilized to control the huge crowd—a final scene worthy of Michael Jackson.

BEETHOVEN'S MUSIC

Today Beethoven's music continues to enjoy great popular favor. Statistics show that his symphonies, sonatas, and quartets are performed in concert and on radio more than those of any other classical composer. These works are tender but powerful, sometimes carefully controlled, sometimes exploding with musical violence. And just as Beethoven the composer struggled to overcome personal adversity—his growing deafness—so his music imparts a feeling of struggle and ultimate victory. It has a sense of rightness, even morality, about it. It elevates and inspires all of us.

Historians have traditionally divided Beethoven's music into three periods: early, middle, and late. In many regards, his work belongs to the tradition of the Classical Viennese style. Beethoven employs Classical genres (symphony, sonata, concerto, string quartet, and opera) and Classical forms (sonata–allegro, rondo, and theme and variations). Yet even in compositions from his early period, Beethoven projects a new spirit in his music, one that foreshadows the musical style of the Romantic era (1820–1900). An intense, lyrical expression is heard in his slow movements, while his allegros abound with pounding rhythms, strong dynamic contrasts, and startling orchestral effects. Although Beethoven largely stays within the bounds of Classical forms, he pushes their confines

FIGURE 21–1

A somewhat glamorized portrait of 1819 showing Ludwig van Beethoven at work on his *Missa Solemnis*. In reality, Beethoven had a pock-marked face and was usually unshaven.

© Beethoven Haus, Bonn/The Bridgeman Art Library

to the breaking point, so great is his urge for personal expression. Though a pupil of Haydn and a lifelong admirer of Mozart, he nevertheless elevated music to new heights of both lyricism and dramatic power. For this reason, he can rightly be called the prophet of Romantic music.

THE EARLY YEARS (1770–1802)

Like Bach and Mozart before him, Beethoven came from a family of musicians. His father and grandfather were performers at the court at Bonn, Germany, on the Rhine River, where Beethoven was born on December 17, 1770. Seeing great musical talent in his young son, Beethoven's father, a violent alcoholic, forcibly made him practice at the keyboard at all hours, day and night. Soon he tried to exploit his son as a child prodigy, a second Mozart, telling the world that the diminutive boy was a year or two younger than he actually was. After an abortive attempt to study with Mozart in Vienna in 1787, Beethoven moved there for good in 1792, a year after Mozart's death. As one of his financial backers said at the time, "You are going to Vienna in fulfillment of your long-frustrated wishes . . . you will receive the spirit of Mozart from the hands of Haydn."

When Beethoven arrived in Vienna, he not only took composition lessons from Joseph Haydn but also bought new clothes, located a wig maker, and found a dancing instructor. His aim was to gain entrée into the homes of the wealthy of the Austrian capital. And this he soon achieved, owing not to his woeful social skills, but to his phenomenal ability as a pianist.

Beethoven played the piano louder, more forcefully, and even more violently than anyone the Viennese nobility had ever heard. He possessed an extraordinary technique—even if he did hit occasional wrong notes—and this he put to good use, especially in his fanciful improvisations. As a contemporary witness observed, "He knew how to produce such an impression on every listener that frequently there was not a single dry eye, while many broke out into loud sobs, for there was a certain magic in his expression."

The aristocracy was captivated. One patron put a string quartet at Beethoven's disposal, another made it possible for the composer to experiment with a small orchestra, and all showered him with gifts. He acquired well-to-do pupils; he sold his compositions ("I state my price and they pay," he said with pride in 1801); and he requested and eventually received an annuity from three noblemen so that he could work undisturbed. The text of this arrangement includes the following provisions:

It is recognized that only a person who is as free as possible from all cares can consecrate himself to his craft. He can only produce these great and sublime works which ennoble Art if they form his sole pursuit, to the exclusion of all unnecessary obligations. The undersigned have therefore taken the decision to ensure that Herr Ludwig van Beethoven's situation shall not be embarrassed by his most necessary requirements, nor shall his powerful genius be hampered.

What a contrast between Beethoven's contract and the one signed by Haydn four decades earlier (see p. 164)! Music was no longer merely a craft, and the composer a servant. It had now become an exalted Art, and the great creator a Genius who must be protected and nurtured—a new, Romantic notion of the value of music and the importance of the creator. Beethoven did his best to encourage this belief in the exalted mission of the composer as artist. He would not stand at the beck and call of a master. When one patron demanded that he play for a visiting French general, Beethoven stormed out of the salon and responded by letter: "Prince, what you are, you are through the accident of birth. What I am, I am through my own efforts. There have been many princes and there will be thousands more. But there is only one Beethoven!" What Beethoven failed to realize, of course, is that he, too, owed his success to "the accident of birth": Coming from a long line of musicians, he had been born with a huge musical talent.

Piano Sonata, Opus 13, the "Pathétique" Sonata (1799)

The bold originality in Beethoven's music can be heard in one of his most celebrated compositions, the **"Pathétique" Sonata.** A Classical sonata, as we have seen, is a multimovement work for solo instrument or solo instrument with keyboard accompaniment. That Beethoven himself supplied the title *"Pathétique"* ("Plaintive") for this solo piano sonata suggests the passion and pathos he felt within it. Its great drama and intensity derive in large part from the juxtaposition of extremes. There are extremes of dynamics (from *fortissimo* to *pianissimo*), tempo (*grave* to *presto*), and range (from very high to very low). The piece also requires of the pianist more technical skill and stamina than had any piano sonata of Mozart or Haydn. Displaying his virtuosity, Beethoven frequently performed the *"Pathétique"* in the homes and palaces of the Viennese aristocracy.

© Stock Montage/SuperStock

FIGURE 21–2

A fanciful, yet in many ways accurate, depiction of Beethoven in the midst of creative chaos. Beethoven's domestic surroundings were always in disarray. In many ways, he served as the "poster boy" for the nineteenth-century concept of genius: a solitary, lonely figure who suffered for, and lived only for, his art.

FIRST MOVEMENT

Contemporaries recount how Beethoven the pianist played with "superhuman" speed and force, and how he banged the keys so hard on one occasion that he broke six strings. The crashing C minor chord that opens the *"Pathétique"* Sonata suggests Beethoven's sometimes violent approach to the instrument. After this startling opening gesture, Beethoven the dramatist continues by juxtaposing music of wildly differing moods: the *sforzando* chord is immediately followed by quiet lyricism, only to be interrupted by another chordal thunderbolt. This slow introduction is probably a written-out version of the sort of improvisation at the piano that gained Beethoven great fame in Vienna. The introduction leads to a racing first theme that rises impetuously in the right hand. The sense of anxiety the listener feels is amplified by the bass, where the left hand of the pianist plays broken octaves (the alternation of two tones an octave apart) reminiscent of the rumble of distant thunder.

@ Download a Supplementary Listening Guide for Beethoven's "Moonlight" Sonata, first and third movements, at the text website.

@ Watch a video of Craig Wright's Open Yale Course class session 18, "Piano Music of Mozart and Beethoven," at the text website.

EXAMPLE 21–1

The remainder of the movement now plays out as a contest between the impetuous, racing themes and the stormy chords. But while there is much passion and intensity here, there is also Classical formal control. The crashing chords come back at the beginning of both the development and the coda in this sonata–allegro form movement. Thus the chords set firm formal boundaries and thereby prevent the racing theme from flying out of control. Beethoven's music often conveys a feeling of struggle: classical forms gave Beethoven something to struggle against.

Listening GUIDE

Ludwig van Beethoven
Piano Sonata, Opus 13, the *"Pathétique"*
Sonata (1799)
First movement, *Grave; Allegro di molto e con brio* (grave; very fast and with gusto)

5   **2**
3/1–3   1/23–25

Genre: Sonata

Form: Sonata–allegro

INTRODUCTION

0:00	**1**	Crashing chords alternate with softer, more lyrical ones
0:33	**23**	Softer chords continually cut off by crashing chords below
0:50		Melody builds to climax and then rapid descent

EXPOSITION [ ] = repeats

| 1:24 | [3:08] | **First theme:** Rising agitated melody in right hand against broken octaves in left |

| 1:43 | [3:27] | Transition modulates to new key, thinner texture |
| 1:56 | [3:40] | **Second theme:** Bass, followed by treble, initiates "call and response" |

2:29	[4:12]	**Closing theme, part 1:** Right and left hands race in opposite directions
2:49	[4:32]	**Closing theme, part 2:** Rapid scales in right hand above simple chords in left
2:56	[4:39]	Reminiscence of first theme

DEVELOPMENT

4:54	**2**	0:00	Crashing chords and softer chords from introduction
5:30	**24**	0:36	First theme extended and varied
6:11		1:17	Rapid twisting descent played by right hand leads to recapitulation

RECAPITULATION

6:17	**3**	0:00	**First theme:** Rising agitated melody in right hand
6:28	**25**	0:11	Transition
6:38		0:21	**Second theme:** Call and response between bass and treble
7:05		0:48	**Closing theme, part 1:** Hands move rapidly in opposite directions
7:25		1:08	**Closing theme, part 2:** Scale runs in right hand
7:31		1:14	Reminiscence of first theme

CODA

| 7:49 | | 1:32 | Recall of chords from introduction |
| 8:21 | | 2:04 | Reminiscence of first theme leads to drive to final cadence |

 Listen to streaming music in an Active Listening Guide, available on the text website.

Listening EXERCISE 27

Beethoven

"PATHÉTIQUE" SONATA

⑤   **②**   **@**   To take this Listening Exercise online and receive feedback or email answers to your instructor, go to the text website.

3/1–3   1/23–25

0:00–1:23   **1/23**   **Introduction**

1. The introduction conveys an unsettled, uncertain feeling. What, specifically, does Beethoven *not* do to create this mood?
   a. He puts very loud and very soft sounds in close proximity.
   b. He starts with happy major chords and moves to sad minor ones.
   c. He contrasts high and low ranges of the piano.
   d. He contrasts slow chords with racing descents.

2. (1:18–1:23) The end of the introduction is marked by a long descent. Which hand of the pianist plays this descent?
   a. right hand   b. left hand

1:24–3:07   **Exposition**

3. (1:18–1:24) The descent gives way to the first theme (1:24), and the tempo changes. Which statement is true?
   a. A fast tempo gives way to a slower one.
   b. A fast tempo gives way to an even faster one.
   c. *Grave* (very slow) gives way to *allegro con brio* (fast with gusto).

4. A rumbling broken-octave bass had accompanied the agitated first theme (1:24–1:42). Now here in the transition (1:43–1:55), can these menacing broken octaves still be heard in the bass?
   a. yes   b. no

5. (1:43–1:55) Transitions involve a movement from one theme and key to another. This one effects motion through the use of what?
   a. rising monophony
   b. rising melodic sequence
   c. rising monotony

6. (2:58–3:06) The final cadence of the exposition is marked by a thick texture. How is this created?
   a. The left hand alternates chords in the top and middle ranges while the right plays ascending broken chords.
   b. The right hand alternates chords in the top and middle ranges while the left plays descending broken octaves.

3:08–4:53   Now comes the repeat of the exposition. As you listen, check your answers to questions 4–6.

0:00–1:22   **2/24**   **Development**

7. (0:00–0:38) The development begins with a return to the chords of the introduction and then proceeds with the first theme. Which statement is true about the tempo in this passage?
   a. The music accelerates and then becomes progressively slower.
   b. The music gets progressively slower, almost stopping, and then suddenly becomes fast.
   c. The music proceeds at a moderate pace and then suddenly becomes fast.

8. (1:17–1:22) Does the left hand (bass) rest during the rapid twisting descent at the end of the development? In other words, is this a solo for the right hand?
   a. yes   b. no

0:00–1:31   **3/25**   **Recapitulation**

1:32–2:14   **Coda**

9. (2:09–2:14) How does this movement end?
   a. with the crashing chords of the introduction
   b. with a soft fadeout
   c. with the closing theme

10. If you were fortunate enough to have been invited to the home of one of Beethoven's aristocratic patrons in Vienna and hear the composer himself perform the *"Pathétique"* Sonata, why is it unlikely that you would have fallen asleep? Choose two answers.
    a. You can never relax while listening to this piece: loud contrasts with soft, fast with slow, and lyrical melody with pounding chords.
    b. There is a uniform and constant mood throughout—of theme, of tempo, and of dynamics.
    c. You would want to be awake to see Beethoven break a string.
    d. All of the above.

SECOND MOVEMENT

Eyewitnesses who heard Beethoven at the piano remarked on the "legato" quality of his playing and contrasted it with Mozart's lighter, more staccato style. Beethoven himself said in 1796 that "one can sing on the piano, so long as one has feeling." We can hear Beethoven sing through the legato melodic line that dominates the slow second movement of the *"Pathétique"* Sonata. Indeed, the expression mark he gave to the movement is *cantabile* (songful). The

Listen to "This Night" in the iTunes, Rhapsody, and YouTube playlists at the text website.

Download a Supplementary Listening Guide for Beethoven's "*Pathétique*" Sonata, second movement, at the text website.

Download a Supplementary Listening Guide for Beethoven's *Egmont* overture at the text website.

singing quality of the melody seems to have appealed to pop star Billy Joel, who borrowed this theme for the chorus (refrain) of his song "This Night" on the album *Innocent Man*.

THIRD MOVEMENT

A comparison of the second and third movements of the "*Pathétique*" Sonata will show that musical form does not determine musical mood. Although both the *Adagio* and the fast finale are in rondo form, the first is a lyrical hymn, and the latter a passionate, but slightly comical, chase. The finale has hints of the crashing chords and stark contrasts of the first movement, but the earlier violence and impetuosity have been softened into a mood of impassioned playfulness.

* * * * *

The eighteenth-century piano sonata had been essentially private music of a modest sort—music a composer-teacher like Mozart or Haydn would write for a talented amateur pupil to be played as entertainment in the home. Beethoven took the modest, private piano sonata and infused it with the technical bravura of the public stage. The louder sound, wider range, and greater length of Beethoven's thirty-two piano sonatas made them appropriate for the increasingly large concert halls—and pianos—of the nineteenth century. Beginning in the Romantic period, Beethoven's piano sonatas became a staple of the professional virtuoso's repertoire. But there was a downside: sonatas that had originally been created for all amateurs to play were now becoming too difficult. The virtuoso had begun to run off with the amateur's music, a development that would continue throughout the nineteenth century.

Beethoven Loses His Hearing

Beethoven cut a strange, eccentric figure as he wandered the streets of Vienna, sometimes humming, sometimes mumbling, and sometimes jotting on music paper. Adding to the difficulties of his somewhat unstable personality was the fact that he was gradually losing his hearing—a serious handicap for any person, but a tragic condition for a musician. Can you imagine a blind painter?

Beethoven first complained about his hearing and a ringing in his ears in the late 1790s, and he suffered considerable anguish and depression. His growing deafness did not stop him from composing—most people can hear simple melodies inside their heads, and the gifted Beethoven could generate complex melodies and harmonies in his "inner ear" without need of external sound. However, his condition caused him to retreat even further from society and all but ended his career as a pianist, since he could no longer gauge how hard to press the keys. By late 1802, Beethoven recognized that he would ultimately suffer a total loss of hearing. In despair, he wrote something akin to a last will and testament, today called the **Heiligenstadt Testament** after the Viennese suburb in which he penned it. In this confessional document for posterity, the composer admits that he considered suicide: "I would have ended my life; it was only *my art* that held me back." Beethoven emerged from this personal crisis with renewed resolve to fulfill his artistic destiny—he would now "seize Fate by the throat."

THE "HEROIC" PERIOD (1803–1813)

It was in this resurgent, defiant mood that Beethoven entered what we call his **"heroic" period** of composition (1803–1813; also simply termed his "middle period"). His works became longer, more assertive, and full of grand gestures.

Simple, often triadic, themes predominate, and these are repeated, sometime incessantly, as the music swells to majestic proportions. When these themes are played *forte* and given over to the brass instruments, a heroic, triumphant sound results.

Beethoven wrote nine symphonies in all, six of them during his "heroic" period. These symphonies are few in number in part because they are so much longer and more complex than those of Mozart or Haydn. They set the standard for the epic symphony of the nineteenth century. Most noteworthy are the "Eroica" (Third), the famous Fifth Symphony, the Sixth (called the "Pastoral" because it evokes the ambiance of the Austrian countryside), the Seventh, and the monumental Ninth. In these, Beethoven introduces new orchestral colors by bringing new instruments into the symphony orchestra: the trombone (Symphony Nos. 5, 6, and 9), the contrabassoon (Symphony Nos. 5 and 9), the piccolo (Symphony Nos. 5, 6, and 9), and even the human voice (Symphony No. 9).

@ Download a Supplementary Listening Guide for Beethoven's "Eroica" Symphony, fourth movement, at the text website.

@ Watch a video of Craig Wright's Open Yale Course class session 20, "The Colossal Symphony: Beethoven, Berlioz, Mahler, and Shostakovich," at the text website.

Symphony No. 3 in E♭ major ("Eroica") (1803)

As its title suggests, Beethoven's **"Eroica" ("Heroic")** **Symphony** epitomizes the grandiose, heroic style. More than any other single orchestral work, it changed the historical direction of the symphony. Its length, some forty-five minutes, is nearly twice that of a typical symphony by his teacher Haydn. It assaults the ear with startling rhythmic effects and chord changes that were shocking to early-nineteenth-century listeners. Most novel for Beethoven, the work has biographical content, for the hero of the "Eroica" Symphony, at least originally, was Napoleon Bonaparte.

Austria and the German states were at war with France in the early nineteenth century. Yet German-speaking Beethoven was much taken with the enemy's revolutionary call for liberty, equality, and fraternity. Napoleon Bonaparte became his hero, and the composer dedicated his third symphony to him, writing on the title page "intitolata Bonaparte." But when news that Napoleon had declared himself emperor reached Beethoven, he flew into a rage, saying, "Now he, too, will trample on all the rights of man and indulge his ambition." Taking up a knife, he scratched so violently to erase Bonaparte's name from the title page that he left a hole in the paper (Fig. 21-3). When the work was published, Napoleon's name had been removed in favor of the more general title "Heroic Symphony: To Celebrate the Memory of a Great Man" (Fig. 21-4). Beethoven was not an imperialist; he was a revolutionary.

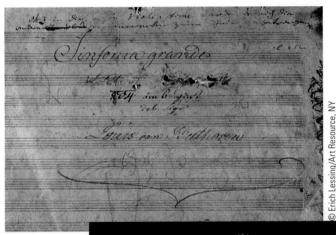

© Erich Lessing/Art Resource, NY

© Burstein Collection/CORBIS

FIGURES 21–3 AND 21–4

(top) The title page of the autograph of Beethoven's "Eroica" Symphony: *Sinfonia grande intitolata Bonaparte.* Note the hole where Beethoven took a knife and scratched out the name "Bonaparte." (right) As a young officer, Napoleon Bonaparte seized control of the government of France in 1799. He established a new form of republican government that emphasized the revolutionary ideals of liberty, equality, and humanity. After Napoleon elevated himself to emperor in 1804, Beethoven changed the title of his Symphony No. 3 from "Bonaparte" to "Eroica." The portrait by Jacques-Louis David shows the newly crowned Napoleon in full imperial regalia. Liberator had become oppressor.

Symphony No. 5 in C minor (1808)

At the center of Beethoven's symphonic output stands his remarkable Symphony No. 5 (see also pp. 8–9). Its novelty rests in the way the composer conveys a sense of psychological progression over the course of four movements. An imaginative listener might perceive the following sequence of events: (1) a fateful encounter with elemental forces, (2) a period of quiet soul-searching, followed by (3) a further wrestling with the elements, and, finally, (4) a triumphant victory over the forces of Fate. Beethoven himself is said to have remarked with regard to the famous opening motive of the symphony: "There Fate knocks at the door!"

The rhythm of the opening—perhaps the best-known moment in all of classical music—animates the entire symphony. Not only does it dominate the opening *Allegro,* but it reappears in varied form in the three later movements as well, binding the symphony into a unified whole.

EXAMPLE 21–2

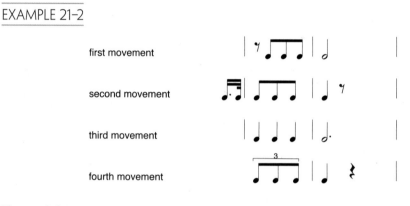

FIRST MOVEMENT

At the very outset, the listener is jolted to attention, forced to sit up and take notice by a sudden explosion of sound. And what an odd beginning to a symphony—a blast of three short notes and a long one, followed by the same three shorts and a long, all now a step lower. The movement can't quite get going. It starts and stops, then seems to lurch forward and gather momentum. And where is the melody? This three-shorts-and-a-long pattern is more a motive or musical cell than a melody. Yet it is striking by virtue of its power and compactness. As the movement unfolds, the actual pitches of the motive prove to be of secondary importance. Beethoven is obsessed with its rhythm. He wants to demonstrate the enormous latent force lurking within even the most basic rhythmic atom, a power waiting to be unleashed by a composer who understands the secrets of rhythmic energy.

To control the sometimes violent forces that will emerge, the music unfolds within the traditional confines of sonata–allegro form. The basic four-note motive provides all the musical material for the first theme area.

EXAMPLE 21–3

The brief transition played by a solo French horn is only six notes long and is formed simply by adding two notes to the end of the basic four-note motive. As expected, the transition carries us tonally from the tonic (C minor) to the relative major (E♭ major).

EXAMPLE 21–4

The second theme offers a moment of escape from the rush of the "fate" motive, but even here the pattern of three shorts and a long lurks beneath like a ticking time bomb.

EXAMPLE 21–5

The closing theme, too, is none other than the motive once again, now presented in a more heroic guise.

EXAMPLE 21–6

In the development, the opening motive returns, recapturing, and even surpassing, the force it had at the beginning. The motive soon takes on different melodic forms, tossed back and forth between instruments, though the rhythmic shape remains constant.

EXAMPLE 21–7

As the motive rises, so does the musical tension. A powerful rhythmic climax ensues and then gives way to a brief imitative passage. Soon Beethoven reduces the six-note motive of the transition to merely two notes, and then just one, passing these figures around *pianissimo* between the strings and winds.

EXAMPLE 21–8

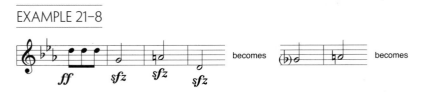

Beethoven was a master of the process of thematic condensation—stripping away all extraneous material to get to the core of a musical idea. Here, in this mysterious *pianissimo* passage, he presents the irreducible minimum of his motive: a single note. In the midst of this quiet, the original four-note motive tries to reassert itself *fortissimo*, yet at first cannot do so. Its explosive force, however, cannot be held back. A thunderous return of the opening chords signals the beginning of the recapitulation.

Although the recapitulation offers a repeat of the events of the exposition, Beethoven has one surprise in store. No sooner has the motive regained its momentum than an oboe interjects a tender, languid, and wholly unexpected solo. A deviation from the usual path of sonata–allegro form, this brief oboe cadenza allows for a momentary release of excess energy. The recapitulation then resumes its expected course.

What is not expected is the enormous coda that follows. It is even longer than the exposition! A new form of the motive appears, and it, too, is subjected to development. In fact, this coda constitutes essentially a second development section, so great is Beethoven's single urge to exploit the latent power of this one simple musical idea.

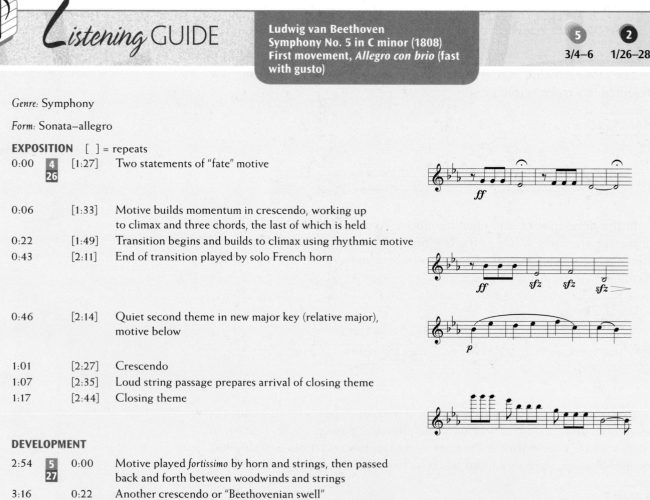

Listening GUIDE

Ludwig van Beethoven
Symphony No. 5 in C minor (1808)
First movement, *Allegro con brio* (fast with gusto)

5 3/4–6   2 1/26–28

Genre: Symphony

Form: Sonata–allegro

EXPOSITION [ ] = repeats

0:00	**4** **26**	[1:27]	Two statements of "fate" motive
0:06		[1:33]	Motive builds momentum in crescendo, working up to climax and three chords, the last of which is held
0:22		[1:49]	Transition begins and builds to climax using rhythmic motive
0:43		[2:11]	End of transition played by solo French horn
0:46		[2:14]	Quiet second theme in new major key (relative major), motive below
1:01		[2:27]	Crescendo
1:07		[2:35]	Loud string passage prepares arrival of closing theme
1:17		[2:44]	Closing theme

DEVELOPMENT

2:54	**5** **27**	0:00	Motive played *fortissimo* by horn and strings, then passed back and forth between woodwinds and strings
3:16		0:22	Another crescendo or "Beethovenian swell"
3:22		0:28	Rhythmic climax in which motive is pounded incessantly
3:30		0:36	Short passage of imitative counterpoint using transition motive
3:40		0:46	Two notes of transition motive passed back and forth
3:51		0:57	Single note passed back and forth between winds and strings; gets quiet
4:03		1:09	Basic four-note motive tries to reassert itself loudly
4:11		1:17	Motive reenters insistently

RECAPITULATION

4:17	**6**	0:00	Return of motive
4:26	**28**	0:09	Motive gathers momentum and cadences with three chords
4:37		0:20	Unexpected oboe solo

4:51	0:34	Motive returns and moves hurriedly to climax
5:15	0:58	Quiet second theme with motive below
5:31	1:14	Crescendo leading to closing theme
5:51	1:34	Closing theme

CODA

5:59	1:42	Motive pounded *fortissimo* on one note, then again step higher
6:15	1:58	Imitative counterpoint
6:30	2:13	Rising quarter notes form new four-note pattern
6:40	2:23	New four-note pattern alternates between strings and woodwinds
7:00	2:42	Pounding on single note, then motive as at beginning
7:21	3:04	Succession of I–V–I chords brings movement to abrupt end

Listen to streaming music in an Active Listening Guide, available on the text website.

Listening EXERCISE 28

Beethoven
SYMPHONY NO. 5 IN C MINOR

5 **2** @

3/4–6 1/26–28

To take this Listening Exercise online and receive feedback or email answers to your instructor, go to the text website.

The first movement of Beethoven's Symphony No. 5 is perhaps the most famous movement in all of classical music. The following questions are designed to show how Beethoven honored, but sometimes broke with, the usual Classical treatment of sonata–allegro form.

0:00–2:53 **4 / 26** Exposition and repeat

1. (0:00–0:43) Which instruments carry the four-note motive and its immediate repetitions?
   a. strings   b. woodwinds   c. brasses

2. (0:46–0:52) Normally in a movement in sonata–allegro form in a minor key, the second theme in the exposition appears in the major mode. Does Beethoven honor that tradition?
   a. yes   b. no

3. (1:17–1:26) Similarly, in a movement in sonata–allegro form in a minor key, the exposition will normally end in a major key and go back to the minor key for the beginning of the repeat of the exposition. Does Beethoven move from major back to minor here?
   a. yes   b. no

4. Consider now the length of the exposition, and compare it to other movements in sonata–allegro form previously studied (see pp. 176–177, 192, 200, and 212). In his Symphony No. 5, Beethoven has constructed an exposition that is what?
   a. similar to the norm in length
   b. remarkably short
   c. remarkably long

0:00–1:22 **5 / 27** Development

5. (0:28–0:35) Consider the rhythmic climax in which the motive is pounded incessantly. This climax occurs where in the movement?
   a. in the first third
   b. in the exact middle
   c. in the last third

6. (1:17–1:22) At the end of the development, the orchestra insistently repeats the motive, and then

(continued)

the recapitulation begins. Beethoven helps announce the recapitulation by using which dynamic level?

a. *fortissimo*   b. *piano*   c. *pianissimo*

0:00–1:41 **6**
         28   **Recapitulation**

7. (0:20–0:33) A solo oboe suddenly interrupts the recapitulation. Was this oboe "cadenza" in the exposition?

a. yes   b. no

8. (0:58–1:13) If Beethoven's treatment of sonata–allegro form honors tradition, he will bring the second theme back in the minor mode. Does the second theme, in fact, come back in minor?

a. yes   b. no

1:42–end **Coda**

9. (1:42–end) Consider the length of the coda. Is it longer or shorter than the exposition?

a. longer   b. shorter

10. Finally, how does Beethoven deviate in this movement from tradition in his treatment of Classical sonata–allegro form?

a. He fails to honor the traditional key format for a sonata–allegro movement in minor.

b. He interrupts the recapitulation with an instrumental "cadenza."

c. He shifts much of the weight of the movement from the exposition to the coda.

d. All of the above.

SECOND MOVEMENT

After the pounding we experienced in the explosive first movement, the calm of the noble *Andante* comes as a welcome change of pace. The mood is at first serene, and the melody is expansive—in contrast to the four-note motive of the first movement, the opening theme here runs on for twenty-two measures. The musical form is also a familiar one: theme and variations. But this is not the simple, easily audible theme and variations of Haydn and Mozart (see pp. 179–183). There are two themes: the first lyrical and serene, played mostly by the strings; and the second quiet, then triumphant, played mostly by the brasses. By means of this "double" theme and variations, Beethoven demonstrates his ability to add length and complexity to a standard Classical form (Fig. 21-5). He also shows how it is possible to contrast within one movement two starkly opposed expressive domains—the intensely lyrical (theme 1) and the brilliantly heroic (theme 2).

FIGURE 21–5

Original autograph of Beethoven at work on the second movement of his Symphony No. 5. The many corrections in different-colored inks and red pencil suggest the turmoil and constant evolution involved in Beethoven's creative process. Unlike Mozart, to whom finished musical ideas came quickly, Beethoven's art was a continual struggle.

© Bildarchiv Preussischer Kulturbesitz/Art Resource, NY

BEETHOVEN AND THE BEATLES: BREAKING THE RULES

Parents try to teach their children the rules of behavior. Colleges and universities teach the rules of grammar, the rules of part writing in music, and the rules of civil procedure in law, for example. Ironically, when it comes time to hold up the great figures in Western arts and ideas, it is usually the rule breakers who are given a place of honor. Shakespeare broke the rules of Greek tragedy (of unity, time, place, and action); Galileo argued that the earth was not the center of the universe, and Einstein said that the universe was not perfectly uniform; Monet and the Impressionists defied the rules of the French Academy; and Bill Gates began his journey to revolutionize information technology by dropping out of college. Conformity and originality, it seems, may not be compatible.

The two most original, creative forces in nineteenth-century classical music and twentieth-century popular music, respectively, were Beethoven and The Beatles. While this may seem an odd pairing, each was a revolutionary force able to take music in a new direction by challenging authority, or at least by defying the authority of tradition. Think of all the radical things that Beethoven did with the symphony and the symphony orchestra: doubled the traditional length of movements (in Symphonies No. 3, 5, and 9), pushed against the wall of form by greatly expanding the coda (Symphony No. 5), brought in new instruments (trombone, contrabassoon, and piccolo in No. 5), mixed musical genres (symphony and oratorio in No. 9), and invented the "holistic" symphony by recalling the themes of earlier movements in the last movement (No. 5 and 9). For each of these iconoclastic acts, an analog can be found in the work of The Beatles: they doubled the length of the traditional three-minute pop song ("A Day in the Life") and sometimes greatly extended the coda ("Hey Jude"), mixed genres by bringing a string quartet or a Broadway chorus into a song ("Yesterday," "The Long and Winding Road"), added instruments not part of the usual rock band (sitar, harpsichord, and Baroque trumpet in "Within You Without You," "In My Life," and "Penny Lane," respectively), and crafted a relationship among all the tracks of an album, thereby creating the "concept album."

Such originality requires stepping outside the box of artistic convention. If society doesn't recognize your radical position and come to value your vision, you are merely a prophet crying in a wilderness, or worse, a lunatic. If it does, you're a genius! Your rules become the new rules—the ruling standard until the next creative genius comes along.

Listening GUIDE

**Ludwig van Beethoven
Symphony No. 5 in C minor (1808)
Second movement, *Andante con moto*
(progressing with movement)**

5
3/7–8

Genre: Symphony

Form: Theme and variations

THEMES

| 0:00 | **7** | Violas and cellos play beginning of theme 1 |

| 0:24 | Woodwinds play middle of theme 1 |

| 0:36 | Violins play end of theme 1 |

| 0:52 | Clarinets, bassoons, and violins play theme 2 |

(continued)

| 1:14 | | Brasses play theme 2 in fanfare style |
| 1:30 | | Mysterious *pianissimo* |

VARIATION 1

1:58		Violas and cellos vary beginning of theme 1 by adding sixteenth notes
2:18		Woodwinds play middle of theme 1
2:31		Strings play end of theme 1
2:48		Clarinets, bassoons, and violins play theme 2
3:10		Brasses return with fanfare (theme 2)
3:26		More of mysterious *pianissimo*

VARIATION 2

3:52	[8] 0:00	Violas and cellos overlay beginning of theme 1 with rapidly moving ornamentation
4:27	0:35	Pounding repeated chords with theme below in cellos and basses
4:44	0:52	Rising scales lead to fermata (hold)
5:04	1:12	Woodwinds play fragments of beginning of theme 1
5:50	1:58	Fanfare (theme 2) now returns in full orchestra
6:36	2:44	Woodwinds play beginning of theme 1 detached and in minor key

VARIATION 3

7:17	3:25	Violins play beginning of theme 1 *fortissimo*
7:43	3:51	Woodwinds play middle of theme 1
7:52	4:00	Strings play end of theme 1

CODA

8:08	4:17	Tempo quickens as bassoons play reminiscence of beginning of theme 1
8:23	4:31	Violins play reminiscence of theme 2
8:34	4:41	Woodwinds play middle of theme 1
8:48	4:55	Strings play end of theme 1
9:11	5:19	Ends with repetitions of rhythm of very first measure of movement

Listen to streaming music in an Active Listening Guide, available on the text website.

THIRD MOVEMENT

In the Classical period, the third movement of a symphony or quartet was usually a graceful minuet and trio (see p. 169). Haydn and his pupil Beethoven wanted to infuse this third movement with more life and energy, so they often wrote a faster, more rollicking piece and called it a scherzo, meaning "joke." And while there is nothing particularly humorous about the mysterious and sometimes threatening sound of the scherzo of Beethoven's Symphony No. 5, it is certainly far removed from the elegant world of the courtly minuet.

The formal plan of Beethoven's scherzo, **ABA'**, derives from the ternary form of the minuet, as does its triple meter. The scherzo, **A**, is in the tonic key of C minor, while the trio, **B**, is in C major. The conflict of major and minor, dark and light, is one of several that are resolved in the course of this four-movement symphony (Fig. 21-6).

FIGURE 21–6

Interior of the Theater-an-der-Wien, Vienna, where Beethoven's Symphony No. 5 premiered on December 22, 1808. This all-Beethoven concert lasted four hours, from 6:30 until 10:30 P.M., and presented eight new works, including his Symphony No. 5. During the performance of the symphony, the orchestra sometimes halted because of the difficulties in playing Beethoven's radically new music. Notice the horses on stage. Beethoven lived during a time of transition, when theaters were used for both public spectacles and music-only concerts.

© Art Archive/Museum der Stadt Wien/Alfredo Dagli Orti

Listening GUIDE

Ludwig van Beethoven
Symphony No. 5 in C minor (1808)
Third movement, *Allegro* (fast)

5
3/9–10

Genre: Symphony

Form: Ternary

SCHERZO A

0:00 **9**		Cellos and basses creep in with theme 1 and pass it on to higher strings
0:09		Repeat
0:20		French horns enter with theme 2
0:40		Cellos and basses return with theme 1
0:55		Crescendo
1:03		Full orchestra again plays theme 2 *fortissimo*
1:25		Development of theme 1
1:52		Ends with theme 2 *fortissimo*, then *piano*

TRIO B

1:59 **10**	0:00	Cellos and basses present subject of fugato
		Violas and bassoons enter with subject
		Second violins enter with subject
		First violins enter with subject
2:14	0:15	Repeat of imitative entries
2:36	0:37	Subject enters imitatively again: cellos and basses, violas and bassoons, second violins, first violins, and then flutes are added
3:04	1:05	Subject enters imitatively again in same instruments and flutes extend it

(continued)

SCHERZO A'

3:30	1:31	Quiet return of theme 1 in cellos and basses
3:39	1:40	Pizzicato (plucked) presentation of theme 1 in cellos accompanied by bassoons
3:50	1:51	Ghost-like return of theme 2 in short notes in winds and pizzicato in strings

BRIDGE TO FOURTH MOVEMENT

4:47	2:48	Long note held *pianissimo* in strings with timpani beating softly below
4:52	2:53	Repeating three-note pattern emerges in first violins
5:23	3:24	Great crescendo leads to fourth movement

Listen to streaming music in an Active Listening Guide, available on the text website.

Now, a stroke of genius on Beethoven's part: he links the third and fourth movements by means of a musical bridge. Holding a single pitch as quietly as possible, the violins create an eerie sound, while the timpani beats menacingly in the background. A three-note motive grows from the violins and is repeated over and over as a wave of sound begins to swell from the orchestra. Here Beethoven is concerned only with volume, not melody, rhythm, or harmony. With enormous force, the wave finally crashes down, and from it emerges the triumphant beginning of the fourth movement—one of the grandest "special effects" in all of music.

FOURTH MOVEMENT

When Beethoven arrived at the finale, he was faced with a nearly impossible task. The last movement of a symphony had traditionally been a light send-off. How to write a conclusion that would relieve the tension of the preceding musical events, yet provide an appropriate, substantive balance to the weighty first movement? To this end, he created a finale that is longer and beefier than the first movement. To bulk up his orchestra, Beethoven adds three trombones, a contrabassoon (low bassoon), and a piccolo (high flute), the first time any of these instruments had been called for in a symphony. He also writes big, bold, and, in most cases, triadic themes, assigning these most often to the powerful brasses. In these instruments and themes, we hear the "heroic" Beethoven at his best. The finale projects a feeling of affirmation, a sense that superhuman will has triumphed over adversity.

Listening GUIDE

Ludwig van Beethoven
Symphony No. 5 in C minor (1808)
Fourth movement, *Allegro* (fast)

⑤

3/11–13

Genre: Symphony

Form: Sonata–allegro

EXPOSITION

0:00 ⑪ Full orchestra with prominent brasses plays first theme

0:33   French horns play transition theme

0:59   Strings play second theme

1:25   Full orchestra plays closing theme

(Repeat of exposition omitted)

DEVELOPMENT

1:56	12	0:00	Loud string tremolo (fluttering)
2:01		0:05	Strings and woodwinds pass around fragments of second theme in different keys
2:24		0:28	Double basses begin to play countermelody against second theme 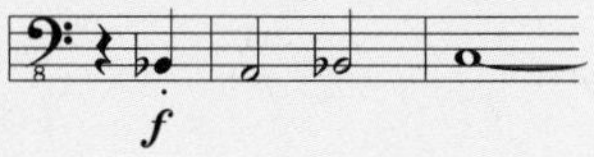
2:31		0:36	Trombones play countermelody
2:59		1:04	Woodwinds and brasses play countermelody above dominant pedal point in cellos and basses
3:15		1:20	Climax and pause on dominant triad
3:35		1:40	Ghost-like theme from scherzo (third movement) with four-note rhythm 

RECAPITULATION

4:09	13	0:00	Full orchestra plays first theme *fortissimo*
4:42		0:33	French horns play transition theme
5:13		1:04	Strings play second theme
5:38		1:29	Woodwinds play closing theme

CODA

6:09	2:00	Violins play second theme
6:19	2:10	Brasses and woodwinds play countermelody from development
6:32	2:23	V–I, V–I chords sound like final cadence
6:40	2:31	Bassoons, French horns, flutes, clarinets, and then piccolo continue with transition theme
7:07	2:58	Trill high in piccolo
7:23	3:14	Tempo changes to *presto* (very fast)
7:47	3:38	Brasses recall first theme, now twice as fast
7:55	3:46	V–I, V–I cadence followed by pounding tonic chord

Listen to streaming music in an Active Listening Guide, available on the text website.

Beethoven's Symphony No. 5 reveals his genius in a paradox: from minimal material (the basic cell), he derives maximum sonority. Climaxes are achieved by incessantly repeating the cell-like motive. Long crescendos swell like tidal waves of sound. Wildly different moods are accommodated within a single movement. In the quiet string music of the *Andante* (second movement), for example, we are never far from a heroic brass fanfare. Everywhere there is a feeling of raw, elemental power propelled by the newly enlarged orchestra. Beethoven was the first to recognize that massive sound could be a potent psychological weapon. No wonder that during World War II (1939–1945) both sides, Fascist as well as Allied, used the music of this symphony to symbolize "Victory."*

THE FINAL YEARS (1814–1827)

By 1814, Beethoven had lost his hearing entirely and had withdrawn from society. His music, too, took on a more remote, inaccessible quality, placing heavy demands on performer and audience alike. In these late works, Beethoven requires the listener to connect musical ideas over long spans of time—to engage in long-term listening. This is music that seems intended not for the audience of Beethoven's day, but rather for future generations. Most of Beethoven's late works are piano sonatas and string quartets—intimate, introspective chamber music. But two pieces, the Mass in D (*Missa Solemnis*, 1823) and the Symphony No. 9 (1824), are large-scale compositions for full orchestra and chorus. In these latter works, Beethoven strives once again to communicate directly to a broad spectrum of humanity.

Beethoven's Symphony No. 9, his last, was the first symphony in the history of music to include a chorus. Here the composer's desire for expression was so great that the instruments of the orchestra alone were no longer sufficient. To make his message obvious to all, Beethoven needed something more: text and voices. The text, *An die Freude* (**Ode to Joy**) by poet Friedrich von Schiller, is a hymn in honor of universal brotherhood, a theme that had been important to Beethoven since his earliest years. Beethoven worked on the melody for this poem, on and off, for nearly twenty years. (The melody and text are given on page 31; the melody serves as the basis of Listening Exercise 5 and can be heard on (intro)/8.)

Ultimately, Beethoven brought his setting of *Ode to Joy* into the last movement of his last symphony, where it provides a theme for a magnificent set of variations. For twenty-five minutes, the music marches toward a grand climax. Beethoven pushes the voices to sing louder and louder, higher and higher, faster than they can enunciate the text. The instrumentalists, too, are driven by the *presto* tempo to go so quickly they can scarcely play the notes. All performers strain to exceed the limits of their physical abilities and accomplish the impossible. The sound is not so much beautiful as it is overwhelming, for the chorus and orchestra speak with one exalted voice. Their message is Beethoven's message: Art will unify all humanity.

EPILOGUE: BEETHOVEN AND THE NINETEENTH CENTURY

The figure of Beethoven towered over all the arts during the nineteenth century. He had shown how personal expression might expand the confines of Classical form with astonishingly powerful results. He had

---

FIGURE 21–7

A drawing of the deceased Beethoven sketched on the morning of March 28, 1827, the day after the composer's death. It was made by Josef Danhauser, the same artist who painted the group portrait that appears on the cover of this book.

© The Cobbe Collection Trust, UK/The Bridgeman Art Library

---

*In Morse code, short–short–short–long is the letter "V," as in "Victory."

given music "the grand gesture," stunning effects like the crashing introduction of the *"Pathétique"* Sonata or the gigantic crescendo leading to the finale of the Fifth Symphony. He had shown that pure sound—sound divorced from melody and rhythm—could be glorious in and of itself. At once he had made music both grandiose and intensely lyrical. His works became the standard against which composers of the Romantic era measured their worth. The painting shown on the cover of this book depicts Franz Liszt at the piano. A bust of Beethoven, larger than life, gazes down at him from Olympian heights, a monument to all that is noble and sublime in art.

A complete Checklist of Musical Style for the Classical period can be found at the text website.

*K*ey WORDS

"Pathétique" Sonata (211)	"heroic" period (middle	"Eroica" ("Heroic")
Heiligenstadt Testament	period) (214)	Symphony (215)
(214)		*Ode to Joy* (226)

The materials on the text website will help you understand and pass tests on the content of this chapter. In addition, you may watch Craig Wright's own lectures at Open Yale Courses and complete this chapter's Listening Exercise interactively, as well as view Active Listening Guides and other materials that will help you succeed in this course.

PART V ROMANTICISM, 1820–1900

© A.K.G. Berlin/SuperStock

| 1820 | 1825 | 1830 | 1835 | 1840 | 1845 | 1850 | 1855 | 1860 |

ROMANTICISM

● 1818 Mary Shelley writes *Frankenstein*

● 1826 Felix Mendelssohn composes *Overture to A Midsummer Night's Dream*

⟵······ ● 1830 Revolution of 1830 in Europe

● 1830 Hector Berlioz composes *Symphonie fantastique* ················⟶

● 1831 Victor Hugo writes *The Hunchback of Notre Dame*

● 1845 Edgar Allen Poe writes poem "The Raven"

● 1848 Revolution of 1848 in Europe

● 1848 Karl Marx writes
The Communist Manifesto

● 1853 Giuseppe Verdi composes
opera *La traviata*

1853–1876 Richard Wagner

The Romantic era was a period in which artists aspired to go beyond the mundane, to the world of the imagination and of dreams. Belief in rational inquiry, an article of faith of the Enlightenment, began to wane. Reason gave way to passion, and objective evaluation to subjective emotion. The Romantics began to see the sublime in art and, most sublime of all, in nature herself. Poets, painters, and musicians depicted surging rivers and thunderous storms in their respective media. Love, too, became an important theme; indeed, from the word *romance*, we derive the term *romantic*. But the Romantic vision also had its dark side, and these same artists expressed a fascination with the occult, the supernatural, and the macabre. This was the age not only of Felix Mendelssohn's playful *Overture to A Midsummer Night's Dream* but also of Mary Shelley's chilling *Frankenstein*.

What was music in the Romantic era? To critic Charles Burney, writing in 1776, music was "an innocent luxury, unnecessary, indeed, to our existence." But to Beethoven, writing in 1812, music was the most important of the arts "that would raise men to the level of gods." Clearly, the very concept of music—its purpose and meaning—had undergone a profound change in these thirty-six years. No longer seen merely as entertainment, music now could point the way to previously unexplored realms of the spirit. Beethoven led the way, and many others—Berlioz, Wagner, and Brahms among them—followed in his footsteps. When the German author E. T. A. Hoffmann wrote that Beethoven's Fifth Symphony "releases the flood gates of fear, of terror, of horror, of pain, and arouses that longing for the eternal which is the essence of Romanticism," he prophesied for much Romantic music to come.

| 1860 | 1865 | 1870 | 1875 | 1880 | 1885 | 1890 | 1895 | 1900 |

ROMANTICISM

- 1860s Otto von Bismarck forges modern state of Germany

- 1861 Final unification of Italy with Rome as its capital

1861–1865 American Civil War

- 1869 Opening of Suez Canal

1870–1871 Franco–Prussian War

- 1876 Johannes Brahms premiers first of his four symphonies

- 1880 Peter Tchaikovsky revises symphonic poem *Romeo and Juliet*

- 1889 Eiffel Tower completed

1898 Spanish-American War

works on his cycle *Der Ring des Nibelungen*

22

INTRODUCTION TO ROMANTICISM

The mature music of Beethoven, with its powerful crescendos, pounding chords, and grand gestures, announces the arrival of the Romantic era in music. The transition from musical Classicism to Romanticism in the early nineteenth century coincides with similar stylistic changes in the novels, plays, poetry, and paintings of the period. In all the arts, revolutionary sentiments were in the air: a new desire for liberty, bold action, passionate feeling, and individual expression. Just as the impatient Beethoven finally cast off the wigs and powdered hair of the eighteenth century, many other Romantic artists gradually cast aside the formal constraints of the older Classical style.

ROMANTIC INSPIRATION, ROMANTIC CREATIVITY

Romanticism is often defined as a revolt against the Classical adherence to reason and rules. Whereas artists of the eighteenth century sought to achieve unity, order, and a balance of form and content, those of the nineteenth century sought self-expression, striving to communicate with passion no matter what imbalance might result. If Classical artists drew inspiration from the monuments of ancient Greece and Rome, those of the Romantic era looked to the human imagination and the wonders of nature. The Romantic artist exalted instinctive feelings—not those of the masses, but individual, personal ones. As the American Romantic poet Walt Whitman said, "I celebrate myself, and sing myself."

If a single feeling or sentiment pervaded the Romantic era, it was love. Indeed, "romance" is at the very heart of the word *Romantic*. The loves of Romeo and Juliet (Fig. 22-1), and Tristan and Isolde, for example, captured the public's imagination in the Romantic era. The endless pursuit of love, the search for the unattainable, became an obsession that, when expressed as music, produced the sounds of longing and yearning heard in so much of Romantic music.

Yet love was only one of several emotions dear to the Romantics. Despair, frenzy, and heavenly exaltation were others expressed in music and poetry. Just how the range of expression was broadened in Romantic music can be seen in the "expression marks" that came into being at this time: *espressivo* (expressively), *dolente* (sadly), *presto furioso* (fast and furiously), *con forza e passione* (with force and passion), *misterioso* (mysteriously), and *maestoso* (majestically). Not only do these directives explain to the performer how a passage ought to be played, they also reveal what the composer wished to express through music.

Romantic musicians eloquently expressed their feelings about nature (Fig. 22-2). As Beethoven proclaimed in 1821, "I perform most faithfully the duties that Humanity, God, and Nature enjoin upon me." In his "Pastoral" Symphony (Symphony No. 6), the first important Romantic "nature piece," Beethoven seeks to capture both nature's tranquil beauty and its destructive fury.

FIGURE 22-1

The Balcony Scene of Romeo and Juliet (1845) by Eugène Delacroix typifies the nineteenth-century fascination with love and with Shakespeare. Berlioz sought to capture the spirit of the play in a five-movement program symphony (*Roméo et Juliette*, 1839); Tchaikovsky tried to do so in a one-movement symphonic poem (*Romeo and Juliet*, 1880).

© A.K.G. Berlin/SuperStock
© A.K.G. Berlin/SuperStock

Schubert's "Trout" Quintet, Schumann's *Forest Scenes*, and Strauss's "Alpine" Symphony are just a few of the many musical works that continue the tradition.

Associated with this desire to be at one with nature was a passion for travel, what the Germans called a *Wanderlust*. Far-off places and people fired the Romantic imagination. The German composer Felix Mendelssohn (1809–1847) journeyed to Italy, Scotland, and the Hebrides Islands to find inspiration for his symphonies and overtures. The English poet Lord Byron sailed to Greece and Turkey and infused his art with a sense of travel and adventure (see boxed essay).

THE MUSICIAN AS "ARTIST," MUSIC AS "ART"

With the Romantic era came the idea that music was something more than mere entertainment and that the composer was more than a hired employee. Bach had been a municipal civil servant, devoted and dutiful, in the town of Leipzig. Haydn and Mozart had served and been treated as domestics in the homes of the great lords of Europe. But Beethoven began to break the chains of submission. He was the first to demand, and receive, the respect and admiration due a great creative spirit. Ultimately, Franz Liszt and Richard Wagner, as much through their literary works as their musical compositions, caused the public to view the artist as a sort of demigod, a prophet able to inspire audiences through the creation of music that was both morally uplifting and beautiful. "To the artist is entrusted the upbringing of mankind," said Liszt. Never was the position of the creative musician loftier than in the mid-nineteenth century.

Just as the musician was elevated from servant to artist, so the music he or she produced was transformed from entertainment to art. Classical music had been created for the immediate gratification of patron and audience, with little thought given to its lasting value. With the mature Beethoven and the early Romantics, this attitude began to change. Symphonies, quartets, and piano sonatas sprang to life, not to give immediate pleasure to listeners, but to satisfy a deep-seated creative urge within the composer. They became extensions of the artist's inner personality. These works might not be understood by the creator's contemporaries, as was true of the late piano sonatas of Beethoven and the orchestral works of Hector Berlioz, for example, but they would be understood by posterity, by future generations of listeners. The idea of "art for art's sake"—art free of all immediate functional concerns—was born of the Romantic spirit.

The newly exalted position of the composer and his art soon brought a more serious tone to the concert hall. Prior to 1800, a concert was as much a social event as a musical experience. People talked, drank, ate, played cards, flirted, and wandered about. Dogs ran freely on the ground floor, and armed guards roamed the theater to maintain at least some order. When people turned to the music, they were loud and demonstrative. They hummed along with the melody and tapped the beat to the music they liked. If a performance

FIGURE 22–2

Man and Woman Gazing at the Moon, by German Romantic artist Casper David Friedrich (1774–1840). The painting projects a sense not only of isolation and a contemplation of nature but also of the slow, evolutionary progress of geological time.

SHELLEY AND THE ROMANTIC POETS

Just as Romantic music is thought to be the emotional core of classical music generally, so the English Romantic poets (Wordsworth, Keats, Byron, and Shelley) are commonly seen as the heart and soul of poetry in the English language. George Gordon Lord Byron (1788–1824) and Percy Bysshe Shelley (1792–1822) led prototypically excessive Romantic lives. Byron had an affair with his half-sister, swam the Hellespont (separating Europe from Asia Minor), and died, at thirty-six, fighting for Greek national independence. Shelley was expelled from Oxford, abandoned his first wife (who later drowned herself in the center of London), and ran off with (and eventually married) Mary Godwin (1797–1851). In the summer of 1816, Percy and Mary Shelley, along with best friend Byron, lived as neighbors in the Swiss Alps, where, as an evening entertainment, she conceived her gothic novel *Frankenstein*. Ultimately, Percy Shelley died at age thirty while sailing on the Italian coast. Shelley's poem "Love's Philosophy" unites the two most powerful forces of the Romantic aesthetic: nature and romance.

© Russell-Cotes Art Gallery and Museum, Bournemouth, UK/The Bridgeman Art Library

© Stock Montage/Super Stock

Mary Godwin and Percy Bysshe Shelley.

> The fountains mingle with the river
> And the rivers with the Ocean,
> The winds of Heaven mix for ever
> With a sweet emotion;
> Nothing in the world is single;

> All things by a law divine
> In one spirit meet and mingle.
> Why not I with thine?—
>
> See the mountains kiss high Heaven
> And the waves clasp one another;
> No sister-flower would be forgiven
> If it disdained its brother;
> And the sunlight clasps the earth
> And the moonbeams kiss the sea:
> What is all this sweet work worth
> If thou kiss not me?

went well, people applauded, not only at the ends of the pieces but also between movements. Sometimes they demanded an immediate encore; other times they hissed their disapproval.

Around 1840, however, a sudden hush came over the concert hall—it became more like a church or temple. With the revered figure of the Romantic artist-composer now before them, the members of the audience sat in respectful silence. A concert-goer who was not distracted socially became a listener who was engaged emotionally. More was expected of the audience, because symphonies and sonatas were longer and more complex. But the audience, in turn, expected more from the music: not just entertainment, but an emotionally satisfying encounter that would leave the attentive listener exhausted yet somehow purified and uplifted by the artistic experience. The painting on the cover of this book, from 1840, suggests how the Romantic imagination wrapped even secular music in a sacred aura. We see a temple of art: the artists are the congregants, Liszt (center) the high priest, the piano the altar, and Beethoven the god.

Romantic Ideals and Today's Concert Hall

Romanticism has kept its grip on the Western imagination. Belief in the artist as hero, reverence toward the work of art as an object of moral inspiration, and the expectations of silence and even formal dress at a concert—all of these attitudes developed in the early Romantic period. What is more, the notion that a particular group of pieces merited repeated hearings gained currency at this time. Prior to 1800, almost all music was disposable music: it was written as entertainment for the moment and was then forgotten. But the generation following Beethoven began to see his best symphonies, concertos, and quartets, as well as those of Mozart and Haydn, as worthy of preservation and repeated performance (see p. 187). These and the best works of succeeding generations came to form a **canon,** indeed a museum, of classical music, and they constitute the core of today's concert repertoire. Thus, what we think about the composer, how we view the work of art, what we can expect to hear at a concert, and even how we dress and behave during the performance are not eternal ideals, with us since time immemorial, but are instead values created during the Romantic period. In many respects, the attitudes about art and music that arose in the early nineteenth century still govern our thinking today.

THE STYLE OF ROMANTIC MUSIC

The Romantic spirit rebelled against Classical ideals in ways that allow us to generalize these two artistic movements in terms of opposites: rational against irrational, intellect opposed to heart, conformity versus originality, and the masses in contradistinction to the individual. Yet in purely musical terms, the works of the Romantic composers represent not so much a *revolution* against Classical ideals as an *evolution* beyond them. The Classical genres of the symphony, concerto, string quartet, piano sonata, and opera remain fashionable, though somewhat altered in shape, throughout the nineteenth century. The symphony now grows in length, embodying the widest possible range of expression, while the concerto becomes increasingly virtuosic, as a heroic soloist does battle against an orchestral mass. The Romantics introduced no new musical forms and only two new genres: the art song (see Chapter 23) and the symphonic poem (see Chapter 24). Instead, Romantic composers took the musical materials received from Haydn, Mozart, and the young Beethoven and made them more intensely expressive, more personal, more colorful, and, in some cases, more bizarre.

Romantic Melody

The Romantic period witnessed the apotheosis of melody. Melodies became broad, powerful streams of sound intended to sweep the listener away. They went beyond the neat symmetrical units (two plus two, four plus four) inherent in the Classical style, becoming longer, rhythmically more flexible, and more irregular in shape. At the same time, Romantic melodies continued a trend that had developed in the late eighteenth century, in which themes became vocal in conception, more singable or "lyrical." Countless melodies of Schubert, Chopin, and Tchaikovsky have been turned into popular songs and movie themes—Romantic music is perfectly suited for the romance of film—because these melodies are so profoundly expressive. They sigh, lament, grow, and wax ecstatic. They start haltingly and then build to a grandiose climax, sublime and triumphant. Example 22-1 shows the well-known love theme from Tchaikovsky's *Romeo and Juliet*. As the brackets show, it rises and falls, only to rise higher again, a total of seven times, on the way to a *fortissimo* climax. (The melody can be heard on **5**3/20 at 2:58.)

EXAMPLE 22–1

Colorful Harmony

Part of the emotional intensity of Romantic music was generated by a new, more colorful harmony. Classical music had, in the main, made use of chords built upon only the seven notes of the major or minor scale. Romantic composers went further by creating **chromatic harmony,** constructing chords on the five additional notes (the chromatic notes) within the full twelve-note chromatic scale. This gave more colors to their harmonic palette, allowing the rich, lush sounds we associate with Romantic music.

Chromatic harmony likewise encouraged bold chordal shifts—a chord with three sharps might be followed immediately by one with six flats, for example. The striking sound that results from these unusual juxtapositions is harmonious with music that seeks to express a wider range of feeling.

Finally, nineteenth-century composers gave a "romantic feel" to music by means of dissonance. Longing, pain, and suffering traditionally have been expressed in music by dissonance. All musical dissonance, so the rules of composition say, must resolve to consonance. The longer the painful dissonance, the greater the desire for resolution. A delay of the resolution intensifies the feelings of anxiety, longing, and searching, all sentiments appropriate to music that often deals with the subject of love.

All three of these qualities of Romantic harmony—chromatic harmony, bold chordal shifts, and prolonged dissonance—can be heard in Frédéric Chopin's Nocturne in C♯ minor (1835). Neither you nor the author can take in all the music given in the following three examples simply by looking at them. (To hear them, turn to **5**4/2 or **2**2/3) We can, however, visualize here some of the music's inner workings—first the bold harmonic shift from a chord with four sharps to one with four flats, then the chromaticism, and finally the prolonged dissonance. In this way, we may begin to understand, when hearing the rich, sensuous sound of Romantic music, how it is created.

EXAMPLE 22–2: BOLD HARMONIC SHIFT AT 2:40

EXAMPLE 22–3: CHROMATIC HARMONY AT 3:20

EXAMPLE 22–4: PROLONGED DISSONANCE AT 5:05

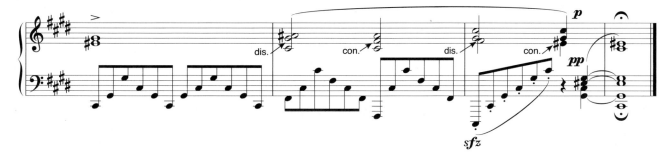

Romantic Tempo: Rubato

In keeping with an age that glorified personal freedom and tolerated eccentric behavior, tempo in Romantic music was cut loose from the restraints of a regular beat. The watchword here was *rubato* (literally "robbed"), an expression mark for the performer written into the score by the composer. A performer playing tempo **rubato** "stole" some time here and gave it back there, moving faster or slower so as to effect an intensely personal performance. The free approach to tempo was often reinforced by fluctuating dynamic levels—ritards were executed with diminuendos, and accelerations with crescendos—as a way of explaining, even exaggerating, the flow of the music. Whatever excesses might result could be excused under license of artistic freedom.

Romantic Forms: Monumental and Miniature

The musical forms that had worked earlier for Haydn and Mozart during the Classical period continued to satisfy the needs of the nineteenth-century composer. Sonata–allegro form, in particular, remained useful because its flexible format could accommodate any number of individual solutions. What developed, then, was not a rush to invent new forms but a trend toward elongating existing ones. Music that expresses longing by definition takes more time. As composers laid out broad and sweeping melodies, indulged in gigantic crescendos, and reveled in the luxurious sound of the enlarged orchestra, the length of individual movements increased dramatically. Mozart's G minor symphony (1788) lasts about twenty minutes, depending on the tempo of the conductor. But Berlioz's *Symphonie fantastique* (1830) takes nearly fifty-five minutes, and Mahler's Symphony No. 2 (1894) nearly an hour and a half. Perhaps the longest of all musical works is Richard Wagner's four-opera *Ring* cycle (1853–1876), which runs some *seventeen* hours over the course of four evenings.

Romantic musicians were not alone in their extended vision. Charles Darwin (*On the Origin of the Species*, 1859) posited that the earth was not merely 7,000 years old, as the Bible suggested, but several million. Painters such as J. M. W. Turner and Casper David Friedrich demonstrated on canvas the slow, inexorable evolution of the earth—Friedrich, by including in his painting (see Fig. 22-2) dying and fallen trees, as well as depicting clear geological strata to show the passing of the ages. The grand, slow gestures we hear in the symphonies of Beethoven, Brahms, and Mahler are all part of the expansive spirit of the age.

Yet, paradoxically, Romantic composers were not interested only in the grandiose; the miniature fascinated them as well. In works of only a brief minute or two, they tried to capture the essence of a single mood, sentiment, or emotion. Such a miniature was called a **character piece.** It was usually written for the piano and often made use of simple binary (**AB**) or ternary (**ABA**) form. Because the character piece passes by in a twinkling of an eye, it was sometimes given a whimsical title, such as bagatelle (a trifle), humoresque, arabesque, musical moment, caprice, romance, intermezzo, or impromptu. Schubert, Schumann, Chopin, Liszt, Brahms, and Tchaikovsky all enjoyed creating these musical miniatures, perhaps as antidotes to their lengthy symphonies and concertos.

EXPRESSIVE TONE COLORS, GREATER SIZE, GREATER VOLUME

Perhaps the most striking aspects of Romantic music are the color and sheer volume of the sound. Sometimes all thematic and harmonic movement stops, and nothing but pure sound remains. Appropriate to an age that indulged in wild mood swings, Romantic composers prescribed greater dynamic extremes. Whereas the range in Classical music extended only from *pp* (*pianissimo*) to *ff* (*fortissimo*), now exaggerated "hyper-marks" such as *pppp* and *ffff* appear. To create sounds as loud as *ffff*, a larger orchestra or a bigger piano was needed. Composers demanded, and received, musical forces equal to the task of expressing the emotional extremes, changing moods, and extravagant gestures of the Romantic spirit.

The Romantic Orchestra

Technology has sometimes profoundly affected the history of music. Think, for instance, of the invention of the electrically amplified guitar, which revolutionized the orchestra or band that accompanied twentieth-century popular and rock songs. The Romantic era witnessed a comparable change in the orchestra. Significantly, it coincided with the Industrial Revolution, which produced new or technologically enhanced musical instruments of every sort. The wood of the flute was replaced by silver, and the instrument was supplied with a new fingering mechanism that added to its agility and made it easier to play in tune. Similarly, the trumpet and French horn were provided with valves that improved technical facility and accuracy of pitch in all keys (Fig. 22-3). These brass instruments were now capable of playing intricate, chromatic melodies, as well as providing the traditional backdrop of sonic support for the rest of the orchestra. The French horn, in particular, became an object of special affection during the Romantic period. Its rich, dark tone and its traditional association with the hunt—and by extension, nature—made it the Romantic instrument par excellence. Composers often called on a solo horn to express something mysterious or distant.

Watch a video of Craig Wright's Open Yale Course class session 20, "The Colossal Symphony: Beethoven, Berlioz, Mahler, and Shostakovich," at the text website.

FIGURE 22-3
A modern French horn with valves, an invention of the 1820s. The valves allow the performer to engage different lengths of tubing instantly, and thereby play a fully chromatic scale.

© Bob Jacobson/Corbis

Besides improvements to existing instruments, several new instruments were added to the symphony orchestra during the nineteenth century (Fig. 22-4). We have seen how Beethoven brought the piccolo (a high flute), the trombone, and the contrabassoon (a bass bassoon) into the orchestra in his famous Symphony No. 5 (1808). In 1830, Hector Berlioz went even further, requiring an ophicleide (an early form of the tuba), an English horn (a low-pitched oboe), a cornet, and two harps in his *Symphonie fantastique*. Berlioz, the embodiment of the Romantic spirit, had a typically grandiose notion of what the ideal symphony orchestra should contain. He wanted no fewer than 467 instruments, including 120 violins, 40 violas, 45 cellos, 35 double basses, and 30 harps! Such a gigantic instrumental force was never actually assembled, but Berlioz's utopian vision indicates the direction in which Romantic composers were headed. By the second half of the nineteenth century, orchestras with nearly a hundred players were not uncommon. Compare, for example, the number and variety of instruments required for a typical eighteenth-century performance of Mozart's Symphony in G minor with the symphony orchestra needed for Berlioz's *Symphonie fantastique* and for Gustav Mahler's Symphony No. 1 (see box). By the end of the nineteenth century, the symphony orchestra had become, in almost all ways, the ensemble of instruments that we see today.

Our reaction to the Romantic orchestra today, however, is very different from the response in the nineteenth century. Our modern ears have been desensitized by an overexposure to electronically amplified sound. But imagine the impact of an orchestra of a hundred players before the days of amplification. Apart from the military cannon and the steam engine, the nineteenth-century orchestra produced the loudest sonic level of any human contrivance. The big sound—and the big contrasts—of the nineteenth-century orchestra were new and startling, and audiences packed ever-larger concert halls to hear them.

The Conductor

Naturally, someone was needed to coordinate the efforts of the enlarged orchestra. Previously, in the days of Bach and Mozart, the orchestra had been led from within, either by the keyboard player of the *basso continuo*, gesturing with his head and hands, or by the chief violinist, directing with his bow. When Beethoven played and conducted his piano concertos, he did so seated at his instrument. When he led one of his symphonies, especially toward the end of his life, he stood before the orchestra, back to the audience, waving his hands. In 1820, the composer Louis Spohr became the first to use a wooden baton to lead the orchestra. Other objects were used as well, including a rolled-up piece of paper (Fig. 22-5), a violin bow, and sometimes even a handkerchief. As symphony orchestras became larger and symphonic scores more complex, every orchestral ensemble needed a leader to keep it from falling apart during performance. In the course of the nineteenth century, this leader evolved from a mere time-beater into an interpreter, and sometimes a dictator, of the musical score. The modern conductor had arrived.

FIGURE 22–4
A large orchestra depicted at Covent Garden Theater, London, in 1846. The conductor stands toward the middle, baton in hand, with strings to his right and woodwinds, brass, and percussion to his left. It was typical in this period to put all or part of the orchestra on risers to allow the sound to project more fully.

FIGURE 22–5
Silhouette of composer Carl Maria von Weber conducting with a rolled sheet of music so as to highlight the movement of his hand.

THE GROWTH OF THE SYMPHONY ORCHESTRA

Mozart (1788)
Symphony in G minor

1 flute
2 oboes
2 clarinets
2 bassoons
2 French horns
1st violins (8)*
2nd violins (8)
violas (4)
cellos (4)
double basses (3)

Total: 36

A satirical engraving suggesting the public's impression of Berlioz conducting his vastly enlarged symphony orchestra.

© Erich Lessing/Art Resource, NY

Berlioz (1830)
Symphonie fantastique

1 piccolo
2 flutes
2 oboes
1 English horn
2 B♭ clarinets
1 E♭ clarinet
4 bassoons
4 French horns
2 trumpets
2 cornets
3 trombones
2 ophicleides (tubas)
1st violins (15)*
2nd violins (14)
violas (8)
cellos (12)
double basses (8)
2 harps
timpani
bass drum
snare drum
cymbals and bells

Total: 89

Mahler (1889)
Symphony No. 1

3 piccolos
4 flutes
4 oboes
1 English horn
4 B♭ clarinets
2 E♭ clarinets
1 bass clarinet
3 bassoons
1 contrabassoon
7 French horns
5 trumpets
4 trombones
1 tuba
1st violins (20)*
2nd violins (18)
violas (14)
cellos (12)
double basses (8)
1 harp
timpani (2 players)
bass drum
triangle, cymbals
tam-tam

Total: 119

*Number of string players estimated according to standards of the period.

The Virtuoso

Appropriate for an era that glorified the individual, the nineteenth century was the age of the solo **virtuoso.** Of course, there had been instrumental virtuosos before—Bach on the organ and Mozart on the piano, to name just two—but now, many musicians began to expend enormous energy striving to raise their performing skills to unprecedented heights. Pianists and violinists in particular spent long hours practicing technical exercises—arpeggios, tremolos, trills, and scales played in thirds, sixths, and octaves—to develop wizard-like hand speed on their instrument. Naturally, some of what they played for the public was lacking in musical substance—tasteless showpieces designed to appeal immediately to the audiences that packed the ever-larger concert halls. Pianists even developed tricks to make it seem as if they had more than two hands (see

Fig. 25-6). Franz Liszt (1811–1886) sometimes played at the keyboard with a lighted cigar between his fingers. The Italian Niccolò Paganini (1782–1840) secretly tuned the four strings of his violin in ways that would allow him to negotiate with ease extraordinarily difficult passages (Figs. 22-6 and 22-7). If one of his strings broke, he could play with just three; if three broke, he continued apace with just one. So great was his celebrity that Paganini's picture appeared on napkins, ties, pipes, billiard cues, and powder boxes. As a composer later remarked, "The attraction of the virtuoso is like that of the circus performer; there's always the hope that something disastrous will happen." The daredevil quality of Paganini's virtuosic music can be seen in Example 22-5, which looks something like a roller coaster. Fortunately, as we shall see, some of these performing daredevils were also gifted composers.

FIGURES 22–6 AND 22–7

(left) Niccolò Paganini. (below) Paganini sleeping while the devil teaches him to play the violin. Paganini's extraordinary powers on the violin led some to believe that he had made a deal with the devil. The highest string of his violin was said to be made of the intestine of his mistress, whom he had murdered with his own hands. None of this was true, and Paganini filed several libel suits to reclaim his honor.

EXAMPLE 22–5: PAGANINI, CAPRICE, OPUS 1, NO. 5

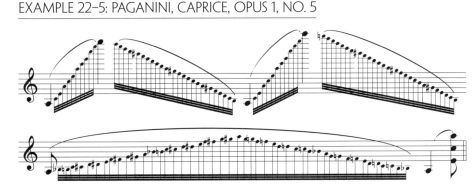

Coda

While this introduction to musical Romanticism treats the major developments of the nineteenth century, there were others. The increased attention paid to literature in the Romantic era inspired new musical genres: the art song (*Lied*), the program symphony, and the related symphonic poem. The technological innovations that fostered the development of the large symphony orchestra also led to the fabrication of a much larger and more powerful piano, as well as a musical literature specifically for it. Finally, political events, which led to the creation of modern nations such as Germany and

Italy, caused musical reverberations in the form of new, nationalistic musical styles. All of these developments—the art song, program music, the Romantic piano, and musical nationalism—will be discussed in the following chapters.

Listening EXERCISE 29

Comparing Orchestral Works of the Classical and Romantic Periods

The transition from the Classical to the Romantic period witnessed a great enlargement of the resources available to a symphonic composer, and this expansion resulted in significant changes in musical style. To appreciate the extent of this change, let's compare two orchestral works: the first movement of Mozart's Symphony No. 40 in G minor (1788) (**5** 2/15–17 or **2** 1/18–20) and the finale of Hector Berlioz's *Symphonie fantastique* (1830) (**5** 3/16–17 or **2** 2/1–2). Listen to the first four minutes of each work and answer the following questions, indicating "M" for Mozart or "B" for Berlioz. If you need help, consult the Listening Guides on pages 192 and 259–260.

1. Which composer begins with pure musical atmosphere, much as in a score for a modern-day motion picture? _____

2. Which composer begins with a clear-cut pair of four-bar antecedent–consequent phrases? _____

3. Which composer exhibits greater "mood swings," in which the music oscillates between louds and softs, and high pitches and low pitches? _____

4. Which composer designates a brass instrument and a percussion instrument to play the melody? _____

@ To take this Listening Exercise online and receive feedback or email answers to your instructor, go to the text website.

5. Which composer requires the violins to present all themes at first appearance? _____

6. Which composer maintains a steady beat throughout (to which you can tap your foot)? _____

7. Which composer maintains a constant tempo throughout (to which you can easily set and maintain a conducting pattern)? _____

8. Accordingly, the work of which composer is more likely to need a conductor during performance, owing to the lack of a clearly audible beat and consistent tempo? _____

9. Which composer drew inspiration for his symphony from events outside of music? _____

10. Which composer had to have a compelling melody because he didn't have the orchestral resources to achieve startling special effects? _____

@ The materials on the text website will help you understand and pass tests on the content of this chapter. In addition, you may watch Craig Wright's own lecture at Open Yale Courses and complete this chapter's Listening Exercise interactively, as well as view Active Listening Guides and other materials that will help you succeed in this course.

Key WORDS

canon (233)
chromatic harmony (234)

rubato (235)
character piece (236)

virtuoso (238)

ROMANTIC MUSIC
THE ART SONG

23

The decade 1803–1813 was perhaps the most auspicious in the history of Western music. In this short span of time were born the composers Hector Berlioz (1803), Felix Mendelssohn (1809), Frédéric Chopin (1810), Robert Schumann (1810), Franz Liszt (1811), Giuseppe Verdi (1813), and Richard Wagner (1813). Add to these the shining figure of Franz Schubert (born 1797) and this brilliant galaxy of Romantic musical geniuses is complete. We call them Romantics because they were part of—indeed, they created—the Romantic movement in music. Perhaps not surprisingly, they were very unconventional people. Their lives typify all that we have come to associate with the Romantic spirit: self-expression, passion, excess, and the love of nature and literature, as well as a certain selfishness and irresponsibility, and even a bit of lunacy. Not only did they create great art, but life, and how they lived it, also became an art.

THE ART SONG

One of the hallmarks of the Romantic era was a quickening interest in literature, especially poetry. Indeed, never were word and tone more closely allied than during the Romantic era. The Romantic poets viewed music as the truest and purest of all the arts, owing to the abstract quality of sound. Composers, in turn, found musical resonance in the poetry of the day and transformed it into song, believing that music could intensify poetic sentiments by expressing things that words alone could not.

Songs inspired by great poetry have appeared throughout human history. But the near frenzy of poetic activity in the nineteenth century inspired Romantic composers to set poems to music with increasing frequency. The English Romantic poets William Wordsworth, John Keats, Lord Byron, and Percy Bysshe Shelley (see p. 232), who burst onto the scene in the early 1800s, had German counterparts not only in the great Johann von Goethe but also in the younger Romantics Joseph von Eichendorff (1788–1857) and Heinrich Heine (1797–1856). Literally thousands of odes, sonnets, ballads, and romances poured from their pens, and many were quickly set as songs by young Romantic composers. In so doing, these musicians popularized a genre called the **art song**—a song for solo voice and piano accompaniment with high artistic aspirations. Because the art song was cultivated most intensely in German-speaking lands, it is also called the *Lied* (pl. *Lieder*), German for "song." Although many composers wrote art songs, none had greater success in the genre than Franz Schubert. His special talent was to fashion music that captured both the spirit and the detail of the text, creating a sensitive mood painting in which the voice, and especially the accompanying piano, expresses every nuance of the poem. Schubert said, "When one has a good poem the music comes easily, melodies just flow, so that composing is a real joy."

Franz Schubert (1797–1828)

Franz Schubert was born in Vienna in 1797. Among the great Viennese masters—Haydn, Mozart, Beethoven, Schubert, Brahms, and Mahler—only he was native-born to the city. Schubert's father was a schoolteacher, and the son, too, was groomed for that profession. Yet the boy's obvious musical talent made it imperative that he also have music lessons, so his father taught him to play the violin, and his older brother the piano. At the age of eleven, Schubert was admitted as a choirboy in the emperor's chapel (this famous group today is called the Vienna Boys' Choir). Proximity to the royal palace brought young Schubert into contact with Antonio Salieri, erstwhile rival of Mozart and still imperial court composer (see p. 166). Schubert began to study composition with Salieri in 1810 and was soon composing his own musical works at an astonishing rate.

After his voice changed in 1812, young Franz left the court chapel and enrolled in a teacher's college. He had been spared compulsory military service because he was below the minimum height of five feet and his sight was so poor that he was compelled to wear the spectacles now familiar from his portraits (Fig. 23-1). By 1815, he had become a teacher at his father's primary school. But he found teaching demanding and tedious, and so after three unpleasant years, Schubert quit his "day job" to give himself over wholly to music.

"You lucky fellow; I really envy you! You live a life of sweet, precious freedom, can give free rein to your musical genius, can express your thoughts in any way you like." This was Schubert's brother's view of the composer's newfound freedom. But as many Romantics would find, the reality was harsher than the ideal. Aside from some small income he earned from the sale of a few songs, he lacked financial support. Schubert, unlike Beethoven, had no circle of aristocrats to provide patronage. Consequently, he lived a vagabond life, helped along by the generosity of his friends, with whom he often lodged when he was broke. He spent his mornings passionately composing music, passed his afternoons in cafés discussing literature and politics, and often spent his evenings performing his songs and dances for friends and admirers.

As Schubert was reaching artistic maturity, the era of the great aristocratic salon was drawing to an end, its role as a primary venue for artistic expression replaced by the middle-class parlor or living room. Here, in less formal surroundings, groups of men and women with a common interest in music, the novel, drama, or poetry would meet to read and discuss the latest developments in these arts. The gatherings at which Schubert appeared, and at which only his compositions were played, were called **Schubertiads** by his friends.

FIGURES 23-1 AND 23-2

(top) Franz Schubert. (bottom) A small, private assembly known as a Schubertiad, named after the composer, at which artists presented their works. The singer before the piano is Johann Vogl, accompanied by Schubert at the piano.

It was in small, purely private assemblies such as these (Fig. 23-2), not in large public concerts, that most of his best songs were first performed.

In 1822, disaster befell the composer: he contracted syphilis, a venereal disease tantamount to a death sentence before the discovery of antibiotics. His lyrical Symphony in B minor of that year, appropriately called the "Unfinished Symphony," was left incomplete. Yet during the years that preceded his premature death in 1828, Schubert created some of his greatest works: the song cycles *Die schöne Müllerin* (*The Pretty Maid of the Mill*, 1823) and *Winterreise* (*Winter Journey*, 1827), the "Wanderer" Fantasy for piano (1822), and the great C major symphony (1828). When Beethoven died in 1827,

Schubert served as a torchbearer at the funeral. The next year he, too, was dead, the youngest of the great composers. The epitaph for his tombstone reads, "The art of music here entombed a rich treasure, but even fairer hopes."

In his brief life of thirty-one years, Franz Schubert wrote eight symphonies, fifteen string quartets, twenty-one piano sonatas, seven Masses for chorus and orchestra, and four operas—a sizable oeuvre by any standard. Yet in his day, Schubert was known almost exclusively as a writer of art songs (*Lieder*). Indeed, he composed more than 600 works in this genre, many of them minor masterpieces. In a few cases, Schubert chose to set several texts together in a series. In so doing, he created what is called a **song cycle** (something akin to a "concept album")—a tightly structured group of individual songs that tell a story or treat a single theme. *Die schöne Müllerin* (twenty songs) and *Winterreise* (twenty-four songs), both of which relate the sad consequences of unrequited love, are Schubert's two great song cycles.

ERLKÖNIG (1815)

To get an idea of Schubert's precocious musical talent, we need only listen to his song *Erlkönig* (*Elf King*), written when he was just seventeen. The text itself is a ballad—a dramatic story told alternately in narrative verse and in dialogue—from the pen of the famous German poet Goethe. It relates the tale of the evil King of the Elves and his malevolent seduction of a young boy. Legend had it that whoever was touched by the King of the Elves would die. This tale typifies the Romantic fascination with the supernatural and the macabre, which is evinced most famously in Mary Shelley's *Frankenstein* (1818).

According to a friend's account, Schubert was reading a book of Goethe's poetry, pacing back and forth. Suddenly, he sprang to a piano and, as fast as he could write, set Goethe's entire ballad to music. From there, Schubert and his friend hastened to the composer's college to play it for a few other friends. In his lifetime, *Erlkönig* became Schubert's best-known song, and one of only a few that earned him any money.

The opening line of the poem sets the frightening nocturnal scene: "Who rides so late through night and wind?" With his feverish son cradled in his arms, a father rides at breakneck speed to an inn in an attempt to save the child (Fig. 23-3). Schubert captures both the general sense of terror in the scene and the detail of the galloping horse; he creates an accompanying figure in the piano that pounds on relentlessly just as fast as the pianist can make it go (Ex. 23-1).

FIGURE 23-3

The ballad of the Elf King depicted by Schubert's close friend Moritz von Schwind. The artist had heard Schubert perform the song at many Schubertiads.

EXAMPLE 23-1

The specter of death, the Elf King, beckons gently to the boy. He does so in seductively sweet tones, in a melody with the gentle lilt and folksy, "um-pah-pah" accompaniment of a popular tune.

EXAMPLE 23-2

(Thou dearest boy, come go with me!)

The frightened boy cries out to his father in an agitated line that culminates in a tense, chromatic ascent.

EXAMPLE 23-3

(Dear father, my father, say, did'st thou not hear the Elf King whisper promises in my ear?)

Begin exploring how this art song by Schubert can be interpreted in very different ways by different performers, in the YouTube playlist on the text website.

This cry is heard again and again in the course of the song, each time at a successively higher pitch and with increasingly dissonant harmonies. In this way, the music mirrors the boy's growing terror. The father tries to calm him in low tones that are steady, stable, and repetitive. The Elf King at first charms in sweet, consonant tones, but then threatens in dissonant ones, as seduction gives way to abduction. Thus each of the three characters of the story is portrayed with distinct musical qualities (though all are sung by a single voice). This is musical characterization at its finest; the melody and accompaniment not only support the text but also intensify and enrich it. Suddenly, the end is reached: the hand of the Elf King (Death) has touched his victim. Anxiety gives way to sorrow as the narrator announces in increasingly somber (minor) tones, "But in his arms, his child was dead!"

Listening GUIDE

Franz Schubert
Erlkönig (1815)

5 2
3/14 1/29

Genre: Art song

Form: Through-composed

0:00 14 29 Piano introduction: pounding triplets in right hand and ominous minor-mode motive in left

Narrator

0:23		Wer reitet so spät durch Nacht und Wind? Es ist der Vater mit seinem Kind. Er hat den Knaben wohl in dem Arm, er fasst ihn sicher, er hält ihn warm.	Who rides so late through night so wild? A loving father with his child. He clasps his boy close with his arm, he holds him tightly and keeps him warm.

Father

0:56		Mein Sohn, was birgst du so bang dein Gesicht?	My son, what makes you hide your face in fear?

Son

1:04	With disjunct leaps but no agitation	Siehst, Vater, du den Erlkönig nicht? Den Erlenkönig mit Kron' und Schweif?	Father don't you see the Elf King— the Elf King with crown and shroud?

Father

1:20	In low, calming tones	Mein Sohn, es ist ein Nebelstreif.	My son, it's only some streak of mist.

Elf King

1:29	With seductive melody in major key	Du liebes Kind, komm, geh' mit mir! gar schöne Spiele spiel' ich mit dir; manch' bunte Blumen sind an dem Strand, meine Mutter hat manch' gülden Gewand.	You dear child, come along with me! I'll play some very fine games with you; where varied blossoms are on meadows fair, and my mother has golden garments to wear.

Son

1:52	Growing agitation depicted by tight chromatic movement in voice	Mein Vater, mein Vater, und hörest du nicht, was Erlenkönig mir leise verspricht?	My father, my father, do you not hear how the Elf King whispers promises in my ear?

Father

2:04	In low, steady pitches	Sei ruhig, bleibe ruhig, mein Kind, in dürren Blättern säuselt der Wind.	Be calm, stay calm, my child, Through wither'd leaves the wind blows wild:

Elf King

2:14	With happy, lilting tune in major key	Willst, feiner Knabe, du mit mir geh'n?	My handsome young lad, will you come with me?

(continued)

		Meine Töchter sollen dich warten schön, meine Töchter führen den nächtlichen Reih'n, und wiegen und tanzen und singen dich ein.	My beauteous daughters wait for you, With them you would join in the dance every night, and they will rock and dance and sing you to sleep.

Son

2:32	Intense chromatic notes, but now a step higher and with minor key suggesting panic	Mein Vater, mein Vater, und siehst du nicht dort Erlkönigs Töchter am düstern Ort?	My Father, my father, don't you see at all the Elf King's daughters over there in the dusk?

Father

2:44	Low register, but more leaps (agitation) than before	Mein Sohn, mein Sohn, ich seh' es genau, es scheinen die alten Weiden so grau.	My son, my son, the form you there see, is only the aging gray willow tree.

Elf King

3:01	Music starts seductively but then turns minor and menacing	Ich liebe dich, mich reizt deine schöne Gestalt; und bist du nicht willig, so brauch' ich Gewalt.	I love you, I'm charmed by your fine appearance; And if you're not willing, I'll seize you by force!

Son

3:12	Piercing cries in highest range	Mein Vater, mein Vater, jetzt fasst er mich an! Erlkönig hat mir ein Leids gethan!	My father, my father, now he's got me, the Elf King has seized me by his trick.

Narrator

3:26	With rising and then falling line	Dem Vater grauset's; er reitet geschwind, er hält in den Armen das ächzende Kind. Erreicht den Hof mit Müh' und Noth:	The father shudders, he rides headlong, holding the groaning child in his arms. He reaches the inn with toil and dread,
3:47	Piano stops, then recitative	in seinen Armen das Kind war todt!	but in his arms, his child was dead!

Listen to streaming music in an Active Listening Guide, available on the text website.

Listening EXERCISE 30

Schubert
ERLKÖNIG

5   **2**
3/14   1/29

@

To take this Listening Exercise online and receive feedback or email answers to your instructor, go to the text website.

Schubert was a master at bringing to life the essential characters and sentiments of the poetry he set to music. This exercise suggests how he used two very basic musical elements—a shift in mode and a change in the accompaniment—to intensify Goethe's dramatic ballad *Erlkönig*.

   1. (0:00–0:22) The opening section presents rapidly repeating notes in the right hand of the accompanist

and an ominous motive below in the left. In which mode is the introduction written?
    a. major   b. minor

   2. (1:29–1:51) When the Elf King enters, is the ominous motive still heard in the accompaniment?
    a. yes   b. no

3. (1:29–1:51) In which mode does the Elf King sing?
   a. major   b. minor

4. (1:52–2:03) As the son reenters, what happens in the piano accompaniment?
   a. Rapidly repeating notes return in the accompanist's right hand, and the mode shifts from major to minor.
   b. Rapidly repeating notes return in the accompanist's left hand, and the mode shifts from minor to major.

5. (2:14–2:30) For the second appearance of the Elf King, which is true?
   a. The rapidly repeating notes in the right hand continue, and the mode is minor.
   b. Arpeggios replace the rapidly repeating notes in the right hand, and the mode is major.

6. (3:01–3:11) For the third and final appearance of the Elf King, which is true?
   a. The accompaniment pattern changes to arpeggios in the right hand, and the mode remains a happy major throughout.
   b. The repeating notes in the right hand continue, and toward the end, the mode changes abruptly from major to minor.

7. (3:47–3:59) How does Schubert emphatically emphasize that the child has died and that there will be no happy ending?
   a. He writes an abrupt V–I cadence in a major key.
   b. He writes an abrupt V–I cadence in a minor key.

8. Excluding the narrator, how many characters are portrayed in Schubert's *Erlkönig*?
   a. one   b. two   c. three

9. How many voices actually sing the *Lied* in performance?
   a. one   b. two   c. three   d. four

10. What must any singer bring to a performance of this art song if it is to be successful?
    a. the ability to sing like a horse
    b. the ability to project a range of voices and styles, almost like an impersonator
    c. the ability to bring a single interpretive mood to the song

Just as the tension in Goethe's poem rises incessantly, from the beginning to the very end, Schubert's music unfolds continually, without significant repetition. Such a musical composition featuring ever-changing melodic and harmonic material is called **through-composed,** and Schubert's *Erlkönig*, accordingly, is termed a through-composed art song. For texts that do not tell a story or project a series of changing moods, however, **strophic form** is often preferred. Here a single poetic mood is maintained from one stanza, or strophe, of the text to the next. Most pop songs are written in strophic form, each strophe consisting of a verse and chorus. For a very familiar example of a nineteenth-century art song in strophic form, revisit the famous Brahms *Lullaby* ((intro)/22).

FIGURE 23–4

Robert and Clara Schumann in 1850, from an engraving constructed from an early photograph.

Robert Schumann (1810–1856)

While some art songs, such as Schubert's *Erlkönig*, were musical arrangements of dramatic ballads, most were settings of lyrical love poems. The subject of love dominates not only Schubert's *Lieder* but also those of Robert and Clara Schumann (Fig. 23-4), whose conjugal life story is itself something of an ode to love.

Robert Schumann was born not to music but to literature. His father was a novelist who introduced him to Romantic poetry and the ancient classics. But the father died young, and Robert's mother determined that her son should take a safe route to prosperity: study law. Reluctantly, Schumann matriculated at the University of Heidelberg, but he attended not a single class, preferring to pass the time with poetry and music. In 1830, determined to become a virtuoso, Schumann moved, with his mother's grudging consent, to Leipzig. But after two years of lessons with the eminent Friedrich Wieck (1785–1873)—during which he practiced seven hours a day—all he had to

@

Download Supplementary
Listening Guides for
Robert Schumann's "Im
wunderschönen Monat Mai"
("In the Wonderful Month
of May"), "Und wüssten's die
Blumen die kleinen" ("And if
the Flowers, the Little Ones,
Knew"), and "Die alten, bösen
Lieder" ("The Old, Accursed
Songs"), from *Dichterliebe*, at
the text website.

show for his labors was a permanently damaged right hand, so he turned his attention to music criticism and composition.

While studying piano with Wieck, Schumann met and fell in love with Wieck's beautiful and talented daughter Clara. Her father vehemently opposed the union, however, and Robert perforce began a legal battle to win Clara's hand. One of Wieck's objections was that Schumann could not support himself, let alone a wife. Inspired by his love of Clara, and perhaps motivated to show that he could earn a living, Schumann turned to writing art songs, then probably the most marketable of musical genres. In 1840, Robert won a legal victory over Clara's father, enabling the couple to marry. That same year, Schumann composed nearly 125 *Lieder*, including settings of poems by major Romantic poets such as Byron, Goethe, and Friedrich Rückert, as well as a few by Shakespeare.

The day Robert Schumann won his court victory for the hand of Clara, he wrote in his diary, "Happiest day and end of the struggle." In this euphoric mood, he completed a setting of eight poems by the German Romantic poet Adelbert von Chamisso (1781–1838) that speak of the hopes and desires of a young middle-class woman. Titled *Frauenliebe und -leben* (*Women in Love and Life*), the eight poems form a unit, moving from the theme of love at first sight, to engagement, to painful separation. Thus the eight collectively form a song cycle. Most of the eight Schumann settings are in **modified strophic form.** In the middle of the cycle, however, comes "Du Ring an meinem Finger" ("You Ring on my Finger"), a five-strophe poem in which the newly betrothed gazes star-struck at her ring. Because strophe 3 is similar to, and strophe 5 identical with, strophe 1, here Schumann chose not to opt for a strophic-form setting but to give the song an **ABACA** (rondo) musical form, providing identical music (**A**) for similar stanzas. The climax comes in strophe (section) **C**, in which the young voice climbs up the scale excitedly as she professes her undying love. Composure returns with the repeat of the lyrical refrain **A**, which is followed by a soft piano epilogue.

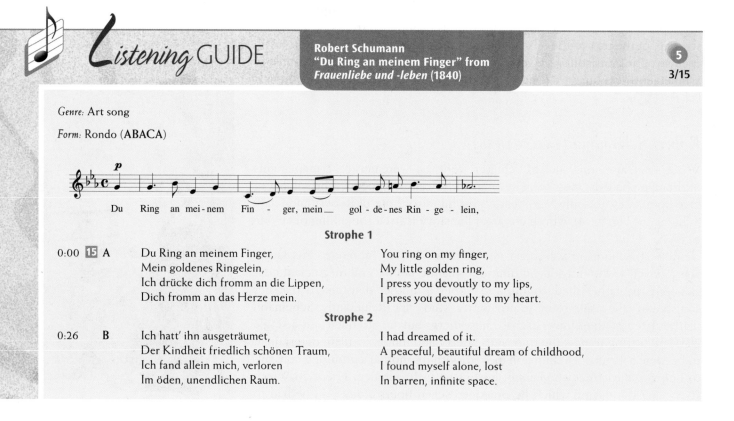

Listening GUIDE

**Robert Schumann
"Du Ring an meinem Finger" from
Frauenliebe und -leben (1840)**

⑤

3/15

Genre: Art song

Form: Rondo (**ABACA**)

Du Ring an mei-nem Fin - ger, mein___ gol - de - nes Rin - ge - lein,

Strophe 1

0:00 **15** A   Du Ring an meinem Finger,   You ring on my finger,
              Mein goldenes Ringelein,   My little golden ring,
              Ich drücke dich fromm an die Lippen,   I press you devoutly to my lips,
              Dich fromm an das Herze mein.   I press you devoutly to my heart.

Strophe 2

0:26 B   Ich hatt' ihn ausgeträumet,   I had dreamed of it.
              Der Kindheit friedlich schönen Traum,   A peaceful, beautiful dream of childhood,
              Ich fand allein mich, verloren   I found myself alone, lost
              Im öden, unendlichen Raum.   In barren, infinite space.

Strophe 3

0:52	A	Du Ring an meinem Finger,	You ring on my finger,
		Da hast du mich erst belehrt,	You have taught me for the first time,
		Hast meinem Blick erschlossen	Have opened my gaze to
		Des Lebens unendlichen, tiefen Wert.	The infinite deep meaning of life.

Strophe 4

1:18	C	Ich will ihm dienen, ihm leben,	I want to serve him, live for him,
		Ihm angehören ganz,	Belong to him entirely,
		Hin selber mich geben und finden	Give myself, find myself
		Verklärt mich in seinem Glanz.	Transformed in his radiance.

Strophe 5

1:39	A	Du Ring an meinem Finger,	You ring on my finger,
		Mein goldenes Ringelein,	My little golden ring,
		Ich drücke dich fromm an die Lippen,	I press you devoutly to my lips,
		Dich fromm an das Herze mein.	I press you devoutly to my heart.

| 2:11 | | Brief coda for piano alone | |

Listen to streaming music in an Active Listening Guide, available on the text website.

Clara Wieck Schumann (1819–1896)

Unlike her husband, Robert, a gifted composer but failed performer, Clara Wieck Schumann (see Fig. 23-4 on p. 250) was one of the great piano virtuosos of the nineteenth century. A child prodigy, she made her debut at the age of eleven in Leipzig, Germany, the city of her birth. She then undertook a concert tour of Europe during which she impressed and befriended several important composers of the Romantic era, including Mendelssohn, Berlioz, Chopin, and Liszt. In Austria, the emperor named her "Royal and Imperial Chamber Virtuosa"—the first time that official title had been given to a Protestant, a teenager, or a woman.

When she married Robert Schumann in 1840, Clara was an international star, and Robert an unknown. Nevertheless, she took up the dual roles of wife to Robert and mother to the eight children she soon bore him. She, too, tried her hand at musical composition, writing mostly art songs and character pieces (see p. 236) for piano. But despite her unmistakable talent as a composer, Clara was ambivalent about the capacity of women, herself included, to excel as creative artists (see boxed essay). As her children grew more numerous, her compositions became fewer. Clara's most productive period as a composer of art songs coincided with the very early years of marriage to Robert.

Clara's "Liebst du um Schönheit" ("If You Love for Beauty") makes a lovely companion piece to husband Robert's "Du Ring an meinem Finger." Composed in 1841, a year after her marriage, Clara's "Liebst du um Schönheit" is a setting of a four-stanza love poem by Joseph Eichendorff (1788–1857). In this wistful, playful text, the poet sets forth three reasons (stanzas 1–3) why the lady should *not* be loved—not for beauty, youth, or money (all three of which Clara actually possessed)—but one (last stanza) for which she *should* be loved—for love alone. Although the melodic and accompanimental figures presented in the first strophe prevail in the subsequent ones, Clara varies the musical setting on each occasion, producing modified strophic form, in this case represented as **AA′A″A‴**. Example 23-4 shows the melody of strophe 1

@ Download a Supplementary Listening Guide for Clara Schumann, "Der Mond kommt still gegangen" ("The Moon Comes Quietly"), at the text website.

WHERE WERE THE WOMEN?

You may have noticed that female composers are poorly represented in this book. We have seen the works of some—Hildegard of Bingen (pp. 70–71) and Barbara Strozzi (pp. 110–111), for example—and we will meet those of Ellen Taaffe Zwilich later (p. 367). But in general, although women have been actively engaged as performers of secular music since the Middle Ages, only rarely, prior to the twentieth century, did they become composers. While the reasons for this are numerous, one stands out above all others: people then had no faith in the capacity, or the propriety, of female creativity. Although a young lady might learn to play the piano in a show of domestic refinement, the woman's function in society was defined as nurturer of children (preferably male) and handmaiden of husband. Fanny Mendelssohn Hensel (1805–1847), the gifted sister of composer Felix Mendelssohn, was fifteen and considering music as a profession when she received the following directive in a letter from her father: "What you wrote to me about your musical occupations, and in comparison to those of Felix, was rightly thought and expressed. But though music will perhaps become his profession, for you it can and must only be an ornament, never the core of your existence. . . . You must become more steady and collected, and prepare yourself for your real calling, the only calling for a young woman—the state of a housewife."

Fanny Mendelssohn in 1829, in a sketch by her husband-to-be, Wilhelm Hensel.

© Mary Evans Picture Library/The Image Works

With no encouragement to become a creative force outside the home, little wonder that self-doubt arose among women of talent. As Clara Schumann wrote in her diary in 1839, "I once believed that I possessed creative talent, but I have given up this idea; a woman must not desire to compose. There has never yet been one able to do it. Should I expect to be that one?"

Composing a symphony or a string quartet is a complex process requiring years of schooling in harmony, counterpoint, and instrumentation. Women did not have access to such formal training in composition. For example, the Paris Conservatory was founded in 1793 but did not admit women into classes in advanced music theory and composition until almost a century later. Women might study piano, but according to a decree of the 1820s, they were to enter and leave by a separate door. (Similarly, women painters were not admitted to the state-sponsored Academy of Fine Arts in Paris until 1897. Even then they were barred from nude anatomy classes, instruction crucial to the figural arts, because their presence was thought "morally inappropriate.") Only in those exceptional cases in which a daughter received an intense musical education at home, as did Fanny Mendelssohn and Clara Schumann, did a woman have a fighting chance to become a musical creator.

and how it is modified in strophe 2. The ever-evolving music gives this art song its remarkable freshness. Did Clara equal or surpass Robert as a composer of *Lieder*? You be the judge.

EXAMPLE 23–4

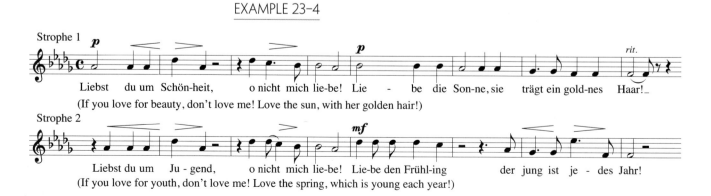

Strophe 1

Liebst du um Schön-heit, o nicht mich lie-be! Lie - be die Son-ne, sie trägt ein gold-nes Haar!_
(If you love for beauty, don't love me! Love the sun, with her golden hair!)

Strophe 2

Liebst du um Ju - gend, o nicht mich lie-be! Lie-be den Frühl-ing der jung ist je - des Jahr!
(If you love for youth, don't love me! Love the spring, which is young each year!)

Listening GUIDE

**Clara Schumann
"Liebst du um Schönheit" (1841)**

intro 23

Genre: Art song

Form: Modified strophic (**AA'A''A'''**)

Strophe 1

0:00 **23** A Liebst du um Schönheit, o nicht mich liebe!   If you love for beauty, don't love me!
       Liebe die Sonne, sie trägt ein gold'nes Haar!   Love the sun, with her golden hair!

Strophe 2

0:34 A' Liebst du um Jugend, o nicht mich liebe!   If you love for youth, don't love me!
       Liebe den Frühling, der jung ist jedes Jahr!   Love the spring, which is young each year!

Strophe 3

1:00 A'' Liebst du um Schätze, o nicht mich liebe!   If you love for money, do not love me!
       Liebe die Meerfrau, sie hat viel Perlen klar!   Love the mermaid, she has many pearls!

Strophe 4

1:27 A''' Liebst du um Liebe, o ja—mich liebe!   If you love for love, oh yes, love me!
       Liebe mich immer, dich lieb' ich immerdar!   Love me for always, and I will love you eternally!

2:04 Brief coda for piano alone

Download an Active Listening Guide, available on the text website.

Listening EXERCISE 31

Comparing Art Songs   (intro) 22   (intro) 23   (5) 3/14   (5) 3/15   (2) 1/29

@ To take this Listening Exercise online and receive feedback or email answers to your instructor, go to the text website.

Who is the best songwriter of recent times: John Lennon, Bob Dylan, Andrew Lloyd Webber, or Elton John? Difficult to say. Who was the best art song composer of the nineteenth century? We have now heard four art songs by four different composers: Schubert and the two Schumanns in this chapter, and Johannes Brahms, a protégé of the Schumanns', in Chapter 6. The following exercise asks you to think about how the four songs were fashioned and how they compare.

1. Which of the four songs is composed in strophic form?
   a. Schubert's
   b. Robert Schumann's
   c. Clara Schumann's
   d. Brahms's

2. Which is in modified strophic form?
   a. Schubert's
   b. Robert Schumann's
   c. Clara Schumann's
   d. Brahms's

3. Which is in rondo form?
   a. Schubert's
   b. Robert Schumann's
   c. Clara Schumann's
   d. Brahms's

4. Which is through-composed?
   a. Schubert's
   b. Robert Schumann's
   c. Clara Schumann's
   d. Brahms's

5. Which of the four is the most dramatic and least lyrical?
   a. Schubert's
   b. Robert Schumann's
   c. Clara Schumann's
   d. Brahms's

6. Knowing that many pop songs are strophic, which art song is closest to a pop song?
   a. Schubert's
   b. Robert Schumann's
   c. Clara Schumann's
   d. Brahms's

(continued)

7. All of these great songs were written by young people, but which one was written by a teenager (someone age seventeen, to be exact)?
   a. Schubert's
   b. Robert Schumann's
   c. Clara Schumann's
   d. Brahms's

8. True or false: Judging from these four works, a piano accompaniment is a traditional part of the nineteenth-century art song, just as is the guitar for a pop song today.
   a. true
   b. false

9. Judging from the texts of these four works, the nineteenth-century art song was directed toward, intended to please, and sung in the homes of whom?
   a. the aristocracy
   b. the clergy
   c. the middle class

10. Which of these four songs did you enjoy most? No correct answer here, but think about the reasons for your preference.
    a. Schubert's
    b. Robert Schumann's
    c. Clara Schumann's
    d. Brahms's

Lives of Tragedy and Fidelity

Robert Schumann was something of a "streak" composer. During the 1830s, he wrote music for solo piano almost exclusively: sonatas, variations, and character pieces. In 1840, he composed almost nothing but art songs. In 1841, he wrote two of his four symphonies, and in 1842, he turned his attention to chamber music, which culminated in a highly regarded piano quintet. The year 1845 saw the composition of the brilliant Piano Concerto in A minor, but after that his creative output diminished.

From his earliest years, Robert Schumann had been afflicted with what psychiatrists now call bipolar disorder (likely exacerbated by doses of arsenic that he had taken as a young man to cure a case of syphilis). His moods swung from nervous euphoria to suicidal depression; in some years, he produced a torrent of music; in others, virtually nothing. As time progressed, Schumann's condition worsened. He began to hear voices, both heavenly and hellish, and one morning, pursued by demons within, he jumped off a bridge into the Rhine River. Nearby fishermen pulled him to safety, but from then on, by his own request, he was confined to an asylum, where he died of dementia in 1856.

Clara Schumann outlived Robert by forty years. She raised the children, and to pay the bills, she resumed her career as a touring piano virtuoso. Dressed in mourning black, she played across Europe into the 1890s. After Robert's death, Clara never composed again and never remarried. Proving that life sometimes imitates art, Clara remained true to the pledge made in her song "Liebst du um Schönheit": "I will love you eternally." Today they rest side by side in a small cemetery in Bonn, Germany, two souls exemplifying the spirit of the Romantic age.

The materials on the text website will help you understand and pass tests on the content of this chapter. In addition, you may complete this chapter's Listening Exercise interactively, as well as view Active Listening Guides and other materials that will help you succeed in this course.

Key WORDS

art song (241)
Lied (pl. *Lieder*) (241)
Schubertiad (242)

song cycle (243)
through-composed (247)
strophic form (247)

modified strophic form (248)

ROMANTIC MUSIC
PROGRAM MUSIC AND BALLET

The Romantic love of literature stimulated interest not only in the art song but also in program music. Indeed, the nineteenth century can fairly be called the "century of program music." True, there had been earlier isolated examples of program music—in Vivaldi's *The Seasons*, for example (see p. 124). But Romantic composers believed that music could be more than pure, abstract sound—that music alone (without a text) could tell a story.

Program music is instrumental music, usually written for symphony orchestra, that seeks to re-create in sound the events and emotions portrayed in some extramusical source: a story, legend, play, novel, or even historical event. The theory of program music rests on the obvious fact that specific musical gestures can evoke particular feelings and associations. A lyrical melody may spur memories of love, harshly dissonant chords might imply conflict, or a sudden trumpet call may suggest the arrival of the hero, for example. By stringing together such musical gestures in a convincing sequence, a composer might tell a story through music. Program music is fully harmonious with the strongly literary spirit of the nineteenth century.

Some Romantic composers, notably Johannes Brahms (1833–1897), resisted the allure of program music and continued to write what came to be called **absolute music**—symphonies, sonatas, quartets, and other instrumental music without extramusical or programmatic references. Most others, however, desiring to convey a clear, coherent message, took advantage of the more overtly narrative character of program music. In 1850, Franz Liszt, a leading advocate of program music, said that a program gave the composer a "means by which to protect the listener against a wrong poetical interpretation and to direct his attention to the poetical idea of the whole." Three of the predominant genres of program music—the program symphony, dramatic overture, and concert overture—were created simply by applying programs to the previously abstract genres of the symphony and overture. A fourth, the symphonic poem, was entirely new to the nineteenth century.

- **Program symphony:** a symphony with the usual three, four, or five movements, which together depict a succession of specific events or scenes drawn from an extramusical story or event. Examples include Berlioz's *Symphonie fantastique* (1830) and Liszt's "Faust" Symphony (1857).
- **Dramatic overture** (to an opera or a play): a one-movement work, usually in sonata–allegro form, that encapsulates in music the essential dramatic events of an opera or play. Many overtures became audience favorites and are today performed at concerts without the opera or play. Examples include Rossini's overture to his opera *William Tell* (1829) and Mendelssohn's *Overture* (1826) to Shakespeare's play *A Midsummer Night's Dream*.
- **Concert overture** (similar to the dramatic overture but *not* designed to precede an opera or play): a one-movement work of programmatic content originally intended for the concert hall. Examples include Tchaikovsky's *The 1812 Overture* (1882) and Mendelssohn's *Hebrides Overture* (1830).

253

- **Tone poem** (also called the **symphonic poem**): a one-movement work for orchestra that gives musical expression to the emotions and events associated with a story, play, political event, or personal experience. Examples include Tchaikovsky's *Romeo and Juliet* (1869; revised 1880), Musorgsky's *Night on Bald Mountain* (1867), and Strauss's *Thus Spoke Zarathustra* (1896). In fact, there is little difference between the tone poem and the concert overture: both are one-movement orchestral works with programmatic content intended for the concert hall.

Two of the best composers of descriptive music were Hector Berlioz and Peter Tchaikovsky.

*H*ECTOR BERLIOZ (1803–1869) AND THE PROGRAM SYMPHONY

Hector Berlioz was one of the most original figures in the history of music (Fig. 24-1). He was born in 1803 near the mountain city of Grenoble, France, the son of a local doctor. As a youth, Berlioz studied mainly the sciences and ancient Roman literature. Although local tutors taught him to play the flute and guitar, he had no systematic training in music theory or composition and little exposure to the music of the great masters. Among the major composers of the nineteenth century, he was the only one without fluency at the keyboard. He never studied piano and could do no more than bang out a few chords; yet he would become one of the greatest orchestrators of all time.

At the age of seventeen, Berlioz was sent off to Paris to study medicine, his father's profession. For two years, he pursued a program in the physical sciences, earning a degree in 1821. But Berlioz found the reality of the dissecting table repulsive and the allure of the opera house and concert hall irresistible. After a period of soul-searching, and the inevitable falling-out with his parents over the choice of a career, he vowed to become "no doctor or apothecary but a great composer."

His dismayed father immediately cut off his living stipend, leaving young Berlioz to ponder how he might support himself while studying composition at the Paris Conservatory (the French national school of music). Other composers had relied on teaching as a means to earn a regular income, but Berlioz, with no particular skill at any instrument, was not qualified to give music lessons. Instead, he turned to music criticism, writing reviews and articles for literary journals. Berlioz was the first composer to earn a livelihood as a music critic, and it was criticism, not composition, that remained his primary source of income for the rest of his life.

Perhaps it was inevitable that Berlioz would turn to writing about music, for in his mind, there was always a connection between music and the written word. As a young man, he read Lord Byron's *Childe Harold's Pilgrimage* and Goethe's *Faust*, works that inspired his viola concerto *Harold in Italy* (1834) and his dramatic symphony *The Damnation of Faust* (1846). But of all literary influences, none was greater than that of Shakespeare.

Shakespeare's dramas first burst upon the literary scene of continental Europe early in the nineteenth century. For Berlioz, the experience was life altering: "Shakespeare, coming upon me unawares, struck me like a thunderbolt. The lightning flash of that discovery revealed to me at a stroke the whole heaven of art." Berlioz devoured Shakespeare's plays and based musical

FIGURE 24-1

Hector Berlioz at the age of twenty-nine.

compositions on four of them: *The Tempest, King Lear, Hamlet,* and *Romeo and Juliet.* The best-known of Berlioz's tributes to the Bard, *Romeo and Juliet,* is a five-movement program symphony in which a chorus and solo voices intermittently paraphrase Shakespeare's own words. The common denominator in the art of Shakespeare and Berlioz is range of expression. Just as no dramatist before Shakespeare had portrayed the full spectrum of human emotions on the stage, so no composer before Berlioz had undertaken to create the widest range of moods through sound.

To depict wild swings of mood musically, Berlioz called for enormous orchestral and choral forces—hundreds and hundreds of performers (see pp. 237–238 and Fig. 24-2). He also experimented with new instruments: the **ophicleide** (an early form of the tuba), the **English horn** (a low oboe), the harp (an ancient instrument that he brought into the symphony orchestra for the first time), the **cornet** (a brass instrument with valves, borrowed from the military band), and even the newly invented saxophone. In 1843, he wrote a treatise on musical instruments, one still used today as a textbook in orchestration classes at music conservatories around the world.

Berlioz's approach to musical form was equally iconoclastic and forward looking; he rarely used such standard forms as sonata–allegro or theme and variations. Instead, he preferred to create forms that flowed from the particular narrative of the story at hand. His French compatriots called his compositions "bizarre" and "monstrous," and thought him something of a madman. Subscribing to the adage "No man is a prophet in his own land," Berlioz took his progressive music to London, Vienna, Prague, and even Moscow, introducing such works as *Symphonie fantastique, Damnation of Faust,* and *Romeo et Juliet.* He died in Paris in 1869, isolated and embittered, the little recognition he received in his native France having come too late to boost his career or self-esteem.

Symphonie fantastique (1830)

Berlioz's most celebrated work, then and now, is his *Symphonie fantastique,* perhaps the single most radical example of musical Romanticism. Its form and orchestration are revolutionary. But what is more, it tells in music a vivid story and, as such, is the first complete program symphony. The story surrounding the creation of the descriptive program of the work is as fascinating as the piece itself.

In 1827, a troupe of English actors came to Paris to present Shakespeare's *Hamlet* and *Romeo and Juliet.* Berlioz, of course, had read some of Shakespeare's plays in French translation, but he was eager to see these works performed on stage. Though he understood little English, he was overwhelmed by what he saw. The human insights, touching beauty, and onstage action in Shakespeare's work far surpassed the virtues found in traditional French theater. Not only was Berlioz smitten by Shakespeare, he also fell in love with the leading lady who played Ophelia to Hamlet and Juliet to Romeo, one Harriet Smithson (Fig. 24-3). Like a lovesick adolescent, Berlioz swooned at her sight and wrote such violently passionate letters that the frightened starlet refused even to meet the student composer. Eventually, his ardor cooled—for a time, he even became engaged to someone else. But the experience of an all-consuming love, the despair of rejection, and the vision of darkness and possible death furnished the stimulus—and story line—for an unusually imaginative symphony.

© Archives Charmet/The Bridgeman Art Library

FIGURE 24-2

A caricature of Berlioz conducting in mid-nineteenth-century Paris, in what became known as "monster concerts" because of the huge forces the composer required. Berlioz would have liked several hundred performers for the premiere of his *Symphonie fantastique* in 1830, but the printed program suggests that he had to settle for about one hundred.

FIGURE 24-3

The actress Harriet Smithson became an obsession for Berlioz and the source of inspiration for his *Symphonie fantastique.* Eventually, Berlioz did meet and marry Smithson. Today they lie side by side in the cemetery of Montmartre in Paris.

Yale Center for British Art/© The Bridgeman Art Library

Berlioz composed his *Symphonie fantastique* in five movements instead of the usual four, an arrangement that may have been inspired by Shakespeare's use of a five-act format. Movements 1 and 5 balance each other in length and substance, as do 2 and 4, leaving the leisurely third movement as the center of the work. But symmetry is not the only element holding the symphony together. Berlioz creates a single melody that reappears as a unifying force, movement after movement, a total of eight times during the symphony. This melody, which represents the protagonist's beloved within the story, became, like Harriet Smithson, the composer's obsession. Berlioz called this musical fixation his **idée fixe** (fixed idea). As the protagonist's feelings about his beloved change from movement to movement, so the *idée fixe* is transformed. The composer alters the pitches, changes the rhythm, and assigns the theme to different instruments, each of which adds its own tone color and feeling. To make sure the listener knows what these feelings are, Berlioz prepared a written program to be read as the music was performed. It tells the story of unrequited love, attempted suicide, imaginary murder, and hellish revenge.

FIRST MOVEMENT: REVERIES, PASSIONS

Program: A young musician . . . sees for the first time a woman who embodies all the charms of the ideal being he has imagined in his dreams. . . . The subject of the first movement is the passage from this state of melancholy reverie, interrupted by a few moments of joy, to that of delirious passion, with movements of fury, jealousy, and its return to tenderness, tears, and religious consolation.

A slow introduction ("this state of melancholy reverie") prepares the way for the first vision of the beloved, who is represented by the first appearance of the main theme, the *idée fixe*.

EXAMPLE 24–1

The movement unfolds in something akin to sonata–allegro form. The "recapitulation," however, does not so much repeat the *idée fixe* as transform the melody to reflect the artist's feelings of sorrow and tenderness.

SECOND MOVEMENT: A BALL

The artist finds himself . . . in the midst of the tumult of a party.

A lilting waltz now begins, but it is interrupted by the unexpected appearance of the *idée fixe* (the beloved has arrived), its rhythm changed to accommodate the triple meter of the waltz. Four harps add a graceful accompaniment when the waltz returns, and toward the end, there is even a lovely solo for cornet. The sequence of waltz–*idée fixe*–waltz creates ternary form.

THIRD MOVEMENT: SCENE IN THE COUNTRY

Finding himself one evening in the country, the artist hears in the distance two shepherds piping. . . . He reflects upon his isolation and hopes that soon he will no longer be alone.

The dialogue between the shepherds is presented by an English horn and an oboe, the latter played offstage to give the effect of a distant response. The unexpected appearance of the *idée fixe* in the woodwinds suggests that the artist has hopes of winning his beloved. But has she falsely encouraged him? The shepherd's tune recurs, but the oboe doesn't respond. In response to the lonely petition of the English horn, we now hear only the rumble of distant thunder in the timpani. The call for love goes unanswered.

FOURTH MOVEMENT: MARCH TO THE SCAFFOLD

Having realized that his love goes unrecognized, the artist poisons himself with opium. The dose of the narcotic, too weak to kill him, plunges him into a sleep accompanied by the most horrible visions. He dreams that he has killed the one he loved, that he is condemned, led to the scaffold, and now witnesses his own execution.

This drug-induced nightmare centers on the march to the scaffold where the artist is to be executed. The steady beat of the low strings and the muffled bass drum sound the steps of the procession. Near the end, the image of the beloved returns in the clarinet, only to be suddenly cut off by a *fortissimo* crash by the full orchestra. The guillotine has fallen.

FIFTH MOVEMENT: DREAM OF THE WITCHES' SABBATH

He sees himself at the witches' sabbath surrounded by a troop of frightful shadows, sorcerers, and monsters of all sorts, gathered for his funeral. Strange noises, groans, bursts of laughter, distant cries echoed by others. The beloved melody returns again, but it has lost its noble, modest character and is now only base, trivial, and grotesque. An outburst of joy at her arrival; she joins in the devilish orgy.

In this monstrous finale, Berlioz creates his personal vision of hell (Fig. 24-4). A crowd of witches and other ghouls is summoned to dance around the corpse of the artist on its way to the inferno. Eerie sounds are produced by the strings, using mutes, and by the high woodwinds and French horn, playing glissandos. A piercing clarinet enters with a horrid parody of the *idée fixe* as Harriet Smithson, now in the frightful garb of a wicked old hag, comes on stage.

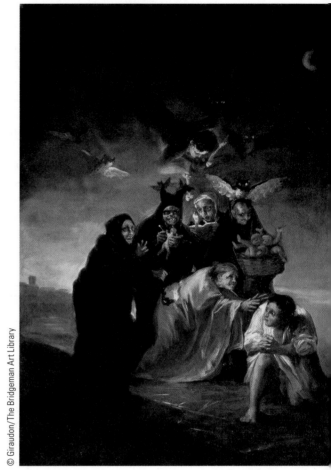

© Giraudon/The Bridgeman Art Library

FIGURE 24-4

Witches' Sabbath by Francisco de Goya (1746–1828) bears the same title as the finale of Berlioz's *Symphonie fantastique*. Both create images of the bizarre and macabre so dear to the hearts of Romantic artists.

EXAMPLE 24-2

@

Download a Supplementary Listening Guide for Berlioz, *Symphonie fantastique*, fourth movement, at the text website.

She is greeted by a joyous *fortissimo* outburst by the full assembly as all proceed to dance to the now perverted *idée fixe*. Suddenly, the music becomes ominously quiet, and in one of the most strikingly original moments in all of classical music, great Gothic church bells are heard. Against this solemn backdrop sounds the burial hymn of the medieval Church, the **Dies irae,** played by ophicleides (tubas) and bassoons. (In more recent years, the *Dies irae* has been used to signal doom and gloom in three movie thrillers: *Nightmare Before Christmas, Sleeping with the Enemy,* and *The Shining.*)

EXAMPLE 24–3

[Di - es i - rae di - es il - la sol - vet sae - clum in fa - vil - la]
[Day of anger, day of wrath, on which the ages will be changed to ash]

Not only is the orchestration sensational, the musical symbolism is sacrilegious. Just as the painter Goya parodies the Catholic Mass in his *Witches' Sabbath*—making babies serve as communion wafers (see Fig. 24-4)—so Berlioz creates a mockery of one of the most venerable Gregorian chants of the Catholic Church. First, the *Dies irae* is played by the horns twice as fast (a process called rhythmic **diminution**). Then the sacred melody is transformed into a jazzed-up dance tune played by a shrill, high clarinet, the entire scene now becoming a blasphemous black mass.

EXAMPLE 24–4

As the ceremony proceeds, the witches begin to dance. But they do so in a strange way: they enter one by one and create a fugato, a fugal passage within a symphonic movement. This successive entry of more and more voices, or dancing witches, creates the effect of a growing tumult around the corpse of the artist.

EXAMPLE 24–5

A climax is reached as the witches' theme, or subject, played by the strings, as well as the *Dies irae* melody, played by the brasses and woodwinds, sound together in different keys, a bizarre example of **double counterpoint.** Stranger still is the sound that follows, for Berlioz instructs the violins to play ***col legno*** (with the wood)—to strike the strings, not with the usual front of the bow, but with the wooden back, creating a noise evocative of the crackling of hellfire.

To the audience that first heard the *Symphonie fantastique* on December 5, 1830, all of this must have seemed incomprehensible: new instruments, novel playing effects, simultaneous melodies in different keys, and a form that is not traditional, like sonata–allegro or rondo, but grows out of the events in a thriller-movie-like program. But it all works. Here again is an instance of a creator, a genius, breaking the rules and stepping outside the box of conventional art; yet he does so in a way that produces a wholly integrated, unified, and ultimately satisfying work. The separate effects may be revolutionary and momentarily shocking, but they are consistent and logical among themselves when heard within the total artistic concept. Had Berlioz never written another note of music, he would still be justly famous for this single masterpiece of Romantic invention.

THE REAL END OF THE PROGRAM

In Berlioz's programmatic *Symphonie fantastique*, art imitates life—he constructs a musical narrative to mirror events (real and imagined) in his young life. But how did the story of Berlioz and his beloved Harriet Smithson really end? In truth, Berlioz did meet and marry Harriet, but the two lived miserably together ever after. He complained about her increasing weight, she about his infidelities. Harriet died in 1854 and was buried in a small graveyard in Paris. In 1864, that cemetery was to be closed and the remains of all the deceased transferred to a new, larger burial ground. It fell to widower Berlioz to remove Harriet's corpse to the new cemetery, as he recounts in his memoirs:

One dark, gloomy morning I set forth alone for the sad spot. A municipal officer was waiting, to be present at the disinterment. The grave had already been

The Parisian painter Eugène Delacroix's depiction of the graveyard scene in *Hamlet* (1829).

© Erich Lessing/Art Resource, NY

opened, and on my arrival the gravedigger jumped in. The coffin was still entire, though it had been ten years underground; the lid alone was injured by the damp. The man, instead of lifting it out, tore away the rotten lid, which cracked with a hideous noise, and brought the contents of the coffin to light. He then bent down, took up the crowned, decayed head of the poor *Ophelia*—and laid it in a new coffin awaiting it at the edge of the grave. Then, bending down a second time, he lifted with difficulty the headless trunk and limbs—a blackish mass to which the shroud still adhered, resembling a heap of pitch in a damp sack. I remember the dull sound . . . and the odor. (Hector Berlioz, *Memoirs*)

Berlioz had begun by playing Romeo to Harriet's Juliet, and ended by playing Hamlet to her Ophelia. He cast his music, and his life, in terms of Shakespearean drama.

Listening GUIDE

Hector Berlioz
***Symphonie fantastique* (1830)**
Fifth movement, "Dream of the Witches' Sabbath"

5 **2**
3/16–17 2/1–2

Genre: Program symphony

0:00	**16** **1**	"Strange noises, groans, bursts of laughter, distant cries" high and low
1:22		Grotesquely transformed *idée fixe* in shrill clarinet
1:29		Joyful, *fortissimo* outburst by full orchestra welcoming now-ugly beloved
1:40		Witches begin dancing to newly grotesque *idée fixe*; bassoons add raucous counterpoint (1:48)
2:33		Sinister transition
2:57		Funeral bells sound
3:23		*Dies irae* heard in tubas and bassoons
3:45		French horns and trombones play *Dies irae* twice as fast
3:55		Woodwinds pervert *Dies irae* chant
4:01		*Dies irae*, its diminution, and its perversion continue
4:25		Tubas and bassoons play *Dies irae* with bass drum reverberation
5:00		Introduction to witches' dance; crescendo

(continued)

5:16		Witches' dance (fugato) begins with four entries of subject

5:45	**17**	0:00	Fugal episode
6:04	**2**	0:20	Three more entries of subject
6:20		0:35	More strange sounds and cries (transition out of fugato)
7:00		1:16	Fragments of *Dies irae*
7:18		1:32	Witches' dance (fugue subject) grows to rapid climax, then *fortissimo* syncopation (2:00)
7:58		2:13	Witches' dance and *Dies irae* combined; trumpets now added
8:30		2:45	Violins use wooden back of bow (*col legno*) to produce crackling sound
8:50		3:05	*Fortissimo* chords
9:07		3:23	Fleeting recall of *Dies irae*
9:20		3:42	More chords with striking harmonic shift
9:30		3:52	Final cadential fanfare

Listen to streaming music in an Active Listening Guide, available on the text website.

Listening EXERCISE 32

Berlioz
SYMPHONIE FANTASTIQUE

5   **2**   **@**

3/16–17   2/1–2

To take this Listening Exercise online and receive feedback or email answers to your instructor, go to the text website.

Imagine that you were among the audience in Paris on December 5, 1830, when Berlioz's *Symphonie fantastique* was first performed. If you had been a dedicated concertgoer up to that time, you might have heard one or two of the latest symphonies of Beethoven. But this would have been the extent of your exposure to "radical" new music. How would you have reacted? The following set of questions asks you to focus upon several aspects of orchestration and form in this astonishingly original work.

1. **16** **1** (0:00–0:23) The opening moments sound eerie because the high strings create "special effects" by means of special string techniques. What two distinctive string techniques are employed?
   a. first tremolo, then ostinato
   b. first pizzicato, then tremolo
   c. first tremolo, then pizzicato

2. (1:22–1:32) The *idée fixe* returns, now transformed. The passage sounds weird because of Berlioz's unusual orchestration. What do you hear?
   a. *idée fixe* in oboe against pounding timpani
   b. *idée fixe* in high clarinet against pounding bass drum

3. (3:23–3:44) Among the instruments that introduce the *Dies irae* is one that Berlioz introduced into the symphony orchestra. Which is it?
   a. high clarinet
   b. cornet
   c. tuba
   d. piccolo

4. (3:45–3:55) The French horns now play the *Dies irae* melody twice as fast as before. What is this sort of reduction in duration in music called?
   a. augmentation
   b. triple
   c. contraction
   d. diminution

5. (5:16–5:41) Now the fugato begins. Its structure is made clear, in part, because the composer cuts off the subject each time so as to announce the next entry. He does this by means of a burst of syncopated chords in the brasses. How many times does this occur?
   a. twice
   b. three times
   c. four times

6. **17** **2** (1:16–1:30) Which instruments play a reminiscence of the *Dies irae* chant?
   a. cellos and double basses
   b. bells
   c. tubas

7. (2:13–2:36) Now the *Dies irae* and the witches' dance (fugue subject) are heard simultaneously. How are they orchestrated?
   a. *Dies irae* in violins, witches' dance in trumpets
   b. *Dies irae* in trumpets, witches' dance in violins

8. (2:13–2:36) When two independent themes or motives sound simultaneously, what process results?
   a. multiple counterpoint
   b. double counterpoint
   c. double play

9. (2:45–3:00) As the strings produce the crackling sound by playing *col legno* (with the wood of the bow and not the horsehair), a melody is heard in the woodwinds. Which is it?
   a. the witches' dance (fugue subject)
   b. the *idée fixe*
   c. the *Dies irae* chant

10. Having now heard a piece of Romantic program music, do you think it is advantageous to have a program? What might be a *disadvantage* of listening to music for which there is a program?
    a. It is easier to get lost with program music than it is with absolute music.
    b. While it is easier to follow the composer's intent, your imagination is restricted; there is only one way to hear the music.

PETER TCHAIKOVSKY (1840–1893) AND THE TONE POEM

The nineteenth century witnessed continued growth in the number and variety of instruments included in the Western symphony orchestra (see pp. 236–238). This expansion worked to the advantage of those composers intent on writing dramatic program music for orchestra, because greater color and volume allowed for ever more dramatic expression. The most prolific writer of late-nineteenth-century program music was Peter Tchaikovsky.

Tchaikovsky was born in 1840 into an upper-middle-class family in provincial Russia (Fig. 24-5). He showed a keen ear for music in his earliest years and by the age of six could speak fluent French and German. (An excellent musical ear and a capacity to learn foreign languages often go hand in hand—both involve processing patterns of sound.) As to his career, his parents determined that law would provide the safest path to success. Thus, beginning in 1852, young Tchaikovsky spent seven years at the School of Jurisprudence in Saint Petersburg and four more years as a clerk in the Ministry of Justice. Then, like Robert Schumann before him, he realized that it was music, not law, that fired his imagination. He made his way to the Saint Petersburg Conservatory of Music, from which he was graduated in 1866. That same year, he went to the newly formed Moscow Conservatory, where he assumed the position of professor of harmony and musical composition.

In truth, it was not his official position in Moscow that supported Tchaikovsky during most of his mature years, but rather a private arrangement with an eccentric patroness, Madame Nadezhda von Meck (Fig. 24-6). This wealthy, music-loving widow furnished him with an annual income of 6,000 rubles (about $45,000 U.S. today) on the condition that she and the composer never meet—a requirement not always easily fulfilled, since the two sometimes resided at the same summer estate. In addition to this annuity, in 1881, Tsar Alexander III awarded Tchaikovsky

FIGURE 24-5

Peter Tchaikovsky.

FIGURE 24-6

Nadezhda von Meck was the widow of an engineer who made a fortune constructing the first railroads in Russia during the 1860s and 1870s. She used her money, in part, to support composers such as Tchaikovsky and, later, Claude Debussy.

Download a Supplementary
Listening Guide for
Tchaikovsky's *1812 Overture* at
the text website.

an annual pension of 3,000 rubles in recognition of his importance to Russian cultural life. Being a man of independent means meant that Tchaikovsky not only was able to travel extensively in Western Europe, and even to America, but also could enjoy the freedom he found so necessary to creative activity.

Tchaikovsky's creative output touched every genre of nineteenth-century classical music, including opera, song, string quartet, piano sonata, concerto, and symphony. But today concertgoers know Tchaikovsky best for his program music and ballets. His extravagant concert overture, *The 1812 Overture* (1882), which commemorates the Russian defeat of Napoleon in 1812, is heard in the United States on the Fourth of July, with Tchaikovsky's musical pyrotechnics usually followed by fireworks in the night sky. Less sensational, but equally compelling, is his tone poem *Romeo and Juliet*. By the end of the nineteenth century, Tchaikovsky was the world's most popular orchestral composer, the "big name" brought from Europe to America when star appeal was needed to add luster to the opening of Carnegie Hall in 1891.

Despite his considerable popular success, Tchaikovsky's life was not a happy one. He was a manic-depressive, a neurotic, and a hypochondriac. He was also a homosexual—and this during a time when there was little tolerance for homosexuality or awareness of its biological causes. He died suddenly in 1893, at the age of fifty-three, after drinking unboiled water during an epidemic of cholera.

Symphonic Poem, Romeo and Juliet (1869; revised 1880)

Tchaikovsky was at his best when writing illustrative music for large orchestra, whether program music or music for ballet. He termed his most overtly programmatic works "overture," "overture fantasy," or "symphonic fantasy." Today we group all of these in the general category of tone poem, or symphonic poem, a title suggesting the literary flavor of these one-movement, programmatic pieces. Tchaikovsky, like Berlioz before him, found that Shakespeare's plays provided the richest source of extramusical inspiration. Of his three tone poems based on the works of Shakespeare—*Romeo and Juliet* (1869; revised 1880), *The Tempest* (1877), and *Hamlet* (1888)—the best is *Romeo and Juliet*.

In *Romeo and Juliet*, Tchaikovsky aimed to capture the spirit, not the letter, of Shakespeare's play, and thus he crafted a free, not literal, representation of its principal dramatic events. In fact, the composer distills these into just three musical themes: the compassionate music of the kindly Friar Laurence, whose plan to unite the lovers goes fatally awry; the fighting music, which represents the feud between the Capulets and Montagues; and the love theme, which expresses the passion of Romeo and Juliet. Most important, whereas Shakespeare's drama unfolds as a continuous linear process, Tchaikovsky sets his themes within the confines of sonata–allegro form, which gives the music a recursive shape: presentation, confrontation, resolution.

The introduction begins with the music of Friar Laurence and concludes with a succession of mysterious chords strummed on a harp, as if Friar Laurence, like a medieval bard, were about to narrate a long, tragic tale. When the exposition begins, we hear angry percussive music, racing strings, and syncopated cymbal crashes, suggesting that we have entered the violent world of the Capulets and Montagues. Soon the fighting subsides and the love theme emerges, precisely where we would expect a lyrical second theme to appear in sonata–allegro form. As appropriate for a pair of lovers, the love theme is in two parts (Exs. 24-6 and 24-7), each of which grows and becomes more passionate when pushed upward in ascending melodic sequences.

EXAMPLE 24–6: LOVE THEME PART 1

viola and English horn

EXAMPLE 24–7: LOVE THEME PART 2

violins

pp

The brief development section pits the feuding families against the increasingly adamant pleas of Friar Laurence. The recapitulation, true to sonata form, begins with the feud music but moves quickly to an expanded, more ecstatic presentation of the love theme (part 2 first, then part 1), which is eventually cut off by a noisy return of the feuding clans. The beginning of the dramatic coda is announced by a foreboding *fortissimo* roll on the timpani. As we hear the steady drumbeats of a funeral procession and fragments of the broken love theme, we know that Romeo and Juliet are dead. A celestial, hymn-like passage (a transformation of the love theme) suggests that the lovers have been united in some higher realm, a feeling confirmed by the return of the love theme in high violins. There only remains to bring the curtain down on the story of the star-crossed lovers, which Tchaikovsky does with seven *fortissimo* hammer-strokes for full orchestra, all on the tonic chord.

Shakespeare wrote *Romeo and Juliet* as a tragedy: "For never was a story of more woe / Than this of Juliet and her Romeo," say the final lines of the play. By incorporating a "celestial conclusion" into his coda—a hymn-like choir of angelic woodwinds followed by the transcendent love theme on high in the violins—Tchaikovsky has changed the final import of the play. True child of the Romantic age, he suggests that the love-death of Romeo and Juliet was, in fact, not a tragedy but a spiritual triumph.

Listening GUIDE

Peter Tchaikovsky
***Romeo and Juliet* (1869; revised 1880)**

5

3/18–21

Genre: Tone poem

Form: Sonata–allegro

INTRODUCTION

0:00 **18**	Friar Laurence theme sounding organ-like in woodwinds	
0:37	Anguished, dissonant sound in strings and French horn	

p

(continued)

1:29		Harp alternates with flute solo and woodwinds
2:11		Friar Laurence theme returns with new accompaniment
2:36		Anguished sound returns in strings with French horn
3:23		Harp strumming returns
3:56		Timpani roll and string tremolos build tension; hints of Friar Laurence theme in woodwinds
4:32		Anguished sound again returns, then yields to crescendo on repeating tonic chord

EXPOSITION

5:16	**19** 0:00	Feud theme in agitated minor; angry rhythmic motive in woodwinds, racing scales in strings
6:04	0:49	Crashing syncopations (with cymbal) running against scales
6:38	1:22	Gentle transition, with release of tension, to second theme
7:28	2:12	Love theme (part 1) played quietly by English horn and viola
7:50	2:33	Love theme (part 2) played quietly by strings with mutes
8:32	3:16	Love theme (part 1) returns with growing ardor in high woodwinds while French horn plays counterpoint against it
9:34	4:18	Lyrical closing section in which cellos and English horn engage in dialogue against backdrop of gently plucked chords in harp

DEVELOPMENT

10:36	**20** 0:00	Feud theme against which horn soon plays Friar Laurence theme
10:56	0:20	String syncopations, again against Friar Laurence theme
11:20	0:44	Feud theme and Friar Laurence theme continue in opposition
12:03	1:27	Cymbal crashes signal climax of development as trumpet blares forth with Friar Laurence theme

RECAPITULATION

12:35	2:00	Feud theme in woodwinds and brasses against racing strings
12:58	2:23	Love theme (part 2) softly in woodwinds
13:35	2:58	Love theme (part 1) sounds ecstatically with all its inherent force and sweep
14:14	3:38	Love theme begins again in strings, with counterpoint in brasses
14:30	3:56	Fragments of love theme in strings, then brasses
14:55	4:20	Love theme begins again but is cut off by feud theme; syncopated cymbal crashes
15:14	4:39	Feud theme and Friar Laurence theme build to a climax
16:12	5:36	Timpani roll announces coda

CODA

16:24	**21** 0:00	Timpani beats funeral march while strings play fragments of love theme
17:19	0:55	Love theme (part 2) transformed into sound of heavenly chorale played by woodwinds
18:20	1:56	Transcendent love theme sounds from on high in violins
18:55	2:31	Timpani roll and final chords

Listen to streaming music in an Active Listening Guide, available on the text website.

Ballet

Ballet, like opera, calls to mind "high-end" culture. Significantly, the origins of ballet are tied to the history of opera, for ballet emerged from a hybrid of the two genres performed at the French royal court of Louis XIV (r1643–1715). Throughout the eighteenth century, no *opera seria*, even one by Mozart, was complete without a ballet or two to provide a pleasant diversion. By the early nineteenth century, however, this dance spectacle had separated from opera and moved on stage as the independent genre we know today. A **ballet** is thus a dramatic dance in which the characters, using various stylized steps and pantomime, tell a story. While ballet first developed in France, during the nineteenth century it gained great popularity, and indeed an adopted homeland, in Russia. Even today, the terms *Russian* and *ballerina* seem inextricably linked.

Early in his career, Tchaikovsky realized that ballet required precisely the compositional skills that he possessed. Unlike Bach, Mozart, and Beethoven, Tchaikovksy was not a "developer"—he was not good at teasing out intricate thematic relationships over long spans of time. Instead, his gift was to create one striking melody and mood after another—to create one vivid scene and then move on to the next. And this is precisely what **ballet music** requires—not symphonic invention or contrapuntal intricacy, but short bursts of tuneful melody and captivating rhythm, all intended to capture the emotional essence of the scene. *Short* is the operative word here; because dancing in a ballet is exhausting; neither the principals nor the *corps de ballet* hold center stage for more than three minutes at most. Tchaikovsky's "short-segment" style proved perfect for the demands of ballet. From his pen flowed *Swan Lake* (1876), *Sleeping Beauty* (1889), and *The Nutcracker* (1892), arguably the three most popular works in the entire repertoire of grand Romantic ballet (Fig. 24-7).

Who among us does not know some of the ballet music from *The Nutcracker* (1892), a holiday ritual as traditional as caroling and gift giving? The story, typical of Romantic-era narratives, springs from a fairy-tale dream. After a Christmas Eve celebration, an exhausted young girl, Clara, falls asleep and sees in her imagination people from exotic places and toys come to life. Fantastical characters parade before us, not merely accompanied but literally brought to life by the music. In "Dance of the Reed Pipes," piping flutes create the mood of the moment. In "Dance of the Sugar Plum Fairy," an instrument new to the orchestra, a keyed percussion instrument called the **celesta,** conjures up an appropriately elfin sound. But ballet music must not only create evocative moods; it must also project a strong, clear metrical pulse to animate—indeed, regulate—the steps of the dancers. If you can't hear the beat, you can't dance, tutu or not!

FIGURE 24-7

A recent production of *The Nutcracker* by the Royal Ballet, showing a *pas de deux* in "Dance of the Sugar Plum Fairy."

© Robbie Jack/CORBIS

Listening GUIDE

Peter Tchaikovsky
"Dance of the Reed Pipes" from
The Nutcracker (1891)

intro
26

Situation: In this portion of the ballet, Clara's dream takes her and the Handsome Prince to exotic places around the globe (China, Arabia, Russia, and Spain among them), and for each, Tchaikovsky creates music that sounds evocative of a foreign locale, at least to Western ears. While in China, we encounter a group of dancing shepherds playing reed pipes—hence the prominence of the flutes.

(continued)

Genre: Ballet music

Form: Ternary

0:00	26		Flutes play melody above low string pizzicato
0:35	A	{	English horn and then clarinet add counterpoint
0:51			Melody repeats with violins now adding counterpoint
1:22	B		Change to minor mode: trumpets play melody above two-note bass ostinato
1:36			Violins join melody
1:57	A'		Return to flute melody (with violin counterpoint) in major mode

Listen to streaming music in an Active Listening Guide, available on the text website.

Listening GUIDE

Peter Tchaikovsky
"Dance of the Sugar Plum Fairy" from
The Nutcracker **(1891)**

5

3/22

Situation: The Sugar Plum Fairy charms the Handsome Prince at the Magic Castle, in a showpiece for any great *prima ballerina.*

Genre: Ballet music

Form: Ternary

0:00	22	Pizzicato strings set beat in duple meter
0:08	A	Celesta enters with melody, as bass clarinet plays amusing descending scale
0:39	B	Tempo increases and scales rise
1:01		Rippling glissandos and static harmony build expectation of return to opening music
1:11	A	Celesta returns with opening melody
1:41		Ballerina scampers away

Listen to streaming music in an Active Listening Guide, available on the text website.

Finally, it is important to keep in mind that ballet music is not program music. Program music is purely instrumental music, in which sounds alone create the narrative. In ballet music, on the other hand, music is an adjunct: the movements, facial expressions, and gestures of the dancers tell the story.

Key WORDS

The materials on the text website will help you understand and pass tests on the content of this chapter. In addition, you may complete this chapter's Listening Exercise interactively, as well as view Active Listening Guides and other materials that will help you succeed in this course.

program music (253)
absolute music (253)
program symphony (253)
dramatic overture (253)
concert overture (253)
tone (symphonic) poem (254)

ophicleide (255)
English horn (255)
cornet (255)
idée fixe (256)
Dies irae (258)
diminution (258)

double counterpoint (258)
col legno (258)
ballet (265)
ballet music (265)
celesta (265)

ROMANTIC MUSIC
PIANO MUSIC

We have all banged away on a piano at one time or another. Some of us were subjected to piano lessons, with the obligatory exercises by Clementi and Craemer, all accompanied by our mother's prediction: "Someday you'll thank me for this!" But did you ever stop to think how the piano came to be? In brief, it was invented around 1700 as an alternative to the harpsichord, as a way of giving more dynamics and shading to the musical line. The piano assumed its modern form—the 3-pedal, 88-key, 1,200-pound grand—during the Romantic period.

Just as the symphony orchestra grew in size and power during the nineteenth century, so, too, did the piano, propelled by the new technology of the Industrial Revolution. Mozart's piano was small (only sixty-one keys), and its frame was made of wood (see Fig. 19-7). Nineteenth-century technology supplied the piano with a frame made of cast iron, allowing for greater tension on the strings. This cast-iron frame supported thicker steel strings, which greatly increased the volume of sound and the punishment the instrument could take. (Recall that the forceful Beethoven had frequently broken strings while playing the older wooden-frame piano—see page 211.) But not only could the Romantic piano support louder and more aggressive playing, it also facilitated a gentler, more lyrical style; its hammers were covered with felt, which allowed the instrument to "sing" with a mellow tone, in contrast to the "ping" of the pianos of Mozart's day. Like the growing nineteenth-century orchestra, the piano could now produce both a very loud sound (*fortissimo*) and a very soft one (*pianissimo*). The instrument's range increased as well: Mozart's five-octave piano of the 1780s had grown to an eight-octave one a century later. Foot pedals were also added in the nineteenth century. On the right side was the **sustaining pedal,** which enabled strings to continue to sound after the performer had lifted his or her hand from the corresponding keys. On the left was the **soft pedal,** which softened the dynamic level by shifting the position of the hammers relative to the strings. Finally, in the 1850s, the Steinway Company of New York began **cross-stringing** the piano, overlaying the lowest-sounding strings across those of the middle register, and thereby producing a richer, more homogeneous sound. By the mid-nineteenth century, all the essential features of the modern piano were in place—the essential design of the piano has not changed in 150 years.

As the piano grew larger and more expressive, it became something of a home entertainment center, a place where the family could gather to play and sing before the days of television and electronic entertainment. Every aspiring middle-class home had to have a piano, both for family enjoyment and as a status symbol—the "high art" instrument in the parlor signified to visitors that they had entered a "cultured" home. Parents made sure their children, especially the girls, received lessons, and publishers, eager to profit from the vogue for the piano, turned out reams of sheet music for pianists of all skill levels.

Spurred by the sudden popularity of the piano, a host of virtuoso performers descended upon the concert halls of Europe with fingers blazing. What

@

Download a Supplementary Listening Guide for piano pieces by Robert and Clara Schumann, at the text website.

they played was often more a display of technical fireworks—rapid octaves, racing chromatic scales, thundering chords—than of musical substance. Happily, however, several of the greatest piano virtuosos of the nineteenth century were also gifted composers.

FIGURE 25-1

A superbly Romantic portrait of Chopin by Eugène Delacroix. It was originally painted with Chopin next to George Sand (see Fig. 25-2). But in 1870, a vandal slashed the double portrait, thereby (unintentionally) creating two canvases.

FIGURE 25-2

Novelist Aurore Dudevant (George Sand) by Eugène Delacroix. Both the painter Delacroix and the composer Chopin often stayed at her summer estate in Nohant in the south of France.

FRÉDÉRIC CHOPIN (1810–1849)

In the compositions of Frédéric Chopin (Fig. 25-1), the piano and its music have their most perfect union. This "poet of the piano," as he was called, was born near Warsaw, Poland, of a French father and a Polish mother. The father taught at an elite secondary school for the sons of Polish nobility, and it was there that Frédéric not only gained an excellent general education but acquired aristocratic friends and tastes as well. He then moved on to the newly founded Warsaw Conservatory, where, between 1826 and 1829, he concentrated on the study of piano and composition. During this period, he composed his first major work, a brilliant set of variations for piano and orchestra on Mozart's duet "Là ci darem la mano" ("Give Me Your Hand") from *Don Giovanni* (on the duet, see p. 206). After this success, Warsaw seemed too small, too provincial, for a young man of Chopin's musical talents. So, in 1830, he departed to seek his fortune in Vienna and Paris. The next year, Poland's fight for independence was crushed by Russian troops; Chopin never returned to his homeland.

After an unsuccessful year in Vienna, the twenty-one-year-old Chopin arrived in Paris in September 1831. His inaugural concerts caught Parisians' fancy, and his imaginative playing soon became the stuff of legend. But Chopin was not cut out for the life of the public virtuoso. He was introverted, physically slight, and somewhat sickly. Consequently, he chose to play at private *musicales* (musical evenings) in the homes of the aristocracy and to give lessons for a fee only the very rich could afford. "I have been introduced all around the highest circles," he said within a year of his arrival. "I hobnob with ambassadors, princes, and ministers. I can't imagine what miracle is responsible for all this since I really haven't done anything to bring it about."

In October 1836, Chopin met Baroness Aurore Dudevant (1803–1876), a writer who under the pen name of George Sand poured forth a steady stream of Romantic novels roughly akin to our Silhouette Romances. Sand, a bisexual, was an ardent individualist with a predilection for wearing men's clothing and smoking cigars (see Sand seated behind Liszt in the painting on the cover and Fig. 25-2). Six years Chopin's senior, she became his lover and protector. Many of the composer's best works were written at Nohant, her summer residence 150 miles south of Paris. After their relationship ended in 1847, Chopin undertook a taxing concert tour of England and Scotland. While this improved his depleted finances, it weakened his delicate health. He died in Paris of tuberculosis at the age of thirty-nine.

Mazurka in B♭ major, Opus 7, No. 1 (1832)

Although Frédéric Chopin spent most of his adult life in France, he maintained strong emotional ties to Poland, and his compositions frequently drew upon musical idioms of his native land. Indeed, the expatriate composer became something of a national hero in Poland, his music embraced as a way of preserving a national heritage. Consciously, Chopin became an avatar of musical nationalism (see Chapter 29).

As a youth, Chopin had vacationed with his family in the Polish countryside, where he was introduced to such traditional Polish dances as the mazurka and the polonaise. The **mazurka** is a fast dance in triple meter with an accent on the second beat. Its melody draws on native folk tunes, some of them of Jewish ancestry, and its harmony suggests the static droning of a village bagpipe. Chopin's Mazurka in B♭ major begins much like a triple-meter waltz, except that the strong accent often falls on beat 2, not beat 1. Yet midway through (in section **C**), the mode switches from major to minor, a strange scale enters in the melody, and a drone appears in the accompanying bass. We have been transported from the world of the Parisian salon to a Polish village, from the familiar to the foreign. In Chopin's day, these mazurkas were experienced as music or as dance: the Parisians listened, the Poles danced.

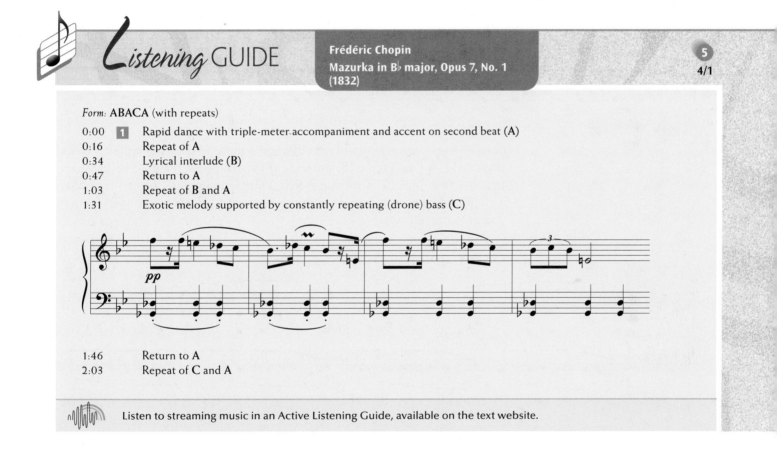

*L*istening GUIDE

Frédéric Chopin
Mazurka in B♭ major, Opus 7, No. 1
(1832)

5
4/1

Form: **ABACA** (with repeats)

0:00	**1**	Rapid dance with triple-meter accompaniment and accent on second beat (**A**)
0:16		Repeat of **A**
0:34		Lyrical interlude (**B**)
0:47		Return to **A**
1:03		Repeat of **B** and **A**
1:31		Exotic melody supported by constantly repeating (drone) bass (**C**)

1:46	Return to **A**
2:03	Repeat of **C** and **A**

Listen to streaming music in an Active Listening Guide, available on the text website.

Chopin was a rarity among Romantic composers—he wrote only for the piano or ensemble pieces (including songs) in which he made the piano figure prominently. His works for solo piano include—in addition to his mazurkas and polonaises—3 piano sonatas, a set of 24 preludes (brief character pieces, one in each of the major and minor keys), 24 etudes (technical studies), and 21 nocturnes. Far better than the other genres for piano, the dream-like nocturnes embody the essence of musical Romanticism.

@

Download Supplementary
Listening Guides for several
more Chopin works, including
a polonaise, etude, and
prelude, at the text website.

Nocturne in C♯ minor, Opus 27, No. 1 (1835)

Want to hear music that is almost painfully beautiful? Download a Chopin nocturne. A **nocturne** (night piece) is a slow, dreamy genre of piano music that came into favor in the 1820s and 1830s. It suggests moonlit nights, romantic longing, and a certain wistful melancholy, all evoked through bittersweet melodies and softly strumming harmonies. To set a nocturnal mood in his Nocturne in C♯ minor, Chopin begins with a tonic C♯ minor chord spun out as an arpeggio in the bass, like a harp or guitar played in the moonlight. The melody (**A**) enters in minor but immediately turns to major, by means of an added sharp. As the opening melody repeats again and again in the course of the work, so, too, the harmony shifts expressively, bending back and forth from minor to major, from dark to light. This twisting of mode is one way that the composer creates the "bittersweet" feeling.

EXAMPLE 25–1

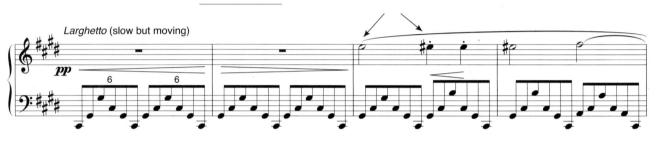

Soon the opening melody breaks off, and a more passionate, agitated mood takes hold. A new theme (**B**) enters and the tempo increases. The bass now begins a long, mostly chromatic ascent. Here Chopin joins a long list of composers who have employed rising chromaticism to create a feeling of anxiety and growing tension.

EXAMPLE 25–2

A climax is reached at the peak of this line, emphasized by a remarkable chord change—a chord with four sharps is immediately followed by one with four flats (see Ex. 22-2). As mentioned earlier (p. 234), the sudden juxtaposition of such distant chords creates bold harmonic shifts of the sort favored by Romantic composers as they strove to fashion a new, more colorful harmonic language. Now a third melody (**C**) enters, which eventually gives way to **A** by means of a descending, recitative-like passage.

The return to **A** is especially rich and satisfying, as the harp-like accompaniment and plaintive melody seem to rise from the depths of the fading bass. Chopin's simple formal plan is now clear: statement–digression–return, each section with its own evocative atmosphere. The "lyrical expressive" (**A**) gives way to the "passionately anxious" (**B** and **C**), which yields to the initial lyricism (**A**). The returning **A** is extended by means of an exquisite little coda. At the very end, a painful dissonance sounds and then resolves to consonance (5:18–5:23), as the fears of the nocturnal world dissolve into a heavenly major realm. As the German poet Heine said of Chopin, "He hails from the land of Mozart, Raphael, and Goethe. His true home is in the realm of Poetry."

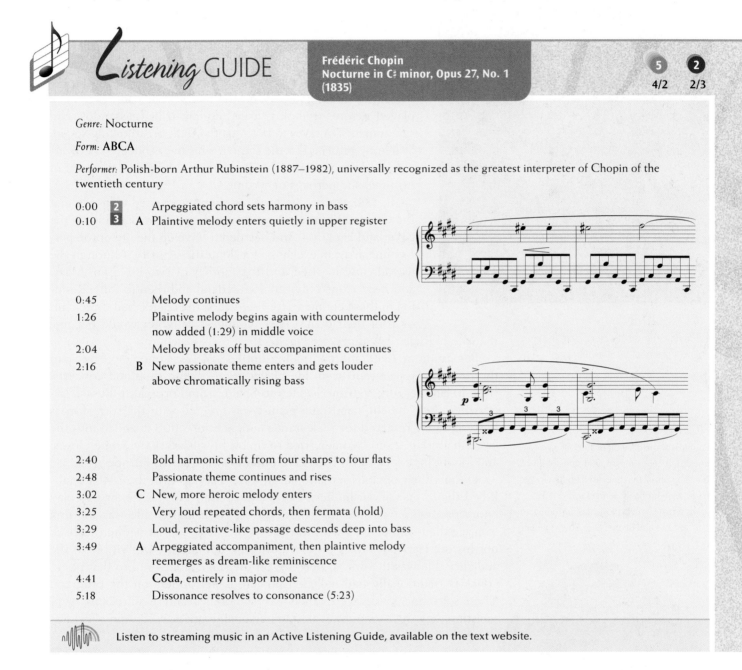

Listening GUIDE

Frédéric Chopin
Nocturne in C♯ minor, Opus 27, No. 1
(1835)

5 2
4/2 2/3

Genre: Nocturne

Form: **ABCA**

Performer: Polish-born Arthur Rubinstein (1887–1982), universally recognized as the greatest interpreter of Chopin of the twentieth century

0:00	**2**		Arpeggiated chord sets harmony in bass
0:10	**3**	A	Plaintive melody enters quietly in upper register
0:45			Melody continues
1:26			Plaintive melody begins again with countermelody now added (1:29) in middle voice
2:04			Melody breaks off but accompaniment continues
2:16		B	New passionate theme enters and gets louder above chromatically rising bass
2:40			Bold harmonic shift from four sharps to four flats
2:48			Passionate theme continues and rises
3:02		C	New, more heroic melody enters
3:25			Very loud repeated chords, then fermata (hold)
3:29			Loud, recitative-like passage descends deep into bass
3:49		A	Arpeggiated accompaniment, then plaintive melody reemerges as dream-like reminiscence
4:41			**Coda**, entirely in major mode
5:18			Dissonance resolves to consonance (5:23)

Listen to streaming music in an Active Listening Guide, available on the text website.

FRANZ LISZT (1811–1886)

Franz Liszt was not merely a musician, he was a phenomenon, perhaps the most flamboyant artistic personality of the entire nineteenth century. Handsome, supremely talented, and equally self-confident, he strutted across the stage as the musical sex symbol of the Romantic era (Fig. 25-3). But he could also play the piano, and like no other.

Franz Liszt was born in Hungary of German-speaking parents. In 1822, his ambitious father took him to Vienna and then Paris to be the next child prodigy, the latest musical *Wunderkind*. But his father died suddenly, and the

© SuperStock/SuperStock

FIGURE 25-3

The young, charismatic Franz Liszt, the pre-eminent pianist of the Romantic era.

FIGURE 25-4

Countess Marie d'Agoult in 1843. She was a novelist in her own right, and some of the tracts on music that appeared under Liszt's name were probably penned by her. Like many female writers of the day, including George Sand and George Eliot, she wrote under a masculine *nom de plume*, Daniel Stern.

© Bridgeman-Giraudon/Art Resource, NY

young pianist's career languished. Liszt's life took a dramatic turn on April 20, 1832, however, when he attended a concert given by the great violin virtuoso Niccolò Paganini (see p. 239). "What a man, what a violin, what an artist! Oh, God, what pain and suffering, what torment in those four strings." Liszt vowed to bring Paganini's technical virtuosity to the piano. Practicing four to five hours a day—unusual dedication for a prodigy—he taught himself to play on the piano what had never been played before: tremolos, leaps, double trills, glissandos, and simultaneous octaves in both hands, all at breathtaking speed. When he returned to the stage for his own concerts, he overwhelmed the audience. He had become the greatest pianist of his time, and perhaps of all time.

In 1833, Liszt's life took another unexpected turn. He met the Countess Marie d'Agoult (at his feet in the painting on the cover and Fig. 25-4) and decided to give up the life of the performing artist in exchange for domestic security. Although she was already married and the mother of two children, Marie and Liszt eloped, first to Switzerland and then to Italy. Residing in these countries for four years, the couple had three children of their own. (Their youngest daughter would become the wife of Richard Wagner; see Fig. 27-3.)

Beginning in 1839, and continuing until 1847, Liszt once more took to the road as a touring virtuoso. He played more than a thousand concerts: from Ireland to Turkey, from Sweden to Spain, from Portugal to Russia. Everywhere he went the handsome pianist was greeted with the sort of mass hysteria today reserved for rock stars. Audiences of 3,000 crowded into the larger halls (Fig. 25-5). Women tried to rip off his silk scarf and white gloves, and fought for a lock of his hair. **Lisztomania** swept across Europe.

Despite their obvious sensationalism, Liszt's concerts in the 1840s established the format of our modern-day piano **recital.** He was the first to play entire programs from memory (not reading from music). He was the first to place the piano parallel with the line of the stage so that neither his back nor his full face, but rather his extraordinary side profile, was visible to the audience. He was the first to perform on the stage alone—up to that point, concerts traditionally had included numerous performers on the program. These solo appearances were called first "soliloquies" and then "recitals," suggesting they were something akin to personal dramatic recitations. As Liszt modestly claimed in his adopted French, *"Le concert, c'est moi!"*

But Liszt was a complex man with many facets to his personality. He thought of himself not only as a showman-pianist but also as a serious composer. So, in 1847, he suddenly quit the lucrative concert circuit and settled in Weimar, Germany, to serve the ducal court as music director and composer-in-residence. Here he concentrated on writing orchestral music. All told, he composed a dozen tone poems, as well as two program symphonies and three piano concertos. In 1861, Liszt again surprised the world: he moved to Rome, entered Holy Orders in the Roman Catholic Church, and took up residence in the Vatican! "Abbé Liszt," as the composer now styled himself, had replaced Don Juan. While in Rome, Liszt wrote the bulk of his sixty religious works including two oratorios. He died at the age of seventy-five in Bayreuth, Germany, where he had gone to hear the latest opera of his son-in-law, Richard Wagner.

Despite Liszt's interest in religious music and programmatic works for orchestra, his reputation as a composer rests primarily upon his sensational piano music, particularly his *Hungarian Rhapsodies*. Liszt had large hands and unusually long fingers with very little web-like connective tissue between them (Fig. 25-6), which allowed him to make wide stretches with relative ease. He could play a melody in octaves when others could play only the single notes of the line. If others might execute a passage in octaves, Liszt could dash it off in more impressive-sounding tenths (octave plus third). So he wrote daredevil music full of virtuosic display.

To build sufficient technique to tackle Liszt's difficult showpieces, performers practiced a musical genre called the "etude." An **etude** is a short, one-movement composition designed to improve one or more aspects of a performer's technique (fast scales, more rapid note repetition, surer leaps, and so on). Before 1840, dozens of composers had published books of technical exercises that became the cornerstone of piano instruction for the burgeoning middle class. Chopin and Liszt took this development one step further. They added beautifully crafted melodies and unusual textures to what previously had been merely mind-numbing finger work, thereby demonstrating that an etude might embody artistry as well as mechanics.

Liszt's most difficult pieces of this sort are his twelve *Transcendental Etudes* (1851). As the title suggests, these works require transcendent, indeed superhuman, technical skill. Ironically, these etudes by Liszt are not useful studies for the average pianist—they are so difficult that the performer must already be a virtuoso to play them! As composer and critic Robert Schumann said, "The *Transcendental Etudes* are studies in storm and dread designed to be performed by, at most, ten or twelve players in the world."

Transcendental Etude No. 8, "Wilde Jagd" ("Wild Hunt"; 1851)

Among the most technically difficult of Liszt's *Transcendental Etudes* is No. 8, "Wilde Jagd" ("Wild Hunt"). The title suggests a nocturnal chase in a supernatural forest of the sort often evoked in German Romantic literature. The similarly "supernatural" demands placed on the pianist are intended to develop skill in playing broken octaves in the left hand and simultaneous chromatic runs in both hands (Ex. 25-3). Occasionally, a lyrical melody shines forth in the dark forest of digital dangers. In these moments, the pianist must project the expressive melody while keeping the difficult accompaniment up to tempo, performing simultaneously the roles of poet and technical virtuoso. Today this etude serves as a "musical Mount Everest"—dozens of young virtuosos can be seen on YouTube trying to scale it.

Lebrecht Music & Arts

FIGURE 25-5

Lisztomania, as depicted in 1842. A recital by Liszt was likely to create the sort of sensation that a concert by a rock star might generate today. Women fought for a lock of his hair, a broken string from his piano, or a shred of his velvet gloves.

Download Supplementary Listening Guides for several more Liszt selections at the text website.

FIGURE 25-6

The aged Liszt, still dazzling audiences and destroying pianos. As a critic of the day said of his slash-and-burn technique, "He is as much a piano slayer as a piano player."

© Mary Evans Picture Library/The Image Works

EXAMPLE 25–3   (0:34)

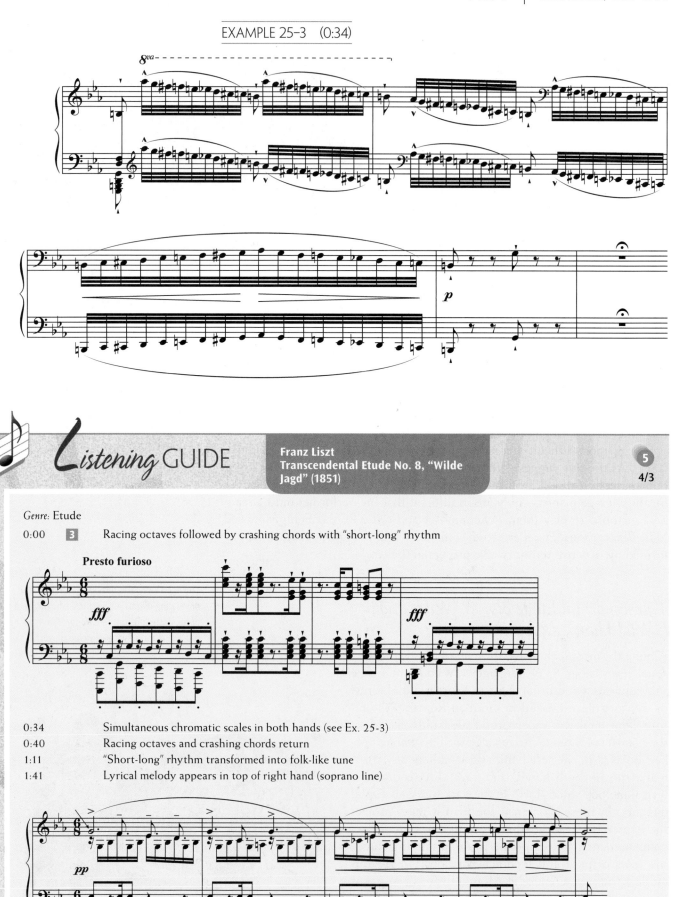

*L*istening GUIDE

Franz Liszt
Transcendental Etude No. 8, "Wilde Jagd" (1851)

5

4/3

Genre: Etude

0:00   **3**   Racing octaves followed by crashing chords with "short-long" rhythm

Presto furioso

0:34   Simultaneous chromatic scales in both hands (see Ex. 25-3)
0:40   Racing octaves and crashing chords return
1:11   "Short-long" rhythm transformed into folk-like tune
1:41   Lyrical melody appears in top of right hand (soprano line)

1:55	Lyrical melody moved octave higher
2:28	Lyrical melody set to more complex accompaniment and grows in intensity
2:56	Racing octaves and crashing chords return and are developed harmonically
3:59	Lyrical melody returns
4:15	Lyrical melody rises in melodic sequence to climax
4:24	Arpeggios ascend and then crashing chords descend to end

Listen to streaming music in an Active Listening Guide, available on the text website.

Key WORDS

sustaining pedal (267)   mazurka (269)   recital (272)
soft pedal (267)   nocturne (269)   etude (273)
cross-stringing (267)   Lisztomania (272)

The materials on the text website will help you understand and pass tests on the content of this chapter. In addition, you may view Active Listening Guides and other materials that will help you succeed in this course.

ROMANTIC OPERA
ITALY

The nineteenth century is often called the "golden age of opera." It is the century of Rossini, Bellini, Verdi, Wagner, Bizet, and Puccini. True, there had been great opera composers before—Monteverdi, Handel, and Mozart, to name just three. But the nineteenth century saw the creation of much of the "core" repertoire of today. Presently, about two-thirds of the productions of the leading opera companies—the Metropolitan Opera in New York and La Scala in Milan, for example—are works created during the years 1820–1900.

Italy, of course, is the home of opera. The Italian language, with its evenly spaced, open vowels, is perfectly suited for singing, and the people of Italy seem to have an innate love of melody. Beginning around 1600, the first operas were created in Florence, Rome, Venice, and Mantua (see Chapter 11). For nearly two centuries, Italian opera dominated the international stage. When Handel wrote operas for London in the 1720s, for example, he composed Italian operas (see Chapter 14), as did Mozart when he created musical theater for the courts of Germany and Austria in the 1770s and 1780s (see Chapter 20).

In the early nineteenth century, the primacy of Italian opera was maintained almost single-handedly by Gioachino Rossini (1792–1868). Surprising as it may seem today, Rossini was the most celebrated composer in Europe during the 1820s, far exceeding even Beethoven in fame. He owed this public favor in large measure to the genre he chose: opera was then the most popular form of musical entertainment. More than the symphony, string quartet, or any other musical genre of the time, opera captured the popular imagination in much the way that cinema does today.

Rossini brought to a glorious close the eighteenth-century tradition of comic opera, or *opera buffa* (see p. 155). Catchy, oft-repeating melodies, vivacious rhythms, and rollicking crescendos were his trademarks. His best-known comic opera, *The Barber of Seville*, has never disappeared from the operatic stage since it first appeared in 1816. Even casual music lovers know a little of this enduring work in the form of the "Figaro, Figaro, Figaro" call from the opening aria for the resourceful barber, Figaro. Rossini could also write in a more serious style, as exemplified in his last opera, *William Tell* (1829). This stormy drama, too, has achieved a measure of immortality, the overture providing the theme music for the radio and film character of the Lone Ranger.

FIGURE 26–1

The reigning opera diva Renée Fleming of Rochester, New York, specializes in *bel canto* opera.

ITALIAN *BEL CANTO* OPERA

Whereas German operatic composers would come to emphasize the dramatic power and instrumental color of the orchestra, Italians after Rossini increasingly focused their energies on melodies for the solo voice—on the art of beautiful singing, or **bel canto.** The two most gifted of the early creators of *bel canto* opera were Gaetano Donizetti (1797–1848) and Vincenzo Bellini (1801–1835). In their works, the orchestra provides merely a simple harmonic support for the soaring, sometimes divinely beautiful, lines of the voice. Look at the opening of the famous aria "Casta diva" from Bellini's *Norma* (1831), in which the heroine sings a prayer to a distant moon goddess (Ex. 26-1). Here the orchestra functions like a giant guitar. Simple chords are fleshed out as arpeggios by the strings while an even simpler bass line is plucked below. All of the musical interest is in the rapturous sound of the human voice. One Italian newspaper of the day declared, "In the theatrical arts it is said that three things are required: action, action, action; likewise, three things are demanded for music: voice, voice, voice."

Watch a video of Craig Wright's Open Yale Course class session 19, "Romantic Opera: Verdi's *La Traviata*, Bocelli, Pavarotti, and Domingo," at the text website.

EXAMPLE 26-1

Ca - sta Di - va, ca - sta Di - va, che i - nar-

(Chaste goddess, who does bathe in silver light these hallowed, ancient trees)

gen - ti que - ste sa - cre, que - ste sa - cre, que-ste sa - cre anti - che pian - te,

Not surprisingly, by placing such importance on the voices of the leading singers, *bel canto* opera fostered a star system among the cast. Usually, it was the lyric soprano—heroine and **prima donna** (first lady)—who held the most exalted position in the operatic firmament. By the 1880s, she would also be called a **diva,** which, as in the aria "Casta diva," means "goddess." Indeed, the diva and her beautiful voice would rule Italian *bel canto* opera throughout the nineteenth century and even down to the present day (Fig. 26-1).

GIUSEPPE VERDI (1813–1901)

The name Giuseppe Verdi is virtually synonymous with Italian opera. For six decades, from the time of *Nabucco* in 1842 until *Falstaff* in 1893, Verdi had almost no rival for the affections of the opera-loving public in Italy and throughout Europe. Even today the best-loved of his twenty-six operas are more readily available—in opera houses, TV productions, DVDs, and webcasts—than those of any other composer.

Verdi was born near Busseto in northern Italy in 1813, the son of a tavern-keeper. He was apparently no musical prodigy, for at the age of eighteen, he was rejected for admission to the Conservatory of Music in Milan because he was already too old and his piano technique faulty. But Verdi stayed on

© Scala/Art Resource, NY

FIGURES 26–2 AND 26–3

(top) La Scala Opera House about 1830. Verdi's first four and last two operas had their premieres at La Scala, then as now the foremost opera house in Italy. (bottom) Verdi's longtime mistress, and ultimately his wife, Giuseppina Strepponi (1815–1897), holding the score of his early opera *Nabucco*. She was instrumental in getting this and other operas by Verdi produced at La Scala in Milan.

© Roger-Viollet, Paris/The Bridgeman Art Library

in Milan to study composition. He returned to Busseto in 1835 to serve as the town's bandmaster and then, four years later, went back to Milan to earn his livelihood as a composer.

To be a composer in nineteenth-century Italy was to be a composer of opera. Verdi's first, *Oberto*, was produced at the famous La Scala Opera House in Milan (Fig. 26-2) in 1839, and it achieved a modicum of success. But his *Nabucco* of 1842 was a popular triumph, receiving an unprecedented fifty-seven performances at La Scala in that year alone (Fig. 26-3). Through subsequent productions in other theaters, Verdi's reputation quickly spread throughout Italy, to the rest of Europe, and even to North and South America. His career had been launched.

The text, or libretto, of *Nabucco*, as well as most of Verdi's other operas of the 1840s, is covertly political. It concerns the suppression of a people (in this case, the Jews) by a cruel foreign power (the Babylonians). By analogy, Verdi thus called attention to the plight of the Italian people, who were then ruled in large measure by the Austrians. Verdi had become a spirited Italian patriot. Normally, we do not think of music as expressing political ideas, but because opera was an important part of Italian mass culture, it could suborn political revolution. Verdi's soloists and choruses (the voice of the people) sang such fiery words as "You may have the universe, so long as I keep Italy" and "Long live Italy! A sacred pact binds all her sons." Partly through such patriotic music and partly by accident, Verdi became a leader in the **Risorgimento,** the movement for a united Italy free of foreign domination. By handy coincidence, the letters of the composer's last name produced an acronym for **V**ittorio **E**manuele **R**e **d'I**talia (King Victor Emanuel being the people's choice for the throne of a united Kingdom of Italy). Thus, cries of "Viva, Verdi!" echoed throughout Italy in hopes of unification. (By coincidence Verdi means "green" in Italian; thus "Viva, Verdi" meant "Long live the Green [Nationalist] Party.") In 1861, after the goal of unification had been largely achieved, Verdi was elected to the country's first parliament, and later, in 1874, to its senate.

But the path to national unity was not an easy one for the Italians. During the 1850s, Verdi became disillusioned with politics and turned his attention from national aspirations to personal drama. In quick order, he composed a trio of works without which no opera house today could function: *Rigoletto* (1851), *La traviata* (1853), and *Il trovatore* (1853). For most of the early-to-mid-1850s, Verdi lived away from Milan, residing in Paris or traveling throughout Europe to oversee the production of his increasingly numerous works. He called these years of toil and intense productivity "my years as a galley slave."

On his return to his homeland in 1857, the pace of Verdi's opera production slackened. He composed only when the subject was of such interest or the money so great that he couldn't refuse. His opera *Aida*

(1871), commissioned to celebrate the opening of the Suez Canal, brought him the astonishing fee of 150,000 francs (about $700,000 in 2010). Verdi had become wealthy, and he retired to his estate in northern Italy to lead the life of a country squire—or so he thought.

But like a performer who feels he owes the audience more, or has something more to prove to himself, Verdi returned to the theater for two final encores: *Otello* (1887) and *Falstaff* (1893), both exceptionally well-crafted operas based on dramas of Shakespeare. The latter work was written when the composer was on the threshold of eighty, a feat without parallel in music history or the annals of the dramatic stage (Fig. 26-4). He died peacefully at his country home in 1901, a much-respected national institution.

Verdi's Dramaturgy and Musical Style

When the curtain goes up on a Verdi opera, the listener will find elements of dramaturgy—construction of the drama—and musical style that are unique to this composer. For Giuseppe Verdi, conflict was at the root of every emotion, and he expressed conflict, whether personal or national, by juxtaposing self-contained, clearly contrasting units of music. A rousing march, a patriotic chorus, a passionate recitative, and a lyrical aria follow in quick succession. The composer aims not at musical and dramatic subtlety but rather at banner headlines of emotion. The emotional states of the characters are so clearly depicted, sometimes exaggerated, that the drama comes perilously close to melodrama, with its excess of sentimentality and sensationalism. But it is never dull. There is action, passion, and intensity, all the things that give an opera mass appeal. In 1854, Verdi said, "There is one thing the public will not tolerate in the theater: boredom."

How does Verdi generate this feeling of intense passion and nonstop action? He does so by creating a new kind of recitative and a new style of aria. As before, recitative still narrates the action, and arias still express the characters' emotional states. But Verdi replaces simple recitative, accompanied only by *basso continuo* (see p. 105), with orchestrally accompanied **recitativo accompagnato.** This allows the action to flow smoothly from orchestrally accompanied aria to orchestrally accompanied recitative and back without a jarring change of texture. As for the aria, Verdi brings to it a new intensity. Yes, he is a composer squarely in the tradition of Italian *bel canto* opera. He focuses his attention on the solo voice and on a lyrical, beautiful vocal line. Indeed, no composer had a greater gift for writing simple, memorable melodies that the audience could whistle on the way out of the theater. Yet Verdi also adds intensity and passion to these arias by pushing the singers to the upper reaches of their range. The tenor is asked to sing up to the B above middle C, while the soprano must sing two octaves (or even higher!) above middle C. The thrilling moments in which the hero (the tenor) or the heroine (the soprano) go right to the top are literally the high points of any Verdi opera.

La traviata (1853)

We may measure the high intensity and passion in Verdi's operas by listening to a portion of his *La traviata* (1853). *La traviata* means literally "The Woman Gone Astray." It tells the story of the sickly Violetta Valery, a courtesan, or "kept

Download a Supplementary Listening Guide for Verdi, "La donna è mobile," from *Rigoletto*, at the text website.

FIGURE 26–4

A photograph of Giuseppe Verdi, taken about 1885, on an early published score of his opera *La traviata*.

© Mary Evans Picture Library/The Image Works

VERDI.
"LA TRAVIATA".

Lebrecht Music & Arts

FIGURE 26–5

Marie Duplessis, the Paris Hilton of the nineteenth century. The end of her brief, scandalous life is the subject of Giuseppe Verdi's opera *La traviata*. So notorious had she become by the time of her death at the age of twenty-three that Charles Dickens said, "You would have thought her passing was a question of the death of a hero or a Joan of Arc."

woman," who first resists and then succumbs to the love of a new suitor, the young Alfredo Germont. For a while, the couple retires from Paris to lead a quiet life in the country. But without explanation Violetta deserts Alfredo, in truth so that her scandalous reputation will not bring disgrace on his respectable family. The hot-tempered Alfredo now publicly insults Violetta, fights a duel with her new "protector," and is banished from France. When the nature of Violetta's sacrifice is revealed, Alfredo rushes back to Paris. But it is too late! She is dying of tuberculosis—her fate dictated by an operatic convention that requires the heroine to sing one last show-stopping aria and then expire.

Verdi based the libretto of *La traviata* on a play that he had seen in Paris in 1852 called *Camille*, by Alexandre Dumas the younger. (His father, Alexandre Dumas senior, wrote *The Count of Monte Cristo* and *The Three Musketeers*.) *Camille* tells the story of the real-life figure, Marie Duplessis (Fig. 26-5), the mistress of the playwright Dumas and, for a short time, of the composer-pianist Franz Liszt as well. Marie served as the model for Violetta in Dumas's play and, a year later, for the same character in Verdi's opera *La traviata*. Like many in this period, Marie died young of tuberculosis, at the age of twenty-three.

We join *La traviata* toward the end of the first act. A gala party is in progress in a fashionable Parisian salon, and here the dashing Alfredo has finally managed to cut Violetta away from the crowd to profess his love to her. He does so in the aria "Un dì felice" ("One Happy Day"), which is lovely, yet somber in tone. The seriousness of Alfredo's intent is underscored by the slow, square, even plodding accompaniment in the orchestra. When Violetta enters, she is supported by the same accompaniment, but the mood of the aria changes radically, becoming light and carefree. Witness Verdi's direct musical characterization at work: Alfredo's slow melody with a hint of minor is replaced by Violetta's flighty sound of high, rapidly moving notes. Eventually, the two join together: he below, somberly proclaiming the mysteries of love; she above, making light of them. What started as a solo aria has become a duet, the voices—and hands—of the principals now intertwined. Once again, music enhances drama by replicating in its own language the action on stage.

*L*istening GUIDE

Giuseppe Verdi
***La traviata* (1853)**
Act I, Scene 4

5

4/4

Characters: Alfredo, a young man of good standing; Violetta, a kept woman leading a wanton life in Paris

Situation: A party in a Parisian salon around 1850; Alfredo professes his love to Violetta, who at first rejects him.

ARIA

0:00 **4**

                Alfredo (tenor)

	Un dì felice, eterea,	One happy day,
	Mi balaneste innante,	you appeared to me.
	E da quel dì tremante	And from this day, trembling, I have
	Vissi d'ignoto amor.	lived in that unspoken love,
	Di quell'amor ch'è palpito	in that love which animates
	Dell'universo intero,	the world,
Shift to minor	Misterioso, altero,	mysterious, proud,
	Croce e delizia al cor.	pain and delight to the heart.

		Violetta (soprano)	
1:22	Violetta changes aria to lighter mood through faster tempo and shorter notes	Ah, se ciò è ver, fuggitemi. Solo amistade io v'offro; Amar non so, nè soffro Un cosi eroico amore. Io sono franca, ingenua; Altra cercar dovete; Non arduo troverete Dimenticarmi allor.	If that's true, leave me. Only friendship I offer you. I don't know how to love or suffer such a heroic love. I'm being honest and sincere. You must find another. It won't be difficult. Just leave me.
DUET		**Alfredo**	
1:48	Alfredo and Violetta together in rapturous duet	Oh amore! Misterioso, altero, Croce e delizia al cor.	Oh love! Mysterious, proud, pain and delight to the heart.
		Violetta	
		Non arduo troverete. Dimenticarmi allor.	It won't be difficult. Just leave me.
2:50	Exuberant vocal flourishes for both	"Ah"	"Ah"

Download an Active Listening Guide, available on the text website.

What started out as a simple dance song has evolved into an almost hysterically virtuosic aria, as Violetta realizes that she will not be able to escape Alfredo's love.

Alfredo kisses Violetta's hand and departs, leaving her alone on stage to ponder her future. She reveals, in a slow strophic aria, "Ah fors'è lui" ("Ah, perhaps he's the one"), that Alfredo may be the one true love she has long desired. But Violetta abruptly rejects the whole idea as impossible. Forget love, she says in an impassioned accompanied recitative: "Folly! Folly! What sort of crazy dream is this!" Recitative leads naturally to aria, and here follows "Sempre libera" ("Always free"), one of the great show arias for soprano voice. It allows Violetta to declare forcefully her resolve to remain free of love's entanglements. This aria, too, helps define through music the character of the heroine—the extraordinary, carefree flourishes on the word "pleasure," for example, reinforce her "live-for-the-moment" approach to life. Violetta's declaration of independence is momentarily broken by the distant voice of Alfredo, who again sings of the mysterious powers of love. This, too, Violetta brushes aside as she emphatically repeats her pledge always to be free.

Verdi has moved quickly from slow aria, to recitative, to fast-concluding aria. Such a three-movement unit is a dramatic convention of Italian opera called a **scena** (a scenic plan made up of diverse movements). So, too, the fast aria at the end of the scena has a name: "cabaletta." A **cabaletta** is a fast-concluding aria in which the increased speed of the music allows one or more soloists to race off stage at the end of a scene or act. Here Violetta, vowing to remain free, dashes off as the curtain falls to end Act I. But, of course, our heroine does not remain free—she falls fatally in love with Alfredo, as Acts II and III reveal. Listen now to the final scene of Act I of Verdi's *La traviata*.

FIGURE 26–6

The great Australian soprano Joan Sutherland singing the role of Violetta, and tenor Luciano Pavarotti as Alfredo, in Verdi's *La traviata*.

Listening GUIDE

Giuseppe Verdi
La traviata (1853)
Act I, Scene 6

5   **2**
4/5–9   2/4–6

Characters: Violetta and Alfredo (outside her window)

Situation: Violetta at first believes Alfredo to be the passionate love she has long sought, but then rejects this notion, vowing to remain free.

ARIA

First Strophe

0:00	**5**	Soprano sings first phrase	Ah, fors'è lui che l'anima Solinga ne' tumulti	Ah, perhaps he's the one whom my lonely heart
0:35		First phrase repeated	Godea sovente pingere De' suoi colori occulti.	delighted often to paint with vague, mysterious colors.
0:59		Voice rises up in melodic sequence	Lui, che modesto e vigile All'egre sogli ascese, E nuova febbre accese Destandomi all'amor!	He who, so modest and attentive during my illness, waited and with youthful fervor aroused me again to love!
1:27		Return of Alfredo's major-key refrain from previous aria	A quell'amor ch'è palpito Dell'universo intero, Misterioso, altero, Croce e delizia al cor.	To that love which animates the world, mysterious, proud, pain and delight to the heart.

Second strophe

2:23	**6** 0:00	Return of first phrase	A me, fanciulla, un candido E trepido desire,	To me, a girl, this was an innocent, anxious desire,
2:57	0:34	First phrase repeated	Quest'effgiò dolcissimo Signor dell'avvenire.	this sweet vision, lord of things to come.
3:21	0:58	Voice rises up in melodic sequence	Quando ne' cieli il raggio Di sua beltà vedea E tutta me pascea Di quel divino error.	When in the heavens I saw rays of his beauty I fed myself completely on that divine error.
3:46	1:23	Return of Alfredo's major-key refrain from previous aria	Sentia che amore è il palpito Dell'universo intero, Misterioso altero, Croce e delizia al cor.	I felt that love which animates the world, mysterious, proud, pain and delight to the heart.
4:44	2:21	Highly ornamental final cadence with lengthy trill		

Situation: But vehemently changing her mind, Violetta instead vows to reject love and always to remain free.

RECITATIVE   Violetta

0:00	**7** **4**	Accompanied by orchestra	Follie! Follie! Delirio vano è questo! Povera donna, sola, abbandonata, in questo popoloso deserto che appellano Parigi. Che spero or più? Che far degg'io?	Folly! Folly! What sort of crazy dream is this! Poor woman, alone, abandoned in this populated desert that they call Paris. What hope have I? What can I do?
0:55		Flights of vocal fancy as she thinks of pleasure	Gioir! Di voluttà ne' vortici perir! Gioir!	Pleasure! Perish in a whirl of indulgence! Pleasure!
1:06		Introduction to cabaletta		

CABALETTA

1:17	**8** 0:00 **5**		Sempre libera degg'io Folleggiare di gioia in gioia,	Always free I must remain to reel from pleasure to pleasure,

			Vo' che scorra il viver mio	running my life
			Pei sentieri del piacer.	along the paths of joy.
			Nasca il giorno, o il giorno muoia,	From dawn to dusk
			Sempre lieta ne' ritrovi,	I'm always happy finding
			A diletti sempre nuovi	new delights that make
			Dee volare il mio pensier.	my spirit soar.

Alfredo

1:58	0:41	Echoes of his previous aria	Amor è palpito	Love that animates
			Dell'universo intero,	the world,
			Misterioso, altero,	mysterious, proud,
			Croce e delizia al cor.	pain and delight to the heart.

Violetta

2:34	1:17	Extravagant flourishes	Follie! Follie!	Folly! Folly!
			Gioir! Gioir!	Pleasure! Pleasure!

CABALETTA RETURNS

3:03 **9** **6**	0:00	This time even more brilliant in its showy, superficial style	Sempre libera . . .	Always free . . .

Download an Active Listening Guide, available on the text website.

Listening EXERCISE 33

Verdi
LA TRAVIATA   **5**   **2**   @

4/7–9   2/4–6

To take this Listening Exercise online and receive feedback or email answers to your instructor, go to the text website.

By the nineteenth century, the castrato had almost entirely disappeared from the operatic stage, and the leading roles of hero and heroine were sung by male tenor and female soprano, respectively. The following questions illuminate the way in which Giuseppe Verdi, working within the tradition of Italian *bel canto* opera, makes the female voice the center of attention. While Verdi from time to time pauses to allow the heroine a luxuriant moment of vocal virtuosity, he nonetheless pushes the opera forward at a rapid pace. Beautiful melody and fast action were the keys to Verdi's success.

1. Which term would *not* have been applied to the singer during the nineteenth century?
   a. diva
   b. prima plata
   c. prima donna
   d. *bel canto* soprano

2. **7** **4** (0:00–0:18) This passage, in which Violetta expresses her fear of being a woman alone and abandoned in the "populated desert" of Paris, is a good example of what?
   a. simple recitative
   b. *secco* recitative
   c. *recitativo accompagnato* (accompanied recitative)

3. What string technique does the orchestra employ to tell us of Violetta's agitated mental state?
   a. tremolo
   b. vibrato
   c. pizzicato
   d. staccato

4. What is the meter of this recitative?
   a. duple (as is appropriate for a march)
   b. triple (as is appropriate for a waltz)
   c. no clear meter (as is typical of recitative)

5. On what word does Verdi engage in extravagant word painting (expressing the meaning of a word through music that sounds like the word)?
   a. Follie!   b. Parigi   c. Gioir!

6. Now Violetta launches into her brilliant cabaletta **8** **5** "Sempre libera." What characteristic identifies this as a cabaletta?
   a. It is a fast-concluding aria that Violetta will use to exit the stage.
   b. The soprano sings in a vocal range called the cabaletta.

(continued)

7. (2:50–3:02) Again Violetta vows to dedicate herself to a life of pleasure ("gioir"). What does the orchestra do during this vocal flourish?
   a. merely plays chordal homophony
   b. creates the "big guitar" effect
   c. nothing

8. Now Violetta repeats "Sempre libera," swearing again to remain free of the snares of love. Where does the vocal high point of "Sempre libera" occur—that is, where does the soprano go to the top of her range?
   a. at the end of the first occurrence of the cabaletta "Sempre libera"
   b. at the end of the reprise of the cabeletta "Sempre libera"

9. To which singing does the term *bel canto* better pertain?
   a. the recitative "Follie! Follie!"
   b. the cabaletta "Sempre libera"

10. Consider now all the portions of *La traviata* you have heard, beginning with the aria "Un dì felice" and ending with the cabaletta "Sempre libera." What can we conclude about this Italian *bel canto* opera?
    a. It is very much an "instrumentalist's" opera focusing on the orchestra.
    b. It is very much a "singer's" opera focusing on the soprano voice.
    c. It is very much a "singer's" opera focusing on the tenor voice.

Key WORDS

The materials on the text website will help you understand and pass tests on the content of this chapter. In addition, you may watch Craig Wright's own lecture at Open Yale Courses and complete this chapter's Listening Exercise interactively, as well as view Active Listening Guides and other materials that will help you succeed in this course.

bel canto (276)
prima donna (277)
diva (277)

Risorgimento (278)
recitativo accompagnato (279)

scena (281)
cabaletta (281)

ROMANTIC OPERA
GERMANY

27

When we go to the opera today, we usually see supertitles in English but hear singing in one of two languages: Italian or German. Before 1820, opera was mainly an Italian affair. It was first created in Italy around 1600 and then, over the next two hundred years, was exported to all parts of Europe. With the onset of the nineteenth century, however, other people, driven by an emerging sense of national pride, developed idiomatic opera in their native tongues. Although Italian opera remained the dominant style, it now had to share the stage, not only with traditional French opera but also with the newer forms of Russian, Czech, and especially German opera.

RICHARD WAGNER (1813–1883)

The composer who realized the dream of a distinct, national German operatic tradition was Richard Wagner (pronounced "REEK-hard VAHG-ner"), a titanic figure in Western cultural history (Fig. 27-1). Wagner was not merely a composer; he was also a philosopher, politician, propagandist, and ardent advocate for his own vision of dramatic music. Not only did he compose operas of monumental scope, he produced a large number of theoretical writings. So controversial are his theories and his art that Wagner has become for some an object of almost religious admiration, a cult figure; yet for others, particularly because of his anti-Semitic statements, he is the most detested composer in the history of Western music. For Wagner, opera was the perfect form of artistic expression, and the opera composer was something of a religious prophet who revealed to his "congregation" (his audience) the wonders of the musical world.

FIGURE 27–1
Richard Wagner in an 1871 photograph.

To be sure, Wagner's music is often inspiring. It contains moments of grandeur unmatched by any other composer. His influence on musical style in the late nineteenth century was enormous. Yet his reception by the musical public at large, then and now, has been divided. Some listeners are left cold, believing the music to be long-winded and the operatic plots devoid of realistic human drama. (Among them was Mark Twain, who quipped famously: "Wagner's music is not nearly as bad as it sounds!") Others (see Fig. 27-4) are immediately converted to adoring Wagnerites at the first sound of the heroic themes and powerful orchestral climaxes.

Who was this controversial artist who has stirred such mixed feelings within the musical public for more than a century? Richard Wagner was born in Leipzig, Germany. Although he studied with the music director of the Saint Thomas Church where Bach had worked (see Fig. 13-6), Wagner was largely self-taught in musical matters. After a succession of jobs as opera director in several small German towns, Wagner moved to Paris in 1839 in hopes of seeing his first opera produced there. But instead of meeting acclaim in Paris, as had Liszt and Chopin before him, Wagner was greeted with thundering indifference. No one could be persuaded to produce his work. Reduced to poverty, he spent a brief stint in debtor's prison.

When Wagner's big break came, it was not in Paris but back in his native Germany, in the city of Dresden. His opera *Rienzi* was given a hearing there in 1842, and Wagner was soon offered the post of director of the Dresden Opera. During the next six years, he created three additional German Romantic operas for the Dresden stage: *Der fliegende Holländer* (*The Flying Dutchman*, 1844), *Tannhäuser* (1845), and *Lohengrin* (1848). In the aftermath of the political revolution that swept much of Europe in 1848, Wagner was forced to flee Dresden, though in truth he took flight as much to avoid his creditors as to escape any repressive government.

Wagner found a safe haven in Switzerland, which was to be his home, on and off, for the next dozen years. Exiled now from the major opera houses in Germany, he began to imagine a complex of music dramas on a vast and unprecedented scale. What he ultimately created was *Der Ring des Nibelungen* (*The Ring of the Nibelung*), a set of four operas, now called the **Ring cycle,** intended to be performed during the course of four successive evenings. *Das Rheingold*, the first, lasts 2½ hours; *Die Walküre* and *Siegfried* each runs nearly 4½ hours; while the finale, *Götterdämmerung* (*Twilight of the Gods*), goes on for no less than 5½ hours. Wagner asked much of the human attention span (and bladder) when he composed this gargantuan epic.

Unlike the great majority of composers throughout music history, Wagner wrote not only the music but also the librettos for his operas. For his four-part *Ring* cycle, he fashioned a single continuous epic by drawing on tales from German mythology. The scene is set in the smoky mists of primeval time, in a land of gods, river nymphs, dwarfs, giants, dragons, and sword-wielding heroes. In many ways, Wagner's *Ring des Nibelungen* is similar to J. R. R. Tolkien's trilogy *The Lord of the Rings* (published in 1954 and 1955; film version, 2001, 2002, and 2003). Both are multipart sagas based on Nordic mythology, both are overrun with fantastic creatures (goblins, wizards, and dragons), and both revolve around a much-coveted ring, which seems to offer its possessor unparalleled power, but which also carries a dark, sinister curse.

But Wagner viewed his *Ring* cycle not as a timeless fairy tale but rather as a timely allegory exploring the themes of power, greed, honor, bravery, and race in nineteenth-century German society. At that time, bravery, power, and national identity were themes with special resonance in Germany, which was then in the process of becoming a unified nation. The German philosopher Friedrich Nietzsche (1844–1900), for a time a friend and confidant of Wagner, modeled his superhero, or superman (see also p. 10), on Wagner's heroic character Siegfried in the *Ring*. In the twentieth century, Adolf Hitler exploited Wagnerian symbolism to foster the notion of a superior German race, fortifying, for example, a Siegfried Line on the Western Front during World War II.

Not surprisingly, publishers and producers were at first reluctant to print or mount the operas of Wagner's *Ring*, given their massive scope and fantastic subject matter. They would, however, pay well for the rights to the composer's more traditional works. So, in the midst of his labors on the *Ring* cycle, the often penurious Wagner interrupted the project for a period of years to create *Tristan und Isolde* (1865) and *Die Meistersinger von Nürnberg* (*The Mastersingers of Nuremberg*, 1868). But these, too, were long and not easy to produce. The bulky scores piled up on his desk.

In 1864, Wagner was rescued from his plight by King Ludwig II of Bavaria, who paid off his debts, gave him an annual allowance, encouraged him to complete the *Ring* tetralogy, and helped him to build a special theater where his giant operas could be mounted according to the composer's own specifications (Fig. 27-2). This opera house, or Festival Theater as Wagner called it, was constructed at Bayreuth, a small town between Munich and Leipzig in southern Germany. The first **Bayreuth Festival** took place in August 1876 with three successive performances of the entire *Ring* cycle. Following Wagner's death in 1883, his remains were interred on the grounds of the Wagner villa in Bayreuth. Still controlled by the descendants of Wagner today, the Bayreuth Festival continues to stage the music dramas of Wagner—and only Wagner. Each summer thousands of opera lovers make the pilgrimage to this theatrical shrine to one of art's most determined, and ruthless, visionaries.

FIGURE 27-2
Bayreuth Festival Theater, an opera house built especially to produce the music dramas of Richard Wagner—and only Wagner.

Wagner's "Music Dramas"

With few exceptions, Wagner composed only operas, ignoring such concert hall genres as the symphony and concerto. But he wanted his opera to be radically different, so he gave it a different name: "music drama." A **music drama** for Wagner was a musical work for the stage in which all the arts—poetry, music, acting, mime, dance, and scenic design—function as a harmonious ensemble. Such an artistic union Wagner referred to as a ***Gesamtkunstwerk*** (total art work). Thus combined, the unified force of the arts would generate more realistic drama. No longer would the dramatic action grind to a halt in order to spotlight the vocal flourishes of a soloist, as often happened in Italian opera.

Indeed, Wagner's music drama differs from conventional Italian opera in several important ways. First, Wagner did away with the traditional "numbers" opera—a string of separate units such as aria, recitative, duet, and the like. Instead, he wrote a seamless flow of undifferentiated solo singing and declamation, what is called "endless melody." Second, he removed ensemble singing almost entirely; duets, trios, choruses, and full-cast finales became extremely rare. Finally, Wagner banished the tuneful aria to the wings. He avoids melodic repetition, symmetry, and regular cadences—all things that can make a tune "catchy"—in favor of long-flowing, nonrepetitive, not particularly song-like lines. As the tuneful aria decreases in importance, the role of the orchestra increases.

With Wagner, the orchestra is everything. It sounds forth the main musical themes, develops and exploits them, and thereby plays out the drama through pure instrumental music. On stage, the words and actions of the singers give the audience supplementary clues as to what the musical drama in the orchestra is all about. In the 1850s, Wagner drank deeply of the philosophy of Arthur Schopenhauer (1788–1860), who wrote that "music expresses the innermost basis of the world, the essence behind appearances." In music drama, what happens on the stage is the appearance; what happens in the orchestral pit below represents the deeper reality, the true drama.

As had Beethoven and Berlioz before him, Wagner continued to expand the size of the orchestra. The orchestra he requires for the *Ring* cycle is massive, especially with regard to the brasses: four trumpets, four trombones, eight horns (four of whom double on tuba), and a contrabass (very low) tuba. Perhaps most remarkable, the score calls for six harps!

A bigger orchestra demanded, in turn, more forceful singers. To be heard above an orchestra of nearly a hundred players, a large, specially trained voice was needed: the so-called Wagnerian tenor and Wagnerian soprano. The voice that typically dominates the operatic stage today—with its powerful sound and wide vibrato—first developed in Wagner's music dramas.

Tristan und Isolde (1865)

Wagner began to compose *Tristan und Isolde* during 1857 when living in Switzerland and supported in part by a wealthy patron, Otto Wesendonck. Although still married, the composer began an affair with Wesendonck's wife, Mathilde—so fully did Wagner the man live his life as Wagner the artist that it was impossible for him to create an opera dealing with passionate love without being passionately in love himself. By 1864, Wagner had made his way to Munich to prepare for the first production of the now finished *Tristan*. Having long since forgotten both Mathilde and his wife, he now fell in love with Cosima von Bülow (Fig. 27-3), the wife of the man scheduled to conduct *Tristan*. Cosima was the illegitimate daughter of Franz Liszt and Marie d'Agoult (see Figs. 25-3 and 25-4), and she and Wagner soon produced three illegitimate children of their own. The first of these, a daughter born on the first day of rehearsals for *Tristan*, was christened Isolde.

The story of *Tristan und Isolde* comes from the medieval legends of King Arthur's England. Briefly, it is the tale of the love between Isolde, an Irish princess, and Tristan, a knight in the service of King Mark of Cornwall (England). Their love, however, is both illicit and ill-fated. They have mistakenly drunk a magical love potion; Isolde forgets her lawful husband (King Mark) and Tristan forgets his royal duty. Despairing of any happy union with Isolde in this world, Tristan allows himself to be mortally wounded in combat and sails off to his native Brittany to die. Isolde pursues him but arrives just in time to have him expire in her arms. Knowing that their union will only be consummated through death, Isolde sings her **Liebestod** (*Love-Death*), an ecstatic vision of their love beyond the grave, and then she, too, expires next to her lover's body. This was the sort of all-consuming, sacrificial love so dear to the hearts of Romantic artists.

Wagner begins *Tristan*, not with a rousing, self-contained overture, but with a simple yet beautiful prelude that sets the general tone of the drama and leads directly to the raising of the curtain. The prelude opens with a plaintive call in the cellos, answered by one in the woodwinds. Each is not so much a lengthy theme as it is a short, pregnant motive. Wagner's disciples called each a **leitmotif** (signature-tune), a brief, distinctive unit of music designed to represent a character, object, or idea, which returns repeatedly in order to

© Mary Evans Picture Library/The Image Works

FIGURE 27-3

Cosima Wagner (daughter of Franz Liszt and Marie d'Agoult), Richard Wagner, and Liszt at Wagner's villa in Bayreuth in 1880. At the right is a young admirer of Wagner, Hans von Wolzogen, who first coined the term *leitmotif.*

@

Download Supplementary Listening Guides for Wagner, Prelude to *Tristan und Isolde*, as well as development of several leitmotifs at the end of Act I, Scene 5, at the text website.

show how the drama is unfolding. Wagner's leitmotifs are usually not sung by the singers but rather are played by the orchestra. In this way, an element of the subconscious can be introduced into the drama: the orchestra can give a sense of what a character is thinking even when he or she is singing about something else. By developing, extending, varying, contrasting, and resolving these representational leitmotifs, Wagner is able to play out the essence of the drama almost without recourse to his singers.

Leitmotifs in *Tristan* are associated mainly with feelings rather than concrete objects or persons. Typical are the leitmotifs representing "Longing," "Desire," and "Ecstasy."

© Craig Wright

FIGURE 27–4

Attending some well-known rock bands are fans who adoringly trek after their heroes; The Grateful Dead have their Deadheads, and Phish their Phish Followers, for example. So, too, lovers of Wagner follow the music of their god, making annual pilgrimages to sites—be it Seattle, New York, or Bayreuth—where a Wagner festival or a performance of the Ring cycle can be heard. Wagnerian groupies are known as Ringnuts, and it isn't difficult to spot them in a crowd. As one recently said in New York, "When the *Ring* takes place, the clan will gather."

EXAMPLE 27–1

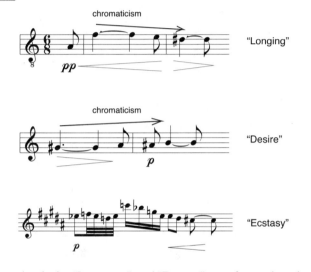

Notice how both the "Longing" and "Desire" motifs involve chromatic lines, the first descending, the second ascending (see arrows). This sort of linear chromatic motion made it easy for the composer to wind continually through many different keys, not stopping long enough to establish any one as a home base, or tonic. This type of intense chromatic harmony (discussed on p. 234) loosened the feeling of key and eventually led to the collapse of tonality as the main organizing force in Western music, as we shall see (pp. 333–334). Here Wagner uses twisting chromatic lines for a specific expressive purpose—to convey a sense of the extreme pain felt by the ill-fated lovers.

As you listen to the final scene of *Tristan*, you can feel Wagner trying to draw you into his all-enveloping world of love, longing, desire, and death. Here Isolde cradles the body of the dead Tristan and prepares to share his fate. As she sings her justly famous *Liebestod*, four leitmotifs sound forth, each heard previously in the opera. They frequently appear in melodic sequences, usually moving upward so as to convey a sense of continual longing and rising tension. Cadences are avoided, thereby increasing the endlessly restless mood. Dissonances are placed at points of climax to heighten the feeling of pain and anguish. At the end, the music reaches one last, glorious climax (**5**4/11 at 0:50 and **2**2/8 at 0:50), and thereafter all is consonance and reduced movement— Isolde has joined Tristan in the world beyond. First, listen to the *Liebestod*, concentrating on the leitmotifs as they are presented by the voice and, to a greater degree, the orchestra. Then listen once more, this time just drinking in, like a love potion, all of Wagner's divinely inspired sound. If there is such a thing as a transcendental experience in Romantic music, you will find it here.

@

Download a Supplementary Listening Guide for another moving farewell—Wotan's farewell to his daughter Brünnhilde, from Wagner's *Die Walküre*—at the text website.

LEITMOTIFS IN *STAR WARS*

The technique of the leitmotif, as developed by Richard Wagner, has been borrowed by many composers of Hollywood film music. To name just one: John Williams, the creator of the music for George Lucas's *Star Wars* series. When Williams wrote the music for *Star Wars, The Empire Strikes Back,* and *The Return of the Jedi,* he composed for each main character (and theme or force) a particular musical motive. Below are two of Williams's leitmotifs, the first signifying the hero Luke Skywalker, and the second (merely an insistent rhythm) the evil Darth Vader.

Like Wagner, Williams sets these leading motives in the orchestra, and thereby tells the audience what the character is thinking or what the future may hold. When young Luke is confined to his uncle's farm, for example,

we learn that greater things await him: the orchestra plays the heroic "Force" leitmotif in the background. In fact, *Star Wars* has more than just leitmotifs in common with Wagner's music dramas. Both Wagner and Lucas started with a core of three dramas and added a fourth as a preface or "prequel" (*Das Rheingold* was prefixed to the *Ring,* and *The Phantom Menace* to *Star Wars*). Lucas, of course, has added three further episodes to his saga, bringing his total to seven, but the leitmotifs remain the same. Both Wagner's cycle and Lucas's saga play out a series of epic battles between larger-than-life heroes and villains, mythical forces for good and evil, warring throughout cosmic time.

Luke's Theme

Darth Vader's Theme

Listening GUIDE

Richard Wagner
Liebestod, **from** *Tristan und Isolde* (1865)

5   2
4/10–11   2/7–8

Characters: The lovers Tristan and Isolde

Situation: Tristan's castle in Brittany; Isolde cradles Tristan in her arms as she prepares to join him in death.

0:00 **10** **7**	Isolde, gazing at Tristan, slowly sings "Love-Death" leitmotif, which is then taken up by orchestra		

Mild und leise wie er lächelt,	Oh how tenderly and gently he smiles
Wie das Auge hold er öffnet—	As he opens his eyes—
Seht ihr, Freunde? Seht ihr's nicht?	Do you see, Friends, don't you see it?
Immer lichter wie er leuchtet,	Ever brighter, how he shines,
Stern-umstrahlet hoch sich hebt?	Glowing in starlight raised on high?

1:10	Orchestra continues with "Love-Death" motif as singer goes her own way	Seht ihr's nicht? Wie das Herz ihm mutig schwillt, Voll und hehr im Busen ihm quillt?

Do you not see it?
How his heart proudly swells,
Full and brave beating in his breast?

1:45	"Ecstasy" leitmotif sounds repeatedly, not in voice, but in high woodwinds and then violins		

	Wie den Lippen, wonnig mild	How from his lips, blissfully tender,
	Süsser Atem sanft entweht—	Sweet breath gently flutters—
	Freunde! Seht!	Do you not see, Friends?
	Fühlt und seht ihr's nicht?	Don't you feel and see it?

2:25   Reappearance of ascending, chromatic "Desire" motif from Prelude

2:35	"Love-Death" motif returns in voice and orchestra, followed by "Ecstasy" motif and then "Desire" motif in voice	Höre ich nur diese Weise Die so wundervoll und leise, Wonne klagend, alles sagend, Mild versöhnend aus ihm tönend, In mich dringet, auf sich schwinget, Hold erhallend um mich klinget?	Do I alone hear this melody Which, so wonderfully and gently, Moaning bliss, expressing all, Gently forgiving, sounding from within Pierces me, soars upwards, Blessedly echoing all around me?

3:43   "Transcendent Bliss" leitmotif appears in violins

	Heller schallend, mich umwallend,	Resounding clearly all around me,
	Sind es Wellen sanfter Lüfte?	Are they waves of gentle air?

3:58 ▮11▮ 0:00 ▮8▮	Tension increases as "Desire" motif rises by chromatic steps in orchestra	Sind es Wolken wonniger Düfte Wie sie schwellen, mich umrauschen, Soll ich atmen, soll ich lauschen? Soll ich schlürfen, untertauchen? Süss in Düften mich verhauchen? In dem wogenden Schwall, in dem tönenden Schall.	Are they clouds of delightful fragrance? As they swell and envelop me, Should I breathe, should I listen? Should I sip them, plunge beneath them? Breathe my last in such sweet fragrance? In the growing swell, the surging sound.
4:48 0:50	Glorious climax with "Transcendent Bliss" motif shining forth in orchestra	In des Welt-Atems wehendem All— Ertrinken, versinken— Unbewusst— Höchste Lust!	In the vastness of the world's spirit To drown, sink down— Unconscious— Supreme bliss!

Orchestra then fades away into silence as curtain descends.

Listen to streaming music in an Active Listening Guide, available on the text website.

Listening EXERCISE 34

Wagner   **5**   **2**   @
LIEBESTOD FROM *TRISTAN UND ISOLDE*   4/10–11   2/7–8   To take this Listening Exercise online and receive feedback or email answers to your instructor, go to the text website.

Isolde's *Liebestod*, which brings *Tristan und Isolde* to a glorious conclusion, is written for soprano voice—indeed, for a dramatic Wagnerian soprano. But even this powerful voice cannot always be clearly heard above Wagner's large, surging orchestra. Imagine a Verdi opera in which the hero or heroine could not be heard! (The recording that follows is a "studio recording," and the soprano voice has been "foregrounded" by the recording engineer to make it more

(continued)

audible.) As some of the following questions suggest, there are several ways in which the German music dramas of Wagner differ from the Italian operas of Verdi.

1. Does the orchestra establish a clear "um-pah" (duple-meter) or "um-pah-pah" (triple-meter) accompaniment in the *Liebestod*?
    10
    7
    a. yes   b.   no

2. When the soprano sings the "Ecstasy" leitmotif (2:58–3:20), she does so to rather square poetry—lines of 4 + 4 syllables with internal rhyme. (Try saying the German to yourself.)

    Wonne klagend,   Moaning bliss,
        alles sagend,   expressing all,
    Mild versöhnend   Gently forgiving,
        aus ihm tönend   sounding from within

    What is the course of the soprano line during this couplet?
    a. It rises.   b. It rises in a melodic sequence.
    c. It falls.   d. It falls in a melodic sequence.

3. Immediately afterwards (3:21–3:39), the music rises toward a climax to reflect the sentiment of the next couplet:

    In mich dringet,   Pierces me,
        auf sich schwinget,   soars upwards,
    Hold erhallend um   Blessedly echoing
        mich klinget?   all around me?

    How is this rising tension brought about in the music?
    a. Tremolos are played by the strings.
    b. There is a gradual crescendo.
    c. The voice rises up chromatically.
    d. All of the above.

4. (0:00–0:40) Wagner now builds to a final climax with the "Desire" leitmotif churning in the orchestra.
    11
    8

    Here the composer employs what tried-and-true method to conjure up a feeling of increasing tension?
    a. He has the powerful orchestra proceed in ever-rising melodic sequence.
    b. He has the powerful orchestra proceed in ever-falling melodic sequence.

5. (1:15–1:51) The great climax has been reached. How does Wagner now musically depict the final words of Isolde "to drown, to sink down, unconscious—supreme bliss"?
    a. The vocal line continually falls.
    b. The vocal line soars up, then falls.
    c. The vocal line falls, then soars up and holds a note.

6. Which leitmotif is heard softly in the oboes (at 2:12) immediately before the final chord?
    a. "Ecstasy"
    b. "Transcendent Bliss"
    c. "Desire"

7. (1:51–end) In this passage, Wagner brings us to the end of the opera. The nature of the music changes to suggest a feeling of winding down. Which one of the following does *not* occur?
    a. The tempo of the music appears to get slower.
    b. The "Transcendent Bliss" leitmotif no longer rises upward.
    c. The orchestra drives toward its own *fortissimo* climax.
    d. The dynamic level gradually changes from loud to soft.

8. Who has the "last word"—that is, who is heard at the very end of the *Liebestod*?
    a. the orchestra   b. the voice

9. Which musical force could be omitted without serious loss to the overall effect of the piece?
    a. the orchestra   b. the voice

10. Which of the following is true about the *Liebestod*?
    a. Wagner places tremendous demands on the singer, in part because the voice has no pauses of more than three seconds until she ceases singing.
    b. Although Wagner places tremendous demands on the singer, requiring mostly *fortissimo* singing, he nonetheless builds in several "breaks" (rests) of about ten seconds duration along the way.

@

The materials on the text website will help you understand and pass tests on the content of this chapter. In addition, you may complete this chapter's Listening Exercise interactively, as well as view Active Listening Guides and other materials that will help you succeed in this course.

Key WORDS

Ring cycle (286)
Bayreuth Festival (287)

music drama (287)
Gesamtkunstwerk (287)

Liebestod (288)
leitmotif (288)

NINETEENTH-CENTURY REALISTIC OPERA

28

Romantic opera, both Italian and German, typically concludes with the lovers eternally united, if not in this world, then in the one beyond. Moreover, the stage is populated by larger-than-life characters or by the well-to-do, people of leisure untroubled by mundane concerns or financial worries. During the second half of the nineteenth century, however, a contrasting type of opera developed in Europe, one more in tune with the social truths of the day. It is called **realistic opera,** because the subject matter treats issues of everyday life in a realistic way. Poverty, physical abuse, industrial exploitation, and crime—afflictions of the lower classes in particular—are presented on stage for all to see. In realistic opera, rarely is there a happy ending.

Realistic opera reflected the social, scientific, and artistic developments of the nineteenth century, which saw the worst effects of the Industrial Revolution, including oppressive factory conditions resulting in widespread social disintegration. The nineteenth century also witnessed the emergence of the theory of evolution, first popularized in Charles Darwin's *On the Origin of Species* (1859), which posits a "dog-eat-dog" world in which only the fittest survive. Painters such as J.-F. Millet (1814–1875) and the young Vincent van Gogh (1853–1890) captured on canvas the life of the downtrodden (Fig. 28-1), as did writers Charles Dickens (1812–1870) and Emile Zola (1840–1902) in their realistic novels. The aim of these artists was to transform the mundane and the

FIGURE 28–1

Vincent van Gogh, *The Potato Eaters* (1885). During his youth, van Gogh chose to live and work in the coal-mining region of eastern Belgium. This grim painting records his impressions of life within a mining family and the evening meal of potatoes and tea.

commonplace into art, to find the poetic and heroic in even the most ordinary aspects of human experience.

Similarly reflecting the credo that art must imitate life, the plots of realistic operas embrace the gritty side of this world. In Bizet's *Carmen* (1875), the heroine is a knife-wielding gypsy girl who works in a cigarette factory; in Leoncavallo's *Pagliacci* (1892), a jealous clown stabs his wife to death; and in Puccini's *Tosca* (1892), an abused singer murders the chief of police. If traditional Romantic opera is usually sentimental and idealistic, nineteenth-century realistic opera is sensational and usually pessimistic.

GEORGES BIZET'S CARMEN (1875)

The first important realistic opera is *Carmen* (1875) by Georges Bizet (pronounced "bee-SAY"). Bizet (1838–1875), who spent his short life entirely in Paris, was primarily an opera composer, and *Carmen* is his masterpiece. Set in nineteenth-century Spain, *Carmen* centers on a sensual young gypsy woman known only as Carmen (Fig. 28-2). This sexually assertive, willful woman holds the populace in her sway. By means of her alluring dance and song, she seduces a naïve army corporal, Don José. Falling hopelessly in love, Don José deserts his military post, "marries" Carmen, and takes up with her gypsy bandit friends. But Carmen, who refuses to belong to any man, soon abandons Don José to give herself to the handsome bullfighter Escamillo. Having lost all for nothing, the humiliated Don José stabs Carmen to death in a bloody ending.

This violent conclusion highlights the stark realism of *Carmen*. The heroine is a woman of easy virtue available to every man, albeit on her own terms. She lives for the moment, surrounded by social outcasts (gypsies), prostitutes, and bandits. All this was shocking stuff for the refined Parisian audiences of Bizet's day. During the first rehearsals in 1875, the women of the chorus threatened to strike because they were asked to smoke and fight on stage. Critics called the libretto "obscene." Bizet's producers asked him to tone down the more lurid aspects of the drama (especially the bloody ending)—to make it more acceptable as family entertainment—but he refused.

Carmen is full of alluring melodies including the well-known Toreador Song and the even more beloved Habanera. In fashioning these tunes, Bizet borrowed phrases from several Spanish popular songs, folk songs, and **flamenco** melodies (songs of southern Spain infused with gypsy elements). The Habanera, which introduces the character Carmen, makes use of a then-popular Spanish song.

Literally, **habanera** means "the thing from Havana." Musically, it is a type of dance-song that developed in Spanish-controlled Cuba during the early nineteenth century. African and Latin influences on its musical style can perhaps be seen in the descending chromatic scale, and certainly in the static harmony (the downbeat of every measure is a D in the bass), as well as in the insistent, repetitive rhythm ($\frac{2}{4}$ ♩ ♪ ♫ | ♩ ♪ ♫). The infectious rhythm of the habanera gives it its irresistible quality—we all want to get up and join the dance. But the habanera is a sensual dance, like its descendant the tango, and this sensual quality contributes greatly to Carmen's seductive aura.

The structure of Bizet's Habanera is straightforward. At first, Carmen sings a descending chromatic line of four 4-bar phrases ("Love is like an elusive bird"). By their nature, highly chromatic melodies often seem to have no tonal center. This one, too, is musically noncommittal and slippery, just as Carmen herself is both ambiguous and evasive. The chorus immediately repeats the chromatic melody, but now Carmen voluptuously glides above it,

FIGURE 28–2

Soprano Leontyne Price, who is heard on our recording of the Habanera from Bizet's *Carmen*, has often sung the title role.

© Bettmann/CORBIS

CARMEN FROM FLOP TO HIP HOP

At its premiere in Paris on March 3, 1875, *Carmen* was a flop—the realistic subject matter was thought too degrading. Despondent over this poor reception, composer Georges Bizet suffered a fatal heart attack exactly ninety days later.

As the nineteenth century progressed and theatrical subjects became increasingly realistic, however, the appeal of *Carmen* grew. Now arguably the world's most popular opera, *Carmen* has been recorded many times and has been transformed into nearly twenty films, including an early silent one of 1915 and an Academy Award–winning production of 1984. In addition, the most popular melodies of *Carmen* serve as background music in countless TV commercials and cartoons, and are sometimes the object of parody (witness the Muppets' hilarious spoof of the Habanera). In an early episode of *The Simpsons*, the family goes

Beyoncé poses with the red dress that she wore in Carmen: A Hip Hopera.

© Frank Micelotta/Getty Images

to the opera where it hears—what else?—*Carmen*, and Bart and Homer sing along. *Carmen* has also been refashioned into an African opera set in Senegal (*Karmen Geï*, 2001), an African-American Broadway musical (*Carmen Jones*, 1954), and an MTV special (*Carmen: A Hip Hopera*, starring Beyoncé Knowles, 2001). Not surprisingly for a realistic opera, *Carmen* is a work that transcends race and class, and that quality accounts in part for its lasting popularity.

@

See a video of the Muppets' Habanera performance, in the YouTube playlist on the text website.

singing the single word *"L'amour"* ("Love"). As her voice soars, like the elusive bird of love, the tonality shifts from minor to major. To this is then added a refrain ("Love is like a gypsy child") in which the melody alternates between a major triad and a minor one. Against this refrain, the chorus shouts, "Watch out!" warning of Carmen's destructive qualities. This same structure—a chromatically descending melody, followed by a triadic refrain with choral shouts—then repeats. Bizet wanted his Habanera to establish the character of Carmen as a sensual enchantress. In every way, the music *is* Carmen. And like Carmen, once this seductive melody has us in its spell, it will never let go.

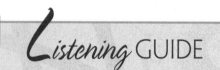

Listening GUIDE   **Georges Bizet**
Habanera from the opera *Carmen* (1875)   ⑤ ②
4/12 · 2/9

Situation: The scantily clad gypsy woman Carmen, exuding an almost primeval sexuality, dances before Don José, soldiers, and other gypsies.

(continued)

peut ap - pri - voi - ser,   Et c'est bien en   vain qu'onl'ap - pel-le,   S'il lui con - vient de   re - fu - ser.

0:00	**12** **9**	Bass ostinato with habanera rhythm; minor mode
0:06		Carmen enters with enticing descending melody

L'amour est un oiseau rebelle	Love is like an elusive bird,
Que nul ne peut apprivoiser;	That cannot be tamed;
Et c'est bien en vain qu'on l'appelle,	You call it in vain
S'il lui convient de refuser.	If it decides to refuse.
Rien n'y fait, menace ou prière,	Neither threat nor prayer will prevail;
L'un parle bien, l'autre se tait;	One man talks a lot, the other is silent;
Et c'est l'autre que je préfère	And it's the latter I prefer,
Il n'a rien dit; mais il me plaît.	He hasn't said a word, but he pleases me.

0:41	Change to major mode; chorus repeats melody; Carmen soars above on "L'amour"
0:57	Carmen sings refrain

L'amour est enfant de Bohème,	Love is like a gypsy child,
Il n'a jamais connu de loi,	Who has never known constraint,
Si tu ne m'aimes pas, je t'aime;	If I love you, and you don't love me,
Si je t'aime, prends garde à toi!	Watch out!

1:14	Chorus shouts, "Prends garde à toi!"
1:37	Chorus sings refrain with Carmen
2:16	Bass ostinato with habanera rhythm
2:21	Carmen enters with enticing chromatic melody

L'oiseau que tu croyais surprendre	The bird you thought you'd surprised
Battit de l'aile et s'envola;	Beat its wings and flew away;
L'amour est loin, tu peux l'attendre;	Love is far away, but expect it;
Tu ne l'attends plus, il est là!	You don't expect it, but there it is!
Tout autour de toi, vite,	All around you, quick!
Il vient, s'en va, puis il revient;	It comes, it goes, and then it returns;
Tu crois le tenir, il t'évite,	You think you've trapped it, it escapes;
Tu crois l'éviter, il te tient!	You think you've escaped it, it traps you!

2:55	Change to major mode; chorus repeats melody; Carmen soars above on "L'amour"
3:11	Carmen, chorus (3:51), and then Carmen (4:09) again sing refrain

Listen to streaming music in an Active Listening Guide, available on the text website.

Listening EXERCISE 35

Bizet
HABANERA FROM *CARMEN*

5 **2**
4/12   2/9

To take this Listening Exercise online and receive feedback or email answers to your instructor, go to the text website.

The enduring popularity of Bizet's *Carmen* can be explained in part by its sensational plot, socially diverse characters, captivating melodies, and rousing choruses, as the following questions suggest.

1. (0:00–0:05) Which older sensual dance has the same **12** **9** rhythmic pattern as the habanera?
    a. the flamenco
    b. the tango
    c. the fandango

2. (0:00–0:39) The sultry mood of the beginning is created in part by the presence of which mode?
    a. major   b. minor

3. (0:06–0:13) What type of scale does the elusive Carmen execute when she first begins to sing?
    a. major   b. minor   c. chromatic

4. (0:22–0:33) How do we sense that Carmen is a sensual creature?
   a. The singer shakes an exotic percussion instrument called the castanet.
   b. The singer recalls her earlier days as a cigar maker in Havana.
   c. The singer does not move from one exact pitch to the next, but slides upward between pitches.

5. (0:41–0:55) When the chorus enters, it sings what?
   a. a flamenco tune
   b. a gypsy melody
   c. the melody just sung by Carmen

6. (0:457–1:37) Carmen now sings the refrain. What is the mode of the refrain?
   a. major   b. minor

7. (2:16–end) Consider the second stanza of the Habanera. Which is true?
   a. It is essentially the same in content and length as the first stanza.
   b. It offers an elaborate variation of the first stanza.

8. Accordingly, what is the form of this habanera?
   a. strophic
   b. theme and variations
   c. through-composed

9. What likely makes Bizet's Habanera such a successful number?
   a. It possesses not one, but two seductive melodies, one major, the other minor.
   b. It combines the beauty of an aria with the power of a chorus.
   c. Despite the sometimes soaring vocal lines, it is firmly grounded on an ostinato bass.
   d. All of the above.

10. Which of the following musicals is *not* a Broadway counterpart of realistic opera?
    a. *Rent*
    b. *West Side Story*
    c. *The Lion King*

GIACOMO PUCCINI'S *LA BOHÈME* (1896)

Italian realistic opera of the late nineteenth century goes by its own special name, **verismo opera** (*verismo* is Italian for "realism"). Yet while it enjoys a separate name, *verismo* opera in Italy was little different than realistic opera elsewhere. Although many Italian composers wrote *verismo* operas, by far the best known today is Giacomo Puccini.

Giacomo Puccini (1858–1924) was the scion of four generations of musicians from the northern Italian town of Lucca (Fig. 28-3). His father and his grandfather had both written operas, and his forebears before them had composed religious music for the local cathedral. But Puccini was no child prodigy. For a decade following his graduation from the Milan Conservatory, he lived in poverty as he struggled to develop a distinctive operatic style. Not until the age of thirty-five did he score his first triumph, the *verismo* opera *Manon Lescaut* (1893). Thereafter, successes came in quick order: *La bohème* (1896), *Tosca* (1900), and *Madama Butterfly* (1904). Growing famous, wealthy, and a bit complacent, Puccini worked less and less frequently. His last, and many believe his best, opera, *Turandot*, was left unfinished at the time of his death from throat cancer in 1924.

Puccini's best-known opera—indeed the most famous of all *verismo* operas—is *La bohème* (*Bohemian Life*, 1896). The realism of *La bohème* rests in the setting and characters: the principals are bohemians—unconventional artists living in abject poverty. The hero, Rodolfo (a poet), and his pals Schaunard (a musician), Colline (a philosopher), and Marcello (a painter), inhabit an unheated attic on the Left Bank of Paris. The heroine, Mimi, their neighbor, is a poor, tubercular seamstress. Rodolfo and Mimi meet and fall in love. He grows obsessively jealous while she becomes progressively ill. They separate for a time, only to return to each other's arms immediately before Mimi's death. If this sounds familiar, there may be a reason: the Pulitzer Prize–winning

FIGURE 28-3
Giacomo Puccini.

musical *Rent* (1996, produced as a motion picture in 2005) is a modern adaptation of this bohemian tale, but here the protagonist dies of AIDS in Greenwich Village, rather than of tuberculosis in Paris.

In truth, there is not much of a plot to *La bohème*, nor is there much character development. Instead, the glorious sound of the human voice (*bel canto* singing) carries the day. Puccini continues the nineteenth-century tendency to lessen the distinction between recitative and aria. His solos typically start syllabically (no more than one note per syllable), as if the character is beginning a conversation. Gradually, the voice grows in intensity and becomes more expansive, with the strings doubling the melody to add warmth and expression. When Rodolfo, for example, sings of Mimi's frozen little hand in the aria "Che gelida manina," ("Ah, What a Frozen Little Hand"), we move imperceptibly from recitative to aria, gradually transcending the squalor of the Left Bank garret and soaring to a better world far beyond. The contrast between the dreary stage setting and the transcendental beauty of the music is the great paradox of realistic opera.

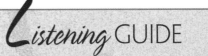

Listening GUIDE

Giacomo Puccini
La bohème (1896)
Aria, "Che gelida manina"

5

4/13

Characters: The poor poet Rodolfo and the equally impoverished seamstress Mimi

Situation: Mimi has knocked on Rodolfo's door to ask for a light for her candle. Charmed by the lovely stranger, he naturally obliges. The wind again blows out Mimi's candle, and amidst the confusion, she drops her key. As the two search for it in the darkness, Rodolfo by chance touches her hand and, then holding it, seizes the moment to tell her about himself and his hopes.

Performer: The tenor here is the famous Placido Domingo, whom you may wish to contrast with the up-and-coming tenor Roberto Alagna heard on **5** 4/4.

0:00	**13**	Rodolfo begins conversationally, much as in recitative	Che gelida manina se la lasci riscaldar. Cercar che giova? Al buio non si trova. Ma per fortuna è una notte di luna, e qui la luna l'abbiamo vicina.	Ah, what a frozen little hand, let me warm it up. What's the good of searching? We won't find it in the dark. But by good luck there is moonlight tonight, and here we have the moon nearby.

(Mimi tries to withdraw her hand)

			Aspetti, signorina, le dirò con due parole	Wait, young lady, I will tell you in two words
1:08		Voice increases in range, volume, and intensity, as Rodolfo explains who he is and what he does	chi son, e che faccio, come vivo. Vuole? Chi son? Sono un poeta. Che cosa faccio? Scrivo. E come vivo? Vivo!	who I am and what I do, how I live. Would you like this? Who am I? I'm a poet. What do I do? I write. How do I live? I live!
1:58		Return to conversational style	In povertà mia lieta scialo da gran signore rime et inni d'amore. Per sogni et per chimere e per castelli in aria, l'anima ho milionaria.	In my delightful poverty I grandiosely scatter rhymes and songs of love. Through dreams and reveries and through castles in the air, I have the soul of a millionaire.
2:32		Voice grows more expansive with longer notes and higher range; orchestra doubles voice in unison	Talor dal mio forziere ruban tutti i gioelli due ladri: gli occhi belli.	Sometimes from the strongbox two thieves steal all the jewels: two pretty eyes.

		V'entrar con voi pur ora,	They came in with you just now
		ed i miei sogni usati	and my usual dreams,
		e i bei sogni miei	my lovely dreams
		tosto si dileguar!	vanish at once!
		Ma il furto non m'accora,	But the theft doesn't bother me,
3:29	Orchestra sounds melody alone; then is joined by voice for climactic high note on "speranza!"	poichè v'ha preso stanza la speranza!	Because their place has been taken by hope!
3:51	As music diminishes, Rodolfo asks for response from Mimi	Or che mi conoscete, parlate voi, deh! parlate. Chi siete? Vi piaccia dir!	Now that you know who I am, Tell me about yourself, speak! Who are you? Please speak!

⌇⌇⌇ Listen to streaming music in an Active Listening Guide, available on the text website.

Key WORDS

realistic opera (293)   habanera (294)   *verismo* opera (297)
flamenco (294)

@

The materials on the text website will help you understand and pass tests on the content of this chapter. In addition, you may complete this chapter's Listening Exercise interactively, as well as view Active Listening Guides and other materials that will help you succeed in this course.

MUSIC AND NATIONALISM

Music does not exist in isolation. As we have seen with realistic opera (Chapter 28), it is often influenced by contemporary social, scientific, and artistic developments. So, too, music can be affected by politics. The nineteenth century was a period in which various European ethnic groups sought to free themselves from foreign domination. During the 1820s and 1830s, the Greeks fought to throw off the rule of the Ottoman Turks, the Poles strove (unsuccessfully) to end control by the Russians, and the Belgians broke free from the Dutch. Simultaneously, lands previously divided into small states became unified nations. In 1861, Italy, once a patchwork of city-states controlled by Austria and Spain, achieved full independence and unification, with Rome as its capital. Ten years later, a German nation, under the political leadership of Chancellor Otto von Bismarck (1815–1898), was formally recognized. Smaller groups, such as the Czechs, Hungarians, Poles, and Finns, sought to break free from more powerful nations, such as Germany, Austria, and Russia. These groups likewise exhibited pride in their national traditions, each highlighting its cultural individuality through artistic expression.

Owing to its emotive power, music naturally gave voice to ethnic and linguistic distinction, a process called **musical nationalism.** A flood of national anthems, native dances, protest songs, and victory symphonies gave musical expression to the rising tide of nationalism. *The Star Spangled Banner,* the *Marseillaise* (French national anthem), and *Italian Brothers, Italy Has Arisen* (Italian national anthem) were all products of revolution and patriotic zeal. National color in music was communicated by means of indigenous folk elements—folk songs, native scales, dance rhythms, and local instrumental sounds. It could also be conveyed by the use of national subjects—the life of a national hero, for example—as the program for a symphonic poem or the libretto for an opera. Among musical compositions with overtly nationalistic titles are *Hungarian Rhapsodies* (Liszt), *Russian Easter Overture* (Nikolai Rimsky-Korsakov), *Slavonic Dances* (Antonin Dvořák), *Má vlast* (*My Fatherland,* Bedřich Smetana), and *Finlandia* (Jean Sibelius). The desire to embrace nationalist musical elements would continue into the twentieth century in the works of such prominent composers as the Russian Stravinsky, the Hungarian Bartók, and the American Ives. For all these composers, a musical signifier (a folk song, for example) served as a badge of both personal identity and national pride.

RUSSIAN NATIONALISM: MODEST MUSORGSKY (1839–1881)

Russia was one of the first countries to develop its own national style of art music, one distinct and separate from the traditions of German orchestral music and Italian and German opera. An early use of Russian subject matter

Download a Supplementary Listening Guide for Smetana's *The Moldau,* from *Má vlast,* at the text website.

can be found in Mikhail Glinka's opera *A Life for the Tsar* (1836). Glinka's nationalist spirit was passed to a group of young composers whom contemporaries dubbed "The Mighty Handful" or, less grandiosely, the **Russian Five:** Alexander Borodin (1833–1887), César Cui (1835–1918), Mily Balakirev (1837–1910), Nikolai Rimsky-Korsakov (1844–1908), and Modest Musorgsky (1839–1881). They dedicated themselves to writing Russian music, free of Western influence, for the Russian people. Of these, the most original and least Western in musical style was Musorgsky (Fig. 29-1).

As with most members of the "Russian Five," Musorgsky (pronounced "moo-SORG-ski") did not at first seem destined for a career in music. He was trained to be a military officer and for a period of four years was commissioned in the Russian army. He resigned his appointment in 1858 in favor of a minor post as a civil servant and more free time to indulge his avocation, musical composition. The next year he said, "I have been a cosmopolitan, but now there's been some sort of regeneration. Everything Russian is becoming dear to me." Unfortunately, his brief, chaotic life was marked by increasing poverty, depression, and alcoholism. During his few periods of creative productivity, Musorgsky managed to compile a small *oeuvre*, which includes a boldly inventive symphonic poem, *Night on Bald Mountain* (1867); an imaginative set of miniatures for piano, *Pictures at an Exhibition* (1874); and an operatic masterpiece, *Boris Godunov* (1874), based on the life of a popular sixteenth-century Russian tsar. Many of Musorgsky's works were left unfinished at the time of his death in 1881.

FIGURE 29–1
Modest Musorgsky.

Pictures at an Exhibition *(1874)*

The genesis of *Pictures at an Exhibition* can be traced to the death of Musorgsky's close friend, the Russian painter and architect Victor Hartmann, who had died suddenly of a heart attack in 1873. As a memorial to Hartmann, an exhibition of his paintings and drawings was mounted in Moscow the next year. Musorgsky was inspired to capture the spirit of Hartmann's works in a series of ten short pieces for piano. To provide unity within the sequence of musical pictures, the composer hit on the idea of incorporating a recurring interlude, which he called *Promenade*. This gave listeners the impression of enjoying a leisurely stroll through a gallery, moving from one of Hartmann's paintings to the next each time the *Promenade* music was heard. Though originally composed as a work for piano, the imaginative sounds of the ten musical pictures begged for orchestration, a task that several composers later undertook. *Pictures at an Exhibition* is best known today in the brilliantly orchestrated version by Maurice Ravel, completed in 1922.

PROMENADE

Here the composer projects himself, and by extension the listener, as wandering through an exposition of Hartmann paintings. Immediately, we are transported musically into a world of purely Russian art. The tempo is marked "Fast but resolute, in the Russian manner"; the meter is irregular, as in a folk dance, with alternating five- and six-beat measures; and the melody is built on a **pentatonic scale,** which uses only five notes instead of the usual Western scale of seven—here B♭, C, D, F, and G. Throughout the world, indigenous folk cultures use the pentatonic (five-note) scale.

To appreciate the power of the pentatonic scale around the globe, watch "World Science Fair 2009: Bobby McFerrin Demonstrates" in the YouTube playlist on the text website.

EXAMPLE 29–1

Allegro giusto, nel modo russico
trumpet solo　　　　　　　　　　　　　　brasses

FIGURES 29–2 AND 29–3

(top) Victor Hartmann, pencil drawing, *A Rich Jew*. The subject wears a comfortable fur skull cap, the symbol of his religion. (bottom) Victor Hartmann, pencil and watercolor, *A Poor Jew*. The subject sits downcast, a sack containing his worldly possessions placed nearby. Musorgsky created appropriately downcast music to characterize this figure.

© RIA Novosti/The Bridgeman Art Library

© RIA Novosti/The Bridgeman Art Library

Now begins a musical depiction of ten paintings. We focus our gaze on numbers 4, 6, and 10.

PICTURE 4: *POLISH OX-CART*

Hartmann's scene is a view of a rickety ox-cart lumbering down a dirt road. The rocking of the cart is suggested by a two-note ostinato. Notice in this brief composition how music can project a sense of time and movement in a way that a painting cannot. In Musorgsky's setting, the viewer remains stationary as the cart appears in the distance (*pp*), moves closer and closer by means of a crescendo (reaching *fff*), and slowly disappears as the orchestra is gradually reduced to playing *ppp*. In addition, Musorgsky was aware of an important acoustical phenomenon: larger sound waves (and hence lower pitches) travel farther than shorter waves (higher pitches). (This is why we hear the bass drum and tubas of an approaching marching band long before we hear the higher trumpets and clarinets; this is also why musicians write fewer pitches for the basses than violins, for example—it takes longer for bass sounds to "clear.") Thus, in *Polish Ox-Cart*, Musorgsky begins and ends with the very lowest sounds (orchestrated with tuba and double basses), to give the impression that the sound comes from a distance and then disappears again into the distance.

PICTURE 6: *SAMUEL GOLDENBERG AND SCHMUYLE: TWO JEWS, RICH AND POOR*

As the title suggests, we are looking here at a pair of Hartmann's drawings, both of which are reproduced (Figs. 29-2 and 29-3). One Jew (Goldenberg) gazes forward confidently; the other (Schmuyle) displays an attitude of despair. They might just as well be two Christians or two Muslims—what counts here is social status, not religion. The oriental quality of Musorgsky's musical setting, however, makes clear that the two hail from Eastern Europe. In particular, the augmented second (here D♭-E), which Musorgsky associates with Goldenberg, recalls the Eastern European folk genre of Jewish klezmer music.

PICTURE 10: *THE GREAT GATE OF KIEV*

The stimulus for the majestic conclusion to *Pictures at an Exhibition* was Hartmann's design for a new and grandiose gate to the ancient city of Kiev, then part of Russia. Musorgsky arranges his thematic material to give the impression of a parade passing beneath the giant gate, in what is tantamount to rondo form (here **ABABCA**). The majestic vision of the gate (**A**) alternates with religious music for a procession of Russian pilgrims (**B**), and even the composer-viewer walks beneath the gate as the *Promenade* theme (**C**) appears, before a final return to a panoramic view of the gate (**A**), now with Hartmann's bells ringing triumphantly.

In this climactic final tableau, Ravel's setting for full orchestra is able to give more powerful expression to all of the local color and grandeur inherent in Musorgsky's original music for piano, just as Musorgsky's musical creation is a more powerful artistic statement than was Hartmann's original design (Fig. 29-4).

FIGURE 29–4

Victor Hartmann's vision *The Great Gate of Kiev*, which inspired the last of the musical paintings in Musorgsky's *Pictures at an Exhibition*. Note the bells in the tower, a motif that is featured prominently at the very end of Musorgsky's musical evocation of this design.

© RIA Novosti/The Bridgeman Art Library

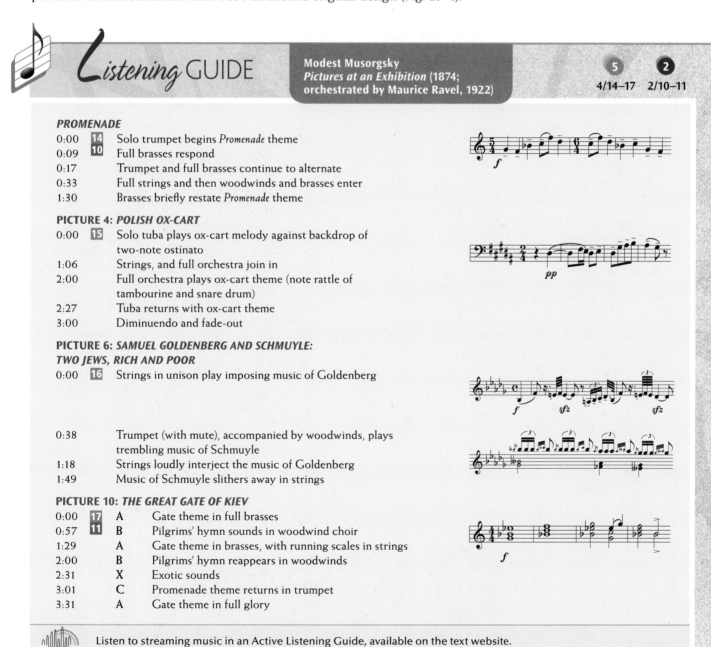

*L*istening GUIDE

Modest Musorgsky
Pictures at an Exhibition (1874; orchestrated by Maurice Ravel, 1922)

5 **2**
4/14–17 2/10–11

PROMENADE

0:00	**14** **10**	Solo trumpet begins *Promenade* theme
0:09		Full brasses respond
0:17		Trumpet and full brasses continue to alternate
0:33		Full strings and then woodwinds and brasses enter
1:30		Brasses briefly restate *Promenade* theme

PICTURE 4: *POLISH OX-CART*

0:00	**15**	Solo tuba plays ox-cart melody against backdrop of two-note ostinato
1:06		Strings, and full orchestra join in
2:00		Full orchestra plays ox-cart theme (note rattle of tambourine and snare drum)
2:27		Tuba returns with ox-cart theme
3:00		Diminuendo and fade-out

PICTURE 6: *SAMUEL GOLDENBERG AND SCHMUYLE:*
TWO JEWS, RICH AND POOR

0:00	**16**	Strings in unison play imposing music of Goldenberg
0:38		Trumpet (with mute), accompanied by woodwinds, plays trembling music of Schmuyle
1:18		Strings loudly interject the music of Goldenberg
1:49		Music of Schmuyle slithers away in strings

PICTURE 10: *THE GREAT GATE OF KIEV*

0:00	**17** **11**	A	Gate theme in full brasses
0:57		B	Pilgrims' hymn sounds in woodwind choir
1:29		A	Gate theme in brasses, with running scales in strings
2:00		B	Pilgrims' hymn reappears in woodwinds
2:31		X	Exotic sounds
3:01		C	Promenade theme returns in trumpet
3:31		A	Gate theme in full glory

Listen to streaming music in an Active Listening Guide, available on the text website.

 **EXERCISE 36**

Musorgsky
PICTURES AT AN EXHIBITION

5 **2** **@**
4/14, 17   2/10–11

To take this Listening Exercise online and receive feedback or email answers to your instructor, go to the text website.

For *Pictures at an Exhibition*, this exercise is limited to *Promenade* and *The Great Gate of Kiev*, both of which are available on the **2-CD** set and the **5-CD** set. Both tableaux have elements of the "exotic Russian East": *Promenade* not only makes use of the pentatonic scale but also has irregular meters typical of Eastern European folk dances, while *The Great Gate of Kiev* has a distinctive section (**C**) that suggests non-Western ways of organizing musical sound.

Promenade

1. (0:00–0:16) Throughout *Promenade*, the meter is **[14] [10]** irregular, which is typical of Eastern European folk music. What is correct regarding the beginning?
   a. The trumpet plays for eleven beats, and the full brasses respond for twenty-two beats.
   b. The trumpet plays for twenty-two beats, and the full brasses for twenty-two beats.
   c. The trumpet plays for eleven beats, and the full brasses for eleven beats.

2. (0:17–0:32) There are two complementary musical phrases. Which is true of each?
   a. The trumpet plays the first eleven beats, and the brasses the next eleven.
   b. The trumpet plays the first seven beats, and the brasses join for the next four.

3. (0:00–0:32) How would you describe the musical texture here?
   a. A monophonic trumpet is followed by polyphonic brass choir.
   b. A monophonic trumpet is followed by a homophonic brass choir.

4. (0:55–1:11) Try to tap your foot and conduct first a duple and then a triple pattern. What do you conclude?
   a. The meter is irregular, shifting back and forth from duple to triple.
   b. The meter is in a consistent duple pattern.
   c. The meter is in a consistent triple pattern.

5. (1:30–end) Which is true about the ending of *Promenade*?
   a. A phrase of eleven beats is followed by a phrase of nine.
   b. A phrase of nine beats is followed by a phrase of eleven.

The Great Gate of Kiev

6. (0:00–0:55) How would you describe the mode and **[17] [11]** texture at the beginning?
   a. major and homophonic
   b. major and polyphonic
   c. minor and homophonic
   d. minor and polyphonic

7. (0:00–0:55) Tap your foot to the music and try conducting, first with a duple-meter pattern and then with a triple-meter one. Which of the following is true?
   a. The music has a regular duple meter.
   b. The music has a regular triple meter.
   c. The music continues the irregular meter of *Promenade*.

8. (2:31–2:53) Exotic sounds, similar to those of Eastern music, are suggested in this passage. Which is *not* one of them?
   a. the sound of a gong and cymbal
   b. Chinese erhu playing the melody
   c. a shimmering tremolo in the strings
   d. a static harmony that repeats in four-beat cycles

9. (4:37–end) To give the conclusion a feeling of majesty, what happens?
   a. The full orchestra plays and the tempo slows.
   b. The full orchestra drives quickly and triumphantly to the end.

10. (4:37–end) Notice the many percussion instruments sounding here at the end: bass and snare drums, cymbal, and (faintly heard) bells. Besides sharpening the rhythmic profile of the music, percussion instruments, as exemplified here, do what?
    a. add clarity and lightness to the music
    b. add intricate melodic counterpoint to the texture
    c. add weight and sonic body to the texture

CZECH AND AMERICAN NATIONALISM: ANTONÍN DVOŘÁK (1841–1904)

In the nineteenth century, the Russians, with their huge army, were capable of dominating their neighbors. The Czechs, on the other hand, were a much smaller ethnic group surrounded, and often controlled, by foreigners. The country we today call the Czech Republic, comprising the provinces of Bohemia and Moravia, historically was dominated by German-speaking countries: Germany to the west and north, and Austria to the south. These larger German nations tended to lure away the best Czech minds: Gustav Mahler and Sigmund Freud were two citizens of Moravia who were drawn to big-city Vienna, for example. But some musicians—namely, Bedřich Smetana (1824–1884), Leoš Janáček (1854–1928), and Antonín Dvořák (1841–1904)—remained at home and succeeded in cultivating a distinctly Czech musical style.

Of these three Czech nationalists, Antonín Dvořák (pronounced "dah-VOR-shock") is today by far the best known (Fig. 29-5). Ironically, at first he was not known at all. Dvořák is a classic case of a "late bloomer"; or, perhaps more accurately, his talent was late to be recognized, owing to the comparative obscurity of the minority culture to which he belonged. The son of a butcher, Dvořák spent the first twenty years of his adult life as a freelance musician in Prague, where he cobbled together a living as a violist and organist, playing in dance bands and opera orchestras and in church. Yet all the while he composed tirelessly—operas, symphonies, and string quartets, almost all of which went unheard.

When recognition came, it did so not through these complex high-art forms, but rather in simpler music that could be played on the piano at home. In 1878, Dvořák published *Slavonic Dances*, a set of eight pieces for piano duet that incorporate the spirit of the folk music of the Czechs (a subgroup of the Slavs). These caught on like wildfire, and Dvořák was soon known throughout Europe. Now even his more ambitious "high art" works were given performances in London, Berlin, Vienna, Moscow, Budapest, and even in the United States, in Cincinnati—which then included a large German and Czech contingent among its population.

In the spring of 1892, Dvořák received an offer he couldn't refuse. He was promised the astonishing sum of $15,000 per year (the equivalent of about $600,000 today) to become director of the newly founded National Conservatory of Music in New York City. And so on September 17, 1892, Dvořák set sail for America and ultimately took up residence at 327 East 17th Street. It was here that he began work on his "American" Quartet and his Symphony No. 9, "From the New World." Instead of returning to Prague that summer, Dvořák and his family traveled by train and carriage to Spillville, Iowa, spending three months among the mainly Czech-speaking people of this rural farming community.

During his three years in America (1892–1894), Dvořák befriended Harry T. Burleigh (1866–1949), a black singer and composer. He also took on a black composition student, Maurice Arnold (1865–1937). From both men, Dvořák came to know the music of African-American spirituals and to believe that the path toward a truly national American music lay in what Dvořák called "Negro melodies." Two such tunes that he directly or indirectly borrowed were the melody of his famous *Humoresque* and that of the slow movement of his Symphony No. 9, "From the New World."

FIGURE 29–5
Antonín Dvořák conducting.

Prove to yourself that you know the tune for Dvořák's *Humoresque* by watching a video of it, in the YouTube playlist on the text website.

Largo *from Symphony No. 9, "From the New World"* (1893)

While an energetic and tuneful first movement and a powerful finale frame the symphony "From the New World," the slow second movement is the emotional soul of the work. A mood of calm strength envelops the opening, a memorable moment for players of brass instruments and listeners alike. Once this solidly serene atmosphere is established, a haunting melody emerges

FIGURE 29-6

An autograph sketch of the famous English horn theme from the second movement of Dvořák's symphony "From the New World." The tempo was later changed from *andante* to *largo* and some of the notes altered to emphasize the pentatonic scale, a traditional signifier of "the folk." For example, compare the sketch to the final version in the Listening Guide below, and notice that the G♭s have been removed.

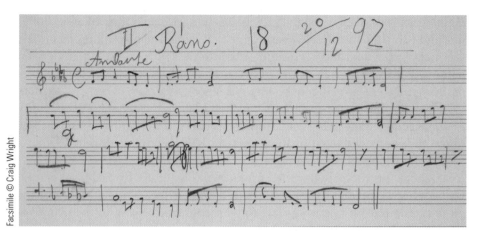

Facsimile © Craig Wright

Download a Supplementary Listening Guide for the first movement of Dvořák's symphony "From the New World," at the text website.

from the English horn (Fig 29-6). Throughout the Romantic period, the English horn was used to suggest a feeling of distance and nostalgia—looking back on a time, place, and people (friends, relatives, countrymen) that are now no more. Sometimes the nostalgia was for an imaginary world that existed only in the mind of the creator. But certainly in the psyche of turn-of-the-century Americans, Dvořák's melody represented "home," because a publisher extracted the tune from the symphony and printed it as a song with words under the title "Goin' Home."

But to *whose* home? Is this a melody composed from scratch by Dvořák in the style of a folk song, or is it one taken from an African-American colleague? Is it distinctly American or Czech? In truth, the melody (see Listening Guide) is built around a pentatonic scale (here D♭, E♭, F, A♭, B♭), which, as we have seen (p. 301), is characteristic of folk music around the world. But this is the power of music: each listener can hear this movement as an avatar of the memories and emotions of a distant home and homeland, no matter where.

Listening GUIDE

Antonín Dvořák
Symphony No. 9, "From the New World"
(1893)
Second movement, *Largo* (Very slow and broad)

⑤

4/18–20

Form: **ABCA**

A Section

| 0:00 | 18 | Solemn introductory chords in low brass choir, then timpani |
| 0:40 | | English horn solo, the "Goin' Home" melody |

1:06	Clarinet joins English horn, then strings join as well
2:20	Introductory chords now played by high woodwinds and French horn, concluded by brasses and timpani
2:48	Strings repeat and extend "Goin' Home" melody
3:44	Melody returns to English horn and is completed by woodwinds and strings
4:25	French horn echoes the melody

B Section

4:48 19 0:00 Faster tempo and new theme (**B1**) in flute and oboe

5:20   0:32 Second new theme (**B2**) in clarinets above bass pizzicato

6:10   1:22 Melody **B1** played more insistently by violins
7:25   2:37 Melody **B2** played more intensely by violins

C Section

8:28   3:40 Oboe introduces chirping of flute and clarinet
8:54   4:06 Brasses play *fortissimo* recall of first theme of first movement
9:10   4:22 Diminuendo and lovely transition back to **A**

A Section

9:23   20   0:00 English horn brings back "Goin' Home" melody
9:47   0:25 Pairs of violins and violas play melody but break off, as if choked by emotion
10:18   0:55 Solo cello and solo violin play melody, then full strings join
10:54   1:31 Quiet soliloquy by violins
11:22   1:59 Final return and extension of opening chords

Listen to streaming music in an Active Listening Guide, available on the text website.

Key WORDS

musical nationalism (300)   Russian Five (301)   pentatonic scale (301)

@

The materials on the text website will help you understand and pass tests on the content of this chapter. In addition, you may complete this chapter's Listening Exercise interactively, as well as view Active Listening Guides and other materials that will help you succeed in this course.

30

LATE ROMANTIC ORCHESTRAL MUSIC

The late nineteenth century was the heyday of the symphony orchestra. Think about how sound was made in those days—there were no iPods or computers, and no amplified surround sound—indeed, no electronically amplified sound at all. To hear an overwhelming sound that would "blow them away," listeners had to attend a concert of a large symphony orchestra. In fact, discounting the noise of a steam engine or a cannon, the highest decibel level (measure of volume) created by humans at this time was that of the symphony orchestra. Ironically, the recent revolution in disseminating sound electronically has been accompanied by a decline in the quality of sound that we hear. Listening to Beethoven or Wagner delivered via compressed MP3 files on speakers or headphones attached to a computer or iPod gives only a vague approximation of the nineteenth-century original. To hear the real thing, we must go to a large concert hall preserving the nineteenth-century architecture.

The period 1870–1910 was a golden age for the construction of large concert halls, not only in Europe but also in the United States. Auditoriums built during this period, such as the Musikverein in Vienna (1870), Carnegie Hall in New York (1893), Symphony Hall in Boston (1900), and Woolsey Hall in New Haven (1901), remain the finest ever built, especially with regard to their excellent acoustics. Thus the recently constructed Schermerhorn Symphony Center in Nashville (2006; see Fig. 1-4) was modeled on those in Vienna and Boston. All of these were built to be large concert halls, seating 2,000–2,700 listeners and accommodating many performers on stage.

The late-nineteenth-century orchestra was large and loud. During the century, more and more instruments were added from top to bottom (see pp. 236–238). The brass section grew especially large (Wagner, for example, sometimes called for eight tubas!), and to balance these additions, more and more string players were needed. The symphonic works of Johannes Brahms (1833–1897), Anton Bruckner (1824–1896), Gustav Mahler (1860–1911), and Richard Strauss (1864–1949) typically required an orchestra (then still all male) that approached a hundred players. The continued growth in the number and variety of instruments made listening to a live symphony orchestra the most powerful aesthetic experience that a citizen of the late nineteenth century could enjoy.

As the symphony orchestra grew in size, the genres of music it performed became more numerous. New kinds of program music had arisen during the Romantic era, including the concert overture, the tone poem, and the program symphony (see pp. 253–254). But the mainstay of the orchestra remained the four-movement symphony and the three-movement concerto, neither with programmatic intent.

THE LATE ROMANTIC SYMPHONY AND CONCERTO

The four-movement symphony originated during the Classical period (1750–1820), principally in the orchestral works of Haydn and Mozart, and remained a favorite with audiences throughout the nineteenth century, except in Italy (obsessed as it was with opera). Symphonic composers in the Romantic period generally continued to follow the four-movement format inherited from their Classical forebears—(1) fast, (2) slow, (3) minuet or scherzo, (4) fast. Yet throughout the nineteenth century, the movements got progressively longer. Perhaps as a consequence, composers wrote fewer symphonies. Schumann and Brahms composed only four; Mendelssohn, five; Tchaikovsky, six; and Dvořák, Bruckner, and Mahler, nine each. No one approached the 40-odd symphonies of Mozart, to say nothing of the 104 of Haydn.

Similarly for the concerto, with expanded length came a reduction in number. A Classical concerto may last twenty minutes, a Romantic one forty; Mozart gave us twenty-three piano concertos, but Beethoven only five. Beethoven, Mendelssohn, Brahms, and Tchaikovsky penned just a single violin concerto, yet each is a substantial showpiece for the soloist. Despite its growing length, the Romantic concerto retained the three-movement plan established during the Classical period—fast, slow, fast.

For a Romantic composer contemplating the creation of a symphony or concerto, no figure loomed larger than Beethoven. Wagner asked why anyone after Beethoven bothered to write symphonies at all, given the dramatic impact of Beethoven's Third, Fifth, and Ninth. Wagner himself wrote only one, and Verdi none. Some composers, notably Berlioz and Liszt, turned to a completely different sort of symphony, the program symphony (see p. 253), in which an external scenario determined the nature and order of the musical events. It was not until the late Romantic period, nearly fifty years after the death of Beethoven, that someone emerged to claim the title of successor to Beethoven the symphonist. That figure was Johannes Brahms.

Johannes Brahms (1833–1897)

Brahms was born in the north German port city of Hamburg in 1833 (Fig. 30-1). He was given the Latin name Johannes to distinguish him from his father Johann, a street musician and beer-hall fiddler. Although Johannes's formal education never went beyond primary school, his father saw to it that he received the best training on the piano and in music theory, with the works of Bach and Beethoven given pride of place. While he studied these masters by day, by night Brahms earned money playing out-of-tune pianos in "stimulation bars" on the Hamburg waterfront. (During 1960–1962, The Beatles went to Hamburg to play in the descendants of these strip joints.) To get his hands on better instruments, Brahms sometimes practiced in the showrooms of local piano stores.

Brahms first caught the public's attention in 1853, when Robert Schumann published a highly laudatory article proclaiming him to be a musical messiah, the heir apparent to Haydn, Mozart, and Beethoven. Brahms, in turn, embraced Robert and his wife, Clara (see Fig. 23-4), as his musical mentors. After Robert was confined to a mental institution, Brahms became Clara's confidant, and his respect and affection for her ripened into love, despite the fact that she was fourteen years his senior. Whether owing to his unconsummated love for Clara or for other reasons, Brahms remained a bachelor all his life.

FIGURE 30–1

Johannes Brahms in his early thirties. Said an observer of the time, "The broad chest, the Herculean shoulders, the powerful head, which he threw back energetically when playing—all betrayed an artistic personality replete with the spirit of true genius."

Disappointed first in love and then in his attempt to gain a conducting position in his native Hamburg, Brahms moved to Vienna in 1862. He supported his modest lifestyle—very "un-Wagnerian," he called it—by performing and conducting. His fame as a composer increased dramatically in 1868 with performances of his *German Requiem*, which was soon sold to amateur choruses around the world. In this same year, he composed what is today perhaps his best-known piece, the simple, yet beautiful art song known among English speakers as "Brahms's Lullaby" (see p. 60 and intro/22). Honorary degrees from Cambridge University (1876) and Breslau University (1879) attested to his growing stature. After Wagner's death in 1883, Brahms was generally considered the greatest living German composer. His own death, from liver cancer, came in the spring of 1897. He was buried in the central cemetery of Vienna, thirty feet from the graves of Beethoven and Schubert.

Vienna was (and remains) a very musical but conservative city, fiercely protective of its rich cultural heritage. That Brahms should choose it as his place of residence is not surprising—Vienna had been the home of Haydn, Mozart, Beethoven, and Schubert, and the conservative Brahms found inspiration in the music of these past masters (Fig. 30-2). Again and again, he returned to traditional genres, such as the symphony, concerto, quartet, and sonata, and to conventional forms, such as sonata–allegro and theme and variations. Most telling, Brahms composed no program music. Instead, he chose to write **absolute music,** chamber sonatas, symphonies, and concertos without narrative or "storytelling" intent. The music of Brahms unfolds as patterns of pure, abstract sound within the tight confines of traditional forms. Although Brahms could write lovely Romantic melodies, he was at heart a contrapuntalist, a "developer" in the tradition of Bach and Beethoven. Indeed, he was to be dubbed the last of the famous "three B's": Bach, Beethoven, and Brahms.

Violin Concerto in D major (1878)

In 1870, Brahms wrote, "I shall never compose a symphony! You have no idea how the likes of us feel when we hear the tramp of a giant like him behind us."

FIGURE 30-2

Brahms's composing room in Vienna. On the wall, looking down on the piano, is a bust of Beethoven. The spirit of Beethoven loomed large over the entire nineteenth century (see also the painting on the cover) and over Brahms in particular.

"That giant," of course, was Beethoven, and Brahms, like other nineteenth-century composers, was terrified by the prospect of competing with his revered predecessor. But Brahms did go on to write a symphony—indeed, four of them, first performed, in turn, in 1876, 1877, 1883, and 1885. In the midst of this symphonic activity, Brahms also wrote his only violin concerto, which rivals the earlier violin concerto of Beethoven.

How do you write a concerto for an instrument that you can't play? How do you know how to make the instrument sound good and what to avoid? Brahms, by training a pianist and not a violinist, did as composers before and after him: he turned to a virtuoso on the instrument—in this case, his friend Joseph Joachim (1831–1907). When the concerto was premiered in 1878, Joachim played the solo part while Brahms conducted the orchestra. One technical "trick" that Joachim surely insisted Brahms employ is the art of playing **double stops.** Usually, we think of the violin as a monophonic instrument, capable of executing only one line of music. But a good violinist can hold (stop) two and sometimes more strings simultaneously and sweep across them with the bow. This imparts a richer, more brilliant sound to the soloist's part. Example 30-1 shows how Brahms incorporates double stops into the melody of the last movement of his concerto.

@

Download Supplementary Listening Guides for movements from Brahms's Symphonies No. 1, 3, and 4, at the text website.

EXAMPLE 30–1

When he arrived at the finale of his Violin Concerto, Brahms the conservative turned to a form traditionally used in the last movement of a concerto: the rondo. Recall that a rondo centers on a single theme that serves as a musical refrain (see p. 183). Here the refrain has the flavor of a gypsy tune, like the Hungarian dances Brahms often heard in Viennese cafés as he sipped beer and chatted with friends. What marks this refrain is its lively rhythm: (). Above this foot-tapping motive, the violin sometimes soars with difficult passage work (scales, arpeggios, and double stops). The makers of the Academy Award–winning film *There Will Be Blood* (2007) chose this movement by Brahms to serve as the background music—whether to represent the tug of war (concerto) between the greedy oil man and the landowners or simply to have an exciting background score is not clear.

*L*istening GUIDE

**Johannes Brahms
Violin Concerto in D major (1878)
Third movement,** *Allegro giocoso, ma non tropo vivace* **(fast and playful, but not too lively)**

⑤   ❷
4/21–23   2/12–14

Genre: Concerto

Form: Rondo

0:00 **21** **12**   A   Refrain played by violin and then by orchestra

(continued)

| 0:50 | | | Transition: racing scales in violin |
| 1:10 | | B | New theme moves up, and then down, a major scale |

| 1:54 | **22** **13** | 0:00 | A | Violin returns with refrain; orchestra repeats it |
| 2:30 | | 0:36 | C | Violin plays more lyrical theme built on arpeggio |

3:28		1:34	B	Rising scale in violin, answered by falling scale in orchestra
4:15		2:19		Elaboration of rhythm of refrain
4:33	**23**	0:00	A	Orchestra plays refrain *fortissimo*
4:59	**14**	0:25		Violin plays very brief cadenza, then rhythm of refrain developed
6:03		1:29		Another brief cadenza
6:17		1:43	Coda	Rhythm of refrain becomes march-like

Listen to streaming music in an Active Listening Guide, available on the text website.

Listening EXERCISE 37

Brahms

VIOLIN CONCERTO IN D MAJOR

5 **2**   **@**
4/21–23 2/12–14

To take this Listening Exercise online and receive feedback or email answers to your instructor, go to the text website.

We derive our term *concerto* from the Italian word *concertare*. A concerto involves a concerted effort, as well as a spirited competition, between a soloist and an orchestra. There is tension between the two forces, though in theory the orchestra is to provide support for the technical display of the soloist. So great were the technical demands placed on the soloist in Brahms's Violin Concerto that one musician of the day complained that the composer had written a concerto, not "for" the violin, but "against" it. To which another virtuoso replied, "Brahms's concerto is not against the violin, but for violin against orchestra—and the violin wins." After listening to this movement, give your own opinion as to who wins.

At the beginning, the refrain is heard three times. In questions 1–3, indicate which is true.

1. (0:00–0:09) First iteration of the refrain _____
   21 **12**
   a. The orchestra has the refrain, and the violin is silent.
   b. The violin has the refrain, and the orchestra accompanies.

2. (0:10–0:18) Second iteration of the refrain _____
   a. The orchestra has the refrain, and the violin is silent.
   b. The violin has the refrain, and the orchestra accompanies.

3. (0:33–0:43) Third iteration of the refrain _____
   a. The orchestra has the refrain, and the violin is silent.
   b. The violin has the refrain, and the orchestra accompanies.

4. (1:01–1:08) At the end of the transition, what is the relationship between the forces?
   a. The orchestra has the melody, and the violin plays counterpoint.
   b. The violin plays runs against pizzicato accompaniment in the orchestra.

5. (1:10–1:15) Now a new theme enters—specifically, a rising scale. Which is true?
   a. There is a true dialogue here: the violin goes up with the theme, and the orchestra comes down with it.
   b. Only the orchestra has the theme, going both up and down with it.

6. (0:18–0:35) Again, there is another transition to a
   22 **13**   new theme. Which is true?

a. The orchestra has the melody, and the violin plays counterpoint.
b. The violin plays difficult arpeggios to a background accompaniment of simple chords in the orchestra.

7. (0:00–0:15) The refrain returns. Which is true?
    23
    14
    a. The orchestra has the melody, and the solo violin is silent.
    b. The solo violin plays the melody in double stops.

8. (0:25–1:00) Now an unusual moment occurs.
    a. The orchestra plays alone, and the violin gradually sneaks back in.
    b. The violin plays entirely by itself, and the orchestra gradually sneaks back in.

9. (1:43–1:49) Following the violin cadenza, the refrain is transformed into a march-like melody. Which of the following is true?
    a. It is played by the orchestra as a single line.
    b. It is played by the orchestra in double stops.
    c. It is played by the solo violin as a single line.
    d. It is played by the solo violin as double stops.

10. Finally, what, in your opinion, is the outcome of this musical context?
    a. Orchestra is dominant.
    b. Violin is dominant.
    c. It's a tie.

Gustav Mahler (1860–1911)

The history of nineteenth-century music can be seen as a development of radically different kinds of music: small-scale private music for the home (mostly piano music and art songs) and large-scale public music for the opera house and concert hall. So great was the attraction of the large symphony orchestra, however, that a domestic genre, namely the art song, gradually found its way to the concert hall, thereby producing a hybrid genre: the orchestral song. An **orchestral song** (or **orchestral *Lied***) is an art song in which the full orchestra replaces the piano as the medium of accompaniment. Because a large orchestra can supply more color and add a greater number of contrapuntal lines, the orchestral song grew to be longer, denser, and more complex than the piano-accompanied art song. In a way, the orchestral song provided the best of both worlds: an intimate poem full of Romantic sentiment along with a colorful, powerful medium with which to express it. Berlioz, Brahms, and Wagner all experimented with the orchestral *Lied* in various ways. Its greatest exponent, however, was Gustav Mahler, who not only wrote orchestral songs but also brought the orchestral song into the symphony.

Gustav Mahler (Fig. 30-3) was born in 1860 into a middle-class Jewish family living in Moravia, now encompassed by the Czech Republic. But as did many other gifted Czechs at that time, Mahler moved to a larger, more cosmopolitan German city to advance his career. At the age of fifteen, he enrolled in the prestigious Vienna Conservatory of Music, where he studied musical composition and conducting. Mahler felt that his mission in life was to conduct—to interpret—the works of the masters ("to suffer for my great masters," as he put it). Like most young conductors, he began his career in provincial towns, gradually working his way to larger and more important musical centers. His itinerary as resident conductor took him, among other places, to Kassel (1883–1884), Prague (1885–1886), Leipzig (1886–1888), Budapest (1888–1891), Hamburg (1891–1897), and finally back to Vienna.

In May 1897, Mahler returned triumphantly to his adopted city as director of the Vienna Court Opera, a position Mozart had once coveted. The next year he also assumed directorship of the Vienna Philharmonic, then and now one of the world's great orchestras. But Mahler was a demanding autocrat—a musical tyrant—in search of

FIGURE 30-3
Gustav Mahler.

an artistic ideal. That he drove himself as hard as he pushed others was little comfort to the singers and instrumentalists who had to endure his wrath during rehearsals. After ten stormy but artistically successful seasons (1897–1907), Mahler was dismissed from the Vienna Opera. About this time, he accepted an offer from New York to take charge of the Metropolitan Opera, and eventually he conducted the New York Philharmonic as well. (The first season alone he earned $300,000 in today's money for three months' work.) Here, too, there was both acclaim and controversy. And here, too, at least at the Met, his contract was not renewed after two years, though he stayed on longer, until February 1911, with the Philharmonic. He died in Vienna in May 1911 of a lingering streptococcal infection that had attacked his weak heart—a tragic end to an obsessive and somewhat tormented life.

Mahler is unique among composers in that he wrote only orchestral songs and symphonies. Songs, however, seem to have come first, both chronologically and psychologically. He began his career as a composer setting various collections of poetry to music: *Lieder eines fahrenden Gesellen* (*Songs of a Wayfaring Lad*, 1883–1885), *Des Knaben Wunderhorn* (*A Youth's Magic Horn*, 1888–1896), *Kindertotenlieder* (*Songs on the Death of Children*, 1901–1904), and the *Five Rückert Songs* (1901). Even when he turned to the traditional four-movement symphony, Mahler did something unusual—he brought the song into the symphony. His collection of single-movement songs served as a musical repository, or vault, to which the composer could return for inspiration while wrestling with the problems of a large, multimovement work for orchestra. Mahler's First Symphony (1889), though entirely instrumental, makes use of melodies already present in his song cycle *Lieder eines fahrenden Gesellen*. His Second (1894), Third (1896), and Fourth (1901) symphonies incorporate various portions of the *Wunderhorn* songs as solo vocal parts. Symphonies Five (1902) and Six (1904) are again purely instrumental, but once more borrow preexisting melodies from earlier songs. Altogether Mahler finished nine symphonies, seven of which make use of his own orchestral *Lieder* or other preexisting vocal music.

Symphony No. 4 (1889–1901)

To see how Mahler incorporated an orchestral song into a symphony, let us consider the genesis of his Symphony No. 4, composed in 1889–1901. To provide a focal point and goal for the standard four-movement symphonic framework, Mahler returned to an art song that he had set for voice and piano back in 1892, titled "Das himmlische Leben" ("The Heavenly Life"), from his *Wunderhorn* settings. Taking the original piano accompaniment, he arranged it for a large (but not huge) orchestra. The arrangement, now for voice and orchestra, was to serve as the final, valedictory movement. The task then was to fashion three brand-new movements that would provide a fitting preface to the climactic finale. So Mahler wrote a lengthy first movement in sonata–allegro form, a scherzo that invokes the figure of the dancing devil of hell, and a double-variation slow movement—all to precede the heavenly finale. Thus the spirit of the symphony expresses a play of opposites: hell and heaven, the demonic and the divine, the macabre and the beautiful.

How do you depict heaven in music? Mahler moves through the four stanzas of the poem almost exclusively in the major, leading the listener through sonic space that is filled with airy melodies, dancing rhythms, light textures, and tinkling percussive sparkles. The most celestial sounds come in the final strophe, in which the composer paints (*Mahler* in German means "painter") the music of the angels: "No music on earth can be compared with ours."

Listening GUIDE

Gustav Mahler
Symphony No. 4 (1889–1901)
Fourth movement, *Sehr behaglich*
(very pleasing)

5
5/1–3

Genre: Symphony

Form: Strophic variation

0:00 **1**	Melody 1 in clarinet with "schmaltzy" slides (typical of Viennese café music) in cellos; other woodwinds take over melody		

STROPHE 1

0:34	Strophe 1 sung to variant of melody 1	Wir geniessen die himmlischen Freuden,	We enjoy heavenly joys,
		D'rum tun wir das Irdische meiden.	And thus shun earthly things.
		Kein weltlich Getümmel	No worldly tumult
		Hört man nicht im Himmel!	Does one ever hear in heaven!
		Lebt alles in sanftester Ruh'!	Everyone lives in harmonious quiet!
1:09	Tempo increases	Wir führen ein englisches Leben,	We lead the life of the angels,
		Sind dennoch ganz lustig daneben;	But a lively one indeed;
		Wir tanzen und springen,	We dance and leap,
		Wir hüpfen und singen,	Hop and sing,
1:33	Music changes to slow and homophonic to become "saintly" at mention of Saint Peter	Sankt Peter im Himmel sieht zu.	While Saint Peter in heaven looks on.
1:48	Sleigh bells begin instrumental interlude		

STROPHE 2

2:22	Strophe 2 sung to melody 2	Johannes das Lämmlein auslasset,	Saint John has released his little lamb,

Jo - han - nes das Lämm - lein aus - las - set,

		Der Metzger Herodes drauf passet.	The butcher, Herod, is to have him.
		Wir führen ein geduldig's,	We lead a meek, mild,
		Unschuldig's, geduldig's,	And innocent,
		Ein liebliches Lämmlein zu Tod.	Lovely little lamb to death.
		Sankt Lucas den Ochsen tät schlachten	Saint Luke slaughters the ox
		Ohn' eninig's Bedenken und Achten.	Without the least thought or care.
		Der Wein kost' kein Heller	Wine costs not a penny
		Im himmlischen Keller;	At the heavenly inn;
2:54	Slow, "saintly," homophonic music returns	Die Englein, die backen das Brot.	The angels bake all the bread.
3:09	Sleigh bells begin instrumental interlude		

STROPHE 3

3:18	Strophe 3 sung to variant of melody 1	Gut' Kräuter von allerhand Arten,	Good things of all sorts,
		Die wachsen in himmlischen Garten,	Grow in the heavenly garden,
		Gut' Spargel, Fisolen	Good asparagus and beans
		Und was wir nur wollen.	And whatever we might want.
		Ganze Schüsseln voll sind uns bereit!	Heaping platters are prepared for us!
		Gut' Äpfel, gut' Birn' und gut' Trauben;	Great apples, pears, and grapes;
		Die Gärtner, die alles erlauben.	The gardener allows us everything.
		Willst Rehbock, willst Hasen,	If you want venison or rabbit,
		Auf offener Strassen	In the public streets
		Sie laufen herbei!	They run right up!
		Sollt' ein Fasttag etwa kommen,	When a fast day arrives,
		Alle Fische gleich mit Freuden ausgeschwommen.	The fish joyfully gather.

(continued)

4:15		"Saintly" music returns	Dort läuft schon Sankt Peter Mit Netz und mit Köder Zum himmlischen Weiher hinein. Sankt Martha die Köchin muss sein.	There goes Saint Peter With net and bait To the heavenly pond. St. Martha must be the cook.
4:41	**2** 0:00	Harp signals beginning of instrumental interlude featuring sleigh bells (0:12)		
5:09	0:28	Harp and English horn ostinato extends instrumental interlude; fragments of melody 1		

STROPHE 4

6:19	**3** 0:00	Strophe 4 sung to variant of melody 1, but slowly to emphasize special nature of music	Kein' Musik ist ja nicht auf Erden, Die uns'rer verglichen kann werden. Elftausend Jungfrauen Zu tanzen sich trauen. Sankt Ursula selbst dazu lacht.	No music on earth, Can be compared with ours. Eleven thousand virgins Begin to dance. Saint Ursula herself laughs at the sight.
7:05	0:46		Kein' Musik ist ja nicht auf Erden, Die uns'rer verglichen kann werden. Cäcilia mit ihren Verwandten Sind treffliche Hofmusikanten! Die englischen Stimmen Ermuntern die Sinnen, Dass alles für Freuden erwacht.	Indeed, there is no music on earth That can compare to ours. [Saint] Cecilia with her followers Are splendid court musicians! The voices of the angels Lift up spirits, So that all is filled with joy.
8:38	2:19	Instrumental postlude with English horn and harp playing reminiscences of melody 1		

 Listen to streaming music in an Active Listening Guide, available on the text website.

@

For a "Mahler heavy" experience, watch a portion of his Symphony No. 5 in the YouTube playlist at the text website.

Gustav Mahler was an extraordinary composer whose greatness came to be recognized only during the second half of the twentieth century. His vision of music—what it can express—is both internal and external, personally introspective yet outward looking. "The symphony is the world; it must embrace everything," he once said. And so he tried to embrace every sort of music within it. At various points in his symphonies, we hear folk dances, popular songs, military marches, off-stage bands, bugle calls, and even Gregorian chant (Fig. 30-4). These musical events, however, do not seem to come in a

FIGURE 30-4

Mahler said, "The symphony is the world; it must embrace everything." This contemporary newspaper caricature suggests the various things that Maestro Mahler threw into symphonies: animal sounds, birdsong, church bells, and military music, among others.

© Imagno/Getty Images

logical or narrative sequence; they do not tell a story. Instead, they sound in an apparently random order, one piling on top of another, creating a dream-like "music of the subconscious"—perhaps not coincidentally, Sigmund Freud and Mahler were acquaintances.

At the same time, Mahler's collage of sound plays outwardly on the grandest scale—achieved, in part, by employing massive forces and a greatly extended sense of time. His Symphony No. 2, for example, calls for ten horns and eight trumpets, and lasts an hour and a half. And the first performance of his Symphony No. 8 in Munich in 1910 involved 858 singers and 171 instrumentalists! With good reason, it has been nicknamed the "Symphony of a Thousand." Thus our Symphony No. 4, requiring only seventy-five or so players, might be rightly termed "Mahler light" and is universally recognized as the most "accessible" of Mahler's nine symphonies.

Gustav Mahler was the last in the long line of great German symphonists that extends back through Brahms, Schubert, and Beethoven to Mozart and, ultimately, to Haydn. What had begun as a modest instrumental genre with a limited emotional range had grown in the course of the nineteenth century into a monumental structure. It had become the equivalent, in Mahler's view, not only of the creator's mind, but also of the entire cosmos.

Key WORDS

absolute music (310)   orchestral song
double stops (311)   (orchestral *Lied*) (313)

For an example of "Mahler heavy," download a Supplementary Listening Guide for his Symphony No. 1, third movement, at the text website.

Watch a video of Craig Wright's Open Yale Course class session 20, "The Colossal Symphony: Beethoven, Berlioz, Mahler, and Shostakovich," at the text website.

The materials on the text website will help you understand and pass tests on the content of this chapter. In addition, you may watch Craig Wright's own lecture at Open Yale Courses and complete this chapter's Listening Exercise interactively, as well as view Active Listening Guides and other materials that will help you succeed in this course.

A complete Checklist of Musical Style for the Romantic era can be found at the text website.

PART VI $\mathcal{M}$ODERN AND POSTMODERN ART MUSIC, 1880–PRESENT

© Musée Marmottan, Paris//Photo © Peter Willi/
SuperStock

| 1880 | 1890 | 1900 | 1910 | 1920 | 1930 | 1940 |

MODERN AND POSTMODERN

◄······● 1894 Claude Debussy composes *Prelude to The Afternoon of a Faun*

● 1907 Pablo Picasso paints *Les Demoiselles d'Avignon*

1908–1914 Charles Ives composes
Three Places in New England

● 1912 Arnold Schoenberg composes
Pierrot lunaire

● 1913 Igor Stravinsky composes
The Rite of Spring

1914–1918 World War I

● 1917 Sergey Prokofiev composes
Classical Symphony

● 1924 Joseph Stalin takes
control of Soviet government

● 1929 Crash of
American stock market

1929–1941 Great Depression

● 1937
Dmitri Shostakovich composes
Symphony No. 5

1939–1945
World War II

Human activity, artistic or otherwise, never occurs within tidy chronological units. Historical periods overlap, and different styles coexist in time. Setting the dates of "modernism" and "postmodernism" is a particularly difficult task. Until recently, historians have usually referred to "modern" music simply as "twentieth-century" music. But modern musical idioms appeared in some Impressionist music of the late nineteenth century, while aspects of musical Romanticism continue to exist even today. Similarly, "postmodernism" may have begun as early as the 1930s and continues to develop during our own times. Recognizing, then, that the terms *modern* and *postmodern* together connote a large, multifaceted musical period, what are a few of the characteristics that mark this epoch?

At the beginning of the twentieth century, composers increasingly turned against the warm sentimentality characteristic of much of nineteenth-century music, replacing this Romantic aesthetic with a harsh, percussive, impersonal sound. Melodies become more angular, and harmonies more dissonant. Simultaneously, the massive compositions of the late Romantic period—perhaps best represented by Gustav Mahler's *Symphony of a Thousand* (1906)—yield to smaller, less extravagant works. The abstract, impersonal quality of modern music is most clearly evident in Arnold Schoenberg's rigid twelve-tone music. In the 1960s, a reaction against the formalism of Schoenberg and his disciples contributed to the increasing popularity of musical postmodernism, which allowed for a diversity of musical genres—electronic music and chance music, for example—performed in unconventional ways. If modernism turned against traditional musical styles, postmodernism, which continues today, often dispenses entirely with conventional musical forms and processes.

1950	1960	1970	1980	1990	2000	2010

MODERN AND POSTMODERN

- 1944 Aaron Copland composes ballet *Appalachian Spring*

- 1945 Atomic bombs dropped on Hiroshima and Nagasaki

- 1945 Béla Bartók composes *Concerto for Orchestra*

1950–1952 Korean War

- 1958 Edgard Varèse composes *Poème électronique* for World's Fair

- 1963 John F. Kennedy assassinated

1963–1973 Vietnam War

- 1985 Ellen Zwilich composes *Concerto Grosso 1985*

- 1986 John Adams composes *Short Ride in a Fast Machine*

- 1991 Fall of Berlin Wall; end of Cold War

- 2000 Tan Dun records score for film *Crouching Tiger, Hidden Dragon*

- 2001 Terrorist attacks in United States

- 2009 Michael Jackson dies unexpectedly

31

IMPRESSIONISM AND EXOTICISM

Romantic music reached its peak during the late nineteenth century in the grandiose works of Wagner, Tchaikovsky, Brahms, and Mahler. But by 1900, this German-dominated musical empire had started to weaken. Some composers outside the mainstream of Romanticism challenged the validity of the predominantly German style, epitomized by the music of Wagner. Not surprisingly, the most powerful anti-German sentiment was felt in France. (France and Germany went to war in 1870 and would do so again in 1914.)

Having first embraced Wagner's music during the 1870s and 1880s, the French avant-garde had, by the 1890s, turned against it. The French began to ridicule the sentimentality of Romanticism in general and the grandiose structures of the Germans in particular. German music was said to be too heavy, too pretentious, and too bombastic, like one of Wagner's Nordic giants. Meaningful expression, it was believed, might be communicated in more subtle ways, in something other than sheer volume of sound and epic length.

FIGURE 31-1

The painting that gave its name to an epoch, Claude Monet's *Impression: Sunrise*, was exhibited at the first group exhibition organized by Monet, Renoir, Degas, and Pissarro in Paris in 1874. The ships, rowboats, and other elements in the early morning light are more suggested than fully rendered. Said the critic Louis Leroy derisively of this painting at the time, "Wallpaper in its most embryonic state is more finished than that seascape."

IMPRESSIONISM IN PAINTING AND MUSIC

The movement that arose in France in opposition to German Romantic music has been given the name **Impressionism** (Fig. 31-1). We are, of course, more familiar with this term as a designation for a school of late-nineteenth-century painters working in and around Paris, including Claude Monet (1840–1903), Auguste Renoir (1841–1919), Edgar Degas (1834–1917), Camille Pissarro (1830–1903), and the American Mary Cassatt (1844–1926). Impressionist painters were not overtly anti-German like their musical counterparts. There was no need to be, because the well-established tradition of French painting was widely considered superior to the German one (see Figs. 22-1 and 25-1). Instead, Monet and his colleagues rebelled against the traditional academic style of their native France. When the French Academy of Fine Arts refused to allow the progressive painters to show their canvases at the official Salon in the early 1870s, they mounted their own exhibition. In the uproar that followed, the artists were disparagingly called "impressionists" for the seemingly imprecise quality

© Musée Marmottan, Paris//Photo © Peter Willi/SuperStock

of their art. The painters accepted the name, partly as an act of defiance against the establishment, and soon the term was universally adopted.

It is ironic that French Impressionism, which once generated such controversy, is now the most popular of all artistic styles. Indeed, judging by museum attendance and reproductions sold, there is an almost limitless enthusiasm for the art of Monet, Degas, Renoir, and their associates—precisely the paintings that the artists' contemporaries mocked and jeered. But what is it about the Impressionist style that initially caused such a furor?

The Impressionists were the first to reject photographic realism in painting. Instead, they tried to re-create the impression that an object produced upon the senses in a single, fleeting moment. The key here is light: the Impressionists saw the world as awash in vibrant rays of light and sought to capture the aura that light-bathed objects created in the eyes of the beholder. To accomplish this, they covered their canvases with small, dab-like brushstrokes in which light was broken down into spots of color, thereby creating a sense of movement and fluidity. Shapes are not clearly defined but blurred, more suggested than delineated. Minor details disappear. Sunlight is everywhere and everything shimmers (Fig. 31-2).

As impressions and sensations became paramount for these painters, not surprisingly, they showed an intensified interest in music. What art form is more elusive and suggestive? What medium allows the receiver—the listener—more freedom to interpret the sensations he or she perceives? Painters began to speak in musical terms. Paul Gauguin (1848–1903) referred to the harmonies of line and color as the "music of painting," and Vincent van Gogh (1853–1890) suggested "using color as the music of tones." Paul Cézanne (1839–1906) painted an "overture" in homage to Wagner, while James Whistler (1844–1903), an American who worked in Paris in the 1860s and 1880s, created "nocturnes" and "symphonies." The painters envied the musicians' good fortune to work in a medium that changes continually—rather than one that required the artist to seize the moment and fix it on canvas.

For their part, musicians found inspiration in the visual arts. Claude Debussy, whose work most consistently displayed the Impressionist style in music, was delighted to be grouped with the Impressionist painters. "You do me great honor by calling me a pupil of Claude Monet," he told a friend in 1916. Debussy gave various collections of his compositions such artistic titles as *Sketches*, *Images*, and *Prints*. Rare are the moments in history when the aesthetic aims of painters and musicians were as closely allied.

FIGURE 31–2

Claude Monet, *Woman with Umbrella* (1886). The Impressionist canvas is not a finished surface in the traditional sense. Rather, the painter breaks down light into separate dabs of color and juxtaposes them for the viewer's eye to reassemble. Here bold brushstrokes convey an astonishing sense of movement, freshness, and sparkling light.

FIGURE 31–3

Claude Debussy at the age of twenty-four.

*C*LAUDE DEBUSSY (1862–1918)

Debussy (Fig. 31-3) was born in 1862 into a modest family living in a small town outside Paris. Since neither of his parents was musical, it came as a surprise when their son demonstrated talent at the keyboard. At the age of ten, he was sent to the Paris Conservatory for lessons in piano, composition, and music theory. Owing to his skill as a performer, he was soon engaged for summer work in the household of Nadezhda von Meck, a wealthy patroness of the arts and the principal supporter of Tchaikovsky (see Fig. 24-6). This employment took him,

@

Watch a video of Craig Wright's Open Yale Course class session 21, "Musical Impressionism and Exoticism: Debussy, Ravel, and Monet," at the text website.

in turn, to Italy, Russia, and Vienna. In 1884, he won the Prix de Rome, an official prize in composition funded by the French government, one that required a three-year stay in Rome. But Debussy was not happy in the Eternal City. He preferred Paris with its bistros, cafes, and bohemian ambience.

Returning to Paris more or less permanently in 1887, the young Frenchman continued to study his craft and to search for his own independent voice as a composer. He had some minor successes, and yet, as he said in 1893, "There are still things that I am not able to do—create masterpieces, for example." But the next year, in 1894, he did just that. With the completion of *Prélude à l'Après-midi d'un Faune* (*Prelude to The Afternoon of a Faun*), he gave to the public what has become his most enduring orchestral work. Debussy's later compositions, including his opera *Pelléas et Mélisande* (1902), the symphonic poem *La Mer* (*The Sea*, 1905), and his two books of *Preludes* for piano, met with less popular favor. Critics complained that Debussy's works were lacking in form, melody, and forward motion.

Today, in hindsight, we see in these works the beginnings of modernism. Debussy hated what he called the German "developmental agenda" and wrote no symphonies. He replaced the warm strings and heavy low brasses of the Romantic orchestra with a variety of woodwinds, which often dominate his textures. He began to separate color (instrumental sound) from line (traditional melody) and then to luxuriate in color alone. Illness and the outbreak of World War I in 1914 brought Debussy's innovations to a halt. He died of cancer in the spring of 1918 while the guns of the German army were shelling Paris from the north.

Prelude to The Afternoon of a Faun (1894)

Debussy spent more of his time in the company of poets and painters than musicians. His orchestral *Prelude to The Afternoon of a Faun*, in fact, was written to precede a stage reading of the poem *The Afternoon of a Faun* by his friend and mentor Stéphane Mallarmé (Fig. 31-4).

Mallarmé was the spiritual leader of a group of versifiers in *fin-de-siècle* Paris called the **Symbolists,** poets whose aesthetic aims were in harmony with those of the Impressionist painters. They worked to create a poetic style in which the literal *meaning* of the word was less important than its *sound* and the associations that that sound might produce. Said Mallarmé, "To name an object is to destroy its poetic enjoyment; the aim is to suggest the object."

Symbolism is certainly at the heart of Mallarmé's evocative *The Afternoon of a Faun*, which applies suggestive language to an ancient Greek theme. The faun of Mallarmé's poem is not a young deer but a satyr (a mythological beast that is half man, half goat), who spends his days in lustful pursuit of the nymphs of the forest. On this afternoon, we see the faun, exhausted from the morning's escapades, reclining on the forest floor in the still air of the midday heat (Fig. 31-5). He contemplates future conquests while blowing listlessly on his panpipes. The following passage suggests the dream-like mood, vague and elusive, that Debussy sought to re-create in his musical setting:

FIGURE 31-4

The poet Stéphane Mallarmé, author of *The Afternoon of a Faun*, as painted by the great predecessor of the Impressionists, Edouard Manet (1832–1883). Mallarmé was a friend and artistic mentor of the composer Debussy.

No murmur of water in the woodland scene,
Bathed only in the sounds of my flute.
And the only breeze, except for my two pipes,
Blows itself empty long before
It can scatter the sound in an arid rain.
On a horizon unmoved by a ripple
This sound, visible and serene,
Mounts to the heavens, an inspired wisp.

Debussy, who did not compose linear, narrative programmatic music in the tradition of Berlioz or Tchaikovsky, made no effort to follow Mallarmé's poem closely. As he said at the time of the first performance in December 1894, "My *Prelude* is really a sequence of mood paintings, throughout which the desire and dreams of the Faun move in the heat of the midday sun." When Mallarmé heard the music, he, in turn, said the following about Debussy's musical response to the poem: "I never expected anything like it. The music prolongs the emotion of my poem and paints its scenery more passionately than colors could."

Significantly, both musician and poet refer to *Prelude to The Afternoon of a Faun* in terms of painting (Fig. 31-5). But how does one create a painting in music? Here a tableau is depicted by using the distinctive colors of the instruments, especially the woodwinds, to evoke vibrant moods and sensations. The flute has one timbre, the oboe another, and the clarinet yet a third. Debussy has said, in effect, let us focus on the sound-producing capacity of the instruments, let us see what new shades can be elicited from them, let us try new registers, let us try new combinations. Thus a solo flute begins in its lowest register (the pipes of the faun), followed by a harp glissando, then dabs of color from the French horn. These tonal impressions swirl, dissolve, and form again, but seem not to progress. As with the poetic language of the Symbolists, in Debussy's musical syntax, units of meaning can come irregularly. There are no repeating rhythms or clear meters to push the music forward. All is languid beauty, a music that is utterly original and shockingly sensual.

FIGURE 31–5

Mallarmé's *The Afternoon of a Faun* created something of a sensation among late-nineteenth-century artists. This painting by Pal Szinyei Merse (1845–1920) is just one of several such representations of the faun and woodland nymphs. Notice that he holds classical panpipes, which Debussy transformed into the sound of the flute.

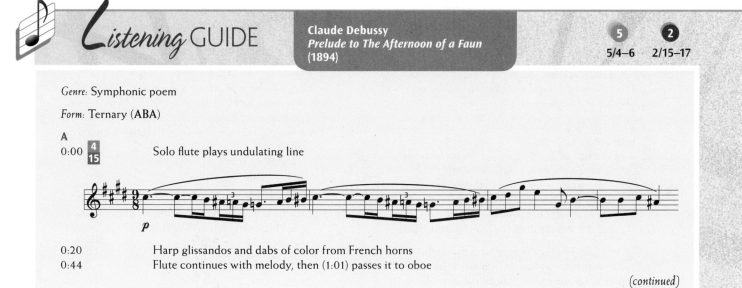

Listening GUIDE

Claude Debussy
Prelude to The Afternoon of a Faun
(1894)

5 2
5/4–6 2/15–17

Genre: Symphonic poem

Form: Ternary (**ABA**)

A
0:00 **4/15**   Solo flute plays undulating line

0:20   Harp glissandos and dabs of color from French horns
0:44   Flute continues with melody, then (1:01) passes it to oboe

(continued)

1:13		Crescendo that disappears before it can climax
1:35		Return of melody to flute

B

2:48 **5/16** 0:00   Clarinet and then flute play rapid chromatic arabesques

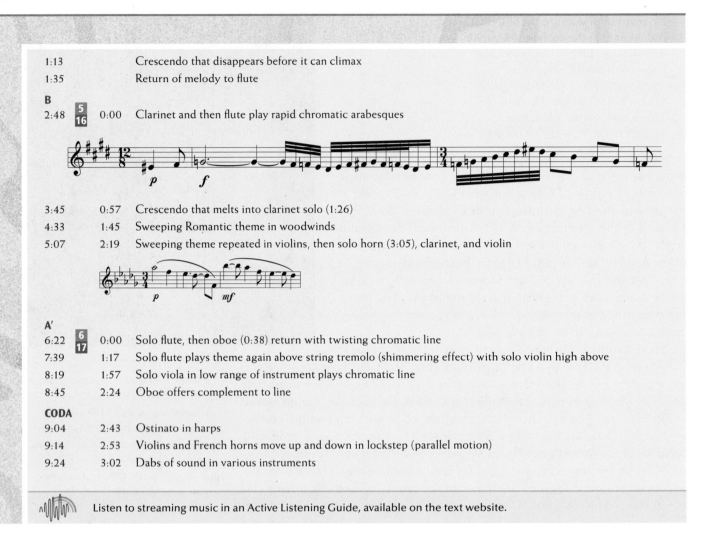

3:45	0:57	Crescendo that melts into clarinet solo (1:26)
4:33	1:45	Sweeping Romantic theme in woodwinds
5:07	2:19	Sweeping theme repeated in violins, then solo horn (3:05), clarinet, and violin

A′

6:22	**6/17** 0:00	Solo flute, then oboe (0:38) return with twisting chromatic line
7:39	1:17	Solo flute plays theme again above string tremolo (shimmering effect) with solo violin high above
8:19	1:57	Solo viola in low range of instrument plays chromatic line
8:45	2:24	Oboe offers complement to line

CODA

9:04	2:43	Ostinato in harps
9:14	2:53	Violins and French horns move up and down in lockstep (parallel motion)
9:24	3:02	Dabs of sound in various instruments

Listen to streaming music in an Active Listening Guide, available on the text website.

Listening EXERCISE 38

Debussy

PRELUDE TO THE AFTERNOON OF A FAUN   **5** 5/4–6   **2** 2/15–17   **@**

To take this Listening Exercise online and receive feedback or email answers to your instructor, go to the text website.

Debussy, as we have seen, was a master of generating new sonorities, as well as creating new, discontinuous orchestrations. The following questions, therefore, pertain mainly to issues of color and orchestration.

1. (0:00–0:18) Which of the following is true about the **4/15** beginning of this piece?
   a. The texture is monophonic, the meter is vague, and the melody has chromaticism.
   b. The texture is polyphonic, the meter is clear, and the melody has chromaticism.
   c. The texture is homophonic, the meter is clear, and the melody does not have chromaticism.

2. (0:44–1:12) The flute returns with the opening line, but now the strings quietly shimmer behind it. Which string technique creates this shimmering effect?
   a. pizzicato   b. obligato   c. tremolo

3. (1:22–1:33) By repeating a motive as it fades away, Debussy avoids any large climax of the sort beloved by Romantic composers. In restating this motive continuously, on the same pitches, Debussy is employing what?
   a. a walking bass
   b. an ostinato
   c. an arpeggio

4. (1:18–1:34) Which dynamic marking does Debussy use to create this feeling of evasion and anticlimax?
   a. crescendo–diminuendo
   b. diminuendo–crescendo

5. (1:36, 1:52, and 2:14) When the flute returns with the twisting chromatic line, which instrument provides a colorful background?
   a. English horn   b. French horn   c. harp

6. (0:00–0:28) Which is a correct description of the music at this point?
   a. The violins sweep forward with a sensuous melody based on a whole-tone scale.
   b. Various instruments dart in and out with tiny motives, creating colorful sonorities but a discontinuous texture.

7. (2:19–3:04) In this beautiful passage, Debussy comes closest to re-creating the lush sentimentality more typical of Romantic than Impressionist music. Which statement is *not* correct?
   a. There is a solo for French horn and then violin at the beginning.
   b. There is a long, sweeping, rhythmically free melody.
   c. The melody is played expressively by the violins.

8. A passage with a prominent flute is stated (0:00–0:37) and then repeated at a lower pitch (0:30–1:16), now featuring an oboe. What happens to the texture and orchestration in the course of each of these two passages?
   a. Polyphonic texture and discontinuous orchestration give way to homophonic texture and unchanging orchestration.
   b. Homophonic texture and unchanging orchestration give way to polyphonic texture and discontinuous orchestration.

9. In a typical orchestral work of the Classical or Romantic periods, it is usually the violins that present most themes. In Debussy's Impressionist *Prelude*, however, the instruments of which family introduce most melodic motives?
   a. strings
   b. brasses
   c. woodwinds
   d. percussion

10. Between 1870 and 1939 France and Germany went to war three times, and Debussy died in the middle one of these three engagements. The emotional effect of his *Prelude to The Afternoon of a Faun* is to turn you into what?
    a. an aggressive, charging warrior
    b. an enervated pacifist

Debussy's voluptuous *Prelude* creates an entirely new world of musical aesthetics, one very different from the German Romantic school of Mendelssohn, Wagner, and Brahms. Where a composer in the German Romantic tradition asserts a strongly profiled theme, a French Impressionist like Debussy instead insinuates a tiny motive. In place of clear meters and regular rhythms, the Impressionist favors constantly shifting accents that obscure the pulse. Rather than working toward a thunderous climax and a strong cadence, the Impressionist prefers to avoid a climax by placing a diminuendo before the cadence, thereby creating an anticlimax. Instead of marching purposefully along a well-directed harmonic progression, the Impressionist chooses to sit on a single static harmony and let the colorful instruments work their magic. Most important, instead of using musical color to reinforce the musical theme, the Impressionist prefers to call on the instruments to demonstrate their sonorities *independent* of theme. In the music of Debussy and the Impressionists, then, beautiful sonorities are allowed simply to exist, without having to progress thematically to some distant goal.

All this was radically modern. Think back to the orchestral music of Beethoven, Brahms, and Tchaikovsky. In these earlier works, new themes are generally introduced by a new instrument or group of instruments. Instrumental color thus reinforces and gives profile to the theme. With Debussy, on the other hand, instruments enter with a distinct color but with no easily discernible theme. Thus, color and texture begin to replace melody as the primary agents in the creation of musical form. Debussy's approach was adopted by the revolutionary figures of twentieth-century music—among them Charles Ives, Edgard Varèse, and John Cage (see Chapters 35 and 36)—who often generate musical form through colors and textures, rather than through thematic development. Not coincidentally, during the peak of Debussy's career (around the turn of the twentieth century), the Impressionist painters began to separate color from line as well (Fig. 31-6).

FIGURE 31–6

In Edgar Degas's *Combing of the Hair* (c1896), the lines of the objects are sometimes only vaguely sketched, and the intense orange color runs beyond the boundaries of the lines. The intensity of color is now a prime emotive force in art, a hallmark of the new modernist style.

@

Download Supplementary Listening Guides for Debussy's *Nuages (Clouds)*, from *Nocturnes*, and *La cathédrale engloutie* (*The Sunken Cathedral*), from *Preludes*, at the text website.

Preludes *for Piano* (1910, 1913)

Debussy's last and most far-reaching attempt at descriptive writing in music is found in the two books of *Preludes* for piano that he published in 1910 and 1913. Here the challenge to create musical impressions was all the greater, for the piano has a more limited musical palette than the multicolor orchestra. The evocative titles of some of these short pieces allude to their mysterious qualities: *Steps in the Snow*, *The Sunken Cathedral*, *What the West Wind Saw*, and *Sounds and Perfumes Swirl in the Night Air*.

Voiles (Sails), from the first book of *Preludes* of 1910, takes us to the sea (Fig. 31-7). As we hear a fluid descent, mostly in parallel motion, we imagine sails flapping listlessly in the breeze. The hazy, languid atmosphere is created in part by the special scale Debussy employs, the **whole-tone scale,** one in which all the pitches are a whole step apart.

EXAMPLE 31–1   WHOLE-TONE SCALE

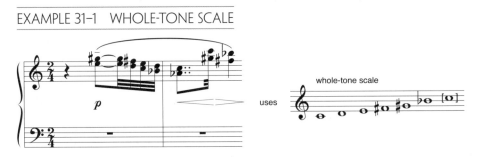

Because in the whole-tone scale each note is the same distance from its neighbor, no one pitch is heard as the tonal center—all pitches seem equally important. The composer can stop on any note of the scale, and it will sound no more central, or final, than any other note. The music floats without a tonal anchor. Then, as if impelled by a puff of wind, the boats seem to rock on the now-rippling waters. Debussy creates this gentle rocking sensation by inserting a four-note ostinato into the texture. Frequently employed by

FIGURE 31–7

Claude Monet's *Sailboats* (1874). The rocking of the boats is suggested by the exaggerated reflections on the water.

Impressionist composers, ostinatos help account for the often static, restful feeling in the harmony. By definition, ostinatos involve repetition and inertia rather than dramatic movement.

EXAMPLE 31–2 OSTINATO

A new ostinato now appears in the upper register (right hand), while a succession of four-note chords sounds in the middle register (left hand). Notice that all four notes of each chord consistently move in what is called parallel motion. In **parallel motion,** all parts move together, locked in step, in the same direction.

EXAMPLE 31–3 PARALLEL MOTION

Parallel motion is the antithesis of counterpoint, the traditional musical technique in which two or more lines usually move in directions opposite to one another. Parallel motion was an innovation of Debussy, and it was one way he expressed his opposition to the German school of Wagner and Brahms, so heavily steeped in counterpoint.

Suddenly, a gust of wind seems to shake the ships as the pianist races up the scale in a harp-like glissando. This scale, however, is different from the preceding whole-tone one. It is a pentatonic scale. There are only five notes

EXOTIC INFLUENCES ON THE IMPRESSIONISTS

At the turn of the twentieth century, Paris was the cultural capital of the Western world, and its citizens were eager to turn their eyes and ears to the East. In 1889, the French government sponsored an *Exposition universelle* (World's Fair) that featured Far Eastern art. It was here that painter Paul Gaugin (1848–1903) first became enamored with the tropical colors of the Pacific. Claude Debussy, too, made several visits. Not only did he see the newly completed Eiffel Tower and newfangled inventions like electric lighting and electric-powered elevators, he also heard for the first time the exotic sounds of the Far East. Colonial governments including those of Cambodia, Vietnam, and Indonesia had sent small ensembles of instrumentalists, singers, and dancers to perform in newly constructed pavilions. The Cambodian pagoda seems to have been the inspiration for a later piano piece called *Pagodes* (*Pagodas*, 1903). Debussy also heard there a colorful gamelan orchestra from Indonesia, as he recalled to a friend some years later: "Do you not remember the Javanese (Indonesian) music that was capable of expressing every nuance of meaning, even unmentionable shades, and makes our tonic and dominant sounds seem weak and empty?" This experience encouraged Debussy to incorporate in his own music the sounds of the East: ostinatos, static harmonies, pentatonic and whole-tone scales, delicately layered textures,

© Alinari Archives/The Image Works

The Cambodian pagoda at the World's Fair in Paris in 1889. Here Debussy heard the music of Cambodia, China, Vietnam, and Indonesia, and began to formulate a musical aesthetic different from the prevailing German symphonic tradition.

and shimmering surfaces. It also suggested to him that music did not always have to progress toward a goal—instead, it might simply exist for the moment.

within each octave, here the five notes corresponding to the black keys on the piano. We have seen before that the pentatonic scale is often found in folk music (see pp. 301 and 306). Debussy first encountered it in the Southeast Asian music he heard at the Paris World's Fair of 1889 (see box).

EXAMPLE 31–4   PENTATONIC SCALE

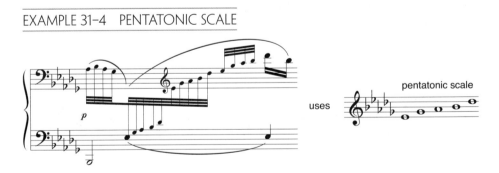

uses   pentatonic scale

Following this energized whirl around the pentatonic scale, the seascape regains its placid demeanor with the return of the whole-tone scale and, ultimately, the descending parallel thirds with which the piece began. At the end, Debussy directs the pianist to push down and hold the sustaining pedal (the right-most of the three pedals). Once the sustaining pedal is pressed and held, all notes sounded thereafter will blur into a vague haze, similar to the hazes and mists that envelop many Impressionist paintings (see Fig. 31-1).

Listening GUIDE

Claude Debussy
Voiles (Sails), **from** *Preludes*, **Book I**
(1910)

Form: Ternary (**ABA'**)

0:00	**7**	**A**	Descending parallel thirds using whole-tone scale
0:10			Bass pedal point enters
1:01			Ostinato enters in middle register
1:38			Ostinato moves into top register; chords move in parallel motion in middle register
2:09		**B**	Harp-like glissandos using pentatonic scale
2:23			Chords moving in parallel motion above pedal point
2:46			Glissandos now employing whole-tone scale
3:16		**A'**	Descending thirds return
3:28			Glissandos blur through use of sustaining pedal

Listen to streaming music in an Active Listening Guide, available on the text website.

EXOTICISM IN MUSIC

One of the magical qualities of music is its capacity to transport us to distant lands. Far-off places can be experienced in our minds, if only through the strange and mysterious sounds we associate with them. Composers at the turn of the twentieth century delighted in such vicarious journeys, and their music is brimming with the "exotic." Claude Debussy was strongly influenced by the art of the Far East (see boxed essay), and so, too, were the famous painters of the time. Impressionist Claude Monet lined the walls of his home in Giverny, France, not with his own canvases, but with prints and water colors from Japan. Their influence can be seen in the startling portrait of his wife in traditional Japanese costume (Fig. 31-8). Modernists like Pablo Picasso (1881–1973) and Georges Braque (1882–1963) began collecting African art in Paris during the years 1905–1908. Some historians believe that the Cubist movement in painting (see p. 333) was born of Picasso's interest in African sculpture and ceremonial masks.

But what was the exotic in music? Briefly, musical **exoticism** was communicated by any sounds drawn from outside the traditional Western European musical experience. It might be a non-Western scale, a folk rhythm, or a musical instrument, like the tambourine or gong that signified the exotic. It might also be an alien subject matter. Giacomo Puccini fashioned operas using stories set in Japan (*Madam Butterfly*, 1904), China (*Turandot*, 1924), and even the American West (*The Girl of the Golden West*, 1910). For the French Impressionists like Claude Debussy and Maurice Ravel, nearby Spain was thought to be exotic. Debussy composed an orchestral piece (*Ibéria*, 1908) and a piano work ("Evening in Grenada," 1903) using Spanish melodies. Ravel wrote his first orchestral work (*Rapsodie espagnole*, 1907) and his last ballet (*Bolero*, 1928), as well as an opera (*The Spanish Hour*, 1911), on Spanish subjects. Yet neither Debussy nor Ravel ever set foot in Spain. In art, the evocative powers of the imagination are often a more potent force than mundane reality.

FIGURE 31–8

Claude Monet, *La Japonaise (Madame Camille Monet in Japanese Costume*, 1876). Europe and America began to show an enthusiasm for things Japanese after the opening of trade with Japan in the 1850s. Fashionable Parisian women wore kimonos and furnished their homes with oriental furniture, prints, and *objets d'art*.

© Interfoto/Alamy

@

Download a Supplementary
Listening Guide for Ravel's
Bolero and Concerto for Piano
and Orchestra in G major, at
the text website.

Maurice Ravel (1875–1937)

"He was the eternal traveler who never went there," said an acquaintance of Maurice Ravel. Indeed, Ravel spent almost all of his life in Paris, an unassuming music teacher and composer earning a modest living. Only through his music did he journey to Spain, Arabia, Greece, and the Far East—all lands he sought to evoke through exotic-sounding elements in his music. Yet there was one exception to Ravel's life of the imagination. In 1928, he embarked on a four-month concert tour of the United States. He heard jazz in Harlem with the American composer George Gershwin (1898–1937) and had breakfast in Hollywood with Charlie Chaplin (1889–1977); he visited Niagara Falls and the Grand Canyon. Having performed and conducted his music in twenty-five American cities, Ravel returned to Paris with what was then the enormous sum of $27,000—in those days, even classical musicians, like pop singers today, could go on lucrative concert tours. It was fortunate for Ravel that he acquired this financial security, for his mental powers soon declined, and he died of Alzheimer's disease in Paris in 1937.

Rapsodie espagnole (1907)

@

Download a Supplementary
Listening Guide for Ravel's
Prelude to the Night, the
first movement of *Rapsodie
espagnole*, at the text website.

Ravel's first composition, written in 1895 at the age of twenty, was a work for piano titled *Habanera*. A habanera, as we have seen (see p. 294), is a slow, seductive dance named after Havana, the capital of the then-Spanish colony of Cuba. The rhythms that mark its progress are, however, West African, a musical legacy of the slave trade to Cuba. In 1907, Ravel arranged his *Habanera* for orchestra and added three additional pieces to it to form his four-movement *Rapsodie espagnole*. Musical elements of the exotic include the habanera rhythm (see the Listening Guide), as well as the presence of a **tambourine**, a small drum with jingles around its rim, from the Basque country (a region of Spain). As you first listen to *Habanera*, you might feel you are witnessing the seductive dance through a screen or filter—it all sounds distant and hazy. There are gossamer glissandos, hints of themes rather than distinct melodies, and lines moving in parallel motion. This is exotic Spain, filtered through the musical sensibilities of a French Impressionist.

Listening GUIDE

Maurice Ravel **Rapsodie espagnole** (1907) **Third movement, *Habanera* (*Assez lent et d'un rhythm las* [rather slow and with a relaxed rhythm])**	5
	5/8

Genre: Habanera

| 0:00 | 8 | Introduction: syncopated habanera rhythm $\frac{2}{4}$ ♪♪♪ ♪♪ ♪♪♪ ♪♪ and glissandos in strings |

| 0:20 | Habanera melody in oboe and English horn |

| 0:44 | Solo violin and viola continue habanera melody |
| 0:56 | French horns move from minor triad to major triad against habanera rhythm |

1:07   Violins play habanera melody in parallel motion

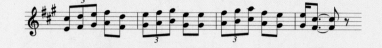

1:32   Woodwinds continue habanera melody with tambourine faintly in background

1:50   Violins continue habanera melody with tambourine in background

1:58   French horns play habanera melody

2:08   Trumpets slide from minor triad to major triad at end

Listen to streaming music in an Active Listening Guide, available at the text website.

Key WORDS

Impressionism (320)

Symbolists (322)

whole-tone scale (326)

parallel motion (327)

exoticism (329)

tambourine (330)

The materials on the text website will help you understand and pass tests on the content of this chapter. In addition, you may watch Craig Wright's own lecture at Open Yale Courses and complete this chapter's Listening Exercise interactively, as well as view Active Listening Guides and other materials that will help you succeed in this course.

32

MODERNISM IN MUSIC AND THE ARTS

The twentieth century might best be called the Age of Extremes. On the one hand, the era was marked by unspeakable tragedies, including two world wars; the systematic extermination of millions of people; the use of chemical, biological, and atomic weapons; and brutal acts of terrorism. On the other hand, scientific advances significantly improved both the quality and length of human life. Such medical advances as antibiotics, organ transplants, and vaccines have saved countless lives. The automobile and airplane profoundly changed the way we travel, offering quick access to virtually the whole world. And important technological innovations—first radio and television, then computers and the Internet—have revolutionized the dissemination of information.

Technological progress has also affected our musical culture. The twentieth century saw steady advances in recording and playback technology, with the respective inventions of the LP record, magnetic tape, compact disc, and MP3 file, which have made popular and classical music alike available to ever-larger segments of the population. These advances, however, have not come without a cost, arguably having discouraged musical education and music-making in the home: Why learn to play an instrument, one might wonder, when you can much more easily hear music on a computer or iPod?

MODERNISM: AN ANTI-ROMANTIC MOVEMENT

The first half of the twentieth century was a particularly horrific time. In World War I (1914–1918), 9 million soldiers were killed on the battlefields. Shocked by the carnage, intellectuals turned away from the predominantly idealistic, sentimental aesthetics of Romanticism—how could one think of love and beauty in the face of wholesale destruction? For writers, painters, and composers alike, disjunction, anxiety, and even hysteria became valid artistic sentiments that reflected the realities of the day.

Musicians of the early twentieth century did not ignore the traditions of classical music. They retained, for example, the genres of opera, ballet, symphony, concerto, and string quartet. The most progressive composers, however, radically transformed the elements of expression *within* these genres, creating new kinds of melody, harmony, rhythm, and tone color.

Radical experimentation in music began quietly enough in the music of the Impressionists—specifically, in Claude Debussy's early separation of color from line (see pp. 325–326). But as World War I approached, a crescendo of protest could be heard in the music of the avant-garde. The progressives renounced the notion that music should be beautiful, pleasing, and expressive or that it

should delight or comfort the listener. Instead, they resorted to distorting traditional musical practices, sometimes violently, with the intention of shocking audiences. Their compositions often achieved the intended effect: Arnold Schoenberg's early experiments with dissonance were received at first with hoots by a hostile public in Vienna in 1913; and Igor Stravinsky's dissonant chords and pounding rhythms caused a riot at the first performance of *Le Sacre du printemps (The Rite of Spring)* in Paris that same year. Such avant-garde composers sought to shake their listeners out of a state of complacency, to yank them out of the Romantic mists and back to harsh reality.

One can see clear parallels between the music and the visual art of this period: early-twentieth-century painters also introduced radical distortions into their works, similarly offending middle-class sensibilities. The increasingly angular melody and discontinuous rhythm of the new music found analogous expression in an artistic style called **Cubism.** In a Cubist painting, the artist fractures and dislocates formal reality into geometrical blocks and planes, as in the famous *Les Demoiselles d'Avignon* (Fig. 32-1), created in 1907 by Pablo Picasso (1881–1973), where the female form has been recast into angular, interlocking shapes. Picasso seems to have found his musical counterpart in Stravinsky—the two friends admired each other's works and occasionally collaborated artistically. Schoenberg, a talented painter himself, found artistic camaraderie in the works of the German Expressionist painters (see p. 344), who so distorted formal reality that objects in their paintings were sometimes barely recognizable. Just as traditional (singable) melody disappeared from early modernist music, so, too, the conventional figure vanished from avant-garde painting (Fig. 32-2).

FIGURE 32–1

One of the first statements of Cubist art, Picasso's *Les Demoiselles d'Avignon* (1907). The ladies of the evening are depicted by means of geometric shapes on a flat, two-dimensional plane. Like much avant-garde music of the time, Cubist paintings reject the emotionalism and decorative appeal of nineteenth-century art.

FIGURE 32–2

The angularity and disjointed quality of much early-twentieth-century melody can also be seen in contemporary painting. In Picasso's *Three Musicians* (1921), for example, the figures are fractured and out of alignment. Compare the disjunct melody of Arnold Schoenberg given in Example 32-1.

$\mathscr{E}$ARLY-TWENTIETH-CENTURY MUSICAL STYLE

The early twentieth century was a period of stylistic diversity and conflict. During these years, Gustav Mahler continued to write his massive symphonies in a predominantly Romantic idiom (see Chapter 30), while Claude Debussy composed in the Impressionist style (see Chapter 31), an early French forerunner of modernism. At the same time, the most progressive composers of art music turned to radical, indeed shocking, new ways of expressing melody, harmony, rhythm, and tone color.

Melody: More Angularity and Chromaticism

Unlike the melodies of the Romantic period, many of which are song-like in style and

therefore easily sung and remembered, there are very few themes in twentieth-century music that the listener goes away humming. In fact, melody per se is less important to the avant-garde composer than is a pulsating rhythm, an unusual texture, or a new sonority. If Romantic melody is generally smooth, diatonic, and conjunct in motion (moving more by steps than by leaps), early-twentieth-century melody tends to be fragmented, chromatic, and angular. The young avant-garde composers went to great lengths to *avoid* writing conjunct, stepwise lines. Rather than moving up a half-step from C to D♭, for example, they were wont to jump down a major seventh to the D♭ an octave below. Avoiding a simple interval for a more distant one an octave above or below is called **octave displacement;** it is a feature of modern music. So, too, is the heavy use of chromaticism. In the following example by Arnold Schoenberg (1874–1951), notice how the melody makes large leaps where it might more easily move by steps and also how several sharps and flats are introduced to produce a highly chromatic line.

EXAMPLE 32–1

Harmony: The "Emancipation of Dissonance," New Chords, New Systems

Ever since the late Middle Ages, the basic building block of Western music had been the triad—a consonant, three-note chord (see p. 34). A composer might introduce dissonance (a nontriad tone) for variety and tension, yet the rules of consonant harmony required that a dissonant pitch move (resolve) immediately to a consonant one. During the late Romantic period, however, composers like Richard Wagner (1813–1883) began to enrich their music with more and more chromaticism. By the first decade of the twentieth century, composers such as Arnold Schoenberg were using so much dissonance that the triad had all but disappeared. Schoenberg famously referred to this development as "the emancipation of dissonance," meaning that dissonance was now liberated from the requirement that it move to a consonance. At first, audiences rebelled when they heard Schoenberg's dissonance-filled scores, but the composer ultimately succeeded in "raising the bar" for what the ear might stand and preparing listeners for a much higher level of dissonance in both classical and popular music. Indeed, the work of Schoenberg and like-minded composers paved the way, albeit indirectly, for the heavy dissonances of today's progressive jazz and the dissonant "metal" styles of Metallica, Slipknot, and others.

Early-twentieth-century composers created dissonance not only by obscuring or distorting the traditional triad but also by introducing new chords. One technique for creating new chords was the superimposition of more thirds above the consonant triad. In this way were produced not only the **seventh chord** (a seventh chord spans seven letters of the scale, from A to G, for example) but also the **ninth chord** and the **eleventh chord.** The more thirds that were added on top of the basic triad, the more dissonant the sound of the chord.

EXAMPLE 32–2

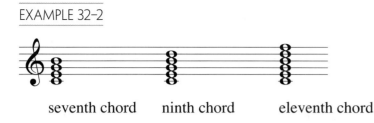

seventh chord   ninth chord   eleventh chord

The ultimate new chord was the **tone cluster,** the simultaneous sounding of a number of pitches only a whole step or a half step apart. Example 32-3 shows a tone cluster created by the American modernist Charles Ives (1874–1954). But you, too, can create this high-dissonance chord simply by striking a group of adjacent keys on the piano with your fist or forearm. Try it.

EXAMPLE 32–3   TONE CLUSTER

Chromatic dissonance, new chords, and tone clusters all weakened the traditional role of tonality in music. Remember that triads had belonged to an interlocking system (key) and that each moved progressively toward a tonic (see p. 35). As the triad disappeared, so, too, did the feeling of a key and the pull of a tonic. What were composers to do without triads, keys, and tonality, all of which had provided a structural framework for music? Simply said, they invented new systems to give structure to music. As we shall see, Igor Stravinsky anchored much of his music in long ostinatos, while Arnold Schoenberg invented an entirely new type of musical structure called the twelve-tone method.

Rhythm: New Asymmetrical Rhythms and Irregular Meters

Most art music before the twentieth century, as well as most of our pop and rock music down to the present day, is built on regular patterns of duple ($\frac{2}{4}$), triple ($\frac{3}{4}$), or quadruple ($\frac{4}{4}$) meter. Romantic music of the previous generation of composers had many qualities to recommend it: direct expression, broad themes, powerful climaxes, and moments of tender lyricism, to name several. But only rarely was Romantic music carried along by an exciting, vital rhythm; instead, it stayed within the comfortable confines of regular accents and duple or triple meter.

At the turn of the twentieth century, composers of art music began to rebel against the rhythmic and metric regularity that had governed most of nineteenth-century music. Musicians such as Stravinsky and Béla Bartók began to write music in which syncopations and measures with odd numbers of beats made it all but impossible for the listener to feel regular metrical patterns. Accents moved from one pulse to another, and meters changed from measure to measure. In abandoning the traditional structures of regular rhythms and consistent meters, these composers mirrored the techniques of modern poets like Gertrude Stein (1874–1946) and T. S. Eliot (1888–1965), who dispensed with traditional poetic meters and repeating accents in favor of free verse.

FIGURE 32–3

Lines of varying lengths can be seen as analogous to measures of different lengths caused by changing meters. Theo van Doesburg's *Rhythms of a Russian Dance* (1918) was surely inspired by the Russian sounds of Igor Stravinsky's *The Rite of Spring* (1913).

Digital Image © The Museum of Modern Art/Licensed by Scala/Art Resource, NY

Tone Color: New Sounds from New Sources

Twentieth-century composers created a brave new world of sound. This came about in large part because many musicians were dissatisfied with the string-dominated tone of the Romantic symphony orchestra. The string sound, with its lush vibrato, was thought to be too gentle, perhaps too mushy and sentimental, for the harsh realities of the modern world. So the strings, which had traditionally carried the melody, relinquished this role to the sharper, crisper woodwinds. Instead of playing a sweeping melody, the violinists might now be called on to beat on the strings with the wooden part of the bow or to take their hands and strike the instrument on its sound box. This preference for percussive effects over lyrical melody was also reflected in the new importance assigned the instruments of the percussion family. Entire pieces were written for percussion instruments alone. Instruments such as the xylophone, glockenspiel, and celesta were added to the group (see p. 50), and objects that produced an unfixed pitch, like the cowbell, brake drum, and police siren, were also heard on occasion. Finally, the piano, which in the Romantic era had been favored for its lyrical "singing" tone, came to be used as an orchestral instrument prized for the percussive way in which the hammers could be made to strike the strings.

Introducing new instruments, or having traditional instruments make new sounds by means of novel playing techniques, was an important innovation. But a more radical development came about as composers began to think of musical color as a wholly independent expressive element. During the Classical and Romantic periods, sounds of different colors were used mainly as a way to demarcate themes, and thus to articulate the form of a composition. The second theme in sonata–allegro form, for example, was often assigned to a new instrument, thereby emphasizing for listeners that a new theme had entered. The use of tone color as a servant of melody came to an end at the turn of the twentieth century, when Claude Debussy began to use color, independent of melody, to give form to a work. But Debussy's innovation was carried to radical lengths by later composers such as Charles Ives (1874–1954), Edgard Varèse (1883–1965), and John Cage (1912–1992), whose works sometimes seem to do nothing but progress from bright tones spaced far apart to dark tones densely grouped. These compositions may have no melody or harmony as traditionally conceived, but instead only clusters or streams of sounds with changing colors. This approach to color and line is, of course, similar to the one taken by avant-garde painters of the early twentieth century, who deconstructed recognizable figures in order to emphasize the emotive power of pure color (Figs. 31-6, 33-3, and 33-4). The bold recognition that color alone can elicit a strong emotional response from the listener or viewer was arguably the most significant development in the history of early modern music and painting.

The materials on the text website will help you understand and pass tests on the content of this chapter. In addition, you may view Active Listening Guides and other materials that will help you succeed in this course.

Key WORDS

Cubism (333)
octave displacement (334)

seventh chord (334)
ninth chord (334)
eleventh chord (334)

tone cluster (335)

EARLY-TWENTIETH-CENTURY MODERNISM

33

Among the composers of the early twentieth century, no two had a greater influence on the course of Western musical history than Igor Stravinsky and Arnold Schoenberg. Each composed masterpieces still performed by orchestras today, and each had his own vision as to the direction modernist art should take. Schoenberg ultimately developed what is called the twelve-tone system of composition, while Stravinsky, after perfecting flamboyant modernist ballet, moved on to a more restrained idiom called Neo-classicism.

IGOR STRAVINSKY (1882–1971)

For three-quarters of the twentieth century, Igor Stravinsky personified the cultural pluralism and stylistic diversity of cutting-edge art music (Fig. 33-1). He created masterpieces in many different genres: opera, ballet, symphony, concerto, church Mass, and cantata. His versatility was such that he could write a ballet for baby elephants (*Circus Polka,* 1942) just as easily as he could set to music a Greek classical drama (*Oedipus Rex,* 1927). Throughout his long life, he traveled with the fashionable set of high art. Although reared in St. Petersburg, Russia, he later lived in Paris, Venice, Lausanne, New York, and Hollywood. Forced to become an expatriate by the Russian Revolution (1917), he took French citizenship in 1934, and then, having moved to the United States at the outbreak of World War II, he became an American citizen in 1945. He counted among his friends the painter Pablo Picasso (1881–1973), the novelist Aldous Huxley (1894–1963), and the poet T. S. Eliot (1888–1965). On his eightieth birthday, in 1962, he was honored by President John F. Kennedy at the White House and, later in the same year, by Russian Premier Nikita Khrushchev in the Kremlin. He died in New York in 1971 at the age of eighty-eight.

Stravinsky rose to international fame as a composer of ballet music. In 1908, his early scores caught the attention of Sergei Diaghilev (1872–1929), the legendary **impresario** (producer) of Russian opera and ballet (Fig. 33-2). Diaghilev wanted to bring modern Russian ballet to Paris, at that time the artistic capital of the world. So he formed a dance company, called the *Ballets russes* (Russian Ballets), and hired, over the course of time, the most progressive artists he could find: Pablo Picasso and Henri Matisse for scenic designs (see Figs. 32-1, 32-2, 33-3, and 33-4), and Claude Debussy, Maurice Ravel, and Stravinsky, among others, as composers. Stravinsky soon became the principal composer of the company, and the *Ballets russes* became the focus of his musical activity for the next ten years. Accordingly, the decade 1910–1920 has become known as Stravinsky's Russian ballet period.

With the onset of World War I and the concurrent disappearance of large symphony orchestras in Europe, Stravinsky, along with others, developed a

FIGURE 33-1
Igor Stravinsky.

FIGURE 33-2
Sergei Diaghilev in New York in 1916.

@

Watch a video of Craig Wright's Open Yale Course class session 22, "Modernism and Mahler," at the text website.

FIGURES 33–3 AND 33–4

(top) In 1909, Henri Matisse painted the first of two canvases titled *Dance*. Here he achieves a raw primitive power by exaggerating a few basic lines and employing a few cool tones. Two years later, he created an even more intense vision of the same scene. (bottom) In *Dance* (1911), Matisse uses greater angularity and more intense colors, and thereby inspires a more intense reaction to this later version of a primitive dance scene.

style called **Neo-classicism,** which emphasized classical forms and smaller ensembles of the sort that had existed in the Baroque and Classical periods. Stravinsky's Neo-classical period extended from 1920 until 1951, when he adopted the twelve-tone technique of Arnold Schoenberg, which he continued to pursue until his death.

Although Stravinsky's style continually evolved over the course of nearly seventy years, a recognizable "Stravinsky sound" is always evident. In simple terms, his music is lean, clean, and cool. Stravinsky's instrumental colors are not "homogenized" sounds, as when the winds and strings together join on a single line, but rather distinctly separate colors. While his orchestra is sometimes large, he downplays the warm strings, preferring instead the tones of piercing winds and brittle percussion. Thus, while his orchestral scores are often opulent, they are rarely lush or sentimental. Most important, rhythm is the vital element in Stravinsky's compositional style. His beat is strong, but often metrically irregular, and he builds complexity by requiring independent meters and rhythms to sound simultaneously (see below). Many of these stylistic traits can be heard in his most famous work, *The Rite of Spring*, a watershed of early musical modernism.

Le Sacre du Printemps (The Rite of Spring, *1913*)

Igor Stravinsky composed three important early ballet scores for Diaghilev's dance company: *The Firebird* (1910), *Petrushka* (1911), and *The Rite of Spring* (1913). All are built on Russian folk tales—a legacy of musical nationalism (see Chapter 29)—and all make use of the large, colorful orchestra of the late nineteenth century. Yet the choreography for these Russian ballets is not the elegant, graceful ballet in the Romantic tradition, the sort that we associate with Tchaikovsky's *Swan Lake* and *The Nutcracker* (see p. 265). These are modern dances with angular poses and abrupt, jerky motions (see Figs. 33-3 and 33-4). To inspire this dance in the modern style, Stravinsky composed rhythms and chords that explode with a primordial force.

Although *The Rite of Spring* has been called *the* great masterpiece of modern music, at its premiere it provoked not admiration but a riot of dissent. This premiere, the most notorious in the history of Western music, took place on an unusually hot evening, May 29, 1913, at the newly built Théâtre Champs-Élysées in Paris. With the very first sounds of the orchestra, many in the packed theater voiced, shouted, and hissed their displeasure. Some, feigning auditory pain, yelled for a doctor, others for two. There were arguments and flying fists as opponents and partisans warred over this Russian brand of modern art. To restore calm, the curtain was lowered momentarily and the house lights were turned on and off. All in vain. The musicians still could not be heard, and consequently, the dancers had difficulty following the pulse of the music. The disorder was experienced firsthand by a visiting critic of the *New York Press*, who reported as follows:

I was sitting in a box in which I had rented one seat. Three ladies sat in front of me and a young man occupied the place behind me. He stood up during the course of the ballet to enable himself to see more clearly. The intense excitement under which he was laboring, thanks to the potent force of the music, betrayed itself presently when he began to beat rhythmically on the top of my head with his fists. My emotion was so great that I did not feel the blows for some time. They were perfectly synchronized with the beat of the music!

In truth, the violent reaction to *The Rite of Spring* was in part a response to the modernist choreography, which sought to obliterate any trace of classical ballet: the dance was just as "primitive" as Stravinsky's musical score. But what aspects, specifically, of Stravinsky's music shocked so many in the audience that night?

PERCUSSIVE ORCHESTRA

First, there is a new percussive—one might say "heavy metal"—approach to the orchestra. The percussion section is enlarged to include four timpani, a triangle, a tambourine, a guiro, cymbals, antique cymbals, a bass drum, and a tam-tam. Even the string family, the traditional provider of warmth and richness in the symphony orchestra, is required to play percussively, attacking the strings with repeated down-bows at seemingly random moments of accent. Instead of warm, lush sounds, we hear bright, brittle, almost brutal ones pounded out by percussion, heavy woodwinds, and brasses.

IRREGULAR ACCENTS

Stravinsky intensifies the effect of his harsh, metallic sounds by placing them where they are not expected, on unaccented beats, thereby creating explosive syncopations. Notice in the following example, the famous beginning of "Augurs of Spring," how the strings accent (>) the second, fourth, and then first pulses of subsequent four-pulse measures. In this way, Stravinsky destroys ordinary 1-2-3-4- meter and forces us to hear, in succession, groups of 4, 5, 2, 6, 3, 4, and 5 pulses—a conductor's nightmare!

EXAMPLE 33–1

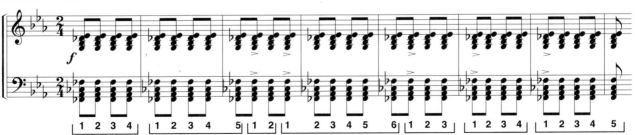

POLYMETER

The rhythm of *The Rite of Spring* is complex because Stravinsky often superimposes two or more different meters simultaneously. Notice in Example 33-2

Download Supplementary Listening Guides for the conclusion of Stravinsky, *The Firebird*, and Scene 1 from *Petrushka* at the text website.

that the oboe plays in $\frac{6}{8}$ time, the E♭ clarinet plays in $\frac{7}{8}$, while the B♭ clarinet is in $\frac{5}{8}$. This is an example of **polymeter**—two or more meters sounding simultaneously.

EXAMPLE 33–2

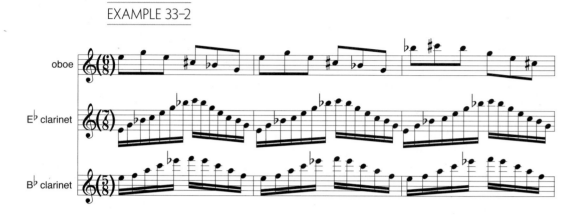

POLYRHYTHM

Not only do individual parts often play separate meters, but they also sometimes project two or more independent rhythms simultaneously. Look at the reduced score given in Example 33-3. Every instrument seems to be doing its own thing! In fact, six distinct rhythms can be heard, offering a good example of **polyrhythm**—the simultaneous sounding of two or more rhythms.

@

To see a demonstration of how various meters can be combined, watch "Extreme Polymetric Ostinato Demonstration" in the YouTube playlist on the text website.

EXAMPLE 33-3

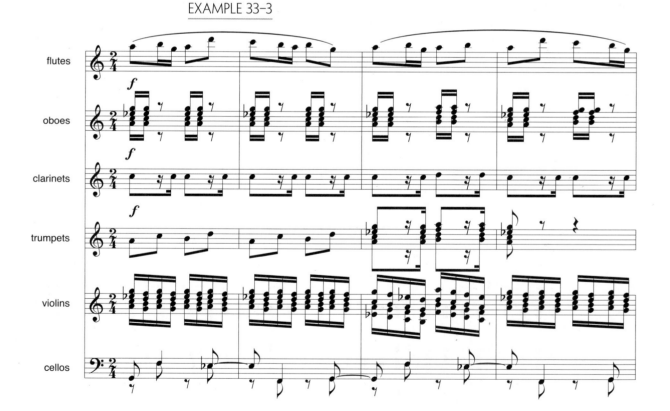

OSTINATO FIGURES

Notice also in Example 33-3 that most of the instruments play the same motive over and over at the same pitch level. Such a repeating figure, as we have seen, is called an ostinato. In this instance, we hear multiple ostinatos. Stravinsky was not the first twentieth-century composer to use ostinatos extensively—Debussy had done so earlier in his Impressionist scores (see p. 327). But Stravinsky employs them more often and for longer spans than did his predecessors. In *The Rite of Spring*, ostinatos give the music its incessant, driving quality, especially in the sections with fast tempos.

DISSONANT POLYCHORDS

The harsh, biting sound that is heard throughout much of *The Rite of Spring* is often created by two triads, or a triad and a seventh chord sounding at once. What results is a **polychord**—the simultaneous sounding of one triad or seventh chord with another (Fig. 33-5). When the individual chords of a polychord are only a whole step or a half step apart, the result is especially dissonant. In Example 33-4, the passage from the beginning of "Augurs of Spring," a seventh chord built on E♭ is played simultaneously with a major triad built on F♭.

EXAMPLE 33–4

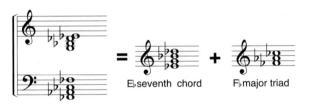

E♭ seventh chord   F♭ major triad

THE PLOT

The plot of *The Rite of Spring* is suggested by its subtitle: *Pictures of Pagan Russia*. Part 1, "The Kiss of the Earth," depicts the springtime rituals of primitive Slavic tribes. In Part 2, "The Sacrifice," a virgin dances herself to death as an offering to the god of spring. Before the curtain rises on Part 1, the orchestra

---

@

Download Supplementary Listening Guides for Stravinsky's *The Rite of Spring*, Part 1, Scenes 2 and 3, and Part 2, at the text website.

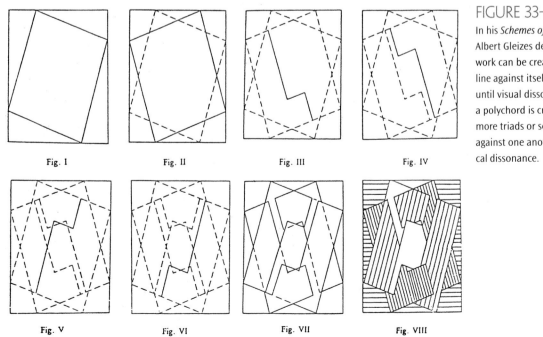

Fig. I   Fig. II   Fig. III   Fig. IV

Fig. V   Fig. VI   Fig. VII   Fig. VIII

FIGURE 33–5

In his *Schemes of Painting* (1922), the artist Albert Gleizes demonstrates that a Cubist work can be created by rotating a figure or line against itself, and then again and again until visual dissonance results. Similarly, a polychord is created by placing two or more triads or seventh chords off center and against one another, thereby creating musical dissonance.

plays an Introduction. This music unfolds gradually but inexorably, from soft to loud, and from one line to many, suggesting the flora and fauna of the earth coming to life with the beginning of spring. The first scene, "Augurs of Spring," features jarring, almost brutal accents (see Ex. 33-1) and pounding dissonance (see Ex. 33-4). Yet there are also lyrical, almost sensuous moments in the score, especially when Stravinsky incorporates folk songs, whether quoting authentic Russian songs or (more commonly) composing his own melodies within this folk idiom. Despite the folkloric element, the bulk of the composition came from within. As Stravinsky declared, "I had only my ears to guide me. I heard and I wrote what I heard. I am the vessel through which *The Rite of Spring* passed."

*L*istening GUIDE

Igor Stravinsky
The Rite of Spring (1913)
Introduction and Scene 1

5   **2**
5/9–10   2/18–19

Genre: Ballet music

INTRODUCTION

(Awakening of earth; curtain still down)

0:00	**9** **18**	Bassoon writhing in high register
0:21		Other winds (bass clarinet, English horn, another bassoon, high clarinet) gradually enter
1:40		Flutes play in parallel motion
1:56		Writhing woodwinds continue
2:40		Ostinato in bass supports gradual orchestral crescendo
3:03		Bassoon melody returns, clarinet trills

AUGURS OF SPRING: DANCES OF THE ADOLESCENTS

(Youthful dancers pound onto stage; male and female groups entice one another; attention shifts to more folk-like dances of girls)

0:00	**10** **19**	Elemental pounding of dissonant string chords punctuated by blasts from French horns and trumpets (see Ex. 33-1)
0:48		Bassoons and then trombones play stepwise motive
1:19		*Fortissimo* chords and timpani blows
1:43		French horn plays folk-like melody
2:05		Flute plays melody
2:20		Trumpets play new folk-like melody
2:54		Gradual orchestral crescendo

🎵 Listen to streaming music in an Active Listening Guide, available on the text website.

Listening EXERCISE 39

Stravinsky

THE RITE OF SPRING

5 **2**

5/9–10   2/18–19

@   To take this Listening Exercise online and receive feedback or email answers to your instructor, go to the text website.

As you listen to the Introduction of *The Rite of Spring*, you may be shocked by its dissonant, seemingly "disorganized" sound. You will find it difficult to identify a tonic pitch or a familiar scale that governs the music. To "stabilize" the music in the absence of a core tonality, Stravinsky employs several ostinatos. These ostinatos not only help hold the music together but also impart a feeling of kinetic energy—energy continually being recycled and renewed, like spring itself. The following exercise asks you to focus on the ostinatos in the Introduction and Scene 1. Hearing these ostinatos will not always be easy. Listen carefully to the inner parts. Are ostinatos present? Answer "yes" or "no" below.

9/18

1. (0:35–0:56) _____
2. (2:12–2:26) _____
3. (2:40–3:02) _____
4. (3:02–3:30) _____
5. (3:31–3:39) _____

10/19

6. (0:25–0:38) _____

7. (1:19–1:25) _____
8. (1:26–1:40) _____
9. (2:15–2:35) _____
10. Judging from your responses, are there more moments in *The Rite of Spring* that make use of an ostinato than those that do not? _____

Following the *succès de scandale* that attended the premiere of *The Rite of Spring*, Stravinsky extracted the music from the ballet itself and presented it as an independent orchestral suite. The music alone was now recognized as an important, if controversial, statement of the musical avant-garde. Later, in 1940, the score of *The Rite of Spring* furnished the music for an important segment of Walt Disney's early full-length animated film, *Fantasia*. For a brief moment, in Disney's *Fantasia*, musical modernism had become mainstream.

ARNOLD SCHOENBERG AND THE SECOND VIENNESE SCHOOL

Ironically, the most radical shoot of musical modernism took root in Vienna, a city with a long history of conservatism. In the early twentieth century, a trio of native Viennese musicians—Arnold Schoenberg (1874–1951), Alban Berg (1885–1935), and Anton Webern (1883–1945)—ventured to take high-art music in a completely new direction. The close association of these three innovative composers has come to be called the **Second Viennese School** (the first, of course, consisted of Mozart, Haydn, and Beethoven—see p. 162).

Arnold Schoenberg, the leader of this group, almost single-handedly thrust musical modernism upon a reluctant Viennese public. Schoenberg was from a Jewish family of modest means and was largely self-taught as a musician. As a young man, he worked as a bank clerk during the day but studied literature, philosophy, and music at night, becoming a competent performer on the violin and cello. He came to know the music of Brahms, Wagner, and Mahler, mostly by playing their scores and attending concerts. Having "left the world of bank notes for musical notes" at the age of twenty-one, he earned a humble living by conducting a men's chorus, orchestrating operettas—the Viennese counterpart of our Broadway musicals—and giving lessons in music theory and composition. Eventually, his own compositions began to be heard in Vienna, though they were usually not well received.

@

Download a Supplementary
Listening Guide for
Schoenberg's *A Survivor from
Warsaw,* at the text website.

Schoenberg's earliest works are written in the late Romantic style, with rich harmonies, chromatic melodies, expansive forms, and programmatic content. But by 1908, his music had begun to evolve in unexpected directions. Strongly influenced by Wagner's chromatic melodies and harmonies, Schoenberg started to compose works with no tonal center. If Wagner could write winding chromatic passages that temporarily obscured the tonality, why not go one step further and create fully chromatic pieces in which there is no tonality? This Schoenberg did, and in so doing created what is called **atonal music**—music without tonality, without a key center (see also the boxed essay).

Schoenberg's contemporaries found his atonal music difficult. Not only was there no tonal center, but the melodies were highly disjunct, and the harmony exceedingly dissonant (see p. 134). Some performers refused to play his music, and when others did, audience reaction was occasionally violent. At one concert on March 31, 1913, the police had to be called in to restore order. Despite this hostility, Schoenberg remained true to his own vision, offering this directive to all creative artists: "One must be convinced of the infallibility of one's own fantasy; one must believe in one's own creative spirit."

Pierrot Lunaire (Moonstruck Pierrot, *1912*)

Pierrot lunaire (Moonstruck Pierrot), Schoenberg's best-known composition, is an exemplary work of Expressionist art. It is a setting for chamber ensemble and female voice of twenty-one poems by Albert Giraud. Here we meet Pierrot, a white-faced clown from the world of traditional Italian pantomime and

EXPRESSIONISM AND ATONALITY

Arnold Schoenberg and his students Alban Berg and Anton Webern were not alone in creating a radically new style of art. As we have seen, there appeared at this same time a powerful movement in the visual arts called Expressionism. **Expressionism** was initially a German-Austrian development that arose in Berlin, Munich, and Vienna. Its aim was not to depict objects as they are seen but to express the strong emotion that the object generated in the artist; not to paint a portrait of an individual but to express the subject's innermost feelings, anxieties, and fears. In Edvard Munch's early Expressionist painting *The Scream* (1893), the subject cries out to an unsympathetic and uncomprehending world. Schoenberg's statement in this regard can be taken as a credo for the entire Expressionist movement: "Art is

The Scream, *by Edvard Munch.*

the cry of despair of those who experience in themselves the fate of all Mankind" (1910). Gradually, realistic representations gave way to highly personal and increasingly abstract expression. Schoenberg was himself a painter and exhibited his works with the Expressionists in 1912. In fact, the music and art of this movement can be described in rather similar terms. The clashing of strong colors, the disjointed shapes, and the jagged lines of the painters have their counterparts in the harsh dissonances, asymmetrical rhythms, and angular, chromatic melodies of Schoenberg and his followers. It is surely not an accident that Schoenberg moved from tonality to atonality in music (1908–1912) at precisely the time that Munch and others turned away from realistic representation to abstract expression.

puppet shows. Yet in this Expressionist poetry, the clown has fallen under the sway of the moon and changed into an alienated modern artist. Pierrot projects his inner anxiety by means of ***Sprechstimme*** (speech-voice), a vocal technique that requires the vocalist to declaim the text more than to sing it. The voice is to execute the rhythmic values exactly; but once it hits a pitch, it is to quit the tone immediately, sliding away in either a downward or an upward direction. This creates exaggerated declamation of the sort one might hear from a lunatic, which is appropriate for Pierrot, given the lunar spell cast upon him.

Poem 6 of *Pierrot lunaire* depicts the protagonist's tormented, hallucinatory vision of the suffering Madonna at the cross. Its poetic form is that of a *rondeau*, an ancient musical and poetic form marked by the use of a refrain (set in boldface type in the Listening Guide). Traditionally, composers had used the appearance of a textual refrain to repeat the melody as well, thereby creating musical unity (see p. 248). However, Schoenberg, the iconoclast, repeats the text but not the music. Thus his music unfolds in an ever-varying continuum, like a stream of consciousness. Perhaps not coincidentally, precisely during the years that Schoenberg was creating this music of intense introspection, Sigmund Freud originated the theory of psychoanalysis, also in Vienna.

The absence of obvious repetition in Schoenberg's music—nothing is allowed to become familiar—places unprecedented demands on the listener. Your first reaction to the dissonant continuum of sound in *Pierrot lunaire* may be decidedly negative. Yet with repeated hearings, the force of the jarring elements of the atonal style begins to lessen, and a bizarre, eerie sort of beauty emerges, especially if you are sensitive to the meaning of the text.

@

Download Supplementary Listening Guides for four more sections of *Pierrot lunaire—Valse de Chopin, Der kranke Mond, Nacht,* and *Der Mondfleck*—at the text website.

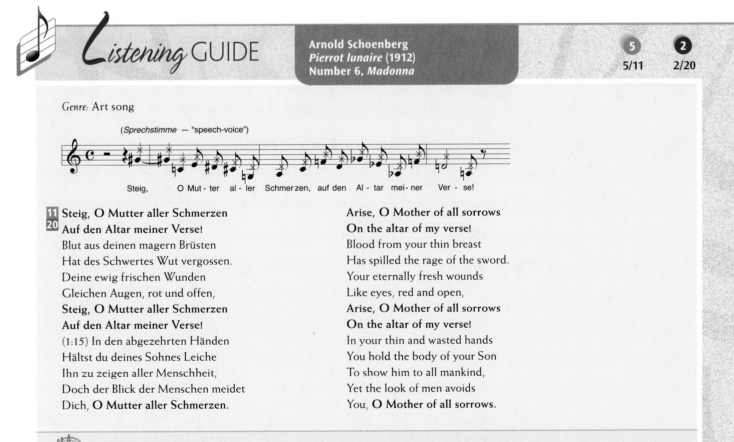

Listening GUIDE

Arnold Schoenberg
Pierrot lunaire (1912)
Number 6, *Madonna*

5 5/11   **2** 2/20

Genre: Art song

(*Sprechstimme* — "speech-voice")

Steig, O Mut - ter al - ler Schmerzen, auf den Al - tar mei - ner Ver - se!

11 20 Steig, O Mutter aller Schmerzen	**Arise, O Mother of all sorrows**
Auf den Altar meiner Verse!	**On the altar of my verse!**
Blut aus deinen magern Brüsten	Blood from your thin breast
Hat des Schwertes Wut vergossen.	Has spilled the rage of the sword.
Deine ewig frischen Wunden	Your eternally fresh wounds
Gleichen Augen, rot und offen,	Like eyes, red and open,
Steig, O Mutter aller Schmerzen	**Arise, O Mother of all sorrows**
Auf den Altar meiner Verse!	**On the altar of my verse!**
(1:15) In den abgezehrten Händen	In your thin and wasted hands
Hältst du deines Sohnes Leiche	You hold the body of your Son
Ihn zu zeigen aller Menschheit,	To show him to all mankind,
Doch der Blick der Menschen meidet	Yet the look of men avoids
Dich, **O Mutter aller Schmerzen.**	You, **O Mother of all sorrows.**

Listen to streaming music in an Active Listening Guide, available on the text website.

Schoenberg's Twelve-Tone Music

When Arnold Schoenberg and his followers did away with tonal chord progressions and repeating melodies, they found themselves facing a serious artistic problem: how to write large-scale compositions in the new atonal style. For centuries, musical structures, like fugue and sonata–allegro form, had been generated by means of a clear tonal plan and the repetition of broad musical themes—repetition created form. But Schoenberg's chromatic, atonal, nonrepeating melodies made traditional musical forms all but impossible. What other formal plan might be used? If all twelve notes of the chromatic scale are equally important, as is the case in atonal music, why choose any one note or another at a given moment?

By 1923, Schoenberg had solved the problem of "formal anarchy"—the absence of form caused by total chromatic freedom. He discovered a new way of creating music that he called "composing with twelve tones." **Twelve-tone composition** is a method of writing that employs each of the twelve notes of the chromatic scale set in a fixed, predetermined order. The composer begins by arranging the twelve notes of the chromatic scale in a sequence of his or her choosing, forming a "tone row." Throughout the composition, these twelve notes must come in the same order. Music in which elements such as pitch, timbre, or dynamics come in a fixed series is called **serial music.** In twelve-tone music, the twelve-note series may unfold not only as a melody but also as a melody with accompaniment, or simply as a progression of chords, since two or more notes of the row may sound simultaneously. Moreover, in addition to appearing in its basic form, the row might go backward (retrograde), or upside down (inversion), or both backward and upside down at the same time (retrograde inversion). While such arrangements might seem wholly artificial and very unmusical, we should remember that composers such as Johann Sebastian Bach in the Baroque era and Josquin Desprez in the Renaissance subjected their melodies to similar permutations. The purpose of Schoenberg's twelve-tone method was to create musical unity by basing each piece on a single, orderly arrangement of twelve tones, thereby guaranteeing the perfect equality of all pitches so that none would seem like a tonal center.

To see a biting satire of Schoenberg's and Berg's twelve-tone music, watch "Twelve Tone Commercial" in the YouTube playlist on the text website.

Trio from Suite for Piano (1924)

Schoenberg's first steps along this radical twelve-tone path were tentative, and the pieces that resulted were very short. Among Schoenberg's first serial compositions was his *Suite for Piano,* a collection of seven brief dance movements, including the Minuet and Trio to be discussed here. The tone row for the *Suite,* along with its three permutations, is as follows:

Row	Retrograde
E F G D♭ G♭ E♭ A♭ D B C A B♭	B♭ A C B D A♭ E♭ G♭ D♭ G F E
1 2 3 4 5 6 7 8 9 10 11 12	12 11 10 9 8 7 6 5 4 3 2 1

Inversion	Retrograde-inversion
E E♭ D♭ G D F C F♯ A G♯ B B♭	B♭ B G♯ A F♯ C F D G D♭ E♭ E
1 2 3 4 5 6 7 8 9 10 11 12	12 11 10 9 8 7 6 5 4 3 2 1

Schoenberg allows the row or any of its permutations to begin on any pitch, so long as the original sequence of intervals is maintained. Notice in the Trio, for example, that the row itself begins on E but is also allowed to start on B♭ (see Listening Guide). In the second part, measures 6–9, the exact serial progression

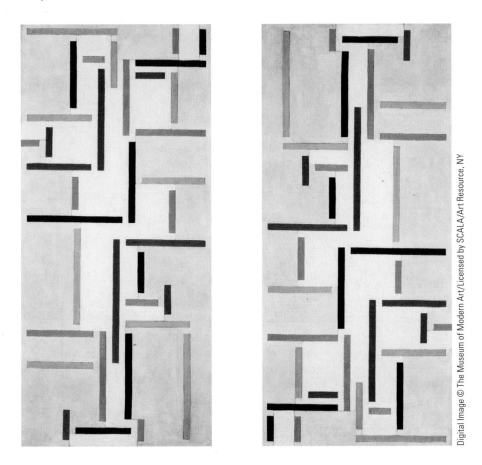

FIGURE 33-6

Artist Theo van Doesburg (1883–1931) often fashioned designs in retrograde motion (see his *Composition IV*, 1917), in which the pattern proceeding downward from the top left was the same as that upward from the bottom right. One can simulate the same effect by comparing his *Rhythms of a Russian Dance* (1918) in upright and rotated orientations.

Digital Image © The Museum of Modern Art/Licensed by SCALA/Art Resource, NY

of the row breaks down slightly. The composer explained this as a "justifiable deviation," owing to the need for tonal variety at this point. Notice as well that the rhythms in which the notes appear may likewise be changed for the sake of variety. As you listen to the Trio, see if you can follow the unfolding of the row and all its permutations. Listen many times—the piece is only fifty-one seconds long! Its aesthetic effect is similar to that of a constructivist painting of an artist like Theo van Doesburg (see Fig. 33-6). If you like the painting, you might well enjoy Schoenberg's twelve-tone piano piece as well.

Listening GUIDE

**Arnold Schoenberg
Trio from *Suite for Piano* (1924)**

5
5/12

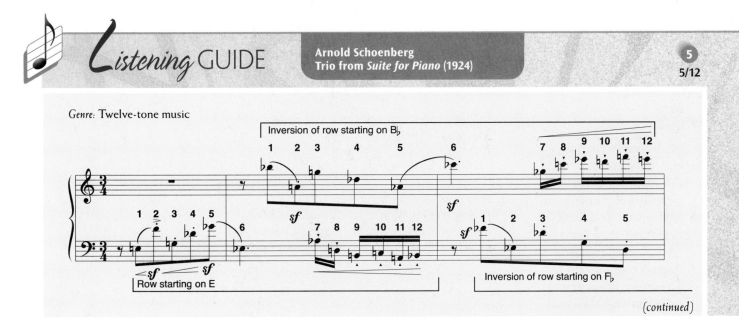

(continued)

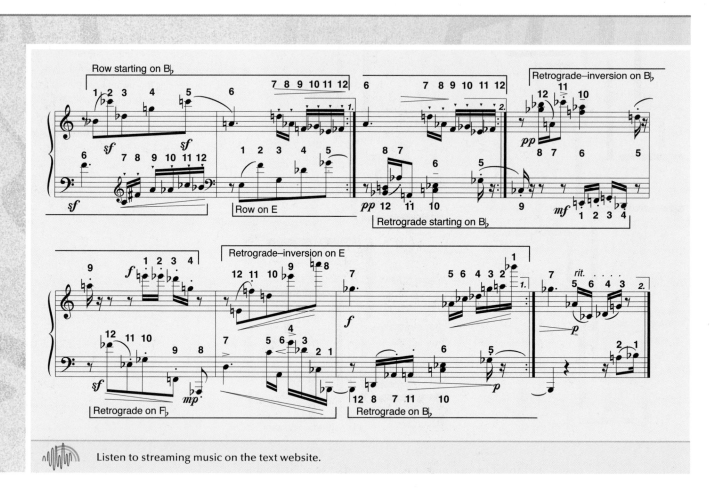

Listen to streaming music on the text website.

As the years progressed, Schoenberg used his twelve-tone method to construct longer compositions for larger forces. By 1932, he had completed most of a full-length opera, *Moses and Aaron,* and in 1947, he finished a long cantata, *A Survivor from Warsaw,* that tells of Nazi atrocities in Poland. Both works are in the twelve-tone style throughout. But the listening public never fully embraced twelve-tone music; the style is as inaccessible as Schoenberg's earlier atonal music. For most listeners, it sounds irrational and arbitrary, completely "out of control." Indeed, the twelve-tone system has been called one of the two great failed experiments of the twentieth century, the other being Communism. Schoenberg was philosophical about the public's general dislike of his music: "If it is art, it is not for all, and if it is for all, it is not art."

The materials on the text website will help you understand and pass tests on the content of this chapter. In addition, you may watch Craig Wright's own lecture at Open Yale Courses and complete this chapter's Listening Exercise interactively, as well as view Active Listening Guides and other materials that will help you succeed in this course.

Key WORDS

impresario (337)
Neo-classicism (338)
polymeter (340)
polyrhythm (340)
polychord (341)

Second Viennese School (343)
atonal music (344)
Expressionism (344)
Sprechstimme (345)

twelve-tone composition (346)
serial music (346)

RUSSIAN AND EASTERN EUROPEAN MODERNISM

34

We naturally tend to assume that Western civilization has been shaped primarily by those events that took place in the West itself. In the early twentieth century, however, several events of great importance to Western history occurred in Russia and Eastern Europe (Fig. 34-1). In 1917, the West was shaken by the **Russian Revolution,** the overthrow of the Russian tsar by the socialist Bolshevik Party. This turn of events paved the way for the establishment of a Communist-ruled Soviet Union in 1922, a development that led ultimately to the Cold War, which dominated Western foreign policy concerns for decades. We likewise tend to credit the military powers of the West with the defeat of Adolf Hitler and his Nazi regime in the Second World War. But while Western soldiers unquestionably played a vital role, the bulk of the fighting took place on the Russian Front. Apart from combat in the Pacific, fully 80 percent of soldiers killed in World War II died on the Russian Front—about 11 million Russians

FIGURE 34-1

Western Russia and Central and Eastern Europe, early twentieth century.

349

and 5 million Germans. Civilian casualties in the East likewise outnumbered those in the West. The number of civilian dead in Russia—victims of war, famine, and government purges—is estimated between 30 and 40 million. These horrors affected all segments of society, including artists, intellectuals, and musicians. Indeed, it is no exaggeration to say that the three composers discussed in this chapter had their lives ruined by the cataclysmic events that rocked Russia and Eastern Europe in these decades. We begin with Russia.

Progressive artists who worked in the Soviet Union during the dictatorship of Joseph Stalin (r1924–1953) did so under conditions that are incomprehensible today. During the 1920s and 1930s, the ruling Communist Party forcefully confiscated the wealth of the well-to-do and redistributed it collectively among the proletariat. Anything that smacked of "elitism"—anything that could not be immediately understood and enjoyed by the masses—was suspect. Heading the list of likely "subversives" were the names of almost all modern artists, including composers, and especially those who wrote in the atonal or twelve-tone style. The Soviet regime encouraged patriotic compositions, in which large choruses sang hymns of praise to the fatherland and to the working class—pieces to promote Communist propaganda. Soviet authorities referred to modern music as **formalism** and branded it "antidemocratic." To be identified as a "formalist" was tantamount to a death sentence. The challenge for a composer working under Stalin was to remain true to a personal artistic vision, yet remain alive.

SERGEY PROKOFIEV (1891–1953)

The career of Sergey Prokofiev is full of contradictions and ironies, caused in part by the place he occupied in Russian history. The son of a well-to-do farm administrator, he fled the Russian Revolution in 1917 but later returned to celebrate in music the most murderous of the revolutionaries, Joseph Stalin. Prokofiev was once known as the dissonant, atonal "bad boy" of the St. Petersburg Conservatory, where he received his musical education, but he later wrote such pleasantly benign works as *Peter and the Wolf* (1936). He thought of himself above all as a serious composer—the author of seven symphonies, six operas, six ballets, five piano concertos, and nine piano sonatas. Today, however, he is remembered mainly for his lighter works: the *Classical Symphony*, *Peter and the Wolf*, and the film scores *Lieutenant Kijé* and *Alexander Nevsky*.

The Russian Revolution (October 1917) has been called "the ten days that shook the world," and it certainly shook Prokofiev's world. With his family's wealth about to be confiscated, he took the Trans-Siberian Express eastward toward Japan and ultimately landed in San Francisco. After four years (1918–1922) as a composer-pianist in America, the vagabond Prokofiev moved to Paris where for a time he worked as a ballet composer for Sergei Diaghilev and his *Ballets russes* (see p. 337). But his career languished. Eager to have illustrious ex-patriots return to the Soviet Union and working through his secret police in Paris, dictator Joseph Stalin lured Prokofiev back home with the promise that a simpler, less dissonant musical style would bring both popular success and governmental approval.

Romeo and Juliet *(1935)*

Prokofiev's first official work as a Soviet composer was the ballet *Romeo and Juliet*, which he wrote for the famous Kirov Ballet of St. Petersburg during the summer of 1935. To conform to a Soviet artistic dictate of the day (no tragic endings), the composer penned a happy conclusion. Before the work could be staged, however, a reign of cultural terror fell upon all Soviet artists in 1936 (see p. 352), and Prokofiev withdrew the work. Not until five years later, in 1940, did the composer feel that the political environment was safe enough to allow the work to be performed.

What could possibly be controversial about *Romeo and Juliet*? Not the age-old story, nor the idea of romance, but rather Prokofiev's musical style. Prokofiev had been a dissonant and occasionally atonal composer before his return to the Soviet Union. Now his task was to meld his modernist tendencies with the required simple, melodious music the government demanded. As we listen to the ball scene from *Romeo and Juliet*, we can hear this modernist-populist dialectic at work. For a courtly dance, we would expect pleasant music. What we get is pleasing but not quite pleasant (bracing would be more accurate)—the initial music is dark (minor), somewhat disjunct melodically, and unstable tonally, sliding from one unexpected chord to another. Yet it has power and energy; we feel ourselves swaying to the beat of the regular, duple-meter bass line. As the *corps de ballet* exits to allow a *pas de deux* ("steps for two," here Paris and Juliet), the music becomes softer (high flutes), and the melody is strangely beautiful, owing to its slightly dissonant cast. Everywhere there is just enough hard edge and bite to Prokofiev's music to prevent this sentimental story from becoming sappy or kitschy. Sentimentality had no place in the modernist aesthetic.

Listening GUIDE

Sergey Prokofiev
"Dance of the Knights" from *Romeo and Juliet* (1935)

5
5/13

Genre: Ballet

Form: **ABCBA**

Situation: The ball scene as represented in Shakespeare's rendition, Act I, Scene 4. The young aristocrats of the Capulet clan dance; Juliet dances with Paris and is observed by an enthralled Romeo.

0:00	**13** A	Heavy, ponderous, yet powerful music in the low register; grows in volume and rises in pitch as more dancers come forward	
1:21		Heavy music of dance continues	
1:46	B	Light melody in triple meter for flutes accompanied by simple pizzicato strings	
2:51	C	Balancing melody in duple meter for solo oboe	
3:07	B	Return to contrasting flute melody	
3:48	A	Return to heavy duple meter dance led first by woodwinds (including saxophones) and then full orchestra and full corps of dancers	

Listen to streaming music in an Active Listening Guide, available on the text website.

Lebrecht Music & Arts

FIGURE 34-2

Dmitri Shostakovich.

FIGURE 34-3

Shostakovich, the "poster boy" for Russian resistance to German aggression, as presented to Americans in 1941.

Lebrecht Music & Arts

Had you been general secretary of the Communist Party at this time, would *you* have banned the music you just heard because its modernist sounds might cause social unrest? In fact, performances of Prokofiev's music were officially outlawed in 1948. That same year, his wife, Lina, was arrested by the secret police for "espionage" and sentenced to an exile of twenty years. With Prokofiev in ill health, his output dwindled to nothing. He died within a few minutes of his nemesis, Joseph Stalin, on the night of March 5, 1953. Yet news of Prokofiev's death was withheld for days so as not to deflect attention from the deceased dictator. No flowers could be bought for the great composer's coffin; the funeral of Stalin had, without exaggeration, claimed them all.

DMITRI SHOSTAKOVICH (1906–1975)

Prokofiev was not the only composer to suffer during Stalin's reign of terror. Dmitri Shostakovich (Fig. 34-2), a few years Prokofiev's junior, experienced even greater trauma.

Born to a musical family, Shostakovich showed exceptional promise from an early age. He had perfect pitch and could play through all of Bach's *Well-Tempered Clavier* by age eleven. In 1919, he entered the St. Petersburg Conservatory, where he studied harmony, orchestration, and composition. After mixed results in his courses at the Conservatory, Shostakovich achieved his first major success in 1925 with the completion and performance of his Symphony No. 1, which earned the composer international acclaim at the age of nineteen. In 1934, Shostakovich attracted widespread attention once again with his realistic opera *Lady Macbeth of the Mtsensk District*. But in 1936, his career prospects took a disastrous turn when Stalin attended a performance of his opera but walked out three-quarters of the way through. Two days later, Shostakovich's music was denounced in the official Soviet newspaper *Pravda* in an article titled "Chaos Instead of Music." As the composer later said, "I'll never forget that day [and] the bitterness that has colored my life gray."

Throughout his career, Shostakovich's relationship with the Soviet government was complex and ever-changing. During the 1930s and 1940s, he was the most popular composer of Russian high-art music. His symphonies were played not only at home but also throughout Europe and in the major cities of the United States and Canada. This international stature gave him a measure of protection; it was difficult for Stalin to exile such a public figure to a work camp, or to execute him, as he did other intellectuals. Indeed, in some years, Shostakovich was "in favor." In 1941, he won the Stalin Medal for service to the state and served as a "poster boy" for the spirit of Russian resistance in the war with Hitler's Germany (Fig. 34-3). But twice, in 1936 and 1948, his music was officially denounced as "formalistic" (see p. 350). After each condemnation, Shostakovich hid his most progressive scores (those with atonal or twelve-tone content) and "toned down" the modernist component in the little music that he did allow to be performed. This game of "cat and mouse"—with Shostakovich as the mouse—continued until the composer died from a heart attack in 1975.

Symphony No. 5 (1937)

In his Symphony No. 5, written the year following his first denunciation at the hands of the Soviet authorities, Shostakovich felt compelled to keep his modernist tendencies largely hidden from view. The work was a huge success when it premiered in November 1937. Here was music that the average listener—Stalin, for example—could understand. In spirit, Symphony No. 5 resembles the symphonies of Gustav Mahler (see p. 314), with their brilliant orchestrations and expressive, emotional character. Yet Shostakovich was fully a citizen of the twentieth century, intent on speaking with a fully modern voice. Here, while the progressive voice is, of necessity, somewhat muted, it can still be heard in the heavy percussion, moderate (but not extreme) dissonance, ostinatos, and "sliding harmonies" of the sort found in Prokofiev's *Romeo and Juliet* (see p. 351). Shostakovich would go on to compose ten more symphonies. While many of these are often performed today, the fifth remains his most popular. The exultant finale seems to signal the ultimate triumph of the human spirit. Yet in light of the circumstances under which it was written, critics still ask: Was the "rejoicing" expressed here truly felt, or was it feigned—forced from the composer? Shostakovich himself suggested the answer when he said, "The majority of my symphonies are tombstones."

Listening GUIDE

Dmitri Shostakovich
Symphony No. 5 (1937)
Fourth movement, *Allegro non troppo*
(fast, but not too fast)

5
5/14–16

Genre: Symphony

Form: Abbreviated sonata–allegro

EXPOSITION

0:00 14	Percussive sounds as low brasses play first theme	
0:32	First theme unfolds continually in brass, strings, and winds	
2:08	Trumpet introduces second theme above swirling mass of strings	
2:33	Violins sweep along with second theme in heroic fashion	
3:04	Low brasses play transition	
3:18	French horn plays lyrical solo (variant of second theme)	

DEVELOPMENT

3:51 15	0:00	Strings and then winds quietly develop second theme and then fragments of first
4:57	1:06	Hints of first theme begin to appear in low strings and then low brasses

ABBREVIATED RECAPITULATION

6:38 16	0:00	First theme returns quietly and somewhat altered with snare drum accompanying
7:30	0:52	First theme grows in intensity

CODA

8:11	1:33	Brasses play first theme slowly; intervals altered to change mode from minor to major
8:34	1:56	Harmony is static, holding on tonic pitch; timpani pounds dominant and tonic pitches

Listen to streaming music in an Active Listening Guide, available on the text website.

@ To take Listening Exercise 40 for this musical selection online and receive feedback or email answers to your instructor, go to the text website.

FIGURE 34–4

Béla Bartók.

FIGURE 34–5

Béla Bartók recording folk songs among Czech-speaking peasants in 1908. The performers sang into the megaphone of a wax-cylinder recording machine invented by Thomas Edison.

BÉLA BARTÓK (1881–1945)

The music of the Hungarian composer Béla Bartók (Fig. 34-4) is decidedly modern, yet distinctly different in sound from that of Stravinsky or Schoenberg. While it can be atonal, like the music of Schoenberg, it is often highly tuneful, making use of sweeping melodies. And while it is frequently percussive and highly rhythmic, like the motor-driven sounds of Stravinsky, Bartók's rhythmic force derives mainly from folk music. Bartók's creative imagination was fired by folk materials of his native Hungary (see Fig. 34-1). He saw the return to the simple, direct style of folk music as a way to counter the tendency in Romantic music toward ostentation and sentimentality.

The life of Béla Bartók was strongly affected by the turbulent events that occurred in Eastern Europe during the first half of the twentieth century. He was born in 1881 in Hungary, but in a part of that nation that was later given over to Romania at the end of World War I. Throughout his life, he was an ardent Hungarian nationalist, and he chose to develop his obvious musical talents at the Academy of Music in Budapest rather than at the German-dominated Vienna Conservatory, to which he had also been admitted. As a student at the academy in Budapest, he studied composition and piano, quickly acquiring a reputation as a concert pianist of the highest quality. By the 1920s, he had achieved an international reputation both as a pianist and as a composer of modernist music. His tours even carried him to the West Coast of the United States, where a local newspaper alerted the public to his coming with the following headline: "Hungarian Modernist Advances upon Los Angeles." As both a Hungarian modernist and nationalist, Bartók was an outspoken critic of the supporters of Nazi Germany who gained control of the Hungarian government in the late 1930s. He called the fascists "bandits and assassins," cut off ties with the German firm that published his music, and banned the performances of his works in Germany and Italy, thereby losing considerable performance and broadcast fees. Ultimately, in 1940, he fled to the United States.

Béla Bartók is rare among composers in that he was as much interested in musical research—specifically, in the study of Eastern European folk music—as in musical composition. He traveled from village to village in Hungary, Romania, Bulgaria, Turkey, and even North Africa using the newly invented recording machine of Thomas Edison (Fig. 34-5). In this way, his ear became saturated with the driving rhythms and odd-numbered meters of peasant dances, as well as the unusual scales on which the folk melodies of Eastern Europe were constructed.

The musical heritage of Eastern Europe is heard throughout Bartók's music, from his first string quartet (1908) to his great final works for

orchestra: *Music for Strings, Percussion and Celesta* (1936), *Divertimento for Strings* (1939), and *Concerto for Orchestra* (1943). This last-named piece was commissioned by the conductor of the Boston Symphony Orchestra for the then-substantial fee of $1,000. It remains Bartók's best-known and most alluring composition.

Download a Supplementary Listening Guide for the third movement of Bartók's *Music for Strings, Percussion and Celesta*, at the text website.

Concerto for Orchestra (1943)

Normally, concertos are written for a single solo instrument—piano or violin, for example—pitted against an orchestra. In Bartók's *Concerto for Orchestra*, however, the composer encourages many instruments to step forward from within the orchestra to serve as soloists from time to time. The spotlight switches from one instrument to another or to a new combination of instruments, each displaying its distinctive tonal color against the backdrop of the full orchestra. There are five movements. The first is "written in a more or less regular sonata form," as the composer says, and makes use of the folk-like pentatonic scale; the second is a colorful parade of pairs of instruments; the third is an atmospheric nocturne, an example of what is called Bartók's "night music," in which the woodwinds slither around chromatically above a misty tremolo in the strings; the fourth is an unusual intermezzo; and the fifth is a vigorous peasant dance in sonata–allegro form. Let us focus our attention on the fourth movement, *Intermezzo interrotto (Broken Intermezzo)*.

An **intermezzo** (Italian for "between piece") is a light musical interlude intended to separate and thus break the mood of two more serious surrounding movements. But here, as the title *Broken Intermezzo* indicates, the light intermezzo is itself rudely interrupted by contrasting music. At the outset of the movement, a charming theme in the oboe establishes a sophisticated mood. As is usual for Bartók, this melody shows the influence of the Hungarian folk song both in its pentatonic construction (the five notes that make up the scale of the melody are B, C♯, E, F♯, and A♯) and in the way the meter switches back and forth between an even $\frac{2}{4}$ and an odd $\frac{5}{8}$. As we have seen (p. 301), the pentatonic scale and irregular meters are marks of the folk.

EXAMPLE 34–1

After the tune is passed among several wind instruments, an even more ingratiating melody emerges in the strings. It, too, is Hungarian in style. In fact, it is Bartók's idealized reworking of the song *You Are Lovely, You Are Beautiful, Hungary*.

EXAMPLE 34–2

But the nostalgic vision of the homeland is suddenly interrupted by a new, cruder theme in the clarinet, and it also tells a tale. Bartók had just heard

Download a Supplementary Listening Guide for the second movement of Bartók's *Concerto for Orchestra*, at the text website.

Dmitri Shostakovich's Symphony No. 7, composed in 1942 as a programmatic work designed to stiffen Russian resistance to the German army, which had invaded the previous year. Shostakovich was a Russian hero at that moment (see Fig. 34-3), and Bartók borrowed the theme that Shostakovich had written to signify the invading Germans, believing its simple quarter-note descent to be appropriately heavy and trite.

EXAMPLE 34–3

Thus Bartók's *Broken Intermezzo* can be heard as an autobiographical work in which, as the composer related to a friend, "the artist declares his love for his native land in a serenade which is suddenly interrupted in a crude and violent manner; he is seized by rough, booted men who even break his instrument." Bartók tells us what he thinks of these "rough, booted men" (the Nazis) by surrounding them with rude, jeering noises in the trumpets and sneering trombone glissandos. Ultimately, he brings back the idyllic vision of the homeland by returning to the two opening themes. As to the soloists in this movement of Bartók's *Concerto for Orchestra*, there are many: oboe, clarinet, flute, English horn, and the entire section of violas.

Listening GUIDE

Béla Bartók
***Concerto for Orchestra* (1943)**
Fourth movement, *Broken Intermezzo*

5

5/17

Genre: Concerto

Form: Rondo

Time			Description
0:00	**17**		Four-note introduction
0:05	A		Oboe introduces folk-like theme
1:00	B		Violas introduce theme
			You Are Lovely, You Are Beautiful, Hungary
1:43	A		Oboe briefly plays folk-like theme
2:06	C		Clarinet introduces theme
			(borrowed from Shostakovich)
2:16			Rude noises in trumpets and
			trombones
2:29	C		Parody of theme in violins
2:37			More rude noises
2:41	C		Theme played in inversion by violins
2:45			More rude noises
2:54	B		Hungarian song returns in violas
3:28	A		Folk-like theme returns in English horn, flute, and clarinet

Listen to streaming music in an Active Listening Guide, available on the text website.

As was true for Prokofiev and Shostakovich, Bartók's last years were not golden. He arrived in New York in 1940 as a refugee from Nazi-dominated Europe and tried to patch together a living by performing and composing. But, aside from his *Concerto for Orchestra,* he had little success and ultimately died of leukemia in New York's West Side Hospital in 1945—a sad ending in an era that brought disillusionment, turmoil, and death to millions.

Key WORDS

Russian Revolution (349)   formalism (350)   intermezzo (355)

The materials on the text website will help you understand and pass tests on the content of this chapter. In addition, you may complete this chapter's Listening Exercise interactively, as well as view Active Listening Guides and other materials that will help you succeed in this course.

35 THREE AMERICAN VOICES

The United States is a highly pluralistic society, home to recent and not-so-recent immigrants, as well as Native Americans. This cultural and ethnic diversity is reflected in the country's many popular musical traditions including blues, ragtime, jazz, rock 'n' roll, traditional Appalachian, bluegrass, and country and western. American art music of the past hundred years was equally varie- gated, exemplified by high-art modernist music of the European type, modernism with a distinctly American flavor, and, most recently, postmodernist music. Unlike the suppressed European composers discussed in Chapter 34, twentieth-century American composers were free to create without governmental constraints. Offering both a "free market" for the exchange of artistic ideas and a safe homeland for ethnic groups from around the globe, the United States has come to enjoy the most diverse and vibrant musical culture in the world. In this chapter, we explore how three composers of high-art music added their very different voices to the diverse chorus of American music.

FIGURE 35-1

Young Charles Ives in the baseball uniform of Hopkins Grammar School, New Haven, Connecticut. A better ballplayer than student, Ives needed an extra year between high school and college to prepare for Yale.

Lebrecht Music & Arts

CHARLES IVES (1874–1954)

Charles Ives was the most original and most radical, and arguably the great- est, of the American composers of art music. He was born in Danbury, Con- necticut, the son of George Ives (1845–1894), a bandleader in the Union army who had served with General Ulysses S. Grant during the Civil War. The senior Ives gave his son a highly unorthodox musical education—at least by European standards. True, there was the obligatory study of the three B's (Bach, Beethoven, and Brahms), instruction in harmony and counterpoint, and lessons on the violin, piano, organ, cornet, and drums. But young Ives was also taught how to "stretch his ears," as he said. In one exercise, for example, he was made to sing "Swanee River" in E♭ while his father accompanied him on the piano in the key of C—a useful lesson in polytonality!

Because his forebears had gone to Yale, it was decided that Charles should enroll there, too (Fig. 35-1). At Yale, he took courses in music with Hora- tio Parker (1863–1919), a composer who had studied in Germany. But Ives's youthful, independent ideas about how music should sound clashed with Park- er's traditional European training in harmony and counterpoint. The student learned to leave his more radical musical experimentations—which included, for example, a fugue with a subject entering in four different keys—outside Parker's classroom. Ives became heavily involved in extracurricular activities, including musicals for the Delta Kappa Epsilon fraternity, and maintained a D+ average (a "gentleman's" mark before the days of grade inflation).

When he graduated in 1898, Ives decided not to pursue music as a pro- fession, realizing that the sort of music he heard in his head was not the kind the public would pay to hear. Instead, he headed for New York City and Wall Street, and in 1907, he and a friend formed the company of Ives and Myrick, an agency that sold insurance as a subsidiary of Mutual of New York (MONY). Ives and Myrick became the largest insurance agency in the United States, and in 1929, the year in which Ives retired, the company had sales of $49 million.

But Charles Ives led two lives: high-powered insurance executive by day, prolific composer by night. During the twenty years between his departure from Yale (1898) and the American entry into World War I (1917), Ives wrote the bulk of his 43 works for orchestra (including 4 symphonies), 41 choral pieces, approximately 75 works for piano solo or various chamber ensembles, and more than 150 songs. Almost without exception, they went unheard. Ives made little effort to get his music performed—composition was for him a very private matter. By the 1930s, however, word of his unusual creations had spread among a few influential performers and critics. In 1947, he was awarded the Pulitzer Prize in music for his Third Symphony, one he had written forty years earlier! In his typically gruff, eccentric way, Ives told the members of the Pulitzer committee, "Prizes are for boys. I'm grown up."

Ives's Music

Charles Ives was an idiosyncratic, quirky man, and his music is unlike that of any other composer. Ives was a modernist of the most extreme sort. Between 1898 and 1917, he independently devised the same radical compositional techniques—including atonality, polymeter, polyrhythm, and tone clusters—that had begun to appear in the works of Schoenberg, Stravinsky, and the other European modernists. Moreover, Ives was the first composer to use polytonality extensively, and he even experimented with **quarter-tone music**—music in which the smallest interval is not the chromatic half step (as is the case on the modern piano) but *half* of a half step. Ives's music places great demands on performer and listener alike. It is full of ear-splitting dissonances and dense, complex textures. At the same time, however, it contains many simple, popular-musical elements, incorporating patriotic songs, marches, hymns, dance tunes, fiddle tunes, rags, and football cheers—this was Ives's musical America. Ives often combines these familiar musical idioms with melodies of his own, piling one tune on top of another to form a new composite. What results is a jarring kind of **collage art**—art made up of disparate materials taken from very different places. In a manner akin to that of an avant-garde artist who reinterprets fragments of reality in surprising ways (Fig. 35-2), Ives takes the familiar and "defamiliarizes" it, thereby making the old sound very modern.

Putnam's Camp, Redding, Connecticut *from* Three Places in New England (*c1908–1914*)

Although he made a fortune in the financial world of Wall Street, Charles Ives was born and died a New Englander. Shortly after his marriage in 1908, he began to compose what he always referred to as his "New England Symphony," though today we call this three-movement programmatic orchestral work *Three Places in New England*. The first movement pays homage to an all-black Civil War regiment honored in a sculptured monument then (and now) on Boston Common, while the third movement depicts a walk on a misty morning in the Berkshire Mountains in

@

Download Supplementary Listening Guides for Ives, *Variations on "America,"* The *Fourth of July,* and Orchestral Set No. 2, third movement ("From Hanover Square North, at the End of a Tragic Day, the Voices of the People Again Arose"), at the text website.

FIGURE 35–2

William Harnett's *Music and the Old Cupboard Door* (1889) creates a satisfying collage of Americana by melding various objects from a closet and the world of music.

©Museums Sheffield, UK/The Bridgeman Art Library

Stockbridge, Massachusetts. The middle movement, *Putnam's Camp*, evokes childhood memories of a Fourth-of-July picnic on the town green in Redding, Connecticut, near Ives's ancestral home. Ives wrote his own narrative program for the movement, and in it, he suggests that this is music as "seen through" the eyes of a child—perhaps the recollections of Ives himself. At first, the boy recalls the games, bands, and singing on Independence Day, but he soon falls asleep and dreams about the American colonial soldiers in the army of General Israel Putnam, who wintered at Redding during 1778–1779. Reawakening, he again hears the colorful, cacophonous sounds of a small-town Fourth of July.

A dream might be termed a "collage of the mind," in which familiar persons and things appear juxtaposed with one another in haphazard sequence. *Putnam's Camp* sounds like a musical dream—tune fragments from many historical periods seem to appear at random. Some of the marches, including "Yankee Doodle" and "The British Grenadiers," date, appropriately, from revolutionary times, but "The Star Spangled Banner" and Stephen Foster's "Massa's in de Cold Ground" were composed much later. In this piece, Ives shows music to be a particularly effective art in which to reassemble random bits of sonic information (here representing the American musical past), in much the same manner that a dream reassembles random bits of personal experience.

Ives's "musical dream" is a bracing, sometimes shocking vision brought about by musical distortion. For example, the composer typically takes a familiar tune and alters the pitches chromatically or changes the rhythm, usually by syncopation. Notice in Example 35-1 how he modifies the tune "The British Grenadiers," thereby making the familiar unfamiliar.

EXAMPLE 35–1

But most jarring is Ives's use of **polytonality,** the simultaneous sounding of two or more keys. Example 35-2 shows how Ives combines the distorted version of "The British Grenadiers" with his own march tune, presenting the first in the key of E♭ major, and the second in the key of C major. Such tonal clashes add a further element of aural disjunction, making the tunes seem out of phase with each other.

EXAMPLE 35–2

Most polytonality is simultaneous (vertical), but Ives also employs polytonality in linear fashion, taking a standard tune and presenting each successive phrase in a different key, as he does with "Yankee Doodle."

EXAMPLE 35-3

key of B♭   key of C   key of B

The following Listening Guide has been prepared with the aid of Ives scholar James Sinclair, whose edition of *Putnam's Camp,* based upon Ives's manuscripts at Yale University, was used in the present recording. The guide attempts to identify the welter of tune fragments Ives drew from his memory of musical America, but even with it and a synopsis of Ives's own narrative program (in italics), *Putnam's Camp* remains a challenging piece. Despite the difficulties, Ives wanted this movement to be fun. As he said to encourage the conductor and instrumentalists prior to a performance in 1931, "The concert will go alright. Just kick into the music—never mind the exact notes or the right notes, they're always a nuisance."

Listening GUIDE

Charles Ives
Putnam's Camp, Redding, Connecticut
Second movement of *Three Places in New England* (1908?–1914)

5
5/18–19

Genre: Program symphony

Form: Ternary (**ABA'**)

A *A boy attends a Fourth-of-July picnic on the village green at Redding, Connecticut.*

0:00 **18** Introduction followed by brisk march tune composed by Ives himself; tune becomes syncopated

0:44   Trumpets and horns play "out-of-phase" fanfare

0:47   Ives's march, to which is added, in flutes and French horn, refrain of Stephen Foster's "Massa's in de Cold Ground"

1:01   "Yankee Doodle"

1:05   Child's song by Ives himself

The boy wanders into a woods in hopes of seeing some old soldiers, but falls asleep.

1:35   Music becomes quiet, and distinctive tunes disappear

B *Dream sequence: Goddess Liberty appears and urges colonial troops to fight on.*

2:01   Shimmering tone clusters

(continued)

Colonial troops begin to desert.

2:22   Music regains rhythmic profile to simulate stirring of mutinous troops

3:03   Trumpets signal deserters' departure; they march away to tune of "The British Grenadiers"

General Putnam appears with his own troops; deserters turn around and march with him back to camp.

3:28   General Putnam's troops march to "Hail, Columbia," played loudly in brass and strings

A' *The boy awakens from the noisy dream and returns to the holiday picnic.*

3:47   **19**   0:00   Return of softer child's song in violins, then another, louder march

4:06   0:19   Three tunes at once: violins play Ives's own march, trombones state his own countertheme, and upper winds present second phrase of "The British Grenadiers"

4:20   0:33   Trumpets play "The British Grenadiers"

4:32   0:45   "Out-of-phase" trumpets reintroduce Ives's own march and altered version of "The British Grenadiers"

4:52   1:05   Musical fireworks go off in explosion of sound

5:09   1:22   Ends with snippet of "The Star Spangled Banner" in low brasses

Listen to streaming music in an Active Listening Guide, available on the text website.

*A*ARON COPLAND (1900–1990)

Composers working in Europe in the nineteenth century sought to establish "national" styles of art music, as if to shout out in sound, "We exist! We matter!" (see Chapter 29). Similarly, in the early twentieth century, the challenge for composers in the United States was to provide this emerging nation with its own distinctive musical identity—to fashion compositions that sounded truly American rather than European. Charles Ives did this within his own unique musical world, one full of American marches, patriotic songs, and hymn tunes. Aaron Copland (Fig. 35-3) did much the same, drawing also on cowboy songs and early jazz. But Copland, in contrast to his older contemporary Ives, set his bits of Americana not within a collage of dissonant polytonality, but instead in a conservative backdrop of generally consonant harmony.

Copland was born in Brooklyn of Jewish immigrant parents. After a rudimentary musical education in New York City, he set sail for Paris to broaden his artistic horizons. In this he was not alone, for the City of Light at this time attracted young writers, painters, and musicians from across the world, including Igor Stravinsky (1882–1974), Pablo Picasso (1881–1973), James Joyce (1882–1941), Gertrude Stein (1874–1946), Ernest Hemingway (1898–1961),

FIGURE 35-3

Aaron Copland.

AP Images/Martell

and F. Scott Fitzgerald (1896–1940). After three years of study, Copland returned to the United States, determined to compose in a distinctly American style. Like other young expatriate artists during the 1920s, Copland had to leave his homeland to learn what made it unique: "In greater or lesser degree," he remarked, "all of us discovered America in Europe."

At first, Copland sought to forge an American style by incorporating into his music elements of jazz, recognized the world over as a uniquely American creation. Then, beginning in the late 1930s, Copland turned his attention to a series of projects with rural and western American subjects. The ballet scores *Billy the Kid* (1938) and *Rodeo* (1942) are set in the West and make use of classic cowboy songs like *Goodbye, Old Paint* and *The Old Chisholm Trail*. Another ballet, *Appalachian Spring* (1944), re-creates the ambience of the Pennsylvania farm country, and his only opera, *The Tender Land* (1954), is set in the cornbelt of the Midwest. It is telling that filmmaker Spike Lee used Copland's music to fashion the soundtrack for his basketball movie *He Got Game* (1998). In the minds of some, the "Copland sound" is as American as basketball!

Download a Supplementary Listening Guide for Scene 1 from Copland's *Billy the Kid,* at the text website.

Copland's Music

In his most distinctly American works, Copland's musical voice is clear and conservative. He uses folk and popular elements to soften the dissonant harmonies and disjunct melodies of European modernism. Copland's melodies tend to be more stepwise and diatonic than those of other twentieth-century composers, perhaps because Western folk and popular tunes are fundamentally conjunct and nonchromatic. His harmonies are almost always tonal and often slow-moving in a way that can evoke the vastness and grandeur of the American landscape. The triad, too, is still important to Copland, perhaps for its stability and simplicity, but he frequently uses it in a modern way, as we shall see, by having two triads sound simultaneously, creating mildly dissonant polychords. But perhaps the most important component in the distinctive "Copland sound" is his clear, luminous orchestration. Copland does not mix colors to produce rich Romantic blends, but keeps the four families of instruments (strings, woodwinds, brasses, and percussion) more or less separate from one another. Moreover, his instrumentation typically features a solid bass, a very thin middle, and a top of one or two high, clear tones. It is this separation and careful spacing of the instruments that creates the fresh, wide-open sound so pleasing in Copland's music.

The clarity and simplicity of Aaron Copland's music is not accidental. During the Great Depression of the 1930s, he became convinced that the gulf between modern music and the ordinary citizen had become too great—that dissonance and atonality had little to say to most music lovers. "It made no sense to ignore them [ordinary listeners] and to continue writing as if they did not exist. I felt that it was worth the effort to see if I couldn't say what I had to say in the simplest possible terms." Thus he not only wrote appealing new tonal works like *Fanfare for the Common Man* (1942) but also incorporated simple, traditional tunes such as *The Gift to Be Simple*, which he uses in *Appalachian Spring*.

Appalachian Spring (1944)

Appalachian Spring is a one-act ballet that tells the story of "a pioneer celebration of spring in a newly built farmhouse in Pennsylvania in the early 1800s." A new bride and her farmer-husband express through dance the anxieties and

FIGURE 35-4

A scene from Martha Graham's ballet *Appalachian Spring*, with music by Aaron Copland. Here Katherine Crockett dances the role of the Bride (New York, 1999).

joys of life in pioneer America. The work was composed in 1944 for the great American choreographer Martha Graham (1893–1991), and it won Copland a Pulitzer Prize the following year (Fig. 35-4). It is divided into eight connected sections that differ in tempo and mood. Copland provided a brief description of each of these orchestral scenes.

Section 1

"Introduction of the characters one by one, in a suffused light." The quiet beauty of the land at daybreak is revealed, as the orchestra slowly presents, one by one, the notes of the tonic and dominant triads.

EXAMPLE 35-4

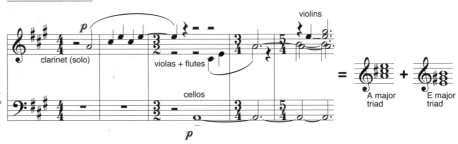

While this overlapping presentation of two triads constitutes a polychord, the effect is only mildly dissonant because of the slow, quiet way in which the notes of the two chords are introduced. The serene simplicity of the introduction sets the tone for the entire work.

Section 2

"A sentiment both elated and religious gives the keynote of this scene." The early calm is suddenly broken by a lively dance with a salient rhythm played aggressively in the strings. The dance has all the modern rhythmic vigor of Stravinsky's music, but none of the extreme polymeter. As the dance proceeds, a more restrained hymn-like melody emerges in the trumpet.

Sections 3–6

Section 3 is a dance for the two principals, a *pas de deux* accompanied by lyrical writing for strings and winds. Sections 4 and 5 are musical depictions of the livelier aspects of country life, with Section 4 including a toe-tappin' hoedown, while Section 6 recalls the quiet calm of the opening of the ballet.

Section 7

"Calm and flowing. Scenes of daily activity for the Bride and her Farmer-husband." For this section, Copland chose to make use of a traditional tune of the Shakers, an extreme religious sect that prospered in the Appalachian region in the early nineteenth century and whose members expressed their spiritual intensity in frenzied singing, dancing, and shaking. Today this tune is famous, having been featured, among other places, in a John Williams piece for Barack Obama's inauguration in 2009. But the melody has become well known only because of Copland's *Appalachian Spring*. The composer plucked it from an obscure book of folk songs in 1944 because he thought the simple, diatonic tune (Ex. 35-5)

fit well with the American character of the ballet, and because the text of the Shaker song is harmonious with what occurs on stage: "scenes of daily activity."

EXAMPLE 35–5

p

'Tis the gift to be simple,
'Tis the gift to be free,
'Tis the gift to come down where we ought to be,
And when we find ourselves in the place just right,
'Twill be in the valley of love and delight.

In the five variations that follow, *The Gift to Be Simple* is not so much varied as it is clothed in different instrumental attire.

Download a Supplementary Listening Guide for Section 8 of *Appalachian Spring*, at the text website.

SECTION 8

"The Bride takes her place among her neighbors." Serenity returns to the scene as the strings play a slow, mostly stepwise descent, as Copland says, "like a prayer." The hymn-like melody from Section 2 is heard again in the flute, followed by the quiet "landscape music" from the beginning of the ballet. Darkness has again descended on the valley, leaving the young pioneer couple "strong in their new house" and secure in their community.

Listening GUIDE

Aaron Copland
Appalachian Spring **(1944)**
Sections 1, 2, and 7

5 5/20–22   **2** 2/21–23

Genre: Ballet music

SECTION 1

0:00	**20** **21**	Quiet unfolding of ascending triads by clarinet and other instruments
0:45		Soft melody descends in woodwinds
1:34		More ascending triads in woodwinds and trumpet, then flute melody (1:46)
2:01		Oboe and then bassoon solos
2:49		Clarinet plays concluding ascending triad

SECTION 2

0:00	**21** **22**	Percussive rhythm (♫ ♩ ♫ ♩) in strings and rising woodwinds
0:17		Rhythm gels into sprightly dance
		mf
0:43		Trumpet plays hymn-like melody above dance
		ff
1:13		Rhythmic motive scattered but then played more forcefully
2:10		Hymn played quietly in strings, with flute counterpoint above
2:45		Rhythmic motive skips away in woodwinds

(continued)

SECTION 7

0:00	**22** **23**	Clarinet presents Shaker tune	

0:33   Variation 1: oboe and bassoon play tune

1:02   Variation 2: violas and trombones play tune at half its previous speed

1:49   Variation 3: trumpets and trombones play tune at fast tempo

2:12   Variation 4: woodwinds play tune more slowly

2:30   Variation 5: final majestic statement of tune by full orchestra

Listen to streaming music in an Active Listening Guide, available on the text website.

Listening EXERCISE 41

Copland

APPALACHIAN SPRING

5 5/20–22   **2** 2/21–23   **@**

To take this Listening Exercise online and receive feedback or email answers to your instructor, go to the text website.

The following exercise asks you to consider the ways Aaron Copland "softens" the more radical aspects of twentieth-century modernist music.

Section 1: Introduction

1. (0:00–0:43) Although the opening involves the over-lap of two conflicting triads, this passage does not sound harshly dissonant. Why not? **20 21**
   a. because the music is quiet
   b. because the notes unfold in succession, rather than sound at once
   c. because the dissonant notes are not all in the same register
   d. all of the above

2. (0:52–1:20) Why does this passage sound more like Romantic than modern music?
   a. A nostalgic-sounding English horn suggests a woodland scene.
   b. An alpine horn call suggests distant mountains.
   c. The strings provide a warm accompaniment, and there are no syncopated rhythms or percussive effects.

3. (1:45–2:45) Which member of the woodwind family does *not* play a solo in this lovely section?
   a. flute
   b. oboe
   c. clarinet
   d. bassoon

4. (2:48–end) In this passage, we hear one of the distinctive aspects of the "Copland sound": the composer spaces the instruments to allow "air" into the middle of the texture. Which is true?

a. The double basses play a pedal point, the strings hold softly in the middle, and the clarinet unfolds a triad above.
b. The double basses play an ostinato, the clarinets hold softly in the middle, and the violin unfolds a triad above.

Section 2: Joys and Anxieties of Pioneer Life

5. The dance theme begins in the strings (0:17), and then the hymn-like tune enters in the trumpet (0:43). When the two are together (0:43–1:13), which sounds more aggressively modern? **21 22**
   a. the strings playing the dance in shorter notes
   b. the trumpet tune moving in long notes

6. (1:28–2:09) Now the lively dance theme dominates. This passage sounds a bit like the music of Igor Stravinsky, a composer whom Copland greatly admired. Which of the following *cannot* be heard in this passage?
   a. strong, irregular accents
   b. a rhythmic ostinato in the flutes and harp
   c. a sweeping melody in the cellos
   d. violent, percussive strokes in the timpani and xylophone

Section 7: Variations on a Shaker tune *The Gift to Be Simple*

7. This section is in theme and variations form. Is this form unique to the twentieth century? Is it a particularly "modern" form? **22 23**
   a. yes   b. no

8. This section is likely the best-known passage in all of Copland's music. Which is true?
    a. It sounds like Romantic music, projecting a pleasing, consonant sound, and a regular meter.
    b. It sounds like modern music, projecting percussive sounds, dissonance, and syncopation.

9. We have said that Copland admired the Russian composer Igor Stravinsky. Which of the following is *not* true?
    a. They both wrote ballet music.
    b. They both spent time in Paris.

c. They both came to the United States as immigrants.
d. They both liked bright, clean, and carefully spaced colors in their orchestrations.
e. They both incorporated folk melodies into their music.

10. Comparing Copland's *Appalachian Spring* to Stravinsky's *The Rite of Spring* (**5** 5/10; **2** 2/19), which of the two scores do you judge to be the more radically modern?
    a. Stravinsky's
    b. Copland's

ℰLLEN TAAFFE ZWILICH (1939–)

By the end of the Second World War, composers such as Ives and Copland had established a uniquely American brand of modernist art music. Consequently, later generations of American composers could work more freely within the tradition of European classical music, without feeling compelled to incorporate distinctively American musical traits. One American composer who might be called, paradoxically, a "traditional modernist" (a modernist working within the European classical tradition) is Ellen Taaffe Zwilich (Fig. 35-5).

The daughter of an airline pilot, Zwilich was born in Miami and educated at Florida State University. She then moved to New York City where she played violin in the American Symphony Orchestra, studied composition at the Juilliard School, and worked for a time as an usher at Carnegie Hall. Zwilich's big "break" came in 1983, when she became the first woman to win the Pulitzer Prize in music. During 1995–1998, she was the first person of either sex to occupy the newly created Composer's Chair at Carnegie Hall—usher had become director. Today Zwilich enjoys a status to which all modern composers aspire: she is free to devote herself exclusively to writing music, sustained by her royalties and commissions. Recently, the New York Philharmonic and the Chicago Symphony Orchestra each paid five-figure sums for a single new composition.

FIGURE 35–5
Ellen Taaffe Zwilich

Courtesy of The Florida State University College of Music

Concerto Grosso 1985 *(1985)*

The tradition of the Baroque concerto grosso lies at the heart of Zwilich's five-movement *Concerto Grosso 1985*. Commissioned by the Washington Friends of Handel, this work honors the composer George Frideric Handel (see Chapter 14), a leading exponent of the concerto grosso. Zwilich borrows a melody directly from Handel (the opening theme of his Violin Sonata in D major). She also embraces several elements of Baroque musical style: a regular rhythmic pulse, a repeating bass pedal point, a walking bass, and a harpsichord. Yet Zwilich adds twisting chromaticism to Handel's melody (see Listening Guide) and sets it to a biting, dissonant harmony. Most important, she demands an insistent, pounding style of playing that would have shocked Handel. Zwilich's concerto, therefore, uses modern idioms to establish a

@

Download a Supplementary Listening Guide for the first movement of Zwilich's *Concerto Grosso 1985*, at the text website.

dialogue with the past. We might call this "Neo-baroque" music—music that is part modern, part Baroque in style. But compositions that heavily reference music from a specific era—be it the Middle Ages, Baroque period, or Classical epoch—are generally referred to as Neo-classical. This is classical music with a distinctly modern twist.

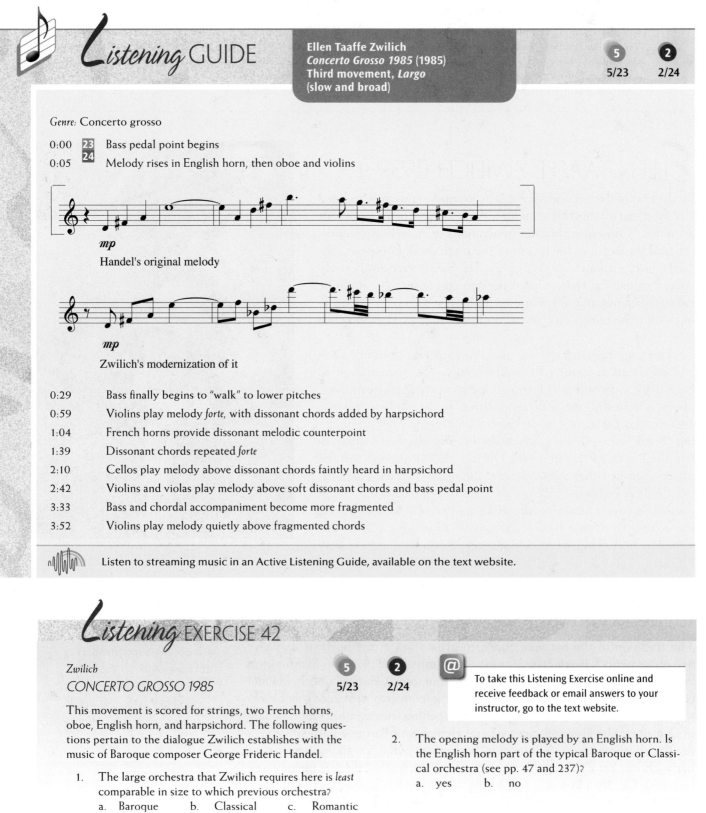

Listening GUIDE

Ellen Taaffe Zwilich
Concerto Grosso 1985 **(1985)**
Third movement, *Largo*
(slow and broad)

5   2
5/23   2/24

Genre: Concerto grosso

| 0:00 | 23 | Bass pedal point begins |
| 0:05 | 24 | Melody rises in English horn, then oboe and violins |

mp

Handel's original melody

mp

Zwilich's modernization of it

0:29	Bass finally begins to "walk" to lower pitches
0:59	Violins play melody *forte*, with dissonant chords added by harpsichord
1:04	French horns provide dissonant melodic counterpoint
1:39	Dissonant chords repeated *forte*
2:10	Cellos play melody above dissonant chords faintly heard in harpsichord
2:42	Violins and violas play melody above soft dissonant chords and bass pedal point
3:33	Bass and chordal accompaniment become more fragmented
3:52	Violins play melody quietly above fragmented chords

Listen to streaming music in an Active Listening Guide, available on the text website.

Listening EXERCISE 42

Zwilich
CONCERTO GROSSO 1985

5   2
5/23   2/24

@ — To take this Listening Exercise online and receive feedback or email answers to your instructor, go to the text website.

This movement is scored for strings, two French horns, oboe, English horn, and harpsichord. The following questions pertain to the dialogue Zwilich establishes with the music of Baroque composer George Frideric Handel.

1. The large orchestra that Zwilich requires here is *least* comparable in size to which previous orchestra?
   a. Baroque   b. Classical   c. Romantic

2. The opening melody is played by an English horn. Is the English horn part of the typical Baroque or Classical orchestra (see pp. 47 and 237)?
   a. yes   b. no

3. (0:00) The music begins with a pedal point in the bass. We first met the pedal point in which period in music history (see p. 130)?
   a. Baroque   b. Classical   c. Romantic

4. (0:59) The harpsichord enters and plays a quiet, chordal accompaniment. In which orchestra is the harpsichord traditionally found?
   a. Baroque
   b. Classical
   c. Romantic
   d. modern

5. (0:59–1:38) Which of the following elements from this passage are *not* a typical element in Baroque music?
   a. the dissonant, disjunct melody
   b. the harpsichord chords
   c. the very regular rhythm pulsations

6. (2:10–2:40) Why does this passage sound less modern and more "romantic"?
   a. The rising cellos play with warmth and sentiment.
   b. The harpsichord plays with much vibrato.
   c. The pedal point sounds with much *rubato*.

7. (2:42) The return of the melody here is comparable to a return of what in a Baroque concerto grosso?
   a. the *rondeau*
   b. the raga
   c. the ritornello

8. (3:52–end) Which of the following is true in this final passage?
   a. The harpsichord plays continuous chords together with a strong bass line, thereby creating the modern equivalent of a *basso continuo*.
   b. The harpsichord plays very different music from the strong bass line, thereby creating the modern equivalent of a *cadenza*.

9. Knowing that Neo-baroque music is simply one type of music within the larger, general category of Neo-classical music, is Zwilich's *Concerto Grosso* a Neo-classical work?
   a. yes   b. no

10. Although there are allusions to music of the Baroque period (the regular rhythm and the presence of the harpsichord, for example), this piece conveys a sense of the anxiety, tension, isolation, and even terror of modern (urban) life. By what means does the composer create this feeling?
    a. a pounding, percussive beat
    b. a separated violin line
    c. prolonged dissonances in a high register
    d. ostinatos that, through repetition, suggest a lack of progress
    e. all of the above

Key WORDS

quarter-tone music (359)   collage art (359)   polytonality (360)

@

The materials on the text website will help you understand and pass tests on the content of this chapter. In addition, you may complete this chapter's Listening Exercises interactively, as well as view Active Listening Guides and other materials that will help you succeed in this course.

36 POSTMODERNISM

Postmodernism is a philosophy of art that came to the fore after World War II. For postmodernists, art is for all, not just an elite few, and all art is of equal potential—Andy Warhol's famous paintings of Campbell's Soup cans or Marilyn Monroe, for example, are just as meaningful as Picassos. Consequently, there is no "high" or "low" art, only art (and maybe not even that). In addition, postmodernism holds that we live in a pluralistic world in which one culture is as important as the next. Indeed, cultural distinctions are seen to be gradually disappearing because of globalization, a process of homogenization made inevitable by instant mass-media communication. Finally, postmodernism is refreshingly egalitarian when it comes to sex and gender, affirming a belief that the creations of, say, gay living black women are just as important as those of straight dead white men.

Postmodernist principles apply to music as well. If all art holds equal potential, then it is no longer necessary to separate classical from popular music—the two styles can even coexist within one and the same composition, as they do, for example, in recent creations of Paul McCartney and Wynton Marsalis. No longer, according to postmodernism, need there be such distinctions between "highbrow" and "lowbrow" music; all music—classical, country, hip hop, folk, rock, and all the rest—is to be prized in equal measure. John Williams's film music is as important as Igor Stravinsky's ballet scores; Michael (Jackson) is as worthy of our attention as Mozart.

Finally, postmodernism brings with it a new agenda as to how to create music. Classical formal models, such as sonata–allegro and theme and variations, are no longer operative. Each musical work must fashion its unique form according to the demands and creative urges of the moment. Music no longer need be "goal oriented"; a particular piece does not have to work progressively to a defined point of arrival or climax. In today's musical culture, amplified instruments and electronic music are commonplace in symphony hall and rock arena alike. Traditional acoustic instruments must share the spotlight with newer electric and electronic ones. While Yo-Yo Ma's Stradivarius cello is a cultural treasure, so, too, is Eric Clapton's electric guitar. Postmodernism embraces an egalitarian, pluralistic musical world in which technology plays an important role.

FIGURE 36–1

Postmodern art takes something of an "in your face" approach to traditional art, as can be seen in this reproduction of Andy Warhol's iconic Marilyn Monroe on the front of the Vancouver Art Gallery. A poster boy for postmodernism, Warhol believed that any "commonly found object"—a photo of Marilyn Monroe, a Campbell's Soup can, or a Coke bottle—might be construed to be art.

EDGARD VARÈSE (1883–1965) AND ELECTRONIC MUSIC

The origins of musical postmodernism can be traced to the 1930s and the experimental compositions of Edgard Varèse. Varèse was born in France but immigrated to the United States in 1915 in search of a less traditional artistic environment (Fig. 36-2). After an accidental fire caused the loss of some of the scores he had brought from Paris, he destroyed the rest intentionally, thereby obliterating all traces of his European musical past. Already an extreme modernist, Varèse showed himself eager to step beyond the boundaries of the Western musical tradition and embrace the postmodernist age. But Varèse was a pioneer, in some ways ahead of his time, and musical postmodernism was not to reach full force until the 1960s. Thus, as with many artistic and cultural eras, modernism and postmodernism overlapped for decades. Indeed, in many ways, the two styles still coexist today.

Significantly, Varèse titled his first work written in the United States *Amériques* (1921), suggesting not only a new geography but also a new world of musical sound. Besides the usual strings, brasses, and woodwinds, the orchestra for *Amériques* also required a battery of new percussion instruments, including sirens and sleigh bells, most of which had never been heard in a symphony orchestra. In earlier centuries, composers had typically called on the percussion to provide accentuation. The thuds, bangs, and crashes of these instruments helped to delineate the climaxes of the musical structure. Like road signs, they pointed the way but did not constitute the essence of the musical journey. By the 1930s, however, Varèse had radically altered the traditional role of percussion instruments. In *Ionization* (1931), the orchestra consists of nothing but percussion instruments, including two sirens, two tam-tams, a gong, cymbals, anvils, three different sizes of bass drum, bongos, various Cuban rattles and gourds, slap-sticks, Chinese blocks, sleigh bells, and chimes. Here, percussive sounds do not *reinforce* the music; they *are* the music.

To grasp the significance of an all-percussion orchestra, remember that most percussion instruments generate sounds of indefinite pitch, rather than one continuous frequency or musical tone. Without discrete tones, two essential elements of traditional music—melody and harmony—have been removed. All that remains is rhythm, color, and texture, which Varèse deployed in original ways. Yet, having created new percussive soundscapes in *Ionization*, Varèse wanted more. As he said in a lecture in 1936, "When new instruments allow me to write music as I conceive it, [then my shifting sound-masses] will be clearly perceived." Two decades later, the "new instruments" Varèse had envisioned—electronic instruments—became available.

FIGURE 36-2

Caricature of composer Edgard Varèse in a futuristic time capsule, surrounded by the unconventional musical instruments that became his signature.

Poème électronique (*1958*)

Most traditional music around the world is played on acoustic instruments (ones made of natural materials). But shortly after World War II, new technology led to the development of **electronic music** produced by a **synthesizer**—a machine that can create, transform, and combine (synthesize) sounds by means of electronic circuitry. Varèse's *Poème électronique* is an early landmark of electronic music. Here the composer combined new electronic sounds generated by a synthesizer with bits of *musique concrète* (see boxed essay), including taped sounds of a siren, a train, an organ, church bells, and a human voice, all altered or distorted in some imaginative way. Varèse created this "poem for the electronic age" to provide music for a multimedia exhibit inside the pavilion of the Philips Radio Corporation at the 1958 World's Fair in Brussels.

ELECTRONIC MUSIC: FROM VARÈSE TO RADIOHEAD

The effect of technology on classical, and especially on popular, music has been nothing short of revolutionary. The earliest experiments with electronic sound—preceding even the first synthesizers—produced something termed *musique concrète*. **Musique concrète** is so called because the composer works, not with sounds written for voice or musical instruments, but with those found naturally in the everyday world. Another term for *musique concrète*, then, is "found sound." A car horn, a person speaking in a room, or a dog's barking may be captured by a tape recorder and doctored in some way—reassembled and repeated (spliced, mixed, and looped) to form an unexpected montage of sound. Edgard Varèse, working in both New York and Paris, was one of the first practitioners of *musique concrète*, his *Poème electronique* (1958) being a landmark in the history of this sort of synthetic music.

Pop artists, too, quickly began to exploit these musical-technical developments. The Beatles' John Lennon used "tape looping" to create a novel background ambience for his song "Revolution 9" (1968). As Lennon recounted, "We were cutting up [tapes of] classical music and making different size loops, and then I got an engineer tape on which an engineer was saying, 'Number nine, number nine, number nine.' All those different bits of sound and noises were all compiled. . . . I fed them all in and mixed them live." Lennon also added *musique concrète* (found sound) to a few Beatles songs. "Strawberry Fields Forever," for example, has a piano crash followed by a dog's whistle played at 15,000 vibrations per second. Not to be outdone, the rock band Pink Floyd incorporated the sounds of a clanging cash register into their song, appropriately titled, "Money" (1973). And filmmakers, too, jumped on the electronic bandwagon. George Lucas used

AP Images/Mark J. Terrill

W. G. "Snuffy" Walden is an eminently successful TV composer, having created the theme for *The West Wing*, as well as scores for *The Drew Carey Show*, *My So-Called Life*, *Friday Night Lights*, *The Wonder Years*, and many others.

banging chains to create the sound of the Imperial Walkers for his *Star Wars* epics. To be specific, he recorded, and then modified and layered, the noise of a bicycle chain falling on a concrete floor—a literal example of the principle of *musique concrète*.

What began as esoteric experiments by a few avant-garde scientists and composers soon transformed the world of popular entertainment. The technological development that made this possible was miniaturization.

Varèse's eight-minute creation was recorded on tape and then played on 425 speakers, again and again, to the 15,000–16,000 people who walked through the structure daily. While the music played, a video montage was projected on the inside walls of the building.

As you listen to *Poème électronique*, you may have one (or more) of the many reactions experienced by those visitors to the Philips Pavilion in 1958: anger, fear, revulsion, curiosity, or awe at the sheer strangeness of the sound. Startling tones come in rapid succession and then disappear quickly; large, dense masses of sound are suddenly succeeded by thin, airy ones. Three mysterious tones rise chromatically. Squawks, honks, swoops, and animal noises come one after another. What is the artist's message? An ardent postmodernist such as Varèse would say that art need not have "meaning." Is *Poème électronique* really music or merely ingeniously contrived noise? Again, the postmodernist would respond that organized *noise* is just as valid an artistic statement as organized *tones* (music).

During the 1960s, the large-console tape machine was reduced to the portable tape recorder, and then, during the 1980s, microprocessors became small enough to power keyboard-synthesizers. In more recent years, the increasing power, versatility, and availability of the personal computer has facilitated revolutionary changes in the way music is composed, produced, and recorded. Today, almost any aspiring composer or rock band can own the hardware required to produce and manipulate their own sounds. Today's computer-driven synthesizer can generate sounds that are almost indistinguishable from those of a ninety-piece orchestra. Consequently, **computer music** has revolutionized the world of commercial music. The computer-equipped recording studio now generates much of the music we hear on radio and television. The opening music for the series *Law and Order*, for example, begins with tones that sound like those of a clarinet. In fact, these are synthesized (artificially fabricated) sounds created by a computer-driven synthesizer.

Technology has facilitated new processes for the production of pop music. In the 1980s, rap and hip hop artists began using a technique called **sampling** whereby the rapper or producer extracts a small portion of pre-recorded music and then mechanically repeats it over and over as a musical backdrop to the text that he or she raps. And in **scratching,** another technique popular in rap and hip hop, a creative DJ with one or more turntables manipulates the needles, scratching on the vinyl of the record while other prerecorded sounds loop continually in the background. Perhaps no contemporary rock group has blended songwriting with the manipulation of electronic audio more extensively than Radiohead. For their albums and concert tours, they use not only analog and

© Frank Micelotta/Getty Images

Musician Thom Yorke surrounded by some of the electronic equipment that gives his band Radiohead its distinctive "electronic" sound.

digital synthesizers but also "special effects" pedals and distortion filters to re-form the audio of their voices and instruments. All these electronic devices and computer processes help give the music of Radiohead its sometimes disembodied, otherworldly quality.

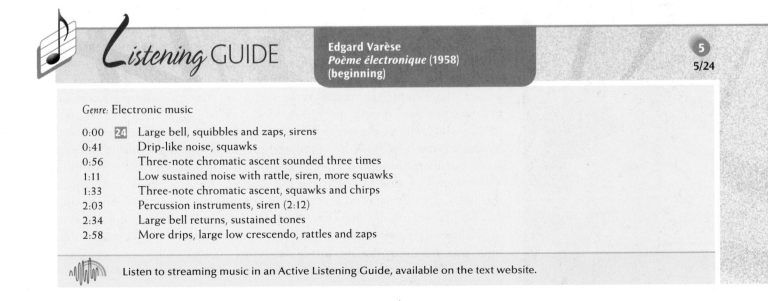

♪ *Listening* GUIDE

Edgard Varèse
Poème électronique (1958)
(beginning)

5
5/24

Genre: Electronic music

0:00	**24**	Large bell, squibbles and zaps, sirens
0:41		Drip-like noise, squawks
0:56		Three-note chromatic ascent sounded three times
1:11		Low sustained noise with rattle, siren, more squawks
1:33		Three-note chromatic ascent, squawks and chirps
2:03		Percussion instruments, siren (2:12)
2:34		Large bell returns, sustained tones
2:58		More drips, large low crescendo, rattles and zaps

Listen to streaming music in an Active Listening Guide, available on the text website.

*J*OHN CAGE (1912–1992) AND CHANCE MUSIC

If, as postmodernists say, music need not progress in an organized fashion toward a goal, why not just leave it to chance? This is essentially what American composer John Cage decided to do. Cage was born in Los Angeles, the son of an inventor. He was graduated valedictorian of Los Angeles High School and spent two years at nearby Pomona College before going to Europe to learn more about art, architecture, and music. Arriving in New York City in 1942, he worked variously as a wall washer at the YWCA, teacher of music and mycology (the science of mushrooms) at the New School for Social Research, and music director of a modern dance company.

From his earliest days as a musician, Cage had a special affection for percussion instruments and the unusual sounds they could create. His *First Construction (in Metal)* (1939) has six percussionists play piano, metal thundersheets, oxen bells, cowbells, sleigh bells, water gongs, and brake drums, among other things. By 1941, he had collected three hundred percussion objects of this kind—anything that might make an unusual noise when struck or shaken. Cage's tinkering with percussive sounds led him to invent the **prepared piano**—a grand piano outfitted with screws, bolts, washers, erasers, and bits of felt and plastic all inserted between the strings (Fig. 36-3). This transformed the piano into a one-person percussion band that could produce a great variety of sounds and noises—twangs, zaps, rattles, thuds, and the like—no two of which were exactly the same in pitch or color. In creating the prepared piano, Cage was merely continuing along the experimental trail blazed by his spiritual mentor, Edgard Varèse: "Years ago, after I decided to devote my life to music, I noticed that people distinguished between noises and sounds. I decided to follow Varèse and fight for noises, to be on the side of the underdog."

Cage's glorification of everyday noise began in earnest during the 1950s. Rather than engage in a titanic struggle to shape the elements of music, as had Beethoven, he decided to sit back, relax, and simply allow noises to occur around him. In creating this sort of intentionally purposeless, undirected music, Cage invented what has come to be called chance music, the ultimate postmodernist experimentation. In **chance music,** musical events are not carefully predetermined by the composer, but come instead in an unpredictable sequence as the result of nonmusical decisions such as following astrological charts, tossing coins, throwing dice, or shuffling randomly the pages of music to be played. In *Music Walk* (1958), for example, one or more pianists connect lines and dots in any fashion to create a musical "score" from which to play. Such "scores" suggest only vaguely what the musician is to do. The musical "happening" that results is the sort of spontaneous group experience that was to flower during the 1960s. More radical still is Cage's work *0'00"* (1962), which allows the performer total artistic freedom. When performed by Cage himself in 1962, he sliced and prepared vegetables at a table on a stage, put them through a food processor, and then drank the juice, all the while amplifying and broadcasting the sound of these activities throughout the hall. Cage's declaration that the ordinary noise made by food processing can be "art" is virtually identical in intent to Andy Warhol's glorification of the Campbell's Soup can: both typify the kind of postmodernist creation that took hold in New York City during the 1960s.

Naturally, music critics called Cage a joker and a charlatan. Most would agree that his "compositions," in and of themselves, are not of great musical

---

To hear the sounds of a prepared piano, listen to "John Cage Sonata V" in the YouTube playlist on the text website.

FIGURE 36–3

John Cage "preparing" a piano. By putting spoons, forks, screws, paper clips, and other sundry objects into the strings of the piano, the composer changes the instrument from one producing melodic tones to one generating percussive impacts.

© New York Times Co./Getty Images

value in traditional terms. Nevertheless, by raising profound questions regarding the relationships between human activity, sound, and music, his compositions eloquently articulate his own musical philosophy. By focusing on the chance appearance of ordinary noise, Cage aggressively asks us to ponder the basic principles that underlie most Western music: Why must sounds of similar range and color come one after the other? Why must music have form and unity? Why must it have "meaning"? Why must it express anything? Why must it develop and climax? Why must it be goal-oriented, as is so much of human activity in the West?

See and hear a random performance of Cage's chance music *0'00"* in the YouTube playlist on the text website.

4'33" (1952)

The "composition" of Cage that causes us to focus on these questions most intently is his *4'33"*. Here one or more performers carrying any sort of instrument come on stage, seat themselves, open the "score," and play nothing. For each of the three carefully timed movements, there is no notated music, only the indication *tacet* (it is silent). But as the audience soon realizes, "absolute" silence is virtually impossible to attain. With no organized sound to be heard during the four minutes and thirty-three seconds that follow, the listener gradually becomes aware of the background noise in the hall—a creaking floor, a passing car, a dropped paper clip, an electrical hum. Cage asks us to embrace these random everyday noises—to tune our ears in innocent sonic wonder. Are these sounds not of artistic value, too? What is music? What is noise? What is art?

Needless to say, we have not filled your CDs with four minutes and thirty-three seconds of background noise. You can create your own, and John Cage would have liked that. Sit in a "quiet" room for 4 minutes and 33 seconds and notice what you hear. Perhaps this experiment will make you more aware of how important willful organization is to the art we call music. If nothing else, Cage makes us realize that music, above all, is a form of organized communication from one person to the next and that random background noise can do nothing to express or communicate ideas and feelings.

Listening GUIDE

John Cage
4'33" (1952)

Genre: Chance music

0:00–0:30	First movement—silence (?)
0:31–2:53	Second movement—silence (?)
2:54–4:33	Third movement—silence (?)

JOHN ADAMS (1947–) AND MINIMALISM

Western classical music—the music of Bach, Beethoven, and Brahms—is typically constructed of large, carefully placed units. A movement of a symphony, for example, has themes, which come in a hierarchy of importance, and sections (development and coda, for example), which must be heard in

FIGURE 36-4

John Adams. In 2003, Lincoln Center, New York, held an eight-week "Absolutely Adams" festival to go along with its annual "Mostly Mozart" program.

a particular order. A compelling sequence of events leads to a desired end and conveys a message from composer to listener. But what would happen if composers reduced the music to just one or two simple motives and repeated these again and again? What would happen if they focused on what things *are*, rather than on what these things might *become*? Such is the approach taken by a group of American postmodernist composers called the Minimalists.

Minimalism is a style of postmodern music, originating in the early 1960s, that takes a very small musical unit and repeats it over and over to form a composition. A three-note melodic cell, a single arpeggio, two alternating chords—these are the sort of "minimal" elements a composer might introduce, reiterate again and again, modify or expand, and then begin to repeat once more. The basic material is usually simple, tonal, and consonant. By repeating these minimal figures incessantly at a steady pulse, the composer creates a hypnotic effect—"trance music" is the name sometimes given this music. The trance-like quality of Minimalist music has influenced rock musicians (Velvet Underground, Talking Heads, and Radiohead) and led to a new genre of pop music called "techno," or "rave" music. Minimalism, in both art and music, has been mainly an American movement. Its most successful musical practitioners are Steve Reich (1936–), Philip Glass (1937–), and John Adams (1947–) (Fig. 36-4).

John Adams (no relation to the presidents) was born in Worcester, Massachusetts, in 1947 and educated at Harvard. As a student, he was encouraged to compose in the twelve-tone style of Arnold Schoenberg (see p. 346). But if Adams counted twelve-tone rows by day, he listened to The Beatles in his dorm room at night. Moving to San Francisco after graduation, Adams developed his own eclectic musical style that blended the learned with the popular and added increasing amounts of Minimalism, which was then gaining popularity in California. Some of Adams's early scores of the 1980s are strict Minimalist works, but later ones become more all-embracing; from time to time, an operatic melody or a funk bass line, for example, will creep into his constantly repeating, minimal sonorities. In 2003, Adams received the Pulitzer Prize in music for his *On the Transmigration of Souls*, which commemorated those killed in the World Trade Center terrorist attacks. Ironically, although Adams is a Minimalist composer, he has been able to extend his ever-repeating blocks of sound into lengthy operas, the best known of which are *Nixon in China* (1987) and *Doctor Atomic* (2005), Minimalist operas that achieve maximum effect. As a creature of the postmodernist age, Adams feels squeezed between the classical tradition and the all-powerful world of pop culture:

I have bad days when I really feel that I'm working in an art form [classical music] that's just not relevant anymore, that had its peak in the years from Vivaldi to Bartók, and now we are just fighting over the crumbs. A really good recording of mine might sell 50,000 copies; that's very rare in classical music. For a rock group, 50,000 CDs sold would be a disaster. (*Harvard Magazine*, 24 July 2007)

Short Ride in a Fast Machine *(1986)*

To experience postmodern Minimalism quickly, we turn to an early work by Adams, one commissioned in 1986 by the Pittsburgh Symphony. *Short Ride in a Fast Machine* is scored for full orchestra and two electronic keyboard synthesizers. Example 36-1 shows how the music is composed of short (mostly four-note) motives that continually repeat. There are five sections to this work (we'll call them laps). In each lap, the machine seems to accelerate, not because the tempo gets faster but because more and more repeating motives are added. The effect created is that of a powerful, twentieth-century engine firing on all cylinders. As Adams has said about his Minimalist work, "You know how it is when someone asks you to ride in a terrific sports car, and then you wish you hadn't?"

EXAMPLE 36–1

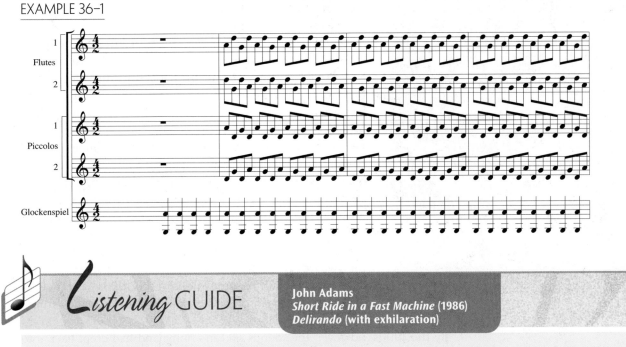

*L*istening GUIDE

John Adams
Short Ride in a Fast Machine (1986)
***Delirando* (with exhilaration)**

5
5/25

0:00	25	Lap 1: Woodblock, woodwinds, and keyboard synthesizers begin; brasses, snare drum, and glockenspiel gradually added
1:04		Lap 2: Bass drum "backfires"; motives rise in pitch and become more dissonant
1:43		Lap 3: Starts quietly with sinister repeating motive in bass; syncopation and dissonance increase
2:30		Lap 4: Two-note falling motive in bass
2:53		Lap 5: Trumpets play fanfare-like motives (this is "victory lap")
3:50		Musical vehicle begins another lap but suddenly breaks down

Listen to streaming music in an Active Listening Guide, available on the text website.

*T*AN DUN (1957–) AND GLOBALIZATION

The signs of **globalization**—the development of an increasingly integrated global economy—are everywhere. Computers, cell phones, and MP3 players—all Western inventions—have brought Western, and particularly American, culture to the Far East. The youth of China, for example, can watch most of the newest American films and TV programs, and listen to latest American music, as instantaneously as can students in the United States. Traditional Western musical culture has also infiltrated the Far East. Music students in conservatories in Japan, China, and Korea now study Western classical music as much as they do their native musics. They learn, for example, how to play the piano, a uniquely Western instrument, performing Bach's fugues and Beethoven's sonatas. Today, nearly as many CDs of Western classical music are sold in Japan as in the United States. But commerce—and cultural

FIGURE 36–5

A poster promoting the film *Crouching Tiger, Hidden Dragon*.

@

To hear strains of Tan and Beethoven in *Internet Symphony No. 1 "Eroica,"* go to the YouTube playlist on the text website.

FIGURE 36–6

Tan Dun.

influence—inevitably flows in two directions. The shorts, socks, and shoes we wear likely came from China, and the automobile in which we ride probably was made (or designed) in Japan. So, too, traditional Chinese music has also made inroads in the West, most emphatically with the Grammy Award–winning film score to *Crouching Tiger, Hidden Dragon* (2000) with music by Tan Dun (Fig. 36-5). As economic barriers are removed, the flow of ideas accelerates, and cultural distinctions begin to blur.

No one better personifies "musical globalization" than Tan Dun (Fig. 36-6). Tan was born in Hunan, China, in 1957 and raised in a rural environment full of music, magic, and ritual. During the **Cultural Revolution** (1966–1976) of Mao Zedong, he was sent to a commune to cultivate rice but was later summoned to play fiddle and arrange music for a provincial troupe of the Beijing Opera. He first heard Beethoven's Symphony No. 5 when he was nineteen and began to dream of becoming a composer. In 1978, owing to his exceptional knowledge of Chinese folk music, Tan was admitted to the Central Conservatory in Beijing, China's most prestigious music school, where he remained for eight years. In 1986, he received a fellowship to study at Columbia University in New York, and at this time, he came under the sway of the most progressive styles of modernism. Indeed, some of Tan's compositions of the 1980s have the sort of atonal, dissonant sound that would have made Arnold Schoenberg smile.

By the 1990s, however, the sounds of Tan's homeland had crept back into his scores: the pentatonic scale, microtonal pitch slides, scratchy string bowings, vibrant percussion sounds, and the nasal timbres of the Beijing Opera style. Tan's own opera *Marco Polo* (1996) earned him the Grawemeyer Award, classical composition's most prestigious prize. Two years later, he wrote the music for the American thriller *Fallen*, starring Denzel Washington. To create his Oscar- and Grammy Award–winning score for *Crouching Tiger, Hidden Dragon*, Tan worked with Yo-Yo Ma (also of Chinese descent). Ma played the cello solos, which were recorded in New York; these were later patched into the full sound track, which was recorded in Shanghai by a Western-style orchestra supplemented by traditional Chinese instruments—a truly global enterprise! Most recently, Tan Dun has worked with Yo-Yo Ma on a series of concerts and recordings called *The Silk Road Project*—a continuing program designed to highlight and integrate the music and instruments of China with those of the Western tradition. In 2009, Google commissioned Tan to compose *Internet Symphony No. 1 "Eroica"* to be performed collaboratively by the YouTube Symphony Orchestra.

Marco Polo (1996)

Tan Dun's opera *Marco Polo* is an excellent vehicle through which to experience his music and explore the process of musical globalization. It was financed and coproduced by opera companies in Amsterdam, Munich, and Hong Kong, where the first three "premieres" occurred simultaneously. Moreover, the subject of Marco Polo, an Italian explorer who traveled the Silk Road to China in the thirteenth century, offered Tan the opportunity to present the music of several different cultures: Western, Middle Eastern, Indian, Tibetan, Mongolian, and Chinese. In the scene "Waiting to Depart," Marco Polo stands before the sea, looking eastward. The figures of Water and Shadows beckon him to begin the journey of time and space. Marco exists in the present (Western Europe) but envisions the future (the Far East). This we know not from reading the sparse libretto, but from listening to the orchestra. What composer Tan has said about this opera in general applies particularly well to this scene: "I think sounds and different musical cultures guide my own development, leading me through a deeper journey. . . . From Medieval [Western] chants, from Western Opera to Beijing Opera, from orchestra to sitar, pipa and Tibetan ritual horns—the fusion of musical sounds from all corners of the globe is the definition of *Marco Polo* to me."

@ Watch a video of Craig Wright's Open Yale Course class session 23, "Review of Musical Style," at the text website.

@ A complete Checklist of Musical Style for the modern and postmodern eras can be found at the text website.

Listening GUIDE

Tan Dun
"Waiting to Depart" from *Marco Polo*
(1996)

13

Genre: Opera

Situation: Marco Polo stands at the edge of Piazza San Marco in Venice, about to embark on his physical and spiritual journey to the East.

0:00	**13**	Low string drone, like Tibetan chant, and then high string sounds sliding between pitches
0:29		"Reedy" flute plays melody around outline of pentatonic scale (E, F♯, G♯, B, C♯, E)
1:09		(Western) cello continues with melody based on same pentatonic scale
1:42		Romantic-sounding (Western) French horn plays same pentatonic scale
2:02		Voice of Water says, "Listen," accompanied by Chinese pipa (see p. 418)
2:14		Voice of Marco says, "Maintain"
2:22		Voices of Water and two Shadows say, "Now journey; listen; now maintain; the journey onward"
3:07		Voice of Marco says, "Preserve; question; read; see"
3:23		Others repeat "Journey," in style of early Western parallel organum
3:45		Drum and gong enter, then full chorus *fortissimo* with dissonant tone clusters: "Go; hurry; into; join"
4:34		Low string drone returns, suggesting mystery and vast distances of East

Key WORDS

electronic music (371)
synthesizer (371)
musique concrète (372)
computer music (373)

sampling (373)
scratching (373)
prepared piano (374)
chance music (374)

Minimalism (376)
globalization (377)
Cultural Revolution (378)

@ The materials on the text website will help you understand and pass tests on the content of this chapter. In addition, you may watch Craig Wright's own lecture at Open Yale Courses and complete this chapter's Listening Exercise interactively, as well as view Active Listening Guides and other materials that will help you succeed in this course.

Glossary

||: :|| : indication to performer to repeat the music

absolute music: instrumental music free of a text or any preexisting program

a cappella: a term applied to unaccompanied vocal music; originated in the expression *a cappella Sistina,* "in the Sistine Chapel" of the pope, where instruments were forbidden to accompany the singers

accelerando: a tempo mark indicating "getting faster"

accent: emphasis or stress placed on a musical tone or a chord

accidental: a sharp, flat, or natural sign that alters the pitch of a note a half step

accompagnato: see *recitativo accompagnato*

acoustic instruments: instruments that produce sounds naturally when strings are bowed or plucked, a tube has air passed through it, or percussion instruments are struck

acoustic music: music produced by acoustic instruments

adagio: a tempo mark indicating "slow"

Alberti bass: a pattern of accompaniment whereby, instead of having the pitches of a chord sound all together, the notes are played in succession to provide a continual stream of sound

allegretto: a tempo mark indicating "moderately fast"

allegro: a tempo mark indicating "fast"

allemande: a stately dance in $\frac{4}{4}$ meter with gracefully interweaving lines

alto (contralto): the lower of the two female voice parts, the soprano being higher

andante: a tempo mark indicating "moderately moving"

andantino: a tempo mark indicating "moderately moving" yet slightly faster than *andante*

antecedent phrase: the opening, incomplete-sounding phrase of a melody; often followed by a consequent phrase that brings the melody to closure

anthem: a composition for chorus on a sacred subject; similar in design and function to a motet

aria: an elaborate lyrical song for solo voice

arioso: a style of singing and a type of song midway between an aria and a recitative

arpeggio: the notes of a triad or seventh chord played in direct succession and in a direct line up or down

Art of Fugue, The: Bach's last project (1742–1750), an encyclopedic treatment of all known contrapuntal procedures, set forth in nineteen canons and fugues

art song: a genre of song for voice and piano accompaniment with high artistic aspirations

atonal music: music without tonality; music without a key center; most often associated with the twentieth-century avant-garde style of Arnold Schoenberg

augmentation: the notes of a melody held for longer than (usually double) their normal duration

backbeat: a drumbeat or cymbal crash occurring regularly after a strong beat, as on beats 2 and 4 in a measure with four beats

ballet: an art form that uses dance and music, along with costumes and scenery, to tell a story and display emotions through expressive gestures and movement

ballet music: music composed to accompany a ballet, with short bursts of tuneful melody and captivating rhythm, all intended to capture the emotional essence of the scene

Ballets russes: a Russian ballet company of the early twentieth century led by Sergei Diaghilev

bandoneon: a square-cut woodwind instrument much like an accordion, except that it is played by pushing buttons rather than keys

bar: see *measure*

baritone: a male voice part of a middle range, between the higher tenor and the lower bass

Baroque: term used to describe the arts generally during the period 1600–1750 and signifying excess and extravagance

bas instruments: a class of soft musical instruments, including the flute, recorder, fiddle, harp, and lute, popular during the late Middle Ages

bass: the lowest male voice range

bass clef: a sign placed on a staff to indicate the notes below middle C

bass drum: a large, low-sounding drum struck with a soft-headed stick

basso continuo: a small ensemble of at least two instrumentalists who provide a foundation for the melody or melodies above; heard almost exclusively in Baroque music

bassoon: a low, double-reed instrument of the woodwind family

basso ostinato: a motive or phrase in the bass that is repeated again and again

bass viol: see *viola da gamba*

Bayreuth Festival: still controlled by the descendants of Wagner, a festival that continues to stage the music dramas of Wagner—and only Wagner—at the Bayreuth Festival Theater, an opera house built especially for that purpose

beat: an even pulse in music that divides the passing of time into equal segments

bel canto: (Italian for "beautiful singing") a style of singing and a type of Italian opera developed in the nineteenth century that features the beautiful tone and brilliant technique of the human voice

binary form: a musical form consisting of two units (**A** and **B**) constructed to balance and complement each other

blues: an expressive, soulful style of singing that emerged from the African-American spiritual and work song at the end of the nineteenth century; its texts are strophic, its harmonies simple and repetitive

bongo drum: a pair of small Afro-Cuban single-headed drums created in Cuba c1900; often heard in Latin American dance bands

Brandenburg Concertos: set of six concerti grossi composed by J. S. Bach between 1711 and 1720, and subsequently dedicated to Margrave Christian Ludwig of Brandenburg

brass family: a group of musical instruments traditionally made of brass and played with a mouthpiece; includes the trumpet, trombone, French horn, and tuba

bridge: see *transition*

bugle: a simple brass instrument that evolved from the valveless military trumpet

cabaletta: the concluding fast aria of any two- or three-section operatic scene; a useful mechanism to get the principals off the stage

cadence: the concluding part of a musical phrase

cadenza: a showy passage for the soloist appearing near the end of the movement in a concerto; usually incorporates rapid runs, arpeggios, and snippets of previously heard themes into a fantasy-like improvisation

canon (of Western music): a core repertoire, or the "chestnuts," of classical music performed at concerts continually since the eighteenth century

canon (round): a contrapuntal form in which the individual voices enter and each in turn duplicates exactly the melody that the first voice played or sang

cantata: a term originally meaning "something sung"; in its mature state, it consists of several movements, including one or more arias, ariosos, and recitatives; cantatas can be on secular subjects and intended for private performance (see *chamber cantata*) or on religious subjects such as those of J. S. Bach for the German Lutheran church

caprice: a light, whimsical character piece of the nineteenth century

castanets: percussion instruments (rattles) of indefinite pitch associated with Spanish music

castrato: a male adult singer who had been castrated as a boy to keep his voice from changing so that it would remain in the soprano or alto register

celesta: a small percussive keyboard instrument using hammers to strike metal bars, thereby producing a bright, bell-like sound

cello (violoncello): an instrument of the violin family but more than twice the violin's size; it is played between the legs and produces a rich, lyrical tone

chamber cantata: a cantata performed before a select audience in a private residence; intimate vocal chamber music, principally of the Baroque era

chamber music: music, usually instrumental music, performed in a small concert hall or private residence with just one performer on each part

chamber sonata: see *sonata da camera*

chance music: music that involves an element of chance (rolling dice, choosing cards, etc.) or whimsy on the part of the performers; especially popular with avant-garde composers

chanson: a French term used broadly to indicate a lyrical song from the Middle Ages into the twentieth century

character piece: a brief instrumental work seeking to capture a single mood; a genre much favored by composers of the Romantic era

chorale: the German word for the hymn of the Lutheran Church; hence a simple religious melody to be sung by the congregation

chord: two or more simultaneously sounding pitches

chord progression: a succession of chords moving forward in a purposeful fashion

chorus: a group of singers, usually including sopranos, altos, tenors, and basses, with at least two and often many more singers on each vocal part; in Tin Pan Alley songs and Broadway tunes, the main melody of the song; jazz musicians often improvised around it

chromatic harmony: harmony utilizing chords built on the five chromatic notes of the scale in addition to the seven diatonic ones; produces rich harmonies

chromaticism: the frequent presence in melodies and chords of intervals only a half step apart; in a scale, the use of notes not part of the diatonic major or minor pattern

chromatic scale: scale that makes use of all twelve pitches, equally divided, within the octave

church cantata: see *cantata*

church sonata: see *sonata da chiesa*

clarinet: a single-reed instrument of the woodwind family with a large range and a wide variety of timbres within it

classical music: the traditional music of any culture, usually involving a specialized technical vocabulary and requiring long years of training; it is "high art" or "learned" music that is enjoyed generation after generation

clavier: a general term for all keyboard instruments including the harpsichord, organ, and piano

clef: a sign used to indicate the register, or range of pitches, in which an instrument is to play or a singer is to sing

coda: (Italian for "tail") a final and concluding section of a musical composition

collage art: art made up of disparate materials taken from very different places

collegium musicum: a society of amateur musicians (usually associated with a university) dedicated to the performance of music, nowadays music of the Middle Ages, Renaissance, and Baroque era

col legno: (Italian for "with the wood") an instruction to string players to strike the strings of the instrument not with the horsehair of the bow, but with the wood of it

color (timbre): the character or quality of a musical tone as determined by its harmonics and its attack and decay

comic opera: a genre of opera that originated in the eighteenth century, portraying everyday characters and situations, and using spoken dialogue and simple songs

computer music: the most recent development in electronic music; it couples the computer with the electronic synthesizer to imitate the sounds of acoustic instruments and to produce new sounds

concertino: the group of instruments that function as soloists in a concerto grosso

concerto: an instrumental genre in which one or more soloists play with and against a larger orchestra

concerto grosso: a multi-movement concerto of the Baroque era that pits the sound of a small group of soloists (the concertino) against that of the full orchestra (the tutti)

concert overture: an independent, one-movement work, usually of programmatic content, originally intended for the concert hall and not designed to precede an opera or play

conga drum: a large Afro-Cuban single-headed barrel drum played in Latin American dance bands

conjunct motion: melodic motion that proceeds primarily by steps and without leaps

consequent phrase: the second phrase of a two-part melodic unit that brings a melody to a point of repose and closure

consonance: pitches sounding agreeable and stable

continuo: see *basso continuo*

contrabassoon: a larger, lower-sounding version of the bassoon

contrast: process employed by a composer to introduce different melodies, rhythms, textures, or moods in order to provide variety

cornet: a brass instrument that looks like a short trumpet; it has a more mellow tone than the trumpet and is most often used in military bands

cornetto: a woodwind instrument, developed during the late Middle Ages and early Renaissance, that sounds like a hybrid of a clarinet and trumpet

Council of Trent: two-decade-long (1545–1563) conference at which leading cardinals and bishops undertook reform of the Roman Catholic Church, including its music

counterpoint: the harmonious opposition of two or more independent musical lines

Counter-Reformation: movement that fostered reform in the Roman Catholic Church in response to the challenge of the Protestant Reformation and led to a conservative, austere approach to art

courante: a lively dance in $\frac{6}{4}$ with an upbeat and frequent changes of metrical accent

crescendo: a gradual increase in the volume of sound

cross stringing: a practice popularized by the Steinway Company whereby the lowest strings of the piano ride up and across those of the middle register, thereby giving the piano a richer, more homogenized sound

Cubism: early-twentieth-century artistic style in which the artist fractures and dislocates formal reality into geometrical blocks and planes

Cultural Revolution: Chairman Mao Zedong's social and political reformation of the People's Republic of China between 1966 and 1976

cymbals: a percussion instrument of two metal discs; they are made to crash together to create emphasis and articulation in music

da capo **aria:** an aria in two sections, with an obligatory return to and repeat of the first; hence an aria in ternary (**ABA**) form

da capo **form:** ternary (**ABA**) form for an aria, so called because the performers, when reaching the end of B, "take it from the head" and repeat A

dance suite: a collection of instrumental dances, each with its own distinctive rhythm and character

decrescendo (diminuendo): gradual decrease in the intensity of sound

development: the center-most portion of sonata–allegro form, in which the thematic material of the exposition is developed and extended, transformed, or reduced to its essence; often the most confrontational and unstable section of the movement

diatonic: pertaining to the seven notes that make up either the major or the minor scale

Dies irae: a Gregorian chant composed in the thirteenth century and used as the central portion of the Requiem Mass of the Catholic Church

diminished chord: a triad or seventh chord made up entirely of minor thirds and producing a tense, unstable sound

diminuendo: a gradual decrease in the volume of sound

diminution: a reduction, usually by half, of all the rhythmic durations in a melody

disjunct motion: melodic motion that moves primarily by leaps rather than by steps

dissonance: a discordant mingling of sounds

diva: (Italian for "goddess") a celebrated female opera singer; a prima donna

Doctrine of Affections: early-seventeenth-century aesthetic theory that held that different musical moods could and should be used to influence the emotions, or affections, of the listener

dominant: the chord built on the fifth degree of the scale

doo-wop: type of soul music that emerged in the 1950s as an outgrowth of the gospel hymns sung in African-American churches in urban Detroit, Chicago, and New York; its lyrics made use of repeating phrases sung in a cappella (unaccompanied) harmony below the tune

dotted note: a note to which an additional duration of 50 percent has been added

double bass: the largest and lowest-pitched instrument in the string family

double counterpoint: counterpoint with two themes that can reverse position, with the top theme moving to the bottom, and the bottom to the top (also called *invertible counterpoint*)

double exposition form: a form, originating in the concerto of the Classical period, in which first the orchestra and then the soloist present the primary thematic material

double stops: a technique applied to string instruments in which two strings are pressed down and played simultaneously instead of just one

downbeat: the first beat of each measure; indicated by a downward motion of the conductor's hand and usually stressed

dramatic overture: a one-movement work, usually in sonata–allegro form, that encapsulates in music the essential

dramatic events of the opera or play that follows

drone: a continuous sound on one or more fixed pitches

duple meter: gathering of beats into two beats per measure, with every other beat stressed

dynamics: the various levels of volume, loud and soft, at which sounds are produced in a musical composition

electronic instruments: machines that produce musical sounds by electronic means, the most widespread instrument being the keyboard synthesizer

electronic music: sounds produced and manipulated by magnetic tape machines, synthesizers, and/or computers

eleventh chord: a chord comprising five intervals of a third and spanning eleven different letter names of pitches

encore: (French for "again") the repeat of a piece demanded by an appreciative audience; an extra piece added at the end of a concert

English horn: an alto oboe, pitched at the interval a fifth below the oboe, much favored by composers of the Romantic era

Enlightenment: eighteenth-century period in philosophy and letters during which thinkers gave free rein to the pursuit of truth and the discovery of natural laws

episode: a passage of free, nonimitative counterpoint found in a fugue

"Eroica" Symphony: Beethoven's Symphony No. 3 (1803), originally dedicated to Napoleon but published as the "Heroic Symphony"

Esterházy family: the richest and most influential among the German-speaking aristocrats of eighteenth-century Hungary, with extensive landholdings southeast of Vienna and a passionate interest in music; patrons of Haydn

etude: a short one-movement composition designed to improve one aspect of a performer's technique

exoticism: use of sounds drawn from outside the traditional Western European musical experience, popular among composers in late-nineteenth-century Europe

exposition: in a fugue, the opening section, in which each voice in turn has the opportunity to present the subject; in sonata–allegro form, the principal section, in which all thematic material is presented

Expressionism: powerful movement in the early-twentieth-century arts, initially a German-Austrian development that arose in Berlin, Munich, and Vienna; its aim was not to depict objects as they are seen but to express the strong emotion that the object generates in the artist

falsetto voice: a high, soprano-like voice produced by adult male singers when they sing in head voice and not in full chest voice

fantasy: a free, improvisatory-like composition in which the composer follows his or her whims rather than an established musical form

fermata: in musical notation, a mark indicating that the performer(s) should hold a note or chord for an extended duration

figured bass: in musical notation, a numerical shorthand that tells the player which unwritten notes to fill in above the written bass note

finale: the last movement of a multimovement composition, one that usually works to a climax and conclusion

flamenco: a genre of Spanish song and dance, with guitar accompaniment, that originated in southern-most Spain and exhibits non-Western, possibly Arab-influenced, scales

flat: in musical notation, a symbol that lowers a pitch by a half step

flute: a high-sounding member of the woodwind family; initially made of wood, but more recently, beginning in the nineteenth century, of silver or even platinum

folk-rock: a mixture of the steady beat of rock with the forms, topics, and styles of singing of the traditional Anglo-American folk ballad

folk song: a song originating from an ethnic group and passed from generation to generation by oral tradition rather than written notation

form: the purposeful organization of the artist's materials; in music, the general shape of a composition as perceived by the listener

formalism: modern music, according to Soviet authorities in the 1920s and 1930s, who branded it as "antidemocratic"

forte (𝆑): in musical notation, a dynamic mark indicating "loud"

fortepiano (*pianoforte*): the original name of the piano

fortissimo (𝆑𝆑): in musical notation, a dynamic mark indicating "very loud"

free counterpoint: counterpoint in which the voices do not all make use of some preexisting subject in imitation

free jazz: a style of jazz perfected during the 1960s in which a soloist indulges in flights of creative fancy without concern for the rhythm, melody, or harmony of the other performers

Freemasons: fraternity of the Enlightenment who believed in tolerance and universal brotherhood

French horn: a brass instrument that plays in the middle range of the brass family; developed from the medieval hunting horn

French overture: an overture style developed by Jean-Baptiste Lully with two sections, the first slow in duple meter with dotted note values, the second fast in triple meter and with light imitation; the first section can be repeated after the second

fugato: a short fugue set in some other musical form, such as sonata–allegro or theme and variations

fugue: a composition for three, four, or five parts played or sung by voices or instruments; begins with a presentation of a subject in imitation in each part and continues with modulating passages of free counterpoint and further appearances of the subject

full cadence: a cadence that sounds complete, in part because it usually ends on the tonic note

furiant: an exuberant folk dance of Czech origin in which duple and triple meter alternate

galliard: fast, leaping Renaissance dance in triple meter

genre: type of music; specifically, the quality of musical style, form, performing medium, and place of performance that characterize any one type of music

Gesamtkunstwerk: (German for "total art work") an art form that involves music, poetry, drama, and scenic design; often used in reference to Richard Wagner's music dramas

Gewandhaus Orchestra: the symphony orchestra that originated in the Clothiers' House in Leipzig, Germany, in the eighteenth century

gigue: a fast dance in $\frac{6}{8}$ or $\frac{12}{8}$ with a constant eighth-note pulse that produces a gallop-like effect

glissando: a device of sliding up or down the scale very rapidly

globalization: development of an increasingly integrated global economy

glockenspiel: a percussion instrument made of tuned metal bars that are struck by mallets

gong: a circular, metal percussion instrument of Asian origin

grave: a tempo mark indicating "very slow and grave"

great (grand) staff: a large musical staff that combines both the treble and the bass clefs

Gregorian chant (plainsong): a large body of unaccompanied monophonic vocal music, set to Latin texts, composed for the Western Church over the course of fifteen centuries, from the time of the earliest fathers to the Council of Trent (1545–1563)

ground bass: the English term for *basso ostinato*

guiro: a scraped percussion instrument originating in South America and the Caribbean

habanera: an Afro-Cuban dance song that came to prominence in the nineteenth century, marked by a repeating bass and a repeating, syncopated rhythm

half cadence: a cadence at which the music does not come to a fully satisfying stop but stands as if suspended on a dominant chord

half step: the smallest musical interval in the Western major or minor scale; the distance between any two adjacent keys on the piano

harmony: the sounds that provide the support and enrichment—the accompaniment—for melody

harp: an ancient, plucked-string instrument with a triangular shape

harpsichord: a keyboard instrument, especially popular during the Baroque era, that produces sound by depressing a key that drives a lever upward and forces a pick to pluck a string

hauts instruments: a class of loud musical instruments, including the trumpet, sackbut, shawm, and drum, popular during the late Middle Ages

Heiligenstadt Testament: something akin to Beethoven's last will and testament, written in despair when he recognized that he would ultimately suffer a total loss of hearing; named after the Viennese suburb in which he penned it

"heroic" period: a period in Beethoven's compositional career (1803–1813) during which he wrote longer works incorporating broad gestures, grand climaxes, and triadic, triumphant themes

hip hop: larger genre, encompassing rap music, in which the vocal line is delivered more like speech than like song and in which a wide variety of rhythmic devices are used

homophony: a texture in which all the voices, or lines, move to new pitches at roughly the same time; often referred to in contradistinction to polyphony

horn: a term generally used by musicians to refer to any brass instrument, but most often the French horn

hornpipe: an energetic dance, derived from the country jig, in either $\frac{3}{2}$ or $\frac{2}{4}$ time

humanism: Renaissance belief that people have the capacity to create many things good and beautiful; it rejoiced in the human form in all its fullness, looked outward, and indulged a passion for invention and discovery

idée fixe: literally, a "fixed idea"; more specifically, an obsessive musical theme as first used in Hector Berlioz's *Symphonie fantastique*

idiomatic writing: musical composition that exploits the strengths and avoids the weaknesses of particular voices and instruments

imitation: the process by which one or more musical voices, or parts, enter and duplicate exactly for a period of time the music presented by the previous voice

imitative counterpoint: a type of counterpoint in which the voices or lines frequently use imitation

impresario: renowned producer

Impressionism: late-nineteenth-century movement that arose in France; the Impressionists were the first to reject photographic realism in painting, instead trying to re-create the impression that an object produces upon the senses in a single, fleeting moment

incidental music: music to be inserted between the acts or during important scenes of a play to add an extra dimension to the drama

intermezzo: (Italian for "between piece") a light musical interlude intended to separate and thus break the mood of two more serious, surrounding movements or operatic acts or scenes

interval: the distance between any two pitches on a musical scale

inversion: the process of inverting the musical intervals in a theme or melody; a melody that ascends by step, now descends by step, and so on

invertible counterpoint: see *double counterpoint*

jazz-fusion: a mixture of jazz and rock cultivated by American bands in the 1970s

jazz riff: a short motive, usually played by an entire instrumental section (woodwinds or brasses), that appears frequently, but intermittently, in a jazz composition

key: a tonal center built on a tonic note and making use of a scale; also, on a keyboard instrument, one of a series of levers that can be depressed to generate sound

key signature: in musical notation, a preplaced set of sharps or flats used to indicate the scale and key

Köchel (K) number: an identifying number assigned to each of the works of Mozart, in roughly chronological order, by Ludwig von Köchel (1800–1877)

Kyrie: the first portion of the Ordinary of the Mass, and hence usually the opening movement in a polyphonic setting of the Mass

largo: a tempo mark indicating "slow and broad"

La Scala: the principal opera house of the city of Milan, Italy, which opened in 1778

leading tone: the pitch a half step below the tonic, which pulls up and into it, especially at cadences

leap: melodic movement not by an interval of just a step, but usually by a jump of at least a fourth

legato: in musical notation, an articulation mark indicating that the notes are to be smoothly connected; the opposite of staccato

leitmotif: a brief, distinctive unit of music designed to represent a character, object, or idea; a term applied to the motives in the music dramas of Richard Wagner

lento: a tempo mark indicating "very slow"

libretto: the text of an opera

Liebestod: (German for "love death") the famous aria sung by the expiring Isolde at the end of Richard Wagner's opera *Tristan und Isolde*

Lied: (German for "song") the genre of art song, for voice and piano accompaniment, that originated in Germany c1800

Lisztomania: the sort of mass hysteria, today reserved for pop music stars, that surrounded touring Romantic-era pianist Franz Liszt

London Symphonies: the twelve symphonies composed by Joseph Haydn for performance in London between 1791 and 1795; Haydn's last twelve symphonies (Nos. 93–104)

lute: a six-string instrument appearing in the West in the late Middle Ages

lyrics: text set to music

madrigal: a popular genre of secular vocal music that originated in Italy during the Renaissance, in which usually four or five voices sing love poems

madrigalism: a device, originating in the madrigal, by which key words in a text spark a particularly expressive musical setting

major scale: a seven-note scale that ascends in the following order of whole and half steps: 1-1-½-1-1-1-½

Marseillaise, La: a tune written as a revolutionary marching song in 1792 by Claude-Joseph Rouget de Lisle and sung by a battalion from Marseilles as it entered Paris that year; it subsequently became the French national anthem

Mass: the central religious service of the Roman Catholic Church, one that incorporates singing for spiritual reflection or as accompaniment to sacred acts

mazurka: a fast dance of Polish origins in triple meter with an accent on the second beat

measure (bar): a group of beats, or musical pulses; usually, the number of beats is fixed and constant so that the measure serves as a continual unit of measurement in music

melisma: in singing, one vowel luxuriously spread out over many notes

melismatic singing: many notes sung to just one syllable

melodic sequence: the repetition of a musical motive at successively higher or lower degrees of the scale

melody: a series of notes arranged in order to form a distinctive, recognizable musical unit; most often placed in the treble

meter: the gathering of beats into regular groups

meter signature: see *time signature*

metronome: a mechanical device used by performers to keep a steady tempo

mezzo-soprano: a female vocal range between alto and soprano

middle C: the middle-most C on the modern piano

Minimalism: a style of modern music that takes a very small amount of musical material and repeats it over and over to form a composition

Minnesinger: a type of secular poet-musician that flourished in Germany during the twelfth through fourteenth centuries

minor scale: a seven-note scale that ascends in the following order of whole and half steps: 1-½-1-1-½-1-1

minuet: a moderate dance in $\frac{3}{4}$, though actually danced in patterns of six steps, with no upbeat but with highly symmetrical phrasing

mode: a pattern of pitches forming a scale; the two primary modes in Western music are major and minor

moderato: a tempo marking indicating "moderately moving"

modified strophic form: strophic form in which the music is modified slightly to accommodate a particularly expressive word or phrase in the text

modulation: the process in music whereby the tonal center changes from one key to another—from G major to C major, for example

monody: a general term connoting solo singing accompanied by a *basso continuo* in the early Baroque period

monophony: a musical texture involving only a single line of music with no accompaniment

motet: a composition for choir or larger chorus setting a religious, devotional, or solemn text; often sung a cappella

motive: a short, distinctive melodic figure that stands by itself

mouthpiece: a detachable portion of a brass instrument into which the player blows

movement: a large, independent section of a major instrumental work, such as a sonata, dance suite, symphony, quartet, or concerto

music: the rational organization of sounds and silences as they pass through time

musical nationalism: see *nationalism*

music drama: a term used for the mature operas of Richard Wagner

musique concrète: music in which the composer works directly with sounds recorded on magnetic tape, not with musical notation and performers

mute: any device that muffles the sound of a musical instrument; on the trumpet, for example, it is a cup that is placed inside the bell of the instrument

nationalism: a movement in music in the nineteenth century in which composers sought to emphasize indigenous qualities in their music by incorporating folk songs, native scales, dance rhythms, and local instrumental sounds

natural: in musical notation, a symbol that cancels a preexisting sharp or flat

Neo-classicism: a movement in twentieth-century music that sought to return to the musical forms and aesthetics of the Baroque and Classical periods

New Age music: a style of nonconfrontational, often repetitious music performed on electronic instruments that arose during the 1990s

ninth chord: a chord spanning nine letters of the scale and constructed by superimposing four intervals of a third

nocturne: a slow, introspective type of music, usually for piano, with rich harmonies and poignant dissonances intending to convey the mysteries of the night

nonimitative counterpoint: counterpoint with independent lines that do not imitate each other

oboe: an instrument of the woodwind family; the highest-pitched of the double-reed instruments

octave: the interval comprising the first and eighth tones of the major and minor diatonic scale; the sounds are quite similar because the frequency of vibration of the higher pitch is exactly twice that of the lower

octave displacement: a process used in constructing a melody whereby a simple, nearby interval is made more distant, and the melodic line more disjunct, by placing the next note up or down an octave

Ode to Joy: An die Freude by poet Friedrich von Schiller, set to music by Beethoven as a hymn in honor of universal brotherhood and used in the finale of his Symphony No. 9

opera: a dramatic work in which the actors sing some or all of their parts; it usually makes use of elaborate stage sets and costumes

opera buffa: (Italian for "comic opera") a genre of opera featuring light, often domestic subjects, with tuneful melodies, comic situations, and happy endings

opera seria: a genre of opera that dominated the stage during the Baroque era, making use of serious historical or mythological subjects, *da capo* arias, and lengthy overtures

operetta: a light opera with spoken dialogue and numerous dances involving comedy and romance in equal measure

ophicleide: a low brass instrument originating in military bands about the time of the French Revolution; the precursor of the tuba

opus: (Latin for "work") the term adopted by composers to enumerate and identify their compositions

oral tradition: the process used in the transmission of folk songs and other traditional music in which the material is passed from one generation to the next by singing, playing, and hearing without musical notation

oratorio: a large-scale genre of sacred music involving an overture, arias, recitatives, and choruses, but sung, whether in a theater or a church, without costumes or scenery

orchestra: see *symphony orchestra*

orchestral dance suite: a dance suite written for orchestra

orchestral Lied: see *orchestral song*

orchestral score: a composite of the musical lines of all of the instruments of the orchestra and from which a conductor conducts

orchestral song: a genre of music emerging in the nineteenth century in which the voice is accompanied not merely by a piano but by a full orchestra

orchestration: the art of assigning to the various instruments of the orchestra, or of a chamber ensemble, the diverse melodies, accompaniments, and counterpoints of a musical composition

Ordinary of the Mass: the five sung portions of the Mass for which the texts are unvariable

organ: an ancient musical instrument constructed mainly of pipes and keys; the player depresses a key, which allows air to rush into or over a pipe, thereby producing sound

organum: the name given to the early polyphony of the Western Church from the ninth through the thirteenth centuries

oscillator: a device that, when activated by an electronic current, pulses back and forth to produce an electronic signal that can be converted by a loudspeaker into sound

ostinato: (Italian for "obstinate") a musical figure, motive, melody, harmony, or rhythm that is repeated again and again

overtone: Extremely faint sound, in addition to the fundamental sound of an instrument, caused by fractional vibrations of a string or air column within a pipe

overture: an introductory movement, usually for orchestra, that precedes an opera, oratorio, or dance suite

parallel motion: a musical process in which all of the lines or parts move in the same direction, and at the same intervals, for a period of time; the opposite of counterpoint

part: an independent line or voice in a musical composition; also, a section of a composition

pastoral aria: aria with several distinctive musical characteristics, all of which suggest pastoral scenes and the movement of simple shepherds attending the Christ Child

"Pathétique" Sonata: one of Beethoven's most celebrated compositions for piano

pavane: slow, gliding Renaissance dance in duple meter performed by couples holding hands

pedal point: a note, usually in the bass, sustained or continually repeated for a period of time while the harmonies change around it

pentatonic scale: a five-note scale found often in folk music and non-Western music

phrase: a self-contained portion of a melody, theme, or tune

pianissimo (pp): in musical notation, a dynamic mark indicating "very soft"

piano (p): in musical notation, a dynamic mark indicating "soft"

piano: a large keyboard instrument that creates sound at various dynamic levels when hammers are struck against strings

pianoforte: the original name for the piano

piano transcription: the transformation and reduction of an orchestral score, and a piece of orchestral music, onto the great staff for playing at the piano

piccolo: a small flute; the smallest and highest-pitched woodwind instrument

pickup: a note or two coming before the first downbeat of a piece, intending to give a little extra push into that downbeat

pitch: the relative position, high or low, of a musical sound

pizzicato: the process whereby a performer plucks the strings of an instrument rather than bowing them

plainsong: see *Gregorian chant*

point of imitation: a distinctive motive that is sung or played in turn by each voice or instrumental line

polonaise: a dance of Polish origin in triple meter without an upbeat but usually with an accent on the second of the three beats

polychord: the stacking of one triad or seventh chord on another so they sound simultaneously

polymeter: two or more meters sounding simultaneously

polyphony: a musical texture involving two or more simultaneously sounding lines; the lines are often independent and create counterpoint

polyrhythm: two or more rhythms sounding simultaneously

polytonality: the simultaneous sounding of two keys or tonalities

popular music: a broad category of music designed to please a large section of the general public; sometimes used in contradistinction to more "serious" or more "learned" classical music

prelude: an introductory, improvisatory-like movement that gives the performer a chance to warm up and sets the stage for a more substantive subsequent movement

prepared piano: a piano outfitted with screws, bolts, washers, erasers, and bits of felt and plastic to transform the instrument from a melodic one to a percussive one

prestissimo: in musical notation, a tempo mark indicating "as fast as possible"

presto: in musical notation, a tempo mark indicating "very fast"

prima donna: (Italian for "first lady") the leading female singer in an opera

program music: a piece of instrumental music, usually for symphony orchestra, that seeks to re-create in sound the events and emotions portrayed in some extramusical source: a story, a play, a historical event, an encounter with nature, or even a painting

program symphony: a symphony with the usual three, four, or five movements in which the individual movements together tell a tale or depict a succession of specific events or scenes

Proper of the Mass: the sections of the Mass that are sung to texts that vary with each feast day

qin: an ancient seven-string Chinese dulcimer played with two bamboo sticks

quadrivium: a curriculum of four scientific disciplines (arithmetic, geometry, astronomy, and music) taught in medieval schools and universities

quadruple meter: music with four beats per measure

quarter note: unit of musical duration that most often represents the beat; normally moves at roughly the rate of the average person's heartbeat

quarter tone: the division of the whole tone, or whole step, into quarter tones, a division even smaller than the half tone, or half step, on the piano

rap: a style of popular music closely associated with hip hop that became popular in the United States in the 1980s, mostly among urban African-Americans; it usually involves rapping along with audio processing (sampling and scratching)

realistic opera: a general term for those operas of the nineteenth and early twentieth centuries that deal with everyday, gritty subjects; includes Italian *verismo* opera

rebec: a medieval fiddle

recapitulation: in sonata–allegro form, the return to the first theme and the tonic key following the development

recital: a concert of chamber music, usually for a solo performer

recitative: musically heightened speech, often used in an opera, oratorio, or cantata to report dramatic action and advance the plot

recitativo accompagnato: a recitative accompanied by the orchestra instead of merely the harpsichord; the opposite of simple, or *secco*, recitative

recorder: an end-blown wooden flute with seven finger holes, played straight out instead of to one side

relative major: the major key in a pair of major and minor keys; relative keys have the same key signature, for example, E♭ major and C minor (both with three flats)

relative minor: the minor key in a pair of major and minor keys; see *relative major*

repetition: process employed by a composer to validate the importance of a section of music by repeating it

rest: a silence in music of a specific duration

retransition: the end of the development section, where the tonality often becomes stabilized on the dominant in preparation for the return of the tonic (and first theme) at the beginning of the recapitulation

retrograde: a musical process in which a melody is played or sung, not from beginning to end, but starting with the last note and working backward to the first

rhythm: the organization of time in music, dividing up long spans of time into smaller, more easily comprehended units

Ring cycle: a cycle of four interconnected music dramas by Richard Wagner that collectively tell the tale of the Germanic legend *Der Ring des Nibelungen*

Risorgimento: the name given to the political movement that promoted the liberation and unification of Italy in the mid-nineteenth century

ritard: a gradual slowing down of the tempo

ritardando: in musical notation, a tempo mark indicating a slowing down of the tempo

ritornello form: form in a Baroque concerto grosso in which all or part of the main theme—the ritornello (Italian for "return" or "refrain"—returns again and again, invariably played by the tutti, or full orchestra

romance: a slow, lyrical piece, or movement within a larger work, for instruments, or instrument and voice, much favored by composers of the Romantic period

rondeau: see *rondo form*

rondo form: classical form with at least three statements of the refrain (**A**) and at least two contrasting sections (at least **B** and **C**); placement of the refrain creates symmetrical patterns such as **ABACA**, **ABACABA**, or even **ABACADA**

rubato: (Italian for "robbed") in musical notation, a tempo mark indicating that the performer may take, or steal, great liberties with the tempo

Russian Five: a group of young composers (Borodin, Cui, Balakirev, Rimsky-Korsakov, and Musorgsky) centered in St. Petersburg, whose aim was to write purely Russian music free of European influence

Russian Revolution: overthrow of the Russian tsar by the socialist Bolshevik Party in 1917

sackbut: a brass instrument of the late Middle Ages and Renaissance; the precursor of the trombone

Salzburg: mountain town in Austria, birthplace of Mozart

sampling: reusing (and often repeating) portions of a previous sound recording in a new song

Sanctus: the fourth section of the Ordinary of the Mass

sarabande: a slow, elegant dance in $\frac{3}{4}$ with a strong accent on the second beat

scale: an arrangement of pitches that ascends and descends in a fixed and unvarying pattern

scena: a scenic plan in Italian opera involving a succession of separate elements such as a slow aria, a recitative, and a fast concluding aria

scherzo: (Italian for "joke") a rapid, jovial work in triple meter often used in place of the minuet as the third movement in a string quartet or symphony

Schubertiad: a social gathering for music and poetry that featured the songs and piano music of Franz Schubert

score: a volume of musical notation involving more than one staff

scratching: sound processing that involves the rhythmical manipulation of a vinyl record

secco recitative: see *simple recitative*

Second Viennese School: a group of progressive modernist composers centered around Arnold Schoenberg in Vienna in the early twentieth century

sequence: a Gregorian chant, sung during the Proper of the Mass, in which a chorus and a soloist alternate; see also *melodic sequence*

serenade: an instrumental work for a small ensemble originally intended as a light entertainment in the evening

serial music: music in which some important component—pitch, dynamics, rhythm—comes in a continually repeating series; see also *twelve-tone composition*

seventh chord: a chord spanning seven letter names and constructed by superimposing three thirds

sforzando: a sudden, loud attack on one note or chord

sharp: a musical symbol that raises a pitch by a half step

shawm: a double-reed woodwind instrument of the late Middle Ages and Renaissance; the precursor of the oboe

simple recitative: recitative accompanied only by a *basso continuo* or a harpsichord, and not the full orchestra

sinfonia: (Italian for "symphony") a one-movement (later three- or four-movement) orchestral work that originated in Italy in the seventeenth century

Singspiel: (German for "singing play") a musical comedy originating in Germany with spoken dialogue, tuneful songs, and topical humor

Sistine Chapel: the pope's private chapel within his Vatican apartments

snare drum: a small drum consisting of a metal cylinder covered with a skin or sheet of plastic that, when played with sticks, produces the "rat-ta-tat" sound familiar from marching bands

soft pedal: the left pedal of the piano, which, when depressed, shifts the keyboard in such a way that the hammers strike fewer strings, making the instrument sound softer

solo: a musical composition, or portion of a composition, sung or played by a single performer

solo concerto: a concerto in which an orchestra and a single performer in turn present and develop the musical material in the spirit of harmonious competition

solo sonata: a work, usually in three or four movements, for keyboard or other solo instrument; when a solo melodic instrument played a sonata in the Baroque era, it was supported by the *basso continuo*

sonata: originally, "something sounded" on an instrument as opposed to something sung (a "cantata"); later, a multi-movement work for solo instrument, or instrument with keyboard accompaniment

sonata–allegro form: a dramatic musical form that originated in the Classical period involving an exposition, development, and recapitulation, with optional introduction and coda

sonata da camera (**chamber sonata**): a suite for keyboard or small instrumental ensemble made up of individual dance movements

sonata da chiesa (**church sonata**): a suite for keyboard or small instrumental ensemble made up of movements indicated only by tempo marks such as *grave, vivace*, and *adagio*; originally intended to be performed in church

song cycle: a collection of several songs united by a common textual theme or literary idea

soprano: the highest female vocal part

Sprechstimme: (German for "speech-voice") a vocal technique in which a singer declaims, rather than sings, a text at only approximate pitch levels

staccato: a manner of playing in which each note is held only for the shortest possible time

staff: a horizontal grid onto which are put the symbols of musical notation: notes, rests, accidentals, dynamic marks, etc.

stanza: a poetic unit of two or more lines with a consistent meter and rhyme scheme

statement: presentation of important musical idea

step: the interval between adjacent pitches in the diatonic or chromatic scale; either a whole step or a half step

stomp: a piece of early jazz in which a distinctive rhythm, with syncopation, is established in the opening bars, as in the opening phrases of the "Charleston"

stop: a knob (or key) on a pipe organ that, when pulled (or pushed), allows a particular group of pipes to sound, thereby creating a distinctive tone color

string bass: see *double bass*

string instruments: instruments that produce sound when strings are bowed or plucked; the harp, the guitar, and members of the violin family are all string instruments

string quartet: a standard instrumental ensemble for chamber music consisting of a single first and second violin, a viola, and a cello; also, the genre of music, usually in three or four movements, composed for this ensemble

strophe: see *stanza*

strophic form: a musical form often used in setting a strophic, or stanzaic, text, such as a hymn or carol; the music is repeated anew for each successive strophe

style: the general surface sound produced by the interaction of the elements of music: melody, rhythm, harmony, color, texture, and form

subdominant: the chord built on the fourth, or subdominant, degree of the major or minor scale

subject: the term for the principal theme in a fugue

suite: an ordered set of instrumental pieces, usually all in one key, intended to be played in a single sitting (see also *dance suite*)

sustaining pedal: the right-most pedal on the piano; when it is depressed, all dampers are removed from the strings, allowing them to vibrate freely

syllabic singing: a style of singing in which each syllable of text has one, and only one, note; the opposite of melismatic singing

Symbolists: group of poets in late-nineteenth-century Paris whose aesthetic aims were in harmony with those of the Impressionist painters; they worked to create a poetic style in which the literal *meaning* of the word was less important than its *sound* and the associations that that sound might produce

symphonic poem (tone poem): a one-movement work for orchestra of the Romantic era that gives musical expression to the emotions and events associated with a story, play, political occurrence, personal experience, or encounter with nature

symphony: a genre of instrumental music for orchestra consisting of several movements; also, the orchestral ensemble that plays this genre

symphony orchestra: the large instrumental ensemble that plays symphonies, overtures, concertos, and the like

syncopation: a rhythmic device in which the natural accent falling on a strong beat is displaced to a weak beat or between the beats

synthesizer: a machine that has the capacity to produce, transform, and combine (or synthesize) electronic sounds

tambourine: a small drum, the head of which is hung with jangles; it can be struck or shaken to produce a tremolo effect

tam-tam: an unpitched gong used in Western orchestras

tango: a genre of popular urban song and dance originating in Cuba and Argentina in the nineteenth century; marked by a duple meter with syncopation after the first beat and a slow, sensuous feel

tempo: the speed at which the beats occur in music

tenor: the highest male vocal range

ternary form: a three-part musical form in which the third section is a repeat of the first; hence **ABA**

terraced dynamics: a term used to describe the sharp, abrupt dynamic contrasts found in the music of the Baroque era

texture: the density and disposition of the musical lines that make up a musical composition; monophonic, homophonic, and polyphonic are the primary musical textures

theme and variations: a musical form in which a theme continually returns but is varied by changing the notes of the melody, the harmony, the rhythm, or some other feature of the music

through-composed: a term used to describe music that exhibits no obvious repetitions or overt musical form from beginning to end

timbre: see *color*

timpani (kettle drums): a percussion instrument consisting usually of two, but sometimes four, large drums that can produce a specific pitch when struck with mallets

time signature (meter signature): two numbers, one on top of the other, usually placed at the beginning of the music to tell the performer what note value is carrying the beat and how the beats are to be grouped

toccata: a one-movement composition, free in form, originally for solo keyboard but later for instrumental ensemble as well

tonality: the organization of music around a central tone (the tonic) and the scale built on that tone

tone: a sound with a definite, consistent pitch

tone cluster: a dissonant sounding of several pitches, each only a half step away from the other, in a densely packed chord

tone poem: see *symphonic poem*

tonic: the central pitch around which the melody and harmony gravitate

transition (bridge): in sonata–allegro form, the unstable section in which the tonality changes from tonic to dominant (or relative major) in preparation for the appearance of the second theme

treble: the uppermost musical line, voice, or part; the part in which the melody is most often found

treble clef: the sign placed on a staff to indicate the notes above middle C

tremolo: a musical tremor produced on a string instrument by repeating the same pitch with quick up-and-down strokes of the bow

triad: a chord consisting of three pitches and two intervals of a third

trill: a rapid alternation of two neighboring pitches

trio: an ensemble, vocal or instrumental, with three performers; also, a brief, self-contained composition contrasting with a previous piece, such as a minuet or a mazurka; originally, the trio was performed by only three instruments

trio sonata: an ensemble of the Baroque period consisting actually of four performers, two playing upper parts and two on the *basso continuo* instruments

triple meter: gathering of beats into three beats per measure, with every third beat stressed

triplet: a group of three notes inserted into the space of two

trivium: a literary curriculum of three disciplines (grammar, logic, and rhetoric) taught in medieval schools and universities

trobairitz: female poet-musician of medieval southern France

trombone: a brass instrument of medium to low range that is supplied with a slide, allowing a variety of pitches to sound

troubadour: a type of secular poet-musician that flourished in southern France during the twelfth and thirteenth centuries

trouvère: a type of secular poet-musician that flourished in northern France during the thirteenth and early fourteenth centuries

trumpet: a brass instrument of the soprano range

tuba: a brass instrument of the bass range

tune: a simple melody that is easy to sing

tutti: (Italian for "all") the full orchestra or full performing force

twelve-bar blues: a standard formal plan for the blues involving a repeating twelve-measure harmonic support in which the chords can progress I-IV-I-V-I

twelve-tone composition: a method of composing music, devised by Arnold Schoenberg, that has each of the twelve notes of the chromatic scale sound in a fixed, regularly recurring order

unison: two or more voices or instrumental parts singing or playing the same pitch

upbeat: the beat that occurs with the upward motion of the conductor's hand and immediately before the downbeat

variation: process employed by a composer to alter melody or harmony in some way

vaudeville: an early form of American musical theater involving songs and dances, comedy skits, etc.; a precursor of the musical comedy of Broadway

verismo opera: "realism" opera; the Italian term for a type of late-nineteenth-century opera in which the subject matter concerns the unpleasant realities of everyday life

vibrato: a slight and continual wobbling of the pitch produced on a string instrument or by the human voice

vielle: medieval fiddle

Viennese School: group of Classical composers, including Haydn, Mozart, Beethoven, and Schubert, whose careers all unfolded in Vienna

viola: a string instrument; the alto member of the violin family

viola da gamba (bass viol): the lowest member of the viol family; a large six- or seven-string instrument played with a bow and heard primarily in the music of the late Renaissance and Baroque eras

violin: a string instrument; the soprano member of the violin family

virtuosity: extraordinary technical facility possessed by an instrumental performer or singer

virtuoso: an instrumentalist or singer with a highly-developed technical facility

vivace: in musical notation, a tempo mark indicating "fast and lively"

vocal ensemble: in opera, a group of four or more solo singers, usually the principals

voice: the vocal instrument of the human body; also, a musical line or part

volume: the degree of softness or loudness of a sound

walking bass: a bass line that moves at a moderate pace, mostly in equal note values, and often stepwise up or down the scale

waltz: a popular, triple-meter dance of the late eighteenth and nineteenth centuries

Well-Tempered Clavier, The: two sets of twenty-four preludes and fugues compiled by J. S. Bach in 1720 and 1742

whole step: the predominant interval in the Western major and minor scale; the interval made up of two half steps

whole-tone scale: a six-note scale each pitch of which is a whole tone away from the next

woodwind family: a group of instruments initially constructed of wood; most make their sound with the aid of a single or double reed; includes the flute, piccolo, clarinet, oboe, English horn, and bassoon

word painting: the process of depicting the text in music, be it subtly, overtly, or even jokingly, by means of expressive musical devices

xylophone: a percussion instrument consisting of tuned wooden bars, with resonators below, that are struck with mallets

Index